Treaties with American Indians

Treaties with American Indians

An Encyclopedia of Rights, Conflicts, and Sovereignty

VOLUME I

Donald L. Fixico
EDITOR

Santa Barbara, California • Denver, Colorado • Oxford, England

Library of Congress Cataloging-in-Publication Data
Treaties with American Indians: an encyclopedia of rights, conflicts, and sovereignty / Donald L. Fixico, editor.
p. cm.
Includes bibliographical references and index.
ISBN 978-1-57607-880-8 (hard copy: alk. paper)—ISBN 978-1-57607-881-5 (ebook)
1. Indians of North America—Legal status, laws, etc.—United States—Encyclopedias.
2. Indians of North America—United States—Treaties—Encyclopedias. 3. Indians of North America—Government relations. I. Fixico, Donald Lee, 1951–
KF8203.6.R74 2008
342.7308'72—dc22
2007027797

12 11 10 09 08 1 2 3 4 5 6 7 8

Senior Production Editor: Vicki Moran
Editorial Assistant: Sara Springer
Production Manager: Don Schmidt
Media Editor: Caroline Price
Media Resources Coordinator: Ellen Brenna Dougherty
Media Resources Manager: Caroline Price
File Manager: Paula Gerard

ABC-CLIO, Inc
130 Cremona Drive, P.O. Box 1911
Santa Barbara, California 93116-1911

This book is also available on the World Wide Web as an ebook. Visit www.abc-clio.com for details.

This book is printed on acid-free paper. ♾

Manufactured in the United States of America

This important study of Indian treaties is dedicated to the people of my tribes, who have suffered, endured, and now prosper again:

To the Shawnee,
To the Sac and Fox,
To the Seminole, and
To the Muscogee Creek

—Donald L. Fixico

Board of Advisors

Dr. Duane Champagne (Turtle Mountain Chippewa), former Director of American Indian Studies Center, University of California at Los Angeles

Ms. Ada Deer (Menominee), Director of American Indian Studies, University of Wisconsin-Madison, and former Assistant Secretary of Interior of Bureau of Indian Affairs

Dr. Clara Sue Kidwell (Choctaw), Director of American Indian Center, University of North Carolina, Chapel Hill

Dr. Colin Calloway, Director of Native American Indian Studies, Professor of History, and Samson Occom Professor of Native American Studies, Dartmouth College

Dr. Sharon O'Brien, Co-Director of Tribal Law Center and Professor of Political Science, University of Kansas

Contributors

Donna L. Akers
University of Nebraska, Lincoln
Dancing Rabbit Creek, Mississippi
LeFlore, Greenwood
Pushmataha

Joseph P. Alessi
United States Military Academy
Old Briton
Washakie (Pina Quahah, Scar Face)

Laurie Arnold
The Newberry Library
House Concurrent Resolution 108, 1953
Public Law 280, 1953
Termination

Dewi I. Ball
University of Wales, Swansea
Doctrine of Discovery
Government-to-Government Relationship
Indian Removal
McClanahan v. Arizona State Tax Commission, *1973*
Mille Lacs Band v. Minnesota, *1999*
Puyallup Tribe v. Department of Game of Washington, *1968*
Puyallup Tribe v. Department of Game of Washington, *1977*
Sovereignty
Treaty
United States v. Wheeler, *1978*
Warren Trading Post Co. v. Arizona Tax Commission, *1965*
Winters v. United States, *1908*

Helen M. Bannan
University of Wisconsin, Oshkosh
Wauneka, Annie Dodge

William Bauer
University of Wyoming
California, Eighteen Unratified Treaties, 1851–1852

Jean Bedell-Bailey
Martin, South Dakota
People v. LeBlanc, *1976*

Yale D. Belanger
University of Lethbridge
Aboriginal Title

Brant, Joseph
Crowfoot
Inuvialuit Final Agreements–June 1984

Phil Bellfy
Michigan State University
Constitution Act (Canada), 1982
LaDuke, Winona
Métis
Pontiac
Robinson Superior Treaty (First Robinson Treaty)–September 7, 1850
Sault Ste. Marie, Michigan and Ontario

Sally Colford Bennett
Johnson County Community College
Black Hawk
Chouteau, Auguste
Forsyth, Thomas
Fort Harrison, Indiana
Gaines, Edmund Pendleton
Greenville, Ohio
Jesup, Thomas S.
St. Joseph, Michigan
St. Louis, Missouri
Tippecanoe River, Indiana
Vincennes, Indiana
Wabash River, Indiana
Wells, William

Donald R. Bennie
University of Guelph
Constitution Act (Canada), 1867

Ned Blackhawk
University of Wisconsin, Madison
Opechancanough

Robert D. Bohanan
Jimmy Carter Library
Watie, Stand

Robyn Bourgeois
University of Toronto
Self-Government Agreements (Canada)

John P. Bowes
Dartmouth College
Caldwell, Billy
Pokagun
Treaty with the Chippewa, Etc.–September 26, 1833

Daniel L. Boxberger
Western Washington University
California, Hawaii, and the Pacific Northwest

Jay H. Buckley
Brigham Young University
Clark, William
Lewis, Meriwether

Charles W. Buckner
University of Memphis
Deer, Ada E.
William Campbell
McMaster University
Gadsden, James

Jack Campisi
Mashantucket Pequot Museum and Research Center
Colonial and Early Treaties, 1775–1829

Roger M. Carpenter
National Museum of the American Indian
Riel, Louis
Uncas

Martin Case
Minneapolis, Minnesota
Cass, Lewis
Prairie du Chien, Wisconsin
Traverse des Sioux, Minnesota

Rene Casebeer
University of Washington
Camp Stevens (Walla Walla), Washington
Medicine Creek, Washington

Alexandria E. Casey
Michael S. Casey
Graceland University
Geronimo (Goyathlay)

Phillippe Charland
Université de Québec à Montréal
Canonicus

Anjali Choksi
Hutchins Grant & Associés
Connolly v. Woolrich *(Canada), 1867*
Pre-Confederation Treaties (Canada)
Specific Claims (Canada) (with Lysane Cree)

Ryan L. Church
Los Angeles, California
Allotments
Oliphant v. Suquamish Indian Tribe, *1978*

C. Blue Clark
Oklahoma City University Law School
Relevant Court Cases Related to Treaties

D. Anthony Tyeeme Clark (Meskwaki)
University of Illinois
Harjo, Suzan Shown

Richmond Clow
University of Montana
Spotted Tail

Gavin Clarkson
University of Michigan
Curtis Act, 1898
Morton v. Mancari, *1974*
Rice v. Cayetano, *2000*

Michael C. Coleman
University of Jyvaskyla, Finland
Treaties and American Indian Schools in the Age of Assimilation, 1794–1930

Chip Colwell-Chanthaphonh
Center for Desert Archaeology
Eskiminzin
Sacred Sites

Lysane Cree
Hutchins Grant and Associés
Blondin-Andrew, Ethel Dorothy
Federal Power Commission v. Tuscarora Indian Nation, *1960*
Modern Treaties/Comprehensive Land Claim Agreements (Canada)
Sahtu Dene and Métis Comprehensive Land Claim Agreement–September 6, 1993
Specific Claims (Canada) (with Anjali Choksi)

Steven L. Danver
Journal of the West
Burke, Charles H.
Indian Water Rights and Treaties
Little Turtle
Mankiller, Wilma Pearl
Menominee Tribe of Indians v. United States, *1968*
Ouray
Trust Responsibility

Leigh Darbee
Indiana Historical Society
Harrison, William Henry
Tecumseh

Jennifer Nez Denetdale
University of New Mexico
Barboncito
Manuelito
Treaty with the Navajo–June 1, 1868

David H. DeJong
Prima-Maricopa Irrigation Project
Deloria, Vine, Jr.

S. Matthew DeSpain
University of Oklahoma
Doaksville, Oklahoma
Jerome, David H.
Pike, Albert

Sonia Dickey
Albuquerque, New Mexico
Carson, Kit
Long Walk, 1864

Alan C. Downs
Georgia Southern University
Aquash, Anna Mae Pictou
Canyon de Chelly, Arizona
Massasoit
Wounded Knee Occupation, 1973

Antonie Dvorakova
University of Chicago
Black Kettle
Treaty with the Cheyenne and Arapaho–October 28, 1867
Treaty of Fort Laramie with the Sioux, Etc.–September 17, 1851

R. David Edmunds
University of Texas at Dallas
Northeast and the Great Lakes

C. S. Everett
Vanderbilt University
American Indian Policy Review Commission
Blount, William
Doak's Stand, Mississippi
Lea, Luke

Angela Firkus
Cottey College
Leupp, Francis Ellington
Meriam Report, 1928
Oshkosh

Andrew H. Fisher
College of William and Mary
*Boldt Decision (*United States v. Washington*), 1974*
Hunting, Fishing, and Gathering
Sohappy v. Smith *and* United States v. Oregon, *1969*
Sohappy, David, Sr.

Donald L. Fixico
Arizona State University
Bureau of Indian Affairs (BIA) Public Apology, 2000
Cobell *Case, 1996*
Indian Tribal Energy and Self-Determination Act, 2005
National Museum of the American Indian, 2004
Sand Creek Massacre Site Return, 2002
Seminole Tribe of Florida Purchase of Hard Rock Café, 2007

Hugh W. Foley, Jr.
Rogers State University
Atoka Agreement, 1897
Bearskin, Leaford
Harjo, Chitto

Andrew Frank
Florida Atlantic University
McIntosh, William, Jr.

Ritu Gambhir
New York University
Inuit
Nunavut Land Claims Agreement–May 25, 1993

Granville Ganter
St. John's University
Red Jacket

Tim Alan Garrison
Portland State University
Southeast and Florida

Deborah Gilbert
State University of New York, Stony Brook
Dawes Commission (Commission to the Five Civilized Tribes)
Ridge, John Rollin

Bradley J. Gills
Arizona State University
Doolittle Committee
Trail of Tears

Carole Goldberg
University of California, Los Angeles
Federal Policy and Treaty Making: A Federal View

Kevin Gover
Arizona State University
Statutes as Sources of Modern Indian Rights: Child Welfare, Gaming, and Repatriation

Pamela Lee Gray
Purdue University
Boudinot, Elias
Fort Sumner, New Mexico
New Echota, Georgia
Red Cloud (Makhpiya-Luta)
Ridge, Major

S. Neyooxet Greymorning
University of Montana
Treaty with the Delaware–September 17, 1778

Kimberly Hausbeck
Nova Southeastern University
Domestic Dependent Nation
Indian Country
Plenary Power

Karl S. Hele
University of Western Ontario
Bagot Commission (Canada)
Deskaheh
Dumont, Gabriel
Manitoba Act (Canada), 1870
Royal Proclamation of 1763
Treaty of Montreal–August 7, 1701

Troy Henderson
Loyola University of Chicago
Treaty with the Chippewa–January 14, 1837
Treaty with the Chippewa–October 4, 1842
Treaty with the Chippewa–September 30, 1854

Ross Hoffman
Trent University
Indian Act of Canada, 1876

Tom Holm
University of Arizona
Reservations and Confederate and Unratified Treaties, 1850–1871

Arthur Holst
Philadelphia, Pennsylvania
Bureau of Indian Affairs (BIA)
Commerce Clause and Native Americans
Fort Pitt, Pennsylvania

Chris Howell
Red Rocks Community College
Battle of Fallen Timbers, 1794
Battle of Horseshoe Bend (Tohopeka), 1814
Battle of the Thames, 1813

Stephanie Irlbacher-Fox
University of Cambridge
Alaska Native Claims Settlement Act, 1971
Gwich'in Comprehensive Land Claim Agreement–April 1992
Canadian Indian Treaty 11–June 27 to August 30, 1921

Cornelius J. Jaenen
University of Ottawa
Canada

Bruce E. Johansen
University of Nebraska, Omaha
Canassatego
Captain Jack
Dull Knife
Emathla, Charley
Handsome Lake (with Barbara A. Mann)
Hendrick
Jackson, Helen Hunt
Johnson, William
Kicking Bird
Metacom
Seattle (Seath'tl)
Standing Bear (Mo-chu-no-zhi)
Tibbles, Susette LaFlesche (Bright Eyes, Inshta Theamba)
United States v. Kagama, *1886*

Theodore J. Karamanski
Loyola University of Chicago
Chicago, Illinois
Michilimackinac, Michigan

Anne Keary
University of Utah
Indian Rights Association (IRA)
Longest Walk, 1978
Watkins, Arthur V.

Michael J. Kelly
Creighton University
Jefferson, Thomas
Native American Graves and Repatriation Act, 1990
Supremacy Clause
Treaty with the Cherokee–November 28, 1785
United States v. Dion, *1986*
United States v. Sioux Nation, *1980*
Williams v. Lee, *1959*

Penelope M. Kelsey
Rochester Institute of Technology
Treaty with the Six Nations–November 11, 1794

Clara Keyt
Arizona State University
Banks, Dennis
Means, Russell

Clara Sue Kidwell
University of North Carolina, Chapel Hill
Indian Appropriations Act, 1871
Cooper, Douglas H.

Joyce Ann Kievit
Tempe, Arizona
Opothleyahola
Reconstruction Treaties with the Cherokee, Choctaw, Chickasaw, Creeks, and Seminole–April 28–July 19, 1866
Treaty with the Choctaw–September 27, 1830
Treaty with the Cherokee–December 29, 1835

C. Richard King
Washington State University
Indian Gaming Regulatory Act, 1988

Annie Kirby
University of Wales, Swansea
Collier, John
General Allotment Act (Dawes Act), 1887
Indian Reorganization Act, 1934

Phil Konstantin
San Diego, California
Hawkins, Benjamin

Helen M. Krische
Watkins Community Museum of History
American Indian Self-Determination and Education Act of 1975

Janne Lahti
University of Helsinki, Finland
Fort Laramie, Wyoming

Denise Lajetta
The Kluge-Ruhe Aboriginal Art Collection of the University of Virginia
Alcatraz Occupation, 1964 and 1969

Amanda Laugesen
Australian National University
American Indian Movement (AIM)
Indian New Deal
Trail of Broken Treaties, 1972

Laurie Leclair
Toronto, Ontario
Canadian Indian Treaty 3–October 3, 1873

Lloyd L. Lee
Arizona State University, West Campus
Executive Order Reservations
Guardianship/Wardship

Stacy Leeds
University of Kansas
Indian Treaty Making: A Native View

Peter D. Lepsch
Monteau and Peebles
Trust Land

Tamara Levi
University of Nebraska, Lincoln
Annuities
Pratt, Richard Henry

Anne-Marie Libério
University of Paris IV, Sorbonne
Hitchcock, Ethan Allen

Fred Lindsay
San Francisco, California
Adair, William P.
Adams, Hank

Cherokee Tobacco *Case, 1870*
Jemison, Alice Mae Lee
Joseph
Osceola
United States v. Creek Nation, *1935*

Patricia A. Loew
University of Wisconsin, Madison
Buffalo
Sandy Lake, Minnesota
Treaty with the Sioux, Etc.–August 19, 1825

Brad D. Lookingbill
Columbia College of Missouri
Lone Wolf (Guipähgo)
Sitting Bull

Jean-François Lozier
University of Toronto
Articles of Capitulation of Montreal, September 1760

Priscilla MacDonald
Toledo, Ohio
De La Cruz, Joseph Burton

Barbara A. Mann
University of Toledo
Handsome Lake (with Bruce E. Johansen)

Kurt T. Mantonya
Topeka, Kansas
Council Grove, Kansas
Federally Recognized Tribes
Indian Civil Rights Act, 1968

Patricia S. Mariella
Arizona State University
Property: Land and Natural Resources

Aliki Marinakis
University of Victoria
Erasmus, George Henry

Robert O. Marlin IV
University of Houston, Clear Lake
Treaty of Guadalupe Hidalgo, 1848
Elk v. Wilkins, *1884*

Ron McCoy
Emporia State University
Crazy Horse (Tašunka Witko)
Sitting Bear (Setangya or Satank)

James McIntyre
Moraine Valley Community College
Fort Harmar, Ohio
Knox, Henry

Mark Edwin Miller
Southern Utah University
Federal Acknowledgment Process (FAP)
Nonrecognized Tribes
State-Recognized Tribes

John Bear Mitchell
University of Maine
Maine Indian Claims Settlement Act of 1980 (with Micah Pawling)

Bradford W. Morse
University of Ottawa
Canadian Indian Treaties

Daniel S. Murphree
University of Texas, Tyler
McGillivray, Alexander

Caryn E. Neumann
Ohio State University
Cherokee Nation v. Georgia, *1831*
Pitchlynn, Peter
Worcester v. Georgia, *1832*

Greg O'Brien
University of Southern Mississippi
Indian Removal and Land Cessions, 1830–1849

Sharon O'Brien
University of Kansas
Indian Treaties as International Agreements

Caoimhín Ó Fearghail
University of Maryland
Ex Parte Crow Dog, 1883

Knut Oyangen
Iowa State University
Battle of Tippecanoe, 1811
St. Clair, Arthur
Wayne, Anthony

Vera Parham
University of California, Riverside
Oakes, Richard

Linda S. Parker
San Diego State University
Alaska, Hawaii, and Agreements

Micah Pawling
University of Maine
Maine Indian Claims Settlement Act of 1980 (with John Bear Mitchell)

Larry S. Powers
University of Memphis
Indian Territory

Jay Precht
McNeese State University
Indian Claims Commission Act, 1946
Indian Claims Commission (ICC)

Edward D. Ragan
Old Dominion University
Powhatan

Akim D. Reinhardt
Towson University
Tribal Government Authority versus Federal Jurisdiction (with John R. Wunder)

Martin Reinhardt
Reinhardt & Associates, Brighton, Colorado
Trust Doctrine

Jon Reyhner
Northern Arizona University
Dodge, Henry Chee
Southern Plains and the Southwest

Justin B. Richland
University of California, Irvine
Mitchel v. United States, *1835*

Barnett Richling
University of Winnipeg
British-Labrador Inuit Peace Treaty–April 8, 1765

Chad Ronnander
University of Wisconsin, Eau Claire
Dodge, Henry

Paul C. Rosier
Villanova University
Northern Plains

Ezra Rosser
Loyola University of New Orleans
Cohen, Felix S.
Johnson v. M'Intosh, *1823*
Nixon's Message to Congress, July 8, 1970

Bruce A. Rubenstein
University of Michigan, Flint
Chivington, John Milton

Deborah Rubenstein
St. Clair County Community College
Dearborn, Henry
Schoolcraft, Henry Rowe

Susan Sánchez-Barnett
Baltimore County Public Schools
Lone Wolf v. Hitchcock, *1903*
Tee-Hit-Ton Indians v. United States, *1955*

John Savagian
Alverno College
Aupaumut, Hendrick

Daniel Edward Shaule
Toronto, Ontario
Williams Treaties with the Chippewa and the Mississauga–October to November 1923

Bradley Shreve
University of New Mexico
Bellecourt, Clyde
Cochise
Santa Fe, New Mexico
Williams, Roger

Steven E. Silvern
Salem State College
Lac Courte Oreilles Band of Chippewa Indians v. Voight et al., *1983*
Reserved Rights Doctrine

Michael A. Sletcher
Yale University
Albany Conferences of 1754 and 1775
Treaty of Albany with the Five Nations–July 31, 1684
Washington's Address to the Senate, September 17, 1789

Eric R. Smith
University of Illinois, Chicago
Great Lakes Indian Fish and Wildlife Commission
Right of Conquest
Right of Occupancy/Right of the Soil

Gregory E. Smoak
Colorado State University
Treaty with the Eastern Band Shoshone and Bannock–July 3, 1868

Elizabeth Sneyd
Royal Military College of Canada
Nacho Nyak Dun Final Agreement–May 29, 1993
Vuntut Gwitchin Final Agreement–May 29, 1993

Scott L. Stabler
Grand Valley State University
Parker, Ely S. (Do-He-No-Geh-Weh)

Michael A. Stewart
University of Oklahoma
Treaty of Ghent, 1814

Gordon Stienburg
University of Toronto
Canadian Bill of Rights, 1960

Paul H. Stuart
Florida International University
Legislation, Treaty Substitutes, and Indian Treaties

April R. Summitt
Arizona State University, Polytechnic Campus
Cornplanter
Satanta

Céline Swicegood
University of Chicago
Indian Removal Act, 1830

Andrew J. Torget
University of Virginia
Jackson, Andrew
Parker, Quanah

Tracey L. Trenam
Aims Community College
Assimilation

Özlem Ülgen
University of Sheffield
Calder v. Attorney-General of British Columbia *(Canada), 1973*
Delgamuukw v. British Columbia *(Canada), 1997*
Hamlet of Baker Lake v. Minister of Indian Affairs and Northern Development *(Canada), 1980*
James Bay and Northern Quebec Agreement–November 11, 1975
Nisga'a Final Agreement–April 27, 1999
Northeastern Quebec Agreement–January 31, 1978
St. Catherine's Milling & Lumber Company v. The Queen *(Canada), 1887*
R. v. Van der Peet *(Canada), 1996*

Tim Watts
Kansas State University
Ross, John

Gray H. Whaley
Western Michigan University
Dalles, The, Oregon

Charles E. Williams
Clarion University
Treaty Conference with the Six Nations at Fort Stanwix–November 1768

Waziyatawin Angela Wilson
University of Victoria, British Columbia
Little Crow

John R. Wunder
University of Nebraska, Lincoln
Tribal Government Authority versus Federal Jurisdiction (with Akim D. Reinhardt)

Jason M. Yaremko
University of Winnipeg
Canadian Indian Treaties 1 and 2–August 1871
Canadian Indian Treaty 4–September 15, 1874
Canadian Indian Treaty 5–September 24, 1875
Canadian Indian Treaty 6–August 28, September 9, 1876
Canadian Indian Treaty 7–September 22, December 4, 1877
Canadian Indian Treaty 8–June 21, 1899
Canadian Indian Treaty 9 (James Bay Treaty)–November 6, 1905, October 5, 1906
Canadian Indian Treaty 10–September 19, 1906, August 19, 1907

Gayle Yiotis
National Museum of the American Indian
Dawes, Henry Laurens

Contents

Volume I

Introduction, xxi

Thematic Essays

Regional Essays

Introduction

PEACE AND FRIENDSHIP is the most commonly used phrase in the language of Indian treaties. The intent of the United States as a young country was to persuade Indian communities to deal only with the United States. Many things were unsettled following the American Revolution, and the tribes found themselves in the middle of it. In the early years of U.S.-Indian relations, the tribes also had common interest with the British, the French, and the Dutch.

Indian agents and other government officials in the United States negotiated more than four hundred treaties and agreements with American Indians; treaty talks occurred for more than one hundred years. Interestingly, Indian and white leaders met at various sites that often had been the meeting places for previous trading and council meetings. Negotiating in Native languages and English through interpreters was difficult, although some Native people spoke some of the white man's tongue. Beginning in 1778 with the Delaware, when the United States negotiated its first successful treaty with an Indian tribe and ratified it, a historic precedent was set, one that has made Native Americans a unique minority in their own country. For the record, Indian tribes in what is now the United States also made treaties with the British, the French, the Confederate States during the Civil War, and with other Indian tribes.

In Canada, the federal government negotiated seventeen treaties with the First Nations peoples, starting in 1871 and ending in the twentieth century. These consist of thirteen numbered treaties plus the four Robinson and Williams treaties.

The mid-nineteenth century represented the zenith of treaty making; during the next twenty years, the practice sharply declined. A rider attached to a congressional appropriations act in 1871 ended the Indian treaty-making business in the United States, although agreements were negotiated until 1917. The Act of 1871 did not end the recognition of Indian treaties, however; it merely halted the treaty-making process.

U.S.-Indian treaties often included more than one tribe, and some tribes signed many treaties. There are 374 ratified treaties and 16 agreements. The first treaty was concluded in 1778; the last one, during the late nineteenth century. The shortest treaty is with the Kickapoo in 1820. The treaty is 16 lines long, with 8 Kickapoo leaders and 6 American officials who signed, involving $2,000 to be paid for Kickapoo removal. The longest treaty is the Treaty with the New York Indians of 1838 at Buffalo Creek in New York; that treaty is 15 pages long. The Potawatomi signed the most treaties of any tribe, a total of 26. The biggest gathering was the council held at Medicine Lodge, Kansas, during October 1867, at which 500 soldiers met with more than 15,000 Plains Indians gathered from the Cheyenne, Arapaho, Apache, Kiowa, and Comanche. The largest number of treaties were signed in 1825 and 1836, 20 each year; 19 treaties were signed in 1855, 18 in 1865, and 17 in 1832.

In regard to categories, 229 treaties involve ceded lands; 205 are about payments and annuities; 202 include the phrase *peace and friendship;* 115 are about boundaries; 99 address reservations; 70 include civilization and agriculture; 59 are about roads and free passages; 52 address the sovereignty or the authority of the United States or tribes; 49 include allotment and guaranteed lands; 47 contain gifts, goods, or presents; 38 contain provisions on education; 34 contain provisions on hunting, fishing, and gathering rights; 28 authorize forts and military posts; 25 include trade; 12 address railroads; several include agents for the tribes; and a few treaties deal with one or more of the following: stolen horses, returning prisoners, slavery, returning criminals, intruders, scalping, alcohol, missions, and mail routes.

Treaties between Indian tribes and the United States are binding agreements. For Native peoples, each step of the negotiation was important, not just the resulting words on a piece of paper. Indian agents, military officials, and officials of the Indian Office met with Native leaders to begin negotiations, which usually began with a council held at a previously agreed-upon site. To Native people, the chosen site was important, and the talk itself was just as significant as the resulting treaty or agreement. The site itself, such as the one near Medicine Lodge in southwestern Kansas and Prairie du Chien in western Wisconsin, set the tone of the council. Medicine Lodge has made a lasting impression and is reenacted every five years.

The first meeting, or council, between Indian and white leaders likely made or broke the tone of the talks. The council was a fundamental concept among the Indian nations, and tribal protocols varied from tribe to tribe. Unsure of how to approach the various tribes, federal officials depended upon local whites, guides, and traders to introduce them to the tribes in their areas. Familiar with the ways of the Indian tribe, these individuals advised officials how to approach Native leaders.

In learning the protocol for dealing with tribes, federal officials experienced difficulty in meeting with more than one tribe at the same time. They made the mistake of trying to get enemy tribes to meet at the same council. Even tribes who met only sometimes, such as the Plains Indians, who gathered annually during the summer to hold the Sun Dance, had a mutual understanding of the importance of the arrival at camp, as exemplified by the Medicine Lodge Council in 1867. Dressed in their finest ceremonial garb, a tribe also sometimes wanted to be the last to arrive so that other tribal groups would acknowledge that an important group had arrived.

Protocol is involved in any type of summit, council, or important discussion involving conflicting interests, especially if there are deep differences between cultures. In the general situation of treaty talks, white officials learned a lot about the importance of kinship relations in forming an agreement, especially if it resulted in an alliance between the two sides. Early treaties—those concluded before the mid-nineteenth century—were often peace treaties, for the United States wanted tribes to acknowledge their relationship with the new nation and abrogate relations with the British and the French. Bringing about peace following a battle or other conflict created balance between two opposites, and this tranquil state of existence fostered mutual respect between the two parties and a need for ceremonial acknowledgement. Thus, smoking the pipe was germane to solidifying the new relationship of nonconflict.

The language barrier between the two sides caused great skills in diplomacy to be exercised. During the height of contact between Indians and whites in the seventeenth and eighteenth centuries, more than 250 indigenous languages were spoken. The role of interpreters, both Indian and white, became crucial to treaty negotiations. The varying protocols among tribes for holding councils compelled American officials to learn about tribal leaders before talks of a serious nature began. Cultural differences added to language barriers as problems arose, often intensifying the clashing views of Indians and whites over land. One perceived land and what it meant economically, and the other understood the earth philosophically and celebrated it with ceremonies. The same commodity became homeland for both sides, and ensuing treaties named who owned the land. A new culture of treaty making emerged from the older Indian way of holding council and talking.

Gift giving played a crucial role in the early contact and negotiations between Indian and white leaders. Federal officials typically brought gifts of inexpensive items such as mirrors, metalwork, and beads to get the Indians into a peaceful frame of mind that would lead to the discussion of bigger issues, such as land cessions. As mentioned, at least forty-seven treaties contained provisions for giving gifts and presents. Officials understood the importance of generosity and sharing among Native peoples and used this against them, hence the "Great White Father" in Washington held a position of respect and generosity.

The cultural difference between Indians and whites proved to be enormous. In addition to the language barriers, both sides operated from different mind-sets; each held different ideas about what was important for the negotiations and what the negotiations meant. Native leaders and federal officials had a challenging situation to overcome before they could begin successful discussions. It is said that, on one occasion Osceola, the noted leader of the Seminole in Florida, disagreeing with tribal leaders who signed the Treaty of Fort Gibson in 1833, stabbed his knife through the two pieces of paper on the table. This was his angry response to all treaties, letting others know that his mind was set on going to war. It is likely that this did happen since there is a hole in the original treaty kept in a vault at the National Archives in Washington.

"Touching the pen" became a common occurrence during Indian treaty making. Native leaders were unable to write their names because they did not know the English language, and therefore white officials asked Native leaders to "make their

mark"—which was of little importance to American Indians, who believed that the spoken word was superior to any words on a piece of paper, which might be blown away by the wind or destroyed; the spoken word would always be remembered. Several treaty councils witnessed impressive oratory articulated by tribal leaders. This was not the white way. The majority of Indian treaties verify the marks made by the tribal leaders. In other situations, the leaders refused to hold the white man's writing instrument, and the federal officials asked the Native leaders to touch the pen after the names were written by the official in charge.

The most important concern for Native peoples in treaty negotiations was their sovereignty. Sovereignty is an important issue of concern resulting from the U.S.-Indian and Canada-First Nations agreements. The signing of a treaty creates binding responsibilities between both sides and includes the respectful recognition of each for the other. Theoretically, the relationship between the two sides is one of a sovereign forming an agreement with another sovereign—that is, government-to-government in a lateral relationship of similar status. The status is one of international law and based on each party to the treaty having faith in the agreement and recognizing each other as being sovereign.

Trust is a meaningful legal responsibility between two nations and their people, and treaties established this reciprocal relationship. Both sides of a treaty agreement must abide by the provisions and must continue to fulfill the responsibilities outlined in the document. That trust responsibility continues into this century, in the hands of the assistant secretary of the Department of the Interior, who supervises the Bureau of Indian Affairs for all tribes in the United States.

Treaties were a systematic procedure for dealing with Indian tribes. By examining the history of these agreements, some assessment can be made about them in stages or phases. For example, treaty negotiations, talks, or councils were the first step in this system of agreements. During these important gatherings, significant Indian individuals were recognized and acknowledged so the representatives of the United States would know who they were dealing with. In some cases, such as the Prairie du Chien meeting, "making chiefs" occurred; this happened more than once when government officials persuaded certain individuals to sign for their tribes as leaders. The federal government operated on the political philosophy that a head of state represented a nation, thus an Indian nation must have one significant leader or chief. This was not the case with many tribes, such as the Muscogee Creek, the Ojibwa, and others, who had leaders for each town or village and settlements scattered over a vast region of the country.

Discussion of the treaty's provisions was another critical phase of Indian treaty making. Both sides met with an agenda of needs, according to their thinking, and they lobbied to obtain agreement from the other side. Some acute Native leaders saw that education was an important part of the future of their people and wanted educational assistance in the form of teachers. Common provisions included goods and annuities over a number of years and perhaps blacksmiths. Most of all, large sums of money were paid to the tribes for their lands.

The next phase consisted of the results of treaties—some of which caused important changes, such as the exchange of enormous tracts of land for perpetual gifts, or changes in fishing or hunting rights on ceded lands. The treaties led to a new era in Indian-white relations and actually marked the decline of the strength of Indian nations. This decline became evident as tribes such as the Potawatomi, Delaware, Chippewa, and others signed several treaties with the United States. After 1800, the federal government almost always had the leverage in treaty talks.

Strategies of treaty-making involve several motives, all of which resulted in the decline of the Indian nations. These strategies involved introducing the idea of one nation, one leader; setting boundaries; manipulating leadership; making chiefs; courting treaty signers; and giving gifts to influence tribes and their leaders. Such actions almost always were directed toward Indian men, not toward women (although, in many tribes, women held the authority to select their leaders).

Peace was the main objective in the early U.S. treaties until about 1850. The federal government found it much easier to make peace with the Indian nations than to fight them, which proved costly, especially as great effort was needed just to find them. The United States signed 374 treaties but fought more than 1,600 wars, battles, and skirmishes against Indian tribes. The Navajo Treaty of 1849 and the Fort Laramie Treaty of 1851 were negotiated with peaceful objectives in mind rather than more land cessions. The Fort Laramie agreement involved multiple groups of the Northern Plains, Sioux, Gros Ventre, Mandan, Arikara, Assinaboine, Blackfeet, Crow,

Cheyenne, and Arapaho. Boundaries were set to keep them apart, with additional provisions for roads and military posts included as part of the treaty.

The establishment of boundaries for tribes was another goal for government officials as they treated with Indian leaders. Many tribes hunted over vast territories; government officials were able to contain tribes within certain areas, and they reminded leaders of the boundaries established in the agreements. Officials introduced Native peoples to the idea of land ownership and individual ownership. In 1858, the Sisseton and Wahpeton Sioux signed a treaty in Washington, D.C., agreeing to new reservation boundaries. This led to the surveying of the tribal land for division into individual eighty-acre allotments. In this way, tribal lands were reduced in size.

At times, the United States undermined and manipulated leadership to get the lands it wanted. The importance of kinship played a vital role in treaty making between Indians and the United States. Federal officials learned of the importance of kinship and symbolic bonds in tribal communities and used this knowledge to develop a tribal dependence on the "Great White Father" in Washington. When the leaders of tribes refused to negotiate, federal officials sought out other Indians who were more easily persuaded to sign treaty documents.

Land acquisition was the principal reason for treaties and was pursued to such an extreme extent that, by the end of the nineteenth century, American Indians held less than 2 percent of the land that they had once possessed totally. The unleashed white settler became an uncontrollable force to consume Indian lands. Such was the settlers' greed that federal officials were forced to deal with tribes, which resulted in many Indian removal treaties or war. A domino effect occurred as eastern tribes moved onto lands of interior groups, who moved onto lands of western tribes, and so forth.

Expansion of the United States was another goal of government officials. During the Civil War, federal officials negotiated, and the government ratified, eighteen treaties that called for expanding the territory held by the Union. During the three years between March 1862 and March 1865, federal officials concluded treaties with the Kansa, Ottawa, Chippewa, Nez Percé, Shoshone, Ute, Klamath, Modoc, Omaha, Winnebago, and Ponca Nations. These agreements included land cessions and further diminished the territories of the tribes. Indian lands were further reduced by the systematic creation of "permanent" reservations.

Control of tribal movements was the final strategy and result of the treaties. With treaties in place and with military power greater than that of the tribes, the United States could enforce control over the weakened Indian nations. Once the leaders were undermined and control exerted over them, Indian superintendents controlled the Indians and conditions on the almost two hundred reservations throughout Indian country.

Land was the central issue of U.S.-Indian treaties. As more settlers arrived from England and other countries, the need for more Indian land placed considerable pressure on the Indian tribes. A domino effect began to occur as eastern seaboard tribes of the Atlantic coast retreated inland, thereby encroaching on the hunting domains and farming areas of tribes nearby to the west. The expansion of white settlement across the Appalachian Mountains caused the newly formed United States to treat with the inland tribes. British agents and traders worked among the Indian nations to gain their allegiance and convince them to reject the proposed talks of federal officials.

At the same time, other European interests in the form of French, Scots, and Irish traders proved successful in obtaining acceptance among tribes. These trading activities made it more difficult for the United States as more Americans pushed into the Ohio Valley and the back country of the Southeast.

The most obvious kind of treaty called for tribes to surrender their lands. In less than thirty years, from 1801 to 1829, federal officials made thirty-one treaties with the Chickasaw, Choctaw, Muscogee Creek, Cherokee, and Florida tribes. These cession treaties extinguished Indian title to all of the area east of the Mississippi River from the Ohio River to the Gulf of Mexico.

Officially, treaties had to be ratified by the U.S. Congress and signed by the president of the United States. Congressional ratification was most active during the 1800s, as federal officials met with Native leaders at an increasing rate. Treaty making fell into a pattern: More and more treaties were negotiated with eastern tribes, who were thus forced to keep moving westward; the Delaware, for example, were forced to remove at least nine times.

Unratified treaties were agreements not confirmed by the U.S. Congress. Naturally, many agree-

ments were submitted to Congress; most submissions were ratified, and some had their provisions amended. It is estimated that between forty-seven and eighty-seven treaties were unratified. Most Native leaders did not understand the ratification process and believed that all the agreements they made were official.

Organization of the Encyclopedia

This encyclopedia is intended as a comprehensive reference tool for anyone interested in American Indian treaties with the United States. In these three volumes, the larger number of U.S.-Indian treaties, their lengths and complexity, and the complexity of Canada-Indian treaties are described. The volumes are organized in sections. The first volume consists of major essays that explain various perspectives on Indian treaties, and regional treaties. In the second volume, entries are included that describe each treaty; short entries address treaty sites and terms; and there are primary source documents of many treaties. The third volume contains a historical chronology, brief biographies of noted individuals involved in the treaties, and a section on treaty-related issues.

Acknowledgments

This three-volume project has been the work of many people. I have often felt like an academic Sisyphus, facing the enormous task of rolling the big boulder up the mountain. More than three hundred people have helped, supported, and written entries or essays for this encyclopedia. I am grateful for the help of the following individuals, who assisted with this project in the early years at the Center for Indigenous Nations Studies at the University of Kansas: research assistants Viv Ibbett, Melissa Fisher Isaacs, David Querner, and Elyse Towey. I appreciate the support given my work by Chancellor Robert Hemenway, Provost David Shulenburger, former Associate Dean Carl Strikwerda, and former Dean Kim Wilcox at the University of Kansas.

I would like to express appreciation to the following individuals at Arizona State University, who have been helpful in the completion of this project over the last two years: President Michael Crow; Executive Vice President and Provost Elizabeth Capaldi; former Provost Milton Glick; Vice President David Young, Divisional Dean Debra Losse; former Chairperson Noel Stowe of the History Department; and Chairperson Mark von Hagen. I am grateful for the support from the ASU Foundation, which sponsors my Distinguished Professorship of History, and for ASU as a leading university that supports scholarship in American Indian history. I especially want to thank Clara Keyt as a research and editorial assistant. I thank my research assistants during the final phase: Matt Garrett, Cody Marshall, and Kristin Youngbull; they have helped to track down a lot of information as well as doing other chores. With their help, after I moved to Arizona, the boulder was pushed the rest of the way to the top of the mountain in the sun with a smile.

Appreciation is also expressed to all the contributors who wrote entries and the noted scholars who wrote the essays for the encyclopedia. Nor would this project have been possible without the patience, effort, and tremendous understanding of my good friend and editor, Steven Danver. Thank you to Caroline Price for the tremendous illustrations; and to April Wells-Hayes for the thorough copyedit of the manuscript. I wish all editors were like Vicki Moran who guided this project smoothly through all its production stages. I am especially grateful to my wife, Professor April Summitt, whose words of support encouraged me to complete this project. I am also grateful to my son, Keytha Fixico, who has patiently waited for me so that we could go to a movie and do other son-and-dad stuff. Always, I am grateful for the support of my parents, John and Virginia Fixico; and I want to acknowledge my four tribes—the Shawnee, Sac and Fox, Seminole, and Muscogee Creek—to whom this three-volume encyclopedia is dedicated.

Donald L. Fixico
Arizona State University

Treaties with American Indians

Thematic Essays

Governments and Treaty Making

Indian Treaty Making: A Native View

Like other peoples, American Indians have always been concerned with preserving their cultural autonomy, retaining their land, and maintaining political sovereignty. One way tribes have preserved their legal rights is by entering into treaties and agreements with other sovereigns. Approximately 370 Indian treaties were ratified by the United States (Deloria, V., and DeMallie 1999, 181). A number of other treaties that resulted from negotiations between the United States and Indian tribes were never ratified by the U.S. Senate and remain unenforceable.

Indian tribes entered into treaties with other sovereigns for different reasons and with varying results. Treaties created military and political alliances, authorized trade, defined political and jurisdictional boundaries, divided natural resources, established and maintained peace, ensured community survival, and at times provided for the final dissolution of tribal governments.

As a matter of tribal law and policy, a treaty is a binding agreement between two or more nations. Treaties are legal agreements that Indians expected to be binding (Wilkinson and Volkman 1975, 612). Although not every tribe negotiated treaties with the United States, the political consequences of treaty making and the legal principles that flow from court cases involving treaty interpretation continue to define the legal status of tribal governments within the United States today (Monette 1994, 617–618). Even the tribes that never entered into treaties with the United States benefit from the resulting legal framework of Indian nations as sovereigns. Today, there are more than 560 federally recognized tribes within the United States, including Alaska Native villages. Treaties were the foundation of federal recognition of Indian tribes as sovereigns (Porter 2004, 1601).

Although treaties were common among the tribes in the southeastern United States, the Woodlands (eastern United States), the Great Plains, and the Northwest, many tribes in other regions did not routinely negotiate treaties with the United States. For example, few ratified treaties will be found between the United States and tribes in California or between the United States and the Pueblos of the Southwest (Brann 2003, 754–755). The United States did not enter into treaties with any of the Alaska Native sovereigns (Case and Voluck 1978, 16–17).

Treaties are legally binding agreements between sovereigns; they are also called *compacts, covenants, conventions*, and *memoranda of understanding*. Regardless of the nomenclature, these treaties have been a critical part of the American Indian past and are of continuing importance to tribal governments today. In fact, tribal governments continue to negotiate treaties and agreements with various sovereigns, particularly state and local entities (Deloria, P., and Laurence 1994, 381).

U.S. federal policy ended treaty making with tribes in 1871. In March of that year, Congress placed a rider on an appropriations bill that ended the practice of Indian treaties in the United States (25 U.S.C. § 71). Prior to that date, the executive branch would negotiate treaties with the tribes, and the Senate would either ratify the treaty or not. Some treaties involved monetary payments to tribes, for which Congress needed to appropriate funds. The House of Representatives objected to this process because they were being asked to fund items included in treaties despite the fact that the House had played no role in treaty negotiations. Although the legislation of 1871 prohibited the federal government from negotiating further treaties with Indian tribes, the law on the books differs from what actually happened.

Tribes continued as sovereigns, with territorial control over lands and natural resources. The federal government continued to have a government-to-government relationship with tribes, and political negotiations continued, although not by means of formal treaties as they had before.

As a practical matter, the United States continued to negotiate formal agreements with tribal governments well into the 1910s; however, rather than being submitted to the Senate for ratification, these new agreements were presented to Congress and adopted or rejected by both the Senate and the House of Representatives. In this form, the post-1871 agreements with tribes took the form of congressional enactments rather than ratified treaties. The most common examples of these agreements are the tribally specific enactments to implement allotment on particular reservations. After lengthy negotiations with tribal governments, federal agents prepared formal allotment agreements with the consent of tribal officials. These agreements were formally presented to Congress and adopted as legislation

instead of ratified as treaties. The federal-tribal diplomatic process, followed by tribal consent and federal approval, was essentially the same as the treaty-making process prior to 1871.

Modern tribal governments continue to enter into agreements with other tribes and with state and local governments. Tribal and state governments frequently negotiated cross-deputization agreements between each other as two sovereigns. These agreements address the jurisdictional ambiguities of law enforcement in Indian country and typically involve shared law enforcement authority in otherwise-disputed areas. The agreements permit tribal police officers to make arrests on lands that would otherwise be under the jurisdiction of the state, and vice versa. In some areas of the country, where state and tribal jurisdiction depends on the ownership of neighboring parcels of land, these ongoing agreements are necessary to public safety and effective policing (Pommersheim 1995, 161).

Tribes and states also enter into revenue-sharing agreements as a means of resolving conflicts of taxation jurisdiction (Fletcher 2004, 5–7). These agreements are typically referred to as *compacts.* Where tax jurisdiction is ambiguous or where collection of tax revenues proves burdensome, tribes and states have negotiations compacts in lieu of federal court litigation. One sovereign agrees not to pursue tax claims in court, whereas the other sovereign agrees to share tax revenues with the first sovereign. In some compacts, the sovereigns agree how the funds are to be spent in a mutually beneficial manner both for citizens of the state and for citizens of the tribe.

Treaty Making Past and Present

For more than five hundred years, tribes have entered into treaties with the United States and with other international governments. Tribes entered into various treaties with Great Britain, Spain, and other European sovereigns prior to the American Revolution (Deloria, V., and DeMallie 1999, 103).

For centuries prior to European contact, tribes negotiated with other tribes agreements akin to the treaties they would later negotiate with European countries and ultimately with the United States. By the time Europeans arrived, tribes were already skilled in negotiating treaties and agreements for a variety of purposes. Tribes had formed military alliances and political confederations for centuries.

Tribes also had elaborate trade routes that required access to vast territories, including lands owned or controlled by other tribes. Tribes reached agreements that recognized boundaries between tribal lands and passage between those territories. All these negotiations predated European contact and influence. In fact, much of the Indian treaty-making process was passed from the tribes to their European counterparts, who freely adopted Indian treaty-making procedures and diplomatic decorum in the negotiations that followed.

For instance, Indian treaty negotiations often involved long ceremonial meetings, during which past transgressions were set aside, friendships renewed, and gifts exchanged between the parties as a sign of goodwill (Deloria, V., and DeMallie 1995, 685). These formalities and ceremonial gestures preceded any discussion of new parameters or terms of agreement. In this regard, American Indians influenced the manner in which future negotiations would take place, and federal negotiators embraced many of these concepts.

The influence of European and subsequent U.S. treaty-making traditions also altered the way Indian tribes negotiated. There was a shift away from reliance on oral agreements toward a focus on written documents. Prior to European contact, the treaty negotiations of tribes were committed to memory, with the entire discussion constituting the binding agreement of the parties. The non-Indians' insistence on memorializing agreements in writing altered the treaty-making process and, over time, changed the way tribes entered into the negotiating process. The result was a shift in focus: today, many Indian people might know the words of the treaty document but not the context in which the negotiations arose.

Indians and non-Indians alike initially approached the early treaty negotiations with little or no knowledge of each other's traditions or beliefs. The language barrier routinely would have made fluid communications nearly impossible, yet agreements were made. In coming together, each side influenced the treaty process of the other sovereign, and a unique system of negotiations emerged that included elements of both the Indian and the European traditions.

The first treaty between America and an Indian tribe was completed during the Revolutionary War, the Treaty of Fort Pitt (Treaty with the Delaware) in 1778. The Delaware made a formal alliance with the American revolutionaries, and the tribe permitted colonial troops free movement across their territory. In exchange, the Americans agreed to build a fort inside the Delaware Nation to

protect the community when soldiers were elsewhere engaged. Beyond its historical significance, this treaty was important because it established that tribes were sovereign entities with the power of diplomacy. It also established, in a legal context, that tribes were property owners with full dominion over territory, including the right to exclude others from their territory. The Delaware were in a position of strength when negotiating with the colonies.

The relative strength of the Delaware diminished over time, and the tribe later found itself in a much weaker diplomatic position. Yet whether in strength or in weakness, the Delaware continued to negotiate treaties with other sovereigns to accomplish their goals.

In 1867, the Delaware entered into a treaty with the Cherokee Nation that arguably led to a political dissolution of the Delaware (Treaty between the Cherokee and Delaware–April 8, 1867). The Delaware negotiated citizenship rights within the Cherokee Nation to preserve legally protected status for the Delaware people and to ensure a friendly place to settle.

The Delaware story is important because it demonstrates how a sovereign can enter into treaties for various purposes at various times. Sometime tribes are in a position of strength, and sometimes tribes face political or physical annihilation. In each circumstance, the sovereign made a contextual decision and chose to negotiate a treaty to protect its interests or to mitigate a situation. Just as there was no uniform Delaware approach to treaty making over time, there is no uniform Native perspective on treaty making.

In 1867, the Cherokee and the Delaware were both in politically weak positions relative to the United States. In fact, both tribes were pressured to enter into the intertribal treaty by the United States, and the treaty was executed by both tribes, not in Delaware or Cherokee territory, but in Washington, D.C., in the presence of, and for the benefit of, federal officials.

The Delaware were being removed by the United States from their territory and relocated inside Indian Territory. Most of the Indian Territory lands had been accounted for, and the federal government needed land to implement the Delaware relocation. In a treaty with the United States, the Cherokee Nation agreed to accept the Delaware along with the Shawnee. The Cherokee agreed both to the relocations and to the inclusion of the Shawnee and Delaware people as citizens of the Cherokee Nation as a result of a post–Civil War treaty with the United States. The Cherokee Nation, like the Osage, the Muscogee Creek, the Seminole, and other Indian nations, entered into treaties of alliance with the Confederate States in 1861. When the Civil War was over, the United States reestablished ties with the Cherokee Nation, but the Cherokee Nation agreed to several concessions, including the settlement of other tribes on Cherokee lands. These post–Civil War treaties were among the last official treaties between Indian nations and the United States. The post–Civil War treaty with the Cherokee is unique because it precipitates additional treaties between tribes on the request of the United States. Rather than using force to require the Cherokee Nation to accept the relocation of other Indian tribes, the United States acknowledged that the tribes would work out the terms of relocation and new citizenship in an intertribal treaty. This illustrates how, even toward the end of formal treaty making with the United States, tribes were viewed as sovereigns who negotiated with each other and with the United States as a means of diplomacy.

The United States officially ended treaty making between the federal government and tribal governments in 1871 (25 U.S.C. § 71). The United States continued to make formal agreements, although they were not considered treaties, with tribes well into the twentieth century. One of the most common subjects of these agreements was the allotment of tribal lands.

In the late 1800s and early 1900s, the federal government pushed for Indian lands to be allotted. Rather than holding land in a contiguous land base with a property law system governed by tribal law, the United States pressured tribes to divide their lands and allow individual Indians to own lands without the control or oversight of the tribes. The U.S. Congress passed the General Allotment Act as a statement of federal policy; however, the federal allotment policy was not self-executing (Royster 1995, 7–15).

Allotment of reservation lands was generally implemented only after elaborate negotiations and treaty making with the affected tribes. Some tribes were successful in avoiding the allotment of their lands altogether. The majority of tribes were pressured to allot their lands, and the details were outlined in tribal agreements with the United States.

In fact, more than twenty agreements between the United States and tribal governments were made in the years 1876–1895. The United States did not

stop making treaties; it simply relabeled the process and extended ratification rights to both houses of Congress rather than to the Senate alone.

During this period, the tribes did not have the same political and military strength they once had had. By this time, tribes had typically been relocated to reservations or to diminished land bases. Even though very few tribes were militarily conquered by the United States, in previous treaties many tribes had agreed to become protectorates of the United States and had thereby abandoned any effort to maintain their own troops.

With no military threat and with increased economic dependency of tribes on the federal government, the United States continued to gain political power over the tribes. With increased political power, the United States began to interfere with matters that had previously been internal to the tribe, including how the tribes governed themselves. Increased federal involvement in internal tribal matters quickly led to an effort by the federal government to change the land tenure systems inside Indian country.

As such, the allotment agreements were heavily coerced by the federal government, and the tribes were powerless to demand many concessions. The tribes felt that, if they did not participate in the agreements, the federal government would unilaterally act to allot their lands. The tribes were faced with two options: either to allow Congress to pass a law permitting allotment of tribal lands without tribal consent or input, or to enter into negotiations with the federal government for the allotment of tribal lands on terms more agreeable to the tribes. Those tribes that entered into negotiations with the federal government for the allotment of tribal lands did so under duress. Although the tribes vehemently opposed allotment, they negotiated allotment to avoid being completely voiceless in the process. Tribal input in the allotment process was better than no negotiation at all (Leeds 2005, 64–66).

The federal perspective in negotiating the allotment agreements was that allotment would end tribalism and prepare Indian people for ultimate citizenship in the United States. This would make Indian people members of a national minority and end the notion of tribal sovereignty. Therefore, many of the allotment agreements included provisions that dissolved tribal governments and provided for U.S. citizenship.

The Atoka Agreement of the Choctaw and Chickasaw Nations in 1897 is a prime example. The agreement divided tribal lands into individual allotments and provided for the ultimate dissolution of the tribal government as a condition precedent to the extension of U.S. citizenship to tribal members.

Several shifts in federal policy occurred after allotment. Since the 1960s, there has been a consistent trend away from the termination of tribal existence toward a policy of respecting tribal self-determination. Tribal governments have rebounded and have resumed the exercise of their inherent sovereign powers, including the right to negotiate treaties and agreements with other sovereigns.

Indian treaty making continues throughout Indian country today. Many tribes continue to make agreements with state and local municipalities and with other tribes.

Historically, the Cherokee Nation has completed twenty-two treaties since 1721, first with Great Britain and then with the United States. The contemporary Cherokee Nation continues to make treaties and currently maintains more than twenty ongoing agreements with state, county, and city law enforcement agencies. Most of the agreements were negotiated in the 1990s, and additional negotiations for new agreements are pending.

The Navajo Nation and the State of Arizona have negotiated agreements to control the distribution of tax revenues between the two sovereigns and to cooperate in the delivery of youth and family protective services. The Navajo Nation is geographically located within three states, and each of the sovereign states has engaged in negotiations with Navajo Nation officials.

Tribes in the Puget Sound and Great Lakes areas have recently negotiated intertribal agreements that ensure equitable rights to fish and wildlife harvests. Tribes throughout the country are currently engaged in intertribal cooperatives to restore buffalo herds, manage water resources, and clarify jurisdiction.

A foundational principle of federal Indian law has been the role of the federal government in Indian affairs, to the exclusion of the states. Early cases and federal statutes preclude states from negotiating treaties with tribal governments. However, when formal federal treaty making came to an end, states and local governments increased their willingness to negotiate with tribes, realizing that treaties and agreements are mutually beneficial.

In at least three areas, the federal government has authorized states to enter into agreements with tribes: (1) law enforcement, (2) the care and custody of Indian children, and (3) gaming. Tribes that

engage in casino-style gaming routinely negotiate with the states compacts that dictate revenue sharing, maintenance of roads, and other governmental infrastructure. These agreements routinely lead to shared law enforcement responsibilities and clarify jurisdiction of tribal and state courts.

Tribes do not need authorization from the federal government to negotiate agreements with other sovereigns. The right to negotiate and make treaties is an important component of inherent sovereign powers, and tribes will continue to exercise this power into the future. Indian treaties are hardly relics of the past. The ability to negotiate and reach valid legal agreements with other sovereigns is a critical and active component of modern tribal sovereignty.

The Diversity of Tribal Perspectives

The Native perspective of treaty making is diverse. More than 560 federally recognized tribal governments have entered into several hundred treaties, both ratified and unratified, with the United States. Many other treaties have been negotiated with tribes, states, and foreign countries. The sheer number of negotiations and resulting treaties suggests there is no single Native approach to treaty making. From tribe to tribe, the customs, laws, languages, and philosophies greatly differ. It follows that the concepts of treaty making and diplomacy are distinctive as well.

Many differing factors lead to negotiations, depending on the tribes involved. Many tribes never entered into treaties with the United States. Other tribes entered into multiple treaties with multiple sovereigns. The Cherokee Nation, for example, has negotiated treaties with Great Britain, the United States, and the Confederacy, and with several Indian tribes, most notably the Shawnee and the Delaware. The Choctaw Nation entered into treaties with Spain prior to entering into multiple treaties with the United States. The Kashaya Pomo tribe in California entered into a treaty with Russia in 1817. Other tribes have entered into treaties with Mexico and Canada (Deloria, V., and DeMallie 1999, 106–108.)

Tribes sometimes negotiated treaties that were never ratified either by the United States or by their tribal citizens. The U.S. Senate failed to ratify eighteen Indian treaties after the tribes had agreed to all the provisions (Prucha 1994, 244). But in other circumstances, negotiations ended so that tribal leaders could return home to get the proper assent from their tribal constituents.

Tribes approached the treaty-making process in vastly different ways, according to the political, social, and cultural contexts. Tribal peoples, like their counterparts throughout the world, make political and diplomatic decisions for innumerable reasons. The viewpoints and motivations of the Indian leaders who negotiated and signed treaties are equally diverse. Like sovereigns the world over, tribes have leaders who fall into different camps. Some leaders are true statesmen who represent their people in difficult situations and make the tough decisions based on what they sincerely believe to be in the best interest of their constituents, with or without popular support. Other leaders succumb to greed and allow personal gain to influence their decisions, even to the detriment of the people they represent. Indian country has had a host of leaders in both camps.

The Indian treaty-making process involved leaders who made sincere assessments of the difficulties faced by their nations and made decisions to enter into treaties even though the will of the people did not wish to enter into treaties. Other leaders entered into treaties that directly benefited them personally. In the Treaty of Dancing Rabbit Creek of 1830 (Treaty with the Choctaw), Chief Greenwood LeFlore of the Choctaws consented to have the Choctaw people removed from their ancestral lands and relocated to Indian Territory. Nonetheless, he was permitted to remain in Mississippi and to maintain ownership of his lands (Foreman 1934, 26). Other tribal leaders received favorable land allocations and monetary payments in exchange for signing treaties that bound their nations to opposite fates.

From the perspective of the United States, treaty making is a power of the executive branch of government subject to Senate ratification. Federal agents were sometimes sent out into Indian country to negotiate treaties. At other times, tribal representatives went to Washington, D.C., or other destinations outside their home territories to negotiate.

From the tribal perspective, the authority of individuals or groups within the tribe to participate in negotiations varied. In several instances, the individuals recognized by the federal government as having the power to sign treaties were not the individuals who had the right to speak on behalf of the tribes. As a result, many tribal communities have not recognized certain treaties that the United States has ratified and implemented. The federal government has sometimes declared individual Indians chiefs for the purpose of obtaining signatures, regardless of whether the individuals were recognized by the tribes as the official leaders. The United States continued this practice well into the 1960s by appointing tribal leaders for purposes of securing signatures on leases and other legal documents. In these instances, the federally appointed "chiefs" were not popularly elected by the tribal communities.

Some tribes had treaty councils or treaty delegations that were clearly sanctioned by the tribal people as spokespersons. The Chickasaw Nation, in the 1890s, issued official notarized certificates from the tribal government to individuals who were official delegates to Washington (Viola 1995, 81). These individuals had the right to negotiate on behalf of the people and the ability to enter into treaties and bind the people they represented. But unlike their federal counterparts, many of those who had the apparent authority to negotiate treaties were limited in terms of the subject matter they could concede and were limited in their powers.

Some tribes had elaborate property law schemes of their own and would freely engage in land cessions and land trades. Contrary to some historical accounts, it was not a foreign concept to some tribes to purchase or exchange lands. Many of the tribes in Indian Territory in the late 1800s maintained elaborate property journals as a matter of official tribal government records. These journals are similar to the current county land records in which are recorded deeds and various types of land transactions, such as leases, easements, and land sales transactions. In these tribes, individual citizens could own the surface of the land and were free to alienate those lands to other tribal citizens. The underlying estate, however, was owned by the tribe to preserve the contiguous land base and protect territorial sovereignty from outside encroachment.

Other tribes viewed land as a sacred object that could not be traded, sold, or otherwise negotiated. On this philosophy, the Lakota people have refused to accept money judgments due to them from federal court decisions in which they prevailed on staking claims. They view return of the land as the only solution. Tribes that embraced this philosophy historically would not have conveyed their lands to the United States through treaties. For such tribes, the authority of the tribal leaders would have been limited to other subject areas in diplomacy. Those tribal leaders might have possessed delegated authority from their people to speak and negotiate with other sovereigns in matters of trade, war and peace, and political relationships, but they likely would have lacked the authority to convey real property.

Other tribes did not believe that a small group of people had the authority to represent the full body politic of the tribe, and instead required the approval of general councils before decisions could be made. For instance, some treaties had provisions that affirmatively required subsequent amendments to the treaty to be submitted to a popular vote of the tribal people. A single delegate would not have had the authority to bind the tribe to treaty amendments (Treaty with the Kiowa and Comanche of 1867; *Lone Wolf v. Hitchcock,* 187 U.S. 553 1903). Still other tribes were required to consult particular groups of community constituents, such as elders or women, before a final decision or deal could be completed (Berger 2004, 105).

The Treaty as a Negotiation Process

In the early days of treaty making with Europeans and then with the Americans, the process of treaty negotiation was of more importance to the tribes than the legal document that followed. The tribal representatives tended to place more importance on the discussions between the negotiators, the context that brought the parties together, the fellowship and interaction between the people involved, and the oral representations and positive assurances made by the parties (Sullivan 2004, 684–686).

Following the negotiations, the federal representatives would typically create a written document that constituted the agreement of the parties. Given the fact that few tribal representatives spoke English—the written language used in most Indian treaties—it was the spirit of the negotiations that were important to tribal communities, not the piece of paper that followed. Tribal leaders who could not read or write English routinely placed their marks in the form of an X on the treaty document to register assent to the terms of the document, despite the fact that they were relying on oral promises rather than on an independent review of the treaty text. Promises and affirmations that were made during the negotiations were as binding, from the Native perspective, as the document that followed.

Therefore, tribes that later sought compliance with oral promises of negotiations were disenchanted with the non-Indians' strict reliance on the words of the final, written version of the treaty. From the Native perspective, the spirit of the treaty should prevail over the treaty document itself. The spirit of the treaty was the crux of the promises made in good-faith negotiations and not the technical interpretation of words on paper.

The federal courts, when first reviewing the treaties in legal proceedings, tended to agree that the negotiations and historical context were important in addition to the treaty text. The federal courts adopted a set of interpretive rules, to be applied in treaty cases, that give accord to the Native perspective of treaty making. These interpretive rules, known as the canons of Indian treaty construction, have been the basis for tribal legal victories for treaty enforcement. The canons require that Indian treaties and agreements be liberally construed in favor of the Indians. The canons require that the treaty be interpreted not literally but as the tribe would have understood the treaty at the time the agreement was made. In essence, the federal courts that have applied the canons of Indian treaty construction give life to the spirit of the treaty rather than relying solely on a strict interpretation of the text (Wilkinson and Volkman 1975, 623–634).

Although the federal courts began developing these canons in the 1830s with the legal opinions of Justice Marshall, the canons have been applied recently to take into account the Native perspective and the negotiations themselves. In a recent U.S. Supreme Court case, *Minnesota v. Mille Lacs Band of Chippewa Indians,* various treaties with the Chippewa were interpreted to preserve the right of certain tribes to hunt, fish, and gather in lands that were otherwise ceded to the United States. Relying on the canons, the Court concluded that the tribal rights survived despite the fact that, in the treaty, the Chippewa agreed to "fully and entirely relinquish and convey to the United States, any and all right, title, and interest, of whatsoever nature the same may be, which they may now have in, and to any other lands in the Territory of Minnesota or elsewhere" (*Minnesota v. Mille Lacs Band of Chippewa Indians,* 526 U.S. 172 1999).

Strictly interpreted, the treaty language could be viewed as a full cession of all rights to the land. The Court, however, went beyond the written words in the treaty and considered the larger context, giving weight to the tribe's perspective. The tribe would not have understood, at that time, that they were giving up their right to hunt and fish. The case involved several treaties with Chippewa Indians in the Great Lakes region: the Treaty with the Chippewa–October 4, 1842; the Treaty with the Chippewa–August 2, 1847; and the Treaty with the Chippewa–September 30, 1854.

The Force and Effect of Treaties

Many of the guarantees in Indian treaties are promises that were intended in perpetuity. They are typically not limited by time. The Treaty with the Choctaw, 1830, contains language typical of the time period to indicate that the treaty was final and that no further territorial incursions would occur:

> The Government and people of the United States are hereby obliged to secure to the said Choctaw Nation of Red People the jurisdiction and government of all the persons and property that may be within their limits west, so that no Territory or state shall ever have a right to pass laws for the government of the Choctaw Nation of Red People and their descendants; and that no part of the land granted them shall ever be embraced in any Territory or State. (ibid. at Article 4)

Despite the permanent language in the treaties that suggests the treaties will live on forever, the United States has failed to comply with most treaties, at least in part. History tells us that the United States always breaks treaties but that Indians believed that a treaty was sacred and could not be broken. This story is far too simplistic. Context and circumstances change for tribes just as they change for sovereigns the world over. And, although the federal government's history of unilaterally breaking treaties is well documented, changing tribal circumstances and reversals of tribal diplomatic decisions should also be noted. Tribes, too, have abrogated treaties unilaterally.

As previously noted, some tribes entered into treaties with competing factions in order to secure a favorable stance with the victor of a foreign war. During the American Revolution, tribes entered into treaties of alliance with both Great Britain and the colonies. Allegiances change, and treaties are renegotiated. During the American Civil War, tribes with long histories of relations with the federal government entered into treaties with the Confederacy.

Conclusion

The treaty-making process between the United States and Indian tribes has evolved over the centuries and continues today in various forms. The most important legacy of Indian treaties is the legal framework they created. American Indian tribes are governments that have negotiated with other sovereigns in an array of political contexts. Modern tribal governments are the outgrowth of indigenous nations with centuries of experience in diplomacy both internationally and domestically.

Stacy Leeds

References and Further Reading

Berger, Bethany R. 2004. "Indian Policy and the Imagined Indian Woman," 14 *Kansas Journal of Law and Public Policy* 103.

Brann, Amy C. 2003. "Comment, Karuk Tribe of California v. United States: The Courts Need a History Lesson," 37 *New England Law Review* 743.

Case, David S., and David A. Voluck. 1978. *Alaska Natives and American Law.* Fairbanks: University of Alaska Press.

Clark, Blue. 1999. *Lone Wolf v. Hitchcock: Treaty Rights and Indian Law at the End of the Nineteenth Century.* Lincoln: University of Nebraska Press.

Debo, Angie. 1970. *A History of the Indians of the United States.* Norman: University of Oklahoma Press.

Deloria, P. S., and Robert Laurence. 1994. "Negotiating Tribal-State Full Faith and Credit Agreements: The Topology of the Negotiation and the Merits of the Question," 28 *Georgia Law Review* 365.

Deloria, Vine, Jr., and Raymond J. DeMallie. 1999. *Documents of American Indian Diplomacy: Treaties, Agreements, and Conventions, 1775–1979*, vol. 1. Norman: University of Oklahoma Press.

Fletcher, Matthew L. M. 2004. "The Power to Tax, the Power to Destroy, and the Michigan Tribal-State Tax Agreements," 82 *University of Detroit Mercy Law Review* 1.

Foreman, Grant. 1934. *The Five Civilized Tribes.* Norman: University of Oklahoma Press.

Kappler, Charles J., ed. 1975. *Indian Treaties 1778–1883.* New York: Interland Press.

Leeds, Stacy. 2005. "By Eminent Domain or Some Other Name: A Tribal Perspective on Taking Land," 41 *Tulsa Law Review* 51.

Monette, Richard A. 1994. "A New Federalism for Indian Tribes: The Relationship between the United States and Tribes in Light of Our Federalism and Republican Democracy," 25 *University of Toledo Law Review* 617.

Pommersheim, Frank. 1995. *Braid of Feathers: American Indian Law and Contemporary Tribal Life.* Berkeley: University of California Press.

Porter, Robert. 2004. "The Inapplicability of American Law to Indian Nations," 89 *Iowa Law Review* 1595.

Prucha, Francis Paul. 1994. *American Indian Treaties: The History of a Political Anomaly.* Berkeley: University of California Press.

Richter, Daniel K., and James H. Merrell, eds. 2003. *Beyond the Covenant Chain: The Iroquois and Their Neighbors in Indian North America 1600–1800.* University Park: Pennsylvania State University Press.

Royster, Judith V. 1995. "The Legacy of Allotment," 27 *Arizona State Law Journal* 1.

Sullivan, Julie E. 2004. "Legal Analysis of the Treaty Violations That Resulted in the Nez Perce War of 1877," 40 *Idaho Law Review* 657.

Viola, Herman J. 1995. *Diplomats in Buckskin: A History of Indian Delegations in Washington City.* Norman: University of Oklahoma Press.

Wilkinson, Charles, and John M. Volkman. 1975. "Judicial Review of Indian Treaty Abrogation: 'As Long as the Water Flows, or the Grass Grows Upon the Earth—How Long a Time is That?'" 63 *California Law Review* 601.

Williams, Robert A., Jr. 1996. "'The People of the States Where They are Found Are Often Their Deadliest Enemies,' The Indian Side of the Story of Indian Rights and Federalism," 38 *Arizona Law Review* 981.

Federal Policy and Treaty Making: A Federal View

For nearly one hundred years of federal treaty making with the Indians, from 1778 to 1869, the federal government's main objective remained constant: acquisition of as much Indian land as possible while minimizing the cost in American lives and dollars. The U.S. Senate ratified more than 365 Indian treaties during this period in pursuit of Indian land and other resources. The federal government chose treaties as the primary vehicle for Indian relations, not only because the European powers that settled North America had established such a tradition but also because treaties were deemed the most effective instrument for achieving American land acquisition goals while minimizing the loss of non-Indian lives. Other objectives of federal treaty making changed over time, corresponding to changes in broader federal Indian policy. For example, in the early years, an important policy aim was to ensure the loyalty of Indian nations to the Americans rather than to compete with European powers such as England and Spain. During the middle period, the goals of peace and land acquisition were pursued through a policy of removing Indian nations to reservations far from non-Indian communities. Toward the end of the treaty-making period, when tribes could no longer threaten alliance with European powers and non-Indian settlement westward made separation impossible, treaty provisions to facilitate assimilation of tribal members into non-Indian society became more central to the treaty-making process.

Establishment and Conduct of Indian Relations through Treaties

When America declared its independence from Great Britain in 1776 and embarked on the war to free itself from British rule, one of its major challenges was to ensure that tribal forces would become allies or at least remain neutral. To attack British troops positioned on the St. Lawrence and the Great Lakes, the Continental Army needed to cross through territory of the Haudenosaunee (Iroquois Confederation) and the Lenni Lenape (the Delaware) in New York and the Ohio valleys. But the obstacles to securing the friendship or neutrality of these Native nations were formidable. During the pre–Revolutionary War period, Britain had been far more respectful of tribal sovereignty and property than had the colonists. In particular, settlers from the colonies had persistently encroached on tribal lands and engaged in fraudulent trade practices with the Indians, prompting violent Indian response and calls from the colonists for British military aid. Britain intervened to prevent such offenses to the tribes because the alternative was involvement of British troops in costly warfare, and because otherwise the Indians might favor France or Spain, which also had interests in North America. Not surprisingly, the Indian nations viewed Great Britain more favorably than they did the new government representing the settlers.

To deal successfully with the tribes, the former colonies knew that unity was essential. Tribes could all too easily exploit rivalries among the colonies through separate dealings. Indeed, British policy had long been to take advantage of divisions among the tribes. Thus, although individual colonies had interests in land acquisition and trade that drew them toward individual arrangements with Indian nations, the newly confederated colonies made collective overtures. And because of tribal expectations born of decades of relations with the British, the form such overtures took was predetermined.

Appointed representatives of the newly united colonies, known as commissioners, invited large numbers of tribal representatives from particular regions to assemble for what was sometimes called a *council* or a *treaty.* The Continental Congress, which appointed these commissioners, assigned three different groups to deal with Indians in the north, south, and middle areas of the new nation. In each sector, the commissioners carried on Native-inspired ceremonial practices first introduced by the British, such as condolence ceremonies expressing grief over one another's losses, presentation of gifts and strings of wampum, and speeches of goodwill. Out of these first councils emerged an informal alliance with the Oneida and a formal written treaty with the Delaware, signed and sent to Congress in 1778. This treaty was the first the Americans concluded with an Indian nation and the only one entered into during the Revolutionary War. Due to wartime exigencies, the Treaty of Fort Pitt (Treaty with the Delaware) focused more on military and political relations than on land acquisition. But even that treaty addressed property issues, as it acknowledged and guaranteed the territorial rights of the tribe.

During the brief period of the Articles of Confederation, from 1781 to 1787, American treaty making continued, but the government's practices during that time did not set precedents for subsequent government policy. Although most Indian nations had remained allied with the British during the Revolutionary War, the tribes had not participated in the treaty of peace in 1783 between the United States and Britain. Weakened by war but no longer immediately threatened by the British, the American government wanted to dictate terms of peace to the Indians while still minimizing further hostilities. The dominant view in Congress was that the Indians had been conquered and therefore surrendered their lands and other claims. Secretary of War Henry Knox warned, however, that forcing terms on the tribes would require military engagement that risked either defeat or a bad reputation abroad.

Congress again chose treaties as the preferred means of dealing with the tribes and again appointed commissioners to "negotiate" with the tribes. This time, however, the commissioners' directions were to insist on treaty terms involving land cessions and prisoner return rather than to secure the assent of the tribes. Commissioners abandoned most of the pretense of adhering to Native ceremonies associated with treaty making. As a result of this approach, although the Continental Congress concluded eight treaties with Indian nations during this period, Indian dissatisfaction with treaty terms precluded the possibility of a real and lasting peace.

Furthermore, complicating and defeating American treaty-making initiatives during this period was uncertainty about the role of states in negotiating treaties with the Indians. The provision in the Articles of Confederation dealing with control of Indian affairs was ambiguous, at once declaring and then disclaiming congressional power over Indians who were "members of the states." To add to the confusion, the section ended with a proviso that "the legislative right of any State within its own limits be not infringed or violated." States such as New York took this language to mean that they had authority, under the Articles of Confederation, to make their own treaties and proceeded to seek land cessions on their own, capturing lands that settlers had occupied in violation of congressional bans and federal treaty terms.

When Native resentment over the post–Revolutionary War treaties began to manifest itself in pantribal alliances and threats of war, Congress and the administration reassessed their approach to treaties. Framers of the new Constitution of 1787 strongly affirmed exclusive federal power over Indian affairs. In Article I, Section 8, known as the commerce clause, the Constitution linked congressional control over Indian relations to similar authority over relations with foreign nations and among states. Implicit in this linkage was the view that Indian tribes, like foreign countries and states, were governments and to be dealt with as such. The Constitution did not directly specify, however, that these dealings with Indian nations were to be by treaty. Its references to treaties were more general. The Constitution authorized the president "by and with the Advice and Consent of the Senate, to make Treaties, provided two thirds of the Senators present concur"; prohibited states from making treaties; and acknowledged that properly made treaties would be the supreme law of the land.

In his first administration, however, George Washington continued the pattern of conducting most Indian relations via treaty and instituted the same ratification process for Indian treaties that was used for foreign treaties. Until the Senate provided its ratification by two-thirds vote, the treaties could not take effect. A remaining question was how much the Senate would become involved in the treaty negotiations themselves. President Washington made some early attempts to engage the Senate in planning for treaty negotiations. Because the treaties entailed significant U.S. financial commitments for land purchases, gifts, payment of Indian debts to traders, and other purposes, as well as drawing of boundaries in which settlers and speculators had an intense interest, political support was essential. President Washington soon realized, however, that securing detailed advance instructions from the Senate would be cumbersome and detrimental to U.S. strategic interests. Later in his administration, he limited his requests to more general guidance.

The return to bilateral, treaty-based Indian relations under the new Constitution reflected a hard-nosed calculation of the relative costs of war and land purchases. Washington's secretary of war, Henry Knox, estimated that the cost of fighting the Indians would be at least $2 million and the loss of lives immeasurable. In contrast, eliminating the Indians' cause for grievance by compensating them for land confiscated under earlier treaties would cost less than $20,000. Knox's analysis is manifest in the earliest treaties of this period. Notably, land that the United States had claimed by right of conquest of the Iroquois and the Northwest tribes in the Treaties of Fort Stanwix (Treaty with the Six Nations) and Fort McIntosh (Treaty with the Wyandot, Etc.) of 1784 and 1785 were purchased from those same Indian nations via the two Treaties of Fort Harmar in 1789 (Treaty with the Wyandot, Etc.; Treaty with the Six Nations).

During this early period under the Constitution, federal legislation accompanied treaties as a means of conducting Indian affairs but did not really detract from bilateral agreements as the primary means of carrying on relations with the tribes. The only major piece of legislation, the Non-Intercourse Act of 1790, aimed its mandates at non-Indians more than at the tribes. It prohibited trade with the Indians absent a federal license, required federal approval of all land transactions with the tribes, and applied federal criminal laws to Indian country except where the crimes were committed by one Indian against another or where an Indian offender had already been punished by the tribe itself. These provisions actually facilitated treaty relations by removing causes for conflict between the United States and the tribes, such as fraudulent trading deals and improperly authorized land transactions. Many violations of the Non-Intercourse Act were simultaneously treaty violations.

The fact that the United States chose to deal with Indian nations via treaties does not really answer the question of whether these treaties were truly voluntary, bilateral agreements. It was important to the federal government, both to avoid hostilities with the tribes and to present an honorable face to European nations, to deal with Native nations on a consensual basis. At the same time, the political pressure from settlers and speculators was intense to expand the territory available for white settlement. And the United States, saddled with Revolutionary War debts and a new nation to build, was eager to gain control of tribal lands so it could resell to the settlers and speculators at a profit.

From the earliest years of English settlement, it had been accepted legal doctrine that the tribes had some kind of property claim to the lands they occupied, one that must be extinguished before Europeans and their descendants could take full title. Presumably, that meant that the Indians could refuse to sell. And the federal government, like its British colonial predecessor, had decreed that no land could be transferred without its permission. Thus, the burden of overcoming Indian resistance to sale fell upon the federal government. The settlers and speculators did not really care how the land became available for non-Indian settlement and purchase; they just wanted more land at low cost and without the hazards of war. Because Indians were not U.S. citizens capable of voting, the federal government was politically accountable only to the non-Indian population and adopted methods suited to meet the settlers' and speculators' demands.

Federal treaty negotiators resorted to an array of sharp or unsavory methods for obtaining Indian treaties. They also took advantage of government policies, as well as practices by settlers and traders, that undermined tribal resistance. Finally, the United States used its superior control over its own populace to give itself the sole power to purchase Indian land, in what is known as a *monopsony*. The cumulative result of these stratagems was the wholesale transfer of tribal lands to the federal government via treaty, with minimal compensation to the tribes.

The shadier methods of acquiring land by treaty included taking advantage of superior knowledge of the English language, dealing with individuals or groups that were unauthorized to sell, offering secret "gifts" to tribal leaders, playing off one tribe against another, and threatening force. The Cherokees complained, for example, that in their treaty of 1791 the federal negotiator had inserted rights for the Americans without the Cherokees' knowledge. They further charged that the negotiator had bribed the interpreter to recite the land cession as involving a smaller amount of land than was actually inserted in the treaty and the payment for the land as twice the amount written in the treaty.

The United States frequently tried to locate the most agreeable tribal leader to conclude land cessions, paying little attention to tribal political organization or the legitimate authority of the individual(s) involved. Fortunately for the United States, the tribes lacked any effective mechanisms for restraining unauthorized individuals from making such deals. In 1825, after the head chiefs of the Muscogee Creek Nation had refused to sell tribal lands and had departed the treaty council, the treaty commissioners nonetheless pronounced the council a legal one and proceeded to make an agreement with a minor chief. The fact that the treaty offered protection to the signer suggests that the treaty commissioners knew their transaction was with a person of dubious authority to bind the Muscogee Creek Nation. In 1835, with the United States determined to fulfill its promise to Georgia to remove the Cherokee from that state, the United States deliberately chose to treat with Major Ridge, the leader of a minority bloc of Cherokee supporting removal, rather than with John Ross, the staunch opponent of removal who had a majority following. The treaty that was concluded with the Ridge faction specified that it would not be binding unless approved by the Cherokee Nation in council. But after the council met and rejected the treaty, the United States sent notice to the Cherokees to meet with federal negotiators to conclude a new treaty. This notice provided that any Indians who did not attend would be deemed to have approved any treaty signed by the negotiators. When the Ross party boycotted the gathering, leaving only a small number of Ridge supporters, the United States signed a treaty with them anyway—the Treaty of New Echota (Treaty with the Cherokee–December 29, 1935). The preamble to the treaty justified U.S. reliance on only a small portion of the Cherokee Nation by noting the history of negotiations with the Cherokee and the prior warning that nonattendance would be treated as assent to the council's actions. After outraged Cherokee leaders complained of the methods used to secure the treaty, Senator Henry Clay sought to prevent its ratification, proposing that the Senate refuse to approve it based on the absence of authority on the part of the Cherokee who signed it. The Senate rejected this proposal by nearly two to one.

Sometimes the United States bought off the legitimate tribal leaders with side deals, which might or might not be acknowledged in the language of the treaty. In 1790, for example, the Treaty of New York with the Creeks ceded most of the Creek lands in Georgia to the United States. "Secret articles" in the treaty guaranteed a perpetual salary of $1,200 per year to the head chief of the Creek and perpetual salaries of $100 per year to lesser chiefs. The Chickasaw treaty of 1805 entailed federal payments of nearly $5,000 to assorted tribal leaders, a common feature of treaties made at that time. And a treaty of 1855 with Pacific Northwest coast tribes (Treaty with the Dwamish, Suquamish, Etc.–January 22, 1855) (Kappler 1975, 669–673) used special cash annuities for the chiefs to overcome tribal hostility and secure concessions of land. American leaders such as Andrew Jackson understood, however, that the bribery must be kept secret, or the influence of the chiefs would be destroyed.

Another frequently successful strategy of the United States was to exploit intertribal conflicts over claims to land. Sometimes overtly, sometimes implicitly, the United States would warn tribes that, if they did not enter into treaties of cession for particular tracts, the federal government would make a treaty for the same land with a competitor tribe. Thus, the Muscogee Creeks were surprised to learn that the United States had purchased their lands from the Choctaws. And in 1818, the United States sought to persuade the Cherokees to sell by threatening to make a deal for the very same land with the Chickasaws. William Henry Harrison was a notoriously successful practitioner of this strategy, taking advantage of the fact that villages sometimes included members of several tribal groups that shared common areas. He would induce representatives of one group to make a cession, threatening others that they would get nothing if they refused to go along. That is how he secured a cession of Piankashaw lands in southwestern Indiana in 1804. Theoretically, the tribe that had not made the first deal could have held out for a separate payment. But the United States stuck to a policy of paying less for later claims. And in any event, once settlers entered the land following the first sale, the land became depleted of game and less valuable to the remaining tribe.

Not only did the United States seek to impress the tribes with its economic and military might by sending troops along with treaty negotiators, it sometimes resorted to threats of force to secure treaty cessions of land. In negotiations with the Choctaw in 1820, Andrew Jackson found the tribal leaders adamantly opposed to selling their land. He informed them that the United States would wage war, destroy them, and remove them despite their opposition. More circumspectly but no less effectively, in 1809 William Henry Harrison informed the reluctant Miami that, if they continued to refuse to sell their land, he would "extinguish the council fire." Such threats are antithetical to the notion of a free exchange.

The federal government also took advantage of private non-Indian practices that made treaty making and land cessions more advantageous for the American side. Prominent among those practices were illegal settlement by non-Indians on tribal lands and trading with the tribes that resulted in hefty Native debts.

Illegal settlement by non-Indians weakened the Indians' position in treaty bargaining in two ways.

First, the presence of non-Indians on tribal lands brought new microbes, to which the Natives had little resistance. Death and disease left the tribal lands abandoned or worth little to those Natives who remained. Second, non-Indian presence and settlement, especially agricultural pursuits and animal husbandry, depleted the game that supplied an important component of the Natives' livelihood. Land cleared for agriculture diminished the forest habitat for wild game, non-Indians hunted the game, and domesticated livestock competed with the game for food. After the game disappeared or fled elsewhere, the lands held less value for the tribes, and the Indians were far more willing to enter into treaties of cession. For the settlers, the lesson was clear: trespassing on tribal lands would ultimately be rewarded by the availability of new land. It is difficult to imagine a greater incentive for illegal non-Indian settlement on lands previously guaranteed to the tribes. Illegal settlement persisted despite the federal prohibitions on such settlement and the concern of the United States that squatters would infuriate the Indians and precipitate costly wars. Of course, legal settlement had some of the same impact as illegal settlement—non-Indians reaching the furthermost reaches of land purchased from the tribes would also spread disease and thin the game, yielding further land cessions. And the United States encouraged such settlement by selling lands purchased from the Indians at a discount, hoping for large benefits down the line through future land sales.

The other private practice that the United States saw as a boon to treaty negotiations was the trading that took place between non-Indians and tribe members. Contact with Europeans had left the Indians dependent on trade goods such as guns and cooking utensils; and after the decline of the fur trade due to depleted stocks of game, land was the major asset the tribes could use to exchange for such goods. As Indian trade debts accumulated, the traders pressed the United States to arrange land cessions that would put cash in the hands of the Indians, who would in turn be obliged to use the funds to repay their debts. Alternatively, traders recommended cutting out the middle step and giving the cash directly to them. For example, by the end of the eighteenth century a single trading firm, Panton, Leslie and Company, had acquired many of the debts owed by members of the southeast tribes. Panton, Leslie lobbied the U.S. government to make treaties in which the Americans would pay off tribal debts in exchange for cessions of land. The treaties of 1805 between the United States and the Cherokee, Chickasaw, Choctaw, and Creek, in which the United States acquired eight million acres of land, conformed to this pattern. After 1825, nearly all the treaties signed with tribes in the Old Northwest Territories, including the Sac and Fox, the Miami, and the Ottawa, allowed for traders' claims. The United States was sometimes skeptical of the amounts the traders claimed, demanding investigations and insisting on documentation. And disputes over the traders' practices sometimes precipitated conflict with the tribes, leading the United States to place limits on the exchanges through the Non-Intercourse Acts and otherwise. But the accumulation of debts provided incentives both for the Indians to cede lands in the treaties and for traders to lobby for such treaties.

Perhaps the most powerful factor producing land cession treaties with the Indians was the federal government's effective control over who could purchase lands from the tribes. Like the British, the United States determined that it would be highly advantageous to the non-Indian population as a whole to restrict the market for Native lands. Partly it was a military calculation. Speculators and other private parties that had done business with the tribes in the early decades of European settlement sometimes cheated the Indians, misstating boundary lines or providing defective goods in exchange for the land. The tribes often responded to such practices with attacks on local settlers, and the settlers expected the U.S. military to come to their rescue. Requiring federal permission for the sale of tribal lands, as provided in the Non-Intercourse Acts, helped prevent such outbreaks.

From a business point of view, the absence of multiple bidders for tribal lands left the tribes at the mercy of the federal government. Once the War of 1812 eliminated the opportunity for Native dealings with Great Britain or any other European power, the United States had a monopsony—a buyer's monopoly. Freed from the possibility of bidding wars, the non-Indian population could benefit from rock-bottom sales prices to the United States, so long as the United States was willing to forgo substantial profits. In fact, the United States was in such a superior bargaining position by virtue of its monopsony that it could afford a 5,000 percent markup on the land and still sell at prices advantageous to the settlers. As Missouri senator Thomas Hart Benton noted in 1826, the United States was buying land from the Indians at two cents or less per acre and selling it to settlers for $1.25 per acre or more. Some tribes did better, especially as they came to value their remaining land and to resist parting with it. But the Senate was vigilant in amending treaties to reduce the size or duration of payments, and the U.S. Claims Commission, more than one hundred years later, awarded more than $800,000,000 to tribes mostly for "grossly inadequate and unconscionable" payment for ceded lands.

The treaty system of pressure, trickery, and hard bargaining, coupled with the outward form of bilateral, consensual relations, suited American interests well. Straightforward conquest would have cost too much in lives and dollars. Bargaining in accordance with honorable principles of contract would have cost too much as well and would have taken more time than eager settlers, speculators, and traders were willing to tolerate. The treaty policy the United States adopted required some Indian wars and took longer than some U.S. citizens wished. It reflected a compromise between the rough-and-tumble frontiersmen, who preferred swift seizure of tribal lands at the risk of war, and the interests of well-placed easterners who wanted to treat the Indians more honorably and respect their property rights.

Indian treaties represented such peculiar bargains that influential Americans began to question their use altogether. Georgia's governor, speaking in 1830 at the height of the Cherokee removal controversy, declared that "treaties were expedients by which ignorant, intractable, and savage people were induced without bloodshed to yield up what civilized peoples had a right to possess by virtue of that command of the Creator delivered to man upon his formation—be fruitful, multiply, and replenish the earth, and subdue it." Congress expressed a similar view, stating that payment for tribal lands was "but the substitute which humanity and expediency have imposed, in place of the sword, in arriving at the actual enjoyment of property claimed by the right of discovery, and sanctioned by the natural superiority allowed to the claims of civilized communities over those of savage tribes."

By the middle of the nineteenth century, even those who viewed themselves as friends of the Indians raised doubts about the treaty system, calling it a farce. Henry Whipple, Episcopal bishop of Minnesota in the 1860s, urged the United States to deal with the tribes as wards rather than as independent nations. The real purpose of the treaties, he observed, was to pay worthless debts of the Indian traders and to create jobs for political cronies, not to compensate the Indians or provide for their future well-being. Ultimately, however, federal treaty making ended because the House of Representatives became resentful of demands that it appropriate money to fulfill obligations contained in treaties it had had no part in ratifying. A particular source of irritation was a provision in the Osage treaty of 1868, replicated in some other treaties that ceded Indian lands directly to the railroads rather than to the government for addition to the public domain and resale to needy settlers. But members of the House were also unhappy with treaties of 1867 and 1868 involving tribes of the plains along with the Navajo, complaining that they supplied the tribes with too much money over too long a period of time, thereby delaying the day when tribe members would feel pressure to give up their tribal affiliations, accept non-Indian "civilization," and become self-reliant. Attacking the treaty-making system more broadly, one representative asserted that "the idea of this Government making treaties with bands of wild and roving Indians is simply preposterous and ridiculous. It is not good judgment or statesmanship; it is child's play, nothing more and nothing less." Beginning in 1868, the House refused to appropriate funds to fulfill promises made in the 1867 and 1868 treaties, despite the fact that the Senate had ratified the treaties. Finally, in 1871, the impasse between the houses of Congress ended when they agreed upon legislation that would affirm the validity of past treaties but declared that "hereafter no Indian nation or tribe within the territory of the United States shall be acknowledged or recognized as an independent nation, tribe, or power with whom the United States may contract by treaty." Henceforth, agreements might be made with the tribes, but they would only become law when enacted into legislation by both houses.

Specific Treaty Objectives and Provisions from a Federal Perspective

The only treaty made during the Revolutionary War, the Treaty of Fort Pitt with the Delaware Nation (1778), manifests the fledgling American nation's desire to gain support in its conflict against Great Britain. Each signer agreed to assist the other in times of war, and the Delaware specifically agreed to allow free passage to U.S. troops across its lands. The United States, in turn, agreed to build a fort so that the Delaware elders, women, and children could be protected while the warriors "engaged against the common enemy." The sovereignty of the Delaware is acknowledged in a requirement that representatives from both nations, sitting together, be empowered to try individual wrongdoers, either Indian or non-Indian. So eager was the United States for a Delaware alliance that it also promised to guarantee the territorial integrity of Delaware lands and to allow friendly tribes, under the leadership of the Delaware, "to form a state whereof the Delaware nation shall be the head, and have a representation in Congress." This treaty made little difference during the war, and the Indian representation in Congress never came to pass.

With so many tribes having sided with Britain during the Revolutionary War, the earliest postwar Indian treaties aimed at land acquisition and the return of prisoners but also at affirming the exclusive loyalty of the tribes to the United States and maintaining peace with the tribes. Convinced that it had conquered the tribes when it defeated the British, the new federal government believed it could use the treaties to demand additional tribal lands of the Six Nations, the tribes of the Old Northwest, and the southeastern nations. Thus, treaties such as those at Fort Stanwix, Fort McIntosh, Fort Harmar, and Hopewell set boundary lines, with Indian settlement allowed on one side and outlawed on the other. These treaties also included acknowledgements by the tribes that they were "under the protection of the United States and of no other sovereign whatsoever." To assure the dominance of the United States and to avoid sources of conflict, these treaties also reserved lands for U.S. military forts and trading posts, denied American protection to illegal settlers on Indian lands, and required that the tribes deliver up Indians who committed certain crimes against American citizens.

The simultaneous goals of peace with the Indians and acquisition of their lands were difficult for the federal government to maintain, however. The tribes resented their dispossession under the treaties, and the land-hungry settlers ignored even those boundaries, establishing themselves on lands allocated to the Indians. Furthermore, in the years before the War of 1812, the British remained a persistent threat to the fledgling United States, and the possibility of an Indian-British alliance worried American political leaders. Concerned about the possible outbreak of war with the Indians, Congress announced its intention to deal with the Indians on the basis of "good faith" and directed its Indian agents to reduce such sources of irritation to the tribes as fraudulent traders and encroaching settlers. The result was a series of treaties, exemplified by the Treaty of Holston with the Cherokee, made in 1790 and reaffirmed in 1794, and the Treaty of Canandaigua with the Iroquois, made in 1794. These treaties more clearly recognized that the Indian nations were reserving their own lands; clarified boundaries where they had been in dispute; increased the amount of compensation through annuities, goods, and otherwise to be paid to the Indians; and, in the case of the Iroquois, affirmed that the United States would not claim any Indian lands unless the Indians wished to sell them. War with the Indians erupted nonetheless in the Northwest Territory, as the Indians appeared to be unifying under the leadership of Tecumseh (Shawnee), among others. It was not until the Battle of Fallen Timbers, in 1794, when the British demonstrated their reluctance to come to the aid of the Indians, that the United States was able to achieve the larger treaty cessions of land that non-Indian settlers craved. In the Treaty of Greenville, which followed that conflict, the Indians relinquished their claims to the southern two-thirds of Ohio and a small part of what is now Indiana in exchange for compensation and continued hunting rights in the ceded lands. But because the United States remained militarily weak, with isolated forts dotting a far-reaching boundary along the Ohio, it continued to pursue diplomacy with the Indians rather than attempting to subdue them through brute force. Indeed, both the Treaty of Canandaigua and the Treaty of Greenville were concluded through ceremonies showing respect for Indian ways, returning to Indian-preferred vocabulary, such as "Great Father" for the United States.

Even the boundaries created by these more substantial treaties of cession were difficult for the United States to maintain, however, given the political pressures from non-Indian settlers. So, in these early decades of the nation, leaders such as Washington's secretary of war, Henry Knox—and, later, Presidents Thomas Jefferson, James Madison, and James Monroe—held out hope that the Indians could be persuaded to part with even larger tracts of land if the men would only give up hunting as a way of life and take up agriculture, which had heretofore been the province of women. As Jefferson said in 1803, "[W]hile the Indians are learning to do better on less land, our increasing numbers will be calling for more land, and thus a coincidence of interests will be produced between those who have land to spare and want other necessities and those that have necessities to spare and want land." The treaties of this time reflected that objective. Thus, for example, the Treaty of Greenville (Treaty with the Wyandot, Etc.–August 3, 1795; Kappler 1975, 39–45) specified that a tribe could ask that a part of its annuity be paid out in the form of "domestic animals, implements of husbandry, and other utensils convenient for them, and in compensation for useful artificers who may reside with or near them, and be employed for their benefit."

Indian debts to traders also figured into the treaties of the young United States. As the numbers of game and fur pelts on Indian lands diminished due to non-Indian encroachment, Indians had much less to exchange for the manufactured goods to which they had become accustomed, and found themselves in greater and greater debt to traders. As of 1803, for example, the Creeks alone owed $113,000. The only thing of value that the Indians had to offer was their land. But given the federal government's restrictions on transfer of Indian lands to private parties, the Indians could not settle their debts by giving land directly to the creditors. So the non-Indian traders began to pressure the U.S. government to negotiate land cessions with the tribes, with the expectation that federal compensation to the tribes would quickly be diverted to satisfy the mounting obligations. Thus, debt satisfaction and land acquisition proved to be comfortable companions as U.S. treaty aims. President Jefferson even suggested that the Indians be encouraged to run up such debt at U.S. factories that they would become impelled to "lop them off" with land cessions.

In the first decade of the nineteenth century, the United States pursued these aims with an emphasis on proper diplomacy; Jefferson's secretary of war, Henry Dearborn, urged his negotiators to use "all prudent means in your power . . . to reconcile [the Indians] and to remove every obstacle to their mutual friendship." In addition to seeking land and debt repayment, Jefferson wanted to obtain rights-of-way through Indian country for roads that would knit the growing nation together, to consolidate the newly acquired western territory of the Louisiana Purchase, and to secure the Mississippi valley against foreign invasion. The Spanish presence in Florida was a particular concern; Jefferson noted in 1808 that the United States needed a strong buffer of militia between Indians and Spanish-controlled Florida.

Jefferson's negotiating team produced mixed results, with the Cherokees and the Creeks reluctantly ceding as little land as possible and the Chickasaws and the Choctaws offering more. The Treaty of Mount Dexter with the Choctaws, made in 1805, illustrates the treaty terms most sought by the United States during this period. In exchange for a large cession of lands in southern Mississippi Territory, the United States paid $50,000, $48,000 of which was to enable the tribe "to discharge the debt due to their merchants and traders. . . ." Jefferson focused heavily on the location of the ceded lands in relation to U.S. military objectives in the South. A treaty the same year with the Creeks included allowance of a horse path through Creek country as well as the sought-after land cession, but compensation paid was not specifically targeted for debt repayment.

In the Northwest Territory, then governed by a young William Henry Harrison, the federal government's objective was to prevent Indian wars by removing non-Indian settlers trespassing on Indian lands and to facilitate cessions by resolving boundary disputes among the many tribes in that area and fostering Indian assimilation. As traditional means of subsistence declined for the tribes, treaties on such terms became easier to achieve. In the 1809 Treaty of Fort Wayne with the Delaware, Potawatomi, Miami, and Eel River tribes, for example, the United States acquired more than two and a half million acres at less than two cents an acre, giving the United States control over the land in the Old Northwest. In words that ring hollow in hindsight, Harrison assured the Indians that "[t]he United States would always adhere to their engagements. To do otherwise would be offensive to the great spirit and all the world would look upon them as a faithless people." This expressed concern about world opinion probably counted for little with federal officials, because the European powers of the day were busy conducting their own colonial campaigns. For them to condemn the United States in its treatment of the Indians would have been hypocritical and contrary to their own interests.

Other treaties of this era, such as the treaty with the Osage made in 1808 and ratified in 1810, affirmed that the Indians would not sell lands to any foreign power or to citizens of the United States without approval of the federal government, and offered certificates redeemable for trade at the factory or fort, but only to Indians who remained friendly to the United States. The treaties of this decade reflect the growing inequality of power between the United States and the Indian nations, the tribes acknowledging the friendship and protection of the federal government and the treaties themselves establishing terms that were less and less accommodating to the tribes. At the same time, these treaties also acted as a relatively new form of political recognition of the tribes. By attesting to the legitimacy of the Indian tribes with whom it signed formal treaties, as well as the tribes' "Indian title" to their lands, the United States was consolidating the status of Indian nations as distinct political entities. Although the U.S. negotiators may not have intended this result of governmental recognition, the ingrained practice of dealing through treaties led the United States along that path.

Although the Treaty of Fort Wayne (Treaty with the Delaware, Etc.–June 7, 1803) succeeded in shifting land from tribes to the United States, it did not produce peace with the Indians, many of whom considered its Indian signers unauthorized to make such an agreement. Siding with the British in the War of 1812, these Indians also suffered the consequences of U.S. victory. Indeed, Francis Paul Prucha, who has written definitive works on Indian treaties, describes the War of 1812 as "a watershed in the history of treaty making with the Indians." With defeat of the British in 1812 and the Creeks in 1814, the Indians no longer posed a serious threat east of the Mississippi, and the United States assumed the dominant position in North America. Postwar treaties with Indian tribes confirmed this arrangement through terms that were less and less accommodating to the tribes. For example, the punitive 1814 treaty with the Creeks at Fort Jackson ceded immense Creek land holdings, roughly twenty million acres in Alabama and Georgia, without compensation. Under the treaty, the land was deemed "an equivalent for all expenses incurred in prosecuting the war to its termination." The treaty also gave the United States rights to establish military and trading posts and roads within Creek territory, and all hostile Creeks who had fought against the United States were to be surrendered.

Over the next fifteen years, treaties with the Indians produced larger and larger land cessions. With lands now available west of the Mississippi through the Louisiana Purchase, the United States began to seek relinquishment of all Indian lands east of the river and removal of the tribes to guaranteed lands in the West. Although this idea did not originate after the War of 1812, it was only after the war that provisions for removal of the Indians, entailing exchange of lands east of the river for lands to the west, found their way into the treaties. One illustration of this new thrust was the treaty of 1817 with the Cherokee, in which they gave up two large tracts in Georgia and North Carolina for land of equivalent size on the Arkansas and White rivers. Eleven years later, the same group of western Cherokee signed another treaty moving them beyond the western boundary of the Arkansas Territory, with emphatic language promising them a "permanent home, . . . that shall never, in all future time, be embarrassed by having extended around it the lines, or placed over it the jurisdiction of a Territory or State. . . ." Although many Cherokees steadfastly resisted this plan, a significant number had chosen to move west.

Along with the dissenting group of eastern Cherokees, many other tribes were unwilling to exchange lands and remove. So, with them, the United States settled for cession of the largest tracts possible, reserving small domains for the tribes and heavily promoting the tribes' shift to agrarian pursuits.

One interesting issue that arose with regard to these reserves was whether the reserved lands could be held by the Indians in private ownership, or fee simple. A treaty in 1817 negotiated with the Wyandot, Delaware, Shawnee, Seneca, and others at the Rapids of the Miami incorporated such a scheme. But this form of tribal landholding threatened the legally questionable but rapidly exploding private market for rights to acquire former Indian lands once the United States extinguished the Indians' right of possession. These "rights of preemption" would be valueless if the Indians acquired full ownership through the treaty. So the treaty had to be modified before the Senate would ratify it; and this treaty, as well as future treaties with other tribes, specified that reserved lands would be held "in the same manner as Indian reservations have been heretofore held."

With little room to bargain in this immediate postwar period, the Indians focused on the form and amount of their compensation. A particular concern of the United States was to avoid perpetual annuities as much as possible, because they were inconsistent with the U.S. goal of assimilation. Like rehabilitative alimony in modern-day divorce cases, payments to Indians were to be made only for the period of time it would take, as treaty negotiator William Clark wrote, "to teach them to subsist themselves by the arts of civilized life. . . ." In the treaty of 1825 that

Clark negotiated with the Osages, for example, livestock, farming utensils, and technical assistance were primary elements. A treaty of 1826 with the Potawatomi, typical for its time, promised annual sums for the education of Indian youth.

Toward the end of the 1820s, as positions of power and tactics changed, U.S. negotiators began to suggest that treaties were not the best way of dealing with the tribes. In the South, Andrew Jackson, who had risen to prominence in wars with the Creeks, argued that Indians have only "possessory rights to the soil, for the purpose of hunting and not the right to domain," concluding that "[C]ongress has the full power, by law, to regulate all the concerns of the Indians." Jackson rejected the idea that Indians were independent nations with rights of sovereignty, a position echoed in the statement of the secretary of war, Henry Calhoun, that "it is perfectly absurd to hold treaties with those within our limits, as they neither are, nor can be, independent of our government." This critique of treaty making was to gain force over time; but the practice continued for more than another forty years, with more than sixty-seven Indian treaties ratified while Jackson himself was president.

Treaties of the Jacksonian period of the 1830s pressed hard on the Indians to remove from areas in the East that were occupied or coveted by non-Indians. In the Old Northwest, a majority of the treaties provided for the reduction of the land base without removal. But several provided for permissive removal and eight for obligatory removal. Some of these treaties reserved land for chiefs or other individuals or bands that refused to migrate beyond the Mississippi.

In the South, even more powerful storm clouds of removal gathered. The best-known treaties during this time involve the Cherokee, whose national sovereignty and right to refuse sale of their lands had been recognized in the Treaties of Hopewell (Treaty with the Cherokee, 1785) and Holston (Treaty with the Cherokee, 1791). When Georgia boldly extended its laws over Cherokee territory, and the federal government could not persuade the remaining Cherokees to sell their land and leave for the Indian Territory, the stage was set for a national debate on the sanctity of Indian treaties. A bill to remove the Cherokee without their consent made its way through the Congress, prompting angry protests and avid defense.

Protestant minister Jeremiah Evarts was the most vocal and eloquent proponent of keeping treaty promises to the Indians, arguing that the very signing of these treaties implied that Indian communities had governments of their own not subject to the laws of the United States. Not only did the Constitution require adherence to the treaties, but so did Christian morality, which made it a sin to violate one's solemn commitments.

Georgia and its supporters, including Baptist missionary Reverend Isaac McCoy and Georgia politician Wilson Lumpkin, contended in response that treaties had been a huge mistake and were nothing more than a mockery and a farce. How, Lumpkin asked, could a guardian make a government-to-government agreement with its own ward? Those sharing his view pointed to the treaty provisions acknowledging the Cherokees' dependence on the United States, as well as the reality of changed circumstances. Although agreements are made precisely to protect against changed circumstances, that fact did not appear to give Lumpkin or the others of his ilk any pause. In the end, the Cherokee bill passed; Jackson signed it into law on May 28, 1830. Unwilling to acquiesce, the Cherokee made passionate appeals to Congress and pursued their cause through litigation before the U.S. Supreme Court. In two decisions rendered by Chief Justice John Marshall in 1832, the Court affirmed the Cherokees' status as a "domestic dependent nation" (*Cherokee Nation v. Georgia*) occupying and governing a territory that was not subject to Georgia state law (*Worcester v. Georgia*). These decisions established rules of interpretation, or canons of construction, for Indian treaties. Among those rules were requirements that treaties be interpreted as the Indians would have understood them and that ambiguities in treaty language be resolved in favor of protecting the Indians' sovereignty and property. In effect, the Court established, as a general default position, that treaties would not defeat preexisting Indian rights, whether inherent in the tribes or recognized in earlier treaties, unless Congress was clear in expressing its intent to do so. These principles reflected basic rules of contract interpretation that favored the much weaker party in negotiations, especially when that party is forced to negotiate in a foreign language. They also may have stemmed from the Court's awareness that Indians were not sewn into the constitutional fabric in any way that resembled consent.

The Jackson administration snubbed Chief Justice Marshall's decision and continued to foist removal treaties on the Cherokee and other south-

ern tribes. Even as the debate over Cherokee removal swirled about the Capitol, the Choctaw capitulated to what they believed was inevitable, signing the Treaty of Dancing Rabbit Creek (Treaty with the Choctaw, 1830). Indeed, Jackson's negotiators had told them that, if they refused to move west, state law would be imposed on them, and their tribal existence would no longer be recognized. The treaty offered many inducements and reassurances to secure the Choctaws' land cessions and emigration. Departing from past practice, the new lands west of the Mississippi were granted to the tribe in fee simple, "to inure to them while they shall exist as a nation and live on it." Furthermore, the United States promised that, in exchange for removal, it would secure to the Choctaws "the jurisdiction and government of all the persons and property that may be within their limits" and would prevent the establishment of any state or federal territory upon their lands. Protection against unauthorized intruders as well as domestic and foreign enemies was included as well. And additional annuities and schooling for Choctaw youth were also part of the package, along with houses for the chiefs. For those who could not bring themselves to leave, individual lands would be allotted in fee within the ceded territory.

The treaty with the Choctaw was followed over the next three years by similar treaties with the Chickasaw, the Creeks, and the Seminoles. But the Cherokees, most of whom had refused to leave for the West under the 1817 and 1828 treaties, tried to resist removal, staking their position on the favorable ruling they had received from the U.S. Supreme Court. At this point, the United States was able to exploit a division within the Cherokee Nation, one that pitted the Treaty Party, made up of those who wanted the best bargain possible in light of inevitable removal, against a group of adamant removal opponents. Only 350 Cherokee among the nearly 20,000 remaining in Georgia supported the Treaty of New Echota in 1835, which was tailored much like the Choctaw Treaty of Dancing Rabbit Creek, ceding eastern lands in exchange for new lands in the West to be held in fee simple. While the payment amounts differed, the only major distinction between the Cherokee and Choctaw treaties was that the Cherokee agreement did not allow individual allotments within the ceded lands.

More than 15,000 Cherokees signed a petition protesting the treaty of 1835 and attesting to its illegitimacy. Nonetheless, President Jackson forcibly and brutally carried out the removal. Although the suffering of the Cherokee was immense, it was redeemed to some extent by the treaty provisions affirming political autonomy and land rights of the Indian nations, born of the Cherokees' victory in *Worcester v. Georgia* and the forceful pro-treaty rhetoric of Jeremiah Evarts and others. Even President Jackson could not abandon treaty making, though he thought it a farce. The practice was too embedded in American and Native thinking about proper ways of conducting relations.

During this same period, outside the South the same pressures for removal prevailed, and U.S. treaty policy took a similar form. However, in the Old Northwest, the tribes were smaller and had been moved about on numerous occasions already, leading to some variations from the southern treaties. Thus, although groups of the Ho-Chunk and Potawatomi tribes entered into relatively standard removal treaties, some other tribes managed to stay put. The western bands of Chippewa, for example, made the treaty of 1837, signed at Fort Snelling, in which they gave up large wooded tracts in eastern Minnesota and north central Wisconsin in exchange for annuities, settlement of traders' claims, payoffs to powerful leaders, and retention of hunting, fishing, and rice-gathering rights on the ceded lands "during the pleasure of the President of the United States." Although President Zachary Taylor tried to effect removal in 1850, the Chippewa remained in place, and the unilateral nature of the removal order ultimately led the Supreme Court to declare it void.

Removal fever also found its way into treaties with the New York tribes. A powerful land company held preemption rights to the Indian lands and wanted the Indian title extinguished. Furthermore, the City of Buffalo was eager to expand into areas then part of the Iroquois territory. Treaties in 1831 and 1832 with the Menominee tribe of Wisconsin had provided land for westward-migrating Oneidas. But the Treaty of Buffalo Creek in 1838 with the Seneca and other New York Indians succeeded in achieving land cessions without actually resettling the tribes on the territory in Kansas that was set aside for them. The Seneca and the Oneida remaining in New York stayed on in the state, albeit on tracts much smaller than before.

The removal plan, premised as it was on the potential for complete separation of Indian from non-Indian populations, broke down in the 1840s and 1850s as improved transportation, acquisition of new territories in the Southwest and Northwest, and increased immigration caused non-Indian settlement to catch up with the Indians' western lands, destroying their traditional means of subsistence. Suddenly, federal treaty policy had to contend with new clashes between settlers and the tribes and had to find ways the two groups could coexist. Many of the newly encountered tribes violently resisted encroachment on their lands, and combating them stretched the capacity of the relatively young nation. Moreover, the legal apparatus that accompanied some of these new tribes, especially the fee land title of the Pueblo tribes formerly under Mexican rule, presented new challenges. Treaties continued to be the preferred mode of conducting Indian relations during these years, and dozens were ratified; but there were notable exceptions and breakdowns in the process, and the types of treaty terms began to shift.

Treaties of the 1840s and 1850s focused less on removal west and more on confining the western Indians on smaller and smaller reservation tracts so that non-Indian migration and settlement would not be impeded. The alternative possibilities of curtailing emigration or protecting the Indians against trespass were politically difficult for a U.S. government accountable only to the non-Indians; and the old policy of removing the tribes to an area beyond white immigration and settlement was no longer physically possible. Confinement on small reservations was the preferred solution simply because there was no place further west to move the Indians that had not already been settled by non-Indians or occupied by other tribes.

Sometimes the demands of non-Indian settlers were so great that multiple tribes had to be collected, more or less arbitrarily, onto a single reservation. Thus, for example, in the Pacific Northwest most of the treaties were made with "confederated tribes and bands" in order to limit the amount of territory set aside for the Indians. The experience in California was even more extreme. After the Treaty of Guadalupe Hidalgo ended the war with Mexico in 1848, the U.S. Senate refused to ratify any treaties at all with the California Indians, because the lands that the proposed treaties had set aside for them were considered too valuable by the whites, and there was nowhere else to place the reservations. Only after several decades had passed and sympathy for the "landless" California Indians had mounted did Congress and the executive branch establish small reservations, or *rancherias*.

Elsewhere in the West, however, treaty making was actively under way during this period of the 1840s and 1850s. On the plains, for example, the destruction of buffalo herds that accompanied western settlement prompted the commissioner of Indian affairs, William Medill, to seek relocation of the Indians into "colonies" north and south of the main routes of migration. The Indians would also be compensated for the rights-of-way and for loss of the buffalo. Thus arose the Treaty of Fort Laramie of 1851 with the Sioux, Cheyenne, Arapaho, Crow, Assiniboine, Gros Ventre, Mandan, and Arikara, in which boundaries were set among the tribes and with the United States, and the Indians pledged peace with the United States and cessation of hostilities among themselves. The tribes further agreed to allow the United States to build forts and roads within their territories and to pay restitution to non-Indians harmed while lawfully passing through the Indian lands. For its part, the United States promised generous annuities of $50,000 per year for 50 years and to protect the Indians from predation by the whites. This treaty was later superseded by others less favorable to the tribes.

A few years later, in negotiations with tribes west of Missouri and Iowa, another commissioner of Indian affairs, George W. Manypenny, made a concerted policy of including treaty provisions for allotment of reserved lands. This new policy of allotment was designed to break up the tribal estate by converting tribal ownership into private ownership title held by individual tribal members. Although some federal policymakers tried to argue that private ownership would benefit the Indians, a powerful reality was that allotment served non-Indian interests in land acquisition. Once in private ownership, the lands became much more accessible to non-Indians through tax sales, adverse possession, and sharp dealing. Foreshadowing Congress's enactment of the General Allotment Act of 1887, this treaty policy of allotment also envisioned termination of tribal existence in the near future. Another feature of Manypenny's treaty policy was an end to permanent annuities as a form of payment for land cessions. Under his treaties, the Indians were required to relinquish all claims to funds owed under previous treaties, and newly promised payments were to be paid to the tribes on a rapid timetable. This new method of payment was consistent with the plan for near-term termination of tribal entities. Among the many treaties made on this basis were those with the

Otoe and Missouria tribes in 1854 and the Shawnee in the same year.

A series of treaties made during this period with the tribes of the Pacific Northwest, negotiated by territorial governor Isaac Stevens, largely adhered to the framework of the Manypenny treaties. Nonetheless, they had to take into account the tribes' resistance to moving from their ancestral lands and giving up their traditional fishing practices. So Governor Stevens strategically located the reservations so as to avoid non-Indian settlements while protecting the tribes' means of subsistence. Furthermore, he included provisions reserving to the tribes, on their ceded lands, "[t]he right of taking fish, at all usual and accustomed grounds and stations . . . in common with all citizens of the Territory. . . ." In a series of later cases, the federal courts eventually ruled that this provision guaranteed one-half the catch from these areas to the tribes, decisions that provoked angry outcries from non-Indian commercial and sport fishers.

Notwithstanding the recognition of traditional fishing practices in the Stevens treaties, most treaties of the 1840s and 1850s, and even more so those of the 1860s, focused on transforming Indians into agriculturalists. Some treaties, such as those with the Mescalero and Jicarilla Apache in 1853, actually included agreements by the Indians to settle on the lands allotted to them and to "cultivate the soil and raise flocks and herds for a subsistence." However, this plan was not always backed up by establishment of reservations with soil and water adequate for successful farming. Non-Indian settlers were reluctant to see rich agricultural lands in Indian ownership and pressed the United States to exclude them from the reservations.

Indian treaty making slowed somewhat during the Civil War. Yet during this time, a powerful debate over the desirability and utility of Indian treaties emerged within the federal government, reaching a crescendo in 1864. Military leaders such as General John Pope wanted to employ the overwhelming force of the United States to end the treaty system, stop the flow of annuity payments under earlier treaties, and manage the Indians regardless of their consent. The commissioner of Indian affairs, William Dole, strongly resisted this approach, arguing instead that the United States should continue its long-standing policy of using force only to the point where the Indians could be induced to agree to treaty terms. Otherwise, the Indians would more strongly resist any "civilizing" efforts by the United States.

Dole's position won out, but only for the next five years. Skirmishes with the Indians along the emigrant trails and fears for the security of the newly constructed transcontinental railway led the United States to sponsor the Peace Commission in 1867, giving over treaty-negotiating authority to a specially qualified group of civilian and military leaders. Its charge was to minimize the causes for war among the Indians while securing the routes west and moving the Indians toward greater assimilation. Typical of the treaties that emerged from that process were those with the Sioux and the Navajo, both made in 1868. These treaties attempted to allay the Indians' concerns about loss of land and sovereignty by securing tracts to them for their "absolute and undisturbed use and occupation" and positing that no cessions of land shall be valid "unless executed and signed by at least three-fourths of all the adult male Indians occupying the same." The United States also agreed to arrest and punish "bad men among the whites" who committed wrongs on the Indians and to compensate those Indians who were thus injured. At the same time, the Indians agreed to turn over to the United States, for punishment, any "bad men among the Indians" who committed wrongs against outsiders. Most of the provisions in these treaties, however, were devoted to pressing the Indians toward lives as farmers and ranchers. The United States obligated itself to build schools, to provide agents and teachers who would live on the reservation, and to allocate tracts for farming, seed, and agricultural implements to any tribal member so inclined. The Indians, in turn, agreed to compel their children up to the age of sixteen to attend school. For the Navajos in particular, a major inducement for signing the treaty was the opportunity to return from exile to their ancestral homeland in the Southwest.

The End of Treaty Making

Although non-Indian opposition to Indian treaties had surfaced during the Jackson administration, fueled by the views of Jackson himself, antagonism toward such instruments became more pointed and widespread at the end of the 1860s. The reasons were manifold. Some pointed to the inability of the U.S. military, stretched thin across the growing nation, to make good on American promises to protect boundary lines established in the treaties. As Episcopal bishop Henry Whipple wrote, "We send ambassadors to make a treaty as with our equals, knowing that every provision of that treaty will be our own, [and] that those with whom we make it cannot compel us to observe it. . . ." Many spokesmen of the time contended that it was a farce to treat with Indians as if they were separate and sovereign nations when they had no effective governments and laws of their own. Although such statements ignored the traditions of dispute resolution and social control that remained alive within tribal communities, they also reflected the deterioration of many such institutions under the impact of non-Indian settlement and Indian administration.

Ultimately, in 1871, the Congress abolished future treaty making with the Indians. Among other things, the House of Representatives had become frustrated over the fact that it was required to appropriate funds to fulfill treaty obligations but did not have a voice in the decision to ratify those treaties. Although the United States continued to make agreements with the Indian nations and to enshrine those agreements in legislation, the era of treaty making had come to an end because treaties no longer served federal policy objectives. The United States had already acquired vast quantities of Indian land and didn't need treaties to finish the job.

Carole Goldberg

References and Further Reading

Andrew, John A., III. 1992. *From Revivals to Removal: Jeremiah Evarts, the Cherokee Nation, and the Search for the Soul of America*. Athens: University of Georgia Press.

Banner, Stuart. 2005. *How the Indians Lost Their Land: Law and Power on the Frontier.* Cambridge, MA: Harvard University Press.

Jones, Dorothy. 1982. *License for Empire: Colonialism by Treaty in Early America.* Chicago: University of Chicago Press.

Kades, Eric. 2000. "The Dark Side of Efficiency: *Johnson v. M'Intosh* and the Expropriation of American Indian Lands," 148 *University of Pennsylvania Law Review* 1065–1190.

Kappler, Charles J., ed. 1904. *Indian Affairs: Laws and Treaties*, vol. 2, *Treaties*. Washington, DC: Government Printing Office.

Kappler, Charles J., ed. 1975. *Indian Treaties 1778–1883*, 3rd ed. New York: Interland.

Newton, Nell Jessup, ed. 2005. *Cohen's Handbook of Federal Indian Law.* Newark, NJ: LexisNexis.

Prucha, Francis Paul. 1994. *American Indian Treaties: The History of a Political Anomaly.* Berkeley: University of California Press.

Richter, Daniel K. 2001. *Facing East from Indian Country: A Native History of Early America.* Cambridge, MA: Harvard University Press.

Satz, Ronald. 1975. *American Indian Policy in the Jacksonian Era.* Lincoln: University of Nebraska Press.

Trennert, Robert A., Jr. 1975. *Alternative to Extinction: Federal Indian Policy and the Beginnings of the Reservation System—1846–51.* Philadelphia: Temple University Press.

Legislation, Treaty Substitutes, and Indian Treaties

Legislation affecting the indigenous tribes and peoples in the United States included laws that stated general policy directions, laws that established and regulated the burgeoning Indian Service, laws that authorized appropriations, and laws that appropriated funds to carry out Congress's intent. All these laws were significant for the dealings of the United States with Indian tribes and peoples. During the treaty period, the laws provided a framework for the U.S. representatives who met with the Indian tribes to negotiate treaties. Legislation delineated Indian policy, provided the framework for Indian treaties, and appropriated funds to carry out federal policy. Indian legislation expressed Congress's sense of the nature of contemporary American society, and the progression of Indian legislation reflected the progression of American social organization more broadly considered. After Congress ended treaty making with the Indian tribes in 1871, legislation provided the framework for the negotiation of the agreements that substituted for treaties in the late nineteenth century. These treaty substitutes were subsequently ratified as statutes rather than as treaties; both houses of Congress voted on the agreements, not only the Senate as is the case for treaties. During the twentieth century, intergovernmental agreements between the tribes and the United States and individual states again became an important way of regulating the relations between the United States and the Indian tribes.

In the United States, Indian legislation has included congressional statements of general Indian policy, laws creating and regulating the Indian Service, laws and treaties dealing with specific tribes or groups of tribes, and appropriations acts that provided the funds to carry out Indian policy. Most studies of federal Indian policy have concerned statements of general Indian policy, legislation directed at specific groups of Indians, and the implementation of these statutes. The laws creating and regulating the agencies responsible for carrying out Indian affairs, and appropriation acts, although less studied, have been important in determining the course of Indian affairs.

General Indian legislation at times shaped events in the field and at times responded to them. But general Indian legislation was even more profoundly influenced by the general trend of federal legislation. This is because an objective of Congress in framing Indian legislation has been to influence the direction of development of Indian communities. The desired direction has been influenced by developments in American society and by prevailing assumptions about the likely directions for development. Indian legislation followed trends in the society, including general laws enacted by Congress to apply to all citizens. In America, Harold Hyman has suggested that five laws contributed to a singularly American development of public policy: the Land Ordinance of 1785 and the Northwest Ordinance of 1787, enacted by the Continental Congress before the ratification of the Constitution; the Homestead and Land Grant College Acts of 1862, enacted by the first Civil War Congress; and the GI Bill of 1944, enacted in anticipation of the end of World War II (Hyman 1986). Each of these laws was important in shaping Indian policy, although none was specifically directed toward Native American people.

Trade and Intercourse

Prior to American independence, colonial legislatures and royal provincial governors dealt with tribes within the confines of their territories. After the French and Indian War, the Crown preempted management of relations with the tribes of the Ohio valley. Article IX of the Articles of Confederation, adopted in 1778 during the American Revolution, gave the Continental Congress the power to deal with Indian tribes located in the West on a government-to-government basis; the states were in charge of relations with local tribes.

The Land Ordinance of 1785 provided for a rectangular survey of the area west of the Appalachian Mountains, with one 640-acre section in each township to be devoted to support of the public schools. The Northwest Ordinance of 1787 specified the methods of sale and settlement of the surveyed lands. By providing for the organization of new states in the territory north and west of the Ohio River, the ordinance contemplated the organization of the western territories on the model of

the eastern states. The ordinance promoted and accelerated the westward expansion of the United States.

The source of federal authority in Indian affairs is the Constitution, which gives the Congress plenary power in Indian affairs. The commerce clause (Article I, Section 8) provides that "Congress shall have the power . . . to regulate commerce with foreign nations, and among the several states, and with the Indian tribes." The supremacy clause (Article VI) provides that the "Constitution, and the laws of the United States which shall be made in pursuance thereof; and all treaties made, or which shall be made, under the authority of the United States, shall be the supreme law of the land." Initially, as implied in the commerce clause, the emphasis of congressional legislation was on regulating trade with the Indian tribes. The Indian Trade and Intercourse Acts, enacted between 1790 and 1834, provided for the disposal of Indian lands and the regulation of Indian trade.

The Indian Intercourse Acts went beyond the regulation of trade, however. Congress attempted to regulate the legal relations between Indians and whites and, most significantly, to promote the "civilization" or acculturation of the Indians by providing material assistance and instruction in agriculture. Perhaps necessary in an era when the United States contended with such European powers as Great Britain, Spain, and France for domination of the North American continent, the Indian Intercourse Acts were designed to insure adherence to United States hegemony in North America on the part of the Indian tribes. The conclusion of the War of 1812 served to secure the northern frontier of the United States. Although the war did not result in American expansion to the north as some Americans had hoped it would, competition with European powers for domination of the North American continent diminished. The Indian Civilization Fund Act of 1819 (3 *Stat.* 516) portended future developments in Indian affairs. The act, which remained in force until 1873, authorized annual appropriations to the Civilization Fund, from which "benevolent societies," for the most part Protestant missions to the Indians, received funds to acculturate Native Americans by instructing Indian adults in the European American style of agriculture and Indian children in reading, writing, and arithmetic. Many of the treaties negotiated by the United States with the Indian tribes during this period included provisions for education and training in agriculture along with regulation of trade and commercial relations with whites.

Removal

In 1800, the United States comprised sixteen states: Vermont (admitted in 1791), Kentucky (admitted in 1792), and Tennessee (admitted in 1796), in addition to the original thirteen colonies. By 1830, an additional seven states had joined the union, including Louisiana (admitted in 1804) and Missouri (admitted in 1821), the first states to be organized with territory west of the Mississippi River. In addition, by 1830 territorial governments had been organized for Michigan (in 1805), Arkansas (in 1819), and Florida (in 1822). The population of the United States, enumerated at 5.3 million at the 1800 census, had grown to 12.8 million by 1830. Growing population and the organization of territorial and state governments in the West and South put pressure on Indian people living east of the Mississippi River.

Removal, the forced or voluntary relocation of Indians from tribal lands occupied at contact to new lands in the West, began before Congress enacted the Indian Removal Act of 1830 (4 *Stat.* 411). Sometimes removal was voluntary, as tribes moved west to avoid European Americans or in search of increased opportunity. But often removal was coerced, as whites harassed Indians and as many favored removal because they believed that the isolation of Indians from whites would promote acculturation to European American culture, or "civilization."

The Indian Removal Act envisioned the exchange of Indian lands east of the Mississippi River for new lands to the west. Eastern Indians were to be resettled at the western frontier of white settlement. The act resulted in the negotiation of removal treaties with most of the eastern tribes and forced and voluntary relocations to "Indian country" west of the Mississippi River during the 1830s and 1840s. Some foresaw the development of a "permanent Indian frontier" to the west of Missouri and Arkansas. However, the migration of U.S. citizens to northern Mexico, followed by the establishment of the Texas Republic (1836) and the Mexican War (1846–1848), together with the resolution of the "Oregon Question" (1846), stimulated westward expansion by white Americans and limited the extent of Indian country to present-day

Oklahoma and the Dakotas. Only isolated reservations remained in Kansas and Nebraska as a result of a second round of removals in the 1850s.

Concentration

During the 1840s, the United States acquired a vast inland empire. The acquisition of territory in the Northwest following settlement of the Oregon Question (1846) and in the Southwest following the annexation of Texas (1845), as well as the American victory in the Mexican War (1848), provided the United States, at the beginning of the 1850s, with an expanded western empire. A large number of Indians, who were increasingly likely to conflict with whites, lived in the newly acquired territories. But Congress contemplated a civilian administration of Indian affairs as part of its regulation of the new interior regions of the continent. When Congress created a "Home Department," the Department of the Interior, in 1849, it transferred Indian affairs to the new department, along with the General Land Office, the Patent Office, and the Pension Office ("An Act to Establish the Home Department," 9 *Stat.* 395).

The Treaty of Guadalupe Hidalgo (1848) ended the war with Mexico. Mexico ceded a significant amount of land to the United States, amounting to the northern third of the nation. Article IX of the treaty provided that citizens of Mexico residing in the ceded territory would become citizens of the United States. This provision affected the Pueblo Indians of New Mexico, who had been recognized as citizens of Mexico. The treaty provided the United States with a vast inland empire and stimulated the continued development of the West.

Prior to the Civil War, the objectives of removal of Indians from the path of white settlement and concentration of the tribes in isolated areas guided U.S. Indian policy. In the 1850s, the concentration of Indians on reservations (limited geographic territories reserved for Indian tribes) replaced the old objective of simple removal. On the reservations, Indians would be protected from whites and helped by Indian agents to adapt to white civilization. Thus, for example, the Treaty of Fort Laramie of 1851 (11 *Stat.* 749) provided for a reservation for the western Sioux, and the treaty of 1854 with the Chippewa (10 *Stat.* 1109) reserved lands in northern Wisconsin and Minnesota for the Ojibwe. These and other treaties freed land for settlement by white Americans even as politicians of the new Republican Party pressed for more liberal land measures to facilitate westward expansion by whites.

The early reservation system depended upon the army to enforce compliance with the new boundaries and prevent armed conflict between tribes and between Indians and whites. It also required an efficient administration of the Indian Office, which had the responsibility of administering the reservations and, increasingly, of providing food rations to substitute for hunting grounds given up by the tribes. The Indian Office's responsibilities increased as a result of the many treaties negotiated during the 1850s. However, little improvement in Indian Office administration followed the decade's rash of treaty making. The coming of the Civil War exacerbated administrative problems. Although the pace of white westward movement hardly slowed, the army withdrew troops from frontier areas to fight the Confederacy, and Congress and the president devoted primary attention to the war rather than to Indian administration.

Four laws enacted in 1862 by the first Civil War Congress set the stage for the development of the West and influenced subsequent federal Indian legislation. The Homestead Law of 1862 (12 *Stat.* 392) provided for the distribution of the public lands, in quarter-section parcels of 160 acres each upon payment of a nominal fee, to settlers who would agree to improve the land and live on it for five years. The size of the homesteads, larger than the minimum required for subsistence farming, signaled Congress's intention that the West would be settled by entrepreneurial farmers, who would raise cash crops. The Morrill or Land Grant College Act (12 *Stat.* 503) provided for education in the "agricultural and mechanic arts" to the children of homesteaders. The Pacific Railroad Act (12 *Stat.* 489) would provide a means to transport goods to market, whereas the Department of Agriculture Act (12 *Stat.* 387) provided for the development of a research agency that was to investigate the best methods of agricultural production. When the Pacific Railroad was completed in 1869, thereby increasing traffic between the East and the West, pressure on Indian lands intensified.

After the Union victory in the Civil War (1865), the United States established a new federal agency, the Freedmen's Bureau, to provide limited support to African American former slaves who had been freed as a result of the war ("An Act to Establish a Bureau for the Relief of Freedom and Refugees,"

1865, *13 Stat.* 507). These efforts were supported by missionary associations, including several that were also involved in missions to the Indians supported by the Civilization Fund. In the Indian Territory, tribes that had supported the Confederacy were forced to sign Reconstruction treaties. The treaties with the Cherokee, Choctaw, Chickasaw, Creek, and Seminole tribes (1866) freed the slaves held by those tribes, granted freedmen tribal membership, and subjugated the tribes to authority of the federal government. The Cherokee Reconstruction Treaty of 1866 (14 *Stat.* 799), for example, in Article IX declared that Cherokee freedmen and "all free colored persons who were in the country at the commencement of the rebellion . . . shall have all the rights of native Cherokees."

The end of the Civil War increased the pace of Indian removals from the states of Kansas and Nebraska and from the western Great Plains. In the decade and a half following the end of the Civil War, the Indian Office removed a large number of tribes to Indian Territory, including such plains tribes as the Kiowa, the Comanche, the Cheyenne, and the Arapahoe, and tribes formerly settled on reservations in Kansas and Nebraska, including the Sac and the Fox, the Potawatomi, the Wichita, the Osage, the Pawnee, the Iowa, and the Otoe.

Postwar treaties with noncombatant tribes reflected renewed federal power. The Navajo treaty of 1868 (15 *Stat.* 667) permitted the Navajo, who had been removed from their homeland to eastern New Mexico in 1864, to return to familiar territory to the west but within defined reservation boundaries. The treaty also provided for the distribution of land to individuals "wishing to commence farming" (Article V), compulsory education for Navajo children (Article VI), and the construction of railroads across the new reservation (Article IX).

In 1865, Congress created a joint special committee "to conduct an inquiry into the condition of the Indian tribes and their treatment by the civil and military authorities" (13 *Stat.* 572). The Doolittle Committee, so named after its chairman, Senator J. R. Doolittle of Wisconsin, was a congressional response to the Indian wars and the political turmoil resulting from them. The committee found that the Indians were decreasing in population due to disease, wars, and loss of hunting grounds; it recommended against the transfer of the Indian Office to the War Department, a solution to the agency's administrative problems favored by some. Instead, the committee advocated the creation of boards of inspection to oversee civilian administration. Later in 1867, reporting to the Senate on "Indian hostilities on the frontier," Commissioner of Indian Affairs Nathaniel Taylor recommended an intensified program of tribal consolidation on reservations. Warlike tribes would be confined on large reservations from which all whites except government employees would be excluded, and an intensive acculturation program would be attempted.

Congress created the Indian Peace Commission, headed by Taylor, in 1867 (16 *Stat.* 319). The commission negotiated with many of the western tribes treaties that embodied the consolidation doctrine. A clear line should be drawn between civil and military responsibilities, the commission recommended. Opposed to transferring Indian affairs from the Interior Department to the War Department, the commission recommended a revision of the laws regulating intercourse with the Indians and administrative reforms to ensure "competent and faithful" personnel.

The recommendations of the Indian Peace Commission, together with the ongoing processes of removal and concentration, provided the Grant administration, which took office in 1869, with its Indian reform policy. Hailed by contemporaries as a new departure in Indian affairs, the Peace Policy, as the Grant reforms were known, attempted to improve administration rather than to reformulate the goals of federal activity. Two major elements of the Grant administration's program, church nomination of Indian Service officials and the creation of the Board of Indian Commissioners, were administrative changes. The third element was expressed as "Peace on the reservations, war off." Indians remaining on the reservations were to be subject to a purely civil administration; those leaving without permission were assumed to be at war with the United States and were to be subject to military discipline.

Congress created the Board of Indian Commissioners (BIC) in 1869 (16 *Stat.* 40). Similar to the boards of inspection called for by the Doolittle Commission, the BIC was no doubt modeled on the state boards of charities created by a number of states, beginning with Massachusetts in 1863. Like the state boards of charities, the BIC was an unpaid advisory body that visited Indian reservations, compiled statistics, and made recommendations on Indian administration. BIC members wanted to abolish reservations, the Indian Service, and tribalism. The Dawes Act of 1887 and subsequent Indian legislation to World War I reflected this point of view.

In a provision of the Indian Appropriations Act of 1871 (16 *Stat.* 566), Congress ended the treaty relationship with the tribes. Although the precipitating cause was the unwillingness of the House to be left out of the process of treaty making, terminating the treaty relationship was consistent with the spirit of the reservation policy, in which the domination of the United States was emphasized. The ending of the treaty relationship symbolized the federal government's objective of breaking up the tribal relationship and individualizing the Indians. Eli Parker, Grant's first commissioner of Indian affairs, had earlier requested an end to the "fiction" of treating the tribes as independent nations in his annual report for 1869.

As was true for all nineteenth-century social policy in the United States, work was favored over idleness. Congress viewed Indian labor as an essential part of the process of Indian "civilization." In 1875, in Section 3 of the Indian Appropriations Act, Congress attempted to make Indian labor a requirement for the receipt of rations. The act provided that

> [f]or the purpose of inducing Indians to labor and become self-supporting . . . the [Indian] agent shall require all able-bodied male Indians to perform service upon the reservation and the allowances provided for such Indians shall be distributed to them only upon condition of the performance of such labor. (18 *Stat.* 420)

Criminal jurisdiction remained an area of tribal autonomy. In *Ex Parte Crow Dog* (1883), the Supreme Court found that Indian tribes retained criminal jurisdiction over their members. In response, in a section of the Indian Appropriations Act of 1885 known as the Major Crimes Act (23 *Stat.* 385), Congress placed Indians accused of committing the crimes of "murder, manslaughter, rape, assault with intent to kill, arson, burglary, and larceny" under the jurisdiction of the United States, thus overriding tribal or other Indian authority.

Assimilation and Allotment

By the early 1880s, the concentration policy had to be abandoned as unworkable. There were fewer truly isolated regions to which Indians could be removed. Further, the results of removals, particularly of Northern Plains tribes to the Indian Territory, were unacceptable. Unaccustomed to the climate, Indians died at an increasing rate on the new reservations. When tribes such as the Ponca resisted removal, they found an increasingly sympathetic audience in white reform groups.

After the abandonment of removal as a policy, diminutions in the Indian land base resulted from such factors as the discovery of mineral resources on reservations and from the early experiments in allotment, in which surplus land remaining after each Indian had received an allotment of land was opened to settlement by whites. The discovery of gold in the Black Hills of Dakota Territory resulted in the Sioux Agreement of 1876, which removed the hills from the Great Sioux Reservation, opening them to white settlement and exploitation. Similarly, the discovery of gold and silver on the Ute Reservation in 1879, combined with an uprising against their agent, resulted in the removal of the Ute from their Colorado home. Although some reformers protested the Ute removals, they ultimately acquiesced. Albert B. Meacham, a prominent Indian reformer, served on the Ute Commission, which supervised the removal. White reformers supported land reduction schemes in part because they wanted Indians to adopt land use patterns similar to those of European Americans. In addition, white pressures on Indian lands were so great that reformers believed that the Indians "would have to give up most of their land to retain title to any" (Hagan 1976, 165).

If a tribe held good farmland, white pressures for removal led reformers to advocate allotment even where mineral resources were not discovered. They viewed allotment as doubly beneficial. The experience of property ownership would encourage civilization and acquisition by the Indians of the habits of hard work, thrift, and acquisitiveness, which were presumed to characterize the white population at its best. In addition, by providing protections for the Indian title, commonly a prohibition against alienation for a twenty-five-year period, allotment would forestall efforts at removal and enable the Indians to retain at least a portion of their homeland.

On the reservations of central and western Indian Territory, which were better suited to cattle grazing than to cultivation, a different pattern of white intrusion developed. The contractors who supplied the agencies with beef allowed the issue herds to graze on Indian lands. Texas cattlemen who began driving their herds north to Dodge City, Kansas, in the 1870s similarly exploited reservation grasslands. In the late 1870s, agents at the

Cheyenne, Arapahoe, and Kiowa-Comanche Reservations began to charge ranchers grazing fees, using the proceeds to supplement meager congressional appropriations for supplying the Indians with rations. Although the grazing fees were of doubtful legality, sporadic attempts by Washington officials to regulate their collection were ineffective until Congress legalized leasing allotments held by old or disabled Indians in 1891 (26 *Stat.* 794).

Allotment, the division of Indian lands held by a tribe in common into individually owned tracts, had a long history. The allotment of Indian lands was practiced as early as the seventeenth century in the American colonies. Before the Civil War, reservations in Alabama and Mississippi were allotted as a means of facilitating the sale of Indian lands to whites. After the war, the allotment of Indian reservations was employed as an expedient to prevent the removal of tribes to more remote areas, by demonstrating the willingness of tribal members to become civilized. Thus, the Santee Sioux of Nebraska, threatened with the loss of their reservation on the Niobrara River and removal to Indian Territory, petitioned the commissioner of Indian affairs in 1869 to allot their reservation so that they might hold secure tenure on it. Similarly, when the Omaha tribe of Nebraska was threatened with removal to Indian Territory in 1882, Alice C. Fletcher, the pioneer American ethnologist, proposed allotment as an alternative. Miss Fletcher was visiting the Omaha. She went to Washington to argue against the tribe's removal, carrying a petition requesting allotment. Successful in her mission, Miss Fletcher returned to supervise the allotment of the reservation. After the passage of the General Allotment Act of 1887, she was to supervise the allotment of several other plains reservations.

The frequency of special allotment acts applied to specific tribes both before and after the passage of the General Allotment Act led historian William T. Hagan to suggest that the course of policy development was little affected by the act. In his view, reservations would have been allotted with or without a general allotment law. Most of the treaties negotiated in the 1860s included provisions for eventual allotment; similarly, Congress in 1875 provided that Indians severing their relations to their tribes could homestead on public lands under the provisions of the Homestead Law (18 *Stat.* 402). The possession of private property, especially the separate farm, came to be viewed as the key to Indian civilization and to the maintenance of an Indian land base.

The General Allotment Act of 1887 (24 *Stat.* 388), also known as the Dawes Act after its sponsor, Senator Henry Dawes of Massachusetts, provided for the division of reservation lands, at the discretion of the president, into allotments, which became the property of individual Indians. Each allotment was a quarter section (160 acres) in area. Upon allotment, the Indian became a citizen. The title to the allotment was held in trust by the United States for twenty-five years. At the end of this period, the allottee received a fee simple patent to his allotment. Henceforth, he or she would enjoy full control of the allotted land, which became subject to property taxes. "Surplus" lands, those remaining after all Indians on a reservation had received their allotments, were to be sold by the United States in units not to exceed 160 acres. The objective of the act was the integration of the Indians into American society as independent farmers. Not coincidentally, through the surplus land sales and through an 1891 amendment (26 *Stat.* 794) permitting the leasing by non-Indians of allotments held by elderly and disabled Indians, the allotment policy facilitated the penetration of the remaining Indian lands by white ranchers and farmers. In general, the act, like the Homestead Act of 1862 that it resembled, reflected a land ideology that favored small landholdings and opposed in principle the ownership of units of land too large to be worked by an individual entrepreneur.

The Dawes Act made special provisions for railroad rights-of-way across reservations and for modifications in areas suitable only for grazing. The act probably accelerated the process of allotment, even though in many cases Congress enacted special legislation based on agreements with the affected tribes. For example, the Great Sioux Agreement of 1889 (25 *Stat.* 888), which created the Sioux Reservations of North and South Dakota, provided for their allotments. The Five Civilized Tribes of Indian Territory had been exempt from the provisions of the General Allotment Act. In 1893, however, Congress created a commission to negotiate the dissolution of the tribal governments and the allotment of tribal lands in "the Cherokee Nation, the Choctaw Nation, the Chickasaw Nation, the Muscogee (or Creek) Nation, [and] the Seminole Nation" (27 *Stat.* 557). The retired Senator Henry Dawes, the author of the General Allotment Act, served as the commission's first chairperson. The commission supervised the enrollment of members of the five tribes and attempted to negotiate allotment. When the tribes resisted, Congress enacted the Curtis Act of 1898 (30 *Stat.* 498). The Curtis Act

authorized the allotment of tribal lands, dissolved the tribal governments, and paved the way for the eventual admission of Oklahoma as a state.

The Dawes Act made no provision for the leasing of allotments. When Congress approved the leasing of allotments made to old people and the disabled in 1891 (26 *Stat*. 791), it also modified the size of allotments, providing for the allotment of one-eighth of a section (eighty acres) to each eligible individual and for double allotments of lands suited only for grazing. A series of additional congressional actions in the 1890s extended the scope of leasing. In 1894, Congress authorized the leasing of unsold surplus lands for farming as well as for grazing purposes (28 *Stat*. 305). Sections 13 and 23 of the Curtis Act of 1898 authorized the leasing of Indian Territory allotments and provided for mineral leases as well (30 *Stat*. 495). Congress broadened the criteria for permitting the leasing of allotments again in 1900, providing "inability," in addition to age and disability, as a ground for leasing (31 *Stat*. 229). The leasing provisions, combined with the surplus land provisions of the Dawes Act, permitted extensive white intrusion into what had been reservation lands.

The Burke Act of 1906 modified the citizenship provisions of the Dawes Act by deferring citizenship until expiration of the trust period (34 *Stat*. 182). However, the secretary of the interior could authorize the issuance of a fee simple patent to allottees he found to be competent before the end of the twenty-five-year trust period. For allottees found incompetent at the end of the twenty-five-year trust period, the trust period could be extended upon the order of the secretary. The immediate effect of the Burke Act, however, was probably to hasten the end of the trust period for many allottees. Competency commissions, particularly active during the Woodrow Wilson administration (1913–1921), were active in ending the trust period ahead of schedule.

A Transitional Period

The Buy Indian Act, Section 23 of the Act of June 23, 1910 (36 *Stat*. 861), provided that the Indian Service should buy Indian products and contract with Indian laborers in preference to non-Indian sources. This Progressive Era legislation was intended to promote the integration of American Indians into the economy of the United States and would become important a half century later as Indian tribes attempted to promote economic development. Congress amended the act during the 1980s and 1990s to promote federal government use of Indian energy sources and to allow Indian firms to participate in the Department of Defense's Mentor-Protégé Program (P. L. 100–581, 1988, 102 *Stat*. 2940; P. L. 103–345, 1994, 108 *Stat*. 4572). The Snyder Act of 1921 (42 *Stat*. 208) provided explicit authorization for federal expenditures "for the benefit, care, and assistance of the Indians throughout the United States," including education, health care, industrial development, the maintenance of water sources, and general expenses of government. The act represented a change in government policy because it departed from reliance on treaty provisions for the support of American Indians and represented the first recognition of a general federal obligation to Indian people.

Another post–World War I statute, the Indian Citizenship Act of 1924 (43 *Stat*. 253) made all Indians born in U.S. territory citizens of the United States. Citizenship as a status had long represented the goal of assimilationist white Indian reformers. The Indian Citizenship Act represented the high point of assimilation, as it envisioned the integration of Indian people into American society as individuals. Later Indian legislation would move away from the assimilationist goal and strengthen tribes.

Forty years of experience with the Dawes Act led to the recognition that it had failed to deal adequately with the "Indian problem." By the late 1920s, American Indians had not taken their places alongside white American farmers as independent entrepreneurs. Rather, the allotment policy had led to an even more drastic diminution in the Indian land base than had been envisioned by its framers. Unable to secure credit and inexperienced in farming, holding allotments in many cases too small to be economically viable, allottees sold or leased their holdings or lost their lands through nonpayment of state and local taxes. Allotments that remained in trust status became fragmented as the original allottees died and interest in allotments was divided among an increasing number of heirs.

In 1926, President Calvin Coolidge's secretary of the interior, Hubert Work, asked the Institute for Government Research (soon to become the Brookings Institution) to conduct a survey of Indian affairs with recommendations for administrative action. The report of the institute, known as the Meriam Report (after Lewis Meriam, the technical director of the survey), was published in 1928. Together with Laurence F. Schmeckebier's *The Office of Indian Affairs*, published in 1927 as Number 48 of the institute's *Service*

Monographs of the United States Government, the Meriam Report was the most comprehensive survey to date of the Indian programs of the federal government. The report blamed the unanticipated consequences of the allotment policy on the government's insistence on allotting land to tribes that were unprepared for the individual ownership of property. It recommended that the wishes of the Indians involved be taken into account prior to allotment. The report concluded that the goal of work with the Indians should be integration into white society if they desired it. But if they did not, the goal should be to enable the Indians "to live in the presence of [the prevailing] civilization at least in accordance with a minimum standard of health and decency."

The Indian New Deal

Early New Deal legislation, a response to the stresses of the Great Depression, provided for the corporate organization of the U.S. economy. The National Industrial Recovery Act of 1933 (48 *Stat.* 195) created the National Recovery Administration (NRA) and provided for the organization and regulation of the economy by industry councils representing owners, workers, and the government. Until the Supreme Court ruled the act unconstitutional in 1935, the NRA represented the Roosevelt administration's major effort to promote economic recovery.

Two days after the enactment of the National Industrial Recovery Act, Congress passed the Indian Reorganization Act (IRA; 48 *Stat.* 984). The Wheeler-Howard Act, as the IRA was known, stopped further allotments of tribal land and enabled tribes to organize themselves as governments and as corporations for purposes of economic development. The act had been drafted in the Department of the Interior by John Collier, Franklin D. Roosevelt's commissioner of Indian affairs, and his associates. Collier wanted to restore and preserve Indian communal life and Indian culture while improving the economic status of the Indians. He saw the act as a means of doing so. Corporate development would provide an economic basis for Indian life, while tribal governments would provide the basis for a separate political order. As tribal governments and corporations became viable, the Indian Office's role would become consultative and advisory. Other provisions of the act enabled the secretary of the interior to restore unsold surplus lands to the tribes, to extend the trust period of allotments indefinitely, and to provide for the purchase of lands to be added to the reservations. A credit fund enabled the tribes to get capital to finance economic development projects. Thus, tribes were to be organized as business corporations, even as the national economy was to be organized industry by industry.

The Termination Movement

The Servicemen's Readjustment Act, or GI Bill, of 1944 (58 *Stat.* 284), provided educational benefits for a generation of World War II veterans. The law revolutionized higher education in the United States. The GI Bill also provided health care for veterans and gave them access to credit for homeownership and business development. The law established the basis for a postwar middle class and an increasingly suburban society. In Indian affairs, Congress followed a similar course, emphasizing investment in individuals and their economic and social development. During World War II, Congress reduced funding for the Indian Service's community-based activities and increased funding for health and education services directed toward individual Indians. The Indian Service promoted Indian migration to urban areas to work in defense plants.

In 1946, in order to "streamline" administration, Congress authorized substantial delegation of authority from the secretary of the interior to the commissioner of Indian affairs and from the commissioner to subordinate officials in the field (60 *Stat.* 939). In 1947, an administrative reorganization resulted in the creation of five regional headquarters, or area offices, in Minneapolis, Billings, Portland, Phoenix, and Oklahoma City. Also in 1946, Congress created the Indian Claims Commission Act (ICC; 60 *Stat.* 1049). The ICC was established to hear claims against the United States arising from treaty disputes, thereby streamlining the claims process. The Indian Office was officially designated the Bureau of Indian Affairs (BIA) in 1947.

Following the conclusion of World War II, a movement for the termination of federal responsibility to the Indians and for the transfer to the states of the federal government's health, education, welfare, and law enforcement functions dominated Indian affairs. The movement was supported by the Hoover Commission on the reorganization of the federal government in 1949, based on its rejection of the Collier position of separate development of the tribes. The Hoover Commission called for the integration of the Indians into American life, transfer of the bureau to the proposed successor to the Federal Security Agency, and the transfer, as rapidly as possible, of federal services to state auspices.

In 1953, Congress endorsed the Hoover Commission's program of federal disengagement and Indian integration. The Termination Resolution, as House Concurrent Resolution No. 108 (67 *Stat.* B132) was known, called for the termination of federal responsibility for American Indians as quickly as possible. Congress terminated federal responsibility for a number of tribes during the 1950s, notably the Klamath tribe of Oregon (P. L. 83–587, 1954, 68 *Stat.* 718), the Menominee tribe of Wisconsin (P. L. 83–399, 1954, 68 *Stat.* 250), and the Paiute tribe of Utah (P. L. 83–762, 1954, 68 *Stat.* 1099). Other legislation provided for the removal of restrictions on the sale of alcoholic beverages to Indians (P. L. 83–277, 1954, 67 *Stat.* 586), for the transfer of responsibility for Indian health from the Bureau of Indian Affairs to the U.S. Public Health Service, and for a relocation program to encourage Indian migration to urban areas. Public Law 280 (67 *Stat.* 588), also passed in 1953, enabled the states to extend law enforcement jurisdiction to Indian reservations without consulting the tribes involved. All of these measures attempted to solve the "Indian problem" by promoting the integration of the Indian into American society through the removal of special services and special protections. The National Congress of American Indians, an organization of tribal governments established under the provisions of the Indian Reorganization Act, and some white-led reform groups opposed the termination movement of the 1950s.

The Hoover Commission had recommended transferring services of the Bureau of Indian Affairs to agencies that provided similar services to the general population. The Transfer Act of 1954 (P. L. 568, 68 *Stat.* 674) transferred Indian health services from the Bureau of Indian Affairs to the Public Health Service in the Department of Health, Education, and Welfare. Legislators intended this and related acts to be a prelude to the termination of special status and services for Indians, but the results were quite different. The Public Health Service moved to improve the health status of Indian people and during the 1960s competed with the Bureau of Indian Affairs to provide an increasing array of services to Indian reservations.

Self-Determination

Although the termination movement moved the federal government away from the principles of the Indian New Deal after World War II, the basic legislation was not repealed, and the tribal governments continued to function. The new Democratic administration of 1961 brought an end to the termination movement. Stewart Udall, secretary of the interior under Presidents John Kennedy and Lyndon Johnson, disavowed the policy in 1961. Presidents Johnson and Nixon both explicitly rejected termination in special Indian messages to Congress in 1968 and 1970. Ultimately, federal responsibility for the American Indians would be reduced through the economic development of the tribes.

The Economic Opportunity Act of 1964 (P. L. 88–452, 78 *Stat.* 508) strengthened the tribal governments established under the Indian Reorganization Act, as they designated themselves Community Action Agency (CAA) Boards. Consequently, the War on Poverty increased the power of the existing tribal governments on the reservations rather than creating new power centers, as it often did in urban areas. Tribal governments began to administer a wide variety of welfare and economic development programs. During the late 1960s, a number of Great Society programs established "Indian desks." Tribal governments became increasingly sophisticated in shopping for federal agencies willing to finance pet projects. The *Catalog of Federal Domestic Assistance Programs*, similar in size and format to the catalogs of the large mail-order houses, was a fixture in every tribal office library.

Still, the federal programs of the 1960s failed to improve the relative position of the American Indians. By the end of the decade, they were still the nation's most deprived minority group, whether the measure was nutritional level, educational accomplishment, median income, or morbidity and mortality rates. In part, the effects of the Economic Opportunity Act on the tribes were deceptive. The act provided the illusion of local control, while the effect of federal guidelines was to create a tribal bureaucracy controlled in large part by the "memorandum writers" who occupied the Indian desks of the federal granting agencies. Guidelines also resulted in a uniformity of programs across the many supposedly locally controlled CAAs.

The African American civil rights movement of the early 1960s had little effect on Indian people; the nationalist movements of the latter part of the decade, however, evoked a stronger response. This was particularly true among the relocated Indians of the cities, who were increasingly critical of the goal of assimilation, whether by termination or by tribal economic development. They were also critical of the tribal governments, which they viewed as corrupt political machines. On the Pine Ridge Reservation, by the early 1970s urban militants had allied with conservative older Indians who had opposed the Indian Reorganization Act in the mid-1930s. They called for a return to the situation that had prevailed before the passage of the Dawes Act. Then, they said, the government dealt with Indian tribes as units without attempting to influence their internal affairs. Political power within the tribes would be based on ascribed status: family ties, age and wisdom, demonstrated leadership.

The Indian Civil Rights Act of 1968 (82 *Stat.* 77) extended the protections of the Bill of Rights to American Indians by restricting tribal governments' dealings with their citizens. The act prohibits tribal governments from interfering with religious freedom, freedom of speech, and freedom of the press. The statute provides most of the restrictions on government action included in the first ten amendments to the U.S. Constitution. As an exercise of Congress's plenary power in Indian affairs, this legislation provides an exception to the general expansion of tribal powers after 1960.

In 1973, Congress passed the Menominee Restoration Act (P. L. 93–197, 87 *Stat.* 770), reversing the termination of the Menominee tribe nearly twenty years earlier. The next year, Congress created the American Indian Policy Review Commission (P. L. 93–580, 88 *Stat.* 1910). The Indian Education Assistance and Self-Determination Act (P. L. 93–638, 88 *Stat.* 2206), enacted in 1975, finally ushered in the era of self-determination that Presidents Lyndon Johnson and Richard Nixon had called for. The law made it possible for tribes to contract with federal agencies to provide services to their members and to subcontract with other entities to deliver those services. The law encouraged devolution of implementation authority from the federal government to tribal governments and gradually resulted in an expansion of tribal government organizations. The final report of the American Indian Policy Review Commission, issued in 1977, supported the self-determination policy. Other laws enacted during the decade also strengthened tribal governments—notably, the Indian Child Welfare Act of 1978 (P. L. 95–608, 92 *Stat.* 3069) gave tribal courts primary jurisdiction in cases involving Indian children and provided funding to tribes for child welfare services.

Later congressional legislation emphasized economic development, returning to the business organization provisions of the Wheeler-Howard Act of 1933. The Indian Mineral Development Act of 1982 (P. L. 97–382, 96 *Stat.* 1940) authorized tribes to contract with energy companies and others to develop the mineral resources on Indian reservations. In the Indian Gaming Regulatory Act of 1988 (P. L. 104–330, 102 *Stat.* 2467), Congress attempted to strike a balance between state and tribal interests. The act reflected the growing importance of gambling as a source of tribal economic development. Congress recognized tribal interests in gaming but required tribes to negotiate with states before providing Class III gambling—that is, gaming that goes beyond traditional tribal games and bingo. The law established the National Indian Gaming Commission to oversee negotiations between tribes and states.

Paul H. Stuart

References and Further Reading

Commission on Organization of the Executive Branch of the Government. 1949. *Indian Affairs: A Report to the Congress.* Washington, DC: Government Printing Office.

Commission on the Rights, Liberties, and Responsibilities of the American Indian. 1966. *The Indian: America's Unfinished Business.* Norman: University of Oklahoma Press.

Institute for Government Research. 1928. *The Problem of Indian Administration: Report of a Survey made at the request of Honorable Hubert Work, Secretary of the Interior, and submitted to him February 21, 1928.* Baltimore: Johns Hopkins Press.

Hagan, William T. 1961. *American Indians,* rev. ed. Chicago: University of Chicago Press.

Hagan, William T. 1976. "The Reservation Policy: Too Little and Too Late." In *Indian-White Relations: A Persistent Paradox,* ed. Jane F. Smith and Robert M. Kvasnicka, 157–169. Washington, DC: Howard University Press.

Hyman, Harold L. 1986. *American Singularity: The 1787 Northwest Ordinance, the 1862 Homestead and Morrill Acts, and the 1944 G.I. Bill.* Athens: University of Georgia Press.

Joint Special Committee. 1867. "Condition of the Indian Tribes," *U.S. Senate Reports,* 39th Congress, 2nd Session, No. 156, Serial 1279.

Kelly, Lawrence C. 1975. "The Indian Reorganization Act: The Dream and the Reality," *Pacific Historical Review* 44 (August): 291–312.

Prucha, Francis Paul. 1984. *The Great Father: The United States Government and the American Indians.* 2 vols. Lincoln: University of Nebraska Press.

Schmeckebier, Lawrence F. 1927. *The Office of Indian Affairs: Its History, Activities, and Organization.* Baltimore: Johns Hopkins Press.

Stuart, Paul. 1977. "United States Indian Policy: From the Dawes Act to the American Indian Policy Review Commission," *Social Service Review* (September): 451–463.

Stuart, Paul. 1990. "Financing Self-Determination: Federal Indian Expenditures, 1975–1988," *American Indian Culture and Research Journal* 14(2): 1–18.

Relevant Court Cases Related to Treaties

Treaty law is one of the major underpinnings of federal Indian law. Throughout the history of the United States, courts have interpreted, misinterpreted, dismissed, and denied the terms of treaty articles signed with Indian tribes. Treaties have long-standing implications for national and international relationships; their impacts sometimes have a wide reach. American Indian treaties with the U.S. government are one of the major characteristics that make the Indian experience unique for the American nation. Because indigenous nations met the earliest Europeans and subsequent immigrants, American Indians have had a long and continuing relationship with both the European predecessors and the descendants of the American republic's founders. Treaties with indigenous nations became a major vehicle for Native land cessions for the later American republic.

For American Indians, land cessions at first were viewed simply as a temporary accommodation for guests. Natives approached bilateral agreements from a perspective radically different from that of European Americans. How they concluded treaties had a bearing on their interpretation of treaty law. Indigenous peoples strove to strike bargains between kinfolk. Outsiders could be turned into fictive relatives through elaborate adoption and welcoming rituals. Rituals involving the sacred pipe were called *calumet ceremonies.* There were numerous tribal variations on the form of the rituals (Sabo 1992). Once converted into a kinship relationship, the parties to a sacred agreement shared mutual obligations and responsibilities for reciprocity. Once made brothers, kinfolk did not betray the fealty of a brother without the direst of consequences. That was especially true when the supreme creative force of the universe had sanctioned the agreement through the proper performance of ceremonies.

Indigenous people and their nations did not fit easily or comfortably into normal political or legal arenas for the American republic's leaders. Justices who dealt with the topic early in the history of the United States referred to the legal situation as a peculiar relationship. The judiciary deemed the entire relationship of tribes to the United States "an anomalous one" (*U.S. v. Kagama* 1886, 381). One scholar who devoted his career to an examination of Indian policy issues in the United States summarized his research into Indian treaties with the assessment that they were "a political anomaly" (oddity) in the nation's history because the documents and the ties did not fit neatly into European American historical categories (Prucha 1994, 1, 289). Native nations preceded the European American presence; Indian tribes were neither foreign nations nor domestic states but entities in between in their interaction with the federal government. The leading Indian scholar of the last century placed treaties at the very bedrock of the entire federal-Indian relationship (Deloria 1996, 970–971).

The interpretation of treaty rights frequently drives much contemporary litigation that focuses on Indian sovereignty and rights. Controversies often focus on American Indian treaties and claims of the violation of treaty rights. Across the nation, local conflicts involved controversies over long-standing treaty obligations toward descendants of the original signers of Indian treaties. American Indians continue to raise treaty rights as the basis for their claims to hunt, to fish, or to regain lost territory, such as the Black Hills for the Sioux. American courts have recognized the long-term implications of Indian treaties for Native rights. Treaties created a trust relationship with the U.S. government that is the heart of federal-Indian policy. Provisions of some treaties signed between the federal government and American Indians are still in effect. Other provisions sometimes are revived in court opinions to have renewed impact upon contemporary events. The recognition of historic treaty rights to resources, lands, and position within the national republic contributes to the rich legacy that helps constitute Indian country. Indian treaties have an impact not only within the United States but also internationally. During the colonial period, tribes in the eastern and southwestern portions of the United States concluded alliances with European nations, and some claim a continuous relationship. Emigration, migratory wildlife, whaling, and more are affected. American Indian treaties make up a significant part of the ongoing demands from Native peoples for acknowledgement of their sovereignty and their rights.

Powers of Treaty Making

Courts point to the U.S. Constitution as the fundamental source guiding the judiciary's examination and determination of the impact of treaties. Article II, Section 2, clause 2 of the Constitution declares, "The President shall . . . have power, by and with the advice and consent of the Senate, to make treaties, provided two-thirds of the Senators present concur. . . ." In the Constitution, Article VI, Section 2 provides that "[t]his Constitution, and the laws of the United States which shall be made in pursuance thereof; and all treaties made, or which shall be made, under the authority of the United States shall be the supreme Law of the land; and the Judges in every State shall be bound thereby, any thing in the Constitution or laws of any State to the contrary notwithstanding." The United States dealt with Indian tribes as "distinct, independent political communities" (*Worcester* 1832, 559) through treaties. Chief Justice John Marshall and the Court, in the famous *Worcester* decision of 1832, voided Georgia state laws impinging upon the Cherokee Nation because the laws were repugnant to treaties, to the U.S. Constitution, and to the laws "giving effect to the treaties" (ibid., 562). Still earlier, the same justice, in a majority opinion, referred to the phrase in the commerce clause of the Constitution. That clause gave Congress the power to "regulate commerce with foreign nations, and among the several states, and with the Indian tribes" (Article III, Section 8). The decision found tribes to be neither foreign nations nor domestic states, deeming Indian tribes to be "domestic dependent nations" with a relationship to the United States that "resembles that of a ward to his guardian" (*Cherokee Nation v. Georgia* 1831, 17). Justice Smith Thompson's noteworthy dissent in 1832 favored Indian nation status in part based upon the treaty interaction (ibid., 50).

Scholars have argued that American Indian sovereign rights should be recognized in a new era as reserved rights under the terms of treaties (or agreements), as well as under the Tenth Amendment of the U.S. Constitution, which contains the wording "All powers not granted in this Constitution shall be reserved to the States, or to the people" (Wilkins and Lomawaima 2001, 120; Deloria 1996, 972). Tribes still retain sovereignty and still exercise inherent rights of self-government. Those powers have existed since time immemorial. Some tribal leaders seek renegotiated treaty terms, insisting on more inclusive advantages, territorial acquisitions, and recognition of expanded rights.

Colonies negotiated with tribes, and European nations concluded agreements with indigenous nations, to secure amity, trade, allies, and land cessions. After the declaring of American independence in 1776, the rebellious colonies sought Indian allies, or at least Native neutrality, during the Revolutionary War. Following the successful revolution, which secured independence, the fledgling American government also entered into agreements with tribes to secure peace, to identify borders, and to make allies for the postwar period.

Courts have interpreted treaties with Native tribes in a variety of ways throughout U.S. history, but they have always recognized treaties as superior to the law of any individual state. In 1905, the Supreme Court set out the historical fact of treaty making with tribes, acknowledging that an Indian treaty is "not a grant of rights to the Indians, but a grant of rights from them—a reservation of those not granted" (*U.S. v. Winans* 1905, 381). A treaty did not give rights to Indians; rather, through their treaty, Indians granted away rights they already had. Ideally, treaties are agreements negotiated between equals. Like the federal powers set forth in the Constitution, Indian tribes possess inherent powers, not ceded through treaties, that are not articulated until needed. Tribes retain or reserve sovereign powers unless expressly granted away by treaty or expressly taken from the tribe through federal statute. Sometime treaties simply acknowledged rights that Indians "from time immemorial . . . always had and enjoyed" (*Makah Indian Tribe v. McCauly* 1941, 78). The Court has reasoned that a treaty between the negotiators for the United States and an Indian tribe is essentially a contract between two sovereign nations. The judiciary has acknowledged the varying circumstances under which treaty negotiations have taken place through the nation's history. Most often, agreements arose out of unequal relationships. Obviously, treaties made under threat were inherently unfair and one-sided. Sometimes, U.S. negotiators sidestepped American Indian opposition to the terms they presented and simply affixed signatures or Xs to the document or, in the case of the Kiowa in 1892, returned to the nation's capital and added the marks to the end of the document (Clark 1999, 48). It was a fraudulent tactic but an expedient one. At other times, U.S. authorities reacted to Indian opposition by passing laws seizing Indian territory, such as Black Hills legislation in 1877 or allotment in severalty acts. Over time, as the relative power position between the United States and Indian nations changed, the U.S. government imposed terms on disparate groups that allegedly represented entire Indian nations, and then the Senate quickly ratified the "treaty" as if it had come from the wellspring of the demands of a whole Native nation.

Around the time of the American Civil War, a growing clamor arose among government agents, missionaries, and other leaders, calling for an end to treaty making with tribes. Part of the expressed concern arose from ongoing conflicts between government agencies over which branch, military or civilian, would control Indian affairs. Another reason related to U.S. insistence on reflecting the changed situation between the national government and tribes. Pressure from business interests that believed they were hampered in their dealings with Native peoples as a result of the constraints of treaties added another excuse. Other people sought more Indian lands, believing treaties stood in their way. The clash between the houses of Congress over ultimate control of Indian affairs, involving executive branch privileges, helped determine the outcome. Congress responded to the call and in 1871 enacted an amendment to an Indian appropriations bill that halted treaty making with tribes (Act of 3 March 1871, 16 *Stat.* 566, sect. 1). The act stated that treaties made prior to 1871 were not affected, that ". . . no obligation of any treaty lawfully made and ratified with any such Indian nation or tribe prior to March 3, 1871, shall be hereby invalidated or impaired." In the future, the president could authorize executive agreements with consenting tribes, agreements that would be ratified by both houses of Congress (Prucha 1984, I, 527–533; Wunder 1985). Agreements that could be ratified by both houses of Congress continued to be made until 1911. Thereafter, Congress authorized numerous measures that directly dealt with Indian lands and rights, but the enactments were not officially termed treaties. Two examples are the federal acknowledgement, in the contemporary era, of the Mashantucket Pequot in their land claims settlement act in the state of Connecticut, and recognition of the Ysleta del Sur Pueblo (usually called the Tigua) within the state of Texas in 1988 (former, 25 U.S.C. § 1751, 1988; latter, 101 *Stat.* 666). Although such measures are called land settlement acts now, they are in reality agreements negotiated with tribal governments, once termed Indian treaties. Contemporary tribal compacts with state and local governments perform the same function as historic bilateral treaties.

Treaty terms varied widely in the length of time they ran and the effects they had. Courts sometimes have ruled that the terms of a particular article of a treaty no longer hold. Some treaty terms, such as the payment of annual annuities to Pawnee tribal members, are still in effect. At other times, courts have recognized Indian treaty rights long after the original historical circumstances had radically changed. Beginning in the late 1960s, federal courts upheld the Northwest tribes' treaty "right of taking fish" in the region (*U.S. v. Washington* 1975, 683). Other examples occurred in the 1980s and in 1999, when the Supreme Court ruled that Chippewa Indian band members retained their rights for hunting, fishing, trapping, and gathering, both on and off their reservation (the latter are called *usufructuary rights*), that were guaranteed to them under their treaty (*Lac Courte Oreilles v. Voigt* 1983; *Minnesota v. Mille Lacs* 1999, 176; Wilkinson 1991). From time to time, Congress also enacts legislation to implement terms of past treaties. One example is the Pacific Salmon Treaty Act, passed in 1985 (P. L. 99–5, 99 *Stat.* 7). The measure established a U.S.-Canadian commission that included Indian representation to oversee the protection of tribal treaty international fishing stocks. The commission tries to address problems arising from the multinational impact of North Pacific fishing resource questions. Additional challenges are posed by the enforcement of treaty terms and congressional appropriation of funding to support the implementation of treaty terms.

The Canons of Treaty Construction

Ambiguous Expressions Must Be Resolved in Favor of Indians

The conditions under which two sides negotiated treaties left much to be desired, as a result of power differentials, language and cultural barriers, and a host of other problems. Discerning what a figure in history thought or believed with certainty is next to impossible, given the lapse of time and the difficulties of documentation. Jurists have struggled through the years with the basic question of how to interpret treaty language and how to reconcile treaty rights with congressional and court desires, local and state demands, to end the terms of treaties. Courts established rules under which treaties could consistently be interpreted for a period of time. The rules regarding treaties are called *canons of construction* (or guidelines). Judges have held that any significant ambiguities in interpretation of treaty rights must be resolved in the favor of Indians because of language barriers and as a result of cultural differences. When brothers erected fishwheels on the

Columbia River, relying on their state license to permit them to take a large amount of fish, Yakima Indians objected because of the rapid depletion of fish resources. The Indians insisted on recognition of their treaty right to fish. In 1905, the Supreme Court ruled that treaties must be interpreted as the Indians would have understood them. The Indians could fish on the river (*U.S. v. Winans* 1905, 371). In *Winters v. U.S.* (1908, 576), the same Court ruled that, if ambiguities occur in the interpretation of agreements and treaties, "ambiguities will be resolved from the standpoint of the Indians." "Doubtful expressions are to be resolved in favor of the weak and defenseless people who are wards of the nation, dependent upon its protection and good faith" (*Carpenter v. Shaw* 1930, 367). In part, the Court reasoned that American Indians could discern neither the meaning of English phrases as a foreign language nor the disguised meaning of English words and phrases, even if the Natives spoke some English (*Winters* 1908, 577). Moreover, the *McClanahan* decision of 1973 asserted, in a case that examined state taxation of a reservation resident's income, that the Indians' dire circumstances surrounding the forced signing of a treaty in 1868 lent credence to the interpretation of the document in favor of the Indians (*McClanahan* 1973, 174). This canon of construction has wide application. It has been applied to Indian grazing rights that carried with them priority rights within a national forest even though the Indian treaty and subsequent agreement made no mention of those specific rights (*Swim v. Bergland* 1983, 716–718). In 1999, the Court also upheld such a reading of treaty rights in a decision dealing with Chippewa Indians' hunting and fishing rights across a swath of the southern Great Lakes region (*Mille Lacs* 1999, 200, 206).

Treaties Must Be Interpreted as Indians Understood Them

Although court opinions have weighed in on all sides of treaty interpretation, one of the mainstays of viewing an Indian treaty has been that the document must be interpreted according to what the Indians thought the articles meant. This is another major canon of treaty construction. As an example, the Choctaw treaty of 1830 provided that "in the construction of this Treaty wherever well founded doubt shall arise, it shall be construed most favorably towards the Choctaws" (Treaty of 27 Sep. 1830 at Dancing Rabbit Creek, 7 *Stat.* 333, Article 18). After all, the United States sought out Native tribes for negotiations. The federal government often coerced tribe members into negotiating. "The Indian Nations did not seek out the United States and agree upon an exchange of lands in an arm's-length transaction. Rather, treaties were imposed on them and they had no choice but to consent" (*Choctaw Nation v. U.S.* 1970, 630–631). Just before the turn of the twentieth century, the Supreme Court restated an earlier decree that an Indian treaty "therefore must be construed, not according to the technical meaning of its words to learned lawyers, but in the sense in which they would naturally be understood by the Indians" (*Jones v. Meehan* 1899, 11; *Choate* 1912, 675; *Washington v. Washington Fishing Assn.* 1979, 676). In 1979, the Court examined fourteen treaties among four Puget Sound tribes in the Pacific Northwest, involving the issue of treaty negotiations over rights to territory and to fish; the Court ruled, "It is absolutely clear, as Governor [Isaac] Stevens himself said, that neither he nor the Indians intended that the latter 'should be excluded from their ancient fisheries,' and it is accordingly inconceivable that either party deliberately agreed to authorize future settlers to crowd the Indians out of any meaningful use of their accustomed places to fish. That each individual Indian would share an 'equal opportunity' with thousands of newly arrived individual settlers is totally foreign to the spirit of the negotiations. Such a 'right,' along with the $207,500 paid the Indians, would hardly have been sufficient to compensate them for the millions of acres they ceded to the Territory [of Washington]" (ibid.). In a shocking pronouncement, if treaties were signed between roughly equal sovereigns, the Court reasoned, then each side was due roughly half the fish harvest (ibid., 687). Because the tribes' populations had dwindled while the settlers' numbers had exploded, the smaller tribes received as much of the fish harvest as the much larger surrounding non-Indian populace.

Treaties Must Be Construed in Favor of Indians

The Supreme Court has held repeatedly that treaties are to be interpreted liberally in favor of the Indians when there is disputed language about the implementation of the terms of a treaty (ibid., 676, 678; *Choctaw Nation v. U.S.* 1970, 432; *Mille Lacs* 1999, 200). This is yet another major canon of construction. One of the most generous interpretations of Indian treaty language was in the *Winters* decision of 1908, in which a federal district court held that it was implicit in the treaties that sufficient waters for tribal use were preserved, preceding and preempting any other rights subsequently established by state law or use. The Supreme Court affirmed the opinion. The tribe not only had treaty rights guaranteed to it but also had reserved to it all the rights necessary to carry out the purpose of the treaty, including the first use of scarce water for Indian agriculture. Courts have rendered similarly supportive rulings in favor of Indian rights under other treaties (*Swim* 1983, 716; *Grand Traverse Band* 1998, 639). This canon of construction also has broad application to other areas of Indian country. An appeals court in 1998 applied the liberal interpretation of a treaty from 1855 to grant Yakima Indian truck drivers who were hauling reservation timber over state highways immunity from state vehicle permit fees (*Cree v. Flores* 1998, 769, 771). The same year, another appellate court proclaimed that members of a Chippewa band could anchor their commercial fishing vessels at a public dock on the shore of a lake, as a result of construing Indian treaties from 1836 and 1855 liberally in favor of the Indians, even though the documents did not say anything specifically about commercial mooring rights (*Grand Traverse Band* 1998, 638–639).

Court pronouncements have extended the maxims for benefiting Indians when interpreting treaties to the examination of federal statutes. The canons of treaty construction have been applied broadly to federal statutes dealing with American Indians. A unanimous Court in 1974 found that administrative rules and regulations should favor tribes in interpreting treaty law (*Morton v. Ruiz* 1974, 229). Furthermore, where Indians are concerned, the normal rules of interpretation for statutes do not apply: ". . . federal statutes are to be construed liberally in favor of Native Americans, with ambiguous provisions interpreted to their benefit" (*EEOC v. Cherokee Nation* 1989, 939). Similarly, the usual deference shown in court for agency administrative interpretation of ambiguous statutes also does not apply to American Indians (*Muscogee [Creek] Nation v. Hodel* 1988, 1444–1445; *Montana v. Blackfeet Tribe* 1985, 766; *Oneida County* 1985, 247; *Connecticut v. U.S. Dept. of the Interior* 2000, 92; *Ramah Navajo Chapter* 1997, 1462). Two additional examples illustrate the trend. A circuit court in 1982 held that the secretary of the interior had violated the Bureau of Indian Affairs' regulations regarding petroleum leases, and any doubt over interpreting the regulations had to be resolved in favor of the Indians (*Jicarilla v. Andrus* 1982, 1332). An appeals court applied the same sentiment to BIA interpretation of an ambiguous statute regarding complicated educational funding formula calculations in 1997 and found in favor of the Indians. The court stated that "if the [Act] can reasonably be construed as the Tribe would have it construed, [then] it must be construed that way" (*Ramah* 1997, 1432; *Muscogee v. Hodel* 1988, 1445).

Plenary Power

The U.S. Congress gave to itself the political authority, also called *plenary power,* to enact laws altering Indian policies. Plenary power also has an effect upon Indian treaties. In its major statement on the subject, the Supreme Court ruled, in the infamous decision involving the Kiowa leader Lone Wolf, that the commerce clause of the U.S. Constitution gave Congress sweeping power over American Indians. Indeed, Indian treaties were similar, in the Court's view, to federal statues (*Lone Wolf v. Hitchcock* 1903, 568; *Warren v. Tax Comm* 1965, 380.) As such, under this approach Congress has the authority to limit rights promised to Indian tribes in treaties. Going back in time, after the American Civil War, amid a growing chorus to open Indian lands to pioneer settlement, Supreme Court justices reasserted congressional plenary power in a decision regarding tobacco manufactured just inside the boundary of the Cherokee Nation. Article 10 of the Cherokee treaty of 1866 had clearly pledged that the Cherokee could sell merchandise without paying "any tax thereon which . . . may be levied by the United States" (15 *Stat.* 167). In its decision, the Court recognized congressional authority to modify an Indian treaty and to enact a measure in direct violation of the treaty "as if the treaty were not an element to be considered" (*Cherokee Tobacco* 1870, 621). The Court relied upon what is called the "last-in-time" rule, under which a congressional statute that is the latest enactment in time supersedes a previous treaty. Among succeeding examples is the Court's ruling in 1882 that legislation creating the State of Colorado in 1875 "repeals . . . any existing treaty" blocking its path (*U.S. v. McBratney* 1881, 623). Fourteen years afterward, the Court also stated that Indian treaties "should not be made an instrument for violating the public faith by distorting the words of a treaty," thereby jeopardizing the rights of citizens in Wyoming fully to regulate hunting (*Ward v. Race Horse* 1896, 516). Since the latter could be amended or repealed, therefore, Congress could alter the terms or even abolish the terms of treaties with tribes. Still later, the same high tribunal ruled that it was unfortunately "too late" for the president

of the United States to protect the Indians in their treaty rights and left the Natives to the fate of congressional whim (*U.S. v. Winans* 1905, 75).

Takings

The most notorious decision regarding the outright seizure of Indian Territory is the *Tee-Hit-Ton Indians v. U.S.* opinion of 1995. In that pronouncement, the Court voiced the draconian assumption that the United States could take Indian lands, even those protected by treaties. Moreover, the Court decreed, under the Fifth Amendment the United States could seize Tlingit lands in Alaska without payment because of the false contention in the ruling that "the savage tribes of this continent were deprived of their ancestral ranges by force" used by the conqueror (*Tee-Hit-Ton* 1955, 289). The Tee-Hit-Ton band had no treaty relationship with the United States. Congress had not enacted legislation recognizing their lands or status. No recognition, no rights. As Congress had not authorized ownership, Indian occupancy "may be extinguished by the Government without compensation" (ibid., 288). Tribes lost their land rights because the conqueror took them. If unprotected by a treaty or a federal statute, then, the Court ruled, the United States could take Indian lands without due process of law, without just compensation, and without concern for the usual requirement that such a taking of the land needed to be for a public purpose. Constructing federal statutes so they state congressional intent to abrogate treaty rights, including vested property rights for which compensation must be paid under the Fifth Amendment, avoided the obligation for financial payment. Through its decision in *Shoshone v. U.S.* (1937), the Supreme Court announced that treaty rights are a form of property and as such are under the protection of the Fifth Amendment to the U.S. Constitution, specifically, the just compensation clause. If those rights are taken away, then compensation must be paid.

In 1980, the Court repudiated the taking of Indian lands without compensation at the same time the jurists also repudiated the most flagrant exercise of plenary power where American Indians are concerned. In *U.S. v. Sioux Nation*, the Court held that just compensation must be paid under the Fifth Amendment if treaty rights are violated (*U.S. v. Sioux Nation* 1980, 408). When seizing more than 20 percent of the Tuscarora Indian reservation for a hydroelectric project, the Court invoked slim evidence that Congress intended to abrogate the American Indian title to Seneca land coveted for the Allegheny Reservoir. The Kinzua Dam project created the reservoir. The Court concluded that Congress must have known and considered the catastrophic impact of flooding 10,000 acres of Indian land, as well as using the remaining 2,300 acres for highway access to serve the reservoir (*Seneca Nation v. U.S.* 1965, 56; Josephy 1984). When the Court approved the seizure of Tuscarora Indian land for a hydroelectric project that would drown Native land, Justice Hugo Black wrote a stinging dissent. He diverged from his colleagues' determination that public utilities, acting under license from the Federal Power Commission, could condemn Tuscarora lands for a power project. Alarmingly, the Court ruled that "general Acts of Congress apply to Indians as well as to others in the absence of a clear expression to the contrary" (*FPC v. Tuscarora* 1960, 120). Justice Black remarked that "great nations like great men should keep their word" (ibid., 142)

Abrogation

To end or take away a treaty's effect is to abrogate it. Courts have ruled that treaty terms may be violated or altered if new circumstances arise that necessitate the change. Lawmakers have also rationalized the abrogation of Indian treaties when the delegates wanted to open Indian lands to further sale and settlement. In its clearest expression of opposition to Indian treaties, at the start of the twentieth century in the *Lone Wolf* decision, the U.S. Supreme Court held that congressional plenary power granted to that body full rights to end the terms of any Indian treaty when Congress deemed it necessary to carry out national policies. Judges drew from earlier Court edicts such as *Cherokee Tobacco* and *Kagama*. The *Lone Wolf* opinion announced, "The power exists to abrogate the provisions of an Indian treaty. . . . [It] was never doubted that the power to abrogate existed in Congress, . . . particularly if consistent with perfect good faith towards the Indians" (*Lone Wolf* 1903, 568). The Court subsequently chipped away at the *Lone Wolf* doctrine, but the pronouncement has never been fully repudiated and remains established law.

Justice Edward Douglass White's "good faith effort" in the decision set a standard for violating Indian treaty rights and taking Indian land that successive courts tried to follow. Courts looked for evidence that congressional deliberations considered some impacts from the abrogation of a treaty's terms. The high court has upheld the rule that Congress must clearly express its intent to abrogate an Indian treaty (*Missouri v. Holland* 1919, 417, 421; *Mattz v. Arnett* 1973, 505).

The decision of 1968 regarding the Menominee tribe of Wisconsin supported Indian treaty rights and found that the pertinent legislation, such as the tribe's termination act in 1954 (68 *Stat.* 250) and Public Law 280 in 1953 (67 *Stat.* 588) passed by the same Congress, did not specifically mention Indian hunting and fishing rights falling under state jurisdiction. The Supreme Court applied the "not lightly implied" test and ascertained that the Menominee Termination Act did not abrogate those rights. Moreover, the Court, in a remarkably solicitous attitude, reported it did not believe that Congress intended to abrogate Native treaty rights in "a backhanded way" (*Menominee* 1968, 412). Building upon that decree, the Court later added that it felt "extreme reluctance to find congressional abrogation of Indian treaty rights in the absence of explicit statutory language so directing" (*U.S. v. Washington* 1975, 689).

In a more recent announcement, the Supreme Court ruled that, when Congress enacted legislation to protect the endangered bald eagle and required permits for Indians to take eagles for religious purposes, such action reflected Congress's belief "that it was abrogating the rights of Indians to take eagles" even under treaty guarantees (*U.S. v. Dion* 1986, 743; Laurence 1991; Townsend 1989). Earlier, the Court attempted to clarify its stance when it said, in the Menominee decision in 1968, that treaties cannot be abrogated "in a backhanded way." Instead, the Court held that there must be clear and explicit language to abrogate Indian treaties when Congress enacts legislation. In 1986, however, the Court opinion lessened the requirement and expanded the impact. The Court held that there need be only "clear evidence that Congress actually considered the conflict between its intended action on the one hand and Indian treaty rights on the other, and chose to resolve that conflict by abrogating the treaty" (*U.S. v. Dion* 1986, 740; *U.S. v. Santa Fe Pacific Railroad* 1941, 354).

Courts have sanctioned the violation of treaty rights in a variety of other ways. Courts have seen fit to permit the violation of Indian treaty rights under the so-called conservation necessity standard for states to impose regulations on Indian hunting, fishing, and gathering rights in the interest of enforcement of state conservation regulations (*Puyallup Tribe* 1968, 398; *Antoine* 1974, 207–208). More disturbing, on occasion courts have held that, even if not stated at all, the mere enactment of a statute violating a treaty meant that Congress had considered all the consequences and intended to alter the treaty. This is termed "implied abrogation." In its decision of 1986, justices surmised that "the [C]ourt believes that Congress would have" circumscribed Native hunting and treaty rights. To the Court there was clear evidence—however, never stated—that Congress had considered the consequences of violating treaty rights. In the clash over Indians' use of feathers of species protected under federal and international wildlife enactments, the most noteworthy pronouncement involved two Yankton Sioux Indians. The Court held that legislation to protect endangered bald eagles and the requirement for permits for Natives to take eagles for religious purposes reflected Congress's belief "that it was abrogating the rights of Indians to take eagles" even under treaty guarantees (*Dion* 1986, 740, 743). Justices assumed that Congress must have discussed the consequences and must have known the impact. Opinions following in time have taken the presumption in a different direction. Jurists have held that, if an old treaty or agreement did not specifically mention a modern need, then it was neither permitted nor reserved to the tribe (*Oregon Department* 1985, 754, 767, 770). In 1991, a district judge in Wisconsin ruled that rights for Chippewa Indians reserved under 1837 and 1842 treaties did not include the right to harvest timber commercially (*Lac Courte Oreilles* 1991, 700). In 2001, the Court added a bitter twist to the usual interpretation of statutes in favor of Indians when it ruled that any tax exemption arising from Indian gaming must have been clearly and explicitly expressed, turning the canon of construction on its head (*Chickasaw Nation v. U.S.* 2001, 90).

During the term of Chief Justice William Rehnquist, the Court drastically narrowed many rights for Indian tribes. Brusque opinions sidestepped tribal sovereignty in favor of state intrusions into Native governmental activities. Throughout U.S. history, American Indians have faced local and state opposition to Native rights. Local and state authorities have sometimes ignored Indian rights or at other times actively enforced local and state regulations that violated indigenous rights. State officials have eroded or denied Indian rights to fish, hunt, and gather for seasonal needs. That line of reasoning echoes in court opinions. Anti-Indian groups, when not slinging vitriol over the subject of Indian rights, advocate either terminating tribes and abolishing tribal rights or severely restricting those rights (Williams and Neubrech, 1976). Some of the assumptions are reflected in Court rulings. In 1998, a majority opinion remarked that American Indian tribal rights will "fade over time" (*South Dakota* 1998, 798). The chief justice, in a biting 1999 dissent, acidly commented that Indian treaty rights are only "temporary and precarious" (*Mille Lacs* 1999, 219–220).

C. Blue Clark

References and Further Reading

Court Cases

Antoine v. Washington, 420 U.S. 194 (1974).
Carpenter v. Shaw, 280 U.S. 363 (1930).
Cherokee Nation v. Georgia, 30 U.S. (5 Pet.) 1 (1831).
Cherokee Tobacco, 78 Wall. 616 (1870).
Chickasaw Nation v. U.S., 534 U.S. 84 (2001).
Choate v. Trapp, 224 U.S. 665 (1912).
Choctaw Nation v. U.S., 397 U.S. 620 (1970).
Connecticut v. U.S. Department of Interior, 228 F. 3d 82 (2d Cir., 2000).
Cree v. Flores, 157 F. 3d 762 (9th Cir., 1998).
Equal Employment Opportunity Commission v. Cherokee Nation, 871 F. 2d 937 (10th Cir., 1989).
Federal Power Commission v. Tuscarora Indian Nation, 362 U.S. 99 (1960).
Grand Traverse Band of Ottawa and Chippewa Indians v. Director of Michigan Department of Natural Resources, 141 F. 2d 635 (6th Cir., 1998).
Jicarilla Apache Tribe v. Cecil Andrus, 697 F. 2d 1324 (10th Cir., 1982).
Jones v. Meehan, 175 U.S. 1 (1899).
Lac Courte Oreilles Band of Lake Superior Chippewa Indians v. Lester Voigt, 700 F. 2d 341 (1983).
Lac Courte Oreilles Band of Lake Superior Chippewa Indians v. State of Wisconsin, 758 F. Supp. 1262 (W.D.Wis., 1991).
Lone Wolf v. Hitchcock, 187 U.S. 553 (1903).
Makah Indian Tribe v. McCauly, 39 F. Supp. 75 (1941).
Mattz v. Arnett, 412 U.S. 481 (1973).
McClananan v. Arizona Tax Commission, 411 U.S. 164 (1973).
Menominee Tribe v. U.S., 391 U.S. 404 (1968).
Minnesota v. Mille Lacs Band of Chippewa Indians, 526 U.S. 172 (1999).
Missouri v. Holland, 252 U.S. 416 (1919).
Montana v. Blackfeet Tribe, 471 U.S. 759 (1985).
Morton v. Ruiz, 415 U.S. 199 (1974).
Muscogee (Creek) Nation v. Hodel, 851 F. 2d 1439 (D.C. Cir., 1988).
Oneida County v. Oneida Indian Nation of New York State, 470 U.S. 226 (1985).
Oregon Department of Fish and Wildlife v. Klamath Indian Tribe, 473 U.S. 753 (1985).
Puyallup Tribe v. Department of Game of Washington, 391 U.S. 392 (1968).
Ramah Navajo Chapter v. Lujan, 112 F. 3d 1455 (10th Cir., 1997).
Seneca Nation of Indians v. U.S., 338 F. 2d 55 (2d Cir., 1964); cert. denied, 380 U.S. 952 (1965).
Shoshone v. U.S., 304 U.S. 111 (1937).
South Dakota v. Yankton Sioux Tribe, 118 S. Ct. 789 (1998).
Swim v. Bergland, 696 F. 2d 712 (1983).
Tee-Hit-Ton Indians v. U.S., 348 U.S. 272 (1955).
U.S. v. Dion, 476 U.S. 734 (1986).
U.S. v. Kagama, 118 U.S. 375 (1886).
U.S. v. McBratney, 104 U.S. 621 (1881).
U.S. v. Santa Fe Pacific Railroad, 314 U.S. 339 (1941).
U.S. v. Sioux Nation, 448 U.S. 371 (1980).
U.S. v. Washington, 520 F. 2d 676 (1975).
U.S. v. Winans, 198 U.S. 371 (1905).
Ward v. Race Horse, 163 U.S. 504 (1896).
Warren Trading Post v. State Tax Commission, 380 U.S. 685 (1965).
Washington v. Washington State Commercial Passenger Fishing Vessel Association, 443 U.S. 658 (1979).
Winters v. U.S., 207 U.S. 564 (1908).
Worcester v. Georgia, 31 U.S. (6 Pet.) 515 (1832).

Books and Articles

Chambers, Reid P. 1975. "Judicial Enforcement of the Federal Trust Responsibility to Indians." *Stanford Law Review*, 27 (May): 1213–1248.
Clark, Blue. 1999. *Lone Wolf v. Hitchcock: Treaty Rights and Indian Law at the End of the Nineteenth Century.* Lincoln: University of Nebraska Press.
Cohen, Fay. 1986. *Treaties on Trial: The Continuing Controversy over Northwest Indian Fishing Rights.* Seattle: University of Washington Press.
Cohen, Felix. 1942. "Indian Treaties." In *Handbook of Federal-Indian Law*, ed. Felix Cohen, 33–67. Washington, DC: Interior Department/Government Printing Office. [Repr. by Interior Department, 1958; UNM, 1972; ed. by Rennard Strickland, Mitchie, Bobbs-Merrill, 1982].
Deloria, Vine, Jr. 1996. "Reserving to Themselves: Treaties and the Powers of Indian Tribes." *Arizona Law Review*, 38, 3 (Fall): 963–980.
Deloria, Vine, Jr., and David E. Wilkins. 1999. *Tribes, Treaties, and Constitutional Tribulations.* Austin: University of Texas Press.
Jones, Dorothy V. 1982. *License for Empire: By Treaty in Early America.* Chicago: University of Chicago Press.
Josephy, Alvin, Jr. 1984. "Cornplanter, Can You Swim?" In *Now That the Buffalo's Gone*, ed. Alvin Josephy, Jr., 127–150. Norman: University of Oklahoma Press.
Laurence, Robert. 1991. "The Abrogation of Indian Treaties by Federal Statutes Protective of the Environment." *Natural Resources Journal*, 31 (Fall): 859–886.

Prucha, Francis Paul. 1984. *The Great Father: The United States Government and the Indians.* 2 vols. Lincoln: University of Nebraska Press.

Prucha, Francis Paul. 1994. *American Indian Treaties: The History of a Political Anomaly.* Berkeley, Los Angeles, and London: University of California Press.

Sabo, George. 1992. "Rituals of Encounter: Interpreting Native American Views of European Explorers." *Arkansas Historical Quarterly,* 51 (Spring): 54–68.

Townsend, Michael. 1989. "Congressional Abrogation of Indian Treaties: Reevaluation and Reform." *Yale Law Journal,* 98 (February): 793–812.

Wilkins, David E., and K. Tsianina Lomawaima. 2001. *Uneven Ground: American Indian Sovereignty and Federal Law.* Norman: University of Oklahoma Press.

Wilkinson, Charles F. 1991. "To Feel the Summer in the Spring: The Treaty Fishing Rights of the Wisconsin Chippewa." *Wisconsin Law Review* (May-June): 375–414.

Wilkinson, Charles F., and John M. Volkman. 1975. "Judicial Review of Indian Treaty Abrogation: 'As Long as Water Flows, or Grass Grows Upon the Earth'—How Long a Time Is That?" *California Law Review,* 63 (January): 601–661.

Williams, C. Herb, and Walt Neubrech. 1976. *Indian Treaties: American Nightmare.* Seattle, WA: Outdoor Empire.

Williams, Robert A., Jr. 1997. *Linking Arms Together: American Indian Treaty Visions of Law and Peace, 1600–1800.* Oxford: Oxford University Press.

Wunder, John R. 1985. "No More Treaties: The Resolution of 1871 and the Alteration of Indian Rights to Their Homelands" in *Working the Range: Essays on the History of Western Land Management and the Environment,* ed. John R. Wunder, 39–56. Westport, CT: Greenwood Press.

Indian Treaties as International Agreements

Development of the European Nation State and International Law

Communities of peoples have negotiated agreements with one another for thousands of years. Treaties dating from Babylonian, Assyrian, and Hittite times still exist, written in cuneiform on clay tablets and laying out terms of peace, land exchange, and trade. First applied to the negotiation process rather than to the document, the term *treaty* ultimately came to mean an agreement made by the highest authority, or sovereign, as opposed to sponsions and other agreements made without the full commission of the sovereign (Grotius 1925, 391). The current understanding of treaties, as documents negotiated to establish relations among states and as a primary source of international law, developed as Europe moved from the Middle Ages to the Renaissance.

In the fifteenth century, the Catholic Church, despite its history of corruption and schisms, retained its preeminent power as the religious and secular European authority. The pope, considered God's representative, possessed the authority to crown and dispose of secular rulers, to settle disputes, to excommunicate individuals from the body of the Church and from everlasting salvation, and to bestow legitimacy on new ideas and fields of knowledge or declare them heretical. Three hundred years later, technological advancements, discoveries of new lands and resources, and the rise of the nation-state had severely undermined the authority of the Catholic Church.

The introduction of multiple masts and sails and construction of the caravel (a small, three-masted ship) allowed European rulers to expand their trade and commerce and to sail to new parts of the world, where they found lands of untold resources, sizes, and possibilities. Johannes Gutenberg's invention of movable type around 1450 opened education and knowledge to those beyond the Church. The adoption of gunpowder from China between 1500 and 1600 created a military revolution, allowing European rulers the means to solidify and expand their control over their lands in continental Europe and in the newfound territories.

All these technological improvements assisted the Portuguese and the Spanish in their rediscovery of Africa and the Western Hemisphere. In 1420, under the direction of Prince Henry the Navigator, the Portuguese reached the Madeira Islands and ushered in the European age of exploration. Seven years later, Portuguese explorers had reached the Azores; in 1456, the Cape Verde Islands.

Four years before Bartholomeu Dias sailed around the southernmost tip of Africa in 1488, King John of Portugal had declined to support Christopher Columbus's proposal to sail eastward. Acquiring the support of Queen Isabella of Spain, Columbus rediscovered the Western Hemisphere in 1492. To avoid conflict with Portugal, Queen Isabella requested that Pope Alexander VI divide these newly discovered oceans and lands between the two nations. In 1494, Pope Alexander VI, following negotiations between King John II and Queen Isabella, issued the Treaty of Tordesilla of 1494, dividing the earth by drawing a demarcation line 370 leagues west of the Cape Verde Islands.

As the wealth from these new lands swelled the Spanish and Portuguese coffers, the French and English explorers, disputing the pope's authority to divide the earth, sent their own explorers to claim new lands. Papal authority came under decided political attack in 1576 when the French jurist and natural law philosopher Jean Bodin published *The Six Books of the Commonwealth.* Contained within these essays was the new philosophical concept of sovereignty. Sovereignty, Bodin argued, was the existence of a unified authority in a political community. As the sovereign, the French king held absolute and perpetual power within the French state (Bodin 1576). The monarch derived this total authority to govern from God, not from the pope. As sovereign, the king possessed the authority to make laws binding on its subjects, to declare war and peace, to establish state offices, and to act as the final court of redress.

As the political, economic, and military powers of the developing European nation-states grew and the pope's authority declined, monarchs recognized the need to regulate their interactions through the development of binding international legal principles and documents, which bore an assortment of names, including *treaty, agreement, act, statute,* and *covenant,* among many others. By 1739, Jean Barbeyric had listed sixty subjects of treaties. A reference in the 1427 British Rolls of Parliament is the first known European use of the term *treaty* (Meyers 1957, 579). Approximately a quarter century later, the printing of papal bulls in 1461 is recorded as the first publication of an international document. The first collection of treaties was published in 1643, five years before the negotiation of the Treaty of Westphalia, identified by many scholars as the first modern treaty leading to the development of modern international relations (Liverani 1980, 50).

International law at this time had no prescribed procedure or format for treaty making. As long as the appropriate sovereign authority had approved the negotiations and provisions, the agreement constituted a treaty, whether written or oral. In 1758, Emmerich de Vattel, a Swiss jurist, published the *Law of Nations,* considered the first textbook on international law. In the *Law of Nations,* Vattel defined a treaty as "[a] compact entered into by sovereigns for the welfare of the State, either in perpetuity or for a considerable length of time . . ." (Vattel 1916, 160). The highest state authority could only enter into treaties (ibid., 160). In Sections 220–221, Vattel emphasized the principle that became a fundamental rule of international law, *pacta sunt servanda,* that treaties are "sacred" and must be upheld. States that violate "the faith of treaties"—a faith that is sacred—violates the law of nations. Treaties, the European theorists agreed, created international norms that are binding and inviolable.

Treaty Negotiation between European Powers and Indian Nations

The Spanish monarchs, who were highly religious as well as legalistic, held innumerable discussions and councils to determine the proper treatment of these newly discovered inhabitants and their lands. Laws were published and revised, and conquests stopped for various periods as the most highly regarded intellectuals of the Spanish realm debated any number of issues. Were these Natives a natural part or a new branch of animals or humanity? Did their nature as heathens allow the Spanish to enslave them, to take their lands, to make war and conquer them, and to forcibly convert them to Christianity?

Spanish laws and policies toward the Native inhabitants and their lands initially allowed the unspeakable annihilation of Native communities and confiscation of their lands and resources. Theologians such as Bartolomé de Las Casas, Francisco Suárez, and Francisco de Vitoria (the latter two known as among the first proponents of international law) vociferously argued against Spanish policies in the Western Hemisphere, raising questions and putting forth principles relating to just war, the proper means of obtaining title to inhabited lands, statehood, and the just treatment of peoples. Often referred to as the father of human rights, Vitoria argued that the proper mode for relating to the Native inhabitants was through negotiations and treaties. Only if the Native inhabitants refused to conclude treaties establishing a relationship with Spain could the Spanish legally and morally go to war. Slowly but eventually, Spanish laws in theory (but not always in practice) reflected the ideas and principles espoused by these thinkers.

As explorers and settlers traveled to the Western Hemisphere, increasing the competition among the European powers, rulers directed their representatives to negotiate with the Indian nations for access to land, resources, and trade and to form military alliances. As suggested by Vitoria, the negotiation of treaties proved the most effective procedure for accomplishing these objectives. The total number of treaties concluded by Spain and the other European nations with the Indian nations is unknown. Many early treaties were oral, their existence known only through descriptions written at the time of the councils and the subsequent agreements. Over time, European representatives, needing to prove the existence of these agreements to their competitors, formalized the agreements in written form. Many of these documents have disappeared or remain hidden in state and personal archives and personal collections throughout the world.

As discussed below, European states in general regarded the treaties concluded with the Indian powers as equal to and as legally binding as the treaties they concluded with one another. Vattel also addressed this issue in *Law of Nations,* stating that "faith of treaties has no relation to the difference of religion, and cannot in any manner depend upon it." As for treaties concluded with infidels, Vattel, citing Grotius, states that only natural laws and not spiritual law were to govern the "Rule of treaties of Nations" (ibid., 162). Grotius, too, had earlier referred to this issue, pointing out that treaties made between equal sovereigns and those made between unequal sovereigns differed in subject matter, not validity. Treaties between equal sovereigns generally dealt with the return of captives, the restoration of property, commerce arrangements, and mutual

assistance. Treaties between strong and weak heads of states, in which an impairment of sovereignty resulted, discussed indemnities, withdrawal from territory, and the surrender of fortresses.

Treaty making, no matter the time or culture, involves a negotiation process followed by a symbolic acceptance of the agreed-upon terms. As did most societies, the Indian nations of North, Central, and South America possessed their own traditional forms of negotiating agreements, resolving disputes, and ending wars. Vine Deloria, Jr., and Raymond J. DeMallie, in their important two-volume work, *Documents of American Indian Diplomacy: Treaties, Agreements, and Conventions, 1775–1979,* describe two of these procedures. The Indian nations in the Great Lakes area solidified their agreements with the exchange of wampum and gifts. Other Indian nations employed special and sacred ceremonies that, once performed, signified the end of hostilities and the restoration of mutual peace. Among the Sioux people, the sacred pipe ceremony restored peace among enemies. DeMallie and Deloria (1999) also provide a general overview of Indian treaty-making procedures. No matter the tribe's particular negotiation procedure or the ultimate symbol of acceptance, the tribal parties, like the western world, regarded the negotiations and ensuing agreements as binding.

Although the Native and the western worlds both regarded their negotiated agreements as legitimate and valid, Deloria and DeMallie (1999) point out a subtle but important distinction between the two cultures in their understanding, approach, and ultimate responsibility to these agreements. Among Native communities, agreements— especially those ending a state of conflict—represented a sacred commitment by each side to alter their relationship with one another. The agreement to establish peace was a decision to actively create "a distinct state of being." It was not, as understood in western society, simply an agreement to desist from certain practices that caused conflict. From a cultural perspective, Indian nations understood treaties and agreements as sacred. The words, whether spoken or written, were living representations of each party's commitment to the other.

The western approach to treaty making was of a different and far more practical magnitude. Although, as Vattel emphasized, states were bound by natural law to honor their treaty commitments—otherwise they were of little benefit—the treaty process was an efficient procedure and treaties a practical vehicle for obtaining one's objectives through give-and-take. Although they supposedly remained legally binding, the treaty procedure and document, once concluded, had fulfilled their purpose.

This differing cultural understanding of agreements further affected the two cultures' choices of negotiation procedures. Given the sanctity and totality with which many tribal peoples imbued their decisions, the agreement had to be thoroughly considered and supported. In many tribes, those given the authority to negotiate did not possess the power to ratify. Depending upon the particular tribal arrangement, decisions may have required the support of clan leaders, the approval of related bands, or full tribal consensus. This decision-making process often proved lengthy and infuriating to the Europeans and (especially later) to the Americans, who preferred to settle issues quickly and smoothly.

The Dutch negotiated one of the first known treaties in North America, with the Iroquois in 1613 (Van Loon 1968, 22–26). D'Arcy McNickle discusses an important treaty concluded between the Mohawks and Dutch in 1643 that may have played a role in the Mohawks' annihilation of the Huron Nation in 1645. France concluded many treaties with tribes, including a treaty of friendship with the Onondaga on June 2, 1622, two with the Six Nations in 1633 and 1635, and two with the Huron Nation in 1641 and 1645 (McNickle 1973, 130). The total number of pre–Revolutionary War treaties concluded by England and the colonies with the Indian nations is unknown. Benjamin Franklin published thirteen treaties concluded by the Pennsylvania colony with various tribes from 1738–1762 (Boyd 1938). Later, on Canada's behalf, Great Britain concluded eleven treaties with Indian nations living within Canadian boundaries. It is interesting to note that Canada did not receive the authority to negotiate treaties as a sovereign entity until the passage of the Statute of Westminster in 1931. Another fifty-four treaties concluded between the English colonies and the eastern tribes from 1677 to 1768 appear in a 1917 collection by H. DePuy (DePuy 1917). Deloria and DeMallie include information on another five treaties that England concluded with various non-Iroquoian tribes, such as the Chippewa, the Potawatomi, the Ottawa, and others, between 1777 and 1798.

The treaty of 1752 between Governor Peregrine Thomas Hopson and the Micmac Indians serves as an example of the many treaties concluded during the pre–Revolutionary War period. The treaty comprised eight articles, the first of which renewed former treaties. The second article established an alliance between the parties, and the third and fourth articles detailed the signatories' agreements on trade and hunting and fishing practices. The fifth and sixth articles stipulated the payment, agreed to by the English, to the tribe in return for their negotiations. In the seventh article, the tribes agreed to assist shipwrecked mariners, and the final article provided a procedure for resolving disputes (DePuy 1917, 30).

Two years later, in October 1754 in Philadelphia, the Massachusetts, Connecticut, and Pennsylvania colonies negotiated one of their most important treaties with the Six Nations (McNickle 1973, 137). In a treaty of military alliance, the Six Nations agreed to align themselves with the English in their war against France—an alliance that may have saved England's claim to the eastern half of the United States (ibid., 132.). A final example is a multilateral treaty negotiated in 1758 among the Pennsylvania and the New Jersey colonies and the Six Nations, the Delaware, the Minnisink, and other Indian tribes to settle a land dispute between New Jersey and the Minnisink Indians and to cede formerly purchased lands back to the Six Nations (DePuy 1917, 44).

Spain, as mentioned earlier, concluded a number of treaties with Indian nations throughout the Western Hemisphere. Within the area that became the United States, DeMallie and Deloria list two groups of Spanish treaties negotiated with the Indian nations. The first list includes treaties reached between Spain and the southeastern Creek, Seminole, Chickasaw, Choctaw, and Cherokee nations between 1784 and 1802. The second group covers treaties negotiated between Spain and the Comanche, the Navajo, and the Apache from 1786 to 1819 (DeMallie and Deloria 1999, 106–107).

The Spanish treaties with the southeastern Indian nations are particularly interesting for their insight into the Europeans' view of Indian treaties. Following British cession to Spain of its claims to Florida, the Muscogee Creek chief, Alexander McGillivray, wrote to the Spanish governor, asking that Spain accept the Creek Nation as a protectorate:

> If in the event of war Britain has been compelled to withdraw its protection from us, she has no right to transfer us with their former possessions to any power whatever contrary to our inclination and interest. We certainly as a free Nation have a right to choose our protector . . . (Caughey 1938, 64–65)

Spain agreed, and in the treaty signed at Pensacola on June 1, 1784, the Creeks promised to "maintain an inviolable peace and fidelity toward Spain" and agreed to the formation of a mutual defense alliance (*American State Papers,* 279). This treaty was the first of several that Spain concluded with tribes in western Florida for military alliances and for small land cessions for the construction of Spanish forts and trading stations (Holmes 1969, 140–154).

Although the Creeks promised in the Pensacola treaty to obey the "sovereign orders" of the province's commandant, the Spanish clearly did not consider the Creeks to be stripped of the external sovereignty. In 1786, the Muscogee Creek Nation, without consulting their Spanish allies, waged war on Georgia for refusing to stop settlers from moving onto the Creek lands. The Creeks reminded their protector that the Pensacola treaty provided for a mutual alliance, and Spain contributed arms and ammunitions to the Creek's war.

Six years later, changes in the political and commercial climate persuaded the Creek Nation to sign the Treaty of New York with the newly formed United States on August 14, 1791. Though displeased, the Spanish governor conceded that he was powerless to alter the situation, as the Creeks were an independent nation and could treat with whom they pleased. In the treaty, the United States agreed to pay the Creeks for lands taken by Georgia citizens. In return, the Creeks offered friendship and accepted protection from the United States over Creek lands located with the American sphere of influence. The Creeks refused, despite U.S. objections, to relinquish Spanish protection over those Creek lands within the Spanish sphere. The Creeks also rebuffed the American offer to establish trade relations with the United States, preferring to maintain the services of the English. Article 2 of the treaty further illustrates the Creeks' decision to maintain their external independence. In this article, the Creeks agreed not to negotiate with any individual, state, or citizen of a state. They did not, however, agree to refrain from treating with other foreign nations. Two years after the Treaty of New York, the Creeks, along with the Alibamon, Choctaw, Chickasaw, and Talapuche nations, signed another treaty with Spain to protect their boundaries against American encroachment and to provide the tribes with certain necessities. In Article 19, the tribes agreed to maintain an offensive and defensive alliance among the Chickasaw, Creek,

Choctaw, Talapuche, Alibamon, and Cherokee Nations.

Mexico's independence from Spain did not end the use of treaty making as a vehicle for settling disputes among the various tribes and between the provincial and national governments, especially along the southern border areas. Annual reports of the commissioner of Indian affairs in 1872 and 1874 refer to Mexico's efforts to secure its borders by negotiating agreements with the Apache. DeMallie and Deloria list more than twenty treaties, an estimated one-third of the treaties Mexico negotiated from 1821 to 1850, with Indian nations currently found within the U.S. boundaries. Even Russia, which settled only briefly in the continental United States, signed a treaty in 1817 with the Pomo Indians, located north of present-day San Francisco.

Early American Treaties with the Indian Nations

As the outbreak of war appeared imminent, England and the new revolutionary government engaged in a flurry of negotiations with the Indian nations, each seeking military allies or, at minimum, Indian neutrality in the war. Not surprisingly, the new American government, operating under the Articles of Confederation, adopted the English procedure of negotiating with the Indian nations through treaties. This tradition, in fact, directly affected the colonies' agreement over the treaty-making power in Article IX of the Articles of Confederation. Fearful that the new Congress would negotiate unfavorable treaties concerning land cessions, southern representatives to the Constitutional Convention insisted that all treaties required the support of nine states for approval.

The new government concluded its first treaty in 1778, with the Delaware Nation. Differing little in subject and tone from treaties later concluded with European nations, the United States promised peace and friendship with the Delaware Nation, established trade between the two nations, and instituted a procedure for punishing transgressors. Of particular interest was Article 6, which guaranteed that, if the Delaware, in concert with other tribes, wished to form a state within the Union, the Delaware would be appointed leaders of the congressional delegation. Of further importance was the treaty's forthright response to British charges that the United States planned to seize Indian lands illegally and violate its promises to honor prior treaties:

> Whereas, the enemies of the United States have endeavored by every artifice in their power, to possess the Indians . . . with an opinion, that it is the design of the states (to) take possession of their country; to obviate such false suggestions, the United States do engage or guarantee to the aforesaid nations of Delawares, and their heirs, all their territorial rights, in the most fullest and ample manner, as it hath been bounded by former treaties. (*Article Six* 1975, 3)

The success of the United States in negotiating with the Delaware was significant, for most eastern tribes, having found their dealings with the colonists less than honorable, aligned with the British. The Americans did succeed in obtaining the support of the Oneida and the Tuscarora Nations—an alliance that effectively split the Iroquois Confederacy and at least reduced, if not ensured, the time frame to American victory.

By the late 1780s, Congress had recognized the failure of the Articles of Confederation as a governing document. In 1789, the states ratified the Constitution, establishing a stronger central government with control over a federal system. Article II, Section 2, clause 2 granted to the president "[the] Power, by and with the Advice and Consent of the Senate, to make Treaties, provided two thirds of the Senators present concur." On May 25, 1789, President George Washington directed Secretary of War Henry Knox to deliver two treaties to the Senate for its first action of advice and consent. President of the Senate John Adams received in Knox's package two treaties that the Continental Congress had negotiated with Indian nations at Fort Harmar. On June 12, the Senate selected a three-member committee to consider these treaties. On September 8, the Senate Executive Journals noted that the Senate had adopted a resolution advising the president "to execute and enjoin an observance of" one of the two treaties, the treaty with the Wyandot and other Indian nations.

After receiving the Senate's approval, President Washington sent another communication to the Senate, asking the Senate to clarify whether Indian treaties required Senate approval:

> The treaties with certain Indian Nations, which were laid before you with my message of the 25th of May last, suggested two questions to my mind, viz: 1st, Whether those treaties were to be considered as perfected, and, consequently as obligatory, without being ratified. If

not, then 2ndly, whether both, or either, and which of them, ought to be ratified? (Ralston 1920, 15)

The Senate assigned the question to another three-member committee. The following day, the committee reported its conclusion that Indian treaties did not require Senate approval. The full Senate rejected the recommendation and responded to Washington that the Constitution required Senate ratification of all treaties negotiated with Indians.

For the next three years, representatives and government officials remained at odds over the Constitution's intent regarding the extent and form of the Senate's advice prior and during the negotiation process. To Washington's dismay, during the first few years the Senators took it upon themselves to play an integral role in the negotiation process. In 1794, the Senate issued its first refusal to consent to a treaty transmitted from the executive branch. This "first" also involved an Indian treaty—a treaty that the executive branch had concluded with the Illinois and Wabash nations without advance Senate involvement. It is unclear whether the Senate's refusal to consent to the treaty arose from their objections to the treaty's terms or from their lack of prior involvement.

The United States adopted similar procedures whether negotiating with European powers or the Indian nations. International law requires that a valid treaty must be negotiated on the authority of the highest sovereign. Every nation has developed its own diplomatic procedures and documentation to assure the negotiation authority of other parties. In 1786, Congress authorized the War Department to manage Indian relations. The executive branch continued this procedure under the new Constitution, placing the Indian Office (the precursor of the Bureau of Indian Affairs) under the authority of the War Department. From 1824 until the creation of the Department of the Interior in 1849, the Department of War regulated Congress's relationship with the Indian nations. Once the president or Congress requested the negotiation of a treaty and Congress appropriated the necessary funds, the secretary of war issued a document or commission to the negotiators outlining the government's objectives for the treaty. Whether the government's interest lay in land cessions, trade, alliances, or other matters, these documents provided general instructions concerning the promises made and the funding allowed.

Over time, the treaties concluded by the United States with the Indian nations became increasingly formal and legalistic, using the style and form and covering the subject matter common to all treaties of the time. Indian treaties, written in the same lofty language, were divided into preamble, body, and salutation. The treaty concluded between the United States and the Creek Nation in 1790 at New York opens with the following preamble:

> The parties being desirous of establishing permanent peace and friendship between the United States and the said Creek Nation, and the citizens and members thereof, and to remove the causes of war by ascertaining their limits, and making other necessary, just and friendly arrangements: the President of the United States, Secretary for the Department of War, whom he hath constituted with full powers for these purposes, by and with the advice and consent of the Senate of the United States and the Creek Nation, by the undersigned kings, chiefs and warriors, representing the said nation, have agreed to the following articles: . . .

The salutation reads, "In witness of all and whole Creek nation, the parties have hereunto set their hands and seals, in the City of New York, with the United States, this seventh day of August, one thousand seven hundred and ninety," after which each participant affixed his signature.

In keeping with Grotius's (1925) discussion of international treaties, Indian treaties dealt with the fixing of boundaries (Treaty of January 21, 1785; Treaty of November 28, 1785; Treaty of August 19, 1825), the promise of mutual assistance (Treaty of January 9, 1789; Treaty of July 22, 1814), the exchange of prisoners and hostages (Treaty of October 22, 1784; Treaty of January 21, 1785; Treaty of November 28, 1785), and the establishment of garrisons and forts (Treaty of June 16, 1802; Treaty of November 10, 1808). Also included as subjects of negotiations, were provisions on passports (Treaty of July 2, 1791; Treaty of August 7, 1790), extradition (Treaty of July 2, 1791; Treaty of March 12, 1858; Treaty of June 19, 1859), white immigration onto Indian lands (Treaty of May 24, 1835; Treaty of March 6, 1861), and the right to declare war and conclude treaties with third powers (Treaty of August 24, 1835; Treaty of May 26, 1837).

The new government's decision to entrust the State Department to maintain copies of Indian treaties among their files of other international agreements further illustrates that the United States regarded Indian treaties as international agreements. Listed first in State Department records is a treaty in 1722 between the Six Nations and New York and Pennsylvania. In 1837, the State Department commissioned Samuel D. Langtree and John Louis O'Sullivan to publish the Indian treaties concluded between 1789 and 1813.

Further evidence exists that, in addition to using international treaty standards of procedure, form, and tone in negotiating Indian treaties, the United States regarded Indian treaties as having an international impact on its domestic and foreign policy decisions. As noted above, Indian treaties determined the structure of treaty making under the Articles of Confederation. Indian treaties constituted the first set of treaties delivered to the Senate and rejected by the Senate under the new Constitution. The precedent for obtaining Indian lands through treaties ultimately allayed concerns that President Thomas Jefferson had overstepped his executive authority in concluding a treaty with France for the Louisiana Purchase in 1803. The necessity to subject Indian treaties to the same international legal standards as all treaties also affected U.S. foreign policy decisions. In 1795, England expressed concern to the United States that an American treaty signed that year with several Indian nations had abrogated part of the Jay Treaty of 1794 negotiated between England and the United States the previous year.

The Treaty of Peace ending the American war of independence had left several outstanding issues. Until France's declaration of war on England in 1792, another war appeared imminent between England and the United States. Now anxious to neutralize American involvement in this war, England agreed to sign the Treaty of Amity, Commerce, and Navigation, referred to as the Jay Treaty, with the United States in November 1794. This treaty resolved several key conflicts between the two nations by creating a joint commission to settle boundary disputes, reestablishing American trade with the West Indies, providing for British withdrawal from forts in the Old Northwest, and reaffirming the rights of Indian nations vis-à-vis the new American boundary.

The Indian nations had fought alongside the British in the war as their equals and were incensed at their exclusion from the Treaty of Peace negotiations. Joseph Brandt, chief of the Mohawk, in particular voiced his opposition to the treaty, pointing out that King George had given his personal guarantee that the British would protect the Mohawks' aboriginal lands in New York State and Canada. Anxious to reduce their allies' concerns, in Article 3 of the Jay Treaty the British negotiated an agreement that the Indian nations could freely travel and trade goods across the new border.

The following year, the U.S. government concluded a treaty with several Indian nations, including, among others, the Wyandot, the Miami, the Delaware, the Shawnee, and the Chippewa. During this period, the relations that traders established with the Indian nations often determined and symbolized the tribes' relationship with Americans. Given that the United States possessed no jurisdiction over Indian lands, the U.S. government had no control over traders admitted onto Indian lands. In an effort to control traders and commerce with Indian nations, the government included, as a point of negotiation with tribes, an article that requested tribes to admit only those traders who had obtained the proper license from the U.S. government. Upon hearing of this treaty stipulation, Great Britain expressed concern that this provision violated Article 3 of the Jay Treaty. The following year, the United States agreed to negotiate an explanatory note, a document recognized under international law as having the status of a binding treaty, reaffirming the stipulations of the Jay Treaty by stating that the treaty concluded with the tribes at Greenville, August 3, 1795, "can not be understood to derogate in any manner from the rights of free intercourse and commerce, secured by the third article . . ." (*Respecting the Liberty* 1794).

The U.S. recognition of the international legitimacy of the treaties concluded between the Indian nations and other European powers is further illustrated in Article 6 of the 1803 treaty concluded between the United States and France for the Louisiana Cession:

> The United States promise to execute such treaties and articles as may have been agreed between Spain and the tribes and nations of Indians until by mutual consent of the United States and the said tribes or nations other suitable articles shall have been agreed upon. (Treaty with France 1803)

The Treaty of Peace of 1776, the Jay Treaty of 1794, and the Explanatory Note of 1796 did not end the competition and suspicion between the United States and England. By 1812, war had again broken out between the two powers, and again both sides sought the alliances of the Indian nations. The great Shawnee chief Tecumseh clearly foresaw the danger that the United States posed to Indian people and worked tirelessly to create a confederacy of tribes from Canada to Florida to fight with the British. A brigadier general in the British army, Tecumseh expressed disgust upon hearing of Britain's capitulation to the Americans two years later.

At the peace negotiations concluding the war, England sought recognition from the United States of an independent Indian buffer state. In a treatise written before the negotiations, Nathaniel Atcheson laid out nine points on which Great Britain should negotiate the treaty, emphasizing that the Indian nations were "independent both of us and of the Americans" and that their independence should be secured. Three of the nine points dealt with the status and security of the Indian nations: a new boundary line for the Indian Territory; that the Americans not be allowed to erect forts, military posts, or other public property in Indian Territory; and that Great Britain guarantee the boundaries of the Indian state (Atcheson, 1814).

For months, negotiations stalled over the Americans' refusal to recognize an Indian buffer state. The British finally relented upon the agreement of the United States in Article 9 to restore tribal rights to the 1811 status quo. After ratification of the Treaty of Ghent, ending the War of 1812, both the United States and England negotiated new treaties with their former Indian enemies during the war, restoring recognition of tribal rights to their prewar status.

The War of 1812 ended the Indian nations' ability to serve as a master player in the international intrigues of the East. With the East in firm control, the United States turned its attention to the Mexico Gulf and Florida region, where General Andrew Jackson fought against the English, the Spanish, and their military allies, the Muscogee Creek Confederacy, for final control of the region.

From the British, the United States had inherited the right to treat with and secure lands from the Indian nations of the Old Northwest. Over the next several decades, U.S. forces solidified their control of this area by negotiating with the tribes in groups, pairs, and individually. By the late 1820s, the public clamor, especially from the southern states, to move all eastern tribes to lands west of the Mississippi had become an important political platform for presidential hopeful Andrew Jackson. A few of the southern states, such as Georgia, had passed state laws assuming jurisdictional control over tribally held lands. Now president, Jackson introduced legislation in Congress giving the tribes the choice to move west or stay in the South and submit to the state laws. The tribes and their supporters loudly protested passage of this removal bill, pointing out that the United States possessed no jurisdiction over the Indian nations and that such legislation violated previous treaties and laws recognizing Indian sovereignty and title to their lands.

Well known among European powers as an American leader with little integrity in warfare and even less honor in upholding promises, Jackson had no use for the niceties of law, whether domestic or international. Jackson's philosophy was based entirely on necessity; whatever was necessary to expand the glory of the American republic was just. Congress passed the removal bill by a mere five votes.

The Cherokee Nation responded to the bill's passage by filing an injunction before the U.S. Supreme Court as a foreign nation. As a foreign state, the tribe's attorney, former U.S. attorney general William Wirt, argued that the State of Georgia possessed no authority to execute "certain laws [that] . . . go directly to annihilate the Cherokees as a political society and to seize for the use of Georgia the lands of the nation which have been assured to them by the United States in solemn treaties . . ." (*Cherokee* 1831). The Cherokees, Wirt stated, had been sovereigns from time immemorial, "acknowledging no earthly superior."

The *Cherokee Nation v. Georgia* case proved especially inconvenient for John Marshall. A political opponent of Andrew Jackson, Marshall fully realized that Jackson would ignore any Supreme Court decision that contravened his political agenda (*Cherokee* 1831). For a president to ignore a Supreme Court decision so early in the nation's history would jeopardize the Court's future role in U.S. politics, a role not well articulated by the constitutional authors. Wishing to avoid a showdown with Jackson, Marshall sought to have the case dismissed.

By cleverly employing domestic law to answer questions of international law and manipulating the very meaning of treaties, Marshall ruled that the Cherokees had no standing to bring the case directly to the Supreme Court as a foreign nation. The treaties signed between the Cherokee Nation and the United States, Marshall argued, had placed the Cherokees under the protection of the United States. Through this action, Marshall concluded, the Cherokees had given up their foreign status and had become "domestic, dependent nations."

In his dissent, Justice Smith Thompson refuted Marshall's analysis that the Cherokees had placed themselves under U.S. protection. By comparing the sixth article of the Treaty of Hopewell with the Cherokees in 1785 with the twenty-seventh article of the U.S. treaty with England in 1794, Thompson argued that both provisions dealt with the extradition of wanted criminals from Cherokee and English territory, respectively.

> The necessity for the stipulation in both cases must be, because the process of one government and jurisdiction will not run into that of another; and separate and distinct jurisdiction . . . is what makes governments and nations foreign to each other in their political relations. (*Cherokee* 1831)

The Cherokees refused to give up. The following year, Samuel Worcester, Elizur Butler, and two other missionaries deliberately broke a Georgia law requiring a state license to live on Indian lands. Georgia officials arrested the men, who were sentenced to four years in prison at hard labor. Once again, William Wirt appeared before the Supreme Court to argue the inapplicability of Georgia's laws over Cherokee lands. This time, Wirt based his case on the argument that the Constitution granted "the regulation of intercourse with the Indians" exclusively to the federal government. The government, Wirt argued, exercised this power through treaties and congressional acts. Any attempts by states to alter or void federal law violated the Constitution.

Marshall agreed with the plaintiffs, finding the Georgia laws to be an unconstitutional interference with the treaties concluded between the United States and the Cherokees. To support his ruling, Marshall discussed the proper legal interpretation that should be accorded to Indian treaties. In analyzing the first negotiated treaty of the United States with the Delaware Nation, Marshall found that "[in] its language and in its provisions, [the treaty] is formed, as near as may be, on the model of treaties between the crowned heads of Europe." The treaties concluded by the United States with the Indian tribes in general, as Marshall pointed out, arose from the "same necessity and on the same principle" as those treaties concluded with France (*Cherokee* 1831).

> The words *treaty* and *nation* are words of our own language, selected in our diplomatic and legislative proceedings, by ourselves, having each a definite and well-understood meaning. We have applied them to Indians, as we have applied them to the other nations of the earth; they are applied to all in the same sense. (*Worcester* 1832)

In *Cherokee Nation*, Marshall had used Indian treaties in part to prove that Indian nations were not foreign states. In *Worcester,* he had applied international legal principles to show how Cherokee treaties proved Cherokee sovereignty and independence. Within two years, Marshall had cleverly manipulated and interpreted the role and status of Indian treaties to serve conflicting purposes—a masterful feat not lost on future generations of American judges.

The *Worcester* victory provided the tribes with no practical protection. Hoping to find a new life free of white interference, many tribes negotiated treaties with the United States to move their people west. The U.S. military forcibly "assisted" those individuals and groups who were too reluctant or too slow. The removal of the eastern tribes slowed the government's hunger for tribal lands only briefly.

Looking for new lands, the United States had attempted on more than one occasion to purchase Texas from Mexico. In 1836, Texas declared her independence from Mexico. During her nine years as an independent republic, Texas concluded twelve treaties with various indigenous tribes, including the indigenous Tonkawa, Comanche, Wichita, and Apache, as well as with immigrant bands from the Cherokee, Delaware, and Shawnee nations, fleeing white encroachment of their aboriginal lands.

Congress annexed Texas in 1845 and a year later added the Oregon Territory. Victory in the Mexican War added the entire Southwest in 1848. The discovery of gold in California (1849) and Colorado (1858) brought waves of settlers across tribal lands in the West. Five years later, the Gadsden Purchase completed the present exterior boundaries of the United States. In ten short years, the country's population increased by 32 percent and its size by 70 percent. Between 1830 and 1860, eight states and five territories were added to the Union. To open up this newly acquired territory to settlement, the government embarked on a negotiating frenzy with tribes, securing 174 million acres of land in fifty-three treaties with tribes between 1853 and 1857.

For a period, the Civil War interrupted the western exodus as the North fought to preserve the Union. After declaring its independence from the United States, the Confederacy quickly entered into treaty negotiations with the Indian nations in the important border regions. The politics between the Union and the Confederacy proved especially disastrous among the Indian nations referred to as the Five Civilized Tribes: the Cherokee, the Choctaw, the Chickasaw, the Creek, and the Seminole. In each of these tribes, a handful of tribal citizens, primarily the wealthier mixed bloods, had adopted the southern agricultural system, which required slave labor in order to be economically efficient. Casting their lot with the Confederacy, these groups seceded from their own tribal nations and established rebel governments.

To solidify their relationship, especially their military and economic contributions, the Confederacy signed approximately nine treaties with these rebel governments and several western tribes. The Confederate treaties were quite liberal in the Confederacy's recognition of tribal authority, land, and resources. In return, the rebel groups accepted the protection of the Confederacy but retained the authority to make treaties with other Indian nations.

In the meantime, the de jure tribal governments, arguing the principle of *pacta sunt servanda* (treaties must be upheld), continued to support and fight for the Union, frequently in battles against their own people. After the war, the United States demanded that the Five Civilized Tribes renegotiate their treaties with the federal government. The resulting treaties, supposedly in retaliation for the tribes' treason, were actually negotiated with the southern tribal representatives, who were far more willing to grant away tribal rights and lands than were those who had fought and died for the Union.

Until the Civil War, treaty negotiations with individual tribes often followed a typical cycle. The earliest treaties dealt with peace, friendship, alliances, and land cessions. As immigrants flooded to new western frontiers that encroached on tribal lands, hostilities multiplied. To avoid costly battles, the American government pressured tribes to cede increasingly large areas of land—cessions containing lands often already sold to settlers by eastern speculators. As America's strength grew and the powers of tribes declined, treaty commissioners demanded changes in traditional negotiation and approval procedures, including prohibiting the participation of Native women and demanding that tribal councils forgo their time-consuming consensus building and provide immediate, on-site decisions. Commissioners were also not above appointing any group of Indians as tribal chiefs and investing them with the authority—that is, coercing them with alcohol— to sign treaties. Although treaties signed under duress, or without the sovereign's authority, are illegal, on only a few occasions did Congress refuse to ratify the Indian treaties placed before them. Living under corrupt agents and with little access to food, many tribes increasingly were forced to sign successive treaties that ceded more of their lands, required their children to attend manual labor schools, and allotted communally held lands to individual owners.

In still other instances, tribes negotiated treaties in good faith with U.S. representatives, only to find later that Congress had refused to ratify them or had altered their provisions without tribal approval. The most egregious example involved more than twenty treaties that the California tribes had negotiated with the federal Treaty Commission in 1851. The gold rush had started, and the government directed the Treaty Commission to treat with the Indians to secure title and access to their lands. Convinced that the remaining lands the tribes had reserved for their use also contain gold, the California representatives prevailed upon their colleagues to leave the treaties unratified. For the next fifty years, the physical location of these documents, now referred to as the "lost treaties," was unknown. Without proof of the areas they had ceded and those they had retained as reservation lands, the tribes (except for those in the northern part of the state) were left dependent upon the government to provide them with a land base.

The End of Treaty Making

Initially responsible for enforcing the treaty-established boundaries between Indian and white lands, the military's role changed from defending tribal lands from the encroachment of white settlers to suppressing tribes and often evicting them from their own lands. As the western wars escalated, President Ulysses S. Grant in 1867 appointed the Peace Commission to study the situation. The commission reported that the western hostilities primarily derived from the government's refusal to keep its treaty commitments and from its repeated demands for more tribal land cessions. Other government officials, such as Commissioner of Indian Affairs Ely Parker, a Seneca, pointed to the treaty process as the root of the problem, arguing that Congress should stop making treaties with the tribes and pass legislation to civilize them and open their lands to settlement.

Except for a few remaining Plains and Southwest tribal groups, governmental policies and actions had subdued and weakened most tribes, lending some credence to the argument that tribes no longer possessed the political power to negotiate treaties as equals. Justice Department officials countered vigorously that treaty making remained an effective tool for negotiating with tribes and maintained that ending treaty making without tribal consent was both illegal and dishonorable.

Whether tribes retained the capacity to negotiate treaties was of less concern to most policymakers than was the potential control that outside interests stood to gain from a change in the treaty-making policy. Under the current system, the executive branch took the lead in negotiating treaties, leaving the Senate only with the authority to confirm or refuse the treaty. The House of Representatives, jealous of the Senate's role, was left to appropriate funds for decisions into which they had had little input. Which tribes were contacted, which lands were purchased, and which resources were acquired led to decisions that had immeasurable impact on the representatives' constituents and the economic fortunes of their districts. Once again, Indian tribes became unwitting pawns in a competitive power play among the various branches of government and officials representing competing railroad, mining, livestock, and land speculation interests, among others.

In 1871, the House of Representatives attached the following rider to an appropriations bill: ". . . [T]hat hereafter no Indian nation or tribe within the territory of the United States shall be acknowledged or recognized as an independent nation, tribe, or power, with whom the United States may contract by treaty" (16 *Stat.* 566). Senator Eugene Casserly of California eloquently pinpointed the reason for the rider's passage:

> I know what the misfortune of the tribes is. Their misfortune is not that they are red men; not that they are semi-civilized, not that they are a dwindling race, not that they are a weak race. Their misfortune is that they hold great bodies of rich lands, which have aroused the cupidity of powerful corporations and of powerful individuals . . . I greatly fear that the adoption of this provision to discontinue treaty making is the beginning of the end in respect to Indian lands. It is the first step in a great scheme of spoliation, in which the Indians will be plundered, corporations and individuals enriched, and the American name dishonored in history. (McNickle 1973, 208)

The amendment in 1871 did not end the federal government's negotiations with tribes for lands and other matters. In the place of treaties, the government negotiated agreements, documents that were similar to treaties in content and effect but required the approval of both congressional houses before the president's signature. By the close of the nineteenth century, the United States had negotiated more than five hundred ratified and nonratified treaties with various Indian nations.

The end of treaty making allowed the government new freedom to legislate and establish policies and programs designed to educate and assimilate Indian people into the dominant society. Supportive of the rider and eagerly waiting in the wings to assist the government in their endeavors were the eastern reformers, philanthropists, and churches. In 1874, Congress passed a bill requiring tribal members to perform "useful labor" in return for their annuities, even though annuities represented payments for lands already ceded. The following year, in a prelude to the Dawes Act, individual Indians were encouraged to obtain land under the Homestead Act. In 1879, Congress instituted the rudiments of an Indian educational system with the establishment of the Carlisle Indian School, whose intentions were cogently summarized by the school's director in testimony before Congress: "We accept the watchword, let us by patient effort kill the Indian in him and save the man" (Gates 1885, 131).

As traditional tribal society broke down with the education of the young, the rise in power of the Indian agent, and the teaching of Christianity, the government increasingly supplanted Native practices with the Anglo system. Congress authorized Indian police forces and an Indian court of appeals. In 1886, through the passage of the Seven Major Crimes Act, the federal government assumed jurisdiction of major crimes committed by Indians. A year later, Congress passed the most assimilative piece of legislation to date, the Land in Severalty Act, or the Dawes Act, as it became known. Far surpassing any previous infringement on tribal life, the

Dawes Act provided for the allotment of reservation lands among tribal members, with individuals receiving either 40 acres of farmland or 160 acres of grazing land. Land left after the allotment process was sold to white settlers as surplus. Within less than 20 years, Congress had moved from treating with the tribes as national entities and acknowledging their rights to their land and internal sovereignty to restructuring the tribes' internal affairs and attempting to dissolve their reservations.

Tribes were not consulted about these governmental changes and policies, and many leaders protested and lobbied strongly against their imposition. Eventually, some tribes took their complaints to the Supreme Court, asking the Court to determine on what authority the federal government justified its assumption of such widespread authority over a sovereign people. The question was not easily answered. The U.S. Constitution clearly established the federal government as a government of enumerated powers, meaning that the federal government could exercise only those powers granted by the Constitution. Heretofore, the federal government had regulated its relationships with the Indian nations primarily through the treaty process, which affirmed that each sovereign possessed exclusive authority to make and enforce its own laws in its own land. The treaties negotiated between the U.S. government and the tribes dealt with national issues of trade, land, and military alliances. With few exceptions, tribes had not given the United States the authority to enter their lands or to enforce their laws. When tribes had delegated authority to the United States, it was to improve the lives of their community. For example, Indian governments in Indian Territory had for years protested to the surrounding governments that the latter's failure to control lawlessness had caused the problem to spill into tribal lands. Tribal governments had neither the resources nor the inclination to handle what they perceived as an outside problem. Eventually, tribes gave the United States the authority to enter tribal lands in pursuit of these criminals, a fact that the courts later used to justify U.S. authority over Indian lands.

For the federal government to claim individual control over Indian people would require the courts to "domesticize" the previously international legal principles that had regulated the treaty relationship between the United States and the various tribes. But, as John Marshall had illustrated, a little judicial ingenuity, creativity, and manipulations could provide the government with virtually any legal angle necessary.

The first major challenge to the U.S. assumption of authority came in the 1886 *U.S. v. Kagama* decision (*Kagama* 1886). The previous year, Congress had tacked the Seven Major Crimes Act onto an appropriations bill. The legislation provided the federal government with the authority to assume criminal jurisdiction over Indian individuals who had committed one of seven major crimes on Indian lands. Until then, tribes had handled violations of their laws according to their own codes and processes. On what basis could the federal government claim to have this authority? Tribes had not delegated this specific authority to the federal government in any of their treaties.

The government spuriously claimed that Congress's authority to pass the Major Crimes Act fell naturally under its authority to regulate commerce with the tribes. The commerce clause, Justice Samuel F. Miller ruled, was not the source of the government's authority. The government had recognized the tribes as semi-independent, "not as States, not as nations, but as separate people, with power of regulating their internal social relations and thus not brought into the laws of the Union or of the States within whose limits they resided," Miller acknowledged; but Congress had now decided to govern the tribes through federal legislation (*Kagama* 1886, 381–382). The tribes' dependent condition warranted this change in procedure, Miller asserted. Admitting that the actions of the federal government had weakened the tribes, they were, nonetheless, now wards of the nation, and the United States had a responsibility to care for its wards. In a masterful and convoluted reinterpretation of treaty law, Miller reasoned that the source of U.S. authority to care for the tribes derived from the very treaties the tribes had negotiated with the United States. The United States had offered its protection to tribes in their treaties. Legislation such as the Major Crimes Act fulfilled this promise of protection.

To conclude that Indian treaties, which tribes had negotiated as protection against the federal government and unwanted governmental incursions, had now become the ultimate source of the government's authority over tribes, has to be one of the most tortuous reinterpretations of law yet found in American history. Marshall had stressed in *Worcester* that Indian treaties represented the government's acknowledgement and agreement to protect tribal self-government; they did not imply the destruction of the protected. After the *Kagama* decision, the protections that tribes thought they had negotiated to preserve were nonexistent.

In 1903, in the *Lone Wolf v. Hitchcock* decision, the Supreme Court indicated the extent to which the government was prepared to divest tribes of their guaranteed treaty provisions (*Lone Wolf* 1903). Article 12 of the Treaty of Medicine Lodge stipulated that Congress could not dispose of certain reservation lands without the consent of three-fourths of the adult males. Unable to secure the necessary votes, the government took the land and sold it. Lone Wolf, on behalf of himself and other members of the Kiowa, Comanche, and Apache tribes, charged the government with disposing of tribal property in violation of the Treaty of Medicine Lodge and the protections afforded by the Fifth Amendment of the U.S. Constitution.

In an unbelievable decision, the Court reasoned that the tribes had misconstrued their treaty and had overlooked their dependent status and the government's role as their guardian. To hold Congress to the treaty would limit the government's authority to care for and protect the Indians. The Court conceded that previous courts had described tribal land rights as sacred as fee simple, but these cases had involved protecting tribal lands from the states and individuals. The treaties could not constrain the federal government because of the federal government's responsibility to care for its wards. Citing an earlier case, the Court ruled that the federal government was limited only by those ". . . considerations of justice as would control a Christian people in their treatment of an ignorant and dependent race" (*Beecher* 1877). Within less than a hundred years, the U.S. courts had legally manipulated or "domesticized" international legal principles that recognized and protected international independence, sovereignty, and treaties into domestic sources of authority that allowed the federal government unlimited control over Indian people.

Indian Treaties in the Twentieth Century

The United States closed the nineteenth century having abrogated treaties, forcibly taken Indian lands and lives, and destroyed tribal cultures through brute force and legal manipulations. Indian communities embarked on the twentieth century greatly diminished in numbers, land, and resources and having experienced one hundred years of war, diseases, famine, and cultural genocide. Against all odds, they had survived, bringing into the century an understanding of their identities, their nationhood, and the values their ancestors had fought to protect.

Over the next hundred years, the U.S. government continued its unrelenting attempt to convince indigenous peoples to forgo their cultures, wisdom, and communal identities by embracing and disappearing into the American maelstrom. By doing so, Indian people would become materially and socially self-sufficient, as had the millions of immigrants who had accepted American ideals. As had their ancestors before them, Indian people in large measure refused. The general U.S. population and its public officials possessed little comprehension and even less patience for this refusal, imposing assimilationist and terminationist policies on Indian people in various forms without their consent throughout the twentieth century.

In the eighteenth and nineteenth centuries, the treaty process had managed the relationships of the United States with the Indian nations. In the twentieth century, the very existence of Indian treaties provided an unbreachable psychological, legal, symbolic, and historical link between the United States and its indigenous peoples, between the past and the future, and between the legal and truly moral.

As the preceding discussion illustrated, Congress and the courts can and have legally reinterpreted, misinterpreted, and ignored Indian treaty rights and histories to meet broader domestic policies and objectives. American constitutional law is replete with Supreme Court decisions, such as *Cherokee Nation v. Georgia, U.S v. Kagama,* and *Lone Wolf,* that deftly manipulated the existence, status, and protections afforded by treaties to protect Indian nations and individuals.

As discussed previously, tribes, especially in later years, were often at a considerable disadvantage during the treaty negotiation process. Federal negotiators either purposefully or ignorantly negotiated binding agreements with individuals not authorized to represent the tribe, at times resorting to bribery or to intoxicating pliant tribal members as "chiefs." Because agreements were written in English, tribes were often totally dependent upon the facility and the honor of the individual translator.

In some instances, government officials threatened to withhold rations or annuities owed by earlier treaties until the tribe agreed to the provisions of a new treaty. Other tribal leaders found themselves with the choice of agreeing to a treaty or facing the threat of war or starvation. In other instances, tribes had negotiated and upheld their agreements in good faith, only to find years later that the Senate had struck out provisions, added new ones, or refused to ratify the treaty and compensate the tribe for their land cessions. In at least thirteen cases, when notified that Congress had altered the treaty, tribes rejected it upon its return for approval.

To assist in adjudicating a particularly complex legal area, the courts frequently develop a series of relevant principles or tests to guide judicial analysis. To compensate for these inequalities in the negotiation process and for the lack of precise language, and to ensure a balanced interpretation of the rights at issue, the Supreme Court has established several principles or canons of construction for use in adjudicating Indian treaty issues. The canons include these principles: that ambiguities in treaties must be resolved in favor of the tribes; that Indian treaties must be interpreted as the Indians would have understood them; that Indian treaties must be construed liberally in favor of the Indians; and that reserved rights must be explicitly extinguished by later treaties or congressional action. The following cases exemplify these standards: *Carpenter v. Shaw*, 280 U.S. 363, 367 (1930); *DeCoteau v. District Court*, 420 U.S. 425, 447 (1975); *Bryan v. Itasca County, Minnesota*, 426 U.S. 373, 392 (1976); *Jones v. Meehan*, 175 U.S. 1, 10 (1899); *U.S. v. Shoshone Tribe*, 304 U.S. 111, 116 (1938); *Choctaw Nation v. Oklahoma*, 397 U.S. 620, 631 (1970); *Tulee v. Washington*, 315 U.S. 681, 684–685 (1942); *Washington v. Washington State Commercial Passenger Fishing Vessel Ass'n*, 443 U.S. 658, 690 (1979); and *County of Oneida v. Oneida Indian Nation*, 470 U.S. 226, 247 (1985). Each tribe, tribal history, and negotiated treaty is unique, the Supreme Court emphasized in the *Minnesota v. Mille Lacs* decision (*Minnesota* 1999). The proper interpretation of a particular treaty requires an in-depth historical investigation of the era in which the tribe negotiated the treaty, including but not limited to an examination of government policy, archival records of congressional debates and treaty negotiations, and tribal oral and written histories.

Not surprisingly, a review of the Court's application of the canons of construction in Indian treaty cases over the last half century or so reveals a rather uneven and judicious use of the canons, depending upon the importance of the issue in question. During the 1970s, a time of stated congressional policy to restore tribal sovereignty and tribal governmental powers, several cases pointed to tribal treaties as proof of inherent tribal powers. In three important cases decided between 1959 and 1973, the Supreme Court ruled in favor of Navajo sovereignty based on the protections inherent in their 1868 treaty with the United States.

In the *Williams v. Lee* case in 1959, the Court held that the Navajo treaty of 1868 protected the Navajos' authority to exercise control over internal issues—in this instance, the tribal courts' exclusive jurisdiction over a non-Indian's collection of a debt from an Indian on the reservation (*Williams* 1959). In the *Warren Trading Post v. Arizona Tax Commission* case, the treaty of 1868 also prevented the State of Arizona from collecting state taxes from non-Indians whose businesses lay within reservation boundaries (*Warren* 1965). In the *McClanahan v. Arizona State Tax Commission* case of 1973, noting that Indian sovereignty provided "a backdrop" against which to interpret Indian treaties and federal policies, the Court ruled that Arizona could not collect state taxes from Indians whose "income was derived from reservation sources" (*McClanahan* 1973).

The Supreme Court also invoked the existence and protection of Indian treaties in two of its most resounding victories for tribal sovereignty. In 1974, in *Morton v. Mancari*, the Supreme Court ruled that the Bureau of Indian Affairs policy of providing special preference for Indians did not constitute racial discrimination in violation of the Equal Employment Opportunity Act (*Morton* 1974). Federal laws regarding Indians were passed to fulfill the government's unique political relationship with tribes. This relationship, the Court emphasized, was illustrated in part by its "history of treaties" with tribes.

Four years later, in *United States v. Wheeler*, the Supreme Court considered whether the U.S. Constitution's bar against double jeopardy precluded a Navajo man's trial in federal court on a charge arising out of the same offense for which the Navajo tribal court had convicted him (*U.S.* 1978). The federal courts were not prohibited from trying the individual, the Court concluded. The Navajo had not given up their "jurisdiction to charge, try, and punish members of the Tribe for violations of tribal law" in either their 1849 or their 1868 treaty with the United States. Therefore, the man had broken the laws of two sovereigns and could be tried by both sovereigns.

The federal court's willingness to employ its canons of construction in Indian treaty cases has proven essential in protecting tribal hunting and fishing rights. Among many tribes, hunting and fishing represented far more than economic subsistence. Hunting and fishing symbolized and taught cultural values and one's responsibilities and orientation to one's surroundings. Over time, outside developments and populations crowded out many tribal peoples, preventing them from pursuing the hunting and fishing rights guaranteed by their ancestors. In the 1960s through the early 1990s, tribal peoples moved to reclaim these treaty rights, first through fish-ins and protests and later through court battles. Non-Indian fishing interests, representing the sport and commercial industries, responded to the tribal actions with harassment, violence, and lobbying efforts.

In general, courts from the Northwest to the Great Lakes have concluded that tribal ancestral leaders intended to preserve tribal fishing and hunting rights for their descendants in the treaties they negotiated with the United States more than a hundred years ago. In the *United States v. Michigan* case of 1979, for example, Judge Joel Fox ruled that Michigan tribes preserved their right to fish in Lake Michigan in their treaties of 1836 and 1855 (*U.S.* 1981). Tribes in Wisconsin and Minnesota won similar lawsuits based on interpretation of historic treaties (*Menominee* 1968; *Minnesota* 1999). In a series of northwest fishing cases involving the Treaty of Medicine Creek of 1854 (Treaty with the Nisqually, Puyallup, Etc.), the courts interpreted "The right of taking fish, at all usual and accustomed grounds and stations, is further secured to said Indians in common with all citizens of the Territory . . ." to allow treaty tribes with 50 percent of the allowable salmon catch (*Washington* 1979).

The courts have failed to apply their canons of construction consistently when interpreting Indian treaty provisions. Perhaps not surprisingly, the majority of these cases have occurred when such applications would result in Indian ownership of former lands now needed for economic development and the finding that tribes retained jurisdiction to handle non-Indian criminal activities within tribal lands. For example, in the *Federal Power Commission v. Tuscarora Indian Nation* case of 1960, the Supreme Court, by ignoring its own canons of construction and reinterpreting history, concluded that three treaties negotiated in the 1700s to protect tribal lands conveniently did not include Tuscarora lands. The ruling allowed for the submersion of traditional Tuscarora lands beneath a lucrative energy project. In a strongly worded dissent to the decision, Justice Hugo Black wrote, "I regret that this Court is to be that governmental agency that breaks faith with this dependent people. Great nations, like great men, should keep their word" (*Federal Power Commission* 1960). This ruling was also relevant in the *DeCoteau v. District County Court for the Tenth Judicial District* case (*DeCoteau* 1975).

Two weeks before the Supreme Court handed down the *Wheeler* decision, which emphasized that tribes possessed inherent sovereign powers predating those of the United States, the Supreme Court ruled in the *Oliphant* case that tribes did not possess the authority to exercise criminal jurisdiction over non-Indians (*Oliphant* 1978). The case arose from the Suquamish tribal court's conviction of two men for disturbing the peace during Chief Seattle days. The convictions were invalid, the men argued, as the Suquamish possessed no jurisdiction over non-Indians. In line with previous case law and canons of construction, the Court should have determined whether the Suquamish had forfeited their rights in treaties to handle criminal matters within their own lands, or whether Congress had expressly removed such authority from the tribes. After a selected review of congressional legislation from 1834 to the present, the Court rationalized that Congress had intended to preempt the field. Previously, the Court had operated on the principle that tribes retained their inherent governing rights and rights to resources unless specifically removed or limited through treaties or by Congress. The new rule now read that tribes could not legislate on matters limited by treaties or statutes (old test) or in areas that conflicted with the overriding interest of the United States as the superior sovereign. Exactly what was considered to be in the "interest of the overriding sovereign" the Court did not say, beyond stating that the federal government had a responsibility to protect its (non-Indian) citizens.

The 1981 *Montana v. United States* decision, like the *Lone Wolf* decision in 1903, illustrated the Supreme Court's willingness to mangle previously established Indian law and tests. This case involved the right of the Crow Nation to regulate hunting and fishing rights within their reservation boundaries, in this instance the regulation of non-Indians on nonmember lands. As the Crow Nation's attorney argued, without the right to control all hunting and fishing within reservation boundaries, it was impossible to establish and administer legitimate conservation measures. Furthermore, the Crow had

never given up their authority to regulate any aspect of their reservation hunting and fishing rights, and no federal legislation had extinguished their right.

The Crow Nation, the Court ruled, did not possess the right to regulate non-Indians fishing and hunting on non-Indian lands within the reservation boundaries. To support this tenuous claim, the justices relied on their interpretation of the Treaty of Fort Laramie (Treaty with the Sioux, Etc.) of 1851, finding that nowhere was it "suggested that Congress intended to grant authority to the Crow Tribe to regulate hunting and fishing by nonmembers on nonmember lands" (*Montana* 1981). The Court could only arrive at such an interpretation by completely ignoring its own tests that required Indian treaties to be interpreted as the tribes would have understood them (few people envisioned in 1851 the problem of whites fishing on Crow land), to contain an express extinguishment of authority, and to resolve any ambiguities in favor of the tribe.

Despite periods of egregious failures and the courts' tendency to interpret Indian treaty rights in line with the national political agenda and climate, the United States has refused to completely abandon the guarantees and promises that it negotiated as a young nation. Even after two hundred years of conflictual history, the United States legally regards Indian treaties as the supreme law of the land. As contracts between sovereigns, the supremacy clause of the Constitution governs the legal status of Indian treaties within U.S. law, mandating that Indian treaties possess the same effect and force of federal law and supersede state law. States did not—and still do not—possess the requisite sovereignty to enter into treaty relationships.

Congress and the courts today recognize tribes as domestic dependent nations possessing a government-to-government relationship with the federal government—a status supported by the continuing viability of Indian treaties. The treaties and agreements negotiated by Indian nations with the United States will continue to play a critical role in the recognition of tribal sovereignty and in the protection of Indian lands and resources.

Sharon O'Brien

References and Further Reading

"Act Ending Treaty Making," March 3, 1871, *U.S. Statutes at Large,* 16: 566.

American State Papers, Foreign Affairs, vol. 1. *1832–1861.* Washington, DC: Gales and Seaton.

Article Six, Treaties between the United States and the Several Indian Tribes from 1778 to 1837. 1975. Millwood, New York: Kraus Reprint.

Atcheson, N. 1814. *A Compressed View of the Points to be Discussed in Treating with the United States of America.* London: Rie.

Beecher v. Wetherby, 95 U.S. 517 (1877).

Bodin, J., 1576. *The Six Books of the Commonwealth.* Abridged and translated by M. J. Tooley. Oxford, England: Basil Blackwell, 1955.

Boyd, Julian P., ed. 1938. *Indian Treaties Printed by Benjamin Franklin, 1738–1762.* Philadelphia: Historical Society of Pennsylvania.

Caughey, John W. 1938. *McGillivray of the Creeks.* Norman: University of Oklahoma Press.

Cherokee Nation v. Georgia, 30 U.S. 1 (1831).

DeCoteau v. District County Court for the Tenth Judicial District, 420 U.S. 425 (1975).

Deloria, Vine, Jr., and Raymond J. DeMallie, eds. 1999. *Documents of American Indian Diplomacy: Treaties, Agreements, and Conventions, 1775–1979,* vols. 1–2). Norman: University of Oklahoma Press.

DePuy, H. 1917. *A Bibliography of the English Colonial Treaties with the American Indians: Including a Synopsis of Each Treaty.* New York: Lennox Club.

Federal Power Commission v. Tuscarora Indian Nation, 362 U.S. 99, 137–138 (1960).

Gates, Merrill. 1885. "Land and Law as Agents in Educating Indians," *Journal of Social Science,* 113–146, quote by Captain Henry Pratt.

Grotius, H. 1925. In Livy, Book IV, in *De Jure Belli Ac Pacis Libri Tres* (The Classics of International Law), J. Scott (ed.). Oxford: Clarendon Press.

Holmes, Jack. 1969. Spanish Treaties with West Florida Indians, 1784–1802. *Florida Historical Society,* 48 (140–154).

Liverani, Mario. 1980. *International Relations in the Ancient Near East, 1600–1100 BC.* New York: Palgrave MacMillan.

Lone Wolf v. Hitchcock, 187 U.S. 553, 23 S. Ct. 216, 47 L. Ed. 299 (1903).

McClanahan v. Arizona State Tax Commission, 411 U.S. 164 (1973).

McNickle, D'Arcy. 1973. *Native American Tribalism.* London: Oxford University Press.

Menominee Tribe of Indians v. United States, 391 U.S. 404 (1968).

Meyers, D. P. 1957. "The Names and Scopes of Treaties." *American Journal of International Law:* 51, 579.

Minnesota v. Mille Lacs Band of Chippewa Indians. 526 U.S. 172 (1999).

Montana v. *United States,* 450 U.S. 544 (1981).

Morton v. Mancari, 417 U.S. 535 (1974).
Oliphant v. Suquamish Indian Tribe, 435 U.S. 191 (1978).
Prucha, Francis Paul. 1994. *American Indian Treaties: The History of a Political Anomaly.* Berkeley, Los Angeles, and London: University of California Press.
Ralston, Hayden. 1920. *The Senate and Treaties, 1789–1817.* New York: Macmillan.
Respecting the Liberty to Pass and Repass the Borders and to Carry on Trade and Commerce. 1974. Explanatory Article to the 3rd Article of the Treaty of November 19, 1794.
Toscano, M. 1966. *The History of Treaties and International Politics.* Baltimore: The Johns Hopkins Press.
Treaty of October 22, 1784, with the Six Nations, 7 *Stat.* 15.
Treaty of January 21, 1785, with the Wyandots and others, 7 *Stat.* 16.
Treaty of November 28, 1785, 7 *Stat.* 18.
Treaty of January 21, 1785, 7 *Stat.* 16.
Treaty of November 28, 1785, 7 *Stat.* 18.
Treaty of January 9, 1789, with Wyandot, 7 *Stat.* 28.
Treaty of August 7, 1790, 7 *Stat.* 35.
Treaty of July 2, 1791, 7 *Stat.* 39.
Treaty of June 16, 1802, 7 *Stat.* 68.
Treaty of November 10, 1808, 7 *Stat.* 107.
Treaty of July 22, 1814, with Wyandot, 7 *Stat.* 118.
Treaty of August 19, 1825, 7 *Stat.* 272.
Treaty of May 24, 1835, 7 *Stat.* 450.
Treaty of August 24, 1835, 7 *Stat.* 47.
Treaty of May 26, 1837, 7 *Stat.* 533.
Treaty of March 12, 1858, 12 *Stat.* 997.
Treaty of June 19, 1859, 12 *Stat.* 1037.
Treaty of March 6, 1861, 12 *Stat.* 1171.
Treaty with France for the Cession of Louisiana, April 30, 1803, 8 *Stat.* 200, TS 86.
U.S. v. Kagama, 118 U.S. 375 (1886).
U.S. v. Michigan, 653 F. 2d277 (6th Cir. 1981).
U.S. v. Wheeler, 435 U.S. 313 (1978).
Van Loon, L.G. 1968. "Tawagonshi: Beginning of the Treaty Era." *Indian Historian,* June, 22–26.
Vattel, E. 1916. *The Law of Nations, The Classics of International Law.* Ed. J. Scott. Washington, DC: Carnegie Institution of Washington.
Vitoria, Francisco de. 1917. *De Indis and De Jure Belli Reflectiones.* Sec. 2, titles 6 & 7, "On the Indians and on the Law of War," ed. Ernest Nys, trans. John Pawley Bate. New York: Oceana, 1964. Originally published Washington, DC: Carnegie Institution.
Warren Trading Post v. Arizona Tax Commission, 380 U.S. 685 (1965).
Washington v. Washington State Commercial Passenger Fishing Vessel Association, 443 U.S. 658 (1979).
Williams v. Lee, 358 U.S. 217 (1959).
Worcester v. Georgia, 31 U.S. (6 Pet.) 515 (1832).

Historical Periods

Colonial and Early Treaties, 1775–1829

For the first fifty years of the republic, the United States, in its relations with the Indian tribes within its borders, focused its diplomatic and political energies on ending wars and establishing peaceful relations, controlling trade, asserting supremacy, extending its criminal and civil jurisdiction, and securing titles to the tribal lands. To achieve these goals, the United States entered into 159 treaties with Indian tribes between 1775 and 1829 (Deloria and DeMallie 1999, 183–190). In doing so, it adopted the precedent established nearly two hundred years earlier by European sovereigns—that of negotiating treaties with Native polities. Under the prevailing international law, the land belonged to the sovereign in whose name it was discovered, but the Indian tribes that occupied the land had a perpetual right of use. This right could be extinguished only by abandonment, by a "just war," or by purchase, the last being the most common means. These legal principles were enunciated by the Spanish jurist Francisco de Vitoria in 1532 and quickly became the law of nations.

The treaties negotiated in the half century covered by this essay may be divided into three time periods: the united colonies during the Revolutionary War, the Continental Congress under the Articles of Confederation, and the United States under the Constitution. The last time period began with the United States engaged simultaneously in war and in diplomacy: war in the Northwest Territory, war and diplomacy in the South, and diplomacy in western New York, all resulting in peace treaties and land cessions. The same pattern was followed during the first three decades of the nineteenth century: wage war when necessary, treat with tribes as policy required, and, above all, secure land cessions either as war reparations or sales. The Northwest and the South remained foci of federal attention, and although western New York ceased to be a concern, it was replaced after 1803 with the lands west of the Mississippi River.

The United Colonies during the Revolutionary War

From the first skirmish at Concord and Lexington in April 1775, Revolutionary War leaders were aware of the threats posed by the Indian tribes within and on the borders of the thirteen colonies. In writing the Declaration of Independence, the committee of Thomas Jefferson, Benjamin Franklin, John Adams, Robert Livingston, and Roger Sherman made special note of the tribal threats to colonial survival: "He [King George III] has excited domestic insurrections amongst us, and has endeavoured to bring on the inhabitants of our frontiers, the merciless Indian Savages, whose known rule of warfare, is an undistinguished destruction of all ages, sexes and conditions." Although they grossly overstated the situation and expressed it in polemical terms, the Revolutionary War leaders had good reason for concern. At the end of the French and Indian War (1754–1763), a conflict in which most of the Indian tribes bordering the colonies had joined the French, England had established a policy restricting colonial settlement on Indian lands. The restrictions began in 1763, when the Crown issued a proclamation prohibiting settlement west of the Appalachian Mountains. The superintendents for Indian affairs, John Stuart for the southern district and Sir William Johnson for the northern district, negotiated treaties with the various Indian tribes in 1767 and 1768 that established the boundary line envisioned in the Proclamation of 1763. That line ran from a few miles west of Fort Stanwix (in present-day Rome, New York) in the north to the Gulf coast of Florida. There were to be no colonial settlements west of this line. Additionally, the colonies were required to pay a series of taxes to simultaneously recoup the Crown's costs incurred during the French and Indian War and maintain the Crown's continuing protection against Indian attacks—a requirement to which the colonists vehemently and, in some instances violently, objected.

It is not surprising that with few exceptions—most notably the Oneida and the Tuscarora, who supported the colonial cause—the Indian tribes west of the property line of 1768 were more sympathetic to the English than to the colonials. Some twenty years before, the English had represented the principal threat to their lands, and consequently an alliance with the French served their collective purpose. Now roles had changed. England appeared ready to protect Indian lands against American incursions.

In this situation, the most the American officials could hope for was that the tribes would remain neutral and perhaps give some quiet support. To accomplish this goal, the Continental Congress entered into seven treaties or agreements with the following tribes:

Six Nations, Delaware, and Shawnee (1775)
Seneca, Cayuga, Nanticoke, and Conoy (1776)
Passamaquoddy, Penobscot, and Malecite (1777)
Winnebago (1778)
Fox (1778)
Delaware (1778)
Cherokee (1779)
(Deloria and DeMallie 1999, 183; *ASP* 1832, 61:1, 1).

Except for the Delaware and Cherokee treaties, these were informal agreements. Although the treaties in 1775 and 1776 differ in details, they have in common two elements: an explanation or justification of the rebellion against English authority and an appeal for tribal neutrality concerning the conflict between England and the colonies. Witness the speech of John Walker at the Treaty with the Six Nations, Delaware, Shawnee and Ottawa in October 1775. He pressed the tribes to remain neutral and to recognize that they and the United Colonies had a common destiny.

> *Brothers* we wish to Cultivate so strict a Friendship with you as that your Enemies shou'd be Considered as ours, and our Enemies as yours. . . . *Brothers* you have no doubt heard of the dispute between us and some of our Fathers evil Counsellors beyond the Great Water, in this dispute your Interest is Involved with ours so far as this, that in Case those People with whom we are Contending shou'd Subdue us, your *Lands* your *Trade* your *Liberty* and all that is dear to you must fall with us, for if they wou'd Distroy our flesh and Spill our Blood which is the same with theirs; what can you who are no way related to or Connected with them Expect? (Deloria and DeMallie 1999, 55)

The treaties with the Winnebago and the Fox, negotiated by Colonel George Rogers Clark in August 1778, tied the tribes to an "Alliance and Friendship with the United States of America and [the tribes] Promised to be true and faithful Subjects" (ibid., 78, 79).

The informality of treaties ended with the Delaware treaty in 1778. The treaty contains seven articles: a mutual forgiveness of all prior offenses; a guarantee of peace, friendship, and mutual assistance in cases of war; free passage of American troops across Delaware territory to attack English forts; and fair, impartial trials of Delawares and Americans who violated either nation's laws. In addition, the United States agreed to appoint an agent to regulate trade; guaranteed Delaware territory in perpetuity; and, most interestingly, invited the Delaware Nation "to join the present confederation, and to form a state whereof the Delaware nation shall be the head, and have a representation in Congress" (Kappler 1904, 3; 7 *Stat.* 13). The Cherokee treaty of 1779 contains all the provisions found in the Delaware treaty, with the exception of the statehood offer. Both treaties sought to ally the tribes to the United States in exchange for protections against the two major causes of enmity: dishonesty in trade and incursions on tribal lands.

The Continental Congress under the Articles of Confederation

Although written in 1777, the Articles of Confederation did not become officially operational until 1781. The sticking point was the insistence by the "landless" states—those without claims to western lands—that the "landed" states surrender their claims to the United States. Maryland, in particular, held up acceptance of the articles until Virginia agreed to surrender its claims to the Northwest Territory (the area north of the Ohio River, now the states of Ohio, Indian, Michigan, and Illinois) and what is now Kentucky. Other states with western claims were New York, Massachusetts, Georgia, and North Carolina. Many of the claims overlapped, and all were for lands occupied by a large number of Indian tribes. Further complicating matters, the Articles of Confederation gave the United States sole control over war and peace but a vague mandate over Indian affairs. According to Article IX, the Continental Congress had the "sole and exclusive right and power of . . . regulating trade and managing all affairs with the Indians, not members of any of the states, provided that the legislative right of any state within its own limits be not infringed or violated. . . ." Because a number of states contained sizable areas occupied by Indian tribes, and because these states were anxious

to gain title to these lands, Article IX preserved the rights of states to negotiate with the Indian tribes, even at the risk of a general war and in contravention of the interests of the United States.

But the states were not the only ones to be concerned about the stability of relations between the United States and the Indian tribes. Congress also faced that concern, which for them had its roots in the Treaty of Paris. Although the Treaty of Paris (September 3, 1783) ended the Revolutionary War and established the Mississippi River as the western boundary of the United States as far south as Florida, it made no provision for ending the wars with the Indian tribes that had joined the English, and therefore it furthered the possibility of unstable relations with those tribes. As a result, it was clear to the Continental Congress that peace treaties with the hostile tribes were a necessity.

The crucial question was, What should be the terms of any peace treaties with the warring tribes? General George Washington provided an answer in a September 1783 letter written to James Duane, a delegate to the Continental Congress. Washington expressed concern that, in the absence of a quick resolution of hostilities, the Indian lands would "be over run with Land Jobbers, Speculators, and Monoplisers or even with scatter'd settlers" against the best interest of the United States. Normalizing relations with the tribes was imperative in order to prevent a situation that Washington believed to be "pregnant of disputes both with the Savages, and among ourselves . . ." (Prucha 1994, 1). To this end, Washington felt that the tribes should be informed of the provisions of the Treaty of Paris, should be required to return all prisoners, should agree to a boundary line between the United States and themselves, and should grant to the United States a cession of land. Washington believed that the United States, for its part, should give assurances that it would "*endeavour* to restrain our People from Hunting or Settling" in Indian country as well as prevent dishonesty in trade. Washington concluded his letter by recommending that the lands ceded to the United States be purchased instead of seized by force (ibid.). "In a word there is nothing to be obtained by an Indian War but the Soil they live on and this can be had by purchase at less expence, and without that bloodshed . . ." (ibid., 2).

In the winter of 1784, the Continental Congress completed its plans for ending hostilities with the Indian tribes still at war with the United States. To each tribe, the Congress would offer peace and demand a cession of land as reparations for the costs of the war. The latter demand deviated radically from Washington's recommendation to use the long-established practice of purchasing land from Indian tribes or, more precisely, purchasing the Indian tribes' right of use of the land. However, during the 1780s the United States faced an enormous debt and no means to repay it, as well as a vengeful, restive population intent on settling on the very lands under tribal control. From Congress's point of view, the solution to these two problems was to exact retribution from the hostile Indian tribes via the relinquishment of land.

Between 1784 and 1786, the United States negotiated the following six treaties with hostile tribes:

Treaty at Fort Stanwix with the Seneca, Mohawk, Onondaga, and Cayuga (1784)
Treaty at Fort McIntosh with the Wyandot, Delaware, Chippewa, and Ottawa (1785)
Treaty at Hopewell, South Carolina, with the Cherokee (1785)
Treaty at Hopewell, South Carolina, with the Choctaw (1786)
Treaty at Hopewell, South Carolina, with the Chickasaw (1786)
Treaty at Fort Finney at the mouth of the Great Miami River with the Shawnee (1786)

These treaties have five provisions in common. First, they required the tribes to surrender all prisoners and, in the case of the treaties at Fort Stanwix, Fort McIntosh, and Fort Finney, required the Indian tribes to provide tribal leaders as hostages to assure the prompt prisoner return. The three treaties at Hopewell added the return of property, including slaves. Second, the United States offered the Indian tribes peace and protection, which served to end hostilities and to provide the United States with sole control over the Indian tribes. Third, the United States defined the territorial boundaries of the Indian tribes, reserving land for Indians' sole use and occupancy and taking ownership of the remainder. Fourth, the United States agreed that crimes committed by Americans on the tribal lands would be punished. Fifth, the tribes were to surrender to the United States any Indian who committed crimes against Americans.

A number of treaties contained additional provisions specific to the situations between the United States and particular tribes. In the Fort Stanwix

treaty, the United States guaranteed the lands of the Oneida and Tuscarora in appreciation of their loyalty to the colonial cause during the Revolutionary War. Similarly, the Fort McIntosh treaty restored tribal rights and property to those Delaware who had remained loyal to the United States. The Hopewell treaties with the Cherokee, Choctaw, and Chickasaw contained guarantees of fair trade. Additionally, the Cherokee were offered the opportunity to send a representative to the Continental Congress.

Upon hearing the terms announced by the congressional negotiators at the treaty conferences, the Indian negotiators were nearly unanimous in their opposition. They argued that they had not waged war against the United States without provocation, they had never sued for peace, and they were not empowered to grant the cessions demanded. However, they argued without success. These treaties were not made at arm's length: the terms were dictated by the U.S. commissioners, and the tribes were told to accept them or face annihilation. The words of Richard Butler, who negotiated the treaty with the Shawnee at Fort Finney on behalf of the United States, illustrated the Continental Congress's attitude: "The destruction of your women and children, or their future happiness, depends on your present choice. Peace or war is in your power; make your choice like men, and judge for yourselves" (Downes 1977, 297).

Once the Indian delegates returned home and their tribal leaders and members heard the terms imposed, the Indian tribes rejected the terms. As the news of the high-handed way the Indian tribes at the treaty conferences had been treated, other Indian tribes, not party to the treaties but neighbors and allies of those who were, joined in opposition. The result was a loosely formed confederacy of Indian tribes in the Northwest Territory, the area north of the Ohio River to the Mississippi River and including Ohio, Indiana, southern Illinois, Michigan, and a small piece of western Pennsylvania.

Although mindful of the rejection and opposition by the tribes, the Continental Congress proceeded to legislate for the area as though its title were clear and peace prevailed. In 1785, it passed "An Ordinance for ascertaining the mode of disposing of lands in the Western Territory," which provided for the survey of the lands between the Ohio River and the Great Lakes and their subsequent division into six-mile-square townships. The land was then to be sold to settlers. In 1787, the Congress passed the Northwest Ordinance, providing for a system of governance for the Northwest Territory. The Continental Congress's intention to survey and sell the land in the Northwest Territory, combined with the increasingly frequent incursions on Indian lands by hunters and squatters, made war inevitable.

Within a year of the passage of the Land Ordinance of 1785, the United States began surveying and settling the Northwest Territory. To make the point that the United States considered the land its property and would countenance no interference with its settlement, General George Rogers Clark ordered attacks on Shawnee villages in 1786. Although the attacks resulted in the unremitting hostility of the Shawnee, they had a salutary effect from the American point of view: they served to separate those Indian tribes closer to American territory—Seneca, Delaware, Wyandot, and Chippewa—from those more remote and thus less subject to U.S. intimidation—Shawnee, Miami, Wea, Piankashaw, Potawatomi, and Kickapoo.

Exacerbating the Continental Congress's problems concerning Indian relations were the actions of some of the states with sizable Indian populations. Georgia held treaties with the Cherokee and the Creek in 1783 and again with the Creek in 1785 and 1786. Massachusetts negotiated its claims to what is now the western part of New York State with the Six Nations in 1788. But New York State was by far the most aggressive in securing Indian lands. It negotiated with the Oneida for a large tract of tribal land in 1785, a year after federal guarantees to that land, and again with the Oneida in 1788, as well as with the Onondaga in the same year and with the Cayuga the following year. New York went so far as to send individuals to disrupt the federal Treaty of Fort Stanwix (Treaty with the Six Nations) in 1784, although this effort failed to prevent the signing of the treaty.

In the final days of the Continental Congress, the United States sought to reaffirm its treaties made between 1784 and 1786 with the hostile tribes by signing two treaties at Fort Harmar in January 1789. The first, with the Wyandot, Delaware, Ottawa, Chippewa, Potawatomi, and Sac, repeated the terms of the treaties of Fort McIntosh (Treaty with the Wyandot, Etc., 1785) and Fort Finney (1786; Kappler 1904), but in a shift of policy, the United States made a payment to the Indian tribes of $6,000 in goods for the land taken (Kappler 1904, 16–18). The second treaty, with the Six Nations of New York, repeated the terms of the Treaty of Fort Stanwix (1784), and it, too, contained a payment in goods for land: $3,000. As the Mohawk under Joseph Brant were not in

attendance at the treaty, they were denied any payment. The terms of both treaties were dictated by Arthur St. Clair, governor of the Northwest Territory, who hoped that the treaties would end the warfare. However, most of the tribes in the Northwest Territory had refused to attend; of those who were present, none were represented by their principal chiefs. The treaties were repudiated by the tribes, making war in the Northwest Territory inevitable.

Treaties under the United States Constitution

The United States under the Constitution began functioning in April 1789, beset with a myriad of Indian problems, including an inevitable war with the tribes in the Northwest Territory. However, unlike the Articles of Confederation, the Constitution made the United States supreme in the conduct of Indian affairs. The Congress has the sole power "To regulate Commerce . . . with the Indian Tribes" (Article I, Section 8) and to declare war (Article I, Section 8). It granted to the president the power to make treaties with the advice and consent of the Senate (Article II, Section 2).

The first treaties to reach the president and the Senate were the two negotiated at Fort Harmar. They raised a serious question regarding the handling of Indian treaties. Did Article II, Section 2 of the Constitution apply to treaties between the United States and Indian tribes? Washington proceeded on the assumption that a treaty with an Indian tribe should be treated as any other treaty would under the Constitution. He sent the two treaties, supporting documents, and a report from Secretary Henry Knox to the Senate in May 1789. The following month, the Senate appointed a three-member committee to review the treaty and accompanying materials. The Senate was uncertain of the status of Indian treaties; after much consideration, the Senate advised Washington to carry out the treaty (Prucha 1994, 70–71).

This did not satisfy Washington, and he so informed the Senate. He pointed out that treaties made by subordinates were not official until ratified by the sovereign "and I am inclined to think it would be adviseable to observe it in the conduct of our treaties with Indians . . . It strikes me that this point should be well considered and settled, so that our national proceedings in this respect may become uniform, and be directed by fixed, and stable principles" (as quoted in Prucha 1994, 72). The Senate agreed; Indian treaties were to be treated in the same manner as any other treaty entered into by the United States. Once negotiated, they were submitted to the Senate for its advice and consent, which was given by a two-thirds vote, and then proclaimed by the president.

The Department of War, headed by Secretary Henry Knox, was charged with the implementation of Indian policy. Knox, like Washington, believed it was futile to attempt to take Indian land by force. He advised the president that the best policy was one in which the United States recognized the tribes' rights to the lands they possess and offered to purchase by treaty what they were willing to sell. He was certain that the tribes would be willing to sell sections of land at reasonable cost. He explained, "As the settlements of the whites shall approach near to the Indian boundaries established by treaties, the game will be diminished, and the lands being valuable to the Indians only as hunting grounds, they will be willing to sell further tracts for small considerations" (*ASP* 1832–61:1, 13–14).

But first the nation had to deal with a war in the Northwest Territory, hostilities in the South, and a possible war with tribes of the Six Nations in western New York. To meet these threats, the War Department formulated a threefold approach: First, the United States would wage war on the tribes along the Wabash River, principally the Miami. Second, the United States would carry on negotiations with the southern Indian tribes, particularly the Cherokee, the Chickasaw, and the Creek. Third, the president, with the approval of the Senate, would send a commissioner to settle differences with the Six Nations, principally the Seneca, who were angry over the forced land concessions at Fort Stanwix and Fort Harmar.

The United States made two unsuccessful attempts to defeat the Indian tribes north of the Ohio. In the summer of 1790, General Josiah Harmar led an army of 1,453 militia and regulars against the Miami, and after destroying a number of villages, the army was defeated. The following year, territorial governor Arthur St. Clair assembled an army of 2,770 and marched into Miami country. There he met an army consisting of Miami, Wyandot, Chippewa, and Kickapoo, led by the Miami chief Little Turtle. The results were disastrous for the United States. Of the 1,400 U.S. troops who participated in the battle, more than 900 were killed or wounded. The rest retreated to the safety of Fort Hamilton (now Cleveland, Ohio) (Mahon 1988, 150; Downes 1977, 317–318). After the battle, General Anthony Wayne

replaced St. Clair. Wayne was ordered to raise and train an army to defeat the tribes in the Northwest Territory.

The problems with the Six Nations in New York and the tribes in the South were largely the result of white settlers committing crimes against Indians within tribal territories, dishonest traders who cheated the Indians with shoddy goods and exorbitant prices, and states and citizens who forced or tricked the Indian tribes into selling their lands at paltry rates. To remedy these conditions, Congress in 1790 passed the first of a series of laws known as the Indian Trade and Intercourse Acts. These acts sought to regulate trade by licensing the traders who entered Indian country, making individuals who commit crimes in Indian country subject to state or territorial laws and punishments, and prohibiting the sale of Indian lands to individuals and to states "whether having the right of pre-emption to such lands or not, unless the same shall be made and duly executed at some public treaty, held under the authority of the United States" (1 *Stat.* 137–138). The last provision applied only to the original thirteen states, which were acknowledged to have retained the preemption right, that is, the right to purchase the Indian lands within their borders; however, the United States determined when that right could be exercised, when Indian title could be extinguished. The Act of 1790 was temporary, set to expire in June 1793, but Congress renewed and strengthened the act in March of that year. (Congress continued to renew and revise the act in three-year increments until 1802, when it was made permanent. Although the act was modified throughout the period, the essential provision prohibiting individuals from purchasing Indian land and the restrictions on states doing the same remained.)

President George Washington affirmed the protection of Indian land guaranteed by the Indian Trade and Intercourse Act to the Seneca chiefs Cornplanter, Half-Town, and Great-Tree in December 1790. Responding to a litany of complaints, Washington informed them of the provisions of the act and added, "Here, then, is the security for the remainder of your lands. No State, nor person, can purchase your lands, unless at some public treaty, held under the authority of the United States. The General Government will never consent to your being defrauded, but it will protect you in all your just rights" (*ASP* 1832–61:1, 142). In addition to the assurances Washington gave to the Six Nations that their lands would be protected, he took the further step of appointing Timothy Pickering, with the consent of the Senate, as Indian commissioner to the New York tribes. Between 1790 and 1794, Pickering held a series of conferences with the Six Nations to keep them neutral and to resolve outstanding differences.

While the United States pursued its military efforts in the Northwest and its diplomatic efforts with the Six Nations, it had to contend with frequent border depredations in the South. With its limited resources, the United States could not engage in a war against the Choctaw, Cherokee, Chickasaw, and Creeks, nor could it afford to have these tribes join with the Indian tribes north of the Ohio. In response to the dilemma, Washington chose a diplomatic approach, holding a number of treaty conferences with the southern Indian tribes. In 1790 and 1791, the United States negotiated treaties with the Creeks and Cherokee respectively. The two treaties contained essentially the same provisions: the tribes recognized U.S. protection and "no other sovereign whosoever"; the tribes would return all prisoners; their boundaries would be surveyed and guaranteed by the United States; the tribes were free to punish any citizen or inhabitant of the United States who settled on their land; hunting and entry on tribal land without a passport by citizens or inhabitants of the United States were forbidden; fugitives from justice were to be returned to the United States, and individuals committing crimes on Indian land were to be punished according to the laws of the state or territory where the Indian lands were located; both sides would refrain from retaliation; the tribes would give notice of any threats against the United States; and lastly, so that the Indian tribes "may be led to a greater degree of civilization, and to become herdsmen and cultivators, instead of remaining in a state of hunters," the United States would supply domesticated animals and farm implements. Although these treaties did little to quell the border depredations, their provisions set the tone, format, and language for subsequent treaties.

The year 1794 proved to be a turning point in Indian-United States relations and territorial policy. The previous summer, a U.S. delegation had met with the Ohio tribes to negotiate a settlement but had no success. The tribes insisted that the United States accept the Ohio River as the boundary between the parties, which the U.S. commissioners rejected. Negotiations having failed, Knox directed General Anthony Wayne to begin an offensive to secure the Ohio valley. Wayne waited until the summer of 1794 to begin his campaign, and after building a string of forts on the Maumee and the Great Miami rivers, he moved to meet the Indian army, which numbered some two thousand. Wayne proceeded deliberately toward the Indian camp at Fallen Timbers, which was protected by an English post, Fort Miami. The tribes had been led to believe by English officials in Canada that the English would support them militarily and that war between the United States and England was imminent. But when Wayne, whose forces outnumbered the Indians, attacked, the English took no action. Although the Battle of Fallen Timbers, on August 20, did not destroy the tribes' ability to fight, the failure of the English to help resulted in dissolution of the Indian fighting force. Wayne went on to destroy Indian villages and crops unopposed. The war in Northwest Territory was over, but the United States had yet to negotiate a settlement of all grievances with the Six Nations of New York, the tribes in the South, and those it had defeated in the Ohio valley.

The United States began the process of settling tribal grievances even before the commencement of the offensive in the Northwest. In June 1794, the United States negotiated a treaty with the Cherokee at Philadelphia, Pennsylvania, affirming the boundaries and other provisions of the treaties of 1785 and 1791 and granting the Cherokee annually "goods suitable for their use" worth $5,000 "in lieu of all former sums" (Kappler 1904, 26). Two years later, the United States made a similar treaty with the Creek; they confirmed the boundary provision of the treaty of 1790 and the boundaries set by the treaties with the Chickasaw, the Cherokee, and the Choctaw (1785–1786). In return, the United States made a one-time payment of $6,000 in goods to the Creek.

The efforts of the federal government to prevent the Six Nations of New York from joining the Ohio tribes had been largely successful. By the fall of 1794, Timothy Pickering was ready to settle their grievances, having met in council with the Indian leaders and heard their complaints during the preceding three years. He called for a treaty council at Canandaigua, New York, which lasted some two months and ended in November. The treaty acknowledged the lands of the Oneida, the Onondaga, and the Cayuga in New York State to be theirs; nullified the land cession of the Treaty of Fort Stanwix, returning to the Seneca the land taken, except for a four-mile strip along the east bank of the Niagara River from Lake Ontario to Lake Erie; and granted the Six Nations an annuity of $4,500 in perpetuity. In exchange, the Seneca, Onondaga, Cayuga, and Oneida surrendered all claims to any other land within the United States. The treaty was signed by Timothy Pickering for the United States and by fifty-nine "sachems and war chiefs" of the Six Nations, including Cornplanter, Red Jacket, Farmer's Brother, the Seneca prophet Handsome Lake, and the Stockbridge chief Hendrick Aupaumut.

Although both sides were aware of Wayne's victory at Fallen Timbers months before, this did not greatly affect the final results. The principal U.S. interest in the treaty was to gain an unconditional surrender of any Six Nations claims to land in the Ohio Valley. Pickering justified the return of the Seneca lands in western New York, saying that the United States never had a right to the land because the preemption right belonged to Massachusetts, the lands lay within the boundaries of New York State, and the Seneca would never have agreed to the treaty without the return.

There were other problems concerning tribal land and New York and Massachusetts claims to be resolved, and they presented some knotty legal and political issues. The Indian Trade and Intercourse acts made provision for the original thirteen states and Vermont and Maine, which had been parts of original states, to treat for land with tribes within their boundaries. There were two restrictions on the states: they could only negotiate at a federally held treaty at which a U.S. commissioner was present, and they could only negotiate the price to be paid to the tribe that held the right of use. New York State, under the leadership of Governor George Clinton, aggressively sought the purchase of tribal lands and in 1795 negotiated land sales with the Oneida, the Cayuga, and the Onondaga, much to the consternation of Secretary of War Timothy Pickering. John Jay succeeded Clinton as governor of New York in 1795, and he chose to comply with the Indian Trade and Intercourse Act, resulting in three federally held treaties. The first of these was a treaty in 1796 with the Seven Nations of Canada: Caughnawaga and St. Regis (Mohawk), Lake of Two Mountains (Nippising, Iroquois, and Algonquin), St. Francis (Sokoki Abenaki), Becancour (Eastern Abenaki), Oswegatchie (Onondaga, Oneida, and Cayuga), and Lorette (Huron). By this treaty, the Seven Nations surrendered all their claims to land in New York, except for what is now the St. Regis Reservation in upstate New York along the St. Lawrence River, for "the sum of one thousand two hundred and thirty-three pounds six shillings and eight-pence, lawful money" of New

York State and an annuity of 213 pounds, 6 shillings, and 8 pence. A year later, under the leadership of Joseph Brant and John Deserontyon, the Mohawks surrendered their tribal claims in New York for $1,600. New York State negotiated treaties under federal auspices with the Oneida in 1798 and 1802, although the latter treaty was never ratified by the Senate or proclaimed by President Jefferson.

Finally, in 1802 the United States held two treaties with the Seneca. These were unusual in that they were negotiated for the benefit of individuals, in apparent violation of the Indian Trade and Intercourse Acts, which contained an absolute prohibition against individuals purchasing Indian land. The Seneca lands were a unique case. They were the subject of nearly 150 years of dispute over who held the preemption right, Massachusetts or New York. Massachusetts claimed the right from a grant by King James I to the Plymouth Company in 1621 to all the land, from sea to sea, between the 40th and 48th parallels north. New York based its claim to the Seneca lands on a grant from King Charles II to his brother James II, Duke of York. The dispute lingered until 1786, when representatives of the two states met in Hartford, Connecticut, and agreed to a compromise that gave preemption to Massachusetts and jurisdiction to New York. Massachusetts then sold its preemption right to the 6 million acres of Seneca land to private speculators, who in 1788 purchased from the Seneca 2.6 million acres for $5,000 and an annuity of $500 (New York State Assembly Document 51 1889:16–18).

The owners of the preemption were unable to convince the Seneca to sell any more of their remaining 3.4 million acres until 1797. In that year, Robert Morris, acting as agent for the owners, met with the Seneca under the authority of a U.S. Indian commissioner and negotiated the Treaty of Big Tree, whereby the Seneca sold some 3.2 million acres for $100,000 in Bank of the United States stock, reserving for themselves approximately 200,000 acres on nine reservations in western New York State (ibid., 131–134). In 1802, the Seneca agreed to exchange with owners of the preemption forty-two square miles of land of their Cattaraugus Reservation for an equal amount along Cattaraugus Creek. In a separate treaty negotiated at the same convention, the Seneca sold Little Beard's reservation of two square miles for $1,200. These treaties were signed by the most prominent men in the Seneca Nation, including Cornplanter, Farmer's Brother, Red Jacket, and Handsome Lake.

Two additional transactions to which a U.S. Indian commission was present require mention. In 1823, the owners of the preemption right purchased from the Seneca a tract of land for $4,286, and in 1826 the Seneca sold to the same group a second tract of 86,887 acres for $48,260. Neither sale was ratified by the Senate or proclaimed by the president.

Returning to the Northwest Territory, the Treaty of Greenville, which ended the war in that region, was signed on August 3, 1795, by General Anthony Wayne and chiefs of the Wyandot, Delaware, Shawnee, Ottawa, Chippewa, Kickapoo, Miami (including the Piankashaw, Wea, and Eel River bands), Kickapoo, and Kaskaskia. In all, sixty-nine chiefs incribed their marks on the treaty, including Little Turtle, the great Miami chief, and Blue Jacket, a chief of the Shawnee. The treaty was similar in form to those that had preceded it: it declared the parties to be at peace; required that prisoners be exchanged and that the United States hold ten Indian chiefs hostage until the exchange was completed; included a major cession of land north of the Ohio River, plus specific sessions for forts, trading posts, portages, and so forth; and obligated the tribes to warn the United States of any hostile intent by others. In exchange, the United States gave the tribes $20,000 in goods and a perpetual annuity of $9,500 to be divided among them. The tribes were empowered to expel illegal settlers; trade would be opened with the United States, retaliation restrained, and all former treaties voided.

Treaties and National Territorial Expansion, 1800–1829

Four policy goals defined treaty making during the first decades of the nineteenth century: land acquisition, changing tribes to agrarian-based economies, managing trade, and securing and maintaining peaceful relations. First and foremost was the acquisition of land to satisfy the flood of immigrants and Americans moving westward. This meant the surrender of large sections of tribal land upon which the tribes depended for subsistence. To compensate for the land losses, the United States sought to convince the tribes to give up hunting and adopt European American farming and, by providing funds for schools, to adopt American ways. To supply the tribes with products they could not raise or manufacture, the United States proposed to establish trading posts, sometime called factories, on the diminished tribal lands. This would have the salutary effect of reducing complaints from tribes about the unfair practices of individual traders and would keep out any foreign influences potentially threatening to the United States. It would, in addition, provide the federal government with information concerning tribal affairs, invaluable for treaty negotiations. Finally, the treaties would establish and confirm peace and commit the tribes to recognize the United States as their sole protector. This was of particular importance because Spain, France, and England possessed land on the nation's borders and, through trade and alliances, had great influence with many of the tribes east of the Mississippi River.

The problem of foreign involvement in what the federal government considered internal national issues became particularly acute in 1802, when President Thomas Jefferson learned of Spain's secret transfer of the Louisiana Territory to Napoleon. However, the threat of a French occupation of New Orleans, and thus control of the Mississippi River, was removed when the United States in 1803 purchased France's preemption right west of the Mississippi River, an area of some 828,000 square miles. That left Spain in control of Florida, and the English along the nation's northern border.

Although President Jefferson was initially concerned that the purchase was unconstitutional, in the end pragmatic factors overcame philosophical ones, and Jefferson embraced the purchase. The United States had nearly doubled its size and brought within its boundaries a then-unknown number of tribes, yet it had not cleared its title to the area it had secured from England in 1783 nor settled its relations with the tribes that occupied these lands. Jefferson recognized that the tribes east of the Mississippi River were growing ever more opposed to selling any of their land, while at the same time the demands for land were increasing exponentially. The dilemma for the national government was how to gain title without provoking another series of Indian wars.

Jefferson made no departure from the Indian policy established during Washington's administration. Congress had enacted the Indian Trade and Intercourse Act in 1790 and had renewed and modified the act in 1793, 1796, and 1799. In the 1796 renewal of the act, Congress established a system of government-owned trading posts "for the purpose of carrying on a liberal trade with the several Indian nations, within the limits of the United States" (1 *Stat.* 452). In 1802, Congress made permanent the provisions of the Indian Trade and Intercourse Acts. The act of 1802 contained a description of the boundary between Indian country and the United States, continued the prohibitions against settlement on Indian land, provided for the punishment of crimes committed in Indian country, required the issuance of passports to enter Indian country and licenses to trade, prohibited the sale of alcohol, and authorized the president "in order to promote civilization among the friendly Indian tribes, and to secure the continuance of their friendship, . . . to cause them to be furnished with useful domestic animals, and implements of husbandry, and with goods and money, as he shall judge proper . . ." (2 *Stat.* 139–146).

Achieving what had emerged as national policy—the acquisition of tribal land without resorting to conquest—depended on convincing the tribes to change their lifestyles; to accomplish this, the tribes would have to abandon hunting and adopt agriculture. "The extensive forests necessary in the hunting life will then become useless," Jefferson wrote to Congress in 1803, "and they will see advantage in exchanging them for means of improving their farms and of increasing their domestic comforts." Jefferson saw that federal government trading posts were an essential part of national policy (Prucha 2000, 21). Thus, trade provisions were incorporated in many of the subsequent treaties.

The South

Between 1801 and 1829, the United States made thirty-nine treaties with the Chickasaw, Choctaw, Creek, Cherokee, and Florida tribes. These treaties extinguished Indian title to all of the land east of the Mississippi River from the Ohio River to the Gulf of Mexico, except for specific reservations of land for tribal use and occupancy. The first two treaties were with the Chickasaw and the Choctaw in 1801. Collectively, they gave the United States permission to build a road across tribal territory from Tennessee to "Natchez in the Mississippi Territory." These treaties cut a road diagonally from the northeast to the southwest across the tribal territories. In addition, the Choctaw treaty included a provision for the remarking of the boundary lines set by the English before the Revolutionary War and a relinquishment of land east of the Cumberland Mountains (Royce 1900, Pl. LXII).

For their cessions, the Chickasaw received $700 in goods, and the Choctaw received $2,000 in goods (Kappler 1904:2, 41–43). In 1805, the Cherokee agreed to allow a road to run through their territory to connect Knoxville, Tennessee, with New Orleans. The tribe was paid $1,600 (ibid., 61).

Having gained rights-of-way to the Mississippi River across tribal lands, the United States set out to secure the intervening land. This involved land in four states—Tennessee, Alabama, Georgia, and South Carolina—and in the Territory of Mississippi. The western part of Tennessee belonged to the Chickasaw and the Cherokee tribes. The United States title to Chickasaw land was cleared by three treaties in 1805, 1816, and 1818; Cherokee land was purchased in 1805, 1806, and 1819.

The Choctaw land was located in Alabama and Mississippi. By treaties in 1802, 1803, 1805, 1816, and 1820, the Choctaw surrendered their claims in the two states. In 1814, the Creek sold their land in Alabama. Most of the remaining Creek land was located in Georgia. To clear title to this land, the United States negotiated seven treaties with the Creek for land in Georgia: 1802, 1805, 1818, two in 1821, 1826, and 1827. The Cherokee also occupied land in Georgia, which they sold in 1804 and 1817. In 1816, they also sold a part of their territory in South Carolina. For their land cessions east of the Mississippi River, the four tribes received the following compensation: the Cherokee, $209,500 and $8,000 in perpetual annuities; the Chickasaw, $449,815; the Choctaw, $282,000 and $9,000 in perpetual annuities; the Creek, $1,427,000 and $23,000 in perpetual annuities (Kappler 1904, 2). Included in these totals were funds set aside for the construction and operation of schools for tribal children.

Not all of the money stipulated to be paid by the United States went to the benefit of the tribes. The Choctaw's $50,000 went to cover money owed to traders; $250,000 of the Creek funds were earmarked for a similar purpose. The Cherokee were paid $43,760 to indemnify individual tribal members for damage caused by the U.S. Army and citizens. Payments were made to specific individuals in the tribes, very often chiefs or prominent warriors. George Guess (Sequoyah) received $500 in the Cherokee treaty of 1828 "for the great benefits he has conferred upon the Cherokee people, in the beneficial results which they have are now experiencing from the use of the Alphabet discovered by him" (Kappler 1904:2, 207). The same treaty allocated $1,000 for the purchase of a printing press. The Choctaw chiefs and warriors received $14,972 for the assistance against the Upper Creeks in the Pensacola campaign during the War of 1812.

On the other side of the coin, because of "an unprovoked, inhuman, and sanguinary war, waged by the hostile Creeks against the United States" (Kappler 1904:2, 77), the Creek were forced by the treaty of 1814 to surrender more than twenty million acres in Georgia and Alabama (Prucha 1994, 11). The treaty referred to the Creek war of 1813–1814, fought against the United States by an Upper Towns band of the tribe. It took a combined force of American, Cherokee, Choctaw, and Lower Creeks to defeat the Upper Creeks and end the war. No compensation was granted to the Creek tribe in this treaty, even though a part of the tribe had remained loyal to the United States and assisted in the defeat of their fellow tribesmen.

Although the majority of the treaties negotiated with the southern tribes represented the sale of ever-diminishing tribal lands, several made after the Treaty of Ghent in 1814, which ended the War of 1812, provided for the exchange of land east of the Mississippi River for land in the Louisiana Territory. This possibility, a land exchange instead of a sale and reservation, had been foreseen by President Jefferson in 1803 and had been incorporated into law the following year. In 1804, Congress passed legislation establishing a system of governance for the Louisiana Territory. A provision in the act authorized the president "to stipulate with any Indian tribes owning lands on the East side of the Mississippi, and residing thereon, for an exchange of lands the property of the united States, on the West side of the Mississippi, in case the said tribe shall remove and settle thereon . . ." (2 *Stat.* 283).

The Cherokee treaty of 1817 was the first to contain a provision for a land exchange. In exchange for surrendering land in Georgia, those who chose to emigrate were given an equal number of acres in the newly formed Territory of Arkansas. The head of each emigrating household was given a rifle and ammunition, a brass kettle or beaver trap, and a blanket for each member of the family. Those who remained east of the Mississippi River and desired to become citizens were to receive 160 acres of tribal land. The annuities due the Cherokee tribe would be divided proportionately between the two groups. A treaty with the Choctaws in 1820 contains similar provisions: land in the Arkansas Territory for their land in Mississippi, equipment for the emigrating families, and citizenship and land for those remaining in the state of Mississippi.

These treaties ran into immediate opposition from settlers in the Arkansas Territory, so much so

that they required renegotiation. In 1825, the Choctaw were forced to surrender a large portion of the land they had acquired in Arkansas and to accept a cash payment and an annuity of $6,000 instead. In 1828, the Cherokee found themselves in the same situation. They were forced to exchange their seven million acres in Arkansas for an equal amount of land west of the Mississippi River. The treaty described their title in the following terms:

> Whereas, it being the anxious desire of the Government of the United States to secure to the Cherokee nation of Indians, as well those now living within the limits of the Territory of Arkansas, as those of their friends and brothers who reside in States East of the Mississippi, and who may wish to join their brothers of the West, *a permanent* home, and which shall, under the most solemn guarantee of the United States, be, and remain, theirs forever—a home that shall never, in all future time, be embarrassed by having extended around it the lines, or placed over it the jurisdiction of a Territory or State . . . (Kappler 1904:2, 206; emphasis in original)

In addition to the land guaranteed to the tribe, the United States granted the Cherokee "a free and unmolested use of all the Country lying West of the Western boundary" of their reservation, which in 1828 meant all of Oklahoma.

Florida remained under Spanish control until 1819, when the United States completed its purchase. General Andrew Jackson, one of the principal negotiators of treaties with the southern tribes, had invaded the territory in 1818, precipitating the First Seminole War. Although that action caused a diplomatic flap, it allowed the U.S. negotiator, John Quincy Adams, to pressure Spain to sell its preemption right to the land. In 1823, the United States forced the weakened Florida tribes to sign a treaty whereby they surrendered all the territory, except for a small reservation, for $6,000 worth of "implements of husbandry, and stock of cattle and hogs" and a $5,000 annuity for twenty years (Kappler 1904:2, 141).

It should not be assumed that these land transactions were accomplished with the full agreement of the tribes involved; quite the contrary. The Cherokee tribe split over the provision for removal in the treaty of 1817. The National Council of the Creek, led by the Upper Creeks, had passed a law in 1811 making it a capital crime to sell land. Their attitudes further hardened following the Creek war, largely because of sales made by the Lower Creeks. Finally, in 1825, when the leader of the Lower Town Creek, William McIntosh, a supporter of removal and active opponent of the Upper Town Creek, signed the treaty of 1825, the Upper Creeks killed him for ceding Creek land.

Nonetheless, by 1829 much of the tribal land of the Cherokee, Chickasaw, Choctaw, Creek, and Florida tribes had been lost, and many of the tribal members had moved across the Mississippi River. More importantly, tribal governments had been damaged by factional disputes that, in the cases of the Cherokee and Creek, had led to a prolonged and at times violent struggle.

The Northwest and Louisiana Territories

The United States followed the same policy objectives and negotiating procedures with the tribes in the Northwest Territory that it had followed with the southern tribes. However, the problems of dealing with the Northwest tribes were much more complicated and convoluted than in the South. In the Northwest, the United States found multiple tribal claims of ownership to the same lands and a continuing and growing resentment against the United States among members of the affected tribes. Tribal feelings were fed by the land forfeited by the tribes at the Treaty of Greenville in 1795 (Treaty with the Wyandot, Etc.) and by the waves of settlers who showed little concern for the boundaries between Indian land and that belonging to the United States. To be fair, not all the fault lay with the settlers. Although the United States had gained title to a sizable area in the Northwest Territory, the boundaries of the land cession were not well defined, which led inevitably to disputes. The United States endeavored to remedy this in 1803 by entering into a treaty with nine tribes—Delaware, Shawnee, Potawatomi, Miami, Eel River, Wea, Kickapoo, Piankashaw, and Kaskaskia—to define the boundary (Kappler 1904:2, 49), but by then settlements had been established on tribal lands, necessitating new concessions by the tribes.

During the first decade of the nineteenth century, the United States entered into a series of treaties with individual tribes and groups of tribes covering millions of acres of land in Ohio, Indiana, Michigan, and Illinois. The provisions of these treaties were essentially the same: a land cession in exchange for cash or goods and/or an annuity, generally for a specified number of years. A treaty with the Kaskaskia, "originally called the Kaskaskia, Mitchigamia, Cahokia and Tamaroi," in 1803 proclaimed that, because these tribes "from a variety of unfortunate circumstances . . . are reduced to a very small number," the tribe could no longer use its extensive territory and therefore "do relinquish and cede to the United States all the lands in the Illinois Territory." The tribe reserved but 1,630 acres for its own use. For this sale, the tribe had its annuity increased to $1,000, and because a majority of the tribal members were Catholics, the United States agreed to pay $100 to the Catholic priest for seven years (Kappler 1904:2, 49–50). In 1809, the United States signed four treaties; the first, with the Delaware, Potawatomi, Miami, and Eel River Miami, gave the United States a large cession in Indiana. What was unique about this treaty was that a portion of the promised annuity depended upon individual treaties with two tribes that were not parties to the original treaty, namely the Wea and the Kickapoo. They signed separate treaties agreeing to the terms of the treaty of 1809.

Although the language of these treaties and those in the South suggests that they were the product of arms-length agreements, that the U.S. negotiators were sensitive to the needs and interests of their tribal counterparts, nothing could be farther from the truth. From the first opening session of a treaty council, the pressure brought to bear on the tribal negotiators was unremitting. If the presence of U.S. troops at the treaty council and the veiled threats of the U.S. negotiators did not result in the desired land cessions, often tribal negotiators were bribed. It is no wonder that by 1810 the tribes in the Northwest were preparing for war. As early as 1805, two Shawnee leaders were advocating a return to the ways of their forefathers. Led by Tenskatawa (the Prophet) and his brother Tecumseh and supported by the English in Canada, some of the tribes in the Northwest had organized to oppose the United States. Tecumseh's movement split the tribes; those who supported Tecumseh in whole or part were mainly the Shawnee at Prophetstown and the Kickapoo, Ottawa, Chippewa, and Piankashaw; those who joined the Americans included the Wyandot, Sandusky, Seneca, Delaware, Sac, and the main body of the Shawnee. The Miami, one of the most powerful tribes, remained neutral despite attacks on its villages by the Americans. In addition, the tribes farther west, which included the Sioux, Menominee, Fox, Iowa, Winnebago, Kansas, and Winnebago, joined the English. All would face U.S. negotiators at war's end.

The first signs of the impending conflict occurred in 1810 with skirmishes between the two sides. The following year, General William Henry Harrison marched against Prophetstown, Tenskatawa's village on Tippecanoe Creek. Tenskatawa's force came out to meet Harrison's, and although the results were inconclusive, the Prophet lost support among his Shawnee followers. In 1812, the English declared war on the United States and openly joined Tecumseh. Hostilities continued, culminating in the Battle of the Thames in Ontario, Canada, in the summer of 1813, where Tecumseh's forces and their English allies were defeated by the U.S. forces, and Tecumseh was killed.

With the death of Tecumseh, Indian resistance in the Northwest collapsed, but there remained the war with England, which continued for another year. The Treaty of Ghent, signed in December 1814, ended the war between the United States and England. By its terms, the United States agreed to make peace with the warring tribes and to restore to them "all the possessions, rights, and privileges" they had possessed in 1811 before the start of hostilities.

In 1815, President James Madison appointed commissioners to end hostilities with the tribes in the Northwest and Louisiana Territory. In all, the commissioners negotiated twenty treaties with twenty-two tribes on both sides of the Mississippi between 1815 and 1817. These treaties, although they varied slightly in detail, generally speaking contained clauses that established "perpetual peace and friendship" between the parties, recognized past treaties signed by the parties, forgave injuries committed by the parties, and returned any prisoners.

The treaties of peace and friendship were but a prelude to an intensive period of land acquisition. The concerns of the United States were threefold: to complete the acquisition of the land in the Northwest, including Wisconsin and the Upper Peninsula of Michigan; to secure title to land along the west side of the Mississippi River; and to establish relations and supremacy over the tribes farther west. To accomplish the first objective, the federal government made seventeen treaties between 1818 and 1829 (see Table 1). By these treaties, the United States secured most of the Indian title in the area, with the exception of Wisconsin. The nineteen treaties made with the tribes to the west of the Mississippi River

secured for the nation control of the Mississippi River, land for settlement, and a place to move the eastern tribes (see Table 2).

Table 1
Treaties of Cession, by State (Northwest)

State	*Number of Treaties*	*Tribes Involved*
Ohio	4	Potawatomi, Wyandot, Seneca (Ohio), Delaware, Shawnee, Ottawa, Chippewa, Wea, Miami
Indiana	11	Potawatomi, Wyandot, Seneca (Ohio), Delaware, Shawnee, Ottawa, Chippewa, Wea, Miami, Kickapoo
Michigan	9	Potawatomi, Wyandot, Seneca (Ohio), Delaware, Shawnee, Ottawa, Chippewa, Wea, Miami, Winnebago
Illinois	9	Sac, Chippewa, Ottawa, Peoria, Kaskaskia, Potawatomi, Wea, Delaware, Kickapoo, Winnebago
Wisconsin	5	Sac, Chippewa, Ottawa, Potawatomi, Winnebago

Note: Many of these treaties contained cessions of land in more than one state.

Table 2
Treaties of Cession, by State
(West of the Mississippi)

State	*Number of Treaties*	*Tribes Involved*
Louisiana	1	Quapaw
Arkansas	4	Quapaw, Osage
Indian Territory	3	Quapaw, Osage
Missouri	6	Kickapoo, Sac, Fox, Iowa, Osage, Kansa, Shawnee
Kansas	3	Osage, Kansa, Shawnee
Nebraska	6	Kansa
Iowa	1	Sac, Fox

Note: Many of these treaties contained cessions of land in more than one state.

While busy with the land acquisitions just described, the United States began its preparation for the next set of treaties in the 1820s. The first step in the process was to secure treaties of friendship. Again, the treaties followed a set form. The tribes acknowledged the supremacy of the United States and its exclusive right to regulate all trade. For its part, the United States undertook to protect the tribes. In the mid-1820s, the United States made treaties with the Ponca, Sioux, Cheyenne, Arikara, Ministaree, Mandan, Cree, Pawnee, and Omaha. In all, the United States made fifty-three treaties between 1818 and 1829 with the tribes in Michigan, Ohio, Indiana, Illinois, Wisconsin, and west of the Mississippi River.

Conclusion

In the six decades between the commencement of the American Revolution and the election of Andrew Jackson as president, the United States moved its borders across the continent. The policy of incremental acquisition through purchase established during the Washington administration served the national interest throughout the period. Through the treaty-making process, the nation acquired millions of acres from Indian tribes. Besides the loss of their land, the same treaty process also resulted in the displacement of many of the tribes and the change of their status from recognized, fully independent sovereignties to what Chief Justice John Marshall would describe as "domestic dependent nations."

Jack Campisi

References and Further Reading

American State Papers, Foreign Affairs, vol. 1. 1832–1861. Washington, DC: Gales and Seaton.

Deloria, Vine, Jr. and Raymond J. DeMallie. 1999. *Documents of American Indian Diplomacy: Treaties, Agreements, and Conventions, 1775–1979*, vol. 1. Norman: University of Oklahoma Press.

Downes, Randolph C. 1977. *Council Fires on the Upper Ohio: A Narrative of Indian Affairs in the Upper Ohio Valley until 1795*. Pittsburgh: University of Pittsburgh Press.

Kappler, Charles J., ed. 1904. *Indian Affairs: Laws and Treaties*, 2 vols. Washington, DC: Government Printing Office.

Mahon, John K. 1988. *Indian-United States Military Situation, 1775–1848*. In *Handbook of North American Indians*, vol. 4, *History of Indian-White Relations*, ed. William C. Sturtevant, 144–162. Washington, DC: Smithsonian Institution.

New York (State) Legislature. Assembly. 1889. *Report of Special Committee to Investigate the Indian Problem of the State of New York, Appointed by the Assembly of 1888*. Albany, NY: Troy Press.

Prucha, Francis Paul, ed. 1994. *American Indian Treaties: The History of a Political Anomaly.* Berkeley and Los Angeles: University of California Press.

Prucha, Francis Paul, ed. 2000. *Documents of United States Indian Policy.* Lincoln: University of Nebraska Press.

Royce, C. C. 1881. "Cessions of Land by Indian Tribes to the United States: Illustrated by those in the State of Indiana." In *First Annual Report of the Bureau of Ethnology to the Secretary of the Smithsonian Institution, 1879–80*, 247–262. Washington, DC.

"Treaty of Fort Finney or Treaty with the Shawnee, January 31, 1786." 1904. In *Indian Affairs: Laws and Treaties*, vol. 2, comp. and ed. Charles J. Kappler, 16–18. Washington, DC: Government Printing Office.

Indian Removal and Land Cessions, 1830–1849

The Indian removal policy implemented by the U.S. government in the early nineteenth century resulted in dozens of land cession treaties with Indian groups east of the Mississippi River. Under the removal policy, treaties were negotiated with numerous eastern tribes, including the Choctaw, the Chickasaw, the Cherokee, the Seminole, the Muscogee Creek in the South, and more than twenty tribes in New York, the Great Lakes area, and along the Mississippi River north of the Ohio River. These treaties ceded millions of acres of land to U.S. control and forced the relocation of tens of thousands of Indians to Indian Territory. The causes of the removal policy arose from many sources, including American economic growth, the movement of American settlers west and south, racism toward Indians, and the assertion of states' rights. Although most Americans supported Indian removal for one reason or another, some opposed it as an unjust policy. Indians responded to the call for removal in a variety of ways; some accepted the apparent inevitability of removal and negotiated treaties to their best possible advantage, whereas others refused to accept removal by fighting back legally and physically, staying in their homelands, or moving somewhere other than Indian Territory. The impact of the removal treaties was as dramatic as any other episode in the long history of Indian-white relations and continues to shape affairs in Indian country and throughout the United States.

Origins of the Removal Policy

The U.S. government policy that removed Indian groups east of the Mississippi River to Indian Territory in the first half of the nineteenth century stemmed from many causes, but key officials had suggested the eventuality of Indian removal virtually from the moment the United States became a country. War hero George Washington declared in 1783 that "[the] gradual extension of our settlements will as certainly cause the savage, as the wolf, to retire . . ." (Wallace 1993, 38). Under the new Constitution, which went into effect in 1789, government officials increased the push for Indian removal. In 1789, Secretary of War Henry Knox suggested the inevitability of removal, asserting that "in a short period the idea of an Indian this side of the Mississippi will be found only in the pages of the historian . . ." (Getches, Wilkinson, and Williams 1998, 94). A component of early American Indian policy, which began under President Washington and continued under his successors until President Andrew Jackson, was the "civilization" plan. Under this program, the U.S. government urged Indian peoples to adopt American notions of economy, politics, and gender roles. This meant that Indians should abandon hunting as a source of sustenance for agriculture, especially the production of such cash crops as cotton. Differing views about the proper use of land divided Indians and European Americans from the earliest days of contact; eastern Indians pointed out that they already grew vast quantities of corn, squash, beans, pumpkins, and sunflowers. Indian men hunted deer and other animals to provide meat protein for their families' diets and to engage in the fur trade, which the U.S. government sought to manipulate. Indian women farmed among the matrilineal eastern tribes, and Indian men tended to view such work as "women's work," contrary to American understandings of gender roles. The U.S. "civilization" policy sought to turn Indian men into farmers and Indian women into spinners and weavers of cotton, thus challenging Indian cultural concepts at a basic level. In addition, and more to the point of land cessions, the U.S. government insisted that Indians who no longer hunted required far less land and thus should sell their excess acreage to the United States to be sold, in turn, to European American settlers. Indians greeted the "civilization" plan with mixed reactions. A minority of elite and well-connected individuals and families in all the eastern Indian groups adapted rather easily to a market-based economy resting on the production of cotton, wheat, and other commodities. These people instituted cultural modifications such as private property, slave ownership, and constitutional government, in accordance with broader American patterns. Nevertheless, Indian groups as a whole remained staunchly resistant to land cessions, thus negating one of the principal desired effects of "civilization" from the American perspective.

Although he did not put Indian removal into action, Thomas Jefferson was the first president to advocate the possibility of removal. In late 1802 and early 1803, Jefferson wrote several letters and issued official messages urging the creation of federally run trading posts, with the intent, among other purposes, of putting Indians into debt. He realized that the fur trade was a dying practice east of the Mississippi River and that Indians would have to pay their debts by land cessions. Jefferson also suggested that any Indian group offering military resistance to the United States would be driven from the East. He further added that Indians "will in time either incorporate with us as citizens of the United States, or remove beyond the Mississippi . . ." (Getches, Wilkinson, and Williams 1998, 95). In July 1803, word reached Jefferson that the purchase of the Louisiana Territory from France was complete, and he and other government officials recognized immediately that the United States now owned a vast area west of the Mississippi River to which Indian people in the East could be banished. The Louisiana Purchase provided the inspiration and the area for pro-removal advocates to remove eastern Indians and to construct a clear-cut dividing line between Americans and Indians.

The War of 1812 furthered the cause of Indian removal in a number of important ways. Unified eastern Indian resistance to the United States became extremely difficult with the defeat of the pan-Indian movement led by Tecumseh and his brother Tenskwatawa, the Prophet, in the Great Lakes area. Never again would a multitribal force arise east of the Mississippi River to counter American expansion. In the South, Indian groups remained divided, and during the War of 1812 the militant Red Stick Creeks failed in their attempt to stem American expansion and American influences on their people. Andrew Jackson, as major general of the Tennessee militia, led the U.S. and Indian forces that defeated the Red Sticks, who had attacked and killed some four hundred Americans at Fort Mims, north of Mobile. Jackson's forces, aided by Choctaws, Cherokees, and non-Red Stick Creek, defeated the Red Sticks at the Battle of Horseshoe Bend on the Tallapoosa River in 1814. Jackson, at the subsequent Treaty of Fort Jackson, forced all Creeks to cede about twenty-three million acres. Jackson then moved his forces south and defended New Orleans from British attack, earning himself national celebrity.

The United States had found it difficult to enforce its will against Indians as long as another European power, especially Britain, resided in eastern North America and maintained trade with Indians. The War of 1812 essentially eliminated that threat when the United States defeated British forces outside New Orleans and in Canada, thus encouraging American emigration westward, especially into the Old Northwest region of Ohio, Michigan, Wisconsin, Indiana, and Illinois. With the end of the War of 1812, a major economic transformation began, called the Market Revolution by historians, which encouraged Americans of all ranks to seek out profit-making enterprises. That shift from a predominantly subsistence-based lifestyle to one that sought profit by any available means increased pressure on eastern Indians to give up land.

Economic, demographic, and local pressures for Indian removal increased in the early nineteenth century. Eli Whitney's cotton gin, perfected in 1793, and other new cotton processing machines enabled the efficient processing of short-staple cotton that grew well throughout the interior of the Deep South. As a result, European American settlers relocated to the Mississippi Territory, established in 1798 and encompassing present-day Mississippi and Alabama, to cultivate cotton. These newcomers began demanding access to Choctaw, Chickasaw, Creek, and Cherokee lands in those areas. In Georgia, the calls for Cherokee removal reached new heights when gold was discovered on Cherokee lands in the late 1820s. In the north, the completion of the Erie Canal in 1825 across the state of New York encouraged European American emigration to the west and dramatically increased pressures on Indians from New York to Wisconsin to move westward. Other internal improvements, such as railroads and more canals, encouraged American westward migration, resulting in rapid population growth in the newer western territories. The white population north of the Wabash River in Indiana, for example, exploded from 3,380 in 1830 to 65,897 in 1840. The short-lived Black Hawk War in 1832, in which the Sac and the Fox Indians fought white settlers in Indiana and Wisconsin, further sharpened northern voices against Indians remaining in the East. The cries of settlers in the southern and other western states highlighted another major component of Indian removal, the conflict between states and the federal government over Indian relations and control of land. States demanded control over all lands within their borders, while the federal government insisted that, according to the Constitution, it alone could negotiate with Indians who maintained a treaty relationship with the United States. Settlers and elected

officials in the newer western states grew increasingly strident in their denunciation of Indians, and violence sometimes resulted.

No matter how much a particular Indian group became "civilized," Indians encountered uncompromising racism among Americans in the early nineteenth century. One renown western politician, Henry Clay of Kentucky, said he did not "countenance inhumanity towards [Indians]," but he did not "think them, as a race, worth preserving," because they were "essentially inferior to the Anglo-Saxon race" (Garrison 2002, 25). Among European Americans, belief in the unique manifest destiny of the United States and in racial explanations for human behavior became firmly entrenched in the early decades of the nineteenth century. Perhaps more than any other American of the pre-removal generation, Lewis Cass, as governor of the Michigan Territory from 1813 to 1831 and then as secretary of war under Andrew Jackson from 1831 to 1836, formulated the racist moral justification for Indian removal. Conveniently ignoring the horticultural and agricultural reality lived by most eastern Indians, Cass argued that land must be turned over by Indian "hunters" to American agriculturalists, who would make more productive use of it. Only through removal west of the Mississippi, Cass urged, could Indian people acquire the time and space to become "civilized." Cass ridiculed those who "would give to a few naked and wandering savages, a perpetual title to an immense continent," and he insisted that "the Indians shall be made to vanish before civilization, as the snow melts before the sunbeam" (Wallace 1993, 45). Ironically, Indian success under the tenets of "civilization" made them a greater menace to white Americans. The Cherokee, who had formed a constitutional government and aggressively asserted their sovereignty after the War of 1812, had moved far toward economic self-sufficiency by growing and selling cotton, further entrenching their claims to their land. Racial justifications for taking Indian land thus became predominant after 1815, as white Americans greedily sought access to Indian land. Racism surfaced even among Americans who acted in the perceived best interests of Indians. Many American groups who sought to assist Indians, such as Protestant missionaries, eventually supported Indian removal west of the Mississippi, like Cass, as a method of buying time for Indians to become more acculturated to American customs away from the threats of their American neighbors.

Pro-removal forces in America received a boost in 1828, when one of their own, Andrew Jackson, was elected president. A former congressman, senator, and judge from Tennessee, Jackson had gained fame during the War of 1812 when, as head of the Tennessee militia, he led the fight against the Red Stick Creek Indians and then won the Battle of New Orleans. After the War of 1812, Jackson participated in several land cession treaties with the southern Indian groups and urged them to begin migrating west of the Mississippi. By 1820, Jackson's efforts had opened up nearly fifty million acres for American settlement by compelling southern Indians to cede parts of Georgia, Alabama, Tennessee, and Mississippi. In addition, Jackson led an invasion of Spanish Florida in 1818 against the Seminole and the remaining Red Stick Creek Indians, killing several of their chiefs and two British agents whom Jackson accused of inciting the Indians to attack Americans. Jackson then captured Spanish Pensacola, and after Spain sold Florida to the United States in 1819, Jackson briefly became territorial governor of Florida in 1821. By 1823, Jackson was running for president of the United States. He won the most votes but did not gain the needed majority of electoral votes in the election of 1824, which resulted in the "corrupt bargain" that brought John Quincy Adams to the presidency. Nevertheless, Jackson's actions in Indian affairs forced the hands of the Monroe (1817–1825) and Adams (1825–1829) administrations to seek voluntary removal among eastern Indians—a call that select groups of Indians heeded by moving west into Arkansas, Louisiana, and even Texas (part of Spain until Mexican independence in 1821), but that most eastern Indians ignored. In the 1828 election, Jackson and his Democrat Party won easily over Adams, establishing as commander-in-chief of the entire U.S. military the man made famous as an Indian fighter, who possessed a proven record of supporting Indian removal.

State politicians, especially in the South, saw in Jackson a staunch supporter of states' rights, and they responded to his election, even before Jackson was inaugurated as president, by passing laws extending state jurisdiction over Indian lands. Georgia was the first state to do so; on December 20, 1828, it adopted legislation extending state jurisdiction over Cherokee lands in northwest Georgia, although the state delayed enforcement until June 1830 to give Jackson and the federal government time to support their action. Alabama passed a law extending its jurisdiction over Creek Indian lands in January 1829. Mississippi passed a resolution claiming jurisdiction over Choctaw and Chickasaw lands within its borders that was signed into law by the governor on February 4, 1829. Thus, southern states enabled Jackson to mask Indian removal as a solution to the emerging conflict between states' rights and federal jurisdiction and power. In his first State of the Union address in December 1829, Jackson urged eastern Indians to remove west voluntarily or become subject to the laws of the states. After much debate and a close vote in Congress, during which certain Whig politicians—especially the deeply religious Senator Theodore Frelinghuysen of New Jersey—argued against Indian removal on moral grounds, President Jackson signed the Indian Removal Act into law on May 29, 1830.

Jackson defended the Removal Act's passage at the time by emphasizing that this bill "puts an end to the possible danger of collision between the authorities of the General and state Governments, on account of the Indians" (Satz 2002, 44). The act called on the president to negotiate removal treaties with Indian groups and to exchange lands west of the Mississippi River for Indian lands in the east. In his State of the Union speech that December, Jackson applauded the act on humanitarian terms, stating that removal at federal government expense provided Indians with a chance of survival and demonstrated the "humanity and national honor" of the United States in taking action to save "these people" (Wallace 1993, 123). Jackson also insisted that the Removal Act was "so just to the States and so generous to the Indians—the Executive feels it has a right to expect the cooperation of Congress, and of all good and disinterested men" (Satz 2002, 44). Jackson attacked critics of the Removal Act and exposed the ethnocentric and racist essence of the new policy by asking, "[W]hat good man would prefer a country covered with forests and ranged by a few thousand savages to our extensive Republic, studded with cities, towns, and prosperous farms, embellished with all the improvements which art can devise or industry execute, occupied by more than 12,000,000 happy people, and filled with all the blessings of liberty, civilization, and religion?" (Satz 2002, 44). Despite Jackson's generous line of reasoning in support of Indian removal, the Indian Removal Act forced Indians to choose between removal and retaining some autonomy, or subjection entirely to the laws of the state wherein they resided. There was no doubt that the states intended to dispossess Indians of their land. The legal mechanism for removal was in place; all that remained were treaties to be negotiated with each tribe establishing the particulars of their deportation.

The Removal Treaties: The South

Treaty with the Choctaw at Dancing Rabbit Creek, 1830

The first American Indians to have the Indian Removal Act forced upon them were the Choctaw of Mississippi. Certain Choctaw leaders, notably Greenwood LeFlore, responded to Mississippi's extension of state laws over Indians in February 1829 by attempting to negotiate a removal treaty on behalf of all Choctaw before the Removal Act had been passed by Congress. The proposed treaty contained generous compensation for the Choctaw, but it did not reflect the will of most Choctaw people. President Jackson forwarded the treaty to the Senate anyway in May 1830, but the Senate, noting significant Choctaw opposition to the LeFlore treaty, decided not to approve it. Jackson then invited Choctaw representatives to meet him at Franklin, Tennessee, to negotiate a new treaty, but they refused and instead suggested a meeting within Choctaw territory in September 1830. Secretary of War John Eaton and former Indian agent John Coffee, Andrew Jackson's nephew by marriage, represented the United States at the treaty grounds at Dancing Rabbit Creek. Eaton and Coffee, using Jackson's rationalization, warned the approximately five thousand Choctaw in attendance that they could not prevent the state of Mississippi from taking over their lands and that therefore the Choctaw ought to cooperate in removal and gain terms as favorable as possible from the United States. The Choctaw remained deeply divided over removal; after two weeks many of them left the treaty grounds having decided not to give up their lands. American agents convinced the remaining Choctaw, including the three leading chiefs LeFlore, Nitakechi, and Mushulatubbe, to sign the treaty on September 27, 1830. Each of these chiefs, along with several other Choctaw with American connections, received personal sections of land in Mississippi as a form of bribery to ease their resistance to removal. These individuals either stayed in Mississippi, as did LeFlore, or sold their sections for profit.

The Treaty of Dancing Rabbit Creek was ratified by the U.S. Senate on February 24, 1831. According to its provisions, the Choctaw ceded all of their land

east of the Mississippi River in exchange for land, annuities, and other assistance on land west of the Arkansas Territory that became known as Indian Territory. The Choctaw were to leave Mississippi within three years. The vast majority migrated west under situations of near starvation; many died along the way. A few hundred moved that first winter after the treaty was signed, and the rest moved in the next few succeeding years. Individual Choctaw could stay in Mississippi on specific allotted sections of land if they so chose, but all communally held land was dissolved. William Ward, the U.S. agent assigned to manage the allotment process, through fraud and incompetence did not register all of the individual claims, however, and many Choctaws who chose to stay did not receive title to their lands and were forced to relocate anyway. As historians have noted, Choctaw who tried to remain in Mississippi became victims of fraud, intimidation, and land speculation. The early 1830s are known as the "flush times" in Mississippi history, for whites squatted on and seized Choctaw lands with no regard for Indian rights or fair play. Yet a couple of thousand Choctaw managed to stay in Mississippi amid discrimination and poverty and are the basis of the Mississippi Choctaw of today.

Treaty with the Creek, 1832

Muscogee Creek leaders responded to Alabama's extension of jurisdiction over their lands by proposing that they cede lands but retain blocks of private reserves within Alabama under the control of individual families. They took these proposals to Washington, D.C., in March 1832. Secretary of War Lewis Cass disagreed with the size and number of the reserves, but he reached a compromise with the eight Muscogee Creek chiefs on March 24. The resulting treaty was not specifically a removal treaty, for even though the Creek agreed to cede all their lands east of the Mississippi River, they were to receive allotments in Alabama that could be sold or retained under Creek ownership. By April 2, the U.S. Senate had unanimously ratified the treaty. Although the treaty called on the U.S. government both to assist those Creek who wished to emigrate west and to guarantee Creek title to allotted lands in Alabama, the federal government refused to assist Creek in Alabama when whites seized their lands anyway. Land speculators took advantage of the remaining Muscogee Creek and perpetrated frauds resulting in utter turmoil and loss of the Creeks' homes. The Creek wandered around Alabama seeking food and shelter, eventually attacking white settlers and seizing crops and livestock in revenge. In 1836, Cass finally intervened, not as guarantor of Creek rights but instead to forcibly remove the remaining Creeks west of the Mississippi. The U.S. military accomplished what diplomacy could not, and by 1837 almost all of the fifteen thousand or so Muscogee Creek had emigrated to the West.

Treaties with the Chickasaw, 1830 and 1832

Chickasaw leaders also sought to acquire the best terms possible after the passage of the Indian Removal Act. In the summer of 1830, Chickasaw representatives met with U.S. delegates, including President Jackson, at Franklin, Tennessee, and a treaty was signed on August 31. The Chickasaw agreed to cede their lands east of the Mississippi River in exchange for an equal amount of land in the West, but when a suitable area could not be found, this treaty became void. New negotiations for removal were undertaken in 1832 in Chickasaw territory at Pontotoc Creek. On October 20, a treaty was signed that ceded Chickasaw lands to the U.S. government; the lands were to be surveyed and sold immediately, and each adult Chickasaw was to receive a temporary allotment, which would also be sold and all monies therefrom placed in a fund to cover the costs of removal. Whites quickly settled on the Chickasaw lands beginning in 1832, despite a provision of the treaty promising that the U.S. government would prevent white intrusion until the Chickasaw had actually left Mississippi. A suitable new homeland in the West was not found until January 1837, when the Chickasaw and Choctaw met at Doaksville, Choctaw Nation, in Indian Territory, and the Choctaw sold the western part of their new territory to the Chickasaw. Although this agreement between the two tribes was not a treaty with the United States, Jackson submitted it to the Senate for approval anyway, which was accomplished in February 1837. Further details about the exact extent of territory and rights granted the Chickasaw were decided in two additional agreements between the two Indian nations in 1854 and 1855.

Treaties with the Seminole, 1832 and 1833

Florida settlers had long complained about Indian "depredations" committed by the Seminole, and Georgia, Alabama, and Mississippi plantation owners protested that runaway slaves found refuge among these Florida Indians. Border disputes between Americans and the Seminoles had exploded into full-scale war in 1818, when forces led by Andrew Jackson invaded Florida to punish Seminoles and capture African Americans who lived among them. In 1823, after Spain transferred control of Florida to the United States, the Seminole signed a treaty with the United States at Fort Moultrie that ceded the bulk of the Florida peninsula to U.S. control. Discord between the Seminole and Americans continued, however, as the Seminole found living difficult on their reduced acreage. Fulfilling his charge under the new Indian Removal Act, Colonel James Gadsden negotiated a removal treaty with the Seminole Indians at Payne's Landing in northeastern Florida on May 9, 1832. The treaty of 1832 stipulated that removal was conditioned on the Seminoles agreeing to settle in the western territory that the War Department had chosen for them. Under duress, the seven Seminole who journeyed west to inspect their new land signed a new removal treaty with American agents there at Fort Gibson on March 28, 1833. The treaty declared that the Seminole agreed with the location of their new lands, accepted political unification with the Creek Indians, and assented to immediate emigration. Upon their return to Florida, the Seminole agents renounced the Fort Gibson treaty as coerced, and the Seminole refused to abide by the stipulations of either treaty. Meanwhile, a Seminole band that lived along the Apalachicola River signed a separate removal treaty with Gadsden in October 1832, and they migrated to Texas in 1834. The confusion over which Seminoles had authority to accept removal for other Seminoles created an impasse that resulted in a bitter, drawn-out war between the Seminole and the United States that began in 1835 and was often referred to as the Second Seminole War. That war did not end until 1842, when all but a fragment of the Seminoles had been killed or forcibly removed; it cost the United States $30 million–$40 million and 1,500 dead soldiers. Pockets of Seminole and their African American brethren remained in Florida, however, and their descendants are still there.

Treaty with the Cherokee at New Echota, 1835

A few thousand Cherokee had voluntarily moved west after Georgia claimed possession of their lands in December 1828, but the bulk of the Cherokee refused to leave their homeland and instead fought removal through the legal system. In 1830, after the passage of the Indian Removal Act, the Cherokee Nation sued Georgia in the U.S. Supreme Court, asking for an injunction to prevent Georgia's seizure of Cherokee lands. Attorneys for the Cherokee argued that, as an independent nation, the Cherokee could not be subject to state jurisdiction. Chief Justice John Marshall sympathized with the Cherokee position but declined to issue an injunction against Georgia, because Indian nations in the United States were "domestic dependent nations" rather than independent foreign nations; an Indian nation's relationship to the United States therefore "resembles that of a ward to his guardian," thus disqualifying the nation from suing in the Supreme Court. The Cherokee had gained some sympathy for their plight across the United States, and they eagerly pursued another chance to bring the issue of their sovereignty to the Supreme Court. Effective in March 1831, Georgia required any white person living in Cherokee country to have a license issued by the state. Missionaries Samuel Worcester and Elizur Butler ignored this condition, were subsequently arrested by Georgia authorities, and appealed their case to the Supreme Court. In that case, *Worcester v. Georgia* (1832), Marshall declared Georgia's extension of state law over the Cherokee unconstitutional and ordered the release of the missionaries. Georgia refused to abide by the decision, and the executive branch of the federal government had no legal way—short of military intervention—to compel Georgia's compliance had it so desired. The Cherokee won their legal battle, but Georgia's refusal to honor that decision nullified their victory.

After 1832, the Cherokee became less united in their determination to hold onto their lands, and a significant minority, called the Treaty Party, worked to get a removal treaty signed with the U.S. government beginning in 1834. A group of these men signed a removal treaty with Secretary of War John Eaton in Washington, D.C., and Jackson submitted it to the Senate in June 1834. The Senate, however, tabled the treaty, refusing to discuss it. Aware that there existed a group among the Cherokee willing to sign a removal treaty, the Jackson administration sent a representative to the Cherokee Nation in February 1835 to negotiate with them. The "treaty party" was dominated by four related men who aspired to elite status: Major Ridge, his educated son John Ridge, and his two nephews, the brothers Elias Boudinot and Stand Watie. Opposing them were the majority of Cherokee, united under the leadership of principal chief John Ross. Ridge and his relatives signed a removal treaty on March 14, 1835, but it was rejected by the

Cherokee Council and thus nullified. In December 1835, another meeting with U.S. negotiators was held at New Echota; only about two hundred Ridge supporters attended. A removal treaty was signed on December 29. The Cherokee Council condemned the treaty, and Ross appealed to the U.S. Senate to reject it, but the Senate approved it by a one-vote margin. The Treaty Party Cherokee emigrated to Indian Territory immediately, whereas the treaty required the rest of the eastern Cherokee to leave by May 23, 1838. Ross and the more than 15,000 other Cherokee who opposed the treaty appealed repeatedly to have the Treaty of New Echota voided, but they encountered little sympathy in the U.S. government. General Winfield Scott arrived in the Cherokee country in the summer of 1838 to oversee the forced relocation of the Cherokee, which resulted in numerous deaths and the loss of property at the hands of rapacious whites. The split among the Cherokee continued after removal: anti-removal Cherokee killed the two Ridges and Boudinot, and Watie and Ross competed for political power from the late 1830s through the Civil War in the 1860s. Meanwhile, a few hundred Cherokee managed to stay within the mountainous western border of North Carolina, where their descendants live today.

The Removal Treaties: The North

Unlike the large, basically homogenous Indian societies of the South, Indian groups farther north in New York, the Great Lakes, and the Mississippi River Valley were smaller, more splintered societies that in many cases had already migrated dramatically from place to place in the years since the American Revolution. Though their particular histories and circumstances differed from the southern Indians, northern Indian groups confronted the same insistent U.S. government and the same rapacious attitude among white Americans. Negotiating from a position of strength, the United States signed treaties with the numerous northern groups to formalize their removal to the West and to clear up conflicting land claims. From 1829 to 1851, the United States signed eighty-six ratified removal treaties with twenty-six Indian groups in the North. In many cases, removal for the northern tribes was a continuation of their peripatetic history, though that does not mean that they all accepted removal without resistance or that they did not try to acquire the best possible terms.

Treaties with Ohio Valley Indians, 1831–1832

By 1830, many former Ohio Valley Indians had already signed treaties with the state of Ohio requiring them to move north to the Great Lakes or west to the Mississippi River Valley. Various bands of these groups had already moved west of the Mississippi River before 1830, and these final removal treaties sought to remove those who remained in the East and to settle any potential eastern land claims. President Jackson appointed Ohioan James B. Gardiner to negotiate removal treaties with remaining Indian groups in Ohio. In August 1831, Gardiner signed treaties with a group of Shawnee and the Ottawa that ceded all their lands in Ohio in exchange for new lands in the western country beyond Missouri. Profits gained from selling the ceded Ohio lands were to be used for infrastructure improvements, such as mills, in the new lands; the remainder of the money was to be invested on behalf of the Indians. The Wyandot in Ohio insisted that they be allowed to inspect and approve of the new western lands before agreeing to removal. When objectionable reports of the western lands came back, they refused to emigrate. Thus, in the removal treaty signed by Gardiner and the Wyandot on January 19, 1832, the Indians agreed to leave Ohio but "may as they think proper, remove to Canada, or to the river Huron in Michigan, where they own a reservation of land, or to any place they may obtain a right or privilege from other Indians to go" (Prucha 1994, 186–187). In October 1832, several former Ohio Valley Indian groups, including the Piankashaw, Wea, Peoria, and Kaskaskia in Illinois and the Shawnee, Delaware, Menominee, and Kickapoo, who had left Ohio decades earlier and were living at Cape Girardeau and other points along the upper Mississippi River, met with William Clark at St. Louis and signed treaties for their removal west of Missouri.

Treaties with New York Indians, 1831–1842

The various Iroquois and other Indian groups in New York ceded millions of acres to the United States and other interests in the decades after the American Revolution. In 1831 and 1832, additional Oneida, Stockbridge, and Brotherton Indians migrated to former Menominee lands in Wisconsin as a result of treaties involving the Menominee and the United States. In 1838, residents of western New York, particularly Buffalo, insisted that Indians remaining in the state, especially the Seneca, remove west beyond Missouri. A removal treaty with

Seneca and other New York Indians, such as remnant Oneida, Onondaga, Cayuga, Tuscarora, St. Regis, Stockbridge, Brotherton, and Munsee peoples, was signed at Buffalo Creek in 1838. Most Wisconsin land reserved to the New York Indians by previous treaties was also ceded for lands west of Missouri. When President Van Buren submitted the treaty to the Senate in April 1838, there erupted significant opposition to the treaty from the Indians and certain missionary groups, who contended that portions of the treaty were fraudulent and that a truly representative body of Indian chiefs did not sign. Nonetheless, the Senate ratified the treaty, based on certain revisions, made in June, that required the Indians to reapprove the treaty. New signatures by more Indian leaders were obtained by September 1838, and the treaty was sent back to the U.S. government for approval. The Senate and President Van Buren passed the new treaty back and forth, neither seeking to be the sole body authorizing the questionable treaty. When the Senate, seeking the president's recommendation, returned the treaty to his desk, Van Buren responded, "That improper means have been employed to obtain the assent of the Seneca chiefs there is every reason to believe, and I have not been able to satisfy myself that I can, consistently with the resolution of the Senate of the 2d of March, 1839 cause the treaty to be carried into effect in respect to the Seneca tribe" (Prucha 1994, 205). In January 1840, Van Buren again presented the treaty to the Senate, where it was bitterly debated and resulted in several tied votes over the issue of whether or not the Indian signatures had been obtained fraudulently. Eventually, Vice President Richard Johnson broke the tie, and the revised treaty was accepted by simple majority vote in the Senate in March 1840. In spite of its passage, the complicated treaty of 1838 did not result in the movement westward of many New York Indians. A new treaty with the Seneca in May 1842 reestablished their reserves in New York and allowed them to stay there.

Treaties with the Potawatomi, 1832–1836

The Potawatomi negotiated nineteen separate treaties with the United States during the removal period. There were numerous Potawatomi villages and bands possessing fragmented areas of land in Michigan, Illinois, Indiana, and Wisconsin, which resulted in the large number of treaties with them. In total, the Potawatomi still claimed more than five million acres until 1832. Three treaties between the Potawatomi along the Tippecanoe River in Indiana and the United States were signed in October 1832. These agreements resulted in land cessions for the Potawatomi, but they also established around 120 reserves of land east of the Mississippi River for individual Potawatomi families. Because these treaties did not specifically require Potawatomi removal to the west, Lewis Cass insisted on a large treaty meeting with the Potawatomi, calling for their removal; the meeting was held in Chicago in September 1833. Catholic Potawatomi were allowed to remain in Michigan because of their conversion to Christianity, although the Potawatomi did agree to transfer most of their eastern land titles for five million acres west of Missouri. Dozens of Americans insisted that they deserved payment from the sale of eastern Potawatomi lands and government annuities to cover supposed costs for services rendered in the form of trade debts, injuries from conflicts such as the Black Hawk War of 1832, severance pay for old Indian agents and merchants, missionary activities, schools, and so on. President Jackson forwarded the Chicago treaty to the Senate in January 1834, despite concerns about the legitimacy of many of the claims. The Senate approved the treaty that May but changed the area of western land that the Potawatomi were to receive, as Missouri desired the area originally promised to the Indians. The treaty would not be valid until the Potawatomi agreed to the new lands, and the United States did not find any Potawatomi willing to do so until seven representatives signed the revised treaty months later. The Senate ratified the revised treaty on February 11, 1835. Further treaties with individual Potawatomi landholders between 1834 and 1836 resulted in the cession of nearly all their lands east of the Mississippi River. One Potawatomi group in Indiana consisting of around 850 persons refused to move west; they were seized by the U.S. military and forcibly marched west in 1838, and at least 40 Potawatomi died along the way.

Treaties with the Miami, 1833–1841

Much of the U.S. effort to extinguish Miami Indian land title east of the Mississippi was enveloped in similar efforts to remove the Potawatomi, as their lands bordered one another. Coming on the heels of the Black Hawk War of 1832, the United States attempted to get the Miami Indians of Indiana to sign removal treaties in 1833. That initial effort failed, but a treaty was signed with them on October 23, 1834, at the Forks of the Wabash. The Miami ceded most of their remaining lands in Indiana, but individual Miami were allowed to maintain allotments in the state, and the treaty did not explicitly call for Miami removal. President Jackson disapproved of that stipulation and delayed the treaty's hearing by the Senate. His successor, Martin Van Buren, submitted the treaty to the Senate in October 1837, and final approval came in December of that year. Americans in Indiana opposed the treaty because it allowed Miami to remain in the state on individual landholdings, so new treaties were negotiated. In 1838, a treaty between the Miami and the United States assigned individual landholdings in the East. The Miami insisted that only tribal members could get such grants, that grants should not be given to non-Miami who had married into the tribe. Six Miami chiefs also traveled to Kansas to examine new lands. In 1840, Miami chiefs negotiated an unofficial treaty with the Indian agent assigned to their area, seeking financial remuneration in return for their removal to the West. This treaty, although not initiated at the federal level, was submitted to the Senate by President Van Buren anyway and approved on May 15, 1841. Removal for most Miami occurred in 1845–1846, although some Miami continued to own and live on individual land grants in Indiana.

Treaties with the Winnebago, Chippewa (Ojibway), Eastern Sioux, and Menominee, 1829–1851

Treaties with these Indians involved land in Wisconsin and, to a lesser extent, in Michigan and in Minnesota. Henry Dodge, Wisconsin territorial governor and ex officio superintendent of Indian affairs, played the major role in enacting removal treaties among these groups. In 1829 and 1832, the Winnebago signed treaties ceding some land in Wisconsin in exchange for a small strip of land west of the Mississippi River between the Sioux to the north and the Sac and Fox to the south. A portion of the Winnebago population moved west, but this land was untenable, for the neighboring Indian groups warred against each other. A small group of Winnebago who did not have authority to cede lands traveled to Washington, D.C., in 1837 and signed a treaty calling on all Winnebago to abandon their Wisconsin lands and move west. Some Winnebago obeyed the treaty stipulations by moving west and eventually settling in Nebraska; other Winnebago, despite losing title to their lands, stayed in Wisconsin, refusing to abandon their homeland.

In the Pine Tree Treaty of 1837, so named because the United States sought access to timber resources on Chippewa land, the Chippewa ceded millions of acres in Wisconsin and Minnesota, but the treaty did not call for their complete removal from the east, and the Chippewa retained usufructuary rights to the ceded lands. In the Copper Treaty of 1842, named for the copper deposits on Chippewa lands, the Chippewa ceded most of northern Wisconsin to the United States while still retaining usufructuary rights; the area experienced a copper mining boom for the rest of the nineteenth century. In 1850, President Zachary Taylor issued an executive order extinguishing Chippewa usufructuary rights in the ceded lands and ordered their removal to unceded lands in Minnesota. The subsequent forced march of Chippewa west in the winter of 1850–1851 has been termed the "Wisconsin Death March" because more than four hundred Chippewa died. Some Chippewa did manage, however, to retain small tracts of land across northern Minnesota, northern Wisconsin, and the Upper Peninsula of Michigan.

The eastern Sioux ceded their lands east of the Mississippi in Wisconsin at a treaty meeting in Washington, D.C., in 1837. Their remaining lands in Minnesota came under increasing pressure from European American settlement, especially after the Minnesota Territory was created in 1849. In 1851, the eastern Sioux ceded most of their land in Minnesota, but land squatting by settlers and foot dragging by the federal government impeded until 1860 the finalizing of payment for those lands and of the actual boundaries of the Sioux reserves remaining in southern Minnesota.

The Menominee ceded portions of their Wisconsin lands in a series of treaties beginning in 1831, the most spectacular being the 1836 treaty that ceded to the United States more than four million timber-rich acres in eastern Wisconsin. The Menominee disagreed sharply, however, over the legality of these cessions, and many Menominee refused to move for decades—or ever. In October 1848, the Menominee signed a removal treaty exchanging their lands in Wisconsin for territory across the Mississippi River in Minnesota, but they refused to leave and finally relocated along the Wolf River in Wisconsin in 1852.

The amount of land ceded by Indian people as a result of the removal treaties is staggering. In the South, where the largest areas of eastern land under Indian control existed, the Choctaw ceded more than ten million acres in Mississippi; the Chickasaw ceded more than two million acres in Mississippi and Alabama; the Creek ceded about five million acres in Alabama; and the Cherokee ceded almost eight million acres in Georgia, Alabama, Tennessee, and North Carolina. Thus began a land craze in the South, as white venture capitalists, land companies, plantation owners, and small farmers all sought quick access to the newly opened lands. The resulting antebellum South, the South in the period between 1830 and 1860, came to be characterized by rapidly expanding cotton production and African American slavery in the areas abandoned by Indians. The creation of the unified, white-dominated, antebellum South would not have been possible without Indian removal, which had ironic consequences for the relationship between the states and the federal government.

Greg O'Brien

References and Further Reading

Akers, Donna L. 1999. "Removing the Heart of the Choctaw People: Indian Removal from a Choctaw Perspective." *American Indian Culture and Research Journal* 23: 63–76.

Beck, David R. M. 2002. *Siege and Survival: History of the Menominee Indians, 1634–1856.* Lincoln: University of Nebraska Press.

Carson, James Taylor. 1995. "State Rights and Indian Removal in Mississippi, 1817–1835." *Journal of Mississippi History* 57: 25–41.

Clifton, James A. 1987. "Wisconsin Death March: Explaining the Extremes in Old Northwest Indian Removal." *Transactions of the Wisconsin Academy of Sciences, Arts and Letters* 75: 1–39.

DeRosier, Arthur, Jr. 1970. *The Removal of the Choctaw Indians.* Knoxville: University of Tennessee Press.

Edmunds, R. David. 1978. *The Potawatomis: Keepers of the Fire.* Norman: University of Oklahoma Press.

Foreman, Grant. 1932. *Indian Removal: The Emigration of the Five Civilized Tribes of Indians.* Norman: University of Oklahoma Press.

Foreman, Grant. 1946. *The Last Trek of the Indians.* Chicago: University of Chicago Press.

Garrison, Tim Alan. 2002. *The Legal Ideology of Removal: The Southern Judiciary and the Sovereignty of Native American Nations.* Athens: University of Georgia Press.

Getches, David H., Charles F. Wilkinson, and Robert A. Williams, Jr. 1998. *Cases and Materials on Federal Indian Law.* St. Paul, MN: West Group.

Gibson, A. M. 1963. *The Kickapoos: Lords of the Middle Border.* Norman: University of Oklahoma Press.

Green, Michael D. 1982. *The Politics of Indian Removal: Creek Government and Society in Crisis.* Lincoln: University of Nebraska Press.

Horsman, Reginald. 1967. *Expansion and American Indian Policy, 1783–1812.* East Lansing: Michigan State University Press.

Kappler, Charles J. 1904. *Indian Affairs: Laws and Treaties,* vol. 2, *Treaties.* Washington, DC: Government Printing Office.

Lancaster, Jane F. 1994. *Removal Aftershock: The Seminoles' Struggles to Survive in the West, 1836–1866.* Knoxville: University of Tennessee Press.

Perdue, Theda, and Michael D. Green, eds. 1995. *The Cherokee Removal: A Brief History with Documents.* Boston: Bedford Books of St. Martin's Press.

Prucha, Francis Paul. 1962. *American Indian Policy in the Formative Years: The Indian Trade and Intercourse Acts, 1790–1834.* Cambridge, MA: Harvard University Press.

Prucha, Francis Paul. 1984. *The Great Father: The United States Government and the American Indians.* Lincoln: University of Nebraska Press.

Prucha, Francis Paul. 1994. *American Indian Treaties: The History of a Political Anomaly.* Berkeley: University of California Press.

Raffert, Stewart. 1996. *The Miami Indians of Indiana: A Persistent People, 1654–1994.* Indianapolis: Indiana Historical Society.

Remini, Robert V. 2002. *Andrew Jackson and His Indian Wars.* New York: Penguin.

Rogin, Michael Paul. 1975. *Fathers and Children: Andrew Jackson and the Subjugation of the American Indian.* New York: Alfred A. Knopf.

Ronda, James P. 2002. "'We Have a Country': Race, Geography, and the Invention of Indian Territory." In *Race and the Early Republic: Racial Consciousness and Nation-Building in the Early Republic,* Michael A. Morrison and James Brewer Stewart, eds. Lanham, MD: Rowman and Littlefield.

Royce, Charles C. 1899. *Indian Land Cessions in the United States.* Washington, DC: Government Printing Office.

Satz, Ronald. 2001. *Chippewa Treaty Rights: The Reserved Rights of Wisconsin's Chippewa Indians in Historical Perspective.* Madison: Wisconsin Academy of Sciences, Arts and Letters.

Satz, Ronald. 2002. *American Indian Policy in the Jacksonian Era.* Norman: University of Oklahoma Press.

Sellers, Charles. 1991. *The Market Revolution: Jacksonian America, 1815–1846.* New York: Oxford University Press.

Sheehan, Bernard W. 1973. *Seeds of Extinction: Jeffersonian Philanthropy and the American Indian.* Chapel Hill: University of North Carolina Press.

Sleeper-Smith, Susan. 2001. *Indian Women and French Men: Rethinking Cultural Encounter in the Western Great Lakes.* Amherst: University of Massachusetts Press.

Tanner, Helen Hornbeck, ed. 1987. *Atlas of Great Lakes Indian History.* Norman: University of Oklahoma Press.

Wallace, Anthony F. C. 1999. *Jefferson and the Indians: The Tragic Fate of the First Americans.* Cambridge, MA: Harvard University Press.

Wallace, Anthony F. C. 1993. *The Long, Bitter Trail: Andrew Jackson and the Indians.* New York: Hill and Wang.

Washburn, Wilcomb E. 1973. *The American Indian and the United States: A Documentary History,* vol. 4. New York: Random House.

Young, Mary Elizabeth. 1961. *Redskins, Ruffleshirts and Rednecks: Indian Allotments in Alabama and Mississippi, 1830–1860.* Norman: University of Oklahoma Press.

Reservations and Confederate and Unratified Treaties, 1850–1871

From the point of view of U.S. policymakers, Indian reservations were a necessary aspect of American expansion, nationhood, and state building. The creation of reservations, or reserves, aboriginal homelands, or *areas indigena,* was equally the result of the larger European colonial relationship with indigenous peoples in the Americas, Africa, Asia, and Australia. Whatever they were called, the establishment of these defined, often isolated and greatly compressed indigenous living spaces by means of treaties, agreements, and conventions was a distinct phase in the process of American expansion. Often, reservations were simply the remnants of indigenous homelands. The United States, however, removed a number of Native nations from their homelands to distant territories acquired from other indigenous peoples through treaties.

Between 1850 and 1871, when the federal government officially ended the treaty-making process, more than a hundred Native American treaties were ratified, principally to institute some semblance of order on the American frontiers. Most of these were "peace and friendship" treaties concluded to curtail the warfare between the Native peoples who owned the land and the migratory whites who coveted it for themselves. Essentially, the federal negotiators and the governing bodies of the Native American nations mutually agreed that strict boundaries between whites and Indians must be established and maintained before any kind of peace could be realized. Native negotiators were always seeking peace—or, perhaps, the simple absence of war—so that their peoples could enjoy the permanence of a homeland and the security of physically possessing recognized political boundaries. In short, between 1850 and 1871, the United States entered into the phase of colonialism that rested on the ideas of restricting the movements of indigenous peoples, defining the boundaries between the races, and removing any and all obstacles to the placement of European American colonies in the American West.

Reservations

As it came to be used in the period, the term *reservation* applied to nearly every piece of ground occupied by Native nations having formal treaty relations with the United States. Many of these territories were not, strictly speaking, parts of the U.S. public domain that were "reserved for the use of" Native nations. For example, when the Five Civilized Tribes—the Cherokee, Muscogee Creek, Seminole, Choctaw, and Chickasaw Nations—were removed from their traditional homelands in the East, the lands they acquired in the newly established Indian Territory carried titles in fee simple, thus making them relatively well protected from further white encroachment. Many other so-called reservations were in reality greatly diminished homelands that had never become legally a part of the U.S. public domain. Technically, one could argue that Native nations, not the federal government, had by treaty reserved these lands for their own use. Still, as most of the Native nations had concluded some form of diplomatic relations with the United States, the federal government sent agents to the reservations in order to oversee the implementation of treaty provisions and generally to maintain order within their designated areas of responsibility. Agents were also sent as negotiators to the Native nations to acquire more lands. Until 1849, the agents and the implementation of Indian policies were under the bureaucratic control of the U.S. Department of War. Hence, the developing "reservation system" was viewed as a military operation, and in fact many of the agents for years to come were army personnel. The State Department, arguably the agency that should have maintained diplomatic relations with Native nations, had little to do with Indian affairs except to record the final ratified treaties with the tribes.

The reservation system itself became a highly bureaucratic and permanent American institution. After 1849, the Bureau of Indian Affairs, most often referred to as the Indian Office, existed under the Department of the Interior. The "Indian Problem" had essentially boiled down to the impossible administrative predicament of securing more space for non-Indian settlement while at the same time maintaining peace with the Native nations that had to survive on increasingly smaller parcels of land. The Indian Office gained greater discretionary authority over Indian affairs during this period and, by way of administrative fiat, began to emphasize subtle variations in policy. For major Indian policy decisions, Congress, the executive branch, and the

Supreme Court set the agenda and formulated the general approach to Indian affairs. The Indian Office implemented, administered, and evaluated the details of policy and within this particular context was often able to direct or redirect the course of Indian-white relations.

From the very outset of European imperialism, numerous individuals advocated the "civilization" and eventual assimilation of Native Americans into the dominant society. George Washington promoted the notion of "civilizing" Indians in his inaugural address. The idea underpinned the reservation system in one important way. Because the Native nations' land bases were becoming smaller with each new treaty, the Indian Office introduced European American farming methods, livestock production, various home industries such as wool spinning and weaving, and Christianity in the effort to promote "civilization" among the indigenous nations. It was thought that "civilization" and especially its accoutrements—the spinning wheels, livestock, and farm implements—would help Natives survive on what lands they had left. Native peoples, especially on reservations that had been established by treaty, were quickly becoming regarded as "wards" of the U.S. government and, as such, more or less arbitrarily subjected to the caprices of the Indian Office bureaucracy. Ultimately, this system of domestic colonialism deprived Native nations of the ability to experience change on their own terms. The agents enforced cultural and economic changes on the Native peoples so that they could eke out a meager living on their very much smaller domains. Diminished land bases for Native Americans meant, in turn, the opening of more territory for white settlement. White settlement, it was thought, would further encourage civilization and allegiance to the United States among the Native peoples. In this chain of reasoning, the ultimate aim of the reservation system was to fulfill the goal of American Manifest Destiny in as orderly and relatively nonviolent a fashion as possible.

Surplus Lands

The opening of more land for white settlement between 1850 and 1871 also paved the way for the "take-off" period in American industrial growth. It opened greater acreage not only to farmers and ranchers but also to the logging and mining industries. Railroads were building, and especially after the Civil War, large grants of the American public domain, most often acquired through Native land cessions in treaties, went to subsidize the laying of track. The railroads, in turn, fed off the timber, coal, oil, and steel industries. It is little wonder that many of the treaties signed during the period granted railroad rights-of-way through Indian lands, and in most cases the Indian lands that were acquired by the United States went immediately to subsidize the railroad system without ever having been made a part of the public domain.

Between the years 1850 and 1861, a spate of treaties were concluded to open and secure the lands for the United States on the Pacific coast. Throughout the period, gold seekers were pouring into the newly acquired territory of California. From the beginning of the gold rush in 1849, whites had begun an arbitrary but widespread massacre of indigenous populations. The remnants of the California nations that survived the slaughter either fled into isolation to avoid the heavily armed, remorseless, death-dealing whites or sought sanctuary around the old Spanish missions. By 1850, when California was admitted to the Union, most Native leaders would probably have thought it wise to avoid any and all contact with the whites, no matter their intentions.

California had been ceded to the United States under the Treaty of Guadalupe Hidalgo and so claimed title by right of conquest. As a result of the Supreme Court decision in *Johnson v. M'Intosh* (1823), however, the federal government nevertheless recognized that Indians possessed the "right of occupancy" to the land. In consequence, the government sent a three-man commission to California to convince Native Americans to accept the jurisdiction of the federal government and to recognize U.S. sovereignty over California. By January 1852, the commission had negotiated eighteen treaties with 139 Native American bands, towns, confederated groups, and tribal subdivisions. The treaties established reservations and provided for the payment of annuities and the services of teachers and blacksmiths, and promised to provide the Native groups with subsistence in the form of livestock. The negotiations went to naught, however; because the Senate could not grasp the intricacies of California Native sociopolitical organization and because the costs of carrying out the provisions of the treaties were becoming very high, it rejected their ratification.

Federal agents were also occupied with negotiating treaties with the tribes of the Oregon and Washington Territories. The main thrust of treaty

making in the 1850s actually centered on these two potential states of the Union. In 1848, the United States and Great Britain agreed, after years of dispute, to draw a boundary demarcating the line between the United States and Canada. The U.S. claim to what became the Oregon Territory—the present states of Oregon and Washington—was tenuous. There were several trading posts, both British and American, in the region, but until the 1830s white settlement was relatively insignificant. After 1831, American immigrants began to pour into the Willamette Valley in Oregon and the Columbia River basin in what is now Washington. The United States had no legal claim to the territory—either by right of discovery or by conquest in a just war—but they had the numbers. Eventually, Great Britain bowed to the land-hungry Americans, and in 1850 Congress passed the Oregon Donation Act, establishing a special commission to negotiate with and extinguish the land titles held by the tribes of the Oregon Territory. This commission, although abolished in February 1851, nevertheless negotiated six treaties with several bands of the Kalapuya and Molala nations. The law abolishing the Donation Act commission transferred its duties to the superintendent of Indian affairs. As a result, the Donation Act commission's treaties were not ratified. Anson Dart, the superintendent, completed at least thirteen treaties with tribes in western Oregon on which the Senate took no action. While Dart's treaties with the bands of the Tillamook, Clatsop, and Chinook languished in the Senate, the administration and Congress divided the Oregon Territory into the separate territories of Oregon and Washington and gave the power to negotiate with the tribes to the territorial governors.

Unratified Treaties

Many of the settlements negotiated with the Native nations of Oregon and Washington, although still arguably valid and thus operable, nevertheless have been relegated to status of "unratified" or "invalid" treaties. The numerous agreements with these tribes signed in 1851 are cases in point. Dart's treaties of 1851 with the Clatsop, Tillamook, and Chinook bands ceded the entire Willamette Valley of Oregon to the United States. These treaties were negotiated primarily to transfer legally the already white-occupied valley to the U.S. public domain. Because of the change in policy directing the governors of Washington and Oregon to negotiate agreements with the Native nations located in the territories, the Senate did not ratify the Willamette Valley treaties.

In 1906, however, Congress wrote a provision into that year's Indian Appropriation Act authorizing the secretary of the interior to investigate the number of Clatsop, Chinook, and Tillamook people, either signatories of the treaties or their descendants, who were affected by the land cession. In 1851, tribal leaders had negotiated monetary settlements to be paid over the course of ten years. The Native leaders had insisted on the payments because their peoples were in a serious decline as a result of white intrusion and basically did not want the federal government to obtain the land without some kind of exchange or benefit. Because the Senate failed to ratify the treaties, the payments were not forthcoming.

During the first years of the twentieth century, the federal government became interested in clarifying both the status of Native peoples under law and the validity of U.S. land claims. On the one hand, the government was attempting to end the reservation system and extract itself from the "Indian business." On the other, there was a growing interest in protecting what was left of tribal lands so that, as individuals, Native people would possess a level of income that would make their gradual assimilation into American society less abrupt, confusing, and painful. For whatever the reason, Congress prompted a count of the populations of the tribal signatories of the Willamette Valley treaties and in 1913 appropriated \$66,000—a sum greater than the original, agreed-upon remuneration—to pay the surviving tribal members for the loss of their lands.

This compensatory action proved that even "unratified" treaties could indeed become operable. In the case of the Willamette Valley treaties, both parties—the federal government and the Native nations—mutually agreed to reconstitute the membership of the tribes in order to fulfill the treaties' stipulations. The treaties were thus "ratified" bilaterally because both sides actually complied with the provisions of these specific conventions.

The "unratified" treaties with the Chinook, Tillamook, and Clatsop did not provide the United States with clear title to the rest of Oregon and Washington. Over the span of only two years, sixteen treaties were negotiated and eventually ratified with several other nations of the Northwest. In September 1853, the headmen of the Rogue River peoples signed away a large portion of Oregon Territory, from which they agreed to be removed to another "selected" site at a later date. In the same month, the

Umpqua of Cow Creek, also in Oregon, gave up another large tract with the provision that a small section of land be "deemed and considered an Indian reserve until a suitable selection shall be made by the direction of the President of the United States for their permanent residence." In effect, the Umpqua and Rogue River peoples transferred their title to the land to the United States, and a portion was reserved for their temporary use.

The very next year, another Umpqua band and the Rogue River leaders were negotiating new treaties. Under the Rogue River treaty of 1854, a portion of the previously reserved land known as the Table Rock reserve was to be put aside as a reservation for the Rogue River people and for other displaced Native bands. The Table Rock land was to be both a reservation and a refuge until the federal government deemed it necessary to remove the people once again. The Rogue River leaders did, however, secure a provision in the new treaty stipulating that, should a future removal take place, the Nation would share individually the $15,000 payment for their lands, as had been secured in the negotiations of the previous year. In the same month, federal agents negotiated a new treaty with the Cave Creek band of the Rogue River people. The new treaty included the Chasta and Scoton tribes and secured a previously unceded stretch of the Rogue River valley and lay along Applegate Creek. The new Umpqua treaty included the confederated Kalapuya peoples' ceded lands along Calapooia Creek and the Illinois River in Oregon. Like the Rogue River agreement, the treaty provided for a residential reserve and cash remuneration to be paid as annuities. The Chasta of Oregon also negotiated a new treaty in 1854 ceding a large tract of land essentially bordering the lands that had formerly belonged to the Rogue River and Umpqua peoples. Moreover, the Chasta were to be removed to the Rogue River's Table Rock Reservation. The Chastas were promised $2,000 annually for the next fifteen years for the land; thereafter, their payments would be combined in the Table Rock annuities, of which the Chastas would receive a full share. All the negotiations in Oregon in 1854 contained "civilization" provisions. The Native nations were to receive farm implements, blacksmith services, schoolhouses, medical care, and livestock.

The Umpqua treaty furthered the government's "Indian civilization" policy in another important way. It contained a provision for the allotment of reservation lands at the discretion of the president of the United States. Allotment meant the surveying and division of the Umpqua and Kalapuya reserved lands into twenty-, forty-, sixty-, and eighty-acre lots. The lots would be distributed to single males and to families according to the number of immediate members. A single man would receive twenty acres; a family of two would get forty acres; families with three to five members would receive sixty acres; and a family of six or more could claim eighty acres. Families had to work the land, or their allotments would be redistributed to other tribe members. The treaty also stipulated that, when Oregon eventually attained statehood, its legislature could not remove any of the federal restrictions placed on the Indian allotments. Here, in one fell swoop, the federal government attempted to encapsulate the intentions of the "civilization" policy. In the first place, it was thought that the individual or private ownership of property would immediately infuse the allottee with the urge to cultivate the land and thus gain an income. In theory, private property would liberate the allottee from tribal customs and dependence on extended family members and would ultimately promote self-reliance. The preemption of state jurisdiction over the allotments was an equally significant step in the attempt to woo Indians away from their identities as members of separate, sovereign nations. An allottee would, presumably, owe his first allegiance to the federal government as the guarantor of the individual's real property.

Every treaty of the period contained an article that not only established peace but also promised perpetual amity between the signatories. The Native nations that negotiated the treaties literally became protectorates of the United States. As such, their sovereignty, especially in a domestic sense, was not eroded in the least. They did, however, enter into a trust relationship with the United States that has been maintained to this day.

Three ratified treaties negotiated in Oregon Territory were concluded in 1855. In January, the Kalapuya nation entered into another treaty with the United States, one that surrendered more lands along the Columbia River to the Cascade Mountains for the sum of $145,000, to be paid in decreasing amounts over a period of twenty years. The following June, the United States concluded a convention with several bands of Walla Walla and the Wasco Nation at The Dalles in Oregon. Not only did the treaty of The Dalles cede more territory to the Americans, but it also secured for the Walla Walla and Wasco the right to fish in "usual and accustomed stations." This provision essentially said that the Walla Walla and Wasco peoples could take fish even outside the boundaries of their assigned reservations. The treaty in December with the Molala nation extinguished the tribe's "right, title, interest and claim" to the territory bordering the lands surrendered by the Umpqua, Chasta, Scoton, and Rogue River peoples the year before. Except for the Indian reservations, the title to the entire Oregon Territory had shifted to the United States.

The Washington Territory treaties were equally extensive in terms of land surrendered in a relatively short period of time. Between December 1854 and July 1855, the Native nations gave up their "right, title, interest and claim" to the land from the northern border with Canada, to Oregon in the south, and from the Pacific Ocean in the west to the Great Plains in the east. The lands around Puget Sound and along the Columbia River were especially desirable. The fishing, the timber, the fine harbors, the access to the Pacific Ocean whaling grounds, and the fertile farmlands were much too valuable to the Americans for them to remain in Indian hands. The titles to the vast tracts of land surrounding Puget Sound were transferred to the United States in five treaties concluded between December 1854 and June 1855. The Medicine Creek convention, signed with the Nisqally, Puyallup, Steilacoom, Squaxin S'Homamish, Stehchass, Tapeeksin, Squiaitl, and Sahewamish on December 26, 1854, gave up the southern end of the sound. A month later, the Duwamish, the Suquamish, and several other nations agreed to the Point Elliott treaty, which secured the eastern flank of Puget Sound for the United States to a very great depth. In June 1855 came the Point No Point treaty, by which the Clallam, Twana, and Chemakum ceded the lands west of the Point Elliot treaty, thus giving up nearly all of the Olympic Peninsula. The rest of the peninsula was secured in the Neah Bay treaty of June 1855 with the Makah, and the Quinault River treaty of July 1855 with the Quinault, Queets, Hoh, and Quileute peoples. These treaties contained provisions under which the Native nations pledged eternal friendship with the United States and promised not to harbor anyone suspected of breaking the law. The Point Elliot treaties, for example, stipulated that, should any Indian "violate this pledge" and harm an American citizen in any way, the tribe's annuities would be used to compensate the victims. In essence, the Native nations agreed to become protectorates of the United States and assume liability for the actions of their citizens. Federal agents, however, were given the power to judge whether or not American "depredation" claims against the tribes were "satisfactorily proven." Hence, while the Native nations were asserting the sovereign capacity to enter into protectorate status and take up the responsibility for the actions of their peoples, the Americans were assuming an extensive political jurisdiction over the tribes.

In June 1855, several Native nations and the United States negotiated three treaties at Camp Stevens in the Walla Walla valley. The Walla Walla, Cayuse, and Umatilla peoples concluded an agreement whereby, in exchange for $100,000, they ceded a large tract of land in Washington and agreed to be moved to a reservation. These confederated nations were to remove to a reservation chosen by the president of the United States, which was to be surveyed for allotment when the president deemed it in the best interests of the Indians to do so. In separate treaties, the Yakima and Nez Perce agreed to nearly the same stipulations. In July, at Hell Gate in the Bitterroot Valley, the Flathead, Kutenai, and Pend d'Oreille Nations surrendered most of the western half of the territory and agreed to move onto smaller reservations within their former national boundaries. Almost the entire territory of the future state of Washington was in the hands of the United States.

Except for a few provisions dealing with reservation boundaries and amounts of money pledged to the tribes, the treaties negotiated in Washington Territory were all very similar in wording and in form. Treaties in the 1850s were becoming more or less standardized. All of the Washington Territory and a few of the Oregon treaties, however, provided that the Native nations would retain the right to fish in their usual and accustomed "stations" or "grounds" and even to set up buildings in these places to cure the catch and house the fishermen during the seasonal fish or whale migrations. The Native negotiators essentially secured the right to fish even outside the boundaries of their reservations. These fishing rights, guaranteed by treaty with the United States, would later become a long-drawn-out battle between the Native nations and the state of Washington. In the end, the treaties superseded state fish and game regulations, thereby conceding a degree of Native sovereignty.

While a number of officials were sedulously seeking to open up the territories of Oregon and Washington, others were equally preoccupied with securing the land routes over which the whites would come in droves to the northwest coast and

California. One of the first of these was the Navajo (spelled *Navaho* in the original document) treaty of 1849. Under the Treaty of Guadalupe Hidalgo, the Native nations of the Southwest were specifically placed under the "exclusive jurisdiction and protection" of the United States. The Navajo treaty, one of "peace and friendship," ceded no land and established no reservation but bound the Navajo Nation to the U.S. laws governing the trade and intercourse between Indian and American citizens. For the purposes of enforcing these laws, the Navajo Nation was subjected to a jurisdictional annexation to New Mexico Territory. The annexation meant that the Navajos were to repatriate American and Mexican captives and return all property taken in raids. The Navajo were also to deliver to the authorities of New Mexico Territory the murderer or murderers, presumably Navajo, of one Micente Garcia.

According to the reasoning at the time, the United States by right of conquest took the territory from Mexico. Presumably, the Spanish had secured legitimate title to the land of the American Southwest either by way of conquest or by right of discovery, according to the established European means of acquiring new lands. Mexico gained the title from Spain when it rebelled and became an independent state.

On the other hand, U.S. negotiators nevertheless realized that the Navajo Nation, like the Native peoples of California, had, at minimum, a right of occupancy to their lands. In consequence, federal agents negotiated a "free and safe passage through the territory of the aforesaid Indians" so that white immigrants might traverse northern New Mexico Territory in route to California. The treaty also stipulated that a string of military posts be established "to afford protection to all the people and interests of the contracting parties." The right of occupancy also elicited the agreement that the federal government would "at its earliest convenience, designate, settle and adjust" the boundaries of the Navajo national domain.

"Free-passage" treaties were negotiated with the Apache in 1852 and with the Comanche, Kiowa, and Apache (Plains) in 1853. The former treaty was signed at Santa Fe, New Mexico Territory. It established peace and, to enforce the safe passage of whites and maintain order, contained a provision whereby the Apache agreed to the erection of U.S. military posts in their country. They also approved the stipulation that all cases of aggression by whites against them and their property would be referred to U.S. military authority. It was thought, perhaps, that the assumption of U.S. jurisdiction over all white crimes would end the almost constant state of war between white immigrants and the Apache.

The Comanche-Kiowa-Apache treaty of the next year was signed at Fort Atkinson in the Indian Territory. These Native nations agreed to end warfare, both between themselves and against the United States. They agreed, as did the Apache in the Santa Fe treaty, to forgo incursions into Mexico and restore captives to both the Mexican government and the United States. The treaty also carried a free-passage clause and bound the Comanche, Kiowa, and Apache to a provision that called for the laying out of permanent roads through their territories. The Native nations agreed to the erection of military posts and to refer cases of white criminality to military authorities.

The pressing need on the part of the United States to ensure the passage of immigrants to the West Coast led to the demand for the Native nations to surrender more land in what would become the states of Minnesota, Wisconsin, Iowa, Nebraska, and especially Kansas. The list of treaties with the tribes of these areas was remarkably long. Native nations that had been removed from Ohio, Indiana, Illinois, and Michigan and as far away as New York to the "permanent Indian frontier"—a space that roughly covered what today is southern Nebraska and all of Kansas and Oklahoma—were forced to reduce their landholdings once again to tiny reservations or move south into Indian Territory. These land cessions affected the land bases of the Seneca, Delaware, Miami, Mdewakanton, Wahpakoota, Sisseton, and Wahpeton Sioux, Wyandot, Sac and Fox, Oto and Missouri, Shawnee, Omaha, and Iowa Nations. The Miami, Peoria, Kaskaskia, Kickapoo, Chippewa, Winnebago, and Ottawa Nations also surrendered huge amounts of territory, all with the promise of annuity payments, the protection of the federal government, and, most importantly, peace.

The list of unratified treaties that attempted to reduce Native landholdings to the bare minimum and institute peace all along the American frontier was equally lengthy. Some of these treaties were negotiated with nations that had never before dealt with the Americans. Others were stopgap agreements made to quell violence either immediately or until more comprehensive conventions could be worked out. A number of these treaties could, in fact, contain provisions that might be operable simply because Congress has referred to them in other treaties or in making appropriations to fulfill one or another promise made to Native nations.

The Fort Laramie treaty of 1851, like the Navajo treaty of 1849, stands out in this period because it did not call for a land cession on the part of the Native nations. Basically, it was a peace concord that defined the national boundaries of several indigenous peoples of the northern plains. The Sioux, Gros Ventre, Mandan, Arikara, Assiniboine, Blackfeet, Crow, Cheyenne, and Arapaho Nations all participated in the negotiations and agreed not only to the stipulated national borders but also to the building of roads and military posts within these boundaries. Ostensibly, the roads were for the free and safe passage of white immigrants on the trail to the West Coast, and the military posts were erected in order to protect both Indians and whites from each other's potential depredations. The federal government, in compensation, was to pay the Native nations $50,000 a year for fifty years "for their maintenance and the improvement of their moral and social customs."

Land Payments

Probably because no land cession was agreed to in the Fort Laramie treaty, Congress did not pass on it without altering one of its most important provisions. Congress essentially decreased the fifty annual payments to ten, with another five to be paid at the discretion of the president. This sum of money was hardly enough to aid the nearly fifty thousand members of the several Native nations involved in the negotiations; from the point of view of the Native leaders, it was a serious breach of the agreement they had made. The congressional amendment made the treaty's standing hazy at best, even in the eyes of the whites. Charles J. Kappler, in his 1904 compilation of treaties, stated that the Fort Laramie treaty was "never ratified or printed." It was nevertheless valid even in its altered form, and the Native nations, although they voiced concern over the changes made, complied with its provisions.

Four years later, however, some of the Native nations involved in the Fort Laramie treaty, as well as some of those engaged in making agreements with federal agents in Washington Territory, were once again at the negotiating table. The Blackfeet Nation (consisting of, and so recognized by the United States, the Piegan, Blood, and Blackfeet proper); the Gros Ventre from east of the Rocky Mountains; and the Flathead, Upper Pend d'Oreille, Kutenai, and Nez Perce from the west side of the range worked out a new and detailed treaty in 1855. In format much like most of the treaties of the period, the Blackfeet agreement was intended to settle territorial boundaries and maintain order along the northern immigrant trail to Washington Territory. Peace and friendship were declared between the United States and the Native nations as well as between each one of the signatory Native peoples. The Native parties to the treaty also agreed to cease hostilities, except in self-defense, with the Crow, Assiniboine, Cree, Snake (Shoshone), and several Lakota bands. The Blackfeet consented once again to their national boundaries, as had been "recognized and defined by the treaty of Laramie," even though Congress had amended the 1851 convention almost to the point of invalidity.

Perhaps the main point of the Blackfeet treaty was to secure a common hunting ground for the various signatories and to allow whites both to live in and to pass through the large Blackfeet Nation domain. No other tribes were allowed to establish permanent settlements; each Native nation would be allowed to enter the Blackfeet Nation only to use it as a common for the taking of buffalo, and for other purposes only by way of certain designated points of entry. Although the Assiniboine Nation was not party to the treaty, it was specifically mentioned as one of the groups with hunting rights within Blackfeet territory. The treaty went on to stipulate that all Indians were to stay in their respective lands except when on hunting forays. The treaty allowed for the construction of roads "of every description" and the establishment of telegraph lines and military posts. U.S. citizens were allowed the free navigation of all streams and rivers and the permanent use of land, timber, and other natural resources for the erection of "agencies, missions, schools, farms, shops, mills, stations, and for any other purpose for which they may be required." For the effective opening of the Blackfeet Nation to American colonization, the Blackfeet, Piegan, Blood, and Gros Ventre were to receive $20,000 annually for a period of twenty years. The president, however, could increase the annuity to $35,000 should circumstance warrant the increase.

The main thrust of treaty making during the 1850s was to acquire more land and thereby gain political efficacy within the territory claimed by the United States as its national domain. Underlying the acquisition of control over Native territories were strategies calculated to smooth over the hostilities aroused when Native Americans were displaced or

confined to smaller tracts of land. One such strategy was the introduction to Native peoples of the concept of private property by way of allotment in severalty. For example, in 1858 the Sisseton and Wahpeton Sioux penned a treaty in Washington, D.C., that agreed to new reservation boundaries and to having them surveyed with the intent of dividing the reservation into individually owned, eighty-acre plots. The ultimate reason for the acceptance of this new treaty was simply that the U.S. Senate reneged on the Sisseton-Wahpeton agreement of 1851. The Senate unilaterally struck the provision in the treaty of 1851 that set apart a large tract of land for the Sisseton-Wahpeton on the Minnesota River, and instead offered a sum of money "at the rate of ten cents per acre" to the Sisseton-Wahpeton Nation. Other than providing excuses for amending the treaty of 1851, the new convention provided for the same lands to be allotted, which in turn considerably reduced Sisseton-Wahpeton landholdings. Individual tribe members, instead of the Sisseton-Wahpeton Nation, were to hold the land.

Addenda Treaties

The federal government negotiated no fewer than five treaties or addenda to treaties with the Muscogee Creek, Seminole, Chickasaw, and Choctaw in the 1850s. These tribes had been forcibly removed from their homelands in the southeastern United States to the Indian Territory (present Oklahoma) in the 1830s. Not all their tribe members, however, had made the trip. A large number of Choctaws remained in Mississippi, and the Chickasaws had not ceded a four-mile-square parcel of land in Tennessee to the United States. The removal of the Seminole Nation from Florida had started a costly war, and even as late as the 1850s, small bands of Mikasuki Seminoles were still living in the Florida backcountry and fighting American soldiers.

In 1852, the Chickasaw entered into negotiations with the federal government, primarily to settle several of the tribe's claims to particular lands. Additionally, the cost of the Chickasaw removal had far exceeded the funds allocated for the purpose. The treaty of 1852 was intended to clear up the cost of removal, to clear the title of Chickasaw lands that had not been ceded east of the Mississippi River, and to address the allegations of corruption that had resulted in the override of Chickasaw removal funds. The Chickasaw Nation agreed to forgo claims to territories in the east for money to be held in trust by the United States, provided that the secretary of the interior audit the Chickasaw account "from time to time." The Chickasaws would have the "privilege" to review the audit and submit objections to it within a reasonable amount of time. The cost to the United States was ultimately quite low. The four-mile-square parcel in Tennessee, for example, which had been originally set apart as a reservation under the provisions of the Chickasaw treaty of 1818, was to be purchased at a rate of no more than "one dollar and twenty-five cents per acre."

Two years later, the Chickasaws were back at the negotiating table. When removal took place, the Chickasaw and Choctaw were effectively placed together on one large piece of land that made up most of what would become southern Oklahoma. The Chickasaw and Choctaw leaders more or less agreed to this circumstance, very likely because they recognized that, since they were culturally and linguistically tied, the two nations were once one. By 1854, however, the jurisdictional lines between the two peoples had become unclear. The United States was brought into the dispute over the Chickasaw-Choctaw boundaries, and a new treaty was negotiated. Essentially, the two nations agreed to draw a line between themselves: the Chickasaw jurisdiction was established in the western half of the territory, the Choctaw in the east.

The dispute did not end, and the very next year the Chickasaw and the Choctaw agreed to a redrawing of the boundaries between the two nations and to lease their lands west of longitude 98° to the United States. The two nations separated completely. The Choctaw received a sum of money out of Chickasaw funds and ceded all of the land west of 100° longitude. The nations agreed to the establishment of military forts and roads and to railroad and telegraph rights-of-way.

Similar jurisdictional and national disputes had arisen between the Creek and the Seminole. The United States was still attempting to remove the remnants of the Seminole Nation in Florida to the Indian Territory. Those Seminole who had been forcibly removed were moved, again because of linguistic and cultural ties, onto the lands of the Muscogee Creek Nation. The Creek treaty of 1856 essentially ceded a tract of land to the Seminole. A sovereign Seminole Nation was thus established in the hope of getting the Seminole in Florida to cease hostilities and migrate to the Indian Territory. The Seminole Nation West, as it was called, would send a delegation to Florida "to do all in their power to

induce their brethren remaining [in Florida] to emigrate and join them in the west." The usual concessions to the railroads, military posts, roads, and telegraph services were also made. The effort to "induce" the Florida Seminole to remove was not successful. While some Seminole did, indeed, migrate west after the treaty of 1856, the core of the Mikasuki Seminole in the east remained in Florida to this day.

By the end of March 1861, the United States had succeeded in securing the title to nearly all of its claimed territory west of the Mississippi River. Save for a very large tract of land recognized as "the Great Sioux Nation" on the northern plains, most of the Indian Territory (present Oklahoma), a very large portion of New Mexico Territory, and smaller reservations dotting the land, the Americans now held all of what would become the continental United States. The Cheyenne and Arapaho had ceded eastern Colorado in February of 1861, and on March 6, the united Sauk and Fox and Iowa Nations gave up title to most of Iowa and parts of Nebraska.

Confederate Treaties

All of the great land cessions of the 1850s contributed fuel to the oncoming holocaust of the American Civil War. The opening of the entire West Coast, Iowa, Minnesota, Utah, Colorado, Nebraska, Kansas, and much of New Mexico Territory meant the possibility of bringing in several states into the union. Most of these territories, in accordance with several legal compromises, would not become slave-holding states. Southern politicians, of course, saw the organization of states such as Iowa, Minnesota, Nebraska, and Kansas as a threat to their continued power in Congress, to their economic systems, and to their sectional culture, all of which were built on chattel slavery.

When the Civil War broke out in April 1861, the newly formed Confederate States actively began to seek Native American allies. The Confederacy was especially interested in the Indian Territory, which could serve as a buffer between Union Kansas and Confederate Texas, and with the mineral-rich New Mexico and Arizona territories. Albert Pike, whose complete title was commissioner of the Confederate States to the Indians west of Arkansas, negotiated nine treaties with twenty-one Native nations, at four different locations. All of the tribes with which Pike negotiated with were located at the time in the Indian Territory.

The first Confederate treaties were negotiated with the Creek, Choctaw, and Chickasaw in North Fork Town on the Canadian River in the Creek Nation. The Creek treaty, although concluded on July 10, 1861, nevertheless referred to the Seminole treaty of August 7 of the same year in order to clarify the exact boundaries and jurisdictions of both nations. A supplementary article was added to the convention to address the claims of the Apalachicola band. Under two previous treaties with the United States, the Apalachicola still had reserves of land in Florida. The Confederacy acknowledged their claims and agreed to pay for the claims and the property the Apalachicola lost in their removal to the Indian Territory. Remnants of the Apalachicola still living in Florida would be encouraged to move west and reunite with their kinsmen as part of the larger Creek Nation. In the same supplement, the Seminole were guaranteed payments for their lost property and land in Florida "in consequence of their hurried removal west."

The Choctaw and Chickasaw signed a single treaty with the Confederacy. Concluded on July 12, the treaty was lengthy and detailed. It contained more than sixty articles, many of which focused on clearing up the financial arrangements of land sales and annuities. The Confederate government in Richmond essentially took on the U.S. debt to, and assumed the federal trust responsibility for, the Choctaw and the Chickasaw. Moreover, the Confederacy agreed to pay the Chickasaw close to $700,000 as reimbursement for funds invested by the United States in the state bonds of Maryland, Indiana, Tennessee, Illinois, and Arkansas and in stocks issued by the Richmond and Danville railroad and the Nashville and Chattanooga railroad.

The Seminole treaty was agreed to in August at the Seminole Council House, and the Confederate Cherokee convention was concluded in October at Park Hill, Cherokee Nation. The Confederacy had thus made binding agreements with all of the so-called Five Civilized Tribes, establishing itself as the protector of the Indian nations. All these treaties offered the Native nations a good deal more than the Union promised. Native soldiers, who were to be equipped by the South, would not have to fight except in defense of their own territory. The Confederacy would assume all of the Union's debts and annuity payments, in addition to a permanent allocation to pay for certain services, such as schools, insane asylums, health care, and orphanages. The Native nations were also given the option of sending delegates to the Confederate House of Representatives. Most importantly, perhaps, was that the Confederacy pledged its protection from invasion and affirmed each nation's title to its lands in fee simple.

The negotiations at Park Hill produced Confederate treaties with the Osage, confederated Seneca and Shawnee, and Quapaw Nations. Like the treaties made with the Five Tribes, these agreements were somewhat formulaic. The treaties guaranteed annuities, the services of teachers, blacksmiths, and landholdings. The Confederacy also agreed to supply the tribes with arms to be used in their self-protection. The same kinds of guarantees were given in treaties to a number of Native groups in the western Indian Territory, including the Comanche, Wichita, Caddo, Waco, Tawakoni, Anadarko, Tonkawa, and western Shawnee and Delaware tribes. Confederate agents obtained an agreement with the Comanche of the Staked Plains to offer a treaty of friendship with the Kiowa, in order to stop completely raids into Texas.

On the surface, the Confederate treaties promised a remarkably peaceful settlement for most of the Native nations living in or near what is now Oklahoma. The Confederate treaties not only established friendship between the nations and the Confederacy but also between all the Native treaty signatories. Each treaty contained an oath of "perpetual peace and brotherhood" with all the Native nations that made treaties with the Confederacy. The Comanche swore not to raid other Native nations; Cherokee and Osage pledged to end long years of animosity; the Wichita promised to live in peace and forgive those tribes that had threatened them in the past. The Confederacy presumably obtained the safety of its largest state, Texas, and opened the rest of the Southwest for Confederate expansion.

The Confederate-initiated peace in the Indian Territory, however, was not to be. Before the ink was dry on the treaties, Creeks and Seminoles loyal to the Union attempted to escape to Kansas, and numerous Cherokee began to doubt the wisdom of allying themselves with the South. Eventually, fighting erupted between loyal and Confederate Indians all over the territory. All-Indian regiments were raised for both the Union and the Confederacy. These military units were even to go into combat outside the territorial limits of the Native nations. The promise that the nations would not have to fight unless in defense of their own country was quickly made moot. Union and Confederate invasions from Kansas, Arkansas, and Texas left the Indian Territory devastated. And the fighting continued there even after the surrender at Appomattox.

Predictably, war fever engulfed the western territories and states and led to the inflicting of barbarous cruelties on the Native nations. War broke out in Minnesota between the whites and the Santee Sioux. Instead of attempting to use diplomacy, which perhaps could have averted the Santee war, the whites treated genuine Santee complaints as acts of rebellion, eventually trying and convicting many of the Santee men in a military court. California militiamen stormed into Arizona and New Mexico seeking rebels, only to set off a lengthy war with the Apaches and Navajos. The old scout Kit Carson was enlisted to carry on a frightful roundup of the Navajo, which led to their imprisonment at Fort Sumner. In 1864, the Colorado Volunteers attacked and slaughtered the Cheyenne at Sand Creek, notwithstanding the fact that the Cheyenne were peacefully living on the lands guaranteed to them in their 1861 treaty with the United States. The horror of the Sand Creek massacre produced a period of general conflict between the Native nations of the Great Plains and the Union.

From a certain perspective, agents of the United States were indeed attempting to ease the tensions with several Native nations during the war and trying to deal with them diplomatically. The federal government negotiated and ratified eighteen treaties during the war. Between March 1862 and March 1865, exactly three years, treaties were concluded with the Kansa, Ottawa, Chippewa, Nez Perce, Shoshone, Ute, Klamath, Modoc, Omaha, Winnebago, and Ponca Nations. All these agreements included land cessions and further diminished the territories of the tribes involved. Several established "permanent" reservations or removed the nations to smaller concentrations of landholdings. Despite its focus on winning the Civil War, the United States was nevertheless still very much involved in securing title to new lands in the West.

When the fighting between the whites ended, the United States simply resumed its avowed conquest of the western territories, with a side trip to renegotiate treaties with the nations that had signed on with the Confederacy. The United States extracted a heavy price from the nations that signed Confederate treaties, even though large factions within the tribes had repudiated them and had served in Union regiments. The Osage were forced to cede most of their large reservation and confine themselves to the Indian Territory. For the land cession, they were to receive the proceeds of the sale of their lands in Kansas and Missouri, from which the federal government established a fund to build boarding schools. Portions of Osage land were to be directly handed over in fee simple to several individuals. Certain chiefs and mixed-blood citizens of the Osage Nation were awarded direct payments of Osage funds and grants of land. The Osage put themselves under the protectorship of the United States and agreed to be removed from the ceded lands within a six-month period of time. The federal government also extracted railroad rights-of-way through Osage country. Finally, the Osage submitted to a new kind of treaty provision that stated, "Should the Senate reject or amend any of the above articles, such rejection or amendment shall not affect the other provisions of this treaty." The Senate, in other words, could change the treaty as it liked, whereas the Osage were bound to the agreement no matter what.

Reconstruction Treaties

The Five Civilized Tribes each agreed to reconstruction treaties that not only ceded territory but also gave up land for the resettlement of Native nations from Kansas, Nebraska, and Missouri. The Cherokee, Choctaw, Chickasaw, Creek, and Seminole agreed to abolish slavery and admit the freed slaves to citizen status within their respective nations. The new treaties gave away railroad rights-of-way but promised the nations that white intruders would be removed from their territorial boundaries.

The Cherokee treaty of 1866 was perhaps the most comprehensive of the several "reconstruction" treaties. It first contained a provision declaring the Confederate treaty of 1861 null and void, even though the Cherokees had already repudiated it in 1863. Notwithstanding this repudiation, the United States argued that the previously existing Cherokee treaties were nevertheless insufficient. A portion of the Cherokee Nation was set aside for former slaves and for free blacks who had resided in the Cherokee prior to the Civil War, who individually could take 160-acre plots should they desire to move there within a span of two years. This land, however, was not to be "set apart until it shall be found that the Canadian district is not sufficiently large to allow one hundred and sixty acres to each person desiring to obtain settlement under the provisions of this article." The residents of this reserve-within-a-reserve were enabled to elect their own local officers and judges and to have representation in the Cherokee national government. A U.S. court was to be established in the Indian Territory "nearest to the Cherokee Nation" and was to have jurisdiction over all matters civil and criminal involving whites and blacks. The Cherokee court system retained jurisdiction in Cherokee cases only. The Cherokee were also required to take a census of the nation and to participate in an Indian Territory-wide general council in order to regulate intercourse between the Indian nations and with the "colonies of freemen resident in said Territory." The federal government obtained the agreement from the Cherokee to resettle "civilized" Indians in the Cherokee Nation and admit them as citizens (a Delaware and a Shawnee band eventually were so settled). More Cherokee land was to be ceded for the future resettlement of several "friendly" Native nations. The idea of resettling "friendly" Native nations in the Indian Territory marked the beginning of a new round of Indian removal that would continue well into the 1870s, with the relocation of the Ponca, the Pawnee, and numerous other Native nations that had surrendered their lands in Iowa, Minnesota, Kansas, Texas, Nebraska, the Dakotas, and as far away as New York and Oregon.

The years between 1865 and 1868 produced a very long list of Native American treaties with the United States, some ratified, some simply set aside until more comprehensive agreements could be made. Four unratified but very important treaties that fitted the category of stopgap measures were the covenants that ended the Civil War in the Indian Territory. On June 19, 1865, the principal chief of the Choctaw Nation, Peter Pitchlynn, agreed to cease "acts of hostility" against the United States, and four days later, Confederate Brigadier General Stand Watie, who also had taken the title of principal chief of the Cherokee Nation, agreed to do the same. The Chickasaw Nation capitulated on July 14. In September, Union negotiators arranged what was in effect an armistice between Union forces and Confederate and Union Indians in the Indian Territory. Emissaries from the Cherokee, Creek, Choctaw, Chickasaw, Osage, Seminole, Seneca, Shawnee, Quapaw, and Euchee peoples essentially agreed to accept protectorate status under the United States and end any acts of aggression between themselves. That these treaties were not ratified was very likely due to the fact that these groups were seen as combat units rather than as Native nations. Thus, the treaties were thought to be more akin to the surrenders of the individual Confederate armies under Robert E. Lee, Joseph Johnston, and Edmund Kirby Smith. Military leaders, especially those acting in rebellion against the United States, were not heads of state authorized to conduct formal international relations.

Most of the unratified treaties of 1865, 1866, and 1867 were measures under which Native nations surrendered title to vast territories in the West. This round of treaty making was also an effort on the part of the United States to restore its claim to authority over the relations with Native nations. All the Native nations were doubtless aware of the terrible internecine struggle the Americans had just fought and were probably willing to deal with the winner in order to restore orderly relationships with the whites. These treaties, especially those made with the Paiute, Shoshone, Crow, several bands of the Apache, the Arikara, Mandan and Hidatsa, the Assiniboine, the Brule and Oglala bands of Lakota, and the Bannock, were very likely either not even submitted for ratification or had been made by unauthorized military personnel seeking an immediate end to hostilities or by those seeking to earn a measure of fortune or fame for negotiating the surrender of large tracts of Native lands.

Several agreements in the period also went unratified for the same reasons, because they were superseded by subsequent negotiations at the level of formal treaties, or because they were simply nullified by certain events. War was the event that certainly voided most of the agreements and treaties, ratified or not, with several Native nations of the Great Plains and the Southwest. The Apache were embroiled in a continuous war of attrition for their mineral-rich lands in Arizona and New Mexico territories that ultimately would last until the 1880s. The numerous agreements and ratified treaties made with the individual bands of the Lakota Nation, the Yanktonai, the northern and southern branches of the Cheyenne and Arapaho Nations, the Kiowa, Plains Apache, and Comanche in 1865 were but interludes of diplomacy in a lengthy conflict that began with the massacre at Sand Creek and engulfed all of the peoples of the Great Plains.

Because of the continuing violence, Congress created the United States Indian Peace Commission on June 20, 1867. The "Great Peace Commission," headed by Commissioner of Indian Affairs Nathaniel G. Taylor and including famous Civil War generals William Tecumseh Sherman and Alfred Terry, negotiated two of the most significant treaties on the Great Plains: the treaties of Medicine Lodge in 1867 and Fort Laramie in 1868. Neither treaty ended the conflict completely. Their very existence, however, ultimately led to the end of formal treaty making altogether. In a very real sense, the Native nations involved in these treaties negotiated from a position of relative strength, something that the United States was not ready to countenance.

The general warfare on the southern plains was a series of strikes and counterstrikes conducted by the United States and the southern branches of the Cheyenne and Arapaho and the Kiowa, Plains Apache, and Comanche. The Cheyenne Dog Soldiers had carried on an effective hit-and-run campaign against numerous civilian and military targets. The Kiowa and Comanche went on joint raids into Texas and New Mexico and, in the view of American officials, were severely disrupting trade and immigration routes. Although there were a few pitched battles, mostly between small parties of whites and Natives, by and large the war on the Southern Plains between 1865 and 1867 was a costly, confusing, and bitter period of guerrilla warfare. The American press was continually calling for an end to Indian depredations. The army could not find and defeat the tribes in decisive battle, but the continued conflict had begun to wear the Native leaders down. When the Great Peace Commission proposed a meeting that would secure peace at Medicine Lodge Creek in Kansas, many of the Native leaders came with high expectations.

Actually, three treaties were negotiated at Medicine Lodge. The first was with the Kiowa and Comanche. Basically, the price of peace was confinement to a relatively large reservation in southwestern Indian Territory and the withdrawal of opposition to the construction of roads and rail lines into Colorado and New Mexico. Heads of families could select tracts of land not exceeding 320 acres to engage in agricultural pursuits, the boundaries of which would be recorded in the "Kiowa and Comanche land book." The issuance of farming implements, the services of a blacksmith and a physician, and the establishment of reservations schools were promised. Two important provisions in the treaty would eventually become causes for renewed conflicts, one resulting in open warfare and the second in a famous court case.

In Article 11 of the treaty, the Kiowa and Comanche retained the right to hunt the territory south of the Arkansas River "so long as the buffalo may range thereon." With the building of roads and rail lines, immigrant whites, the army, and sportsmen came to these hunting grounds in droves. The great slaughter of the herds had already begun by the time the Native leaders signed the Medicine Lodge agreements. Then, in 1871, a Pennsylvania tannery discovered that bison hides had commercial value. The hides could be used not only for the manufacture of leather goods but also as belting for machinery. Commercial buffalo hunting soon became a leading industry in the West. The Kiowa and Comanche saw the slaughter as a violation of their guaranteed right to hunt, and a war to save the buffalo broke out. It would last until well into the 1870s.

Article 12 of the treaty provided that no further cession of Kiowa-Comanche land could be made without the agreement of three-fourths of the male population of the tribes. When, thirty years later, the federal government moved to allot the Kiowa-Comanche Reservation, leaving surplus land to be set aside for white settlement, no three-fourths majority tribal consent was sought or obtained. A lawsuit, launched on behalf of Kiowa chief Lone Wolf, argued that allotment was in violation of Article 12 of the treaty. The Supreme Court, in *Lone Wolf v. Hitchcock,* decided in 1903 that Congress had plenary authority over the tribes and could therefore abrogate unilaterally the provisions of a prior convention.

The second Treaty of Medicine Lodge was effectively an act of union between the Kiowa, Comanche, and Plains Apache. The Apache agreed to join the Kiowa and Comanche on the reservation and to abide by the same provisions of their comprehensive convention. The third Treaty of Medicine Lodge enjoined the southern Cheyenne and Arapahos to abide by nearly the same provisions as the Kiowa and Comanche but confined them to an area immediately to the north of the Kiowa-Comanche-Apache Reservations.

War on the northern plains centered on a Lakota-led campaign against the illegally occupied military forts along the Bozeman trail in Montana. Under the Oglala leader Red Cloud, the alliance consisting of all of the Lakota bands plus the Yanktonai and Santee Sioux and the northern branches of the Cheyenne and Arapaho Nations soundly defeated the U.S. Army and forced its withdrawal from the forts. Like the Native nations of the southern plains, the Lakota and Cheyenne had disrupted the building of the railroad through Nebraska. When the whites began to invade the Powder River country and erect the forts, however, the alliance launched an all-out and decisive campaign. The army's withdrawal prompted the call to diplomacy and the peace conference at Fort Laramie in 1868.

Again, three treaties were signed. The first was with the Lakota bands, the Yanktonai, the Santee, and the Arapaho. The Great Peace Commission's treaties were remarkably formulaic, worded nearly the same as those signed at Medicine Lodge except for the detailed boundaries of the new Great Sioux Nation in the Dakotas. The Crow Nation, although an enemy of the Lakota-led alliance, signed the second treaty, which established their present reservation in Montana. The Northern Arapaho and Cheyenne penned a separate treaty in which they agreed to relinquish all land claims outside the southern Cheyenne-Arapaho Reservation in Indian Territory, and lands were set aside for them in the Lakota Reservations. The Cheyenne and Arapaho Nations, in short, were left with little choice except to live either with their southern cousins or with their Lakota allies. Later, the northern Arapahos would be moved to a reservation shared with their former enemies, the Shoshone, and the Cheyenne would be removed to the Indian Territory.

Four more ratified treaties were signed in 1868, with the Ute, Cherokee, Navajo, Shoshone-Bannock, and Nez Perce nations. In effect, they were the last treaties of their kind. In 1871, the House of Representatives added a proviso to the Indian Appropriations Act that ended the practice of treaty making with Native nations.

Tom Holm

References and Further Reading

Brown, Dee. 1970. *Bury My Heart at Wounded Knee: An Indian History of the American West*. New York: Holt, Rinehart and Winston.

Cohen, Felix. 1958. *Handbook of Federal Indian Law.* Albuquerque: University of New Mexico Press. Originally published 1942.

Deloria, Vine, Jr., and Raymond J. DeMallie. 1999. *Documents of American Indian Diplomacy, Treaties, Agreements, and Conventions, 1775–1979*. 2 vols. Norman: University of Oklahoma Press.

Deloria, Vine, Jr., and Clifford M. Lytle. 1983. *American Indians, American Justice.* Austin: University of Texas Press.

Jones, Douglas C. 1966. *The Treaty of Medicine Lodge: The Story of the Great Treaty Council as Told by Eyewitnesses*. Norman: University of Oklahoma Press.

Kappler, Charles J., ed. 1904. *Indian Affairs: Laws and Treaties*, vol. 2., Washington, DC: Government Printing Office.

Kickingbird, Kirk, et al. 1980. *Indian Treaties*. Washington, DC: Institute for the Development of Indian Law.

Price, Monroe E., and Robert N. Clinton. 1983. *Law and the American Indian: Readings, Notes and Cases*. Charlottesville, VA: The Michie Company Law Publishers.

Prucha, Francis Paul. 1994. *American Indian Treaties: The History of a Political Anomaly*. Berkeley, Los Angeles, and London: University of California Press.

Statutes as Sources of Modern Indian Rights: Child Welfare, Gaming, and Repatriation

A Statutory History of Federal Indian Policy

As important as treaties are in the history of federal Indian policy, they are second in importance to the statutes enacted by Congress. Statutes, rather than treaties, have come to define the scope of tribal authorities and immunities and the rights of individual Indians. We know that statutes supersede treaties in importance from two pertinent facts. First, every treaty between the United States and the Indian tribes has been broken. Second, the way Congress breaks a treaty with an Indian tribe is by enacting a statute to that effect. Although it may seem odd that a treaty can be done away with so easily, the Supreme Court has held squarely that Congress has the power to break an Indian treaty unilaterally (*Lone Wolf v. Hitchcock*, 1903). The only legal issue of interest regarding the breaking of Indian treaties in any particular case is whether Congress actually intended to do so (e.g., *United States v. Dion*, 1986).

Federal Indian policy has been defined primarily by statute from the beginning. An early order of business for the first Congress was the enactment of the first Trade and Intercourse Act (1 *Stat*. 137, 1790), which forbade transactions affecting Indian land if Congress had not approved the transaction. The act limited the tribes' authority to dispose of their property. Subsequent Trade and Intercourse Acts defined federal policy in the years following the adoption of the Constitution. The federal government alone would treat with the tribes, acquiring tribal land for the growing American nation while reserving land for the ongoing needs of the tribes within the territory of the United States.

The era of forced removal of tribes from the East, South, and Midwest also was defined by a congressional statute. The Indian Removal Act (4 *Stat*. 411, 1830) set the policy. The removal treaties affected the congressional policy, and many tribes were moved west.

With the congressionally mandated end of treaty making in 1871 (16 *Stat*. 566, 1871), statutes became ever more important in defining Indian rights. By 1885, for example, Congress had taken to itself the authority to subject Indians to federal court criminal processes for crimes committed by Indians against other Indians, regardless of the local law of the tribe. The Major Crimes Act (23 *Stat*. 385, 1985) marked the first time Congress had unilaterally extended federal criminal jurisdiction over crimes by and against Indians.

It was in this post-treaty era that the "plenary power" of Congress over Indians and their property was first articulated by the Supreme Court. Decades of failed tribal efforts to prevent encroachment on their homelands had left the Indians confined to reservations and unable to practice their traditional subsistence. They were left utterly dependent on the rations and supplies that had been promised in the various treaties. Ironically, the Supreme Court, in upholding the constitutionality of the Major Crimes Act, cited this tribal dependence on the United States as the source of Congress's power over the tribes:

> These Indian Tribes *are* the wards of the nation. They are communities *dependent* on the United States, dependent largely for their daily food; dependent for their political rights. . . . From their very weakness and helplessness, so largely due to the course of dealing of the federal government with them, and the treaties in which it has been promised, there arises a duty of protection, and with it the power.
>
> The power of the general government over these remnants of a race once powerful, now weak and diminished in numbers, is necessary to their protection, as well as to the safety of those among whom they dwell. It must exist in that government, because it has never existed anywhere else; because the theater of its exercise is within the geographical limits of the United States; because it has never been denied; and because it alone can enforce its laws on all the Tribes. (*United States v. Kagama*, 1886, pp. 383–385)

Having had its power confirmed by the Court, Congress put its power to use in the Dawes General Allotment Act (26 *Stat*. 794, 1887). The Dawes Act was the next of the defining statutes that established federal policy for decades. The dependence and poverty of the tribes, combined with their often-vast reservations, led Congress to believe that the most

beneficent policy toward Indians was to convert them into yeoman farmers and herders, to unsettle them from their tribal relations, and to bring non-Indian settlers among them to teach them the American agricultural way of life (Prucha 1984, 659–671). To that end, Congress authorized the president, in all cases where any tribe or band of Indians has been, or shall hereafter be, located upon any reservation created for their use, "... whenever in his opinion any reservation or any part thereof of such Indians is advantageous for agricultural and grazing purposes, to cause said reservation, or any part thereof, to be surveyed, or resurveyed if necessary, and to allot the lands in said reservation in severalty to any Indian located thereon" (24 *Stat.* 388).

Individual Indians were to receive from the tribal domains individual parcels of land for their use as farms and ranches. These allotted parcels were to be held in trust by the United States for a period of twenty-five years, during which the Indian owners were expected to become self-sufficient farmers and ranchers. Upon the expiration of the trust period, they would receive patents in fee. After receiving their patents in fee, Indians were to "have the benefit of and be subject to the laws, both civil and criminal, of the State or Territory in which they may reside" (24 *Stat.* 390).

The tribal lands remaining after eligible Indians had received their allotments were to be opened for settlement by non-Indians. Significantly, the opening of lands for non-Indian settlement was to be accomplished by negotiation with the tribes. The secretary of the interior was authorized to negotiate with the tribes for the purchase of their reservation lands "in conformity with the treaty or statute under which such reservation is held" and "on such terms and conditions as shall be considered just and equitable between the United States and said tribe of Indians" (24 *Stat.* 389). The agreements negotiated by the secretary would take effect when approved by Congress.

Though nominally requiring the consent of the tribes, the Dawes Act was the centerpiece of a policy of coercive assimilation featuring concerted federal efforts to destroy Indian political and social organization, Indian religion and language, and everything else that made Indians different from white people. Even the requirement that the allotment agreements conform to the relevant tribal treaties proved to be empty. In 1903, the Supreme Court heard Kiowa chief Lone Wolf's challenge to the allotment agreement for the opening of the Kiowa-Comanche-Apache Reservation in Oklahoma Territory. The Treaty of Medicine Lodge Creek of 1867 (Treaty with the Kiowa, Comanche, and Apache) required that three-fourths of the tribal men must consent to any cession of the lands guaranteed by the treaty. Lone Wolf claimed that three-fourths had not consented to the allotment agreement and that many of the consents had been obtained by fraud (*Lone Wolf v. Hitchcock*, 560–561). Notwithstanding the treaty provisions to the contrary, the Supreme Court held that Indian consent simply was not required. The Court did not consider whether Lone Wolf's claims were true, because "[p]lenary authority over the tribal relations of the Indians has been exercised from the beginning, and the power has always been deemed a political one, not subject to be controlled by the judicial department of the government" (ibid., 565). It did not matter that the treaty had been violated:

> The power exists to abrogate the provisions of an Indian treaty, though presumably such power will only be exercised when circumstances arise which will not only justify the government in disregarding the stipulations of the treaty, but may demand, in the interest of the country and the Indians themselves, that it should do so. When, therefore, treaties were entered into between the United States and a Tribe of Indians it was never doubted that the *power* to abrogate existed in Congress, particularly if consistent with perfect good faith towards the Indians. (ibid., 566)

Noting that it had recently held that "full administrative power was possessed by Congress over Indian tribal property," the Court concluded:

> In effect, the action of Congress now complained of was but an exercise of such power, a mere change in the form of investment of Indian tribal property, the property of those who, as we have held, were in substantial effect the wards of the government. We must presume that Congress acted in perfect good faith in the dealings with the Indians of which complaint is made, and the legislative branch of the government exercised its best judgment in the premises. In any event, as Congress possessed full power in the matter,

> the judiciary cannot question or inquire into the motives which prompted the enactment of this legislation. (ibid., 568)

With the Court's decision in Lone Wolf's case, the ascendancy of Congress's unilateral power in Indian affairs was complete. Policy would henceforth be made by Congress through statutes. Congress might seek the consent of the tribes, or it might not. Henceforth, when Congress chose to seek tribal consent, it did so out of benevolence, not legal necessity.

The allotment experiment and the whole policy of coercive assimilation proved disastrous for the tribes. Few of the allotted Indians became self-sufficient, and Congress had to extend the trust period. Most Indians never received their fee patents. Many who did receive their fee patents simply were not prepared for the competitive American economic system, and many soon lost their lands to sharp dealing by unscrupulous non-Indians, to poor federal guardianship of their interests, or to simple misfortune (Prucha 1984, 763–813). Although Congress optimistically made citizens of all Indians (43 *Stat.* 253, 1924), the Indians' poverty and their alienation from the larger society were not overcome. Their tribal systems of support for one another were deliberately suppressed, and they were destitute, ignorant, and ill. New policy was desperately needed.

The new policy arrived in the form of the Indian Reorganization Act of 1934 (48 *Stat.* 984, 1934), yet another super-statute that defined an entire era of Indian policy. The IRA rejected all the assumptions underlying the policies of the allotment era. Rather than suppressing tribal political institutions, tribal governments were to be revitalized through constitutions adopted by the tribes and approved by the secretary of the interior. Rather than promoting exclusively individual self-sufficiency, the IRA prohibited further allotment of tribal lands and sought to establish and capitalize tribal enterprises to develop reservation resources. Rather than trying to destroy tribal cultures, Indians' cultural practices would be accepted, and their arts and crafts would be promoted.

The architect of the new policy, Commissioner of Indian Affairs John Collier, had a vision of tribes as communal economic entities bound together by primordial spiritual understandings of the proper relationships among humans, nature, and the sacred (Philp 1977, 1–3, 159–160). In his idealistic, zealous pursuit of his vision, Collier would alienate many, both Indian and non-Indian, who made a profession of Indian policy. This and the diversion of federal resources to World War II would ultimately defeat the reorganization policy. Still, the IRA had a dramatic impact in some tribal economies and set the stage for the current policy of Indian self-determination by establishing federally sanctioned tribal institutions for the governance of reservation Indians and the provision of services in Indian communities.

But first would come the "termination" policy. The failure of the reorganization policy to deal effectively with poverty on most reservations, along with Collier's oppressive tactics in pressing the policy, alienated key members of Congress. At the same time, the impressive performance of Indian soldiers, sailors, airmen, and marines, as well as Indian workers in war industries, suggested that all that was needed for Indians to achieve self-sufficiency was to free them from the oppressive oversight of the Indian Bureau. Thus, Congress would "terminate" the tribal-federal relationship and leave Indians free to make their way in the world without ongoing federal supervision of their affairs (Fixico 1986, 91–97).

Like its predecessors, the termination policy was defined by congressional enactments: House Concurrent Resolution 108 (67 *Stat.* B132, 1953), and Public Law 83–280 (67 *Stat.* 588, 1953). H.C.R. 108 had no legal effect, but it set the stage for implementation of the termination policy by declaring,

> [I]t is the policy of Congress, as rapidly as possible, to make the Indians within the territorial limits of the United States subject to the same laws and entitled to the same privileges and responsibilities as are applicable to other citizens of the United States, to end their status as wards of the United States and to grant them all the rights and prerogatives pertaining to American citizenship. (p. B132)

H.C.R. 108 directed the secretary of the interior to prepare a report with legislative recommendations for implementing the policy. Praised as a policy of freeing Indians from federal supervision, termination was also a withdrawal of federal programs upon which the tribes had come to rely.

While waiting for the secretary to make recommendations as to which tribes should be terminated, Congress proceeded with another key statute, Public Law 83–280. Consistent with the theme of affording Indians the same privileges and responsibilities as other citizens, Public Law 280 made Indians in several states subject to the criminal jurisdiction of the states in which their reservations were located. Specifically, reservations in Alaska, Minnesota (except the Red Lake Reservation), California, Nebraska, Wisconsin (except the Menominee Reservation), and Oregon (except the Warm Springs Reservation) were subjected to the authority of state courts. The other states were given the option of assuming civil and criminal jurisdiction if they chose. Tribal consent was not required.

Termination began in earnest in 1954. That year the Klamath, Menominee, and several other tribes were the subjects of termination legislation. In 1956, legislation terminated three tribes in Oklahoma, and in 1958, legislation authorized the termination of dozens of California rancherias. In general, termination meant the sale of the tribe's land or transfer of the land to a corporation owned by tribal members. The trust status of the land was terminated, and it was subject to state taxation. Tribal members lost their immunities to state laws and state taxes, and federal programs that had long provided needed social services to Indians were ended. In the case of the largest of the terminated tribes—the Klamath and the Menominee—tribal members shortly fell into poverty and tribal society into disarray (Prucha 1984, 1047–1056).

The best that can be said of the termination policy is that the damage was limited both in scope and in time. Fewer than three percent of the Indian population belonged to terminated tribes, and by the early 1960s, the policy was halted. Many terminated tribes, including the largest ones, have since been restored to federal status as Indian tribes.

The Effects of Past Policy on Modern Tribal Rights

Modern statutes define tribal rights in ways much more favorable to the tribes, as will be discussed in detail following. The older statutes and the treaties, however, continue to define tribal rights, particularly when it comes to the jurisdiction of the tribes and their courts. Chief Justice Marshall in 1831 famously defined tribes as "domestic, dependent nations" (*Cherokee Nation v. Georgia*, 17). The following year, Marshall pursued this thought, saying,

> The Indian nations had always been considered as distinct, independent political communities, retaining their original natural rights, as the undisputed possessors of the soil, from time immemorial . . . The very term "nation," so generally applied to them, means "a people distinct from others." . . . The words "treaty" and "nation" are words of our own language, selected in our diplomatic and legislative proceedings, by ourselves, having each a definite and well understood meaning. We have applied them to Indians, as we have applied them to the other nations of the earth. They are applied to all in the same sense.

As for their status as "dependent" nations, Marshall said that this dependence was not an utter surrender of the sovereign rights of the tribes. To the contrary,

> [T]he settled doctrine of the law of nations is, that a weaker power does not surrender its independence—its right to self-government, by associating with a stronger, and taking its protection. A weak state, in order to provide for its safety, may place itself under the protection of one more powerful, without stripping itself of the right of government, and ceasing to be a state. . . .The Cherokee nation, then, is a distinct community, occupying its own territory, with boundaries accurately described, in which the laws of Georgia can have no force, and which the citizens of Georgia have no right to enter, but with the assent of the Cherokees themselves, or in conformity with treaties, and with the acts of congress. (*Cherokee Nation v. Georgia*, 520)

The history of congressional policy since 1832 has led the Court in a much different direction in modern case law. The Court has been required to synthesize the wildly shifting policies of Congress over two hundred years and to consider the consequences of past policies on tribal authority. This is no small challenge. How is the Court to reconcile policy themes as wildly different as treaty making and coercive assimilation allotment, reorganization and termination?

The truth is that they cannot be reconciled, yet the Court must still decide cases, and its recent decisions tend to dispense with the idea of tribes as independent states. Indeed, the Court, speaking through Justice Thurgood Marshall, remarked on the evolution of the Court's Indian law doctrine in 1973:

> This is not to say that the Indian sovereignty doctrine, with its concomitant jurisdictional limit on the reach of state law, has remained static during the 141 years since Worcester was decided. Not surprisingly, the doctrine has undergone considerable evolution in response to hanged circumstances. . . . [N]otions of Indian sovereignty have been adjusted to take account of the State's legitimate interests in regulating the affairs of non-Indians. . . .This line of cases was summarized in this Court's landmark decision in *William v. Lee:* "Over the years this Court has modified (the Worcester principle) in cases where essential tribal relations were not involved and where the rights of Indians would not be jeopardized. . . . Essentially, absent governing Acts of Congress, the question has always been whether the state action infringed on the right of reservation Indians to make their own laws and be ruled by them." (*McClanahan v. State Tax Commission of Arizona,* 171–172, quoting *Williams v. Lee* 1959)

The Court went on to remark that "[T]he trend has been away from the idea of inherent Indian sovereignty as a bar to state jurisdiction and toward reliance on federal pre-emption. . . . The modern cases thus tend to avoid reliance on platonic notions of Indian sovereignty and to look instead to the applicable treaties and statutes which define the limits of state power." Thus, unlike the findings in the *Worcester* case, the existence of tribal authority does not defeat state authority, even on the reservations. It is the exertion of *federal* power, mostly through congressional statutes, that define tribal authority: "The Indian sovereignty doctrine is relevant, then, not because it provides a definitive resolution of the issues in this suit, but because it provides a backdrop against which the applicable treaties and federal statutes must be read."

The effect of relegating Indian sovereignty to a "backdrop" may be seen in subsequent cases limiting tribal authority. The mold for the future of tribal jurisdiction was made in 1978 in *Oliphant v. Suquamish Indian Tribe.* Commenting on the effect of the history of congressional Indian affairs policy on modern tribal authority, the Court declared, "'Indian law' draws principally upon the treaties drawn and executed by the Executive Branch and legislation passed by Congress. These instruments, which beyond their actual text form the backdrop for the intricate web of judicially made Indian law, cannot be interpreted in isolation but must be read in light of the common notions of the day and the assumptions of those who drafted them" (206). Looking back over the 150 years of policy since the *Worcester* decision, the Court found that Indian tribes were deprived, over time, of any sovereign powers "inconsistent with their dependent status," and that the three branches of the federal government shared an "unspoken assumption" that tribes lacked the authority to try and punish non-Indians for violations of tribal laws.

The *Oliphant* rule has taken on a life of its own and is invoked in any circumstance in which tribes assert authority over persons not members of the tribe. In *Montana v. United States* (1981), the Court ruled that the Crow tribe could not regulate hunting and fishing by a non-Indian on land that was within the Crow Reservation but owned by non-Indians. The Court went on to say that tribes have regulatory jurisdiction over non-Indians on fee lands only in exceptional circumstances. In *Duro v. Reina* (1990), the Court said that tribes did not have jurisdiction to try and punish Indians who are members of other tribes.

A few years later, in *Strate v. A-1 Contractors* (1997), the Court held that tribal courts have no jurisdiction over personal injury actions brought by non-Indians against non-Indians where the accident causing the injury took place on a state-owned highway right-of-way within the reservation. In its decision in *Atkinson Trading Company, Inc. v. Shirley* (2001), the Court said that the Navajo Nation could not tax the guests of a hotel located on non-Indian-owned land within the reservation. And most recently, in *Nevada v. Hicks* (2001), the Court denied a tribal court jurisdiction over a trespass action against a state game warden alleged to have tortiously damaged property owned by an Indian and located on Indian trust land. In each of these cases, the Court said that it was following the policies established by Congress in Indian treaties and Indian affairs statutes.

Even as the Court has restricted tribal authority over non-Indians, it has consistently upheld the application of tribal law to tribal members and prevented the application of state laws to reservation

Indians without explicit congressional consent. Thus, in *Williams v. Lee* (1959), the Court struck down state jurisdiction over an action by a non-Indian against an Indian where the cause of action arose on the reservation. Only the tribal court could hear the action. Similarly, in *Fisher v. District Court* (1976), the Court ruled that state courts could not hear an adoption proceeding where all parties were reservation Indians; the jurisdiction of the tribal court was exclusive. In the area of criminal jurisdiction, the Court held in *United States v. Wheeler* (1978) that tribes retain inherent authority to try and punish their members for violations of tribal law, even where the United States has also exercised jurisdiction over the crime.

States also have been consistently denied authority to tax and regulate reservation Indians. In *Warren Trading Post v. Arizona State Tax Commission* (1965), the Court prohibited the application of state sales taxes to purchases by Indians on the reservation. Similarly, in *McClanahan v. State Tax Commission of Arizona* (1973), the Court held that states may not tax income earned by Indians on their reservations. States may tax non-Indians for their transactions on Indian land in some circumstances (*Cotton Petroleum Corporation v. New Mexico*, 1989), but they may not tax non-Indians where federal policies in support of tribal activities would be adversely affected by such taxation (*White Mountain Apache Tribe v. Bracker*, 1980; *Ramah Navajo School Board v. Bureau of Revenue of New Mexico*, 1982).

Congress has rarely ventured into this jurisdictional maze in recent years, seemingly content to permit the Court to define the extent of tribal authority. From time to time, though, Congress steps in. Recall that in 1953, Congress enacted Public Law 83–280, which authorized states to assume jurisdiction over the reservations whether or not the tribes consented. In 1968, Congress enacted the Indian Civil Rights Act (82 *Stat.* 77), which amended P. L. 280 to require tribal consent to any future extensions of state jurisdiction. The ICRA also placed important conditions on exercises of tribal powers by extending many of the requirements of the Bill of Rights to tribal governments.

Congress occasionally finds it necessary to confirm tribal authority over certain matters. In the Indian Child Welfare Act of 1978 (92 *Stat.* 3069), Congress confirmed the exclusive authority of tribal courts over child custody matters involving reservation Indian children, and gave tribes and Indian parents extraordinary rights in certain state court proceedings regarding custody of Indian children. Most interestingly, Congress has even employed its plenary power to reverse a Supreme Court decision in one instance. Recall that the Court in 1990 ruled that a tribe lacked criminal jurisdiction over an Indian who was a member of a different tribe (*Duro v. Reina*, 1990). In 1991, Congress responded by confirming the authority of tribes to try and punish nonmember Indians for violations of tribal law (105 *Stat.* 646). The Supreme Court recently upheld Congress's authority to do so (*United States v. Lara* 2004).

The scope of tribal powers, therefore, depends less on the inherent sovereign authority of Indian tribes and more on treaties and congressional statutes. Although the treaties remain partially in effect and form the foundation for understanding subsequent developments, statutes have come to play a dominant role in most issues of tribal jurisdiction. Congress has not often employed its Indian affairs authority to explicitly define tribal jurisdiction in recent years, but when it has done so, the results have generally favored the tribes since the end of the termination era. This outcome is consistent with the policies expressed in the flurry of statutes passed since the end of termination. The pressing question in modern Indian policy is, To what extent shall Congress use its plenary power to restore tribal authorities?

Statutes and the Indian Self-Determination Policy

Unlike previous policy eras, no single statute can be said to be the centerpiece of current federal Indian policy. The sheer number of important statutes passed in the last forty years prevents any single statute from dominating the discussion. Even as termination was losing favor, a new policy was being created. President Lyndon Johnson's War on Poverty and Great Society legislation was not addressed primarily to the problems of Indian tribes, but Indian concerns nevertheless received unusual—but appropriate—levels of attention. For example, tribal needs were specifically addressed in the Economic Opportunity Act of 1964 (78 *Stat.* 508, 1964), which made tribes eligible for funding for youth programs, community action programs, and the Volunteers in Service to America (VISTA) program, among others. The Neighborhood Youth Corps, the Job Corps, and Operation Head Start brought new programs and funding to the reservations. And unlike Bureau of

Indian Affairs and Indian Health Service programs, Office of Economic Opportunity (OEO) funds were administered directly by the tribes. Although OEO funds were hardly sufficient to make a dent in the problem of Indian poverty, they had the collateral effect of increasing tribal governments' capacity to administer federal programs and, in turn, increased the desire of tribal governments to take over other federal programs for the reservations (Prucha 1984, 1091–1100).

In March 1968, President Johnson proposed a new Indian policy with a new goal, "a goal that ends the old debate about 'termination' of Indian programs and stresses Self-Determination; a goal that erases old attitudes of paternalism and promotes partnership self-help" (*Public Papers of the Presidents 1968–1969* 1970, 335–344). The new policy was carried on and expanded in the Nixon administration. Indian policy since the allotment era had suffered from a belief that only two policy approaches were possible. One approach, represented by the allotment and termination policies, held that Indians must be de-tribalized and all special federal programmatic support withdrawn. The other, represented by the reorganization policy, held that tribal governments were the proper vehicles for Indian progress and that tribal governments required federal assistance and oversight that were often smothering. In 1970, President Nixon attempted to take the best and reject the worst of each of these policy traditions. In his Special Message on Indian Affairs on July 8 (*Public Papers of the Presidents 1970* 1971, 564–576), President Nixon repudiated both the termination policy and the paternalism that had long characterized the federal government's relationship with the tribes. He concluded that neither termination nor paternalism were acceptable bases for modern policy:

> Self-Determination among the Indian people can and must be encouraged without the threat of eventual termination. In my view, in fact, that is the only way that Self-Determination can effectively be fostered.
>
> This, then, must be the goal of any new national policy toward the Indian people to strengthen the Indian's sense of autonomy without threatening this sense of community. We must assure the Indian that he can assume control of his own life without being separated involuntarily from the tribal group. And we must make it clear that Indians can become independent of Federal control without being cut off from Federal concern and Federal support. (Ibid., 566–567)

In the decade following President Nixon's message, Congress enacted many statutes that fundamentally changed federal Indian policy. Congress's increased level of activity was attributable in part to the reestablishment of a Senate committee specializing in Indian affairs.

The Indian Affairs Committees in both the House of Representatives and the Senate had been abolished in 1946. In 1975, Congress established a commission to review Indian policy. The American Indian Policy Review Commission consisted of three senators, three U.S. representatives, and five Indian private citizens. The commission was charged with a comprehensive review of all aspects of federal Indian law and policy, as well as the administration of Indian programs by federal agencies. In anticipation of receiving the commission's report and recommendations, the Senate in 1977 established a temporary select committee with legislative authority over Indian affairs.

The Select Committee on Indian Affairs was supposed to complete its work in only two years. That proved unrealistic. As more and more issues came before the committee, the life of the committee was extended, and the committee ultimately was made permanent in 1984. The existence of a Committee on Indian Affairs with broad legislative and oversight authority played and continues to play a large role in the great volume of Indian affairs legislation that has been enacted since its establishment.

The Indian affairs statutes enacted since President Nixon urged a policy of Indian self-determination have been impressive in breadth. The last forty years have seen important legislation on topics ranging from social services to cultural resource protection to environmental regulation to tribal administration of federal programs and beyond. Indian policy has been changed fundamentally. Tribal governments now directly administer dozens of service programs previously administered by the Bureau of Indian Affairs and the Indian Health Service. Tribal cultures that were suppressed so aggressively during the allotment era now enjoy federal protection. Tribes regulate reservation environments with federal support. In large measure, tribes and their members have been relieved of the overbearing federal presence of the past with no withdrawal of federal support, just as President Nixon proposed. A review of some of the more important statutes follows.

Restoration Acts and Land and Water Settlement Acts

The rejection of the termination has been quite thorough in the last three decades. The Menominee tribe and the Klamath tribe, the largest of the terminated tribes, were restored to federal recognition in 1973 (87 *Stat.* 770) and 1986 (100 *Stat.* 849), respectively. Several other terminated tribes have been restored as well (Cohen 2005, 168).

Southern and eastern tribes that brought land claims seeking redress for wrongful takings of their land in the eighteenth and nineteenth centuries were able both to resume their status as recognized Indian tribes and to receive cash and property in settlement of their claims. Congress has enacted legislation settling the claims of the Narragansett (92 *Stat.* 813, 1978), Penobscot, Passamaquoddy and Maliseet (94 *Stat.* 1785, 1980), Mashantucket Pequot (97 *Stat.* 851, 1983), Mohegan (108 *Stat.* 3501, 1994), and Gay Head Wampanoag (101 *Stat.* 704, 1987) tribes, among others. These legislative settlements required the tribes to give up their claims to many hundreds of thousands of acres; but, realistically, the tribes were quite unlikely to recover through the judicial process all of the lands they claimed. In exchange for a theoretical legal right to vast portions of the eastern United States, these tribes received statutory assurances of smaller but still valuable territories and ongoing intergovernmental relationships with the United States.

Similarly, a number of western tribes sued to redeem their rights to water for their members and their lands. Since the onset of the self-determination era, Congress has enacted water rights settlements for the Gila River Indian Community (118 *Stat.* 3499, 2004), the Tohono O'odham Nation (96 *Stat.* 1274, 1982), the Pueblo of Zuni (117 *Stat.* 782, 2003), the Paiute tribe of Utah (114 *Stat.* 737, 2000), the Yavapai-Prescott Indian tribe (108 *Stat.* 4526, 1994), the San Carlos Apache tribe (106 *Stat.* 4740, 1992), the Fallon Paiute-Shoshone Indian tribes (104 *Stat.* 3289, 1990), and the Salt River Pima-Maricopa Indian Community (102 *Stat.* 2549, 1988), among others. As with the eastern land claims, these water settlements often required tribes to abandon much larger, but still theoretical, claims to water. These statutory rights are more firm and certain than speculative claims resting on treaties, executive orders, and statutes that created the reservations but made no specific provision for water. For Congress to take pains to ensure tribal water rights in the arid West demonstrates a strong commitment to the futures of these Indian communities.

Tribal Administration of Federal Programs

As noted previously, the Office of Economic Opportunity provided funds directly to tribal governments to operate service programs on the reservations in the 1960s. In 1975, Congress aggressively expanded the concept to include virtually all programs administered by the Bureau of Indian Affairs and the Indian Health Service. The Indian Self-Determination Act of 1975 (88 *Stat.* 2006, 1975) profoundly changed the relationships between tribal governments and the two agencies most responsible for the welfare of Indian tribes. Under the act, tribes may request to contract with the agencies to administer programs on their reservations. The agencies can almost never deny a tribal request. The Self-Determination Act was amended in 1994 by the Tribal Self-Governance Act (108 *Stat.* 4270), which further expands tribal authority in administering service programs on reservations. Congress has also applied the Self-Determination Act model to programs administered by the Department of Housing and Urban Development through the Native American Housing Assistance and Self-Determination Act of 1996 (110 *Stat.* 4016).

Congress has also made substantive reforms to specific programs and created new programs for Indian communities. The Indian Health Care Improvement Act of 1976 (90 *Stat.* 1400), the Indian Law Enforcement Reform Act of 1990 (104 *Stat.* 473), and the Indian Tribal Justice Act of 1993 (107 *Stat.* 2004), established enforceable standards for important health, public safety, and justice programs. The Indian Education Act of 1972 (86 *Stat.* 334), the Indian Elementary and Secondary School Assistance Act (86 *Stat.* 334), the Indian Education Assistance Act of 1975 (88 *Stat.* 2213), and the Tribally Controlled Community College Assistance Act of 1978 (92 *Stat.* 1325) reformed school programs serving Indian students and led to the establishment of dozens of tribal colleges, creating higher education opportunities for reservation residents where none had existed before. These programmatic reforms,

focusing as they do on the key areas of health, education, and law and order, reflect the still-expanding commitment of Congress to improving conditions on reservations. Tribes were consulted throughout the legislative process and helped make these important improvements.

Economic Development

Congress has also attempted to address the poverty that has persisted since the traditional tribal economies were destroyed and the reservations established in the nineteenth century. Much of Indian country remains desperately poor, and no solution has yet been found for most of the largest tribes. Still, progress has been made, and the tribes themselves have been the primary engines of progress on this issue. According to the census bureau, from 2002 to 2004 the Indian poverty rate of 24.3 percent was nearly twice that for all races (12.4 percent) (U.S. Bureau of the Census 2005). The tribes now have ongoing programmatic support from the United States. In 1974, Congress enacted the Indian Financing Act (88 *Stat.* 77). The act created a direct loan program, a revolving loan guarantee fund, and an interest subsidy program to help tribes and Indian business owners borrow money for their enterprises. Congress has also attempted to improve management of both tribal and individually owned lands held in trust for Indians by the United States. The Indian Land Consolidation Act of 1983 (96 *Stat.* 2517) and the American Indian Trust Fund Management Reform Act of 1994 (108 *Stat.* 4239) constitute earnest efforts by Congress to help the tribes make the most of their single largest asset: fifty-five million acres of land.

In like manner, Congress has tried to help the tribes increase their returns on the mineral resources of the reservations. The most significant of these efforts, the Indian Mineral Development Act of 1982 (96 *Stat.* 1938), abandoned the outdated and exploitative model of leasing to outsiders in return for insufficient royalties, authorized more modern and creative relationships between tribes and mineral producers, and reduced federal involvement in tribal decisions.

In 1988, the most important economic development legislation of all was passed: The Indian Gaming Regulatory Act (102 *Stat.* 2467). Since the act's passage, gaming has provided many tribal communities with badly needed discretionary income to support tribal government operations. This landmark legislation is discussed in detail that follows.

Environmental Regulation

Congress has also begun weaving tribal governments into national regulatory regimes, building upon the inherent authority of the tribes over their members and their territories. Federal environmental regulatory laws generally require the Environmental Protection Agency (EPA) to establish and enforce standards for various sources of pollution. The EPA may delegate primary enforcement authority to the states. These federal laws generally apply to Indians, Indian tribes, and their reservations. Before 1986, though, these statutes generally did not provide a regulatory role for Indian tribes, and states generally lack regulatory authority on Indian lands, especially over Indians. Though the EPA had authority to regulate the environment on Indian reservations, the system of delegating authority to local governments broke down when it came to Indian reservations.

Congress therefore amended several major federal environmental statutes between 1986 and 1990. The Clean Water Act, the Comprehensive Environmental Response, Compensation and Liability Act (CERCLA), the Safe Drinking Water Act (SDWA), and the Clean Air Act were amended to permit the EPA to treat tribes in the same manner as it treats states, under certain circumstances and for certain purposes. The national regulatory system thus now involves government-to-government partnerships in which the federal government, states, and Indian tribes play important roles in the establishment and enforcement of environmental standards within and near Indian reservations.

In 1986, Congress amended the Safe Drinking Water Act to authorize the EPA to treat tribes as states under the act (100 *Stat.* 642). The CERCLA was also amended in 1986 so that tribes "shall be afforded substantially the same treatment as a state" (100 *Stat.* 1706). Tribes can enter into cooperative agreements or contracts with the federal government to carry out remedial actions for hazardous waste releases and submit claims to the superfund for damages to tribal natural resources.

Congress amended the Clean Water Act in 1987. Congress authorized the EPA administrator to "treat an Indian tribe as a State" for purposes of establishing water quality standards and issuing National Pollution Discharge Elimination System permits (101 *Stat.* 76). The authorization for tribal regulation refers to waters "within the borders of an Indian reservation." Congress clearly anticipated that all areas within the reservation, including non-Indian-owned lands, would be subject to tribal regulation.

The Clean Air Act was amended in 1990 to authorize tribes to be treated as states for purposes of the act (104 *Stat.* 2464). Like the amendments to the Clean Water Act, the Clean Air Act authorizes the treatment of tribes as states for purposes of the management and protection of air resources "within the exterior boundaries of the reservation."

The amendments to these federal environmental laws mark an important policy decision by the Congress. Rather than leaving the tribes to endure the application of federal or state laws on environmental quality, Congress has created the opportunity for tribes to take that responsibility to themselves. Equally important, the statutes make tribes key threads in a national regulatory tapestry, hardening to at least some degree the place of tribes in American federalism. By doing so, the statutes go beyond the treaties, which envisioned the reservations as islands outside the reach of general federal laws, and tribes as entities unable to participate directly in implementing national policy.

Cultural Resource Protection

From the end of treaty making in 1871 until the reorganization policy of the 1930s, the United States engaged in an organized assault on tribal culture. Modern statutes, though, give favorable attention to Indian cultural and religious practices and languages. In 1978, Congress passed the American Indian Religious Freedom Act (92 *Stat.* 469), which expressed the policy that Native American religions were entitled to constitutional protection. In 1989, Congress passed the National Museum of the American Indian Act (103 *Stat.* 1336), which established a museum on the Capitol Mall in Washington for the presentation of Indian cultures. Finally, in 1990, Congress passed the Native American Graves Protection and Repatriation Act (NAGPRA, 104 *Stat.* 3048), which required that human remains and items of cultural significance in the possession of federally funded museums be returned to the tribes, and created tribal rights in the disposition of human remains and cultural items found on federal and tribal lands. The NAGPRA is discussed in detail that follows below.

The statutes of the self-determination era have expanded tribal authority in numerous respects. The statutes fall well short of acknowledging Indian tribes as independent sovereigns and thus are not like the early treaties made when there was some equality in the federal-tribal relationship. Nor does Congress await formal tribal consent before creating statutory rights for Indians and tribes, as was true of Indian treaties ratified by the Senate. However, statutory rights do resemble treaty rights in some respects. Nearly all the statutes discussed above, especially those that permit tribes to assume responsibility for federal programs, take effect at the option of the tribes. For example, tribes may choose to assume responsibility for BIA and IHS service programs, or they may require the agencies to continue to provide the services directly.

Furthermore, the reestablishment of the Senate Indian Affairs Committee and the ever-increasing and effective participation of tribes in American electoral politics have created a congressional environment in which it is unlikely that major legislation affecting Indians would be enacted over broad tribal opposition. Indeed, most if not all of the self-determination era statutes were passed at the urging of tribal governments. The plenary power of Congress, so frequently engaged to the disadvantage of the tribes in the late nineteenth and early twentieth centuries, has regularly been employed for the benefit of tribes in the last forty years. As discussed shortly, Congress has even used its plenary power to create statutory Indian rights well beyond those of other Americans.

Examples of Statutes Expanding and Protecting Important Tribal Rights

The importance of statutory rights in modern Indian reservation life is easily demonstrated by close examination of three self-determination era statutes: the Indian Child Welfare Act (ICWA), the Indian Gaming Regulatory Act (IGRA), and the Native American Graves Protection and Repatriation Act (NAGPRA).

The Indian Child Welfare Act of 1978

The Indian Child Welfare Act (92 *Stat.* 3269) is a prominent example of modern Indian affairs legisla-

tion. Tribes were concerned with the practices of state and private social service agencies regarding Indian children. These agencies were placing Indian children into white foster families and adoptive families with little or no regard for the wishes of the tribes or the cultural needs of the children. In response to these tribal concerns, Congress passed a statute that gave Indian tribes the primary role in the placement of Indian children, as well as granting the tribes extraordinary authority to prevent state courts from making such determinations in certain circumstances.

Section 2 of the act recites a series of congressional findings that served as the backdrop for the substance of the legislation. Acknowledging the federal responsibility to Indian people and the special place of children in ensuring the future of the tribes, Congress found that

> [A]n alarmingly high percentage of Indian families are broken up by the removal, often unwarranted, of their children from them by nontribal public and private agencies and that an alarmingly high percentage of such children are placed in non-Indian foster and adoptive homes and institutions; and . . . the States, exercising their recognized jurisdiction over Indian child custody proceedings through administrative and judicial bodies, have often failed to recognize the essential tribal relations of Indian people and the cultural and social standards prevailing in Indian communities and families. (92 *Stat.* 3269)

Based on these findings, Congress declared that federal policy would henceforth be to "protect the best interests of Indian children and to promote the stability and security of Indian tribes and families" (ibid). This would be done by promoting the placement of Indian children in foster or adoptive homes that "reflect the unique values of Indian culture," and by providing assistance to Indian tribes in the operation of child and family service programs.

The ICWA went further still, providing for broad tribal jurisdiction over placements of Indian children and, extraordinarily, allowing tribes to preempt states in the exercise of such authority in many circumstances. Indian tribes were given exclusive jurisdiction over custody matters involving Indian children living on reservations. Further, state court cases involving foster care placements of Indian children or terminations of parental rights of Indian parents are required to be transferred to tribal courts, unless either parent objects or unless the state court finds "good cause" not to do so. In proceedings that remain in state court, the child's tribe has the right to intervene at any point in the proceeding. Importantly, judgments of Indian tribal courts in child welfare matters must be afforded full faith and credit by all federal, state, and tribal courts.

The rights of tribes and Indian parents are further expanded in provisions regarding involuntary custody and termination proceedings in state courts. For example, if a state court "knows or has reason to know that an Indian child is involved," the Indian parent or custodian and the Indian child's tribe must be notified of the proceedings and of their right of intervention (92 *Stat.* 3071). No placement or termination proceedings can be held until at least ten days after the parent or custodian and the tribe are notified. If they request additional time to prepare for the proceeding, that request must be granted. Further, if an Indian parent or custodian is indigent, the state court must appoint counsel.

When seeking a foster care placement or termination of parental rights regarding an Indian child, the agency seeking the placement or termination must demonstrate that "active efforts have been made to provide remedial services and rehabilitative programs designed to prevent the breakup of the Indian family and that these efforts have proved unsuccessful" (92 *Stat.* 3072). A foster care placement can be ordered only if the court finds, by clear and convincing evidence, "that the continued custody of the child by the parent or Indian custodian is likely to result in serious emotional or physical damage to the child." A termination of parental rights requires an even stronger showing. Termination may not be ordered unless the evidence shows beyond a reasonable doubt "that the continued custody of the child by the parent or Indian custodian is likely to result in serious emotional or physical damage to the child" (ibid.).

Even when an Indian parent is seeking a voluntary foster care placement or termination of parental rights, the ICWA makes sure that the parents' and the tribes' rights are protected. Such consent must be in writing. The presiding judge must certify that the "consequences of the consent were fully explained in detail and were fully understood by the parent or Indian custodian," and that the parent or custodian either "fully understood the explana-

tion in English or that it was interpreted into a language that the parent or Indian custodian understood" (ibid). Moreover, consents to termination made prior to or within ten days of birth are invalid under the act. In the case of a foster care placement, an Indian parent or custodian may withdraw consent at any time, and the child must be returned. Similarly, even where a parent has agreed to a termination of parental rights or to an adoptive placement of an Indian child, the consent may be withdrawn at any time prior to the entry of a final decree of termination or adoption. If consent is withdrawn, the child must be returned to the Indian parent or custodian. Finally, even after a final decree is entered, a parent may withdraw consent for up to two years if he or she can show that the consent was obtained through fraud or duress. If the court finds such fraud or duress, "the court shall vacate such decree and return the child to the parent" (ibid.) Furthermore, if a foster care placement or termination of parental rights is done in violation of the ICWA provisions described above, the Indian parent or custodian and the Indian child's tribe may petition to have the placement or termination invalidated. Most extraordinarily, perhaps, the child need not actually be a member of an Indian tribe to be an "Indian child" under the act. A child need only be "eligible for membership in an Indian tribe and . . . the biological child of a member of an Indian tribe" for the ICWA to apply (92 *Stat.* 3270).

State court adoptive placements and foster care and preadoptive placements must also comply with substantive standards in the act. Section 105 of the ICWA requires that, in any adoptive placement of an Indian child under State law, "a preference shall be given, in the absence of good cause to the contrary, to a placement with (1) a member of the child's extended family; (2) other members of the Indian child's tribe; or (3) other Indian families" (92 *Stat.* 3073).

Furthermore, any child accepted for foster care or preadoptive placement must be placed in "the least restrictive setting which most approximates a family" and in which any special needs of the child may be met (ibid.). The child must be placed within reasonable proximity to his or her home. Finally, in any foster care or preadoptive placement,

> a preference shall be given, in the absence of good cause to the contrary, to a placement with—(i) a member of the Indian child's extended family; (ii) a foster home licensed, approved, or specified by the Indian child's tribe; (iii) an Indian foster home licensed or approved by an authorized non-Indian licensing authority; or (iv) an institution for children approved by an Indian tribe or operated by an Indian organization which has a program suitable to meet the Indian child's needs. (ibid.)

If the child's tribe establishes a different order of preference, the state court is obliged to follow that order "so long as the placement is the least restrictive setting appropriate to the particular needs of the child" (ibid). The preferences of the child and the Indian parent are to be considered as well.

Congress also permitted tribes to undo state jurisdiction created by Public Law 280.

Under the ICWA, tribes in Public Law 280 states may reassume jurisdiction over child custody proceedings that have been under the authority of state courts. A tribe must petition the secretary of the interior and present a plan for exercising such jurisdiction. The secretary then may approve the plan if, after considering factors specified in the ICWA, he or she finds that the tribe's plan is feasible.

The ICWA is significant in several respects. First and foremost, the specific ousting of the states from jurisdiction over custody proceedings involving Indian children on the reservations is an aggressive use of Congress's plenary power over Indian affairs. Some states and private social service agencies objected to the ICWA, but Congress did not yield, choosing rather to defer to tribal opinions in this sensitive area. Further, the ICWA actually overrides the substantive law of the states. Any state law that is inconsistent with the ICWA is essentially replaced by the relevant ICWA provisions in proceedings involving an Indian child. Family law matters have traditionally been the exclusive domain of the states, and for Congress to intervene so directly to supersede state law in such matters was unprecedented. The plenary power that was used to harm tribal interests a century ago has become a formidable force in the defense of tribal interests now.

Finally, the ICWA seeks to empower tribal governments to assume responsibility for the critical functions of the child welfare system. In addition to the tribal rights listed above, the act authorized the establishment of programs at the Department of the Interior to assist tribes in exercising their authorities under the act. The Department of the Interior was authorized to make grants to tribes to help them to establish licensing systems for foster homes; to operate and maintain facilities for counseling and treating Indian families; to employ child welfare professionals in tribal courts; to provide education relating to child and family assistance; and to provide legal representation for Indian families involved in child custody proceedings. Even off-reservation Indian organizations are eligible for federal funding for programs designed to help assure the appropriate placement of Indian children under the ICWA. In these respects and more, the ICWA marked a major turning point in the willingness of Congress to use its Indian affairs power in ways that favor tribes, even over the objections of states and private interests. For these reasons, it is noteworthy legislation that demonstrates the extent to which tribal rights and powers are increasingly the result of federal statutes.

The Indian Gaming Regulatory Act of 1988

The Indian Gaming Regulatory Act of 1988 (102 *Stat.* 2467) is the most important Indian affairs legislation in recent times. Unlike other self-determination era statutes, the IGRA was passed largely in response to concerns raised by state governments rather than the tribes. In *Cabazon Band of Mission Indians et al. v. California* (1987), the Supreme Court held that Indian tribes could conduct commercial gambling on their reservations so long as similar activities were allowed off the reservations by state law. Because states permitted many types of gambling—from state lotteries to horse racing to charitable bingo to commercial casinos—the *Cabazon* decision opened the door to many forms of commercial Indian gaming. Both Congress and the states were concerned that tribal gaming would be vulnerable to criminal activity. The tribes, on the other hand, were anxious to defend their right to conduct gaming with a minimum of federal and state interference.

In October 1988, Congress enacted the IGRA. The act bore the marks of compromise; fine distinctions were drawn between different types of gambling, and regulatory authority over Indian gaming was divided among the states, the tribes, and the federal government. The purposes of the act included providing a federal statutory basis for the conduct of Indian gaming, empowering the tribes to regulate gaming to prevent infiltration by organized crime, and declaring "that the establishment of independent Federal regulatory authority for gaming on Indian lands [and] the establishment of Federal standards for gaming on Indian lands . . . are necessary to meet congressional concerns regarding gaming and to protect such gaming as a means of generating tribal revenue" (ibid.). To carry out the federal regulatory role, the act establishes the National Indian Gaming Commission, a three-member regulatory commission whose chairman is appointed by the president and approved by the Senate.

The IGRA establishes a three-tier system for the regulation of Indian gaming. Class I gaming, which includes social games and traditional tribal gambling activities, is regulated exclusively by the tribes without federal or state involvement. Class II gaming, including bingo and similar games (and electronic versions of such games) and card games that are specifically permitted by state laws, are subject to both tribal and federal regulation. Class III gaming, which includes most casino gaming and pari-mutuel wagering such as at horse and dog tracks, requires the approval of the state in which a tribe's gaming activity is located and is subject to a complex of federal, state, and tribal regulatory laws.

The act permits tribes to engage in Class II gaming if the gaming is located in a state "that permits such gaming for any purpose by any person, organization or entity (and such gaming is not otherwise specifically prohibited on Indian lands by Federal law)" (102 *Stat.* 2472). The tribe must adopt an ordinance regulating gaming, and the National Indian Gaming Commission (NIGC) must approve the ordinance. The tribal ordinance is required to provide, with only rare exceptions no longer relevant, that the tribe will be the sole owner of the gaming enterprise. Further, the tribal ordinance must limit the uses of tribal gaming revenues to five specific purposes: "(i) to fund tribal government operations or programs; (ii) to provide for the general welfare of the Indian tribe and its members; (iii) to promote tribal economic development; (iv) to donate to charitable organizations; or (v) to help fund operations of local government agencies" (102 *Stat.* 2473). Tribes may pay out gaming revenues to tribe members on an individual basis if the tribe prepares a plan for allocating revenues to the purposes described above and the secretary has approved the tribal plan.

The tribal ordinance must require annual outside audits of the gaming enterprise and must ensure that "the construction and maintenance of the gaming facility, and the operation of that gaming is conducted in a manner which adequately protects the environment and the public health and safety" (ibid). The tribe must also establish a system for licensing gaming employees and conducting background investigations of "primary management officials" and "key employees" of the gaming enterprise. The tribe must notify the NIGC of the results of background investigations before issuing gaming licenses and again when it issues a license. If the NIGC provides to a tribe reliable information establishing that a manager or other key employee is not eligible for a license, the tribe must suspend the employee's license and, after a hearing, may revoke the license. These requirements are to ensure that licenses are not granted to persons "whose prior activities, criminal record, if any, or reputation, habits, and associations pose a threat to the public interest or to the effective regulation of gaming, or create or enhance the dangers of unsuitable, unfair, or illegal practices and methods and activities in the conduct of gaming" (ibid).

Contracts for the management of tribal gaming enterprises must be approved by the commission. Prior to approving such a contract, the chairman of the commission must verify that the contract contains certain terms ensuring that the tribe can adequately regulate the gaming enterprise and that the tribe's financial interests are protected. The contract must provide for a minimum guaranteed payment to the tribe. The term of the contract cannot exceed five years, unless the chairman of the commission finds that the capital investment required for the enterprise and the expected profit justify a longer term of up to seven years. If the manager is to be compensated with a percentage of the revenues from the enterprise, the manager may receive only such a percentage of the net revenues as the chairman of the NIGC determines to be "reasonable in light of surrounding circumstances" (102 *Stat*. 2480). The management fee may not exceed 30 percent of net revenues, unless the chairman finds that the capital investment and income projections for the enterprise justify an additional fee of up to 40 percent of net revenues.

The regulatory process for Class II gaming under the IGRA thus is comprehensive. The process for tribes wishing to engage in Class III gaming is more complicated still. First, the gaming enterprise must be located in a state "that permits such gaming for any purpose by any person, organization, or entity" (102 *Stat*. 2475). The tribe must adopt an ordinance that meets all the requirements of a Class II gaming ordinance as described above, and the ordinance must be approved by the commission. The great difference in the regulation of Class II and Class III gaming is that Class III gaming may be conducted only in conformance with an agreement entered into by the tribe and the state in which the gaming activity is to take place.

This concession to state authority was a controversial provision of the act when it was passed and remains controversial. Tribes sought to prevent state regulation completely, whereas states wanted to regulate all gaming on the reservations, including Class II gaming. Congress did not seem inclined to establish a federal regulatory agency to oversee all of the details of Class III gaming activities, and so the matter was left to agreements—"compacts"—entered into by tribes and states.

The development of a tribal-state gaming compact begins with a tribe's request to a state to commence negotiations. If the negotiations proceed well and produce an agreement, all that remains is for the secretary of the interior to approve the compact. The act authorizes tribes and states to include provision relating to

> (i) the application of the criminal and civil laws and regulations of the Indian tribe or the State that are directly related to and necessary for, the licensing and regulation of such activity; (ii) the allocation of criminal and civil jurisdiction between the State and the Indian tribe necessary for the enforcement of such laws and regulations; (iii) the assessment by the State of such activities in such amounts as are necessary to defray the costs of regulating such activity: . . . (vi) standards for the operation of such activity and maintenance of the gaming facility, including licensing; and (vii) any other subjects that are directly related to the operation of gaming activities. (102 *Stat*. 2476)

The authorization to states and tribes to compact for the application of state laws and state jurisdiction is extraordinary and perhaps unprecedented in federal Indian affairs statutes.

If the parties agree to a compact, there is little reason to object to the process. If the negotiations do not go well, however, the process becomes complex and controversial. At the request of tribes, Congress added a requirement to the IGRA that a state, once asked to start negotiations, must negotiate "in good faith." Should a state fail to do so, the tribe had the option, 180 days after the request for negotiations, to sue the state in federal district court. If the court found that the state failed in its obligation to negotiate in good faith, the court could initiate a process in which the state and tribe were given 60 days to complete a compact. If they failed to agree in that time, they were required to submit their "last best offer" to a mediator appointed by the court. The mediator then selected the compact "that best comports with the terms of" the IGRA and submitted the compact to the parties (102 *Stat.* 2478). If the state consented to the compact selected by the mediator within 60 days, the compact was submitted to the secretary for approval. If the state did not consent, the secretary was authorized to consult with the tribe and to issue "procedures" under which the tribe would be permitted to conduct Class III gaming.

In the years shortly following enactment of the IGRA, this process produced some extraordinary results. Wisconsin and Connecticut, for example, faced with the possibility of a court-ordered mediator, and the possibility that the secretary and the tribes would determine how Class III gaming could be conducted on the reservations, entered into compacts that have left tribes with the exclusive right to own and operate casinos in those states.

As other states faced the same challenge, however, resistance to the IGRA compacting process increased, and the states were ultimately successful in upsetting the process entirely. In *Seminole Tribe of Florida v. Florida* (1996), the Supreme Court ruled that the IGRA provision permitting suits in federal courts against the states was a violation of the states' sovereign immunity.

Although this appeared to give the states the upper hand in dealing with the tribes on gaming issues, the decision in the *Seminole* case has not slowed the explosive growth in Indian gaming. Instead, tribes have managed to use state political processes and institutions to gain the compacts required by the IGRA, even where state officials are reluctant to enter into compacts. In California, for example, tribes persuaded voters to enact changes to the California constitution that left the tribes with the exclusive right to operate slot machines in the state. In New Mexico, the tribes gained sufficient influence in the state's electoral and political processes to persuade the legislature to enact and the governor to approve a new state law that permits tribes to operate casinos on an exclusive basis in the state. Furthermore, the Department of the Interior has issued regulations that establish a process by which a tribe can petition the secretary to issue Class III gaming procedures for the tribe if the state refuses to negotiate in good faith and asserts its sovereign immunity to prevent the federal courts from intervening.

A major consequence of the IGRA—and the most ironic one—is that, because they were required to get the states' permission to conduct Class III gaming, the tribes have had to develop great influence in state political systems. Those processes have been swayed by the financial resources the tribes can now devote to their political efforts. The tribes objected strongly to the requirement of state approval for Class III gaming, yet that requirement has led them to unprecedented influence in state politics.

Violations of the act can result in criminal penalties. Any gambling on reservations not in compliance with the act is a federal crime. Theft from an Indian gaming establishment is criminal as well; theft of more than $1,000 can be punished with a fine of up to $250,000 and a jail term of up to ten years. Theft by employees and holders of gaming licenses can be punished with a fine as large as $1,000,000 and a jail term of twenty years.

The Indian Gaming Regulatory Act is watershed legislation in many respects. Despite its obvious importance when it was being considered, few could have anticipated the truly phenomenal effects it would have in many Indian communities. Between 1995 and 2004, revenues from Indian gaming grew from $5.4 billion to $22.6 billion. Approximately 225 tribes in twenty-eight states are engaged in gaming. Some 250 Class III tribal-state gaming compacts have been approved. Gaming is by far the largest source of revenue for many Indian tribes.

This bounty, however, is not evenly distributed across Indian country. Two hundred tribes in Alaska, for example, are unable to engage in Indian gaming. Tribes in Utah are also unable to conduct gaming because all gaming is prohibited in Utah. Further, most of the largest reservations—such as those in North and South Dakota and Montana—do not generate large amounts of revenue due to their rural locations and the endemic poverty on those reservations. Thus, although gaming has been a successful economic development strategy, most of the largest tribal populations do not receive much benefit.

Still, the Indian Gaming Regulatory Act has widely succeeded in its objective to assist tribes in their efforts at economic development and self-sufficiency. The IGRA is different from most Indian affairs legislation in an important sense. The IGRA seemed to invite state authority onto the reservations in a major way, over the objections of many tribes. Indeed, it seemed to some that the tribal victory in the *Cabazon* case was undone in large part in the IGRA. In truth, however, the Court's *Cabazon* decision was thin soil in which to grow the major industry that Indian gaming has become. It was only with Congress's ratification of the tribes' right to offer commercial gaming that the industry had a firm and comprehensive legal basis. Through ingenuity and persistence, the tribes overcame the hurdles created in the IGRA and have become important players in a major American industry.

The Native American Graves Protection and Repatriation Act

The Native American Graves Protection and Repatriation Act (104 *Stat*. 3048) is another example of the creation and protection of extraordinary rights for Indians. Like the IGRA, the NAGPRA was enacted over the objection of powerful interests unaccustomed to being disadvantaged for the benefit of Indians. In the case of NAGPRA, museums, universities, and other elements of the scientific communities were deeply concerned that congressional limits on their access to Indian graves, antiquities, and cultural objects would inhibit the search for knowledge of the origins and experience of humans in North America. Despite these concerns, Congress enacted a statute intended to empower Indians and Indian tribes seeking to protect the graves of their ancestors and culturally significant property from becoming—or remaining—possessions of non-Indian institutions.

The NAGPRA is meant to ensure that "cultural items" of Native Americans are protected. Cultural items include human remains, "funerary objects" (objects placed in a human grave), "sacred objects" (objects needed by religious leaders for traditional religious practices), and "cultural patrimony" (objects with historical, traditional, or cultural importance to a Native American group or culture, as opposed to property owned by an individual Native American) (104 *Stat*. 3048–49). The NAGPRA increases the protections for Indian graves located on federal and tribal lands and provides for Indian control over cultural items obtained from such lands after the effective date of the statute. With respect to Native American cultural items in the possession of federal agencies and museums, the NAGPRA imposes specific duties on the museums and agencies, most notably the duty to prepare inventories of Native American human remains and associated funerary objects and summaries of the other categories of cultural items, and the duty to repatriate all of these items to culturally affiliated tribes or descendants upon request.

The first key provision of the NAGPRA relates to cultural items found on federal or tribal lands. If human remains and associated funerary objects were or are discovered on federal or tribal lands after November 1990, they belong to the lineal descendants of the deceased. (An *associated funerary object* is an object from a grave, and both the object and the human remains "are presently in the possession or control of a Federal agency or museum." The term also includes items exclusively made for burial purposes or to contain human remains (104 *Stat*. 3048). If the lineal descendants cannot be determined (or if the objects are unassociated funerary objects, sacred objects, or objects of cultural patrimony), and they are discovered on tribal land, they belong to the tribe on whose land they were discovered or to the tribe with the closest cultural affiliation with the object. (An *unassociated funerary object* is an object from a grave, and the remains are not in the possession or control of the federal agency or museum, but the objects can be identified as related to specific individuals or families or to known human remains or as having been removed from a specific burial site of an individual culturally affiliated with a particular Indian tribe.)

If objects are discovered on federal lands, they belong to the tribe whose aboriginal territory (as determined by a judgment of the Indian claims commission or the court of claims) included the land where the objects were discovered, unless another tribe demonstrates a stronger cultural relationship to the objects, in which case they belong to the tribe with the stronger cultural relationship. This establishment of Indian ownership of such items on federal lands is extraordinary in U.S. law. Generally, the owner of land also owns property found on or in the land. The NAGPRA, however, permits Indians and Indian tribes to assert ownership of cultural items found on federal lands.

The statute also protects Indian ownership interests of cultural items found on federal or tribal

lands by allowing their excavation or removal only with a permit issued under the Archaeological Resources Protection Act, and only after consultation with the appropriate tribe. If the cultural items are on tribal land, the tribe must grant consent. The tribe or individual still owns the objects in accordance with the provisions just discussed.

If cultural items are inadvertently discovered, the discoverer must notify the head of the federal agency responsible for the land, as well as the appropriate Indian tribe, of the discovery. Furthermore, if the discovery occurred in the course of an activity such as construction, mining, logging, or agriculture, the activity must cease in the area of the discovery. The discoverer must make a reasonable effort to protect the items discovered before resuming the activity and must provide notice to the appropriate federal agency and Indian tribe. The activities may resume only after the head of the relevant federal agency or the appropriate Indian tribe has certified that notice has been received. Moreover, cultural items inadvertently discovered belong either to individual Indians or to the appropriate Indian tribe, as described previously.

The NAGPRA also is concerned with cultural items in the possession of federal agencies and museums. The act was passed largely in response to the fact that thousands of Native American remains were in museum collections, many of them as the result of a systematic effort to collect such remains in the nineteenth century. The NAGPRA requires federal agencies and museums that receive federal funding (which is nearly every major museum in the country) and have among their collections Native American human remains and associated funerary objects to compile an inventory of such items. They are further required, to the extent possible based on information in their possession, to identify the geographical and cultural affiliation of the items. After compiling the inventory, if the agency or museum determines the cultural affiliation of any particular Native American human remains or associated funerary objects, the agency or museum must notify the affected tribes within six months of completing the inventory.

Similarly, federal agencies and museums receiving federal funding must provide a written summary of any unassociated funerary objects, sacred objects, and objects of cultural patrimony that they have in their collections. The summary must describe the scope of the collection, the kinds of objects included, and references to the geographical locations, means, and period of acquisition and cultural affiliation of the objects, where readily ascertainable.

The purpose of these inventories and summaries is to provide information to Indians and Indian tribes and permit them to determine whether they wish to have the remains and objects returned to them. The NAGPRA establishes standards and procedures for the repatriation of such remains and objects to the individual Indian or tribe to whom they rightfully belong. In the case of human remains and associated funerary objects the cultural affiliation of which has been established, federal agencies and museums are required, upon the request of a known descendant of the Native American or of the tribe, "to expeditiously return such remains and associated funerary objects" (104 *Stat.* 3045). Similarly, with respect to unassociated funerary objects, sacred objects, or objects of cultural patrimony, if the cultural affiliation is shown, the museum or agency must return the objects to the appropriate tribe.

Even where the cultural affiliations of remains and objects have not been established or the items not included, in the inventories or summaries required by the statute, tribes may still have a right to repatriation. In cases involving human remains and funerary objects, a tribe may request repatriation if it can show cultural affiliation "by a preponderance of the evidence based upon geographical, kinship, biological, archaeological, anthropological, linguistic, folkloric, oral traditional, historical, or other relevant information or expert opinion" (ibid.) Upon such a showing, the museum or federal agency must return the item. Furthermore, sacred objects and objects of cultural patrimony must be returned where

> (A) the requesting party is the direct lineal descendant of an individual who owned the sacred object; (B) the requesting Indian tribe . . . can show that the object was owned or controlled by the tribe . . . ; or (C) the requesting Indian tribe . . . can show that the sacred object was owned or controlled by a member thereof, provided that in the case where a sacred object was owned by a member thereof, there are no identifiable lineal descendants . . . or the lineal descendants, upon notice, have failed to make a claim for the object. (104 *Stat.* 3054–55)

Several issues can arise when a museum or agency is requested to repatriate items, and Congress anticipated many of these circumstances. For example, repatriation can be delayed in the case of items that are "indispensable for completion of a specific scientific study, the outcome of which would be of major benefit to the United States" (104 *Stat.* 3055). The return of such items may be delayed until ninety days after the date on which the scientific study is completed.

It is also possible that a museum or agency believes that it came into possession of an item legitimately. In the case of requests for repatriation of unassociated funerary objects, sacred objects, or objects of cultural patrimony, the NAGPRA sets out the method for establishing the validity of the parties' claim to the item. The party requesting repatriation must present evidence supporting the request, and if the evidence, standing alone, would support a finding that the agency or museum did not have the right of possession, then the agency or museum must return the objects "unless it can overcome such inference and prove that it has a right of possession to the objects" (ibid.). An agency or museum has a right of possession when an item was obtained with the voluntary consent of an individual or group that had authority to give the item. Museums and agencies have a right of possession to human remains and associated funerary objects that were obtained "with full knowledge and consent of the next of kin or the official governing body of the appropriate culturally affiliated Indian tribe" (104 *Stat.* 3050).

More than one party might request remains or objects. In such a case, if the agency or museum cannot clearly determine which requestor should receive the item, the agency or museum may retain the item until either the requesting parties agree upon its disposition or the dispute is resolved by a court. The NAGPRA also established a review committee composed of representatives from tribal communities and from museums and scientific groups to monitor the implementation of the statute and advise the secretary. One of the committee's duties is to "facilitate resolution of disputes" among Indian tribes, lineal descendants, museums, and agencies (104 *Stat.* 3056). This is a voluntary process and, although the committee's recommendations are not legally binding, they can be introduced as evidence in later litigation.

The NAGPRA imposes an affirmative duty on agencies and museums to share whatever information they possess regarding an object in question with known lineal descendants and Indian tribes, in order to assist them in making their claim for repatriation. The statute even puts aside any state laws that might prevent a museum from repatriating cultural items by immunizing museums from claims of "breach of fiduciary duty, public trust, or violations of state law that are inconsistent with the provisions of this chapter" (104 *Stat.* 3055).

Finally, the statute imposes penalties. For example, a museum that fails to comply with the statute may be assessed a civil penalty by the secretary of the interior. Persons who knowingly purchase, sell, or transport Native American human remains can be fined or even jailed for up to a year; a subsequent violation increases the possible jail time to five years. Similar punishments can be imposed for selling, purchasing, or transporting cultural items obtained in violation of the act.

The NAGPRA is a remarkable piece of legislation in several respects. First, it created (or perhaps restored) Indian property interests in items that had long since passed out of Indian possession. A few decades ago, there was little reason to believe that Congress might act with sensitivity to ancient claims to cultural items, but the modern era of Indian policy made such a thing possible. The fact that Congress overrode the resistance of powerful and influential scientific institutions such as universities and museums, creating affirmative obligations for these institutions to return precious objects from their collections to the tribes, is no small matter, either. Above all, Congress's rejection of the tendency of science to treat human remains as mere objects of study, and Congress's alignment of itself and the law with the idea of affording these Indian ancestors the dignity that many tribal traditions demand, suggest that the prevailing approach to law and policy in Indian affairs has changed dramatically from the bad old days of allotment and termination.

Conclusion

Statutes have defined U.S. policy toward the tribes from the beginning. The treaties were extensions of the statutes in that they represented the application of prevailing policy to particular tribes and particular situations. Since the end of treaty making in 1871, though, statutes have come to dominate the definition of tribal rights and the rights of individual Indians as members of tribes. The Supreme Court has said that Congress has plenary power over tribes and Indian property. The federal courts do not consider the wisdom or good faith of congressional enactments, so tribal rights exist at the sufferance of Congress.

Federal policies have swung wildly over the years from policies designed to assimilate Indians by coercion and dismantle tribal institutions to policies intended to empower tribal governments. The consequence of inconsistent policies is a body of statutory law and factual circumstances that has led the Supreme Court to limit the authority of tribal governments, particularly over nonmembers. While the Court has simultaneously prevented the application of state laws to Indians on their reservations, the result is a patchwork of jurisdictional authorities, with tribes, states, and the United States all having extensive authority, depending on the particular circumstances.

The current policy of self-determination for tribal governments is also driven by statutes. The statutes of the self-determination era differ from their predecessors in important respects. Most notably, the existence of a Senate Committee on Indian Affairs that is responsive to tribal interests and the growing tribal activism in federal and state electoral politics has given the tribes a strong voice in the federal legislative process. The result is that modern statutes quite often are passed at the urging of tribes, and few if any major statutes are passed in the face of strong tribal opposition.

Thus, the extraordinary authority of the Congress over Indian tribes—the plenary power—right now is being used in ways that favor tribes and in ways that the tribes favor. None can say for how long this will be true. It does appear, however, that tribal statutory rights will continue to exist, and quite possibly to expand, for the indefinite future.

Kevin Gover

References and Further Reading

Court Cases

Atkinson Trading Company, Inc. v. Shirley, 532 *U.S. Reports* 645 (2001).

Cabazon Band of Mission Indians et al. v. California, 480 *U.S. Reports* 202 (1987).

Cherokee Nation v. Georgia, 30 *U.S. Reports* 1 (1831).

Cotton Petroleum Corporation v. New Mexico, 490 *U.S. Reports* 163 (1989).

Duro v. Reina, 495 *U.S. Reports* 676 (1990).

Fisher v. District Court, 425 *U.S. Reports* 696 (1976).

Lone Wolf v. Hitchcock, 187 *U.S. Reports* 553 (1903).

McClanahan v. State Tax Commission of Arizona, 411 *U.S. Reports* 164 (1973).

Mississippi Band of Choctaw Indians v. Holyfield, 490 *U.S. Reports* 30 (1989).

Moe v. Confederated Salish and Kootenai Tribes, 425 *U.S. Reports* 463 (1976).

Montana v. United States, 450 *U.S. Reports* 544 (1981).

Nevada et al. v. Floyd Hicks et al., 533 *U.S. Reports* 353 (2001).

Oliphant v. Suquamish Indian Tribe, 435 *U.S. Reports* 191 (1978).

Ramah Navajo School Board v. Bureau of Revenue of New Mexico, 458 *U.S. Reports* 832 (1982).

Seminole Tribe of Florida v. Florida, 517 *U.S. Reports* 44 (1996).

Strate v. A-1 Contractors, 520 *U.S. Reports* 438 (1997).

United States v. Dion, 476 *U.S. Reports* 734 (1986).

United States v. Kagama, 118 *U.S. Reports* 375 (1886).

United States v. Lara, 541 *U.S. Reports* 193 (2004).

United States v. Anthony Robert Wheeler, 435 *U.S. Reports* 313 (1978).

Warren Trading Post v. Arizona Sate Tax Commission, 380 *U.S. Reports* 685 (1965).

White Mountain Apache Tribe v. Bracker, 448 *U.S. Reports* 136 (1980).

Williams v. Lee, 358 *U.S. Reports* 217 (1959).

Worcester v. Georgia, 31 *U.S. Reports* 515 (1832).

Statutes

American Indian Religious Freedom Act of 1978. Public Law 95-341 August 11, 1978–92 Stat. 469. 95th Congress. Joint Resolution [S.J. Res. 102]. 42 USC 1996

Indian Child Welfare Act of 1978, Public Law 95–608, 92 *U.S. Statutes at Large* 3269, November 8, 1978.

Indian Civil Rights Act of 1986, Public Law 90–284, 82 *U.S. Statutes at Large* 77, April 11, 1968.

Indian Education Act, Public Law 92–318, 86 *U.S. Statutes at Large* 334, June 23, 1972.

Indian Education Assistance Act, Public Law 93–638, 88 *U.S. Statutes at Large* 2213, January 4, 1975.

Indian Elementary and Secondary School Assistance Act, Public Law 92–318, 86 *U.S. Statutes at Large* 334, June 23, 1972.

Indian Financing Act of 1974, Public Law 93–262, 88 *U.S. Statutes at Large* 77, April 12, 1974.

Indian Gaming Regulatory Act, Public Law 100–497, 102 *U.S. Statutes at Large* 2467, October 17, 1988.

Indian General Allotment Act (Dawes Act), Chapter 119, 24 *U.S. Statutes at Large* 388, February 8, 1887.

Indian Health Care Improvement Act, Public Law 94–437, 90 *U.S. Statutes at Large* 1400, September 30, 1976.

Indian Land Consolidation Act of 1983, Public Law 97–459, 96 *U.S. Statutes at Large* 2517, January 12, 1983.

Indian Law Enforcement Reform Act, Public Law 101–379, 104 *U.S. Statutes at Large* 473, August 18, 1990.

Indian Mineral Development Act of 1982, Public Law 97–382, 96 *U.S. Statutes at Large* 1938, December 22, 1982.

Indian Reorganization Act, Chapter 576, 48 *U.S. Statutes at Large* 984, June 18, 1934.

Indian Self-Determination Act, Public Law 93–638, 88 *U.S. Statutes at Large* 2206, January 4, 1975.

Indian Tribal Justice Act, Public Law 103–176, 107 *U.S. Statutes at Large* 2004, December 3, 1993.

Indian Trust Fund Management Reform Act of 1994, Public Law 103–412, 108 *U.S. Statutes at Large* 4239, October 25, 1994.

National Museum of American Indian Act, Public Law 101–185, 103 *U.S. Statutes at Large* 1336–47, November 28, 1989.

Native American Graves Protection and Repatriation Act, Public Law 101–601, 104 *U.S. Statutes at Large* 3048, November 16, 1990.

Native American Housing Assistance and Self-Determination Act of 1996, Public Law 104–330, 110 *U.S. Statutes at Large* 4016, October 26, 1996.

Tribal Self-Governance Demonstration Project Act, Public Law 102–184, 67 *U.S. Statutes at Large* 589, August 15, 1953.

Tribal Self-Governance Act of 1994, Public Law 103–413, 108 *U.S. Statutes at Large* 4250, October 25, 1994.

Tribally Controlled Community College Assistance Act of 1978, Public Law 95–471, 92 *U.S. Statutes at Large* 1325, October 17, 1978.

Books and Articles

Banner, Stuart. 2005. *How the Indians Lost Their Land: Law and Power on the Frontier.* Cambridge, MA: Harvard University Press.

Bernstein, Alison R. 1991. *American Indians and World War II: Toward a New Era in Indian Affairs.* Norman: University of Oklahoma Press.

Canby, William C. 2004. *American Indian Law in a Nutshell*, 4th ed. St. Paul, MN: West.

Clinton, Robert N. 1976. "Criminal Jurisdiction over Indian Lands: A Journey through a Jurisdictional Maze," 18 *Arizona Law Review* 503.

Cohen, Felix S. 1941. *Handbook of Federal Indian Law.* Washington, DC: Government Printing Office.

Cohen, Felix S. 2005. *Handbook of Federal Indian Law.* Newark, NJ: LexisNexis.

Culin, Stewart. 1975. *Games of the North American Indians.* New York: Dover.

Daily, David W. 2004. *Battle for the BIA: G.E.E. Lindquist and the Missionary Crusade against John Collier.* Tucson: University of Arizona Press.

Debo, Angie. 1984. *A History of the Indians of the United States*, Repr., Norman: University of Oklahoma Press.

Debo, Angie. 1940. *And Still the Waters Run: The Betrayal of the Five Civilized Tribes*, Repr., Princeton, NJ: Princeton University Press, 1973.

Deloria, Vine, Jr. 1969. *Custer Died for Your Sins: An Indian Manifesto.* Repr., Norman: University of Oklahoma Press, 1988.

Eadington, William S., and Judy Cornelius, eds. 1998. *Indian Gaming and the Law.* Reno: University of Nevada, Reno Bureau of Business.

Fixico, Donald L. 1986. *Termination and Relocation: Federal Indian Policy, 1945–1960.* Albuquerque: University of New Mexico Press.

Frickey, Philip P. 1996. "Domestic Federal Indian Law," 81 *Minnesota Law Review* 31.

Goldberg, Carole E. 1975. "Public Law 280: The Limits of State Jurisdiction over Reservation Indians," 22 *University of California-Los Angeles Law Review* 535.

Kersey, Harry A., Jr. 1996. *An Assumption of Sovereignty: Social and Political Transformation among the Florida Seminoles 1953–1979.* Lincoln: University of Nebraska Press.

Light, Steven Andrew, and Kathryn R. L. Rand. 2005. *Indian Gaming and Tribal Sovereignty: The Casino Compromise.* Lawrence: University Press of Kansas.

Mason, W. Dale. 2000. *Indian Gaming: Tribal Sovereignty and American Politics.* Norman: University of Oklahoma Press.

Murphy, Mary Lynn. 2001. "Assessing NAGPRA: An Analysis of Its Success from a Historical Perspective," 25 *Seton Hall Legislative Journal* 499.

Newton, Nell Jessup. 1984. "Federal Power over Indians: Its Sources, Scope, and Limitations," 132 *University of Pennsylvania Law Review* 195.

Philp, Kenneth R. 1977. *John Collier's Crusade for Indian Reform 1920–1954.* Tucson: University of Arizona Press.

Pommersheim, Frank. 1989. "The Crucible of Sovereignty: Analyzing Issues of Tribal Jurisdiction," 31 *Arizona Law Review* 329.

Prucha, Francis Paul. 1962. *American Indian Policy in the Formative Years: The Trade and Intercourse Acts 1790–1834.* Cambridge, MA: Harvard University Press.

Prucha, Francis Paul. 1984. *The Great Father: The United States Government and the American Indians.* Unabridged ed. Lincoln: University of Nebraska Press, 1995.

Public Papers of the Presidents of the United States: Lyndon B. Johnson, 1968–1969. 1970. Washington, DC: Government Printing Office.

Public Papers of the Presidents of the United States: Richard Nixon, 1970. 1971. Washington, DC: Government Printing Office.

Riley, Angela R. 2002. "Indian Remains, Human Rights: Reconsidering Entitlement under the Native American Graves Protection and Repatriation Act," 34 *Columbia Human Rights Law Review* 49.

Riley, Thomas. 1988. "Federal Conservation Statutes and the Abrogation of Indian Hunting and Fishing Rights: *United States v. Dion*," 58 *University of Colorado Law Review* 699.

Schlosser, Thomas P. 2001. "Tribal Civil Jurisdiction over Nonmembers," 37 *Tulsa Law Review* 573.

Suagee, Dean. 1998. "Tribal Self-Determination and Environmental Federalism: Cultural Values as a Force for Sustainability," 3 *Widener Law Symposium Journal* 229.

Taylor, Scott A. 1997. "An Introduction and Overview of Taxation and Indian Gaming," 29 *Arizona State Law Journal* 251.

Tellinghuisen, Roger A. 1989. "The Indian Child Welfare Act of 1978: A Practical Guide with [Limited] Commentary," 34 *South Dakota Law Review* 660.

Thomas, David Hurst. 2001. *Skull Wars: Kennewick, Archaeology, and the Battle for Native American Identity.* New York: Basic Books.

Tsosie, Rebecca. 1997. "Negotiating Economic Survival: The Consent Principle and Tribal-State Gaming Compacts under the Indian Gaming Regulatory Act," 29 *Arizona State Law Journal* 25.

Tweedy, Ann. 2005. "Using Plenary Power as a Sword: Tribal Civil Regulatory Jurisdiction under the Clean Water Act after United States v. Lara," 35 *Environmental Law* 471.

U.S. Bureau of the Census. 2005. "Insurance, Poverty, and Health Insurance Coverage in the United States: 2004," *Current Population Reports*, 60–229. Washington, DC: Government Printing Office.

Washburn, Kevin. 2001. "Recurring Problems in Indian Gaming," 1 *Wyoming Law Review* 427.

Washburn, Wilcomb E. 1986. *The Assault on Indian Tribalism: The General Allotment Law (Dawes Act of 1887).* Repr., New York: Krieger.

Washburn, Wilcomb E. 1995. *Red Man's Land/White Man's Law: The Past and Present Status of the American Indian*, 2nd ed. Norman: University of Oklahoma Press.

Wilkins, David E. 2006. *American Indian Politics and the American Political System*, 2nd ed. Boston: Rowman and Littlefield.

Treaty Responsibility and Reserved Rights

Property: Land and Natural Resources

Treaties were the major mechanism for the massive transfer of land from American Indians to European Americans that has occurred in North America over the last three centuries. Even when the United States ceased making formal treaties in 1871, treaty substitutes continued to be used to formalize the dispossession of Indian land into the twentieth century. Land and the natural and biological resources associated with it were the Indian assets of the greatest commercial value to non-Indians; consequently, they have been the greatest source of conflict. Loss of land increasingly made traditional land-based economies impossible, undermining tribal social and political structures that were consistent with these traditional ways of life and jeopardizing traditional religious practices that were deeply tied to tribal homelands.

The first property negotiations between Europeans and Indians on the eastern coast of North America were conducted by individual settlers to obtain small parcels of Indian land, generally in return for trade goods. However, European governments, through their colonial administrations, quickly took control of the land acquisition process by claiming sovereign rights as sole purchasers of Indian land. A major basis of these preemptive claims was that tribes were sovereigns, and negotiations between sovereigns were conducted through treaties. The U.S. government continued to claim the sole right to acquire Indian land parcels, which were then placed in the public domain, divided into smaller parcels, and subsequently sold to individual non-Indians.

The eras of early federal Indian policy are labeled by the key processes through which Indian people were dispossessed of their land: removal, establishment of reservations, and allotment. After the War of 1812, when tribal alliances were no longer critical to the political balance of power among the colonial European nations, the United States forcibly removed entire tribes from their eastern homelands to Indian Territory, west of the Mississippi River. Removal was part of the increasingly coercive process used by the federal government to force tribes to relinquish their land. Although removal was formalized through treaties that guaranteed the remaining land rights of tribes, these guarantees were increasingly ignored when new groups of non-Indians pushed onto Indian lands, established settlements and farms, and prospected for gold and other valuable natural resources.

Between 1850 and 1870, much of the rest of the continental United States passed out of Indian hands. Unlike removal, treaties with tribes west of the Mississippi set aside small pockets of their traditional lands as reservations. These treaties generally included limited payments of goods and services for the land ceded by the tribes. In the 1870s, the federal government began the process of allotting small parcels of land to individual Indian heads of households, ostensibly to assimilate Indian people into the dominant society through small-scale farming. After the small allotments were assigned, the remaining tribal land was deemed surplus and sold. Over time, many Indian families were forced to sell their allotments to pay debts and property taxes. More than two-thirds of the remaining tribal lands were lost to Indian ownership by the time the allotment process was formally ended in 1934 by the Indian Reorganization Act.

Although negotiated by the United States from an increasing position of power, treaties embodied the core legal concept that tribes retained inherent rights to the lands they did not cede—that is, treaties did not give Indian tribes land; instead, treaties were grants of land by tribes that also reserved lands for the practical use of their people. The term *reservation* comes from these reserved rights that were not specifically relinquished in treaty provisions. Reserved rights and the federal government's responsibility as trustee for those rights have been critical to ongoing tribal legal claims to water, timber, and minerals, as well as fossil fuels important to energy production. These rights are also key issues in individual Indian claims against the federal government for mismanagement of oil, gas, and mineral royalties from their land. The termination policy of the federal government in the 1950s and early 1960s was intended to end tribal ownership of land. Part of the local impetus for termination of reservation trust status was the interest of lumber companies in the timber on reservation lands.

From the 1940s through the 1970s, the U.S. Indian Claims Commission attempted to redress the illegal and uncompensated takings of Indian land. Much of the Claims Commission's work involved determination of the fair market value of lands at the time they were ceded, mostly through treaties. However, from a tribal perspective, the value of land as the foundation of society and culture and as having sacred meaning cannot be fully compensated by money.

Traditional Land-Based Economies and Land Tenure

American Indian peoples had long-standing knowledge of the land on which they lived and from which they made a living. As with most indigenous peoples throughout the world, American Indian cultural identity was closely associated with the specific ecosystems and landmarks of tribal homelands. The rich and varied ecosystems of the North American continent provided the basis for the diverse traditional economies of the Native peoples. These systems for making a living included hunting and gathering, harvesting of fish, and agricultural production throughout much of the temperate areas of the continent. These traditional economies varied in the amount of land and population required for subsistence. Most hunting and gathering populations need to move throughout their territories in a seasonal cycle and have relatively low population densities. Much of Native North America had a mixed economy, which included hunting and gathering as well as agricultural production. The crops domesticated by American Indians—primarily the triumvirate of corn, beans, and squash, particularly when supplemented with protein from meat obtained by hunting—provided a balanced and nutritional diet. Indian tribes in the arid Southwest practiced labor-intensive, irrigated agriculture that depended on an adequate supply of surface water and required comparatively dense, sedentary populations.

One significant variable affecting Indian land use and land tenure was the effect of European diseases on the American Indian population. European populations had been exposed for centuries to Old World bacterial and viral infections and had developed substantial immunity to these diseases. American Indians were assaulted by these new pathogens, which led to high mortality rates from disease as each new tribal population was exposed. As Europeans settlers increased in numbers through both immigration and natural population growth, Native populations experienced declines. As a consequence, early agreements by tribal populations permitting small settlements of Europeans within their traditional territories in exchange for trade goods did not put pressures on the access to and use of land. However, as more non-Indians took more land, conflicts increased.

U.S. Indian policy increasingly pushed Indian people toward the most sedentary lifestyles that required the least amount of land. This policy was used to justify the continual renegotiation and dictating of the provisions of treaties and the resulting reduction of tribal landholdings. The federal government intended to force Indian people to assimilate into non-Indian society and to participate in the market economy. This goal was to be accomplished by reducing Indian landholdings and making it impossible to continue the more land-extensive economies that prevailed in much of Native North America. As he negotiated the Louisiana Purchase with France in 1803, Thomas Jefferson wrote that tribes would learn to use less land and that settlers would need more (Jennings 1975). These policies were often justified by rhetoric about the wastefulness of nonsedentary ways of life. In practical terms, without the experience and the resources (money for equipment and seeds, arable land, enough water), Indian people often faced starvation when deprived of the lands, water, plants, and animals upon which they knew how to subsist.

Land as Real Property

European and American Indian societies alike held ideals about how land, water, and natural resources were to be used and allocated. Communal land use was not completely foreign to Europeans, in whose home countries were areas designated as commons, often used by the poor or commoners. General recognition of the tribal system of common land tenure is seen in the congressional reaction to the initial Wyandot treaty of 1817. The initial treaty provided for the land not ceded by the Wyandot to be recorded as fee simple titles to individuals. The Senate Committee on Public Lands expressed concern that this process was unprecedented. They required that the treaty be renegotiated and that the Wyandot land be held "as before," that is, in common (Prucha 1994).

However, by the 1600s the European system of real property consisted overwhelmingly of individual ownership of land with sole legal title. In the Western legal tradition, valuables used in common and to which no individual can claim exclusive rights, such as the oceans or the air, are not considered property. American Indian cultures generally viewed land as commonly held, with recognition of

use rights to extended families, lineages, and clans that worked a particular field, hunted for game, or harvested fish. Many Indian populations also recognized family hunting and trapping territories. Chief Isparhecher of the Muscogee Creek noted to federal officials in the 1890s that the Creek system of land tenure, in which land was held in common, had proven successful and satisfactory throughout their tribal existence. He emphasized that the Creek did not have homelessness or lawsuits about land titles. Similarly, in opposition to proposals to allot their land in Oklahoma, Chief Wilson Jones of the Choctaw explained that the land use system of the Choctaw avoided disputes because the Choctaw people owned the homes and lands of their grandfathers (Banner 2005, 265). In general, the Native systems for use of land tended to be flexible to meet the needs of society as some families and lines grew and others diminished. Some rich ecosystems, such as woodlands and coasts, had territories used by more than one family, band, or tribal group. In some locations, there were buffer zones between Native groups that may have been involved in hostilities over use of land (Sutton 1975). Clearly, when American Indians first entered into land agreements with Europeans, they did so from an economic, social, political, and cultural context different from the one familiar to the non-Indian people with whom they were interacting. It is likely that Indian people intended to provide use rights for, not perpetual sole ownership of, a parcel of land when they were said by Europeans to be "selling" land.

These issues of differing contexts of understanding were exacerbated by basic challenges of communication; in many cases, agreements were reached between representatives who did not speak the same language, and negotiations were conducted through interpreters. Furthermore, tribes used oral tradition and symbolic goods, such as wampum belts, to memorialize agreements and transactions. Europeans and, later, the federal government always used written documents as the final record. The opportunity for abuse, misrepresentation, and gross misunderstanding of legalistic terms was substantial. Many Indian people signed treaties based on what they heard, but non-Indians always held them to what was written (Banner 2005).

Who Had the Right to Sell Tribal Land?

A key question in Indian land deals was, Who had legal authority to negotiate regarding commonly held land? Non-Indians often exploited, and exacerbated for the purpose of acquiring land, the varying interests of different individuals and groups within tribes. Particularly in the early stage of land sales, the individual Indian who first sold a particular parcel of land to non-Indians may have received cash or goods for lands that were considered the territory of a larger group. In the late 1700s, there were complaints within eastern tribes that their sachems and other leaders had become corrupt, accepting bribes and payments for personal gain in negotiations that affected the land of the entire tribal group.

The U.S. Constitution requires the consent of two-thirds of the Senate to ratify treaties, and many federal treaties with Indian tribes contained provisions that required approval by a majority or three-fourths of the adult male members of a tribe. However, Indian peoples had a variety of political structures, which varied from informal forms of leadership within small groups to large-scale political alliances among numerous tribal groups who spoke different languages and had different cultural traditions. But a majority or even super-majority "vote" when members have essentially equal ownership of land certainly seemed unfair to those Indian people who opposed particular negotiations and treaties. Some misunderstandings may have occurred when non-Indians interpreted the political structure of American Indian societies and assumed that some leaders had more authority than they actually had. There were also cases in which non-Indians created authority in individual Indian people that did not practically exist and used it to their advantage in securing treaties for land.

In recognition of the difficulties posed by cross-cultural communication and the standard of responsibility of the federal government as a tribal trustee, the Supreme Court developed rules of treaty interpretation in a series of cases in the 1930s. These rules, or canons, required that ambiguities in treaties be resolved in favor of Indian tribes, that treaties be interpreted as Indian people would have understood them at the time of signing, and that treaties be construed liberally in favor of tribal interests.

Sovereignty and Ownership

When the United States was formed, it claimed sovereignty over huge areas in which it had no on-the-ground governance and where there was no real property ownership by non-Indians. Through the assertion of sovereignty, the development of the laws under which treaties were negotiated, and the

growing power to enforce them, non-Indians increasingly controlled the acquisition of Indian land. This claim of sovereignty by the United States included a preemptive right to purchase title to Indian land and was intended to secure these rights to the exclusion of all other powers. Through preemption, the federal government acquired Indian land, dividing it into smaller parcels and selling it to white settlers. In 1868, the federal government attempted to sell eight million acres of land acquired from the Osage to commercial railroads rather than placing it in the "public domain." Congress would not ratify the treaty, and it had to be renegotiated. The profit made by the United States by purchasing Indian land and selling it to non-Indians, in total the largest land deal in the history of the world, went into the federal treasury. Indian people, however, could only sell or cede their land to the United States, and ownership of land essentially always moved in one direction, from Indians to non-Indians.

President Andrew Jackson argued that the United States should unilaterally take Indian land through the power of eminent domain and provide just compensation rather than negotiate treaties. In 1834, he enforced his view through the power of the U.S. military when he defied Chief Justice John Marshall's rulings in the Supreme Court case *Worcester v. Georgia* and forced the Cherokee on the Trail of Tears to leave their homelands and move to Indian Territory. However, the legal structure of treaties as agreements between sovereigns has proven to be the key source of legal land claims by tribes over time.

Mother Earth: The Value of Land and Natural Resources

Land and the natural and biological resources linked to it were the primary assets Indian people had that were valuable to non-Indians. When Europeans first came to North America, Indian people traded furs, crops, and small parcels of land for the goods they wanted. Indian peoples with exposure to non-Indian society came to understand the unfairness of many land offers and began to ask for more per acre in treaty negotiations. However, within a hundred years after the Revolutionary War, the United States had taken two billion acres of Indian land, approximately one-half purchased by treaty or agreement and much of the rest confiscated by the federal government without compensation or formal action.

Shortly after the Revolutionary War, the U.S. Treasury was nearly exhausted, and the federal government decided that it was much cheaper to buy Indian land through the process of making treaties than to go to war for it. Although the very earliest trades of land for goods may have been voluntary, the transactions became increasingly and profoundly coercive. By the 1850s, the military and political balance of power had shifted dramatically. Congress refused to ratify many treaties negotiated in the field with California tribes because the price was considered too high, even though the California Indians were forced onto mere patches of land and were starving. Overwhelmingly, money, goods, and services paid by non-Indians for land taken from Indian people were worth less than the fair market value of the land, even at the time of purchase. Because it had the power, the government did not pay the fair market value; it paid as little as it could. Some studies of the Indian Claims Commission, which adjudicated tribal land claims between 1947 and 1978, estimate that the United States paid about ten cents per acre for Indian land in the northern plains in the mid-1800s, when the average price paid by white settlers was closer to two dollars (Prucha 1994, 230).

The Constitution of the United States requires the government to pay just compensation for the land it acquires; just compensation is almost always determined through an appraisal based on the market economy. But if the seller does not agree with the price offered, the taking is more a confiscation than a compensation. Can money or goods ever be fair compensation for the land of people whose way of making a living, social structure, and religion are directly tied to the land? Many Indian people over the decades have eloquently expressed the view that monetary value cannot be placed on the land, water, plants, animals, and sacred places. The Native worldview consistently valued the land and the living world not as resources to be exploited or property to be bought and sold but in familial or kinship terms, such as "Mother Earth." Although monetary compensation may have benefited some Indian people individually, loss of land was destructive to tribal ways of life that were closely tied to knowledge of particular ecosystems and territory. These knowledge systems were passed on from generation to generation and were internal to Indian culture and societies. Without tribal homelands, the intergenerational transmission of language and culture was made extremely difficult. Indian people and leaders often expressed their desire to maintain their traditional lifestyles and their independence from white

society and from the markets their independent lifestyles afforded them. Elders of the Fort McDowell Yavapai Nation spoke metaphorically about the relative value of land and money during their struggle to prevent the flooding of their land by the construction of Orme Dam in the 1970s and 1980s: "Land is like diamonds, money like ice. The land stays forever but money melts through your fingers" (Mariella 1990). Similar sentiments have been expressed by Indian people throughout the last two hundred years as they faced the prospect of trying to maintain their identity when they no longer had their homelands.

Treaties between Tribes, Colonial Powers, and the United States before the War of 1812

Colonial governments rapidly took control of the acquisition of land, preempting the right as a sovereign government to negotiate and conclude treaties with the Native peoples. Early treaty making between tribes and European nations and, subsequently, the United States were mechanisms to secure alliances and peace between sovereigns. When the British relinquished their American colonies in the Treaty of Paris in 1783, all the land over which the Crown had claimed sovereignty east of the Mississippi River became part of the United States. Even the tribes who fought with the colonists were legally subsumed, although the treaty said nothing about Indian lands.

The new nation was too weakened militarily and too poor from fighting the Revolutionary War to forcibly acquire Indian lands. Instead, the federal government set about acquiring title to Indian lands through treaties, primarily in exchange for trade goods (e.g., the Treaty of Fort Harmar in 1789, the Treaties of Fort Stanwix in 1768 and 1784, and the Treaty of Fort McIntosh in 1785). Purchases of Indian land were complicated by the sometimes long process of determining boundaries as well as joint ownership.

Removal: Land in Exchange for Land

In 1803, the Louisiana Purchase from France of eight hundred thousand square miles nearly doubled the size of the United States. The federal government encouraged Indian people to move to the new territory, which was isolated from non-Indians. After the War of 1812 and the end of the British threat to the United States, alliances with Indian tribes were no longer critical to the international balance of power on the North American continent. In a pattern that would repeat over the next fifty years, settlers on the frontier who were remote from the political seat of power pushed into the lands of the Cherokee, Muscogee Creek, Chickasaw, Choctaw, and Seminole, the so-called Five Civilized Tribes. These settlers provoked conflict, forcing the federal government to act. With the passage of the Indian Removal Act of 1830, the United States military forcibly removed all the Indian tribes west of the Mississippi to Indian Territory. The southeastern tribes, all farming people, strongly opposed the removal but lacked the military capacity to challenge the army and the political strength to fight the executive power of the president. In 1814, the Creek were forced to surrender twenty-three million acres of land to the federal government and to move to Indian Territory. Subsequently, the Cherokee were forced to sign the Treaty of New Echota, in which they gave up their land east of the Mississippi River in exchange for land in Oklahoma Territory. The move, which was conducted under military escort, is known as the Trail of Tears.

Reservations: Payment for Ceded Lands

The federal government expected that the removal of Indian tribes to Oklahoma Territory would isolate Indians from conflicts with non-Indians. However, when Texas, the Oregon country, and the lands of the Mexican Cession of 1848 became part of the United States, the federal government entered again into treaty making with the many tribes in these frontier territories. Tribes were forced onto relatively small tracts of land, known as *reservations*. Between 1853 and 1856, fifty-two treaties were negotiated, more than in any other period, and close to 174,000,000 acres of Indian land were taken for non-Indian settlers and prospectors. Without any local control to stop them, white settlers put down stakes on Indian lands, creating a de facto ownership that the federal government was subsequently pressured to make permanent. After the Civil War, the Nez Perce were forced to accept the Stevens treaty (Treaty with the Nez Perce–June 9, 1863), which was then delayed in Congress while changes were debated; meanwhile, settlers continued to move into their lands, resulting in further land reductions.

Reservation treaties listed the lands to be ceded to the United States in return for federal promises to provide goods and services and to form the basis for the doctrine of reserved rights established by the Supreme Court in *Winters v. United States* (1908). In addition, these treaties generally contained the federal government's assurance that Indian people could live on their remaining lands in perpetuity or "as long as the water flows, the grass grows upon the earth or the sun rises." Despite the eloquent promises of permanence, many treaties were broken to obtain even more land. By 1860, essentially no tribal lands remained east of the 98th meridian. In the next decade, following the end of the Civil War, most of the Indian lands in the interior of the continent were also taken from tribes.

With passage of the Dawes Act in 1887, Congress ended the practice of making formal treaties with tribes but stated clearly that the provisions of existing treaties remained intact. However, in 1903 the Supreme Court affirmed in *Lone Wolf v. Hitchcock* that Congress had the authority to unilaterally abrogate treaties with Indian tribes as long as land takings were compensated. Later Supreme Court decisions established that reservations created by executive order and by statute have the same legal status as reservations created by treaties.

Allotments: Private Ownership of Land

The General Allotment Act of 1887 (the Dawes Act) was intended to assimilate American Indians into white society and the market economy through small-scale farming. Indian male heads of household were to be allotted land for homesites and farms; after a transition period, often twenty-five years, the land would pass out of reservation trust status and would be held as private property. In contrast, reservation land cannot be sold by tribes or individual Indians; only Congress can authorize the purchase or sale of reservation trust land. The process of dividing tribal reservation lands into small family farms also left acres of tribal land unallotted. The federal government deemed this land surplus, divided it, and sold it to non-Indian homesteaders. Like treaties, the provisions of the Dawes Act of 1887 required that payment be made for any land taken by the allotment process. However, the Department of the Interior rarely lived up to its responsibilities as a trustee, and tribes generally did not receive adequate compensation for their surplus land.

The allotment process left a legacy of complicated land tenure on the reservations that underwent allotment. Once allotments passed out of trust status, individual Indians then had to pay real property taxes, and much of the land was sold to pay taxes and other debts. More than two-thirds of the remaining tribal lands in the continental United States was lost to Indian people during the allotment era. Allotments on a number of reservations remain in trust status, and the lease and homestead rights are inherited. Over many generations, ownership of allotments has become highly fractionated, sometimes with more than one hundred owners for a single acre, making it increasingly difficult for individual allottees and their descendants to make economic use of the allotment rights. The development challenges of fractionated inheritance resulted in the 1982 Indian Land Consolidation Act, in which tribes were given first right of refusal to buy fractionated and privately held land within reservation boundaries. In addition, the historic sale of allotments created checkerboarded land ownership patterns within a number of reservations, in which parcels of Indian land are separated by land owned by non-Indians. These checkerboarded patterns of land ownership on some reservations make it hard for those tribes to conduct regulatory activities and law enforcement.

Some individual Indian people made considerable income from royalties, leasing their allotted lands for economic development; but the transition to the market economy was very difficult for the many individuals who were left without their land and with no money. Without the experience and education to manage money, many individual Indians were not able to create long-term financial security from land sales or lease income. Without tribally held lands, tribal social and political structures were no longer as meaningful, and small parcels of land were not adequate to develop tribal projects that would benefit the tribe as a whole. Uniformly, allotment had deleterious effects on tribal cohesion. Partly in recognition of the harm done to Indian assets and tribal life, the Indian Reorganization Act ended the practice of allotment in 1934.

Termination, Restoration, and the Alaska Native Claims Settlement

With the return of Indian veterans from World War II, federal Indian policy shifted to one of termination, in which treaty rights were ended and trust sta-

tus removed from all the tribal land base. In two key termination cases, involving the Menominee of Wisconsin and the Klamath of Oregon, pressures to terminate the tribes came from interest in the commercially valuable timber on their land. After more than two decades of struggle, tribal status was restored to both tribes in the 1970s.

The most recent treaty-like settlement affecting significant amounts of tribal land in the United States is the Alaska Native Claims Settlement Act of 1971. Alaska Natives did not sign treaties with the federal government, and it had been unclear what aboriginal title meant in Alaska. The Settlement Act gave forty-four million acres to Alaska Natives and provided $962 million for relinquishment of the remainder of their land claims.

Mining

In the 1870s, the discovery of gold in the Black Hills area of what is now western South Dakota, northeastern Wyoming, and southeastern Montana led to a sequence of broken federal treaty promises that stands out even in the lengthy history of treaty abrogation. The impetus behind the relentless pressure to take the land of the Lakota Indians of the northern plains was the commercial value of the gold, silver, and other minerals in the Black Hills. By the late 1850s, the large buffalo herds that had sustained the Plains Indians had been hunted by non-Indians almost to extinction. The loss of the buffalo and the resulting blow to the ability of the Plains tribes to maintain an independent tribal life led to the Treaty of Fort Laramie of 1851. In the initial treaty, the Lakota retained a significant portion of their Black Hills land in the Great Dakota Reservation. The Black Hills were sacred to the Lakota people and were the location of ceremonies, vision quests, and burials. However, government negotiators pressured a group of Lakota to sign a second treaty in 1868 that reduced their land base from sixty million acres to twenty million. This treaty guaranteed the security of the remaining land from the white settlers, who sparked conflicts by constant incursions into the reservation. The federal government viewed the Fort Laramie treaty as a way to force the Plains Indians out of their traditional hunting way of life into small-scale agriculture. But the climate and soils of the arid northern plains presented substantial challenges for sustained agricultural production and was a profoundly different way of life from the buffalo-based culture the Plains tribes knew.

When gold was discovered in the Black Hills in the 1870s, the federal government pressured the Lakota to accept the removal of the Black Hills from their already-reduced reservation by refusing to provide provisions as required by earlier treaties and which were necessary to avoid starvation. In 1877, Congress enacted a new treaty with only 10 percent of the adult male Lakota signing, in direct conflict with the three-fourths requirement of the earlier Fort Laramie treaty. Although the Lakota had been guaranteed by treaty in 1874 that no additional land would be taken, the treaty of 1877 removed the sacred Black Hills from their reservation. Twelve years later, in 1889, Congress again removed half of the reservation acreage and divided the remaining land into six separate reservations. Any resistance to this action was ended with the killing by U.S. soldiers of scores of unarmed Lakota at Wounded Knee in 1890. Between 1904 and 1910, Congress removed additional lands from the six reservations, including three-fourths of the Rosebud Reservation.

In the first year after the Black Hills were taken from the Lakota Reservation, mining companies and prospectors extracted approximately $3.5 million in gold. This figure increased to $4.5 million in 1879 and to $6 million in 1880. The Black Hills also yielded silver, lead, coal, iron, quartz, nickel, and copper. Major mining operations on what once had been Lakota Reservation lands included the Homestake and Gilt Edge Mines, which became some of the most productive and profitable mines in the United States.

Never abandoning their cultural and spiritual relationship to the Black Hills, the Lakota filed a claim in the federal court of claims in 1920 requesting the return of the Black Hills. Despite its authorization to adjudicate claims against the United States under treaties, agreements, or federal laws, the court did not review whether the treaty of 1877 provided just compensation to the Lakota. Not until the establishment of the Indian Claims Commission by act of Congress in 1946 did a new opportunity develop; in 1950 the Lakota filed a claim. In 1967, eight tribes were awarded $12.21 million dollars in compensation from the Claims Commission for twenty-nine million acres taken from them through treaties. The Claims Commission ruled that the United States had used eminent domain to seize their land rather than acting in its role as trustee. Consequently, the United States owed them compensation for the Black Hills.

As the legal efforts were slowly working their way through the Claims Commission and the courts, the State of South Dakota established parks in the Black Hills, making it increasingly difficult for the Lakota to practice their sacred ceremonials. The American Indian Treaty Rights Movement of the 1970s grew out of the Lakota struggle to regain the Black Hills. Members of the American Indian Movement established the Yellow Thunder Camp in the Black Hills to raise awareness of the sacred value of the land, and lawsuits were filed under the American Indian Religious Freedom Act in 1978, claiming that the seizure of hills was a violation of Lakota religious rights.

In 1980, the Supreme Court affirmed the Claims Commission and ruled that the tribes were due cash compensation for the fair market value of the Black Hills at the time land was taken, plus interest—a sum of close to $122.5 million. The fair market value determination did not include the value of minerals extracted from the land by mining corporations, which has been estimated to be close to $4 billion. National news was made when many tribal members refused the compensation, asking instead for the return of the Black Hills. Some attempts were made in Congress in the late 1980s to reach a settlement, but the issue remains unsettled at the time of this writing. Further attention was focused on the Black Hills during the 1980s, when non-Indians, concerned about environmental degradation from strip-mining of coal deposits and leaching of cyanide into groundwater from decades of gold extraction, joined with Native Americans in developing the Black Hills Alliance.

In Oklahoma, the oil boom, which began in the 1890s, had a major impact on Indian lands, including the lands of the Osage tribe. The Osage were forced from their homelands in present-day Missouri and Arkansas into Indian Territory through a series of treaties throughout the 1800s. After ceding close to 45 million acres, the Osage purchased 1.4 million acres in 1870 from the Cherokee for a new reservation in the northeastern portion of Indian Territory. These lands were not sought after by non-Indians until oil was discovered underneath them in 1875. Immediately after the discovery of oil, non-Indians sought leases on the Osage Reservation for mining oil and gas. Many of these initial leaseholders leased substantial portions of land and subleased them. In some cases, these leaseholders made substantially more from the Osage lands than the Osage themselves had. In 1904, the reservation was allotted; each adult Osage male received about 650 acres of surface rights with fee simple title. The individual Osage landowners were able to develop, lease, or sell their land. However, the subsurface mineral rights were held in common, and each Osage received a *headright*—that is, he or she would receive an equal share of all income from oil and gas production from their tribal lands. In the early 1900s, the Osage tribe declared it illegal to sell a headright, which by 1917 was worth $2,719; the value increased to over $8,000 in 1920. As a consequence, individual Osage experienced substantial increases in income. Although some tribe members had the experience and skills to control and manage this income, others spent the money or were manipulated into spending it in ways that did not result in increased quality of life or long-term financial security. The infusion of substantial income from oil headrights also increased conflict and violence within the tribe and attracted a number of non-Indians looking to marry into wealth. The intermarriage with non-Osage further affected tribal cohesion and tribal identity (Fixico 1998).

Today, more than half the nation's coalfields are located west of the Mississippi River; one-third of those western fields are on tribal lands. An estimated 25 to 40 percent of the uranium, one-third of the coal, and 5 percent of oil and gas are on reservations in the western part of the United States, including Black Mesa on the Navajo and Hopi Reservations (Ambler 1990). The federal government, in its role as trustee of tribes, has the responsibility to manage those resources for the primary benefit of those tribes. The poor oversight, poor record keeping, and poor advocacy of the Department of the Interior in approving leasing and royalty arrangements for the historical extraction of the mineral resources of Indian land is the subject of the current Elouise Cobell lawsuit in federal court. With the technical and legal assistance of national organizations such as the Council of Energy Resource Tribes, tribes are increasingly managing their own resources. The building of tribal environmental management and regulatory capacity since the 1980s has supported the goal of protecting land, water, and air quality and ecosystems. However, the power of Congress to override treaty provisions through statute, which was confirmed in *Lone Wolf v. Hitchcock* in 1903, continues to have the potential to affect tribal ability to protect tribal resources. In 2005, Senator Inhofe of Oklahoma added a rider to a national transportation bill that removed the ability of Oklahoma tribes to regulate water quality under federal clean water laws without the approval of the State of Oklahoma.

Timber

The Klamath and Modoc tribes of what is now southeastern Oregon lived, hunted, and fished in the Pacific Northwest coastal region, one of the most productive ecosystems in the United States. The Native peoples of this area were largely sedentary harvesters of the exceptionally rich and reliable fish populations, such as salmon, which spawned annually in the rivers that flowed through their lands. In addition, the homelands of the Klamath included commercially valuable forests of ponderosa pine and mixed conifers. The desire to protect their valuable timberlands was a major reason the Nez Perce treaty of 1863 was reopened, even though settlers were pushing into more of their lands day by day.

The federal government pressured the Klamath into the treaty of 1864, which established their reservation and ceded more than 23 million acres, which included valuable timberlands. Having seriously reduced access to their traditional hunting and fishing resources, the Klamath and the Modoc tribes took up ranching of cattle and horses and developed a small sawmill in 1870. By 1896, sales of Klamath timber were close to 250,000 board feet per year.

Following federal Indian policy of the time and in response to local pressures for more land, the federal government divided the Klamath Reservation into allotments in the 1890s. The allotments were 80 acres of farmland or 160 acres of grazing land per person; the sale of "surplus" reservation land that was not allotted resulted in the additional loss of more than 100,000 acres. By the end of the allotment period in 1934, 10 percent of the land within the reservation was privately owned by individual Klamath Indians; some 860,000 acres were still held in common. As with so many situations in which allotted lands moved out of trust status and into private ownership, Klamath landowners ended up selling or losing 95 percent of their privately owned land. However, on the tribal lands, it was estimated there was $80 million worth of ponderosa pine. The Klamath tribe managed its forests for long-term yield, but the timberlands that had moved out of tribal hands were cut at a faster rate, reducing their ability to sustain healthy wildlife populations and continued logging.

After World War II, local timber interests and some members of the Klamath tribe wanted to remove the trust status protecting the remaining Klamath timber, in order to cut lumber at a faster rate. In 1954, Congress withheld a $2.6 million settlement to pressure for termination of the federal trust status of the Klamath lands. These interests in exploiting the timber in an unsustainable way were part of the drive that led to the termination policy of the 1950s and 1960s, under which both tribal land and allotted land in trust would become individually held, private land. However, most of the tribe members opposed the removal of the trust status, and a Bureau of Indian Affairs report of the time stated clearly that, as a group, the Klamath were not prepared to succeed financially if the trust status were removed. Congress passed the Klamath Termination Act, working with the support of a small segment of the tribal membership. The reservation land was taken by condemnation and the tribal trust status terminated in 1961. Termination released all tribal property that contained rich timberlands, including fifty thousand acres with 3.8 billion board feet of commercial lumber. As a result, significant stands of timber were clear-cut, reducing the long-term productivity of the timberlands but increasing erosion of the soil and pollution of local streams.

Despite the termination of the tribe, in 1974 the Klamath won an initial victory when the federal courts ruled that the Klamath retained treaty rights to hunt, fish, and gather in their traditional territories and had to be consulted in land management decisions when those decisions affected their treaty rights. Then, in 1986, after years of political and legal effort, Public Law 99–398 restored federal recognition of the Klamath tribe as a governmental entity. Like the Klamath, the Menominee tribe of Wisconsin, which has substantial timberlands, was also terminated and then restored to federal tribal status in 1973.

Although restoration of the tribe did not return the Klamath land base to tribal status, the development of the Klamath Economic Self-Sufficiency Plan resulted in the tribe's continued pivotal role in the local economy. Klamath Tribal Forest Management Plans are designed to protect the natural resources of the tribe so that they are not degraded for future generations. This long-term perspective is a core element of a tribal worldview that seeks quality of life for the tribe as a whole.

In the twenty-first century, tribes are buying back land, controlling their own extractive industries, and managing water quality, timber, and other natural resources in a sustainable way that does not

degrade the resources over time. Tribal control of development enables resources to be managed for the future of Native nations for generations to come.

Patricia S. Mariella

References and Further Reading

Ambler, Marjane. 1990. *Breaking the Iron Bonds.* Lawrence: University Press of Kansas.

Banner, Stuart. 2005. *How the Indians Lost Their Land.* Cambridge, MA: Harvard University Press.

Clinton, Robert N., Kevin Gover, and Rebecca Tsosie. 2004. "Introduction." In *Colonial and American Indian Treaties: A Collection.* Tempe: Arizona State University American Indian Law Program.

Debo, Angie. 1966. *And Still the Waters Run: The Betrayal of the Five Civilized Tribes.* New York: Gordian Press. (Orig. pub. 1940).

Fixico, Donald L. 1998. *The Invasion of Indian Country in the Twentieth Century: American Capitalism and Tribal Natural Resources.* Niwot: University Press of Colorado.

Franks, Kenny A. 1989. *The Osage Oil Boom.* Oklahoma City: Oklahoma Heritage Association.

Hughes, J. Donald. 1983. *American Indian Ecology.* El Paso: Texas Western Press.

Jennings, Francis. 1975. *The Invasion of America: Indians, Colonialism and the Cant of Conquest.* Chapel Hill: University of North Carolina Press.

Jorgensen, Joseph G., ed. 1984. *Native Americans and Energy Development.* Boston: Anthropology Resource Center and Seventh Generation Fund.

Lawson, Michael L. 1982. *Damned Indians: The Pick-Sloan Plan and the Missouri River Sioux, 1944–1980.* Norman: University of Oklahoma Press.

Mariella, Patricia. 1990. "Land Like Diamonds, Money Like Ice." *Practicing Anthropology,* 12(2): 8–9.

McNickel, D'Arcy. 1973. *Native American Tribalism.* New York: Oxford University Press.

Parker, Watson. 1982. *Gold in the Black Hills.* Lincoln: University of Nebraska Press.

Prucha, Francis Paul. 1994. *American Indian Treaties: The History of a Political Anomaly.* Berkeley, Los Angeles, and London: University of California Press.

Rollings, Willard H. 1995. *The Osage: An Ethnohistorical Study of Hegemony on the Prairie-Plains.* Columbia: University of Missouri Press.

Stern, Theodore. 1965. *The Klamath Tribe: A People and Their Reservation.* Seattle: University of Washington Press.

St. Germain, Jill. 2001. *Indian Treaty-Making Policy in the United States and Canada, 1867–1877.* Lincoln: University of Nebraska Press.

Sutton, Imre. 1975. *Indian Land Tenure.* New York: Clearwater.

Williams, Robert A. 1997. *Linking Arms Together: American Indian Treaty Visions of Law and Peace, 1600–1800.* New York: Oxford University Press.

Wilson, Terry P. 1985. *The Underground Reservation: Osage Oil.* Lincoln: University of Nebraska Press.

Indian Water Rights and Treaties

In the eastern United States, the states have regulated the use of water by a system of riparian rights that came down from English law, in which all who own land along a water source have the right to the use of the water of that source. However, this system has worked well only in places with average to heavy rainfall, where the utilization of water by upstream users does not have a detrimental effect on downstream users.

In the arid lands of the American West, where most American Indians reside, water rights are governed by state laws founded on the principle of prior appropriation. Prior appropriation can be best summed up by the principle "First in time, first in right." In practical terms, this means that the oldest water right is satisfied in full before later users can have any access to the water supply. In other words, the first to make beneficial use of the water has the right to all the water they originally used. Whatever remains after the first claimant's use of the water is the property of the second claimant, and so on down the line. This worked well in the nineteenth-century West, as the institutions necessary to govern and determine rights in a riparian system were lacking. In a system of prior appropriation, the users themselves were able to determine the first in right, at least initially. The Supreme Court, however, has long recognized that both federal and Indian water rights exist outside of the state-regulated water rights systems and must be satisfied as well, creating a competing system of water allotment.

Water policy, for the majority of American Indians in the West, has been determined by the implementation of two apparently contradictory methods of water allocation: the prior appropriation system and the reserved rights doctrine (also referred to as the *Winters* doctrine). Put succinctly, in signing treaties with the federal government that resulted in the creation of their reservations, Indians agreed to vast land cessions in return for guarantees that their reservation lands would be permanently reserved for Indian use and occupation. The Supreme Court ruled that, when the Indians did this, they reserved to themselves every right not specified in the treaty. Ownership of the land and, implicitly, its resources and all sovereignty not expressly relinquished to the federal government were rights reserved to the Indian nation. The downside of this system, in terms of prior appropriation, is that the "priority date" assigned to the Indians was the date of the congressional act that created the reservation, rather than a date of "time immemorial," which would seem more appropriate, given the lengthy tenure of Indians on their lands.

This system of reserving rights based on reservation status has created some anomalies within Indian country. Land ownership has been the key to New Mexico Pueblo Indians' water rights. The Pueblo nations have early priority dates derived from Spanish land grants and the U.S. Treaty of Guadalupe Hidalgo with Mexico. Because of this, the Pueblos have "aboriginal" water rights. Unlike many other nations, the Pueblos reside on lands they have never left and from which they have never been forced by the United States. Although the United States recognized those prior holdings in the Treaty of Guadalupe Hidalgo of 1848, thereby giving federal protection to the Pueblo rights to land and water, these rights do not depend on any federal action for their existence.

During the twentieth century, however, most Indian nations have had to base their hopes for justice in water rights on federal court decisions. Congress had not passed any definitive, all-encompassing water rights bills supporting or even defining their rights. The decision that formed the most generous basis for Indian water rights, the reserved rights doctrine, and thus the most contention with non-Indian water claimants is *Winters v. United States,* in which the Supreme Court held that, when Indian reservations were established, the Indian nations and the United States implicitly reserved, along with the land, sufficient water to fulfill the purposes of the reservations, which in most cases was farming.

Therefore, according to the *Winters* doctrine, which was derived from the decision, Indian water rights are defined and governed by a body of federal law that recognizes that Indian nations have sovereignty over the water on their reservations. The Supreme Court held that Indian governments have jurisdiction over their members and over activities on the Indian reservations, and this has affected the ways in which Indians can use the water that flows

through or adjacent to their reservations. However, by shortsightedly handing down a decision but failing to provide any way of reconciling it with the prior appropriation system already in use, the Court did more to provoke further conflicts over water between Indian and non-Indian populations than it did to settle them. *Winters* did nothing at all to determine either the scope of its application or the parameters for determining the amount of water Indian nations could claim. Almost from the time the decision was handed down in 1908, and especially during the 1980s and 1990s, many nations have gone to court in an effort to quantify their federal water rights, even though it has often meant a serious diminution of the possible extent of those rights.

Two issues are raised by federal government involvement in protecting Indian water rights and other Indian-held natural resources. First, the ownership of land and water rights is antithetical to many American Indian cultural and religious systems. Secondly, federal involvement raises the issue of the difference between the dependency of Indian nations on the federal government and self-determination with governmental protection. This has long been a difficult distinction to draw. Speaking in purely economic terms, by failing to promote and protect the right of Indian nations to develop their resources, the government perpetuates dependency and poverty. On the other hand, if it protects Indians' interests and Indians' rights to develop their resources, the federal government may be guilty of affecting Indian culture, but it can certainly not be said to be perpetuating dependency. Rather, the federal government would be acting to promote the health of the Indian economies necessary for true self-determination.

The main reason for the continued difficulty in securing water rights under the *Winters* doctrine is that it has constantly come up against prior appropriation, the prevailing method of allocating water claims in the western United States. When the doctrine of prior appropriation is taken to include Indian use, the courts necessarily enter the picture to fix the amounts allocated by right to a given Indian nation as determined by its use of a particular water source. Because Indian reservations were established before most water uses began in the West, Indians often hold the oldest—and thus the most valuable—water rights. Many Indian groups have occupied land since time immemorial and thus also have strong, ancient priority claims to water for Indian uses. State water laws in the West often place a priority on the idea of beneficial use, which, more often than not, has to do with agriculture. Although many southwestern groups, such as the Pueblos, have an agricultural tradition that predates European contact, and others, such as the Jicarilla Apache, have a mixed-subsistence tradition, the factors of modern reservation life do not always mean that the Indian nations will use the water as the state or federal laws would prefer them to.

Because Indian nations are theoretically not held to state laws in these matters, conflicts have continually arisen over which water rights doctrine is applicable to the adjudication of rivers that flow over Indian as well as non-Indian lands. The *Winters* doctrine would seem to support the view that Indians have a right to enough water to irrigate reservation agricultural lands, and yet the doctrine of prior appropriation supports the idea that, if the Indians did not historically irrigate their lands, then non-Indian water claimants would be substantiated. The courts then have to examine what water was reserved for use on the Indian reservations, how Indian water rights are quantified and used, and how these water rights are regulated and enforced. Because of the potential extent and great value of the water that could be claimed by Indian nations under the *Winters* doctrine, especially in the American West, where water has become increasingly scarce, Indian water rights have constantly been under attack in the federal and state courts and in other political arenas as well.

As clearly contradictory as the two dominant systems of allocation (*Winters* and prior appropriation) may appear, the actual situation in practice has been both less contradictory and more confusing than the various federal decisions would make it seem. Historian Daniel McCool pointed out that these two contradictory theories of water allotment created a conflict of interest within the Justice Department. The Justice Department was to be the legal representative for all federal interests, so its official position in favor of prior appropriation in the West was in conflict with the reserved rights doctrine (*Winters* doctrine), which was supposed to determine Indian water rights. The *Winters* doctrine theoretically makes the prior appropriation doctrine irrelevant. In practice, however, federal irrigation and reclamation programs were rarely undertaken in the interests of Indian peoples, even when they were constructed adjacent to Indian lands.

The Bureau of Reclamation, dedicated to the doctrine of prior appropriation and the promotion of non-Indian irrigated agriculture in the West, exercised great power and acted decisively in the interests of its constituents when allocating the waters made useful by its construction projects. Even though the *Winters* doctrine might have given the Indians a theoretically large claim to the waters of the West, battles over access to those waters occupied Indian nations, the federal and state courts, the Department of the Interior (both as the promoter of non-Indian development through the Bureau of Reclamation and as the defender of Indian rights through the Bureau of Indian Affairs), and Congress throughout the twentieth century.

Even where the rights seem plain, the capriciousness of the courts toward Indian nations has meant that the nations have had to enter into lengthy and expensive litigation with no guarantee of success. Since the 1980s, the federal government has promoted negotiated settlements as the best way for all parties to resolve their water claims. Concluded and implemented at both state and federal levels, these settlements have, in many cases, ended the endless decades of litigation and carry with them the promise of delivering real, "wet" water to the Indian nations. Settlement negotiations have usually been started after an Indian nation or the United States has already become involved in a case involving water rights claimed by a state and other non-Indian water users. The negotiation necessary to achieve a water settlement involves the process of alternative dispute resolution, which allows all the interested parties to participate. This type of resolution is most effective when there are factual disagreements on technical data between the parties; therefore, they sometimes rely on court decisions to decide basic legal questions, such as the priority date of the reservation. Rather than seeking final adjudication in the courts, the parties use the court-determined data to achieve a solution that will satisfy some of the desires of all sides rather than all of the desires of one side. Indian water needs are addressed without eliminating non-Indian water uses, although usually neither side is able to achieve all its goals.

Negotiations in a land of limited water like the American West mean that the Indian nations usually do not receive the full share of water determined by the *Winters* doctrine; but in return they often get money for facilities or projects to put to use the water they are allocated. Such federal funding has allowed Indians to secure not only water rights but also delivered water put to beneficial use. At the same time, non-Indians gain the assurance that they will be able to continue using water without the constant threat of an assertion of *Winters* rights on the part of the Indian nations.

Steven L. Danver

References and Further Reading

Burton, Lloyd. 1991. *American Indian Water Rights and the Limits of Law.* Lawrence: University Press of Kansas.

Colby, Bonnie G., John E. Thorson, and Sarah Britton. 2005. *Negotiating Tribal Water Rights: Fulfilling Promises in the Arid West.* Tucson: University of Arizona Press.

Danver, Steven L. 2002. "Land, Water, and the Right to Remain Indian: The All Indian Pueblo Council and Indian Water Rights." In *Water on the Great Plains: Issues and Policies,* eds. Peter J. Longo and David W. Yoskowitz, 141–167. Lubbock: Texas Tech University Press.

Doherty, Robert. 1993. *Disputed Waters: Native Americans and the Great Lakes Fishery.* Lexington: University Press of Kentucky.

DuMars, Charles T., Marilyn O'Leary, and Albert E. Utton. 1984. *Pueblo Indian Water Rights: Struggle for a Precious Resource.* Tucson: University of Arizona Press.

Hundley, Norris, Jr. 1978. "The Dark and Bloody Ground of Indian Water Rights: Confusion Elevated to Principle." *Western Historical Quarterly,* 9: 477.

Hundley, Norris, Jr. 1982. "The 'Winters' Decision and Indian Water Rights: A Mystery Reexamined." *Western Historical Quarterly* 13: 17.

McCool, Daniel. 1987. *Command of the Waters: Iron Triangles, Federal Water Development, and Indian Water.* Tucson: University of Arizona Press.

McCool, Daniel. 2002. *Native Waters: Contemporary Indian Water Settlements and the Second Treaty Era.* Tucson: University of Arizona Press.

Wilkinson, Charles F. 1992. *Crossing the Next Meridian: Land, Water, and the Future of the American West.* Washington, DC: Island Press.

Worster, Donald. 1985. *Rivers of Empire: Water, Aridity, and the Growth of the American West.* New York: Oxford University Press.

Hunting, Fishing, and Gathering

Throughout most of North America, indigenous subsistence traditionally depended on seasonal cycles of hunting, fishing, and gathering. Even among groups that adopted agriculture or pastoralism, wild animals and plants enriched diets while also providing security against the failure of crops or the loss of livestock. In many areas, traditional subsistence practices continued to furnish Indian families with food, clothing, shelter, and tools long after the introduction of European trade goods. Assimilationist policies and ecological changes gradually undermined these activities as white settlement spread across the continent, yet they still occupy an important place in the economic, social, and religious lives of indigenous communities from Alaska to Florida. Many tribes expressly reserved the right to continue hunting, fishing, and gathering on ceded lands through treaties with the U.S. government. Since the late nineteenth century, however, bitter disputes have developed regarding the exact nature and extent of Indian reserved rights. State authorities and private citizens have tried to restrict or prevent Native hunting, fishing, and gathering outside reservation boundaries. Indians have responded with civil disobedience, test cases, and repeated appeals to the federal government. Although the threat of abrogation remains, the federal courts have generally upheld treaty rights since the early twentieth century, and tribes have become co-managers of valuable natural resources.

Tribal regulation of reserved rights and resources is an important element of modern sovereignty, but it also represents a significant departure from aboriginal practice. Before the negotiation of treaties, prime hunting, fishing, and gathering sites traditionally belonged to individuals and kin groups rather than to clearly defined and tightly bounded "tribes." Among the Straits Salish-speaking peoples of Puget Sound, a man could fish wherever he and his wife had relatives, which generally meant anywhere in Straits Salish territory. Specific reef net and weir locations were owned by individuals who managed and maintained them on behalf of larger kin groups. Similarly, in the Columbia River basin, the rights to a particular fishing rock, island, or scaffold descended through inheritance, and the owner had to grant permission for others to use it. Fishing rights thus created a major incentive to marry outside one's own village, as a person could thereby acquire access to several locations across a wide area. Hunting and gathering grounds also belonged to families with recognized usufructuary privileges, which could be more or less exclusive depending on the natural abundance of the resource in question. As one nineteenth-century American observed of the Ottawa and Ojibwe in Upper Michigan:

> The beaver dams . . . all have owners among the Indians, and are handed down from father to son. The sugar camps, or "sucreries," as the Canadians call them, have all an owner, and no Indian family would think of making sugar at a place where it had no right. Even the cranberry patches, or places in the swamp and bush where the berry is plucked, are family property; and the same with many other things.

Such kinship-centered systems of allocation differed significantly from the centralized tribal ownership outlined in treaties and court decisions, as well as from the European American conception of land and natural resources as marketable commodities. Consequently, the post-treaty period witnessed numerous disagreements within and between tribes in addition to disputes with state governments and non-Indian citizens. This essay focuses on the Pacific Northwest and the Great Lakes, which have been the primary arenas of treaty litigation in the United States, but the patterns evident in those regions hold for most others as well.

Native Interpretations of Treaty Rights

At bottom, the determination of Native Americans to defend their treaty rights reflected indigenous conceptions of treaties, land, and natural resources that were fundamentally different from those of European Americans. Indians traditionally viewed animals, fish, and plants as nonhuman persons and potential sources of spiritual power as well as sustenance. To channel that power and to ensure abundant supplies of food, Native people performed ceremonies intended to show respect and gratitude for the assistance and sacrifices of their nonhuman "brothers and sisters." In the Pacific Northwest, for example, many groups held "first-foods" feasts before allowing their members to start hunting, fishing, and gathering. "At the beginning of each season," recalled Vivian Adams (Yakama) in the early 1990s, "a special group of people was selected for the first gathering of the season's offerings." Chosen for their special skills and intimate knowledge of particular resources, these ceremonial leaders fasted and prayed for their people's success in the coming harvest. "Upon return of the group, a feast was held: for the first digging, the first catch, the first picking, and the first kill." Such individual and collective rituals of thanksgiving took place around Native North America, and many are still observed today (albeit in modified form) by Indians committed to traditional subsistence practices. Their ancestors reserved the right to continue those practices because they could not imagine living without them.

U.S. treaty makers found it expedient to placate Indian concerns, but translation problems and differing cultural expectations often produced divergent interpretations of the treaties and the rights they protected. Whereas policymakers assumed that Indians would ultimately assimilate into white society, federal negotiators recognized that tribal leaders would not sign papers that failed to protect their access to important subsistence resources and sites. Therefore, in order to soften the shock of land cessions and ease the expected transition to European American lifeways, many treaties explicitly secured Indian rights to hunt, fish, and/or gather on ceded lands. As early as 1789, the Wyandot treaty stated that "individuals of the said nation shall be at liberty to hunt within the territory ceded to the United States, without hindrance or molestation, so long as they demean themselves peaceably, and offer no injury or annoyance to any of the subjects or citizens of the said United States." The treaties of 1837, 1842, and 1854 with the Lake Superior Ojibwe guaranteed "[t]he privilege of hunting, fishing, and gathering the wild rice, upon the lands the rivers, and the lakes included in the territory ceded . . . during the pleasure of the United States." After Congress unilaterally ended formal treaty making in 1871, some executive orders, federal statutes, and congressional agreements secured Indian hunting, fishing, and gathering rights on ceded lands. In 1891, for instance, an executive order reducing the Colville Reservation in northeastern Washington State provided that "the right to hunt and fish in common with all other persons on [the ceded lands] shall not be taken away or in anywise abridged."

During treaty councils, Indian representatives often specified the subsistence sites they wished to retain for their people. William Yallup, a descendant of a Yakama treaty signer, recalled that each of the chiefs at the Walla Walla council in 1855 "[gave] a description of what they had reserved in the way of food." Their statements went unrecorded but likely echoed those made at the subsequent Wasco council in central Oregon, where several headmen expressed special concern for their food sources. "Our fishing place on the Columbia we wish to keep," declared the Tenino chief Alexis. "The country you have shown us we are glad to live on it. That is all I have to say. I only came to talk of the fishing ground." Simtustus, a Tygh spokesman, likewise explained: "The [Deschutes] have sustained us in fish. The Falls where we catch the fish, we would like to reserve it. You have seen our country where we get our roots, this is the country I spoke about." The Indians had no intention of surrendering their means of survival, and the treaty commissioners consented to provide the necessary protection.

In many cases, however, the provisions that secured Native subsistence rights also sowed the seeds of future controversy. Although the treaties did not *give* the Indians special privileges, as critics later claimed, the language of the documents often restructured indigenous rights in subtle yet significant ways. The treaties of 1854–1855 concluded in the Pacific Northwest offer a case in point. Each of the agreements made in the Oregon and Washington territories contained a virtually identical version of this article:

> The exclusive right of taking fish in all the streams, where running through or bordering said reservation, is further secured to said confederated tribes and bands of Indians, as also the right of taking fish at all usual and accustomed places, in common with the citizens of the Territory, and of erecting temporary buildings for curing them; together with the privileges of hunting, gathering roots and berries, and pasturing their horses and cattle upon open and unclaimed land.

By vesting subsistence rights in "confederated tribes and bands," this clause purported to transform individual and familial entitlements into tribal ones. At the same time, it allowed competition from American citizens and introduced a false distinction between permanent "rights" and temporary "privileges." The treaty commissioners foresaw the continuance of fishing at traditional sites but presumed that the Indians would abandon their other off-reservation activities as assimilation proceeded and whites filled the surrounding country. Indians generally had different expectations, however, and they left the councils with very different understandings of the treaties.

As members of oral cultures, most tribal leaders remembered the verbal explanations of the treaty terms rather than the words written in the official documents. They did not recognize the legalistic difference between rights and privileges, and the commissioners made no such distinction in their descriptions of the "fishing clause." At the Point No Point council in 1854, for example, Washington territorial governor Isaac Stevens simply declared, "This paper secures your fish. Does not a father give food to his children?" The following year, using a chain of mixed-blood interpreters and Indian criers, Stevens informed the Indians at the Walla Walla meeting:

> You will be allowed to pasture your animals on land not claimed or occupied by settlers, white men. You will be allowed to go on the roads to take your things to market, your horses and cattle. You will be allowed to go to the usual fishing places and fish in common with the whites, and to get roots and berries and to kill game on land not occupied by the whites. All that outside the reservation.

At the Wasco council, Oregon superintendent of Indian affairs Joel Palmer assured Native representatives that they "would always have the privilege to hunt, gather roots and berries, and fish." These promises placed all subsistence activities on an equal footing and set no explicit limits on the purpose, time, or method of taking. Insofar as the Indians understood the phrase "in common with the whites," they probably expected to exercise control over American citizens at the fisheries. They certainly never anticipated the imposition of federal, state, and tribal laws on a system regulated by custom and kinship. "The way we understood, the white man wouldn't have any use for salmon, the berries and the roots," recalled John Skannowa, whose uncle signed the Treaty of Middle Oregon; "[T]he white man wouldn't eat that and didn't know what that food was . . . Joel Palmer indicated that there would be no interference with the Indians' fishing rights at all; that the white men just weren't interested in fishing."

The canons of treaty construction established by the U.S. Supreme Court dictate that treaties must be interpreted as the Indians would have understood them at the time, that all doubtful or ambiguous terms must be resolved in favor of the Indians, and that treaties in general must be liberally construed to the benefit of the Indians. In practice, however, the courts have considered only express treaty or statutory language reserving off-reservation hunting, fishing, and gathering rights. Native oral traditions concerning treaties and treaty councils are typically dismissed as hearsay. For Indians steeped in orality rather than literacy, the agreements comprised everything said and solemnized at the councils, not merely the words written in the official documents. Decades later, descendants of treaty signers continued to relate stories of promises made but not recorded on paper. Most importantly, they insisted that their treaty rights had been reserved in perpetuity. As Yakama fishing rights activist David Sohappy, Sr., explained in 1978, his ancestors understood that the treaty would endure "as long as that mountain stood there, as long as the sun rose in the east and long as the grass grows green in the spring and the rivers flow. To me, that meant forever, not to be abrogated or changed or done away with any other way. That's the way the old people talk."

The central issue in most state-tribal disputes has been the extent to which the states can regulate Indian hunting and fishing rights. Faced with declining stocks of fish and game as well as growing pressure from sport and commercial interests, state governments began implementing conservation programs in the late nineteenth century. Many conservation laws favored non-Indian commercial and recreational users over Indians, who found their off-reservation subsistence activities increasingly constrained by a web of regulations governing illegal gear, trespassing, licensing, closed seasons, prohibited areas, catch limits, and the sale of game or fish. When Indians hunted or fished in violation of these laws—knowingly or unknowingly—state authorities arrested and prosecuted them for poaching. Many also had their guns or gear confiscated, adding to the economic and cultural hardships posed by the inability to take traditional resources for subsistence, ceremony, and sale. This concerted assault on their treaty rights confounded traditional Indians and tribal leaders, who generally regarded their foods as sacred gifts from the Creator, not the property of

state governments representing alien intruders. "I was not brought from a foreign country and did not come here," protested Chief Meninock of the Yakama Nation in 1915. "I was put here by the Creator. We had no cattle, no hogs, no grain, only berries and roots and game and fish. We never thought we would be troubled about these things, and I tell my people, and I believe it, it is not wrong for us to get this food."

In their defense, Indians argued that federal treaties protected their rights to hunt and fish without interference from the states. State courts typically dismissed the concept of reserved rights, and the federal government proved an inconstant ally at best. In the case *Ward v. Race Horse* in 1896 (163 U.S. 504), the U.S. Supreme Court held that Wyoming's game laws superseded Shoshone-Bannock treaty rights because of the Constitution's "equal footing" doctrine. According to this line of argument, Indian treaties negotiated during the territorial period were implicitly abrogated when a territory joined the Union with the all rights and powers of the existing states. In the Pacific Northwest, state courts also used the phrase "in common with the citizens of the Territory" to contend that Indians had only the same rights as non-Indians and were thus equally subject to state laws. Treaty tribes in Washington and Oregon repeatedly challenged this interpretation in the federal courts, and Northwest fishing rights cases reached the Supreme Court seven times during the twentieth century. On each occasion, the Court affirmed the existence of Indian treaty rights but failed to foreclose fully the states' power to regulate them. State governments, in turn, continued to cite *Race Horse* and to prosecute Indians for hunting and fishing in violation of state regulations.

Hunting and Fishing Rights in the Pacific Northwest

Fishing rights have been the greatest source of contention in the Pacific Northwest because of their significance in traditional Indian culture and their immense commercial value. Native Americans of the region faced few challenges to their fishing rights before the 1880s. In most places, Indians supplied the small European American market for salmon and continued to use their traditional sites without interference. Following the advent of improved processing technology, however, salmon became a lucrative commodity, and canneries proliferated around Puget Sound and along the lower Columbia River. Native labor remained essential in the formative years of the packing industry, in which Indians worked as both fishers and processors, but its rapid growth and capitalization soon marginalized them. Cannery-operated traps and wheels forced Indians away from their accustomed fishing sites and reduced the need for their labor, while the white commercial fleet expanded dramatically. By the early 1900s, many Indians had lost access to traditional reef and riverine fisheries. As few could afford the equipment necessary to pursue fish at sea, most fell into a state of poverty and dependency that persisted into the 1970s. Although tribal leaders appealed to the federal government for help, the BIA moved slowly and hesitantly because it favored a policy of assimilation based on agriculture. Fishing, hunting, and gathering represented relics of "savagery" that the government wished to stamp out and replace with a "civilized" lifestyle. Therefore, despite the promises made in the treaties, federal officials allowed many of the region's prime fisheries to pass into non-Indian hands.

The first significant victories for Indian treaty rights came along the Columbia River, where conflict erupted when American settlers and packing companies began claiming aboriginal fisheries and impeding Indian access to the river. In 1884, a white homesteader named Frank Taylor ran a barbed-wire fence across the main path to the Tumwater fishery near The Dalles, Oregon, arguing that the barrier was necessary to stop Indians from camping and pasturing horses on his land. The Justice Department responded with a lawsuit on behalf of the Yakama Nation, *U.S. v. Frank Taylor* (3 Washington Territory 88), which reached the Supreme Court of Washington Territory in January 1887. While recognizing the defendant's title to the land, the court held that "the Treaty privilege of the Indians to take fish was an easement upon it at the time the government conveyed the title and that such title did not extinguish the easement." In other words, treaty Indians had the right to cross private property when passing to and from their traditional fishing sites. This opinion reversed the initial ruling of the district court and remanded the case for a new trial, which upheld the treaty and produced an injunction against Taylor in October 1887. Other fishwheel owners ignored the ruling, however, forcing the federal government to bring a second lawsuit in 1897 against Audubon and Linnaeus Winans.

U.S. v. Winans (198 U.S. 371) became a major landmark in the history of federal Indian law. The

Winans brothers, like Taylor, strung a fence across the trail to the aboriginal Tumwater fishery on the Columbia River. They, too, insisted it was essential to protect their crops and pasture from Indian ponies, yet the brothers lost no time in building a fishwheel to harvest salmon. Hoping to overturn the *Taylor* precedent, their attorneys raised several new arguments to bolster the Winans's property rights claim. In addition to citing the U.S. Supreme Court's recent ruling in *Ward v. Race Horse,* the defense contended that the Winans brothers' use of a state-licensed wheel gave them a right superior to that of Native dipnetters, "since wheel fishing is one of the civilized man's methods, as legitimate as the substitution of the modern combine harvester for the ancient sickle and flail." Even when erected at traditional grounds, the defense team alleged, fishwheels supposedly did not deprive Indians of their common right, because it "[applied] to no certain and defined places."

The federal district court agreed with the defense and ruled in favor of the Winans brothers, but the U.S. Supreme Court reversed the lower court's ruling in the spring of 1905. In an eight-to-one opinion delivered by Joseph McKenna, the justices upheld Yakama rights and established two vital principles governing treaty interpretation. The first stated that treaties must be construed as the Indians understood them at the time and "as justice and reason demand" because the United States had exerted superior power over the "unlettered" tribal representatives. The second, known as the reserved rights doctrine, held that treaties were "not a grant of rights to the Indians, but a grant of rights from them—a reservation of those not granted." Putting these principles into action, the Supreme Court declared that members of the Yakama Nation had retained their existing rights to cross the land, to fish at usual and accustomed places, and to erect temporary houses for curing their catches. Neither private property nor superior technology gave the Winans family an exclusive claim to the fishery, and they could not restrict the Indians in their use of it. Before closing, however, the Court added a bit of dictum that kept open the door to controversy. At the same time that it affirmed the Indians' right to fish "at all usual and accustomed places," the ruling did not "restrain the state unreasonably, if at all, in the regulation of that right."

The battle over regulation intensified during the next thirty years as Indians ran afoul of proliferating fish and game laws. In 1915, Washington State implemented its first fisheries code forbidding certain traditional techniques such as spearing and snaring. The following year, the state's supreme court ruled against two Indians convicted of fishing with illegal gear and without state licenses. In both cases, *State v. Towessnute* (89 Wash. 478) and *State v. Alexis* (89 Wash. 492), the justices held that the defendant's treaty right to fish "in common" merely gave him the same privileges as non-Indian citizens. *State v. Wallahee* (143 Wash. 117) applied the same logic to Indian hunting on "open and unclaimed lands" outside reservation boundaries. Although the Office of Indian Affairs urged appeals of *Alexis* and *Towessnute,* the federal government declined to challenge state authority on this issue. The U.S. Supreme Court had recently reaffirmed state regulatory powers in *Kennedy v. Becker* (241 U.S. 556), a case involving Seneca fishing rights in New York, and the prospects for reversal seemed dim. During the 1930s, however, a general shift toward self-determination in Indian affairs created a more favorable climate for tribal claims and assertions of sovereignty. The Columbia River treaty tribes pushed for another test case, and in 1942 the U.S. Supreme Court handed them a qualified victory in *Tulee v. Washington* (315 U.S. 681), which exempted Indians from state license requirements. States could still regulate tribal hunting and fishing for conservation purposes but not by imposing license fees that effectively "[acted] upon the Indians as a charge for exercising the very right their ancestors intended to reserve."

Meanwhile, disagreements within and between the tribes mounted even as they struggled to fend off the common threat of state regulation. With salmon runs sagging and other fisheries disappearing beneath dam reservoirs, many mid-Columbia Indians migrated to the remaining sites between The Dalles and Celilo Falls. The Celilo Fish Committee (CFC), created in 1936 to settle the resulting disputes, provided a forum for competing visions of the fishery. Local residents and people with ancestral fishing stations viewed treaty rights as a legal umbrella beneath which traditional rules still applied. By contrast, newcomers and advocates of tribal control embraced the framework established in the treaties and reinforced through litigation. As Andrew Barnhart explained in 1942,

> I was appointed a fish committeeman from my Umatilla Reservation to protect my tribal rights. I can remember the old people that fished here at Celilo—Wyam Indians. But the white man

> has come here and ruled your location as a tribal relation . . . this Committee will not determine one individual ownership to one location. But we must rule equal right.

The completion of The Dalles Dam in 1957 ended the fishery at Celilo but not the controversy. By 1961, when *Whitefoot v. United States* (293 F.2d 658) expressly defined treaty rights as tribal property, the Warm Springs and Yakama tribes had joined the Quinault and Tulalip of the Washington coast in passing their own fishing ordinances. Traditionalists still objected to the presumption of tribal authority, but their protests were largely drowned out by the climactic confrontation between the tribes and the states.

The battle over Northwest Indian fishing rights peaked in the 1960s and 1970s. Salmon runs had reached record lows after a century of overfishing, habitat destruction, industrial pollution, and dam building. White commercial and sports fishermen generally found it easier to blame each other and the Indians—who took only 5 percent of the catch in 1970—and the regional media often echoed popular claims that tribal fishing endangered the resource. Indian court victories further stoked white resentment of the "special rights" bestowed by the treaties. Building on the precedent set in *Tulee* and *Makah v. Schoettler* (192 F. 2d 224), the decision in *Maison v. Confederated Tribes of the Umatilla Reservation* (312 F. 2d 169) in 1963 established more stringent criteria for state regulation of Indian fishing. The Ninth Circuit Court of Appeals, ruling against the Oregon Game Commission, held that states must prove both the necessity and the indispensability of any conservation regulations imposed on tribal fishing; in other words, Indian treaty rights could be curtailed only if restricting other users had failed to protect the resource. As that case made its way through the court system, however, Washington State cracked down on Nisqually and Puyallup fishers at the southern end of Puget Sound. Indian activists responded with a new tactic, the "fish-in," which triggered violent reactions and moved the fishing rights controversy into the national spotlight.

Fish-ins posed a direct challenge to state authority. Modeled after the contemporaneous sit-ins of the African American civil rights movement, they entailed deliberately breaking the law in order to provoke a response from state authorities, trigger test cases, and publicize the issue of treaty rights. Puyallup fishers Robert Satiacum and James Young pioneered the strategy in 1954, when they violated a ban on set nets after notifying state agencies of their intention to do so. By the mid-1960s, fish-ins had spread to Frank's Landing on the Nisqually River and Cook's Landing on the Columbia, which remained focal points of protest for the next ten years. Activists such as Billy Frank, Jr. (Nisqually), and David Sohappy, Sr., risked arrest numerous times and eventually came to personify the struggle for the non-Indian public. Some tribal members considered fish-ins counterproductive and called the protestors renegades, but they drew increasing support from sympathetic Indians and non-Indians around the country. The National Indian Youth Council sent Hank Adams and Mel Thom to help organize demonstrations, the Native American Rights Fund offered legal assistance, and Janet McCloud (Tulalip) mobilized the Survival of American Indians Association for a major march on the Washington State capitol. Non-Indian allies included the American Friends Service Committee, a Quaker social justice organization; the American Civil Liberties Union, which defended Muckleshoot fishermen in court; and celebrities such as comedian Dick Gregory and actor Marlon Brando, who joined a fish-in in 1964 on the Puyallup River. Brando's arrest, in particular, made the fish-ins national news and encouraged further media coverage.

As protests became more frequent and received more attention, state reactions and local anti-Indian sentiment grew increasingly violent. Some white fishermen vented their anger by cutting nets, stealing fish, setting boats adrift, and even threatening Indians with physical harm. Several Indian fishers complained of being shot at, and in 1971 Hank Adams received a bullet wound from two white men who allegedly said "You . . . Indians think you own everything." State police and game wardens also clashed with tribal fishers during raids on off-reservation fishing sites. Reporters and television crews captured dramatic images of Indians being clubbed, tear-gassed, and dragged across the ground. State patrol boats shadowed Indian fishing canoes and sometimes spilled their occupants into the water to stop them from setting nets. Just as scenes of police brutality in Birmingham, Alabama, galvanized public support for the civil rights movement, media coverage of the fish-ins raised a national outcry and placed mounting pressure on the federal government. In 1966, the Justice Department signaled a shift in policy by declaring that it would accept tribal requests to defend Indians

arrested for fishing off reservation under tribal regulations.

Federal intervention on behalf of the treaty tribes began with *Puyallup Tribe v. Department of Game,* which came to be known as the Puyallup Trilogy because it reached the U.S. Supreme Court on three separate occasions. The case began in 1966, when Washington sued to prevent Nisqually and Puyallup tribe members from fishing contrary to state laws. Federal attorneys filed an *amicus curiae* ("friend of the court") brief in support of the tribes, and the U.S. Supreme Court heard their appeal in 1968. *Puyallup* I (391 U.S. 392) upheld tribal rights to catch both salmon and steelhead, a migratory trout species that the state had classified as a game fish, but it also affirmed the state's power to regulate off-reservation fishing so long as its conservation measures met "appropriate standards" and did not discriminate against Indians. The following year, U.S. District Court Judge Robert Belloni applied these criteria to the Columbia River in the combined cases of *Sohappy v. Smith* (302 F. Supp. 899) and *U.S. v. Oregon.* Going a step further, he also decreed that the treaty tribes must be allowed a meaningful role in the regulatory process and guaranteed "a fair and equitable share" of the catch. While Oregon reluctantly complied with that ruling, Washington continued its vigorous enforcement efforts against the tribes of Puget Sound. In 1970, after a heavily armed force of state wardens and local police attacked a large Puyallup fish camp, the federal government initiated *U.S. v. Washington* (384 F. Supp. 312) to clarify the rights of fourteen treaty tribes (later increased to twenty) that chose to participate in the litigation.

U.S. District Court Judge George Boldt conducted a thorough review of the evidence and arguments with the goal of settling the controversy once and for all. His decision in the first phase of the trial, issued in 1974, shocked state officials and outraged many non-Indians despite the existence of sound legal precedents. Taking into account contemporary dictionary definitions and the probable Indian understanding of the treaties, Boldt interpreted the pivotal phrase "in common with the citizens of the Territory" to mean "sharing equally." Thus, the tribes had a right to 50 percent of the annual salmon and steelhead harvest (excluding fish caught on the reservations and for ceremonial or subsistence purposes) as well as the right to participate in management of the resource. The state could regulate off-reservation fishing only if its measures met appropriate standards, did not discriminate against Indians, and served both "reasonable and necessary" conservation purposes. If the runs could be efficiently preserved by other means, including the restriction of nontreaty fishing "to the full extent," then the Indian fishery could not be regulated at all. Judge Boldt, anticipating resistance to his ruling, followed Belloni's lead in opting to exercise continuing jurisdiction over the case and to issue his own interim plan for management of the fisheries.

As expected, *U.S. v. Washington,* the so-called Boldt Decision, faced massive opposition from Washington State and its large population of commercial and sports fishermen. Many whites signaled their disapproval with a wave of political protests and illegal fishing in violation of court-ordered closures. Some individuals made threats of violence against Indians and tried to interfere with tribal fishing, which led to several tense confrontations on the water, while commercial and sports fishing organizations lobbied for legislation and launched test cases to reverse Boldt. Two such lawsuits, *Puget Sound Gillnetters Association v. Moos* (565 P.2d 1151) and *Washington State Commercial Passenger Fishing Vessel Association v. Tollefson* (571 P.2d 1373), received favorable hearings from the Washington State Supreme Court in 1977. Although the defendant in each case was the state director of fisheries, Washington actually encouraged non-Indian defiance by working aggressively to obstruct and overturn the Boldt Decision. State agencies refused to issue regulations guaranteeing the tribal allocation, the state attorney general pressed for a high court hearing, state courts dismissed citations against white "outlaw" fishers, and the state's congressional delegation introduced several bills to abrogate all treaty rights. Congress rejected those measures, as it had done with earlier state proposals to buy out tribal fishing rights, but the U.S. Supreme Court did agree to review both the *Washington* and *Puyallup* cases, against a backdrop of rising racial animosity.

To the chagrin of Washington State attorney general Slade Gorton, a lifelong opponent of tribal sovereignty, the Court again upheld Indian treaty rights, with only minor qualifications. In 1973, *Puyallup* II (414 U.S. 44) had struck down a state ban on tribal net fishing for steelhead because it discriminated against Indians. Four years later, amid the furor over the Boldt Decision, *Puyallup* III (433 U.S. 165) affirmed the allocation of 45 percent of wild steelhead runs to the tribes. State officials hoped that the Supreme Court would throw out Judge Boldt's 50-50 division, but its decision of 1979 in *Washington*

v. Washington State Commercial Passenger Fishing Vessel Association (433 U.S. 658) merely modified his formula. Whereas Boldt had excluded the ceremonial, subsistence, and on-reservation catch from the Indians' share, the Court held that those fish should be counted against the tribal allocation. Furthermore, the majority opinion fixed 50 percent as a maximum share, intended to secure "so much as, but not more than, is necessary to provide the Indians with a livelihood—that is to say, a moderate living." Although the Court failed to define "a moderate living," it suggested that the tribes' allocation could be reduced due to dwindling membership or economic development that reduced their reliance on fish. For the time being, however, the state had to comply with the district court's order and apportion fish on an equal basis. To do otherwise would violate the supremacy clause of the U.S. Constitution, which describes treaties as "the supreme law of the land" and therefore binding on state governments.

As Washington moved slowly to align its policies with Boldt's initial ruling, Phase II of the trial tackled two outstanding issues: Did the Indian allocation include hatchery fish, and did the treaties imply a right to environmental protection of fish runs and fish habitat? Judge William Orrick, who replaced Boldt upon the latter's retirement in 1979, answered both questions positively. The tribes needed hatchery fish to replace the wild runs destroyed or depleted by environmental degradation, he argued, and the state would have no incentive to rehabilitate salmon habitat or to prevent further destruction if Indians could catch only wild fish. In a concession to non-Indian economic concerns, however, Orrick ruled that the state had only to refrain from degrading the resource to an extent that would deprive Indians of their "moderate living needs." This ambiguous interpretation limited the tribes' ability to enjoin activities that harm fish runs and habitat, and it also failed to define what constitutes a moderate living. They immediately appealed, arguing for the restoration of salmon populations to pre-treaty levels or at least for a higher standard of "no significant deterioration." Meanwhile, the states and various industrial interests tried equally hard to overturn Orrick's ruling, which they deemed a threat to hydroelectric power generation and economic growth. The decision stood, though it has been reviewed several times to clarify its meaning, and "Boldt II" remains one of the most controversial and potentially far-reaching aspects of *U.S. v. Washington.*

Judge Boldt's hope of ending the controversy dimmed further in the 1980s and 1990s due to inter- and intratribal disputes over harvest allocation and the ownership of usual and accustomed fishing sites. Although they have common adversaries and a mutual commitment to preserve the salmon, the tribes also compete for fish and have not shared their portions equally. By the mid-1980s, the Lummi had developed a large ocean fleet capable of catching close to half the entire allocation for the twenty-four treaty tribes in western Washington. Tribes located on southern Puget Sound, with less valuable "terminal" fisheries and little capital with which to "gear up," fear that the Lummi and other northern tribes will intercept and deplete the runs before others have a chance to fish. The Muckleshoot, Nisqually, Puyallup, and Squaxin Island tribes have asked the courts to ensure more equitable shares, while the Skokomish and Klallam tribes have challenged Lummi claims to various fishing areas around Puget Sound. Competition for an already-scarce resource has also led some treaty tribes, such as the Quinault and Tulalip, to oppose the efforts of nontreaty groups seeking federal recognition. Within tribes, tensions have developed over the practice of "double-dipping" (fishing with state licenses on days closed to Indians), challenges to tribal regulation, and control of specific fishing sites. The tribes have worked to develop management strategies more appropriate to their cultures and conceptions of the resource, but the continued decline of salmon populations has made it difficult to avoid both internal and external conflicts.

Since the 1970s, the federal government has generally followed its established pattern of alternately helping and hindering Northwest tribes in the exercise of their rights and the protection of endangered resources. In 1982, federal agents arrested activist David Sohappy and eighteen other Yakama fishers in an anti-poaching sting operation the press later dubbed "Salmonscam." Sohappy and his son ultimately spent five years in prison, despite the fact that government allegations proved vastly overblown, and non-Indians received only fines for the same crime. The Bureau of Indian Affairs then tried to evict the Sohappys and other Indian families from the in-lieu fishing sites where they lived, arguing that the sites were tribal property and not intended for permanent occupancy. Meanwhile, the Army Corps of Engineers dragged its heels in completing additional in-lieu sites promised fifty years earlier when Bonneville Dam inundated traditional

fishing locations in the Columbia River gorge. The corps has also joined the Bonneville Power Administration in opposing tribal efforts to make the dams and the river more hospitable for salmon. The tribes, in turn, have sued several times to force the Commerce Department to reduce the ocean seasons set by the Pacific Marine Fisheries Commission (PFMC). Although the courts have resisted tribal demands, they have required the PFMC and other agencies to work with the tribes in creating mutually acceptable management plans.

The shift toward cooperative management is one of several important legacies of the long struggle over Northwest Indian treaty rights. Most of the tribes concerned in *U.S. v. Oregon* and *U.S. v. Washington* currently operate their own fish hatcheries and employ their own harvest managers, enforcement officers, biologists, and technicians. They also work collectively through the Northwest Indian Fisheries Commission, founded in 1974 to coordinate the regional treaty councils in western Washington, and the Columbia River Inter-Tribal Fish Commission. In addition to providing technical assistance to the tribes and information to the non-Indian public, these organizations consult and negotiate with a bewildering array of state, federal, and international bodies. The tribes have thus become key players in fisheries management and environmental politics, fueling a resurgence of tribal sovereignty to match the economic and cultural revitalization many reservations experienced following the Boldt Decision.

The Makah, whose treaty of 1854 also reserved the right to hunt whales, reported a similar upsurge in tribal pride when they resumed the practice after an eighty-year hiatus. Makah whalers had voluntarily stopped hunting in the 1920s, when gray whales became endangered due to commercial exploitation, but in 2001 the tribe successfully petitioned the federal government and the International Whaling Commission for permission to take five whales per year. The resulting protests and court challenges show that treaty rights and tribal traditions, though now on firmer legal footing, remain poorly understood by much of the non-Indian public.

Hunting and Fishing Rights in the Upper Midwest

The controversy over Indian treaty rights in the Upper Midwest has followed a trajectory similar to the struggle in the Pacific Northwest. Starting in the seventeenth century, the extension of the European fur trade into the Great Lakes region disrupted the aboriginal economy of the Ottawa and Ojibwe (Chippewa/Anishinaabe), gradually drawing them into a market system over which they had little control. Initially, many Indians adapted to this new economic network by integrating wage labor into their subsistence cycle, but the commodification of natural resources eventually undermined Native autonomy and self-sufficiency. By 1900, market hunting and logging had decimated the animal populations and pine forests of northern Michigan, Wisconsin, and Minnesota. Indians maintained a toehold in the fishing industry as wage laborers and continued their seasonal migrations as best they could. As the white fishing industry developed, however, the same capital-intensive operations that forced the Indians off the lakes systematically depleted one native species after another. Industrial pollution and lamprey infestation (caused by the St. Lawrence Seaway) aggravated the effects of overfishing, leading to the complete collapse of the Great Lakes commercial fishery in the 1950s. The surrounding states restocked the waters with popular game fish such as trout and coho salmon, but this lucrative sports fishery soon ran headlong into the rising Native American consciousness of the postwar decades.

The Indian peoples of the Great Lakes, like those of the Pacific Northwest, had long borne the brunt of state conservation efforts in spite of their treaty-reserved rights to hunt, fish, and gather on ceded lands. Wisconsin first proscribed gillnetting in the early 1850s, and in 1868 the state began setting seasons for deer, game birds, and fur-bearing animals. Although these regulations were not strictly enforced until the 1880s, they effectively reduced the land area within which Indians could pursue their traditional economy without breaking the law. The expansion of state hatchery programs and the Northwoods tourist industry in the early twentieth century encouraged fish and game officials to tighten their grip on tribal hunting and fishing. Wisconsin even sought to impose its regulations on certain reservation lands in the 1930s, by which time "violating" had become a way of life and a source of pride for many Indians. Midwestern state courts proved just as unsympathetic to treaty rights as had those in the Northwest. In 1930, in the case *People v. Chosa*, for instance, several members of Michigan's Keweenaw Bay band of Chippewa stood trial for fishing contrary to state regulations. The Michigan Supreme Court concluded that they no longer had

any off-reservation treaty rights because "when one becomes a citizen of the United States [as Indians had in 1924], he casts off both the rights and obligations of his former nationality and takes on those which pertain to citizens of the country."

Native hunters and fishers in Michigan moved from covert evasion to outright defiance of state laws during the 1960s. In 1965, stirred by news of the Northwest fish-ins, William Jondreau of the L'Anse band of Chippewa tested his rights under their 1854 treaty by informing state officials of his intention to net lake trout out of season. Six years later, *State of Michigan v. William Jondreau* (384 Mich. 539) reached the state supreme court, which overruled one of its own opinions (*Chosa*) and upheld the treaty. The implications of Jondreau's victory remained uncertain because few of Michigan's Indians were party to the agreement of 1854, but the ruling helped inspire further litigation. In the case *People v. LeBlanc* of 1976 (399 Mich. 31), brought by Bay Mills band member Albert LeBlanc, the Michigan Supreme Court affirmed Chippewa and Ottawa fishing rights under the treaty of 1836. Citing the precedent set in *Puyallup* I, the court held that the state's ban on gillnetting could only be applied to Indians if the state first showed that it was necessary for conservation and did not discriminate against them. Skeptical of the outcome in the state courts, the Bay Mills Community and the Sault Ste. Marie tribe of Chippewa also took action in federal court. The U.S. Departments of Justice and Interior intervened on their behalf, and their case reached the U.S. District Court in 1979.

U.S. v. Michigan (471 F. Supp. 192) ultimately brought mixed results for the Indians. In the opinion, Judge Noel Fox affirmed Chippewa and Ottawa treaty rights to fish the Great Lakes with modern technology and without regard to state law. "The right is not a static right today any more than it was during treaty times," he wrote, and therefore it was not limited as to the species and origin of fish or the purpose, time, or manner of taking, as long as the Indians obeyed tribal and federal regulations. The U.S. Supreme Court refused to hear the state's appeal. The Michigan Department of Natural Resources (MDNR), in turn, continued to enforce its regulations against Indian fishers and failed to protect them against white vigilantes affiliated with Stop Gill Netting and other anti-treaty groups that sprang up in the wake of the ruling. Spurred by lurid MDNR and press portrayals of Indian fishing as a threat to conservation and tourism, sportsmen harassed tribal fishers and destroyed their gear as state wardens and police looked on. State officials made political hay of the issue and pushed for congressional abrogation of treaty rights. Michigan's intransigence prevented a resolution to the dispute until 1985, when a new judge appointed Francis McGovern to negotiate a settlement out of court. The subsequent Sault Ste. Marie Agreement split the fishery into state and tribal zones and compensated the tribes for their diminished rights, but it offered little to the small-boat Indian fishers who found themselves confined to less productive northern waters.

Similar events transpired in Wisconsin, where Fred and Mike Tribble of the Lac Courte Oreilles (LCO) band of Chippewa initiated a test case in 1974. Following their arrest for spearfishing out of season and off the reservation, the tribe filed a federal suit against Lester Voigt, head of the Wisconsin Department of Natural Resources (WDNR). U.S. District Court Judge James Doyle initially determined that the Indians could not hunt, fish, and gather off the reservation free of state regulation. He contended that, whereas the treaties of 1837 and 1842 had expressly reserved usufructuary rights, the treaty of 1854 had not done so, thereby implicitly suspending them. In 1983, however, the U.S. Court of Appeals overturned Doyle's decision in *La Courte Oreilles v. Voigt* (700 F. 2d 341) and remanded it to the district court for clarification. Commonly known as LCO I or the Voigt Decision, the appeals court ruling held that explicit language would have been necessary to suspend treaty-reserved rights, given their legal standing and the Indians' interpretation of the treaty of 1854. The state could only regulate those rights in the interests of conservation, public health, or safety and then only if the regulations were reasonable and necessary to preserve a particular species, were the least restrictive possible, and did not discriminate against Indians. Judge Doyle's adjudication of the case continued until 1991, producing eight subsequent rulings (LCO II-IX) to define the exact scope of Chippewa rights, while the controversy raged outside the courtroom.

The furor over the Voigt Decision in northern Wisconsin rivaled the earlier backlash against the Boldt Decision. White sportsmen bitterly denounced the court's alleged extension of "unlimited rights" to the Indians under "old treaties," echoing the WDNR's claim that tribal hunting and fishing would destroy the resources. State-sponsored studies have shown that Indian spearfishers and gillnetters normally take less than 3 percent of the annual walleye

and musky harvests on northern lakes, while the tribal deer harvest remains lower than the yearly roadkill rate. Nevertheless, anti-Indian sentiment flared under the influence of economic recession and ill-informed media coverage. Blaming Indians for the decline of the tourist industry, anti-treaty groups such as Protect Americans' Rights and Resources (PARR) and Stop Treaty Abuse-Wisconsin (STA-W) spouted racist rhetoric and encouraged their members to disrupt the spearfishing season. Signs and bumper stickers proliferated, proclaiming, "Save a Walleye, Spear an Indian," and angry crowds gathered at boat landings to hurl rocks and racial slurs at Chippewa fishers. Out on the water, non-Indian boats tried to block lake access, harassed spearfishers with spotlights, and attempted to swamp their vessels. Some Indians even reported receiving death threats or hearing gunshots, yet local police and local courts did little to curtail the protests on the grounds that they were protected by the First Amendment.

Meanwhile, despite Governor Anthony Earl's call for cooperation between state agencies and tribal governments, many bureaucrats and politicians worked hard to obstruct and overturn the Voigt Decision. Early interim agreements, intended to allow for the meaningful exercise of Chippewa rights while litigation continued, proved so restrictive that some tribal leaders considered them a bad joke. The WDNR also imposed excessively low bag limits on non-Indian anglers, sparking increased hostility, which in turn compelled Chippewa fishers to voluntarily reduce their catches. Republican congressman Frank Sensenbrenner introduced an unsuccessful treaty abrogation bill in 1987, while Wisconsin's entire congressional delegation signed a letter threatening tribal governments with drastic budget cuts if they refused to curb off-reservation hunting and fishing. Two years later, a tribal referendum on the Lac du Flambeau reservation rejected a $42 million buyout of the band's rights, proposed by the state attorney general. Other reservations proved more amenable to state leasing proposals, however, and in 1991 the Chippewa collectively agreed not to appeal their loss in LCO VIII (timber rights) or seek back damages if the state would respect the other rulings.

The battle in the courts and on the lakes exposed significant cultural and strategic differences within and among the nine Ojibwe bands in Wisconsin. Following their victorious appeal of LCO I, they formed the Voigt Inter-Tribal Task Force to reach a consensus on the meaning of the decision. Tribal leaders agreed to define treaty rights as tribal and not individual property, but they quibbled over which rights to prioritize and how much to demand from the state. The Lac Courte Oreilles and Lac du Flambeau (LdF) bands took the most aggressive stance. LCO tribal members generally preferred hunting over fishing, though, whereas the Mole Lake band expressed more interest in protecting its rights to harvest wild rice. The St. Croix tribal council initially wanted nothing more than free state fishing licenses, leading LdF spearer Tom Maulson to deride them as the "Zebco tribe" (Zebco being a popular brand of fishing tackle). Maulson's Wa-Swa-Gon Treaty Association organized the fight against the state's buyout proposal, which some tribal members considered reasonable because only a minority of Chippewa still exercised their treaty rights. Wa-Swa-Gon supporters countered this argument by encouraging the revival of cultural traditions and transforming the fishing spear and the torch (historically used to "shine" walleye at night) into key symbols of Chippewa identity. They also advocated a strategy of nonviolence on the lakes and welcomed the presence of non-Indian "Witness in Wisconsin" observers at the landings. Other spearfishers, by contrast, counseled militant self-defense and regarded the witnesses as an unnecessary provocation to local whites.

Minnesota Chippewa have likewise divided at times over the best approach to resolving the treaty rights controversy. In 1988, the Boise Forte, Grand Portage, and Fond du Lac bands negotiated an agreement with the state to settle a lawsuit Grand Portage had brought to affirm its rights under the treaties of 1837 and 1854. By signing the agreement, the bands consented to stop or limit the exercise of certain off-reservation rights in return for an annual payment from the state and cooperative enforcement of fish and wildlife codes. Fond du Lac subsequently withdrew from the agreement, however, choosing to return to court for an adjudication of its rights. The Mille Lacs band also sued the state in 1990, seeking a declaratory judgment that they retained usufructuary rights under the treaty of 1837 and an injunction against state interference with those rights. Nine years later, the U.S. Supreme Court upheld the treaty in *Minnesota v. Mille Lacs Band of Chippewa Indians* (526 U.S. 172) by a narrow five-to-four vote. Six bands of Wisconsin Chippewa intervened in the suit, demonstrating the extent to which the tribes share common interests despite their various differences.

They cooperate through the Great Lakes Indian Fish and Wildlife Commission (GLIFWC) to coordinate conservation and enforcement efforts, disseminate information to the public, gather scientific data, and confront environmental threats such as mercury contamination. Thus, in the Upper Midwest as in the Pacific Northwest, the struggle for treaty rights has stimulated a revitalization of tribal governance and intertribal cooperation as well as renewed interest and pride in Native traditions.

Currently, the criteria for state regulation of Indian hunting and fishing rights depend on the particular treaty or statute and the various federal, state, and tribal interests involved. Generally speaking, tribes may regulate on-reservation hunting and fishing free from state interference. In some cases, however, tribal governments lack the authority to prevent non-Indians from hunting or fishing on reservation lands that are not owned by individual Indians or by the tribe itself. Furthermore some federal conservation laws (e.g., the Eagle Protection Act) preempt both on- and off-reservation treaty rights. State governments may regulate off-reservation hunting and fishing only when they present a sufficient conservation or safety risk. To justify such regulation, the state must demonstrate that a significant hazard exists, that the state cannot meet its objectives by regulating non-Indians alone, and that the regulation is the least restrictive alternative available. Cooperative management has become the new paradigm in resource conservation, and negotiation has gradually replaced litigation as the preferred means of dispute resolution between states and tribes. Tribal governments, in particular, have grown more cautious about going to court, as states' rights and property rights ideologies have resurged within the federal judiciary and the national legislature. Still, having fought so hard to protect their hunting and fishing rights, Indians must continue to fight to ensure that the resources do not disappear. After all, as Judge William Orrick noted in reference to the Boldt Decision, "fifty percent of nothing is nothing."

Gathering Rights

Treaty-reserved gathering rights have generally caused less conflict than tribal hunting and fishing because many food and medicinal plants harvested by Native Americans possess little appeal or commercial value for non-Indians. In cases where competition does exist, or where ecological changes have caused scarcity, gathering rights have become the subject of litigation and legislation. Wild rice (*manoomin*), a staple of the Ojibwe diet since the seventeenth century, offers a prime example of this pattern. All the Chippewa treaties in the Great Lakes region either explicitly or implicitly reserved the right to gather wild rice on ceded lands. Despite federal efforts to replace rice harvesting with "civilized" agriculture, most Chippewa continued to gather manoomin well into the twentieth century, typically taking enough to supply both their own needs and the small non-Indian market. During the 1960s, however, the introduction of combine harvesters and paddy ricing enabled whites to gain control of the expanding industry. Although many Chippewa had readily adopted earlier technological advances, they could not afford the expensive new machines and protested their destructive impact on natural rice beds. Minnesota eventually banned mechanical harvesters and passed conservation laws to protect the resource, but not before overproduction had ruined many rice lakes and glutted the market. Falling prices forced more Indians out of the market, while industrial pollution and resort development contaminated or closed off access to many of the remaining rice beds. By the 1970s, few Chippewa harvested manoomin commercially, though many still gather it for subsistence and ceremonial purposes today.

As with hunting and fishing rights, state regulation of ricing presented a problem for tribes without sizable rice lakes on their reservations. Consequently, several bands have sued to secure their rights to gather off reservation, starting in 1939 with *U.S. v. 4,450.72 Acres of Land* (72 F. Supp. 167). That case, brought by the federal government on behalf of the Minnesota Chippewa, prompted Congress to establish the Wild Rice Lake Reserve for their exclusive use. Under state law, however, Indian harvesters had to pay license fees and accept oversight by the Department of Game and Fish (DGF) even when ricing on the reserve. Many Chippewa simply ignored the license requirement, and DGF harassment became a regular feature of harvest time. The Minnesota Supreme Court upheld the state's regulatory role in *State v. Keezer* (292 N.W.2d 714), a decision in 1980 stemming from the arrest of two Chippewa ricers, but the U.S. Supreme Court's recent ruling in *Mille Lacs* forced the state back to the table. Wisconsin has also entered into negotiations since 1987, when LCO III (653 F. Supp. 1420) affirmed Ojibwe rights to harvest wild plants on all public lands within the bands' ceded territories. Although the state retains some regulatory power over wild rice, numerous other species fall under a memorandum of understanding (MOU) reached between the U.S. Forest Service and ten GLIFWC tribes. A model of cooperative management, this MOU provides for tribal enforcement of tribally approved codes, including a requirement that harvesters obtain annual off-reservation permits.

In the Pacific Northwest, treaty tribes reserved "the privileges of hunting, gathering roots and berries, and pasturing their horses and cattle upon open and unclaimed land." Their subsequent defense of these "privileges" revealed that they applied the phrase "usual and accustomed places" to all subsistence activities—not just fishing—and they logically tried to use rights won in fishing litigation to support their claims to off-reservation gathering sites. At a hearing in 1928 in Washington, D.C., for example, Noah James Saluskin of the Yakama Nation testified that "my forefathers reserved the right to fish and hunt, gather roots outside the reservation on ceded lands and I think I have a right to gather roots and berries." In 1932, when an army of unemployed non-Indians invaded tribal huckleberry fields in the Cascade mountains, local Forest Service officials made an effort to accommodate Yakama claims by setting aside some three thousand acres for exclusive Indian use. This "handshake agreement" has survived into the present, but it took a federal court decision in 1984 (*State of Washington v. Miller*, 689 P.2d 81) to establish that there is "no operative distinction" between treaty-reserved "rights" and "privileges." Fifteen tribes party to *U.S. v. Washington* also returned to court in 1989 to clarify their rights to harvest shellfish on privately owned tidelands. Five years later, U.S. District Court judge Edward Rafeedie held that the treaties' "in common" language meant that the tribes had reserved gathering rights to half of all shellfish from their usual and accustomed places, except those specifically set aside for non-Indian shellfish cultivation purposes. As with hunting and fishing rights, however, securing access to shellfish beds and berry fields does not guarantee that there will be adequate and uncontaminated resources to harvest. Pollution, habitat destruction, and commercial exploitation still threaten to render treaty rights a set of empty promises.

The struggle to preserve these hard-won rights will likely continue in the future as ongoing economic competition and environmental degradation take their toll on indigenous plant, fish, and animal populations. Although relatively few Native Americans in the United States (excluding Alaska) now depend on hunting, fishing, and gathering for subsistence, those activities have become powerful symbols of Indian identity. To those who still exercise them, treaty rights are integral to cultural and religious practices that define what it means to be a tribe member. Accordingly, many elders lament the fact that younger people often express little interest in traditional hunting, fishing, and gathering practices. "Today it's hard to be an Indian person, and it's easy to be white," observed Edward James (Umatilla) during the sesquicentennial commemoration of his tribe's treaty of 1855. "If we don't hunt, fish, dig roots and pick berries then what are we? We're certainly not being *Natitayt* [Indian people]." To protect the old ways, however, Native Americans have also developed the legal, political, and scientific expertise necessary to secure a place at the negotiating table. Contemporary tribal leaders understand that both traditional and modern forms of knowledge must be passed on to future generations and that the battle to uphold their rights has not ended either in the court of law or in the court of public opinion. "There are citizens who believe that the treaties are not living documents, that they are out of date, obsolete and no longer useful," reminded Roberta Conner, director of the Tamastslikt Cultural Institute on the Umatilla Reservation. She warned, "Indeed, treaties were the means through which all others obtained legal title to Indian lands, and it would behoove non-Indians to protect and uphold the treaties today."

Andrew H. Fisher

References and Further Reading

Bentley, Shannon. 1992. "Indians' Right to Fish: The Background, Impact, and Legacy of *United States v. Washington*." *American Indian Law Review* 17(1): 1–35.

Boxberger, Daniel L. 1989. *To Fish in Common: The Ethnohistory of Lummi Indian Salmon Fishing*. Lincoln: University of Nebraska Press.

Bruun, Rita. 1982. "The Boldt Decision: Legal Victory, Political Defeat." *Law and Policy Quarterly* 4: 271–298.

Cohen, Fay G. 1986. *Treaties on Trial: The Continuing Controversy over Northwest Fishing Rights*. Seattle: University of Washington Press.

Danielsen, Karen C., and Jonathan H. Gilbert. 2002. "Ojibwe Off-Reservation Harvest of Wild Plants." In *Nontimber Forest Products in the United States*, eds. Eric T. Jones, Rebecca J. McLain, and James Weigand, 282–292. Lawrence: University Press of Kansas.

DeMallie, Raymond J. 1980. "Touching the Pen: Plains Indian Treaty Councils in Ethnohistorical Perspective." In *Ethnicity in the Great Plains,* ed. Frederick C. Luebke, 38–51. Lincoln: University of Nebraska Press.

Doherty, Robert. 1993. *Disputed Waters: Native Americans and the Great Lakes Fishery.* Lexington: University Press of Kentucky.

Fisher, Andrew H. 1999. "This I Know from the Old People: Yakama Indian Treaty Rights as Oral Tradition." *Montana, The Magazine of Western History* 49: 2–17.

Fisher, Andrew H. 2004. "Tangled Nets: Treaty Rights and Tribal Identities at Celilo Falls." *Oregon Historical Quarterly* 105 (Summer): 178–211.

Fixico, Donald L. 1987. "Chippewa Fishing and Hunting Rights and the Voigt Decision." In *An Anthology of Western Great Lakes Indian History,* ed. Donald L. Fixico, 481–519. Milwaukee: University of Wisconsin-Milwaukee American Indian Studies Program.

Goodman, Edmund Clay. 2002. "Indian Reserved Rights." In *Nontimber Forest Products in the United States,* eds. Eric T. Jones, Rebecca J. McLain, and James Weigand, 273–281. Lawrence: University Press of Kansas.

Landau, Jack L. 1980. "Empty Victories: Indian Treaty Fishing Rights in the Pacific Northwest." *Environmental Law* 10: 413–456.

Nesper, Larry. 2002. *The Walleye War: The Struggle for Ojibwe Treaty and Spearfishing Rights.* Lincoln: University of Nebraska Press.

Satz, Ronald N. 1991. *Chippewa Treaty Rights: The Reserved Rights of Wisconsin's Chippewa Indians in Historical Perspective.* Eau Claire: Wisconsin Academy of Sciences, Arts and Letters.

Ulrich, Roberta. 1999. *Empty Nets: Indians, Dams, and the Columbia River.* Corvallis: Oregon State University Press.

Vennum, Thomas, Jr. 1998. *Wild Rice and the Ojibway People.* St. Paul: Minnesota Historical Society Press.

Wilkins, David E. 1996. "Indian Treaty Rights: Sacred Entitlements or 'Temporary Privileges?'" *American Indian Culture and Research Journal* 20(1): 87–129.

Wilkinson, Charles. 2005. *Blood Struggle: The Rise of Modern Indian Nations.* New York: W. W. Norton.

Tribal Government Authority versus Federal Jurisdiction

On January 16, 2003, the *Omaha World-Herald* carried an obvious truism to those who know the history of law and Native Americans. "Tribes' Jurisdiction 'Complicated'" rang the admonition. A tremendous understatement, complications over indigenous jurisdiction stem from a tangle of laws, court decisions, executive actions (deriving from state, federal and tribal governments), and treaties and other agreements that date back more than two centuries. Within the maze that is Indian law, there are countless inconsistencies, reversals, and contradictions. It should not be surprising, then, that confusion persists over the issue of jurisdiction. However, what represents a new development for Native nations—or perhaps a return to older ways, depending on one's perspective—are greater jurisdictional assertions of sovereignty by tribal governments.

In the summer of 2002, the Omaha Tribal Council authorized its tribal police to conduct a safety check of all vehicles in Pender, Nebraska, a predominantly non-Indian town located on the reservation. A week later, Nebraskans woke up to another headline about jurisdiction, but this time a more incendiary one. "Farmers Oppose Tribal Move" spoke to another jurisdictional tumult. Two white farmers, who worked land on the Winnebago Reservation (which is contiguous with the Omaha Reservation) that had been purchased from an Indian family more than eighty years ago, were furious. The Winnebago and Omaha tribes had both decided to take over the enforcement of laws concerning pesticide handling and application. This had previously been handled by the federal Environmental Protection Agency. The farmers created a group called We the People to protest their rights. Said the head of Thurston County's We the People chapter, "The fear is either they're going to try to regulate us out of business or fine us out of business." Tribal officials see it rather differently. They argue that, because they are close at hand, the tribe should take over. The tribe can improve the response time to clean up spills, and, by assuming jurisdiction, it can also create some reservation jobs. "Basically, our goals are parallel," said John Blackhawk, chairman of the Winnebago Indian tribe. "It won't be the tribe trying to pick on anyone or move anyone off their land. They just don't like the scenario of being in charge." Bad local feelings and lawsuits seem inevitable. Indeed, jurisdiction issues have been a part of life for Native America from time immemorial, and they continue to represent flash points.

Over the last 225-plus years, tribal governments have worked to maintain their jurisdictional authority in the face of expanding encroachment by the U.S. federal government. Native authority has witnessed a series of jurisdictional attacks and retreats on the part of federal, state, and local governments. The steady erosion of Native authority during the nineteenth century reached a low watermark at the turn of that century, which was reversed during the 1930s Indian New Deal. A savage attack on indigenous jurisdiction was sustained in the post–World War II years, only to be turned back in the 1970s. That attack has been revitalized since the 1980s, this time by the U.S. Supreme Court instead of Congress. Despite such obstacles in their paths, Native nations continue to strive for sovereignty. And although they have not regained all of their previous jurisdiction, they have made great strides in that direction.

Native America and Original Jurisdiction

When one considers that the current boundaries of the United States encompass a land mass comparable in size to Europe's, it should come as no surprise that, historically, there has been a wide range of indigenous nations and governments. In fact, the plurality and diversity of Native American nations in precontact times far exceeded the plurality and diversity of Europe. For example, whereas Europe came to be dominated by one form of government (monarchy), Native nations produced a multitude of governing bodies, including democratic systems.

What all these Native political bodies had in common, whether the theocracies of the Southwest, the decentralized structures of the Great Plains, the multinational League of the Haudenosaunee (Iroquois), the family-based polities of the Great Basin, the confederacies of the Southeast, or any other, was that they were all independent, sovereign nations. Their sovereignty met the same definitions as that of other nations all around the world: they were independent, self-governing political organizations.

However, Europeans who began arriving in the Americas at the end of the fifteenth century often dismissed the legitimacy of indigenous governments on the grounds that Indians were neither Christian nor white. But such opinions reflected the biases, prejudices, racism, and imperial ambitions then prevalent in European thought, not the political realities of the Western Hemisphere. Thus, though Europeans might denigrate indigenous governments in one breath, they were forced to confront the reality of Native sovereignty in the next. Contrary to the disinformative stereotypes they promulgated, Europeans stumbled upon neither disorganized Indian populations living in anarchy nor the Edenic and doomed bliss of a childlike people who had yet to tackle complex politics. They encountered a great many forms of Native government, and interaction between Europeans and Indians represented nation-to-nation relations.

Almost from the beginning of contact, Europeans employed a variety of techniques designed to minimize or even obliterate Native sovereignty—brute force. Though European/African/Asiatic diseases were responsible for most of the destruction of Native populations, European aggression also played a substantial role in the diminution of sovereignty among many Native nations.

The Spanish used merciless military might to take control of the southwestern Pueblos at the end of the sixteenth century. Slaughtering resisters and employing terror to subdue the substantially larger Native populations, the Spanish attempted to wipe out Pueblo governments altogether. In the early 1600s, England, France, Holland, and Sweden all jockeyed for influence along the Atlantic coast, none of them having the wherewithal to immediately impose their will upon Native nations. As the European powers competed with each other, they formed alliances with various Native nations in an effort to bolster their position. Likewise, Indian leaders often saw Europeans as potentially potent allies in their own world of Native political and diplomatic rivalries. After all, just as Europe was a sharply divided continent plagued by wars up to the present day, so, too, was North America a place where indigenous nations competed with each other in commerce and warfare. Thus, if a European nation sought to profit by affiliating with the right Native nation, Native nations likewise sought to profit by affiliating with the right European nation.

The legalistic and literate English colonists first began the process of signing titles, deeds, and other contracts with American Indians. Representatives of the Crown went a step further and conducted nation-to-nation negotiations with Native nations that resulted in the signing of treaties. On numerous occasions, the English government made formal agreements with various indigenous parties that did everything to form alliances, begin and end wars, outline commercial transactions (including land purchases), and create centralized jurisdictions.

Whereas a written document was vital to the European understanding of negotiations, Native nations valued other parameters. For many Indians of the Northeast, wampum was the central artifact. Strings of small polished shells or beads were bound together to form a belt. The arrangement of the multicolored beads formed patterns and even images. Wampum had numerous purposes, but within the context of negotiations it served a function similar to the written treaty. At the conclusion of a successful negotiation, a Native nation would often create a new wampum belt, its images recording the agreements that had been made. At future meetings between the parties, that wampum would be presented and recited as reminders of previous accords.

By negotiating, signing treaties, and accepting wampum, the English recognized the sovereignty of indigenous governments, both by their own standards and by those of Native nations. Regardless of English motivations for signing treaties, simply engaging in the process was a tacit acknowledgment of Native sovereignty. When the United States chose to continue that process after achieving its independence, it likewise made that same acknowledgment. And although federal officials often negotiated in bad faith, manipulated proceedings, and subverted Native sovereignty, the results were a double-edged blade. Article VI of the U.S. Constitution explicitly states that treaties are on a par with the Constitution itself, ranking as "the supreme law of the land." To the extent, then, that the United States would continue to use treaties as the legal knife for slicing into Native lands and sovereignty, that knife would cut both ways. Treaties are agreements between nations. Therefore, no matter how much the United States would attempt to usurp the jurisdiction of Native governments in the years to come, it had to recognize the nationhood of every group with which it had signed a treaty. As time passed and the power of Native governments waned in the face of the expanding American empire, many indigenous nations understandably clung to the treaties they had signed, revering the documents that proclaimed their sovereignty.

Although by 1776 a number of indigenous nations had already capitulated beneath the weight of various European invasions, the vast majority of Indian governments were still fully independent sovereignties when the American Revolution broke out. Indeed, many of those west of the Mississippi River and east of modern-day coastal California had had only limited contact, if any, with Europeans by this time. However, the thirteen English colonies that sought to establish their own country in that year generally harbored a rather hostile opinion of Native governments and their citizens. Such hostility was even reflected in their Declaration of Independence from Great Britain. King George III, the rebellious colonists asserted, had done no less than incite "Indian savages, whose known rule of warfare is an undistinguished destruction of all ages, sexes, and conditions." On one level, the statement was a piece of contemporary political propaganda designed to gain European allies and justify a rebellion that many were then interpreting as treason. After all, it was the English (and other Europeans), not indigneous peoples, who had pioneered the mass murder of civilian populations in North America. On another level, though, the statement reflected a basic flaw in the philosophy of the new American nation: Native governments were not seen as the legitimate expressions of the will of Indian people. Rather, the Revolution's leaders publicly dismissed out of hand the legitimacy, effectiveness, and even morality of Indian governments. This meant they could mischaracterize Indian political decisions and actions as the "savage" anarchy of people who lived without "rules." And even though it was obviously and patently untrue, that assertion would come to serve as a powerful rationalization for many misdeeds and acts of bad faith on the part of the United States toward Native nations in the years to come. It would become the fulcrum on which the battle over sovereignty turned.

Although it is unlikely that many indigenous people then knew of the libel contained within the Declaration of Independence, that act of broad character assassination was merely symbolic of what was already apparent to most Indians. Many English colonists had an open disrespect for Native sovereignty and a seemingly endless thirst for Indian lands. If the colonists successfully revolted and escaped the strictures of royal government, their aggressions might go unchecked. It is not surprising, then, that many Native nations chose to side with the British during the war. Particularly in the trans-Appalachian region and throughout much of the South, one indigenous nation after another took up arms to help the British put down the rebellion. These were not the heathen pawns of the English Crown, as the Declaration of Independence had erroneously claimed. These were calculated expressions of Native sovereignty. And despite the colonial rhetoric about Indian savages, the Revolution's leadership knew all too well just how politically sophisticated and militarily imposing many Native nations were.

Faced with these realities, General George Washington placed a high priority on achieving a state of detente with as many Native nations as possible. He knew his cause depended on it. From the outset of the conflict, American diplomats toured eastern America, soliciting councils and working hard to extract promises of neutrality from suspicious Native governments. In fact, early in the conflict, the Continental Congress made a preliminary invitation to the powerful Lenape (Delaware) Indian nation: if they would fight with the colonists, the Lenape Nation could enter the United States as its own state after the war. The Lenape did not immediately accept the proposition, and it was never again offered. Nonetheless, this episode clearly illustrates the strength, independence, and sovereignty of Native nations. Further, it shows that the imperial conquest of Native nations was by no means a forgone conclusion or an inevitable consequence of American independence.

During the Revolutionary War, some Native nations did form open alliances with the American colonists and help them fight the British. In particular, a number of Algonkian nations of New England, whose own political power had diminished significantly during the past sesquicentury, joined with the colonists from the outset. Often, their reward for years of fighting was to return home from the war to find their land squatted on by colonists. Some members of the mighty Haudenosaunee Confederacy also sided with the colonists. Haudenosaunee territory stretched from the Adirondack Mountains in the East to the Great Lakes in the Midwest. Consequently, military and economic concerns as well as historical factors led to political division within the confederacy and even within its various memberships. Generally, the Oneida and Tuscarora (the latter a recent addition to the League) allied with the colonists, and the Onondaga, Mohawk, Cayuga, and

Seneca fought for the British; the confederacy's members at times faced each other on the battlefield. Ironically, the United States generally offered better terms of settlement to Haudenosaunee nations that had fought against it than it did to those that had allied with it.

Early Indian-U.S. Jurisdiction

After the American victory, the new U.S. Congress quickly attempted to establish its exclusive domain over economic and diplomatic relations with Indian governments. But given the decentralized nature and relative weakness of the first U.S. government under the Articles of Confederation, Indian nations frequently found themselves negotiating with individual states as well as the national government.

In 1789, when the United States began the process of replacing the Articles of Confederation with the Constitution, it renewed its effort to certify the federal government's primacy over the states in relations with Native nations. Individual states would no longer have the power to conduct relations with Native nations unless explicitly granted permission to do so by the federal government. This ideal would usually be upheld by U.S. courts over the succeeding years. However, there would be numerous occasions, down to the present, when the federal government would conduct the states' bidding or simply allow states to run amok.

The Constitution's specific mentions of Native nations are sparse but telling. Article I, Section 2, in creating the formula for congressional representation from a state's population, excludes "Indians not taxed." In other words, Native Americans were officially excluded from congressional representation; their outsider status was confirmed. Article I, Section 8, also known as the commerce clause, gives Congress the authority to regulate commerce "with foreign nations, and among the several States, and with the Indian tribes." By differentiating between Indian nations and foreign nations (and referring to them as "tribes" instead of nations), the Constitution alluded to the realpolitik stance that the United States was adopting. The United States would never accord Native nations the same dignity and respect it did nonindigenous nations, and by singling out Native nations, even those beyond its borders, it was attempting to invalidate Native sovereignty and submerge it beneath federal control. Indeed, the U.S. Supreme Court would later cite the commerce clause to justify extending federal jurisdiction over Native nations.

The practical outcome of this policy was the development of federal trading houses. In 1790, Congress passed the first in a series of laws known as the Intercourse Acts. These bills created a system whereby only federally licensed traders could conduct commercial transactions with American Indians. Business would take place at federal trading houses. And one commercial transaction in particular was completely abolished: the purchasing of Indian lands by any U.S. citizen, corporation, or state. Only the federal government would be allowed to acquire title to Native lands.

One of the main goals of the various Intercourse Acts was to eliminate the corruption, theft, and conflict that had often marked business relations between Indians and European Americans, particularly at the far western reaches of the new country. Unregulated trade had featured a bevy of unsavory business practices, most of which disadvantaged Native participants. But in addition to cleaning up the dirtier aspects of international commerce, the Intercourse Acts also impinged upon Native jurisdiction. The very first of these bills declared that, when non-Indians committed crimes against Indians, those cases should be heard in American courts; Native legal systems should have no jurisdiction. Europeans had always sought to have such matters settled through their own legal system, and now the new United States was following that precedent, proclaiming in federal legislation its right to insulate its citizens from Native jurisdictions.

Subsequent Intercourse Acts and related bills passed through the mid-nineteenth century mandated that Indians committing crimes off their reservations be tried in federal courts; that Indians committing crimes against non-Indians should have their cases heard in federal court, even if the crime had been committed on Indian land; that non-Indians traveling to Indian lands needed passports; that Native nations were banned from engaging in diplomacy with nations other than the United States; and that individual Indians were prohibited from criticizing the U.S. government. The imperial nature of these edicts is self-evident. As the nineteenth century opened, the assault on Native jurisdiction was well under way.

Enforcement of the Intercourse Acts was always problematic. Illegal trade continued to flourish beyond the reaches of federal enforcement, and this struck at a basic jurisdictional issue that would haunt U.S.-Indian relations in the century to come. The simple fact was that the U.S. federal government was rather weak. It often had great difficulty enforcing its own laws on a recalcitrant citizenry. That is, in making jurisdictional claims over its own populace, it frequently took on more than it could realistically enforce. However, it was quite successful in insulating its citizens from Native jurisdictions. Local, state, and federal governments consistently refused to recognize the legitimacy of Native jurisdictions. American citizens were generally quite pleased by this development, as they could usually count on racist judges and juries to clear them of charges or impose minimal fines and sentences for crimes committed against Indians. For Native nations, however, it was a challenge to their sovereignty. The battle over jurisdiction had begun, and the balance of power was swinging to the United States.

The Nineteenth Century

During the first one-third of the nineteenth century, the United States implemented a program of ethnic cleansing. Native Americans by the tens of thousands were forcibly removed from their lands east of the Mississippi River. The phrase *ethnic cleansing* did not yet exist, and the official term for the policy was *removal*, but these actions were clearly on a par with more recent episodes of violence and forced migration that we now label ethnic cleansing.

Native nations in the Upper Midwest lost a series of wars that led to their expulsion. In the Southeast, however, circumstances differed. Five larger nations dominated the regions by the opening of the nineteenth century: the Cherokee, Muscogee Creek, Choctaw, Chickasaw, and Seminole. All five nations were potentially formidable military opponents. The difficulty of waging war against them would later crystallize in the First and Second Seminole Wars. Therefore, the federal government developed a different strategy for dispossessing and expelling their populations. On one hand, it stood by as individual state governments illegally usurped Native jurisdictions. Meanwhile, it applied bad-faith economic, political, and diplomatic pressure on the five nations, pressuring them to leave while enticing them with promises of free land and independent sovereignty in the West. Despite all the carrots and sticks, the five nations still resisted. They fought removal in a number of ways, including lobbying Congress, negotiating with presidents, and publishing their views. The Cherokee Nation took matters a step further by going to court. Their resistance marked an important episode in jurisdictional issues between the United States and Native nations.

In 1823, the U.S. Supreme Court heard the case of *Johnson v. M'Intosh*. Congress had begun expanding its jurisdiction over Native nations with the 1790 Intercourse Act. Now the federal judiciary took similar steps. In a remarkable display of audacity, Chief Justice John Marshall ruled that the United States shared title to all Indian lands within the proclaimed boundaries of the United States. Furthermore, he stated, Native Americans could sell their land only to the United States. This was a bold power play by the U.S. government. And there was more to come.

During the 1820s, the State of Georgia made numerous efforts to impose its jurisdiction unilaterally over the Cherokee Nation. It organized Cherokee lands into Georgia counties; it asserted that Georgia state laws applied in Cherokee country; and it even arrested, tried, and executed a Cherokee man for a crime he had committed within the Cherokee Nation. President Andrew Jackson, a strong advocate of removal, actively encouraged Georgia, hoping its actions would pressure the Cherokee to leave the South. The Cherokee appealed to the Supreme Court, seeking an injunction against further outrages by Georgia, and in 1831, the high court heard *Cherokee Nation v. State of Georgia*. In his decision, Marshall ruled that the Court did not have jurisdiction over the case because the Cherokee (and by extension, all Native nations) were not a foreign state. He then fabricated from thin air a new political designation to which he assigned Native Americans. Their governments, he claimed, constituted "domestic, dependent nations." That is, they were nations after all, but they were not foreign nations, for they existed within the proclaimed boundaries of the United States; and they were not independent nations, for they were dependent upon the United States for their continued existence.

Marshall's rationale for his decision was circular, self-referential, ill informed, and condescending. Native nations were not foreign, he asserted, because the commerce clause of the Constitution refers to them separately. This chicken-and-egg logic declared that Native nations were not foreign nations, for no reason other than that the United States said so. With regard to their state of dependence, the chief justice maintained that Indians were in essence pupils, learning to become civilized from their American teachers. Their alleged cultural short-

comings, he reasoned, translated to political and legal shortcomings as well.

In this political atmosphere, Georgia's aggressions ran unchecked. The state went so far as to pass a rather incredible law that attempted to overturn the Cherokee Nation's own democratic elections. Then, Georgia officials marched into Cherokee country and arrested Postmaster Samuel Worcester for violating a Georgia law that forbade all whites from living in the Cherokee Nation. In cahoots with Georgia, President Jackson even went so far as to fire Worcester to prevent him from claiming exemption from arrest on the grounds that he was a federal employee. A third Supreme Court case was in the making.

In *Worcester v. Georgia* (1832), the Court was more sympathetic to Cherokee sovereignty. Justice Smith Thompson had previously authored a strong dissent in *Cherokee Nation,* convincingly arguing that the Cherokee were indeed a sovereign nation, albeit a weak one. Though his opinion had not carried the day in 1831, apparently it influenced the Court after the fact. As he had in *Cherokee Nation,* the Cherokees' counsel again argued that Georgia laws could not apply in Cherokee country because they were superseded by treaties the Cherokee had signed with the federal government, the commerce and contract clauses of the U.S. Constitution, and Cherokee sovereignty. In *Worcester,* Marshall backtracked, proclaiming Indian nations to be like "other nations of the earth . . . distinct, independent political communities, retaining their original natural rights." Although logically this decision should have overturned the "domestic, dependent nation" clause in *Cherokee Nation,* such was not the case. The long-term effect of *Worcester* was to establish the primacy of the federal government over states in relations with Native nations. That is, states had no authority over Native nations except as granted to them by the federal government.

The Cherokee Supreme Court cases are collectively known as the Marshall Trilogy. Despite their highly flawed logic and even contradictory assertions, they still form the foundation for the legal standing of American Indians within the United States. As the United States continued to use brute force to conquer and rule Native nations during the nineteenth century, it continued to dress the colonial process in the niceties of legal sanctions. The basis for those sanctions was, and continues to be, the Marshall Trilogy.

In 1866, the U.S. Supreme Court upheld the primacy of federal jurisdiction. When the State of Kansas attempted to tax Native Americans within its boundaries, Shawnee Indians sought redress. In *The Kansas Indians,* the Court ruled that Kansas could not tax Native Americans because Congress held exclusive jurisdiction over them. The decision did not stop there, however. Chipping away at Native sovereignty, the Court went on to say that states could assume jurisdiction if Indians dissolved their nations or if Congress made them U.S. citizens. Either of these two developments, the Court claimed, would nullify Indian treaties. The decision made no allowance for dual citizenship.

As if taking a cue from *Kansas Indians,* Congress attached a rider to the Indian appropriations bill of 1871 that forbade the signing of any future treaties between the federal government and the United States. Furthermore, it banned individual Indians from signing any contract without the permission of the commissioner of Indian affairs, head of the Office of Indian Affairs. President Ulysses Grant promptly signed the bill into law. The Resolution of 1871 was the capstone on nearly three hundred years of warfare between Native Americans and Europeans and their descendants, and the latter were proclaiming their victory. The United States would no longer sign any treaties with Native nations because it no longer needed their permission for anything. Only a few armed conflicts remained. The United States had established its dominance, and now it was stating, in essence, that might makes right. The one saving grace of the resolution was its acknowledgment that the provisions of all previous treaties would be honored.

As the end of the century drew near, most Native nations had been confined to reservations. A major blow to reservation-bound Native jurisdiction sprung from the U.S. Supreme Court case *Ex Parte Crow Dog* (1883). When a Sichangu Lakota (Sioux) named Crow Dog shot and killed a fellow countryman named Spotted Tail, the Lakota rightfully assumed jurisdiction and handled the matter through their own legal system, which is based on restitution. But Spotted Tail had been on good terms with the Americans, and many of them were outraged; by their standards, Crow Dog was literally getting away with murder. Crow Dog was promptly arrested, tried in federal district court, convicted, and sentenced to death. The Dakota Territorial Supreme Court upheld the sentence. His lawyers appealed to the U.S. Supreme Court, which found in Crow Dog's favor. It ruled that, because Native nations were sovereign, a fact that was supported by the existence of treaties, federal courts had no jurisdiction over crimes committed between Indians on reservations.

On the surface, *Ex Parte Crow Dog* sounds like a long overdue and resounding pronouncement in recognition of Native sovereignty. But such was not the case. With a nudge and a wink to the legislative branch, the Court noted in its opinion that only an act of Congress could change the current situation. Congress took the hint. In 1885, it passed the Major Crimes Act. The bill listed seven crimes for which the federal government could assume original jurisdiction, even if they were committed on a reservation by one Indian against another: murder, manslaughter, rape, assault with intent to kill, arson, burglary, and larceny. In the years since, the act has been amended, and ten more offenses have been added to the list, bringing to sixteen the total number of crimes for which federal courts may assume jurisdiction. The federal government was now free to extend its criminal jurisdiction over Native nations. The Supreme Court upheld the Major Crimes Act the following year in *United States v. Kagama*.

Another congressional bill that struck at Native jurisdiction was the Dawes Severalty Act of 1887, also known as the General Allotment Act. In this bill, the federal government asserted control over Native national lands. Allotment was the process of dividing up reservations into various parcels and then assigning fee patent ownership of those parcels to individual Indians. This was an egregious blow to Native sovereignty in any number of ways. For starters, it gave Congress the power to unilaterally allot reservations, regardless of the tribe's wishes. Many (though not all) nations held their land in common; this would now end. The bill also restricted the rights of the individual owners it created; Indians receiving allotments could not sell or lease them without federal permission. Finally, after allotments were handed out, most of the remaining land, which the federal government termed "surplus," was auctioned off to outside interests. Congress would pass a number of additional severalty bills over the course of the next forty years. This devastating policy wrought no tangible benefits to Native nations, struck at the heart of their sovereignty, and resulted in a massive land grab by Americans.

As the century ended, Native peoples were seeing their sovereignty erode at an alarming pace in the face of U.S. colonialism. Central to this development were the continued efforts of the United States to impose its jurisdiction over indigenous people.

The Office of Indian Affairs

In 1824, the federal government created an agency to deal exclusively with implementing Native policy: the Office of Indian Affairs (OIA). Eventually renamed the Bureau of Indian Affairs (BIA), it would quickly gain a reputation as the least efficient and most corrupt office in the entire federal government. But more telling than the OIA's astounding incompetence was its placement within the federal scheme. As an executive office, it needed to be placed within an existing department. The logical assignment would have been to the State Department, the department in charge of foreign relations. Instead, the OIA landed in the War Department (later renamed the Defense Department). It was clear that the federal government's long-term goal was not to establish and conduct normal relations with Native nations. Rather, it sought the colonial subjugation of Native nations by any means necessary. Equally telling, in 1849, when the United States was a growing empire instead of a teetering, fledgling experiment, it moved the OIA to the Department of the Interior, which is concerned with domestic assets such as natural resources and wild animals.

The very existence of the OIA set a tone for issues of jurisdiction. During the years in which the United States conquered one Native nation after another, the army was the sword, and the OIA was the hammer in that process. After a nation capitulated to the military, the OIA became the instrument of colonial control. The OIA was the federal government's administrative arm, and its roles were many.

The local face of the OIA was the reservation agent. In the years before modern civil service, this was typically a bottom-rung patronage position awarded to the minor supporters of presidential victors and their appointees. Frequently knowing next to nothing about Indian affairs, disappointed in the paucity of their prestige and salary, and assigned to a locale they considered unfavorable, agents were often corrupt and incompetent, and the OIA was plagued by a high turnover rate.

The real job of the OIA agent was the direct colonial administration of Indian reservations. With

few guidelines other than the prevailing racism and ethnocentrism of the day, agents' attitudes and approaches varied widely from case to case. Whether an agent chose to recognize the continued existence of Indian governments was entirely up to that agent. At whim, the agent could tolerate and patronize them or refuse to officially recognize them altogether. The agent could even replace them with his or her own contrivances. In short, the reservation agent was an autocrat.

The OIA agent's dictatorial powers were directly vested by the federal government. Other than the threat of further military intervention, practical power came from his ability to distribute treaty annuities and offer jobs to economically impoverished and dependent subjects. This power often played havoc with Native governing institutions. Although a reservation population might recognize the authority of certain Native leaders, an agent could undermine their authority by playing favorites. He could designate individual Indians to distribute annuities, thereby giving them tremendous power and influence. By the end of the nineteenth century, federal regulations had ended that practice. Instead, the agent and his staff distributed annuities directly, further concentrating their power.

Another potent source of power for the reservation agent came from his ability to hire and arm hand-picked Native Americans as official OIA police. In 1878, Congress began to fund the creation of reservation police forces staffed by local Indians. These men, though members of a Native nation now were paid by, wore the uniform of, and owed their allegiance to the United States. Their boss was the reservation agent, who hired and fired them at his discretion. Thus, by engaging in his own form of patronage, the agent could reshape the reservation's power structure. By 1884, two-thirds of all reservations had an Indian OIA police force. It was another blow to Native jurisdiction.

The jurisdictional control of the reservation agent and his OIA underlings increased further in 1883, when Congress authorized the creation of courts of Indian offenses. During this era, the United States was attempting to commit cultural genocide against Native Americans. It called the policy *assimilation*. Federal legislation outlawed all sorts of indigenous social and cultural practices, including, but not limited to, religious ceremonies, dancing, singing, traditional medical services, and polygamy, to name a few. Congress created the court of Indian offenses to prosecute these "crimes." OIA police were now also certified as judges. They had the power to arrest someone, convict that person, and collect a fine, all in one action.

Federal jurisdiction over Indians was so pervasive that Native people could not sign contracts without permission from the reservation agent and the commissioner of Indian affairs. This restriction, a result of the Indian Appropriations Bill of 1871, was so broad in its reach that American Indians could not even hire a lawyer without said approval. This meant that, if an Indian person were accused of committing a crime against another Indian person on a reservation, not only could the U.S. federal courts claim jurisdiction, but the accused Indian did not even have the freedom to choose his or her own counsel. And if a Native American wished to sue a corrupt OIA reservation agent, he or she could not hire a lawyer without the permission of that agent.

Federal jurisdiction over Native Americans was so profound that the government even set out to control the movement of indigenous peoples. A startling illustration of this is the fact that, by the late 1800s, a Native American could not leave his or her reservation without permission. Enforcement varied from reservation to reservation and could be extreme. The Apache people of the Southwest had only recently surrendered, and when they left their reservation without permission, they were routinely hunted down and killed. Likewise, the massacre of Miniconjou Lakota (Sioux) at Wounded Knee Creek in 1890 on the Pine Ridge Reservation in South Dakota stemmed from several factors, the most immediate of which was that they had disobeyed the agent's orders to stay put. In fact, the Miniconjou had not even left the reservation when the U.S. Cavalry overtook and slaughtered some three hundred of them.

The direct colonialism of the Office of Indian Affairs and the totalitarian powers of the reservation agents would persist until well into the twentieth century. Under these conditions, federal jurisdiction over Native peoples reached its zenith, while Native sovereignty dropped to its nadir.

The Twentieth Century

If the turn of the twentieth century represented a low point for Native sovereignty, the legal embodiment of that situation was the 1903 U.S. Supreme Court decision in *Lone Wolf v. Hitchcock*. Lone Wolf was a Kiowa in Oklahoma who objected to the impending allotment of his reservation. Fortunately for the

Kiowa people, they had previously signed a treaty that mitigated such actions. The Treaty of Medicine Lodge Creek of 1867 stipulated that none of the reservation land, which was held in common by the nation, could be subject to any transactions without the agreement of three-fourths of the adult male population. However, the Supreme Court was about to give official sanction to the naked aggression of U.S. colonialism.

Federal negotiators were unable to procure anywhere near the number of signatures needed for the allotment of the reservation. This failure occurred despite their fraud, which included adding non-Kiowa names to the petition for allotment and striking actual Kiowa people from the official tribal rolls. When federal negotiators fell short despite their perfidy, they simply ignored the treaty's relevant provisions and drew up plans to allot the reservation against the will of most of its resident Indians. Congress eventually accepted the dubious proposal. Lone Wolf then sued the secretary of the interior to prevent the allotment, and the case eventually advanced to the high court.

Peeling the mask of civility from the face of colonialism, the justices rendered the following opinion. Congress had the plenary power to unilaterally abrogate any Indian treaty. Why? Because, despite any irregularities in the process, Congress was the ultimate arbiter of Indian policy; because treaty review was beyond the jurisdiction of federal courts; because Indian lands were under the complete control of the United States; because the binding requirement of Indian consent could be ignored in times of emergency; because the act of 1871 banning further treaties could be interpreted to mean that Congress could also annul previous treaties (even though the act of 1871 explicitly denied that); because Congress acted in the best interests of Native peoples; and because even if Congress worked against the interests of Indian peoples, Congress still had superior authority.

The decision was a firm rebuke of Native sovereignty. It was the official declaration of colonialism. It was indeed a low point for American Indians in their ongoing effort to assert their jurisdiction over their own nations and people. But the assault by the high court was far from over. *United States v. Sandoval* (1913) concerned a man's effort to sell liquor in a pueblo. This violated federal law, which prohibited liquor sales on all Indian lands. Joseph Sandoval's lawyers were initially victorious in federal court, citing a previous Supreme Court decision that had given Pueblos immunity from such laws because the United States had acquired their land after war with Mexico, and no treaties existed between the Pueblos and the United States. The high court now overturned the lower decision. The crux of its logic in so doing was nothing short of racism. Since Pueblo peoples were Indians, it reasoned, they were inherently primitive and inferior. Therefore, they were not entitled to challenge congressional decisions, much less seek immunity from them.

The same year that *Sandoval* sucker punched Native jurisdiction, Congress gave the secretary of the interior the right to approve all wills and testaments of Indian people. In 1914, the secretary gained the power to completely quarantine a reservation during an outbreak of contagious disease(s). Shortly thereafter, the secretary assumed the authority to distribute to individual Indians those tribal funds held in common and to lease to outside interests any and all tribally held lands. In either case, the permission of Native peoples was not required. Even when the federal government attempted to do something positive for Native Americans in the early twentieth century, its high-handed actions led to dubious results. Such was the case with citizenship.

From the inception of the Constitution, American Indians had been denied citizenship rights within the United States. The Supreme Court gave sanction to that stance in *Elk v. Wilkins* (1884) by ruling that Native Americans could not become citizens even if they abandoned their Native nations and assumed residence and employment in the United States. Indians were officially denied the right to citizenship through conventional avenues. But provisions in various allotment acts had foisted citizenship on some Native Americans when they accepted their land. The issue came to a head after World War I.

Though immune to the draft, Native Americans had a higher per capita rate of participation in the U.S. military than any other ethnic group (the same has been true of all twentieth-century wars). When the deep sacrifice and honor of American Indian servicemen came to light, Congress decided to reward Native people. In 1919, it declared all Native American veterans to be citizens. Then, in 1924, it passed the Citizenship Act. The bill unilaterally bestowed American citizenship upon all Native peoples. Although the law was meant to be a show of gratitude, many indigenous people viewed it as another unwanted consequence of colonialism. A number of eastern Indians, in particular, were highly critical of the act. It was, they maintained, an assault on their sovereignty. After all, they were already citizens of their own indigenous nations and had not asked to be members of the ever-encroaching United States. And even at that, the supposed benefits of citizenship were often elusive. Just as African Americans were largely denied the right to vote in the South during this era, numerous states successfully prevented their new Native citizens from participating in American elections.

Two jurisdictional bright spots did appear during this long, dark period. In 1905, the U.S. Supreme Court acknowledged in *United States v. Winans* that the Yakima nation of Washington State did not lose fishing rights simply because it had ceded certain lands. The Court reasoned that Indians did not receive rights in treaties, they relinquished them. Therefore they retained any previously held rights that they did not specifically relinquish. The Yakima could continue to fish on the Columbia River even though it was outside their reservation. Then, in 1908, the Court upheld Native water rights in *Winters v. United States.* Residents of the Fort Belknap Reservation in Montana sued to prevent diversion of the Milk River, their only source of water. Similar to *Winans,* the Court ruled that the Indians of Fort Belknap had not lost their rights to the river when they ceded land adjacent to it. Nonetheless, the assimilation period, which extended from the late 1800s until 1934, was largely an assault on Native sovereignty.

After taking office in 1933, President Franklin Roosevelt appointed John Collier the new commissioner of Indian affairs. Collier's tenure would prove to be a watershed in the ongoing struggle over jurisdiction. A harsh critic of assimilation policies, Collier was more enamored with the experiments in indirect colonialism that Great Britain was conducting in Nigeria and elsewhere. He believed that it would be more efficient and humane if Native Americans were allowed to engage in limited self-government instead of being subjected to the widespread and overbearing authority of the OIA. Collier's reforms were eventually watered down by a skeptical Congress, but to be sure, the secretary did not support the notion of returning full sovereignty to Native nations, entities that he naively and condescendingly romanticized. Rather, he believed that, if infused with a sufficient amount of American-style democracy and subject to federal oversight, Native governments could manage much of the day-to-day affairs of their reservations.

The official and lasting shift in policy came with the passage of the Indian Reorganization Act (IRA) in 1934, also known as the Wheeler-Howard Act. In addition to overturning many of the more odious aspects of the assimilation policy, the bill outlined a plan for reorganization: the installation of new governments on reservations. The vestiges of traditional Native governments would be scrapped altogether and replaced with a new Collieresque model: a combination of American republicanism and the corporate boardroom. From their soon-to-be-formed reservation districts, Indians would elect representatives to sit on a tribal council. They would also elect a tribal chairman (or president) and a vice chairman in a reservation-wide election. In addition, the council would feature an executive committee drawn from among its own ranks. According to the plan, tribes would then create a new constitution and bylaws, and then they would write a charter and incorporate.

Whereas some people have viewed reorganization as nothing short of a revolution, another interpretation is that it merely represents the mixed blessings of some modifications to the colonial system, not an end to it. Either way, the IRA provided good and bad outcomes. For starters, Collier never sought Native advice when developing his plan. Consequently, and perhaps predictably, he was surprised when a number of Indian groups came out against it. Some Indians who had profited from allotment and other assimilation policies considered it unneeded federal interference. Indians who supported their own forms of government saw the IRA as a potentially fatal blow to their own jurisdiction, as yet another violation of treaties that had promised the United States would not interfere in Native governments. Their combined criticisms led to an amendment to the bill that allowed Native nations to opt out of reorganization. Reservation-wide referenda would decide whether or not to reorganize, and if so, whether to adopt constitutions and incorporate. And Oklahoma and Alaska Natives were excluded altogether, falling under separate, milder legislation tailored for them in 1936.

Collier and his staff lobbied heavily for reorganization, mobilizing their resources and exerting tremendous pressure on Indians to reorganize. Nonetheless, it was rejected by 78, or nearly one-quarter of the reservations, including the single most populated, the Navajo Reservation, which covers parts of three southwestern states. The measure was accepted by 174 reservations; of them, only 92 elected to make constitutions, and even fewer wrote charters and incorporated.

For those nations that reorganized, the consequences have varied from reservation to reservation. For example, the Oglala Lakota (Sioux) Pine Ridge Reservation in South Dakota has been a vivid example of reorganization gone awry. The original referendum passed by only the thinnest of margins, with a large percentage abstaining, a traditional form of disapproval in Lakota culture. Since then, the Oglala Sioux Tribal (OST) government has been the source of much controversy, including numerous impeachment hearings and even occasional political violence. The most notable dispute resulted in the seventy-one-day-long siege of Wounded Knee in 1973, an event that attracted international attention and witnessed the shooting deaths of two Indians and the paralysis of one U.S. marshal. As recently as 2006, the OST president was impeached.

On the flip side, the Wind River Reservation in Wyoming has served as an example of smooth adaptation. There, Arapaho politicians found the malleable aspects of reorganization and worked the system to make it conform to many of their traditional governmental offices, procedures, and dynamics. The Arapaho tribal council has governed with great success.

There were definite pros and cons to the system. Among the positives, the IRA ended assimilation's relentless persecution of Native culture and began to reduce the patronizing and omnipotent elements of the OIA. But there were also obvious negatives. In a larger sense, the system is a foreign imposition on Native nations foisted upon them by the United States; the Collier administration simply created a template of what it thought Native government should look like and stamped it on as many reservations as possible. More specific flaws include no distinct executive branch, which leads to a lack of checks and balances, and no staggering of the tribal council election cycle, which can lead to dramatic turnovers in governments every two years.

In 1946, Congress passed the Indian Claims Commission Act. It provided for an Indian Claims Commission (ICC) that would review cases of treaty violations and other outstanding grievances Native nations had against the United States. However, the act stipulated that all judgments (favorable or not) would be final, and in return for financial compensation as determined by the commission, all claims stemming from the original transgression would be canceled. In essence, the federal government was attempting to pay a final bill for past wrongs, or at least those wrongs to which it was willing to admit. Judgments against Native plaintiffs meant that they would have no avenue of appeal within the American system.

The commission was originally chartered for five years. To win their case, plaintiffs had to prove aboriginal title to the lands in question. The ICC would then review the case and assess the amount, if any, that was to be paid in compensation. However, so many claims were filed against it that the commission was continually extended so that it could hear its cases. By the end of the 1950s, it had heard 152 cases and rendered $42 million in judgments. By the time the commission was finally dissolved in 1978, it had heard 484, deciding 285 of them and authorizing more than $800 million in settlements. There were still 133 cases remaining on its docket that it never heard. Those cases were transferred to the U.S. Court of Claims.

If the IRA and the ICC had their ups and downs, the termination and relocation programs of the 1950s and 1960s were mostly down. Termination was nothing short of an all-out assault on Native sovereignty. Formalized as a policy statement in House Concurrent Resolution (HCR) 108 in 1954, termination was, in essence, the return of assimilation policy in disguise, its last, dangerous gasp. The federal government now acknowledged its ongoing shortcomings in living up to its treaty obligations. But instead of offering to fix those problems, termination's solution was to simply end all treaty obligations. The Bureau of Indian Affairs would be disbanded; one by one, the federal government would cease to recognize Native nations; they would be "terminated." It was a blatant attack on the treaty rights of Native nations.

The federal government composed a list of all federally recognized tribes and divided them into three categories: those ready for immediate termination, those requiring some assistance, and those that would need continued federal support for the foreseeable future. However, senatorial politics, more than any rational assessment, often decided on which list a Native nation would find itself. Thus, reservations within states such as Washington, Utah, and Nevada, which were represented by pro-termination senators, were particularly at risk of termination. While nations ostensibly had to agree to termination, various methods were used for obtaining their assent. For example, several tribes were told they would not receive their ICC awards until they agreed to accept termination. For most nations,

termination was an utter disaster. The Menominee of Wisconsin are a case in point.

Targeted for immediate termination, Menominee leaders were misled and strong-armed into acquiescing to federal officials. Final approval was achieved by a "popular" referendum, in which only 8 percent of the reservation participated. After six years of rushed preparations, the Menominee Nation was terminated on April 30, 1961. One of the better-functioning reservations instantly became the poorest county in Wisconsin. The county's tax base was insufficient to pay for services as basic as police, waste disposal, and firefighting. All tribal assets were transferred to a corporation, Menominee Enterprises, Inc. (MEI), and county expenditures quickly gobbled up meager MEI profits, pushing the corporation toward bankruptcy and leading it to sell off property. The reservation hospital, reliant on federal funds, closed. Schools, utilities, and other services either ended or were dramatically scaled back. Menominee assets had been valued at more than $10 million in 1954. By 1964, they had dwindled to $300,000.

From 1954 to 1960, Congress terminated fifty-four tribes, communities, and individual allotments. Some of the latter were solicited by individual Indian landowners, but the majority were implemented against the will of the affected peoples. However, some successfully resisted. The Florida Seminole Nation is an example. A bill to terminate them was introduced in January 1954. But the Seminole people were fortunate to have several members of the Florida congressional delegation support their cause. Of twenty witnesses called at the bill's hearings, only three supported Seminole termination. After the hearings concluded, various Seminole groups continued to lobby Congress, and termination was successfully avoided.

By the late 1960s, few observers could deny that termination had been a disaster, and the policy atrophied. Approximately twelve thousand Indian peoples had been affected by 109 acts of termination. Many of them fought to regain federal recognition of their sovereignty and treaty rights. In 1970, a group called Determination of Rights and Unity for Menominee Stockholders (DRUMS) mobilized on their erstwhile reservation in opposition to termination. They were ultimately successful. On December 22, 1973, President Richard Nixon signed a law restoring the Menominee tribe. Although most terminated nations have been restored—most recently the Northern Ponca of Nebraska in 1990—others are still fighting for it. Although termination policy had been abandoned by the early 1970s, Congress did not officially repudiate it until 1988.

Relocation was a population resettlement plan that worked hand in hand with termination in attacking Native sovereignty. Growing out of a 1948 job placement program, relocation quickly evolved into a national plan for moving Indians off reservations and into large American cities. Using propaganda to lure Native Americans into accepting one-way bus tickets to distant locales, relocation's long-term goal was twofold: to liquidate reservation populations and to make Indians disappear through assimilation into large, faceless, urban populations. Aside from the program's dubious motivations, relocation also was an attack on treaty rights and tribal jurisdiction. It stipulated that anyone relocating off reservation would lose eligibility for numerous Indian-only federal programs, such as access to the Indian Health Service. Because many of these programs in essence are extensions of treaty annuities that were often guaranteed in perpetuity, using relocation as an excuse to end them represented a massive violation of treaty rights against individual Native Americans. Like termination, relocation was largely a failure in any number of ways. The program was all but defunct by the early 1970s.

On the heels of termination and relocation was Public Law 280. Passed by Congress in 1953, P. L. 280 extended state criminal and civil jurisdiction over Indian reservations in Nebraska, Minnesota, Oregon, Wisconsin, California, and, later, Alaska. Additionally, it provided that other states could assume such jurisdiction without the permission of affected reservations either by passing a law or by amending its state constitution. The number of states eventually grew to a dozen. P. L. 280 represents a profound violation of Native sovereignty and treaty rights and an erosion of Native jurisdictions. Treaties signed between Native nations and the United States firmly established nation-to-nation relations between the two sides and the primacy of the federal government over states in those relations. The United States itself has officially reaffirmed this repeatedly, going back to the Marshall Trilogy. Therefore, an individual state within the United States can have no jurisdiction over a Native nation, in much the same way that Alaska could not extend its jurisdiction over France, for example. By allowing states to do so through P. L. 280, the United States clearly failed to uphold its treaty obligations. Like termination and relocation, it was

a colossal failure in its original form. It has since been transformed into something akin to a tense partnership between reservations, county governments, and state governments.

Further attempts by states to extend their criminal jurisdictions over Indian reservations stemmed from the Assimilative Crimes Act. Originally passed in 1825, the bill gives states the right to impose their own "lesser laws" (minor misdemeanors such as traffic violations and the like) upon federal lands that have no local legal code, such as military bases and state parks. Although it seems clear that the law was never intended to apply to Indian reservations, federal courts have allowed this infringement, based on the bill's rather vague language. Any extension of the Assimilative Crimes Act to reservations seems bogus, though it has at least been limited. Only crimes between Indians and non-Indians fall under its discretion. However, while its application has been restricted with regards to ethnicity, it has been wrongly extended in other areas. Generally perceived as not applying to consensual, or "victimless," crimes, the Seventh Circuit Court nonetheless held in *United States v. Sosseur* (1950) that Wisconsin could use its laws to prosecute a Native American who operated slot machines under a tribal license on a reservation.

Contrary to *Sosseur,* the Supreme Court asserted the legal separation between states and reservations in *Williams v. Lee* (1958), one of the few legal bright spots of the 1950s. In ruling against the non-Indian owner of a general store on the Navajo Reservation who attempted to use the Arizona state courts to collect on a debt from a Native customer, *Williams* stated that "the exercise of state jurisdiction here would undermine the authority of the tribal courts over Reservation affairs and hence would infringe on the right of the Indians to govern themselves." The opinion went on to assert that it did not matter that the plaintiff was not Indian. Nonetheless, as recently as 1977 the Ninth Circuit Court of Appeals extended state jurisdiction under the Assimilative Crimes Act when, in *Puyallup Tribe, Inc. v. Department of Game,* it upheld the conviction of Puyallup Indians, under Washington State law, for selling fireworks on their own reservation.

During the 1950s, the U.S. Supreme Court twice addressed treaty issues. As before, the Court was not afraid to directly contradict itself. *United States v. Alcea Band of Tillamooks* (1951) found that Native nations could seek compensation from the United States even if they had not signed a treaty. Just four years later, the Court completely reversed itself in *Tee-Hit-Ton v. United States.* Now it was the Court's stance that Native nations could not receive compensation without a treaty. The Supreme Court was proving to be as frustratingly inconsistent as ever.

When the Navajo Tribal Council outlawed peyote on its reservation (the drug derived from certain cacti is a sacrament in the Native American Church), the Tenth Circuit Court of Appeals presided over *Native American Church v. Navajo Council* (1959). First Amendment protections did not apply on reservations, it decided. The court went so far as to declare that Native governments had a higher status than states. Ironically, what was a setback for the Native American Church was a show of support for Native governments.

The 1960s witnessed a slowing of the attacks on Native sovereignty but by no means an end to them. While the Kennedy administration publicly espoused an end to termination, the government nonetheless moved to terminate the Northern Ponca nation in 1962. Not until the end of the decade would the federal government finally show signs of truly relenting in its post–World War II assault on Indian rights.

In 1968, President Lyndon Johnson suggested a shift in the federal government's Indian policy. He referred to the new approach as "self-determination." Vague on details and soon to leave office, Johnson left it to his successors to outline the change. Embracing the notion of self-determination, Richard Nixon worked with Indian advisors to propose a policy that urged the final end to termination, which he decried as morally and legally unacceptable. His policy also sought to remove much of the BIA's authority over reservation governments by encouraging tribes to contract directly with the federal government for needed services. However, Congress was recalcitrant, and it was not until after Nixon's resignation that it passed the Indian Self-Determination and Education Act and the American Indian Policy Review Commission Act in 1975.

The first bill's legislative mandate acknowledged the failures of federal paternalism and the desire of Native people to assert their sovereignty. In more concrete terms, it gave reservations more control over education, offered hiring preferences to Native people applying for jobs on federal contracts relating to Indian affairs, and pledged to maintain the federal government's trust responsibility.

The commission set up as part of the second bill was dominated by Native Americans, save for the

chair and vice chair. The committee made 206 recommendations in its final report of 1977, including a call for expanded recognition of sovereignty that ranged from issues of civil and criminal jurisdiction to taxation and hunting and fishing rights.

The 1970s featured more gains. The Indian Child Welfare Act of 1978 worked to curb what at times amounted to little more than child theft from Native parents. Private and public agencies alike were now required to prove serious emotional or physical endangerment to Indian children before removing them from their homes. Previously, children could be taken from their parents with little or no justification. Since the bill's passage, various loopholes and enforcement problems have surfaced, but many of the most egregious cases of kidnapping have been stopped.

The American Indian Religious Freedom Act of 1978 was designed to guarantee basic religious liberties that were routinely denied to many Native peoples, including access to sacred sites, the use and possession of sacred objects, and the right to worship in traditional ways. The bill vows to protect Indian religious rights and gives the president the power to order federal agencies to consult with Native religious leaders about removing restrictions detrimental to religious practices.

To the north, Alaskan Natives had never signed any agreements with the United States. Jurisdictional issues received some clarification with the passage of the Alaska Native Claims Settlement Act (ANCSA) in 1971. The federal government recognized Native title to forty million of the sixty million acres they had claimed. Although a boon for Native land claims, it was not as large a victory for Native jurisdiction. The government did not recognize jurisdiction by Native governments over these lands. Instead, it formed thirteen regional Native corporations, in which Native Alaskans received ownership shares, which they could sell to outsiders after a twenty-year moratorium. Alaska's Natives also received separate shares in their individual villages, which were likewise incorporated. These shares could not be sold to outsiders. The difference? The federal government was willing to allow Native Alaskans to firmly secure their control over the jurisdiction of small villages scattered throughout the Alaskan peninsula while passively encouraging them to disenfranchise themselves in vast and lucrative portions of the state that were coveted by mining, lumbering, and tourism interests (most of the twenty-million-acre claim they had not received was set aside for parks and oil interests). Fortunately, Native peoples in Alaska have benefited from history's hindsight. Noting the sometimes disastrous effects of the General Allotment Act and Indian Reorganization Act, they have since moved to strengthen their hold over their lands. They pushed through a 1988 amendment to ANCSA that prohibits the sale of individual shares in the regional corporations without corporate approval. However, corporations are not governments. They can be dissolved or go bankrupt, and so there is still a very tenuous quality to the issue of Native Alaskan jurisdiction. A real issue confronting the latter of those two possibilities was the restrictive caps ANCSA placed on the profits those corporations can receive from non-Native corporations conducting business on their lands.

The self-determination era of the 1970s was clearly an improvement for Native jurisdictional issues over the assaults of the post–World War II years. However, the 1980s ushered in a period of renewed challenges that has featured, in particular, a hostile court system. During the last several decades, American courts have wrought havoc on jurisdictional issues, beginning with a series of Supreme Court decisions.

In the decision of *Sequoyah v. Tennessee Valley Authority* in 1980, the high court permitted the construction of the Tellico Dam, which destroyed an area where Cherokees garnered religious objects and medicine. That same year, the Court decreed in *Badoni v. Higginson* that Navajo religious rights were subsidiary to tourism and local hydroelectric needs. In *Montana v. United States* (1981), the Court ruled that states, not Native governments, have the right to regulate riverbeds running through reservations. It also severely limited reservation jurisdiction over non-Indians by claiming that the tribe can only regulate the actions of non-Indians on the reservation if their actions directly threaten the politics, economics, or physical health of the tribe as a whole. Another blow came with *United States v. Dion* (1986). The Court declared that federal legislation protecting endangered species superseded Native religious freedoms; Native peoples could not kill animals for religious practices if such actions were prohibited by federal legislation. *Lyng v. Northwest Indian Cemetery Protective Ass'n* (1988) overturned a host of lower courts and attacked the American Indian Religious Freedom Act of 1978 when it ruled that the National Forest Service should pave a road and harvest trees in an area of the Hoopa Valley Indian

Reservation sacred to Yurok, Karok, and Tolowa peoples. Even the Forest Service itself told the Court that it agreed with the Indians, but to no avail. The Court judged that the road should be built and the trees should be taken. Furthermore, it insisted that the free-exercise aspect of religious freedom guaranteed to all Americans by the Constitution did not apply to Native Americans. Rather, they would have to meet the restrictive standard of proving that they were coerced into violating their beliefs or penalized for practicing them. In *Cotton Petroleum Corporation v. New Mexico* (1989), the Supreme Court asserted that a state could in fact tax non-Indian corporations doing business on reservations, thereby threatening the profitability of many reservation-based economic development plans. The Court then engaged in baffling legal doublespeak in *Employment Division, Department of Human Resources of Oregon et al. v Alfred L. Smith et al.* (1990). The Court maintained that states can pass laws prohibiting the Native American Church from administering peyote as a sacrament, yet at the same time it insisted that the existing laws in all fifty states prohibiting the distribution of alcohol to minors cannot apply when wine is administered to minors as a sacrament in a Christian church.

State courts have been equally hostile at times. In 1988, the Wyoming Supreme Court decreed that Shoshone and Arapaho members of the Wind River Reservation had no rights to groundwater under their very own reservation. The decision was so outrageous that it led many Native groups to shift their focus from the court system to the federal legislature when seeking redress. But if the last two decades have been difficult times for advocates of Native sovereignty, perhaps solace can be found in the major historical trend that defines federal Indian policy: inconsistency. The tides may yet turn again in the twenty-first century.

Contemporary Issues

In recent years, three issues in particular have attracted national attention: repatriation, gaming, and federal recognition. All these issues strike at the heart of Native jurisdiction.

The debate over gambling took center stage in 1979 when, in defiance of state law, the Florida Seminoles opened a bingo hall that offered prizes of up to $10,000. The state attempted to close them down, but the Seminoles successfully stated their case in federal court. The Supreme Court eventually considered Indian gaming in *California v. Cabazon* (1987), asserting that, despite Public Law 280, any state that offered any legalized gambling of its own could not outlaw Indian gaming.

The following year, however, Congress undercut the Court's decision and Native sovereignty when it passed the Indian Gaming Regulatory Act (IGRA). It defined three classes of gambling. Class III represents the most sophisticated type of casino table gaming (card games, craps, etc.), and Class I is the simplest form of gambling. The act required Indian nations wishing to pursue Class II or Class III gaming to negotiate a compact with the state. In other words, although the Constitution and the courts have affirmed time and time again that the federal government, not the states, has jurisdiction over Native nations, Congress allowed the states to assume jurisdiction over reservation gambling with the passage of the IGRA.

Several stereotypes have since sprouted up around the issue of Indian gaming: that most reservations have casinos; that these casinos are all wildly successful; that gambling casinos are anathema to "traditional" Indian culture and therefore "un-Indian." All these stereotypes are inaccurate and deserve further scrutiny. Because of the requirement to gain state permission for Class III gaming, most Indian casinos around the country do not offer full-fledged casino gambling. Class I and Class II casinos, which most Americans would not identify as true casinos, are much more common. Beyond that, some states have been more amenable than others over the issue. For example, Washington State was initially opposed to Indian gaming, but a change in administrations led to a change in policy. Nebraska has been continually hostile, levying fines of $2,000 per day and threatening military intervention against the Santee Dakota Reservation. In an effort to protect its own lucrative gambling interests, Nevada has actually spent money to campaign against compacts in *other* states. Internal factors also prohibit many reservations from serious gaming enterprises. A lack of startup capital is one frequent problem for impoverished reservations. Another is relative isolation from large population centers from which to draw customers. Finally, some tribes have not embraced gambling simply because they do not feel it represents their best interests. Consequently, only a small number of reservations offer Class III, casino-style gambling, and many offer no gambling at all.

Indians themselves have split over the specific issue of high-stakes gambling. Some have eagerly embraced the opportunity to use gambling to generate income. Various tribes have used gambling profits to offer their members schools, community centers, and health services, college scholarships, housing, care for the elderly, and, of course, jobs. Other nations have rejected gambling altogether for a variety of reasons. Some eschew gambling as a social vice that is contrary to tribal values. Others feel the money promotes corruption. Many are loath to sign a compact with states, believing it undermines their sovereignty. The Diné (Navajos), for example, twice rejected gambling in reservation-wide referenda in 1994 and 1997 before approving it in 2005. Some nations have divided over the issue. The Florida Seminoles not only pioneered Indian casino gambling, they were also the first to witness the division it can cause. Some members were so opposed to the idea that they eventually left to form a separate nation, the Independent Traditional Seminole Nation of Florida. Several Haudenosaunee nations have also seen conflict over the issue. Intimidation, violence, and arson have marred the debate on several reservations.

An equally contentious issue has been the matter of protecting Native remains and sacred and ceremonial cultural artifacts. In an effort to put an end to the grave robbing that had supported enterprises ranging from small-town curio shops to the nation's most elite academic and archival institutions, Congress passed the Native American Graves Protection and Repatriation Act (NAGPRA) in 1990. No longer are amateurs and professionals alike allowed to wantonly exhume Indian remains or steal sacred objects. However, the number of skeletons already in the possession of non-Indians numbered in the hundreds of thousands. The University of California at Los Angeles alone held the remains of some four thousand Indians. Therefore, NAGPRA also outlined criteria and timetables for identifying and returning Native remains and ceremonial objects to their respective communities.

The debate over NAGPRA has at times revolved around the false notion that the bill's mandates limit legitimate scientific inquiry. The bill merely asks the scientific community to apply the same respectful constraints and cultural sensitivity that it already accords other Americans. In the past, it has not. For example, in 1972 when an Iowa road construction crew discovered twenty-six white bodies, one Indian woman's body, and her child's body, the white skeletons were reburied, and the Native remains were shipped off for "research." In fact, the scientific value of Indian remains, most of which are quite recent, is minimal, and the vast majority of Indian remains were simply stockpiling in archives or being exploited by entrepreneurs.

NAGPRA's origins stem from the grassroots activities of groups like American Indians Against Desecration (AIAD), which protested against the ongoing double standard toward remains. And although NAGPRA is a piece of federal legislation, its jurisdiction is limited. Private institutions are not required to return their remains. Thus, the profanity of Indian skeletons on display for a fee persists at curio shops and the like around the country.

Debates over jurisdiction between the federal government and Native nations depend upon an important ingredient: federal recognition of Native nations. There continue to exist a number of Native nations that the federal government refuses to recognize. These nations typically have lived at the margins of American society, some (but not all) of them intermarrying with local populations at a substantial rate. They have nonetheless kept their ethnic identities, cultures, and national consciousness alive. However, since the federal government does not recognize their existence as Indian nations, they have no relationship with the federal government. Consequently, these nations receive none of the benefits that flow from federal recognition, including money from BIA programs, lands held in trust, certain tax exemptions, federal protection from state actions, and the right to sue for past grievances. In search of the same benefits and status that come with federal recognition, a number of them have sought to attain it, with varying success.

There are three methods by which a Native nation may obtain recognition. The first involves a successful action in federal court against the U.S. government. This method is expensive, very risky, and can be extremely time consuming. Often seen as a last resort, no Native nation has received recognition by this means. The second method is congressional legislation. Clearly, this method is highly politicized. Thus far, only three groups have achieved recognition through this route, most recently the Arootsook Micmac Nation in 1991. The final and most common method is through the Department of the Interior's application process. The Federal Acknowledgment Project of 1978 allowed the BIA to recognize previously unrecognized nations. Formalized in January 1994, this process is

highly bureaucratic. It demands that a petitioning nation meet seven requirements: it must establish continuous Indian identity from historical times to the present; establish distinct Indian location or community of a substantial portion of its population; establish tribal political influence or authority over its constituents throughout history to the present; show current governing documents, including membership criteria and governing procedures; show a list of all known members who meet tribal criteria that is acceptable to the secretary of the interior; establish that membership is separate from other Indian nations; and establish that the group has not earlier lost recognition through congressional legislation. Another half-dozen have successfully navigated this process.

Numerous other nations have been unsuccessful in their efforts to achieve federal recognition due to a number of obstacles. All three processes are expensive, time consuming, subject to politics, and degrading, as people are in essence asked to justify their existence. In addition, some previously recognized nations have at times opposed the recognition of more tribes for fear that it will reduce their share of federal money and benefits.

If one of the immediate goals for many, if not all, Native nations is to strengthen their sovereignty by asserting their jurisdiction and working toward a more equitable relationship with the U.S. federal government, then the long-term goal may involve taking such issues to the international stage. More and more indigenous nations (within the current boundaries of the United States and elsewhere) may seek to take their places among the other member nations of the world. Efforts to do so are well established and ongoing.

In 1921, the Haudenosaunee League of Nations sent delegates to London, England, to assert their sovereignty from Canada (the League is artificially divided by the U.S.-Canadian border). Two years later, they went to Geneva, Switzerland, and petitioned for entry into the League of Nations. Their petition was denied, though three sitting members, including Ireland, did vote in favor of it. More recently, Canada has carved a thirteenth province, named Nunavut, which falls under the jurisdiction of its resident Native peoples. Denmark has allowed the colony of Greenland, with its large indigenous population, to assert local jurisdiction (while still restricting its foreign affairs). With regard to U.S. Indians, by the early 1990s seventeen different nations recognized and accepted travel passports issued by the Haudenosaunee League of Nations. In 1992, the United Nations declared that it was the year of indigenous people. A nice-sounding but hollow gesture; a more substantive approach would have been to admit indigenous nations to its body.

Akim D. Reinhardt and John R. Wunder

References and Further Reading

Barsh, Russel Lawrence, and James Youngblood Henderson. 1980. *The Road: Indian Tribes and Political Liberty.* Berkeley: University of California Press.

Burke, Joseph C. 1969. "The Cherokee Cases: A Study in Law, Politics, and Morality." *Stanford Law Review* 21 (February): 500–531.

Burt, Larry W. 1982. *Tribalism in Crisis: Federal Indian Policy, 1953–1961.* Albuquerque: University of New Mexico Press.

Burton, Lloyd. 1991. *American Indian Water Rights and the Limits of Law: Reflections in a Glass Bead.* Lawrence: University Press of Kansas.

Castile, George Pierre. 1998. *To Show Heart: Native American Self-Determination and Federal Indian Policy, 1960–1975.* Tucson: University of Arizona Press.

Cohen, Felix S. 1942. *Handbook of Federal Indian Law.* Washington, DC: Government Printing Office.

Deloria, Vine, Jr. 1971. *Of Utmost Good Faith.* San Francisco: Straight Arrow Books.

Deloria, Vine, Jr., and Sandra Cadwalader. 1984. *The Aggressions of Civilization: Federal Indian Policy Since the 1880s.* Philadelphia: Temple University Press.

Deloria, Vine, Jr., and Clifford Lytle. 1984. *The Nations Within: The Past and Future of American Indian Sovereignty.* New York: Pantheon Books.

Deloria, Vine, Jr., and David E. Wilkins. 1999. *Tribes, Treaties, and Constitutional Tribulations.* Austin: University of Texas Press.

Fairbanks, Robert A. 1977. "A Discussion of the Nation-State Status of Indian Tribes: A Case Study of the Cheyenne Nation." *American Indian Journal* 3 (October): 2–24.

Fixico, Donald L. 1986. *Termination and Relocation: Federal Indian Policy 1945–1960.* Albuquerque: University of New Mexico Press.

Getches, David H., and Charles F. Wilkinson. 1998. *Federal Indian Law: Cases and Materials,* 4th ed. St. Paul, MN: West.

Goldberg, Carole E. 1975. "Public Law 280: The Limits of State Jurisdiction over Reservation Indians." *UCLA Law Review* 22 (February): 535–594.

Green, L. C., and Olive P. Dickason. 1989. *The Law of Nations and the New World.* Edmonton, AB, Canada: University of Alberta Press.

Gross, Emma R. 1989. *Contemporary Federal Policy Toward Indians.* Westport, CT: Greenwood Press.

Harring, Sidney L. 1994. *Crow Dog's Case: American Indian Sovereignty, Tribal Law, and United States Law in the Nineteenth Century.* New York: Cambridge University Press.

Kappler, Charles J., ed. 1904. *Indian Treaties 1778–1883,* 3rd ed. Washington, DC: Government Printing Office; repr., New York: Interland Press.

Metcalf, Richard P. 1974. "Who Should Rule at Home? Native American Politics and Indian-White Relations." *Journal of American History* 61 (December): 651–665.

Philp, Kenneth R., ed. 1986. *Indian Self-Rule: First-Hand Accounts of Indian-White Relations from Roosevelt to Reagan.* Salt Lake City, UT: Howe Brothers.

Price, Monroe E. 1973. *Law and the American Indian.* Indianapolis, IN: Bobbs-Merrill.

Prucha, Francis Paul. 1984. *The Great Father: The United States Government and the American Indians.* 2 vols. Lincoln: University of Nebraska Press.

Quinn, William W., Jr. 1990. "Federal Acknowledgment of American Indian Tribes: The Historical Development of a Legal Concept." *American Journal of Legal History* 34 (October): 331–364.

Stanek, Edward. 1987. *Native People: Their Legal Status, Claims, and Human Rights.* Monticello, IL: Vance Bibliographies.

Stuart, Paul. 1979. *The Indian Office: Growth and Development of an American Institution.* Ann Arbor, MI: UMI Research Press.

Wilkins, David E., and K. Tsianina Lomawaima. 2001. *Uneven Ground: American Indian Sovereignty and Federal Law.* Norman: University of Oklahoma Press.

Wilkinson, Charles N. 1987. *American Indians, Time, and the Law: Native Societies in a Modern Constitutional Democracy.* New Haven, CT: Yale University Press.

Williams, Robert A., Jr. 1997. *Linking Arms Together: American Indian Treaty Visions of Law and Peace, 1600–1800.* New York: Oxford University Press.

Wunder, John R. 1994. *"Retained by The People": A History of American Indians and the Bill of Rights.* New York: Oxford University Press.

Ziontz, Alvin J. 1975. "In Defense of Tribal Sovereignty: An Analysis of Judicial Error in Construction of the Indian Civil Rights Act." *South Dakota Law Review* 20 (Winter): 1–58.

Treaties and American Indian Schools in the Age of Assimilation, 1794–1930

For more than two centuries since the birth of the United States, treaties have been central to the American project of schooling Indian children. Although treaty making with the tribes ended in 1871, and although not all treaty commitments have been faithfully adhered to by the United States, its citizens, or Indians, ratified treaties remain part of U.S. federal law. Many of these treaties provide for educational assistance, thus committing the federal government to an ongoing role in Indians' schooling. From the 1780s until the 1930s, the goal of U.S. and missionary educators was to Christianize, "civilize," and Americanize tribal boys and girls, turning them into white citizens in everything but skin color. This century-and-a-half-long "era of assimilation" is the primary focus of the present essay, but developments since the 1930s are also pertinent. Radical reforms of Indian education began during the New Deal, reforms later extended and deepened from the 1970s until today. In the last three decades especially, the emphasis of government-assisted Indian schooling (reserved for Indian children) has changed, and federal authorities, along with involved tribal peoples, cooperate to reinforce tribal pride and self-determination. The vast majority of Indian children, however, now attend state public schools along with the children of other ethnic groups. Whether at Indian schools or public schools, Native American children were and still are powerfully affected by treaties made between their peoples and the federal government in the first eight decades of the republic.

"You have no education," declared Captain Richard H. Pratt, founder of the famous Indian Industrial School at Carlisle, Pennsylvania, to Spotted Tail of the Lakota Sioux in 1879. Like generations of white Americans before and after him, this dedicated but ethnocentric educator assumed that, because tribal peoples did not educate their children within the four walls of a school building, the children remained uneducated. Yet education was highly institutionalized in traditional Indian societies. Family members (especially older people such as grandfathers and grandmothers), along with specialists in economic activities, warfare, art, and spiritual matters, systematically educate boys and girls into responsible tribal adulthood. In a typical comment on the demands of such an education, Francis La Flesche, an Omaha Indian, wrote, "To us, there seemed to be no end to the things we were obliged to do, and the things we were to refrain from doing" (La Flesche 1963, xvi).

From colonial times until well into the twentieth century, unable to see such apparently unstructured activities as education, European Americans have set out to Christianize and "civilize" Indian peoples through the schooling of their children. In northeastern parts of the present United States and Canada, for example, Roman Catholic Jesuit and Récollet (Franciscan) missionaries, along with Ursuline nuns and other congregations and orders, established far-flung missions, some employing schools and some sending Indian children to live with white people. "Always strive by all manner of methods," declared a royal French instruction in 1671, "to excite all the clergy and nuns . . . to raise among them the greatest possible number of the said children in order that through instruction in the matters of our religion and in our ways they might compose with the inhabitants of Canada a single people and by that means also fortify the colony" (Jaenen 1976, 176). Characteristic of future efforts, whether by French, Spanish, English, or U.S. missionaries and officials, schooling would thus convert children to Christianity but also assimilate them to the dominant culture and assure their political loyalty. Yet getting the desired results was never easy, as an Ursuline mother superior admitted during the same period. Out of a hundred children that her order schooled, "scarcely have we civilized one. We find docility and intelligence in them," she noted magnanimously, but

> when we are least expecting it they climb over our enclosure and go to run the woods [*sic*] with their relatives, where they find more pleasure than in all the amenities of our French houses. (Jaenan 1976, 173)

As later generations of Indian educators would find, keeping the children at their desks required a combination of compulsion, persuasion, and, above all, the convincing of kin and the children themselves that schooling was useful to the people.

"Come over and help us," pleaded the Indian depicted on the seal of the Massachusetts Bay

Colony in 1629, and at least for a minority of English Protestant colonists and for support organizations back in Britain, conversion of the "heathen" became a major rationale of colonization. The "Apostle of the Indians," the seventeenth-century Puritan missionary John Eliot, for example, established fourteen "praying towns" across New England. As with Catholic efforts, schools were central to his mission. Initially quarantined from their "savage" family backgrounds, young Indians would first be saved themselves. They would then return as cultural brokers—the term used by ethnohistorians for mediators between cultures—to carry the Gospel and English culture back to their peoples. Some colonists sent tribal children to England; some, like the French, took them into their homes. A number of young Indians actually attended Harvard and other colonial universities and colleges. Missionaries such as Eliot, generations of the Mayhew family who established schools for Indian peoples of Martha's Vineyard, and Eleazor Wheelock, who founded Dartmouth College and the famous Moor's Charity School (which was attended by almost ninety Indian boys and girls) were undoubtedly sincere in their desire for Indian "uplift" into Christian society. Many fellow colonists, however, regarded such efforts as an economic way of pacifying Indians and of removing them from their lands. Indians themselves quickly learned the game of countermanipulation, seeing schooling of their children as a tactic for individual and group survival in the rapidly changing colonial world.

Although these English colonial ventures reached very few Indian children, they established patterns for assimilationist Indian schooling in the area of the present United States throughout the nineteenth century and into the early twentieth. Protestant colonial and American missionaries, government officials, and, later, "friends of the Indian" fused versions of Christianity and an idealized American lifestyle into an all-embracing, messianic vision. This "Christian civilization" was locked in a deadly struggle against "heathenism," "savagery," and all such supposedly deficient cultural states. Colonial missionaries and, later, educators generally combined an egalitarian and nonracist conviction of the capacity of Indian peoples with a near-absolute ethnocentric conviction that Indians must leave all their old ways behind and accept all of the new way. The school thus became a panacea: many Indians were too old and too set in their ways to change; therefore salvation, both spiritual and secular, would come through the children. Like Eliot, generations of missionary and U.S. government educators thus struggled to separate children from their supposedly corrupting tribal environments, sometimes in large, off-reservation boarding schools. Patterns of Indian countermanipulation of white educators also persisted for the next two centuries once Indian communities came to realize the advantage of schooling to individual and group survival. And just as colonial governments made treaties with Indian peoples, so would the government of the new republic.

In international law, a treaty is a documented agreement negotiated between two sovereigns or more, and it is ratified by the governments of the parties involved. As the United States became more and more dominant on the North American continent, pressure developed to discontinue treaty making with Indian tribes, which Americans no longer recognized as sovereign nations, which led to the end of treaty making in 1871. Treaties served their purpose from an American perspective, for they became "the legal instruments by which the federal government acquired full title to the great public domain stretching west of the Appalachian Mountains." Yet throughout and beyond the period under review, many Americans were adamant that the United States should keep its part of the treaty bargains. To this day, Indian peoples, too, recognize the importance of treaties made over a century ago in holding the government to its commitments. Further, treaties were often more than mere devices for land exchange, and they brought about considerable cultural change to Indian tribes. Thus, they were "civilizing documents," often with a heavy educational component: schooling in exchange for supposedly surplus land (Prucha 1994, 2, 9, 11, 226).

According to the U.S. Constitution, the conduct of Indian affairs was and is the responsibility of the federal government rather than the individual states. Also, the making of treaties is a federal responsibility: the executive branch negotiates a treaty, and the legislative branch (through the Senate, the upper house of Congress) approves or rejects it. Within seven years of its establishment in 1787, the new government made its first Indian treaty that mentioned education. The treaty of 1794 with the Oneida, Tuscarora, and Stockbridge Indians mandated the establishment of mills and the instruction of some young men "in the arts of miller and sawer." A decade later, in 1803, a treaty with the Kaskaskia Indians of Illinois noted that, as most of the people had been baptized into Roman Catholicism, the

United States would provide $100 annually over seven years toward the support of a priest and "to instruct as many of their children as possible in the rudiments of literature" (ARCIA 1885, LXXVIII). Thus was a pattern established: the use of the treaty to extend government support of secular and religious instruction—in this case, not even Protestantism. And in 1819, as we shall see, Congress would reinforce its commitment, one that by the early twentieth century had produced an "educational empire" that included hundreds of day schools as well as on-reservation and off-reservation boarding schools for the children of the tribes.

It is currently fashionable to use emotionally loaded terms such as *genocide* to describe U.S. treatment of Indian peoples. Yet such treaties and legislation indicate that many government officials and concerned "friends of the Indian" sought acceptably humane and Christian methods (by their own standards) by which to free Indian lands of their inhabitants yet preserve Indian people as future citizens of the republic. Even before the war of independence, the Continental Congress (about to become the government of the colonies in revolt) in 1775 appropriated $500 for the education of tribal youth at Dartmouth College (ARCIA 1885, LXXVII). By the early nineteenth century, there was growing concern that Indians would soon vanish from the face of the earth if Christian Americans and their government failed to help Indians adjust to the new civilization that was overwhelming their traditional lifestyles. Few white Americans at the time showed respect for Indian cultures, whether of the hunting and gathering type or, in the case of many Indian peoples, agricultural. But through the schooling of their children, especially, all Indians could be raised into Christian and civilized society and thus could be saved in both this life and the next. As in the colonial period, these goals effortlessly blended a withering contempt for Indian lifestyles with an equally powerful belief in the capacity of the people themselves to respond and to rise into the privileges and responsibilities of American citizenship. Many Americans sought only the disappearance of the tribes, of course, even if this included actual physical extinction. But many others in and out of government sincerely believed that the offer of civilization and Christianity would amply repay Indian peoples for the loss of mostly "useless" tribal lands; thus "uplifted," they would practice American-style agriculture and be absorbed into the population of the republic like other ethnic groups. The school, then, often supported by treaty-mandated funds, would free most of the land of Indians and simultaneously free the Indians of their "savagery," and all would benefit from the exchange.

Further stimulating such thinking were a number of trends. The early nineteenth century witnessed the Second Great Awakening in America, a wave of religious revivals that powerfully stimulated Protestant missionary activity. American Indians—"our own heathens," as a Presbyterian tract called them (Coleman 1993, 39)—were not neglected in this crusade to win the world for Christ. Simultaneously influential was a growing belief in the transforming power of education. This century was to see the rise of the school: the explosive expansion, in nation after nation in the Western world and also in Japan, of state-supported mass elementary education. For the United States, with its increasingly diverse white population, to say nothing of its even more diverse Indian peoples (African Americans, slave or free, rarely figured in this discourse during the early nineteenth century), the school would become the great unifier. Through its presentation of a standardized Christianizing and Americanizing curriculum in thousands of nearly identical classrooms across the land, it truly would create one nation out of many. From the Revolution on, education proved to be an important cultural tool for forming a national identity, maintaining communities, and establishing republican idealism, especially in a nation so diverse, with so many interests represented from different parts of Europe. Such guided change was pertinent for forming a new nation (Green 1990, 171). The school became "a formidable structure of persuasion," inculcating American values, self-control, and Protestant Christianity into young Indians and children of other groups (Finkelstein 1989, 24). Thus transformed, these young cultural brokers from many different ethic groups would return to their communities to help instill American values into still-deficient adult members, be they German, Irish, or Native American.

Beyond inspiring the educational clauses in treaties, this heady mix of idealism, social anxiety, and relentless pragmatism produced the so-called Indian Civilization Act of 1819. This "Act making provision for the civilization of the Indian tribes adjoining the frontier settlements" was sweeping and yet explicit in its goals. Characteristically, it was introduced "for the purposes of providing against the further decline and final extinction of the Indian tribes . . . and for introducing among them the habits

and arts of civilization." It empowered the president, where practicable, "and with their [Indians'] own consent," to embark on Indian schooling. He was "to employ capable persons of good moral character to instruct them in the mode of agriculture suited to their situation, and for teaching their children in reading, writing, and arithmetic . . . " Most significant then and later, an annual sum of $10,000 was appropriated for carrying out the provisions of the act. Further, "an account of the expenditure of the money, and proceedings in execution of the foregoing provisions, shall annually be laid before Congress" (ARCIA1885, LXXVIII–IV). Although the legislature discontinued this specific "civilization fund" in 1873—more than half a century later and two years after the end of Indian treaty making—it continued to appropriate money for Indian education. By 1882, the annual sum had risen to $135,000; by the end of that decade, to about $1,348,000. By 1900, the figure was $3 million—about three hundred times the initial 1819 fund, a massive increase in expenditure, even accounting for inflation (ARCIA 1900: 44). The act of 1819, then, was not a one-time measure. Legislation and treaties together signified a commitment to permanent federal involvement and permanent accounting in Indian education. Like other national governments and American state governments in the early nineteenth century, the U.S. government had gotten itself into mass schooling, but in this case only for a special and supposedly "problem" group within the nation.

At the time of the legislation in 1819, the War Department exercised oversight of Indian affairs, and in 1824 Congress established a unit within it called the Office of Indian Affairs, later the Bureau of Indian Affairs (BIA). Headed from 1832 by the commissioner of Indian affairs, in 1849 the BIA was transferred to the Department of the Interior, where, despite some attempts to return it to the War Department, the BIA has remained to this day. In its first few decades of existence, the new Indian Office used the "civilization fund" to subsidize existing missionary efforts among the tribes rather than to plunge into new school-building ventures. Indeed, a later Indian commissioner, Francis E. Leupp, admitted in 1905 that for the first one hundred years of the republic (until the late 1880s, in other words) the education of Indian children "was practically in the hands of the religious associations" (ARCIA 1905, 34–35). This occurred despite the ideal of church-state separation supposedly so central to American republican ideology. By 1824, there were thirty-two such government-aided mission schools among many different Indian peoples, enrolling more than nine hundred tribal children (Coleman 1993, 39). This apparent continuity with rather haphazard colonial missionary practices is actually misleading. By congressional fiat, the federal government had now become inextricably involved in not only the subsidizing but also the policing of Indian schools—and it would later begin to build and staff such institutions. Indeed, near the end of the period under review, commissioner Robert G. Valentine could describe the functions of the BIA as "primarily educational" in both the broad and the narrow senses of the term. It was, he wrote in 1909, "a great outdoor-indoor school, with an emphasis on the outdoor. The students in this school are 300,000 individuals, ranging in age from babies at the breast to the old men and women of the tribe . . . these 300,000 individuals speak about 250 fairly distinct dialects" (ARCIA 1909, 3).

Furthermore, the government continued to use treaties to achieve educational goals. For example, in a treaty of 1857 with the Pawnees, the government agreed to establish two, possibly four, manual-labor boarding schools (which provided both vocational and literary curricula). The Indians, for their part, agreed to keep each child between the ages of seven and eighteen years in the schools for nine months of every year "or forfeit annuities equal to the value in time of tuition lost"—an acceptance of the principle of compulsory education, which was incorporated into many treaties. The treaty of 1863 with the Nez Perce of the Far Northwest obligated the government to pay $10,000 for the erection of two school buildings "and to employ two assistant teachers and two matrons indefinitely." The treaty of 1867 with the Apache, Kiowa, and Comanche of the Southwest—one of the last Indian treaties—mandated the erection of a schoolhouse and the provision of a teacher for every thirty tribal children of school age until thirty years from the signing of the treaty (ARCIA 1885, LXXX–II).

Again continuing patterns established in colonial times, Native peoples, or at least specific individuals and groups within Indian communities, often exploited schooling for personal and group advancement. Leaders of part-white ancestry, especially among southeastern tribes such as the "civilized" Cherokee and Choctaw, used such treaty funds to subsidize American missionary education for their peoples. Actually, in the pre–Civil War decades, direct government aid, important though it was, amounted to less than 10 percent of the money being poured in to "civilize" Indians. The mission societies raised some of the rest, and Indian treaty money provided the bulk of it (Fischbacher 1967, 65–67). Thus, the government, the missionary societies, and tribal peoples became tied into complex and, indeed, highly symbiotic educational relationships—but increasingly, as we shall see, the BIA would call the tune, at least on the white side.

Throughout the nineteenth century, therefore, Protestant and Catholic missionaries benefited from federal support and from Indian utilization of treaty funds to subsidize schooling; less directly, missionaries also benefited, of course, from the prestige and the increasing military power of the United States. For example, by the 1820s, the schools of the Protestant American Board for Commissioners of Foreign Missions (ABCFM) among the Cherokee of the Southeast had become "an international showpiece" (McLoughlin 1984, 132). At these and other ABCFM schools, and at those run by other Protestant (and Catholic) missionary societies, the regimens and curricula established earlier in the century became characteristic of mission education throughout the period under review and, indeed, of education in the government-controlled schools established during this era of assimilation. Curricula varied according to the size of the school, the availability of teachers, and the ability or English-language level of the pupils. At most mission schools and at government manual labor schools, a "half and half" pattern emerged. Part of the day was spent on common school academic subjects, which ranged from the "three *r*'s" and religion at small schools to highly ambitious academic curricula at large boarding schools, reflecting belief in Indian intellectual capacity. The rest of the day was spent working at vocational skills supposedly appropriate to gender: woodworking, blacksmithing, and farming for boys (although some came from agriculturally proficient tribes); dressmaking, cooking, and other "domestic arts" for girls. In addition, the larger boarding schools later sanctioned an impressive range of extracurricular activities, such as football, basketball, discussion and theater groups, and student-produced newspapers (vetted by the authorities, of course).

From 1819 until the reform of Indian education during the 1930s, missionary and government school curricula were relentlessly ethnocentric. The goal was the destruction of tribal culture and the assimilation of all Indians into American society. "Give the Indian a white man's chance," wrote Indian Commissioner William A. Jones in 1903:

> Educate him in the rudiments of our language. Teach him to work. Send him to his home and tell him he must practice what he has been taught or starve. It will in a generation or more regenerate the race.

Such an education, he concluded bluntly, would "exterminate the Indian but develop a man" (ARCIA 1903, 3). Although some missionaries persisted in employing tribal languages, at BIA schools the language of instruction was English, even to uncomprehending and monoglot children. In 1886, the BIA explicitly forbade the use of Indian languages in its schools. "There is not an Indian pupil whose tuition and maintenance is paid for by the United States Government," declared commissioner J. D. C. Atkins, "who is permitted to study any other language than our own vernacular—the language of the greatest, most powerful, and most enterprising nationalities beneath the sun" (ARCIA 1886, xxiii). In reminiscences and autobiographies, many ex-students recalled the anguish this policy of linguistic chauvinism imposed upon them, especially at the beginning of schooling. "For me it was very hard," recalled Belle Highwalking, a Northern Cheyenne. "No one [of us pupils] spoke English and we couldn't understand the white people when they spoke to us" (Coleman 1993, 105–106). Yet for her and thousands like her, the process of alienation had but begun: the curriculum excluded almost all tribal cultural knowledge (apart from some traditional arts, crafts, and storytelling late in the assimilation period). Thus, unlike young white American or English schoolchildren, who were educated into the values of their own peoples, young Indians simultaneously faced radical deculturation along with intensive enculturation into an alien lifestyle (Coleman 1993, Ch. 6). Finally transformed and imbued with "civilized" and Christian values, the children would return to spread the word among their own peoples. "Soon [Cherokee pupils] will be mingling with their countrymen," declared the ABCFM in a classic description of the cultural broker in 1821, "and imparting their acquired character to others, and they to others still, in a wider and wider range" (Coleman 1993, 40).

Missionary efforts in the Southeast, especially those of the ABCFM, were badly disrupted by the forced removal of most of the Five Civilized Tribes—the Cherokees, Choctaws, Chickasaws, Creeks, and Seminoles—to the Indian Territory of Oklahoma in the 1830s. Despite protest from many missionaries and other "friends of the Indians," and despite an apparently sympathetic Supreme Court decision of Chief Justice John Marshall that the tribes were "domestic dependent Nations" (Prucha 2000, 57–59), most remaining southeastern Indians were forced along the infamous Trail of Tears to the West. But the Indians' adaptive capacity reasserted itself in Oklahoma, as did missionary zeal, and the ABCFM and other missionary societies continued their school-building programs in the new land. In an impressive expropriation of white methods to defend tribal independence and identity, these five peoples also established their own, tribally controlled school systems partly supported through treaty funds. Each tribe built a hierarchy of local schools, boarding schools, and seminaries, and even sent promising scholars to white schools beyond the nation (DeJong 1993, Ch. 6). The five school systems were taken over by the federal government in the early twentieth century (ARCIA 1907, 349–355). Missionary-government educational activities elsewhere in the nation and even in distant areas claimed by the United States continued unhindered during the decades after the removal crisis. By the eve of the Civil War, Protestant and Catholic missionaries had also set up missions and schools among tribes as widely separated as the Omaha of the Midwest and the Nez Perce and Cayuse of the Far Northwest.

Despite its earlier commitment and the educational clauses of many treaties, after the Civil War the federal government attempted to divest itself of its educational responsibilities to the tribes. Perhaps as a result of the exhaustion brought on by the war itself and by attempts to reconstruct the defeated South, and also out of a growing conviction about corruption in the Indian Service, the government attempted to hand over—we might say, hand back—Indian schooling to the missionary bodies. Through its Peace Policy, the administration of President Ulysses S. Grant first invited the Friends (Quakers) to suggest church members as federal agents and teachers to the tribes—a further extraordinary blurring of state-church relationships. In 1870, Commissioner of Indian Affairs Ely S. Parker (himself a Seneca Indian—a highly unusual, early example of the Indianization of the BIA) noted the goal of achieving "a greater degree of honesty in our intercourse with the Indians." He declared that the experiment had been such a success that other denominations would similarly be called upon "to lend their personal and official influences to such educational and missionary or religious enterprises as the societies might undertake." The fused secular and religious goal, according to Parker, was "to combine with the material progress of the Indian race, means for their moral and intellectual improvement." The whole plan, he believed, was "obviously a wise and humane one" rather than a desperate last resort. Noting how Indians tended to pick up the vices rather than the virtues of white people—a common nineteenth-century belief, here regurgitated by a highly acculturated and "successful" Indian—Parker strongly supported the Peace Policy:

> The President wisely determined to evoke the coöperation [*sic*] of the entire religious element of the country, to help, by their labors and counsels, to bring about and produce the greatest amount of good from the expenditure of the munificent annual appropriations of money by Congress, for the civilization and Christianization of the Indian race. (ARCIA 1870, 474–475)

By 1872, for example, Friends (Quakers) had been given ten agencies with more than ten thousand Indians; Presbyterians got nine agencies with a missionary and educational responsibility for thirty-eight thousand Indians; Roman Catholics had received seven agencies with more than seventeen thousand Indians (ARCIA 1872, 460–462). This crass parceling out of human beings produced much resentment among the denominations themselves, and it achieved little obvious "uplift" of the tribes into American civilization. The initially celebrated Peace Policy did not even produce real peace, for some of the most famous Indian wars took place during the 1870s. By the early 1880s, the ambitious yet constitutionally dubious policy had petered out. And although the federal government appeared temporarily to have escaped the Indian school business, in reality this was not fully so. Even during the heyday of the Peace Policy, it was congressional money that subsidized missionary educational ventures, and earlier treaty commitments still held. Ultimately, the government exercised final authority over all such activities, and the BIA accepted and validated the activities of each denomination involved. And it was the government that belatedly decided that the policy had failed for the tribes. The whole program, as Commissioner Parker noted, was established to achieve "the purpose and desire of the Government" (ARCIA 1870, 474).

Indeed, before the late 1870s, even before the Peace Policy and treaty making had been quietly abandoned, the BIA was moving much more forcefully and directly into Indian schooling and would within a few more decades push the Protestant and Catholic missionary societies completely to the margins. As we have seen, yearly appropriations grew rapidly from this decade on. The BIA also began to build and staff its own schools directly under its control. In 1877, there were only 150 such schools, mostly day schools, enrolling about 3,500 pupils. By 1900, the BIA claimed 307 schools of all kinds with a total enrollment of about 21,500 pupils, about half the estimated Indian school-age population at the time. This number included day schools, on-reservation boarding schools, and large, off-reservation boarding schools sometimes great distances from tribal lands (ARCIA 1900, 22–23). Of course, one learns to treat such government statistics with skepticism; but historians generally accept that, despite the ending of treaty making, there was impressive expansion of direct government involvement in Indian schooling during the decades after the Civil War.

Some historians see an intensification of overt American patriotism at the expense of explicitly Christian proselytization at this time. But, just as elementary schooling worked in Britain, Germany, Japan, and other nations to indoctrinate the masses into order and nationalism, so from the beginning of our period to its end, BIA officials and missionaries strove not just to Christianize but also to Americanize their charges. Certainly these educators and "friends of the Indian" admitted to shortcomings in the actions of their nation and were often acutely aware of how individual white Americans could provide un-Christian examples to Indians. Yet no other nation on earth, educators believed, not even Britain, approached so near to the ideal of the Christian civilization. They could express their nationalistic convictions in stark and strident language. "It is of prime importance," declared BIA Commissioner Thomas J. Morgan in 1889,

> That a fervent patriotism should be awakened in their [Indian children's] minds.... They should be taught to look upon America as their home and upon the United States Government as their friend and benefactor. They should be made familiar with the lives of great and good men and women in American history, and be taught to feel a pride in all their great achievements. They should hear little or nothing of the "wrongs of the Indians," and of the injustice of the white race. If their unhappy history is alluded to, it should be in contrast with the better future that is within their grasp. (Coleman 1993, 42)

As the century wore on and the BIA increased its involvement in tribal education, most "friends of the Indian" agreed on broad goals for tribal education. But disagreement sometimes arose over methods. Which form of school would most effectively Americanize Indian children, the local day school, which most then attended, or the distant boarding school? Situated on the reservation, the local day school was obviously cheaper to maintain, but it allowed daily contact with kin and culture and thus dissipated the civilizing message of the teachers. The boarding school, especially the off-reservation boarding school, far more securely quarantined children from the "savagery" of their kin and was to many educators well worth the extra expense. Actually, both kinds of institution, along with an intermediate form, the on-reservation boarding school, persisted from the 1870s until (and beyond) the end of the period under review. Yet in the decades around the turn of the century, the large, off-reservation boarding school seemed to be the most promising tool for Americanization.

Although missionaries had earlier built Indian boarding schools, the new wave of government boarding schools was a product of the vision and energy of Captain Richard Henry Pratt (later General Pratt). In 1879, he founded the Carlisle Indian Industrial School in Pennsylvania—obviously a vast distance from the western tribal areas. An extraordinary man, combining powerful cultural intolerance with a deep sensitivity to Indian needs as he perceived them, Pratt was convinced that only by immersing young Indians for long periods in white civilization could they thus escape their barbarous ways and assimilate into American life. From 1879 until its closure as an Indian school in 1918, Carlisle became a home away from home to thousands of Indian boys and girls from hundreds of different tribal groups. Pratt's example stimulated the opening of many more BIA off-reservation boarding schools. By 1900, there were twenty-five such schools with an average yearly attendance of about six thousand students at widely separated locations such as Chilocco (Oklahoma), Phoenix (Arizona), Santa Fe (New Mexico), Flandreau (South Dakota), and Lawrence (Kansas).

Each school developed its own version of the "half and half" curriculum: literary and vocational education (ARCIA 1900, 15–16). As mentioned previously, many schools also encouraged varied and often popular extracurricular activities. And many also followed Pratt's idea of "outing" students: sending them to work on local white farms during the summer months or even to jobs in urban environments. Thus, near-total separation from tribal society was achieved: first separation from kin and culture; then further separation from all Indians, even fellow pupils, for at least a few months each year.

White educators made no apologies for tearing children from the bosom of the family. Many shared Pratt's conviction that Indian kin arrangements did not merit the sacred appellation "home." In 1863, for example, Commissioner William P. Dole claimed quite characteristically that Indian children who only attended day schools retained "the filthy habits and loose morals of their parents." In a boarding school, however, the children were "under the entire control of the teacher; they are comfortably clothed; fed on wholesome diet . . . in fact, they are raised and educated like white children and on leaving school are found to have acquired a knowledge and taste for civilized habits" (ARCIA 1863, 172). Pratt himself could not have expressed the conviction more succinctly. Control was obviously of central importance: generations of white observers believed that Indian parents failed miserably to control their "wild" children. The schools would provide firm but fair discipline—often military-style discipline, along with uniforms, daily inspections, and drilling for both boys and girls. But more than control was sought. BIA educators sincerely hoped that the boarding schools might become substitute homes for their charges, with good food, comfortable housing, and professional but loving teachers.

By the opening of the new century, then, as obligated by treaties and legislation, the U.S. government had plunged deeply into the complicated task of educating Indian children for assimilation into American life. It was an unusual undertaking by the federal government to assist "a non-white minority" (Hoxie 2002, 69). Indeed, no white ethnic group received such federal attention. But then, no other group within the American nation, white or nonwhite, had made treaties with the federal government. And the figures are impressive: along with the 25 off-reservation boarding schools referred to previously, by 1900 the BIA supported 81 on-reservation boarding schools (with a claimed attendance of 8,000 pupils) and 154 day schools (with a claimed attendance of 3,500 pupils). In addition, there were about 30 schools subsidized through government contracts. Commissioner Jones proudly declared in 1900 that these institutions were "all under complete government control." Furthermore, the BIA still assumed "supervisory care" over mission schools with an enrollment of just under 3,000 pupils (ARCIA 1900, 13–44).

But it was still a loose kind of control that the BIA exercised; there was no centrally imposed hierarchy of schools or standardized examinations. In the late 1880s, BIA Commissioner Morgan had attempted to bring greater order to this collection of schools through establishing a uniform curriculum and standardized textbooks and forms of instruction. He also attempted to inaugurate a graded system of schools through which students would progress: from day school (elementary education) through on-reservation boarding school to Carlisle or other off-reservation boarding school (vocational high school). Although he brought greater coherence to the "system," almost none of the schools, even the most ambitious boarding schools, could claim in this period to have provided more than an elementary education. Indeed, as late as 1928 the BIA admitted that few of its schools offered anything more advanced: "There is not an Indian school in the nation that is strictly a high school" (ARCIA 1928, 13). Furthermore, it was obviously difficult to bring order to what was a loose collection of schools catering to children of diverse tribal cultures, who often spoke no English upon entering school.

To accentuate such problems, nonattendance remained chronic during the whole of the period under review. Runaways—pupils who permanently or temporarily fled the school—especially plagued American Indian educators. In 1900, Commissioner Jones publicly admitted that, out of a possible Indian school-age population of nearly 40,000, only 26,000 Indian children were even enrolled at BIA schools, let alone attending regularly (ARCIA, 1900, 22–23). Absenteeism continued to decline, however, and by the 1920s some schools actually encountered embarrassing problems of overcrowding; but large numbers of Indian children still did not attend any school. By then, too, a new phenomenon had begun to manifest itself: more and more tribal children were attending local state public schools with children from non-Indian ethnic groups. At the turn of the century, only 246 did so, according to BIA figures (ARCIA 1900, 22–23). By 1930, this number had

exploded to almost 40,000—more than half of all Indian children at school (ARCIA 1930, 26–27). Almost all of this latter development took place at the very end of the assimilationist era under review. But the trend, which escalated throughout the twentieth century, merits mention here. The federal government also accepted and continues to accept a measure of responsibility—because of treaties, legislation, and other agreements—for financial assistance to such public-school Indian students.

Problems of absenteeism and runaways provoked continual calls by educators for legal compulsion. As noted above, individual Indian treaties had sometimes included clauses allowing for compulsion, and Congress had earlier passed a number of laws permitting the BIA to compel school attendance on particular reservations. In 1891, the legislature for the first time authorized the BIA to "make and enforce by proper means such rules and regulations as will secure the attendance of Indian children of suitable age and health at the schools established for their benefit" (ARCIA 1891, 67). By 1893, Congress had allowed the withholding of rations and annuities (owed to tribes according to treaties) from parents and guardians who refused to send their children to school. But the next year, Congress partly backtracked and forbade the sending of children to off-reservation boarding schools without parental or kin consent. Congress passed other compulsory laws, and authorities on many reservations tried to coerce parents to send children to school, even employing agency police to round up and carry children off. Many autobiographical narrators tell harrowing tales of such experiences, and their accounts are sometimes corroborated by official reports (Coleman 1993, 45, 61–63). Yet even as late as 1900, the commissioner could write of the need for amendments in existing laws "which will take away from ignorant parents the privilege of continuing their children in a state of savagery and will bring the children into contact with the highest types of civilization" (ARCIA 1900, 35). Indeed, the whole question of compulsion remained controversial even among educators and officials, and a significant proportion of Indian children remained unschooled—not necessarily uneducated—through the 1920s.

Another turn-of-the-century trend deserves attention. Some historians claim that by 1900 the culturally intolerant but racially egalitarian policies of the government began to change. Officials, according to this argument, became somewhat more tolerant of tribal cultural traits but simultaneously more convinced of the racial limitations of the Indians. The schools were thus to lower their sights: to train Indians for work more appropriate to their future condition in life, which would mostly be as lowly manual laborers on the reservation or, for many women, as domestic workers for white families. Most Indians would thus become "hewers of wood and drawers of water"; citizens, yes, but simultaneously wards of the government, forever trapped in this legal limbo, forever limited by their racial "blood" (Hoxie 2002; Riney 1999). Other historians see far more continuity, at least in practice, whatever might be said about policy (Prucha 1984; Coleman 1993). The New Course of Studies (the more vocationally oriented curriculum of 1901) and statements by Indian commissioners and other educators can be read in many different ways and can indeed support either argument. Accounts by narrators who attended BIA schools around the turn of the century suggest that, whatever changes occurred in policy, those at the receiving end noticed few of them. Schools continued to be as culturally intolerant and teachers as humanly varied as ever, but not more explicitly racist in their treatment of Indian pupils. Although the rhetoric did change somewhat, and expressions of biological racism are more prevalent then, perhaps continuity rather than radical change best characterizes the treatment of Indians during this whole period. Whether working with missionaries or building its own school system, the major BIA goals remained unchanged: move them; school them; civilize, Christianize, and assimilate them.

We might expect that ex-pupils of these schools, especially those surviving into the ethnically conscious later twentieth century, would have unanimously decried a system exhibiting such contempt for their own cultural heritage, one that employed rigid discipline and sometimes harsh forms of punishment. From surviving evidence—contemporaneous correspondence between officials, Indian parents, and pupils; and from reminiscences, autobiographies, and interviews—it emerges that Indian children responded in highly diverse ways to this schooling; indeed, the same individual might express strong ambivalence. Large numbers completely avoided attendance (although, as we have seen, by 1930 the vast majority of tribal children were enrolled at some form of BIA or public school). Large numbers began attendance but became either temporary or permanent runaways. Large numbers sickened, and many hundreds died at the schools. The majority—and we can never be sure about

the numbers—suffered, adjusted, accommodated, resisted, and began to use schooling to personal and group advantage. Some, especially the gifted and those able to make fast progress in learning English, thrilled to the new learning, which they saw as an expansion of their horizons rather than a rejection of tribal values. Although many Indian adults strongly opposed schooling, increasing numbers saw its advantage in the new world growing up around them and imbued their offspring with a strong desire to learn white ways. "If you run away from school," one mother warned her daughter, "you'll go *back* faster than you came home" (Horne and McBeth 1998, 31). Another ex-pupil recalled how, in the early 1930s, as the curriculum became more culturally tolerant, her mother was not too impressed when her daughters came home singing Indian songs and doing Indian dances. She had enrolled them "to be educated, and get civilized" (Lomawaima 1994, 36). In fact, for many Indian people schooling became an intensely family affair, with parents and other kin increasingly taking a strong interest in their children's progress, writing letters to them and to their teachers, and visiting the children at nearby schools or even distant ones (Child 1998).

Perhaps surprisingly, some boys and girls came to enjoy the military side of school life, especially the uniforms. Even more surprisingly, some actually began to see the schools as homes, just as authorities had hoped. Esther Burnett Horne, of partly Shoshone ancestry, was both a student and a highly acclaimed teacher at a number of boarding schools during the period under review, and thus she offers the historian invaluable multiple perspectives on the system. She was highly critical of how Indian schools attempted to destroy tribal pride and identity, yet she also saw another side. Reflecting back as an old woman, she believed that the Haskell Boarding School in Lawrence, Kansas, "provided a safe environment for me. The reason it was such a positive experience was that I had security there," especially after her father died, plunging the family into poverty. In a passage with which some, though by no means all, of her fellow students would have agreed, she wrote, "I think also that the sense of community at Haskell was very strong. Among Indian people this is very important. We had pride in our school and in our [football] team, and we had such a strong school spirit." Even in later life, many ex-students kept in touch and had "become part of our extended families" (Horne and McBeth 1998, 52–53).

This sense of belonging, along with such sanctioned extracurricular activities as football, helped Indian children and youth adapt to an alien educational experience. So did the unsanctioned student subcultures that developed at many of the larger schools, each with its own rules, ritual, and slang. Such subcultures could exclude as well as include, but those fortunate enough to become members could enjoy the thrill of resistance, secrecy, and belonging, all of which helped them accommodate the school regimen. Sensitive and gifted teachers, of course, made the school more bearable and even positively memorable for some pupils; indifferent, harsh, or cruel teachers made it equally memorable in the negative sense. Ultimately, it is the resilience of thousands of individual Indian boys and girls across a century and more of assimilationist schooling that has impressed historians. Forced into a bewilderingly new kind of education, most of them "just got used to it." They spent years at the schools—sometimes with hardly a visit home—and returned to their peoples or passed into the dominant culture as American citizens of tribal origin.

Furthermore, we must concede that, by their own criteria, the missionaries and government educators actually achieved a high degree of success during the era of assimilation. True, Indian peoples refused to surrender their tribal identities, identities that remain vibrant today. In addition, some pupils began to develop a complementary sense of pan-Indian identity at the schools. Yet tens of thousands of tribal children, decade after decade, often with kin encouragement, did learn English, reading, and writing, along with so much else of white cultural values and knowledge. Even in retrospect, few autobiographical narrators expressed resentment of the ethnocentric curriculum, which they and their kinfolk regarded from a pragmatic perspective: children go to school for white learning; at home they will learn the knowledge of the people. Ironically, in some ways the children learned too well, and some consequences of schooling were less acceptable from a government perspective. Ex-students could exploit their knowledge in the ways of American civilization, employing the English language, media awareness, American law, and politics in defense of tribal rights. Former students of Carlisle, for example, remembered how the renowned and feared Apache leader Geronimo astutely instructed them to turn white knowledge against its providers. Later, these and other Apaches used their schooling to hire lawyers who presented tribal land claims. Finally, in

1971, the Indian claims court handed down a judgment against the United States of more than $16 million (Ball 1980, 290–291)! General Pratt, the founder of Carlisle, would have enjoyed the irony; according to some Indian accounts, he did not lack a sense of humor.

Ironically, despite the cultural intolerance of the crusade, many tribal people began to identify with the schools. They came to regard them as "our schools" and often opposed late twentieth-century closings of, for example, old boarding schools. Again, Esther Horne well expressed the ambivalence toward and suggested the complex nature of the schools' achievements. "Critics dismiss boarding schools as assimilationist institutions whose intent was to destroy Native cultures," she writes. "While this may be a true generalization, the students and teachers at Haskell will forever be an integral part of who I am as an American Indian" (Horne and McBeth 1998, 52–53).

By the early twentieth century, however, the rigidly assimilationist approach to Indian education began to come under attack. Apart from a few prominent spokesmen or women—Dr. Charles Eastman, for example, an ex-pupil of Indian schools who graduated from Boston University with an MD—tribal people themselves had little voice in the national debate about Indian affairs. But by the 1920s, influential groups of (mostly) white reformers had begun to focus their attentions on the whole question of Indian policy and specifically on Indian education. Rejecting the ethnocentric and optimistic tenor of official reports and reflecting a growing anthropological appreciation of non-Western cultures, groups such as the American Indian Defense Association assailed the wisdom of a century in Native American affairs. The mounting criticism received powerful expression in *The Problem of Indian Administration* (Institute for Government Research, 1928). This huge study is generally referred to as the Meriam Report, as it was produced by a team—including the Winnebago Indian, Henry Roe Cloud—under the directorship of Dr. Lewis Meriam. The carefully researched and calmly written critique devoted more than eight hundred pages to telling the secretary of the interior, to whom the BIA was responsible, just what was wrong with Indian administration. The section on education was written by W. Carson Ryan, Jr., from 1930 to 1935 director of Indian education in the BIA. He was especially critical of government policies and practices in education, rejecting the "civilize or die" maxim and instead insisting that Indians should be allowed to adapt at their own rate to American ways. Almost every aspect of Indian schooling came in for criticism, from its ethnocentric and rigid curriculum—the vocational side of which often degenerated into the exploitation of pupil labor to help support the schools—to the severe health hazards faced by pupils. Influenced also by the so-called progressive education movement, the report advocated more sensitive and community-centered education, the kind that would encourage creativity and help produce adults capable of living full lives in the communities of their choice.

Not only did the Meriam Report make powerful reading, it was also powerfully influential. Even before Franklin D. Roosevelt became president in 1932, Ryan had attempted to put some of these ideas into effect. But Roosevelt's choice of reformer John Collier as BIA commissioner in 1933 led to radical change in many areas of Indian policy and practice. Working initially with Ryan and bringing to the job a passionate and even mystical appreciation of Indian cultures (as he perceived them), Collier wrought changes in many areas of policy and practice, especially in education. Here he drew upon his own experiences (actually quite limited) among Indian peoples, openly utilized the ideas of anthropologists, introduced further progressive ideas, and attempted above all to foster rather than destroy Indian cultural values. By the end of World War II, Collier had been forced from office, and in the 1950s the pendulum in Indian education would temporarily swing back—but not completely—toward older assimilationist thinking.

Yet the 1930s mark the most radical break in Indian educational policies and practices since the beginning of the republic—indeed, since 1492. Despite the apparent defeat of Collier's approach in the 1950s—expressed especially in the Termination Policy, reminiscent of the 1870s Peace Policy, which sought to end federal responsibility for Indian peoples—the tide would turn yet again. By the 1960s and 1970s, BIA thinking on Indian education would swing back toward acceptance of government commitment, along with increased appreciation of Indian culture and increased faith in tribal sovereignty and Indian self-determination.

The shift from BIA schools to state public schools also persisted throughout the twentieth century. By the early twenty-first century, only about 10 percent of tribal children attend Indian schools (reserved for tribal children), and these are often run by their own peoples on BIA grants or contracts. The other 90 percent attend state public schools with American children of other ethnic groups. The BIA still funds seven off-reservation boarding schools (four of which are BIA operated and three tribally operated by contracts). Some older Indians are enrolled at such BIA-operated post-secondary institutes as the Southwestern Indian Polytechnic Institute (SIPI) in Albuquerque, New Mexico, or the Haskell Indian Nations University (HINU), formerly the Haskell Boarding School. Others attend some of the twenty-six BIA-funded, tribally controlled community colleges. Tens of thousands of young men and women attend a variety of white American colleges and universities.

Obviously, in the early twenty-first century, American Indian peoples have far greater control than in 1903 over the education of their children at specific Indian schools. Yet, as during the era of assimilation, the treaty is still central to Indian education of all kinds. "The United States Government," declares the Office of Indian Education Programs (of the BIA) in 2002, "has a unique legal relationship with American Indian Tribal Governments as set forth in the Constitution . . . Federal statutes, treaties and court decisions." Although major public responsibility for education "is reserved respectively for the States, the education of Indian children is an exception" (Hoxie 2002, 2–3). Those 361 treaties ratified before 1871 remain part of federal law, and many of them commit the federal government to subsidization of Indian education. "Treaties are on the book," wrote historian Francis Paul Prucha, "and the courts have supported them" (Prucha 1994, 18). Whereas during the assimilationist period white educators interpreted this responsibility as mandating total control of Indian schooling, including curriculum, today it is exercised in partnership with Indian peoples, often in a government-to-(tribal) government relationship. The BIA and other federal agencies work together with the tribes to encourage the learning of traditional as well as dominant cultural values. Yet considering the imbalance in population and political power—about four million people of Native American ancestry and close to three hundred million other Americans—it is likely that, in the foreseeable future, the tribes will continue to face a peculiar challenge. They must constantly struggle to maintain adequate local control over the education of their children, while simultaneously holding the United States to its commitments—many of them solemnly accepted in treaties—to Native American education.

Michael C. Coleman

References and Further Reading

Adams, David Wallace. 1995. *Education for Extinction: American Indians and the Boarding School Experience, 1875–1928.* Lawrence: University Press of Kansas.

ARCIA (Annual Reports of the Commissioner of Indian Affairs, Bureau of Indian Affairs, Department of the Interior). 1863–1930.

Ball, Eve, with Nora Henn and Lynda A. Sanchez. 1980. *Indeh: An Apache Odyssey.* Norman: University of Oklahoma Press.

Bloom, John. 2000. *To Show What an Indian Can Do: Sports at Native American Boarding Schools.* Minneapolis: University of Minnesota Press.

Child, Brenda J. 1998. *Boarding School Seasons: American Indian Families, 1900–1940.* Lincoln: University of Nebraska Press.

Cogley, Richard W. 1999. *John Eliot's Mission to the Indians Before King Philip's War.* Cambridge, MA: Harvard University Press.

Coleman, Michael C. 1993. *American Indian Children at School, 1850–1930.* Jackson: University Press of Mississippi.

Coleman, Michael C. 2007. *Government Education, American Indians, and the Irish: A Comparative Study.* Lincoln: University of Nebraska Press.

DeJong, David H. 1993. *Promises of the Past: A History of Indian Education in the United States.* Golden, CO: North American Press.

Eastman, Charles A. (Ohiyesa). 1977. *From the Deep Woods to Civilization: Chapters in the Autobiography of an Indian.* Lincoln: University of Nebraska Press.

Ellis, Clyde. 1996. *To Change Them Forever: Indian Education at the Rainey Mountain Boarding School, 1893–1920.* Norman: University of Oklahoma Press.

Finkelstein, Barbara. 1989. *Governing the Young: Teacher Behavior in Popular Primary Schools in Nineteenth-Century United States.* New York: Falmer Press.

Fischbacher, Theodore. 1967. "A Study of the Federal Government in the Education of the American Indian." Unpublished PhD dissertation. Arizona State University.

Green, Andy. 1990. *Education and State Formation: The Rise of Education Systems in England, France and the USA.* London: Macmillan.

Haig-Brown, Celia. 1988. *Resistance and Renewal: Surviving the Indian Residential School.* Vancouver, BC, Canada: Tillacum Library.

Holt, Marilyn Irvin. 2001. *Indian Orphanages.* Lawrence: University Press of Kansas.

Horne, Esther B., and Sally McBeth. 1998. *Essie's Story: The Life and Legacy of a Shoshone Teacher.* Lincoln: University of Nebraska Press.

Hoxie, Frederick E. 2002. *A Final Promise: The Campaign to Assimilate the Indians, 1880–1920.* Lincoln: University of Nebraska Press.

Hyer, Sally. 1990. *One House, One Voice, One Heart: Native American Education at the Santa Fe Indian School.* Santa Fe: Museum of New Mexico Press.

La Flesche, Francis. 1963. *The Middle Five: Indian Schoolboys of the Omaha Tribe.* Madison: University of Wisconsin Press. (Orig. pub. 1900.)

Institute for Government Research. 1928. *The Problem of Indian Administration.* [The Meriam Report]. Baltimore, MD: John Hopkins University Press.

Jaenen, Cornelius. 1976. *Friend and Foe: Aspects of French-Amerindian Cultural Contact in the Sixteenth and Seventeenth Centuries.* Ontario, Canada: McClellan and Stewart.

Lomawaima, K. Tsianina. 1994. *They Called It Prairie Light: The Story of Chilocco Indian School.* Lincoln: University of Nebraska Press.

Lomawaima, K. Tsianina. 2002. "American Indian Education: *By* Indians Versus *For* Indians." In *A Companion to American Indian History,* eds. Philip J. Deloria and Neal Salisbury, 422–440. Malden, MA: Basil Blackwell.

McBeth, Sally J. 1983. *Ethnic Identity and the Boarding School Experience of West-Central Oklahoma American Indians.* Lanham, MD: University Press of America.

McLoughlin, William G. 1984. *Cherokees and Missionaries, 1789–1839.* New Haven, CT: Yale University Press.

Mihesuah, Devon. 1993. *Cultivating the Rosebuds: The Education of Women at the Cherokee Female Academy, 1851–1909.* Urbana: University of Illinois Press.

Miller, J. R. 1996. *Shingwauk's Vision: A History of Native Residential Schools.* Toronto, Canada: University of Toronto Press.

Pratt, Richard Henry. 1964. *Battlefield and Classroom: Four Decades with the American Indians, 1867–1904.* Ed. Robert M. Utley. Lincoln: University of Nebraska Press.

Prucha, Francis Paul. 1979. *The Churches and Indian Schools, 1888–1912.* Lincoln: University of Nebraska Press.

Prucha, Francis Paul. 1984. *The Great Father: The United States Government and the American Indians.* Vols. 1 and 2. Lincoln: University of Nebraska Press.

Prucha, Francis Paul. 1994. *American Indian Treaties: The History of a Political Anomaly.* Berkeley: University of California Press.

Prucha, Francis Paul, ed. 2000. *Documents of United States Indian Policy,* 3rd ed. Lincoln: University of Nebraska Press.

Riney, Scott. 1999. *The Rapid City Indian School, 1898–1933.* Norman: University of Oklahoma Press.

Sekaquaptewa, Helen. 1969. *Me and Mine: The Life Story of Helen Sekaquaptewa. As Told to Louis Udall.* Tucson: University of Arizona Press.

Standing Bear, Luther. 1975. *My People the Sioux.* Ed. E. A. Brininstool. Lincoln: University of Nebraska Press. (Orig. pub. 1928.)

Stearns, Peter N. 1998. *Schools and Schooling in Industrial Society: Japan and the West, 1870–1940.* Boston: Bedford.

Szasz, Margaret Connell. 1988. *Indian Education in the American Colonies, 1607–1783.* Albuquerque: University of New Mexico Press.

Szasz, Margaret Connell. 1999. *Education and the American Indians: The Road to Self-Determination Since 1928.* Albuquerque: University of New Mexico Press.

Trennert, Robert A., Jr. 1988. *The Phoenix Indian School: Forced Assimilation in Arizona, 1891–1935.* Norman: University of Oklahoma Press.

Vincent, David. 2000. *The Rise of Mass Literacy: Reading and Writing in Modern Europe.* Cambridge, England: Polity.

Related Treaty Issues

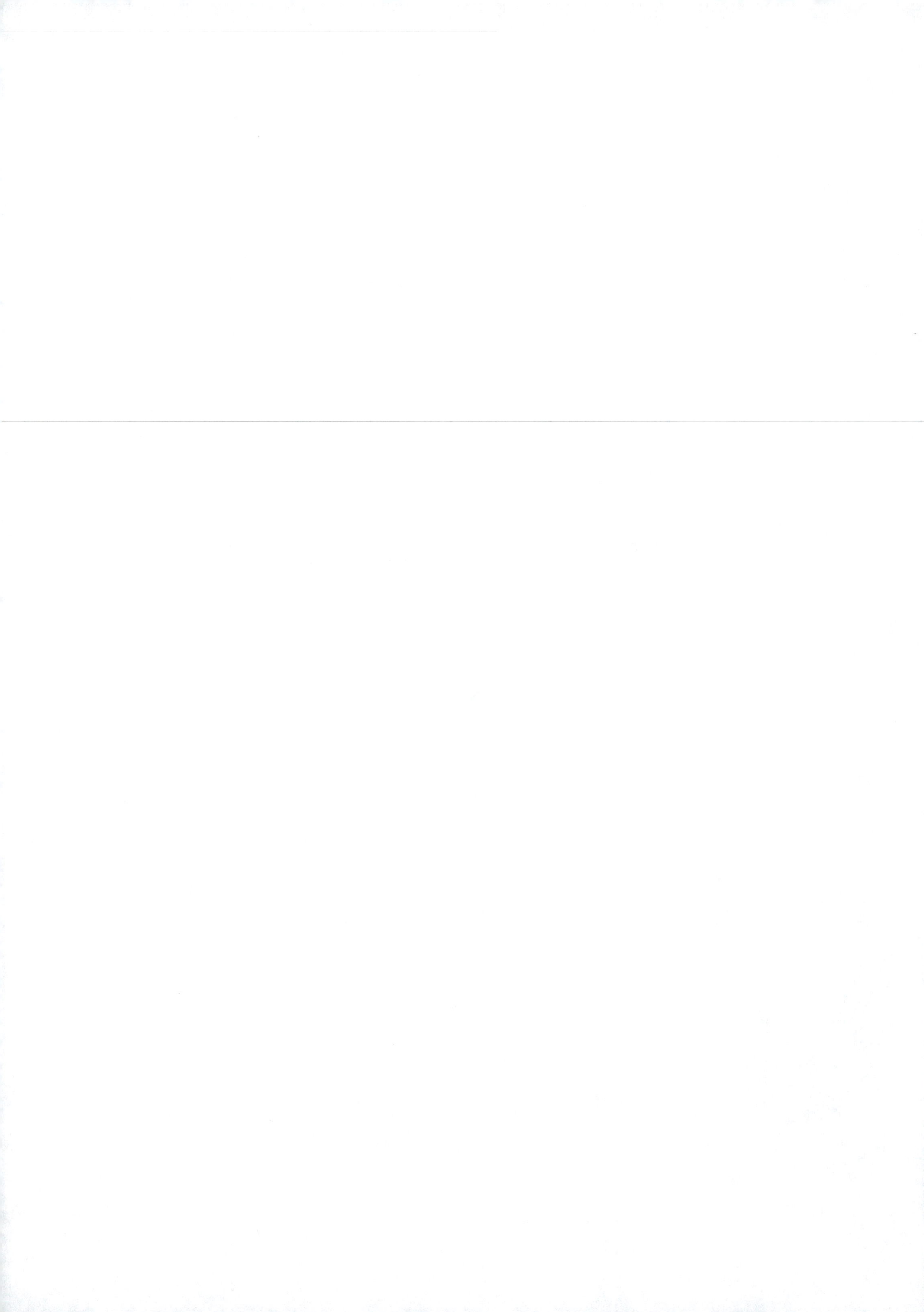

Alaska, Hawaii, and Agreements

Alaska

No Native Alaskan nation ever entered into a treaty with the United States. During the treaty-making era of the United States, which ended in 1871, the lands of the Inuit, the Aleut, and the Athabascan in Alaska were mostly bypassed by the swarms of settlers that uprooted Indians from the lower forty-eight states. Questions of land ownership, with several exceptions, lay dormant for most of the nineteenth and twentieth centuries. It was not until Alaska statehood in 1959 and the discovery of oil at Prudhoe Bay a decade later that Alaska Native lands attained enough economic value to prompt serious congressional attention. In 1971, Congress passed the Alaska Native Claims Settlement Act (ANCSA), a sweeping extinction of aboriginal title in exchange for a land and financial package that federal officials lauded as the richest ever awarded to an American Native group. As with most Indian treaties, a group of representative Native leaders, in this case the Alaska Federation of Natives (AFN), ratified the terms of the agreement.

The Alaska Purchase Treaty of 1867 with Russia provided little guidance for determining the status of Alaska Natives. The comparatively short document stated, "The uncivilized tribes will be subject to such laws and regulations as the United States may, from time to time, adopt in regard to aboriginal tribes in that country" (15 *Stat.* 539). Before 1905, the United States saw little need to reserve for Alaska Natives an "aboriginal status" similar to that recognized for Native Americans of the lower forty-eight states. Early federal land laws within the territory sought to protect both Native and non-Native inhabitants' rights to the land they actively used and possessed. These laws implied that Alaska Natives were entitled only to the land they occupied and, unlike Indians, did not possess an inherent aboriginal title. Neither did the courts, in several early cases, apply the Indian Trade and Intercourse Act to Alaska Natives, for they did not see Alaska as part of Indian country.

The Organic Act for the Territory of Alaska of 1884 specified that federal schools within Alaska be established "without regard to race." Acting within what he probably thought was the intent of the legislation, the solicitor for the Department of the Interior ruled that Alaska Natives did not possess the same relationship with the federal government as did Indians in the lower forty-eight states. Thus, the job of educating Alaska Natives fell upon the federal Bureau of Education rather than the Office of Indian Affairs (later the BIA). Under the guidance of Sheldon Jackson, a Presbyterian missionary appointed general agent for education in Alaska, the Bureau of Education established schools in outlying villages throughout Alaska. These schools, staffed with federal teachers, also provided other services, including health care and law enforcement.

The treatment of Alaska Natives shifted in the direction of federal Indian policy in 1905, when Jackson began to promote the creation of executive order reservations for various uses, including subsistence, reindeer breeding, and schools. Local and federal officials also saw a need to protect Alaska Natives from the diseases and corruption of settlers, as the soon-to-be-completed Alaska Railroad was expected to bring thousands of immigrants to homestead Alaska lands. But only a few Alaska Natives could be persuaded to move onto the reservations. Because the wave of immigrants never came, local and federal officials saw no need to force relocation, an action that had started numerous Indian wars. The reservations nevertheless proved useful, and the executive branch eventually approved more than 150 reservations varying in size from one acre to several hundred thousand.

In 1906, Congress further implied a similarity between Alaska Natives and Indians when it passed the Alaska Native Allotment Act, which allowed any Alaska Native to claim up to 160 acres as a homestead held in trust. Many provisions of the act were similar to the Dawes Act, passed for Indians in 1887. Alienation of land was later allowed with the permission of the secretary of the interior.

As competition over natural resources intensified, some white settlers questioned the authority of the government to create executive order Native reservations. Non-Native encroachment upon these tracts led to several court cases the rulings of which implied a federal relationship similar to the one with Indians. In the most important of the cases, *Alaska Pacific Fisheries v. U.S.*, the U.S. Supreme Court confirmed the exclusive status of these reservations. Based on this decision, the U.S. solicitor general in

1923 reversed Department of the Interior (DOI) policy and acknowledged the similarity in the federal relationship with Alaska Natives and Indians.

After this time, the State of Alaska and much of the public staunchly opposed the creation of any more reservations. However, a few Alaska Native leaders who lived near salmon-rich rivers or coastal areas saw potential in Indian Reorganization Act (IRA) reservations as protected economic zones. Competition from white commercial fishermen depleted the supply of salmon and thus threatened their livelihood. They looked with envy at the prosperous cannery at Metlakatla, a reservation established for the Tsimshian tribe in 1891. Its residents enjoyed an offshore fishing zone protected by federal law that was confirmed by *Alaska Pacific Fisheries v. United States* in 1916. For the next three decades, Haida, Tlingit, and other tribes, with help from the DOI, fought the commercial canneries for the establishment of similar protected reservations. Their efforts fell short due to the post–World War II federal termination policy and the lobby efforts of the State of Alaska. Of three IRA reservations approved by the federal government, two were rejected by tribal vote. A third, at Hydaburg, was approved by the Haida tribe. In 1952, the tribe filed suit to defend its reservation fishing rights, but the district court in *United States v. Libby, McNeill and Libby* (107 F. Supp. 697) invalidated the reservation.

From 1946 to 1966, Congress reviewed several bills that offered limited monetary compensation to Alaska Natives for extinguishment of their aboriginal title. Guided by the federal termination policy, powerful legislators opposed Alaska Natives getting any land except for a few parcels around their villages.

The Fight over Alaska Native Claims

Shortly after statehood, the State of Alaska and various oil companies, miners, and homesteaders rushed to claim Alaska's best federally owned lands. Native village councils, other Native groups, and the BIA opposed many of these selections, claiming aboriginal title. To allow Congress to settle the contested claims, the Bureau of Land Management (BLM) began to withhold approval of the disputed land claim applications in 1963. This "land freeze" became known informally as the Treaty of Caribou Creek. After three years of congressional stalemate, Interior secretary Stewart Udall expanded the land freeze to include applications for oil leases, land titles, rights-of-way, and all other interests in federal lands. Most developers, oil companies, and non-Native Alaskans opposed the land freeze, for it slowed the Alaskan economy and gave the Alaska Natives negotiating leverage.

Contradictory sections of the Alaska Statehood Act of 1959 were partially responsible for the land rights conflict. Section 6 of the act allowed the State of Alaska to claim 103.35 million acres of federal land, whereas Section 4 stated, in effect, that any lands clouded by aboriginal title would remain under federal authority. Because aboriginal title had yet to be extinguished for most of the 375 million acres of federal land in Alaska, Native land claims appeared enormous. The size and unique nature of a prospective settlement required congressional action.

Not long after statehood, Alaska Native leaders and advocates saw the possibility of losing lands critical for subsistence if the state of Alaska were to successfully claim them. Rural and urban Alaska Native groups sprang up to address this issue and its possible congressional settlement; but the great distances within Alaska, the diversity of Alaska Natives, and sometimes disputes among Alaska Native groups presented a formidable barrier to any unified action. In the early 1960s, the establishment of Native news media, particularly the *Tundra Times,* overcame this barrier by informing villagers of land issues and the activities of Native organizations.

In October 1966, the first statewide meeting of Alaska Natives was held in Anchorage. Nearly three hundred Inupiat, Aleut, and Athabascan Indians attended a BIA hearing on land issues and discussed upcoming legislation. Most important, they created an organization, the Alaska Federation of Natives (AFN), to present a united front for negotiating a land deal with Congress and to form a voting bloc to gain leverage in state politics. For the United States, the AFN would add legitimacy to any general settlement that covered a widely scattered, culturally diverse population.

A year later, the DOI wrote a bill that allowed each village to claim up to fifty thousand acres (a total of approximately ten million acres for two hundred villages). The land would be held in trust for twenty-five years, and its use would be controlled by the DOI. It authorized Alaska Native groups to file suit in the U.S. Court of Claims for monetary compensation for land clouded by aboriginal title but not claimed by Alaska Natives. The bill required the court of claims to use the U.S. purchase price of $7.2 million in 1867 as a proper valuation of aboriginal

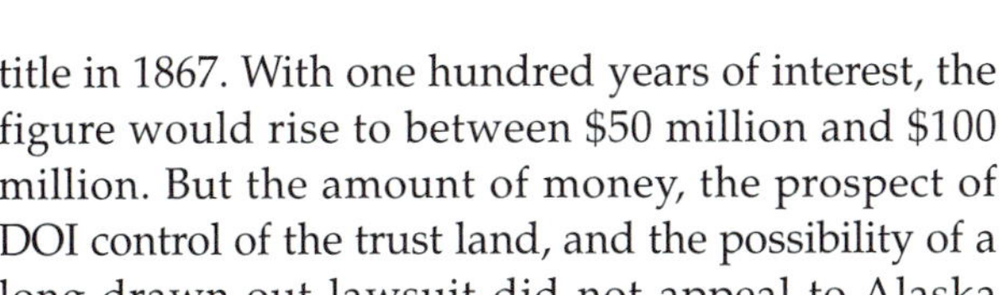

title in 1867. With one hundred years of interest, the figure would rise to between $50 million and $100 million. But the amount of money, the prospect of DOI control of the trust land, and the possibility of a long-drawn-out lawsuit did not appeal to Alaska Native leaders.

Eager to obtain a quick settlement, Alaska governor Walter Hickel led the creation of a state-sponsored task force composed of Native state legislators and AFN leaders. With input from state-sponsored advisors, the task force proposed a novel agreement that included a much larger land and financial award to be distributed under a corporate model. Their draft authorized forty million acres. The monetary settlement comprised an immediate $20 million payment, 10 percent of the oil lease revenue from the continental shelf, and 10 percent of the revenue from the development of state of Alaska lands obtained by selection under the Alaska Statehood Act. Most important, the land and money would be distributed among village and regional corporations chartered under the state of Alaska. Alaska Natives would receive shares that would be inalienable for 150 years.

The bill failed to survive the objections of the DOI, whose officials believed that forty million acres and the continental oil lease money were too generous. The DOI countered with another version of its original bill, offering the same acreage as before but changing the possible money compensation from a court of claims settlement to an up-front payment of $180 million. AFN leaders rejected the DOI bill as insufficient.

By 1971, the clamor for a settlement was especially loud from the oil companies, who wanted to start immediately on a trans-Alaska pipeline, and the state of Alaska, which faced bankruptcy if it did not soon realize oil revenues from the Prudhoe Bay discovery. Due to the land freeze, the state of Alaska had not received title to any federal land, nor had the BLM been able to lease any land to oil companies for the previous five years.

Supporters of a settlement were also threatened by the growing power of a newly emerged conservation group, the Alaska Coalition, who wanted to extend the land freeze (and thus block the Alaska pipeline) until an appropriate land use plan could be implemented for federal lands. The coalition feared the environmental destruction that developers, including the proposed Alaska Native corporations, would cause through abuses such as clear-cutting timberlands, oil spills, or unregulated mining.

Two significant issues blocking settlement were the amount of land (if any) to be awarded and the terms of its ownership. From 1968 to 1971, about a dozen bills and proposals emerged, with acreage awards that varied from zero to sixty million and ownership rights that ranged from trust status to nonexclusive subsistence use. The AFN faced formidable opposition from Senator Wayne Aspinall, chairman of the House Committee of Interior and Insular Affairs, and Senator Henry Jackson, chairman of the Senate Committee of Interior and Insular Affairs. Both senators espoused the 1940s and 1950s termination ideology of assimilation: that tribal existence, reservations, trust lands, and tribal sovereignty impeded what was best for Indians. Senators Jackson and Aspinall favored a smaller, money-only settlement.

The AFN lobbied intensely for forty million acres and substantial monetary compensation. They found support from the Nixon administration and the oil companies, both desperate for an agreement before the Alaska Coalition could muster the votes to add its conservation amendments, which many believed would stall the Alaskan economy with federal red tape. The final version of the bill contained most of the acreage and money that AFN wanted. The AFN also succeeded in getting the settlement administered by regional corporations directed by Alaska Natives. Earlier bills had called for the settlement to be overseen by the DOI or a statewide corporation managed by non-Native Alaskans.

The state of Alaska also won concessions. Congressmen allowed it most of the better lands from which to select, while generally restricting Native selections to less valuable lands around the roughly two hundred Native villages. The biggest winner of land, however, was the Department of the Interior. The late efforts of conservationists won them an amendment that required the federal government to remove eighty million acres for study. DOI land selections took precedence over state or Alaska Native selections.

Although the AFN voted to accept the final version, the settlement was criticized by some delegates who were unhappy that the sixty-million-acre version had not passed. But the loudest dissension came from the Arctic Slope Native Association (ASNA), who represented the sparsely populated north slope region occupied by the Inupiat (the Inuit of Northern Alaska). Because vast reservoirs of oil lay under their land, the Inupiat believed they were entitled to a larger share of the award than the per capita distribution that became law. Opponents of ANCSA did not believe the AFN served their interests, and they especially opposed the inclusion of the populous Tlingit Nation, who rejected a recent and relatively small $7.2 million court award in favor of joining the statewide Native settlement.

The Alaska Native Claims Settlement Act (ANCSA)

ANCSA was the offspring of President Richard Nixon's developing self-determination policy, the old federal policy of termination, and an urgent need for oil companies and the state of Alaska to remove all aboriginal title. Authors of the settlement wanted a solution without "creating a reservation system or lengthy wardship or trusteeship" (43 U.S.C. § 1601b). But they left open the possibility of continued BIA programs and the issue of Alaska Native sovereignty.

Alaska Natives gave up claims to nearly all of Alaska. In return, they received forty-four million acres, or about one-ninth of the state's land, and about $1 billion in payment. An amount of $462.5 million was paid out of the U.S. Treasury, and about $500 million came from a 2 percent royalty from mineral development on federal and state lands. Benefits were generally restricted to people of one-fourth degree or more of Alaska Native blood and/or who were recognized as Alaska Native by their village.

The act created twelve regional corporations, each assigned to a regional area whose resources would be exploited for profit. A thirteenth regional corporation, awarded money but no land, was reserved for Alaska Natives who had moved out of state. Alaska Natives would administer the boards of directors (and thus run the corporations) and would benefit from stock dividends. Each beneficiary received one hundred shares of stock, which would be inalienable until 1991. The corporations could vote to issue new shares to allow for population growth and to prevent inheritance problems.

The act also authorized the creation of around two hundred village corporations, which were to be operated under the supervision of the twelve regional corporations. Like the regional corporations, the village corporations were to be organized under Alaska state laws. The regional and village corporations would select the forty-four million acres from public lands (not already claimed by the state of Alaska, the U.S. Department of the Interior, municipalities, or private interests). The regional corporations retained both surface and subsurface rights to land development, whereas the village corporations kept only surface rights.

The language of ANCSA contained the most thorough extinction of aboriginal title of any U.S. treaty or legislative action dealing with indigenous people. The act extinguished all aboriginal title to land, submerged lands, inland water, or offshore water in Alaska based upon use and occupancy, including any hunting and fishing rights "that may exist." It also nullified any previous federal, state, or foreign treaties or statutes that recognized aboriginal title. The act abolished all reservations (except the Annette Island Reserve) and transferred the land to the corporations. It repealed the allotment acts of 1887 and 1910.

The Aftermath of ANCSA

Given the experimental nature and lack of precedent for the ANCSA, it should not be surprising that the act provided fertile ground for litigation. Some of the subsequent problems involved (1) federal agency interpretation of fuzzy provisions defining how the land and money were to be divided among the corporations; (2) the inalienability of stock, which allowed corporate mismanagement; and (3) the definitions of *Alaska Native* and *Native village.* The continuing evolution of ANCSA resulted in amendments in 1976, 1987, and 1998.

Most of the Native corporations endured a rough start due to the slow pace of the land selection process and to special restrictions, including the inalienability of stock and the need to balance profits with traditional culture. On an operating basis, the twelve regional companies collectively lost much of their $962.5 million award, but special legislation allowed them to sell some of these losses to other companies as tax write-offs. Inept management was also a problem. In 1999, the Alaska legislature audited Alaska's Division of Banking, Securities and Corporations (BSC) for oversight of the Native corporations. The audit revealed a number of deficiencies. Shareholders were misled by inadequate financial disclosure, and their complaints received insufficient attention. The auditors recommended BSC review of proxy materials before their transmission to shareholders, the creation of an independent watchdog group to protect shareholders, remedies for shareholders denied access to corporation records, and more detailed disclosure of compensation for officers and directors. Despite their shortcomings, the Native corporations remain vital to

Alaska's economy, contributing $2.5 billion in revenue and employing more than ten thousand workers (Adams 2002, 6). Their prospects will vary with government policies dealing with Alaska Natives and with prices of natural resources, including oil, coal, timber, and minerals.

Native corporations have had minimal impact upon the conditions of villages, whose locations were determined by the subsistence needs of the Native inhabitants rather than the business needs of the corporations. Comparatively few corporate employees live in the villages and therefore do not contribute their wages to the village economies. Although the influx of federal anti-poverty money in the 1960s and 1970s and oil wealth in the 1980s added material wealth to the villages, social conditions among the inhabitants worsened. The mortality rate is more than three times the national average. Economically, the villages remain dependent on public-sector spending. Despite some growth in incomes and jobs during the 1980s, villages still have much smaller incomes and higher unemployment rates than the state as a whole. The poverty rate is 21 percent, compared to 6.8 percent for all Alaskan families. The depressed economic condition coincides with a mortality rate more than three times the national average and an alcohol-related death rate triple that of non-Native Alaskans. Alaska Natives constitute 32 percent of the prison population, although they represent only 16 percent of the state population. The murder rate is four times the national average (Alaska Natives Commission 1996).

Sovereignty and the Venetie Decision

ANCSA failed to define a process satisfactory to Alaskan Natives of governing and regulating the lands obtained from the act. The settlement granted land titles in fee simple, which conveyed only ownership rights inherent in private property. Even so, many Alaskan Natives believed that the federal government would eventually recognize their nations as possessing the same form of limited sovereignty that allowed Indians of the lower forty-eight states to regulate their lands. In 1998, the Supreme Court decision in *Alaska ex rel. Yukon Flats Sch. Dist. v. Native Village of Venetie Tribal Gov't* (522 U.S. 1998, 520) proved otherwise. At issue was the right of the Native village of Venetie to tax a non-Native business located on its land. In 1987, the village sued to collect more than $160,000 levied against a construction company that had contracted with the State of Alaska to build a school in Venetie. The State of Alaska, which would have had to pay the tax, claimed that the village had no jurisdiction. At issue was whether the ANCSA extinguished the Venetie community's status as a dependent Indian community that encompassed a federal set-aside of land and federal supervision. In other words, was Venetie part of Indian country? After a Native victory in the U.S. Court of Appeals for the Ninth Circuit, the U.S. Supreme Court ruled against Venetie. The Court stated that ANCSA revoked all reservations that had been set aside, and because the land had reverted to fee simple status with no restrictions on alienation, it no longer qualified as Indian country. Its interpretation of ANCSA emphasized the congressional declaration of policy statement (section 1601b), which called for a settlement "without establishing any permanent racially defined institutions, rights, privileges or obligations, without creating a reservation system or lengthy wardship or trusteeship." The decision impacted all Alaska Natives who fell under ANCSA, because the act stipulated that the possession of their land was limited to fee simple ownership. Because they were not part of Indian country, their power to regulate activities within their boundaries was similar to that of a property owner rather than to that of a sovereign governing body. The decision left the Alaska Natives little legal basis for regulating wildlife within their borders, that task falling under the jurisdiction of the State of Alaska and/or the federal government. The inability to tax non-Native businesses seriously cut the revenue of some village corporations. The ruling implied that the villages had no civil or criminal jurisdiction over non-Indians, which left a vacuum of law enforcement, as the nearest authorities were sometimes located at distances requiring one or two days' travel.

Hawaii

During the nineteenth century, the Kingdom of Hawaii approved more than thirty treaties with foreign nations. Its first treaty negotiated with the United States, in 1826, recognized Hawaii's sovereignty and established trade relations. Although the island residents generally acknowledged the treaty, it was never ratified by the United States. As the Hawaiian Kingdom expanded its government and legal system to accommodate western demands, it negotiated treaties with members of the international community, including Great Britain, Japan, France, Samoa, and the United States. By 1850, the settlement of California and Oregon put

Hawaii firmly within the shadow of the United States. In 1875 and 1887, the Hawaiian Kingdom, strongly influenced by American businessmen, agreed to reciprocity treaties that allowed duty-free sugar into the United States. The resulting sugar boom led to a labor shortage and, shortly thereafter, an influx of Asian immigrants that doubled the population of the islands and reduced the Hawaiian component to less than 30 percent. In 1893, a coalition led by American businessmen and descendants of missionaries ousted the monarchy with the aid of the American consulate. Shortly afterward, the United States annexed Hawaii by a unilateral joint resolution of Congress rather than by treaty or agreement with the Native inhabitants. In 1993, Congress approved a resolution offering an apology for U.S. participation in the overthrow, acknowledging the lack of compensation for Native Hawaiians, and urging the executive branch to support reconciliation efforts between the American people and Native Hawaiians.

Early Treaties

In 1826, the United States sent two warships captained by Thomas ap Catesby Jones to protect the property and businesses of American traders and to collect debts owed them by the rulers. Jones extracted an agreement to pay the debts and negotiated what would be Hawaii's first commerce treaty. The treaty, which recognized Hawaiian sovereignty, contained provisions that included the protection of law-abiding Americans in Hawaii, the admission of American ships to Hawaiian ports, and reciprocal "most favored nation" status for import tariffs and trade privileges. This treaty, though never ratified by the United States, was generally recognized by both foreign and Native residents of the islands until it was replaced by the U.S. treaty of 1849.

During the 1830s and 1840s, whaling ships and various businesses began to expand the ports of Honolulu and Lahaina. When businessmen found a lack of Western authority to support their financial or land claims, they turned to their nation's diplomatic representatives, who contacted their governments for help. This period was marked by visits from a series of warships, which empowered their captains and consuls to settle most land claims and debts. On different occasions, foreign marines burned government buildings and heaped countless humiliations upon the Hawaiian government, which was headed by its monarch and a handful of devoted non-Native officials.

The one-sided treaties resulting from these visits made clear the need to establish a government that could cater to the demands of European economics and law. Native Hawaiian leaders turned to the American missionaries to help create such a government. Their combined efforts produced the Constitution of 1840, which incorporated the republican principle of popular representation, a significant departure from the traditional rule of the chiefs. Over the next decade, the new government formed the legal structure for the civil service, the judiciary, and land reform.

In addition to promoting Western law, the Protestant missionaries encouraged religious intolerance. Persecution of the struggling Catholic movement by the chiefs and missionaries brought an expected reprisal from France. In July 1839, Captain C. P. T. Laplace arrived in Honolulu Harbor aboard the frigate *L'Artemise*. A summarized version of his demands included fair treatment of Catholics residing on the islands, compliance with a treaty written by French officials and favorable to the French, and a $20,000 bond to ensure Hawaiian compliance with the terms of the treaty. Under the threat of war, the king signed the document.

The compact was the first of several lopsided treaties that would hamper the fledgling government's economic and political influence for the next two decades. The kingdom's ability to enforce criminal laws was now limited. Frenchmen accused of crimes had to be tried by a jury composed of foreigners who were approved by the French consul. Other nations demanded the same right. In the realm of commerce, the treaty barred Hawaii from forbidding the import of wines and spirituous liquor. This invasion of sovereignty effectively repealed the liquor prohibition instigated by the Protestant missionaries in their efforts to reduce alcohol abuse. The treaty forced the Hawaiian government to grant "most favored nation" status to imported French goods but not to grant similar status for Hawaiian products exported to France. The great powers often imposed this unequal provision during the imperialistic heyday of the nineteenth century.

Shortly after the French seizure of the Marquesas Islands and Tahiti in 1842, many foreign residents believed that Britain or France would soon claim Hawaii. Not surprisingly, a British frigate captained by Lord George Paulet appeared in Honolulu Harbor ostensibly to protect property rights and collect debts owed to British subjects. His demands were backed by the threat of attack and included a cession of land and reparations to the British consul, Richard Charlton, and the extension of British criminal law over British residents. The king reluctantly agreed to these deep impositions upon his sovereignty. When Paulet added new demands, including the overturning of recent court decisions and greatly increased indemnities, the Hawaiian government feared for its credibility. Believing that Paulet was determined to take the islands anyway, the king ceded them to Great Britain, hoping that a review by higher British officials would restore them to the Hawaiian crown. About six months later, Britain, respecting a joint accord with France supporting Hawaiian sovereignty, restored the kingdom but refused to pay for losses or damages caused by Paulet's activities.

In 1844, Hawaiian officials signed a convention similar to the French treaty with Great Britain. They again objected to provisions that limited the government's ability to deal with rowdy foreigners. They also objected to a restriction of their sovereign ability to bar British imports.

The first French and British treaties, although disagreeable to the Hawaiian ministers, did recognize the independence of the Hawaiian government. American residents, who felt bound by the more lenient treaty of 1826, wished to be granted rights similar to those granted by the French and British treaties. The king's written assurances of these rights, however, dissuaded them from pursuing a similar treaty.

After the British convention in 1844, the Hawaiian foreign minister, Dr. Gerrit P. Judd, began a quest for more balanced treaties. New British and French treaties signed in 1846 resembled earlier treaties but contained a small concession for alcoholic beverages that allowed the Hawaiian government import duties but not enough to significantly restrict their importation. Hawaiian officials wanted to restrict alcohol and shortly afterward submitted their own treaties to Great Britain and France, who rejected them.

At this time, U.S. officials petitioned the Hawaiian government to open negotiations for a new treaty. The recent acquisition of California gave the United States a new presence in the Pacific region. But more urgent was a dispute involving a rape accusation against an American citizen, who was not allowed the benefit of a jury selected by his country's consul. As this was a right enjoyed by British and French nationals, the resident U.S. consul, George Brown, accused Hawaiian officials of discrimination.

In 1846, U.S. Secretary of State James Buchanan instructed a new commissioner, Anthony Ten Eyck, to negotiate a treaty. He suggested using the existing British and French treaties as a guide. Instead, Ten Eyck submitted a treaty much harsher to Hawaiian interests. An angry British consul accused the United States of trying to make the islands a dependency. Among the terms Ten Eyck insisted upon was the right of the American consul to nominate juries for civil cases as well as criminal ones. Hawaiian officials objected vehemently. Later, Ten Eyck offered a document similar to the British treaty of 1846, but it was rejected due to resentment over its invasions of Hawaiian sovereignty and, perhaps, Ten Eyck's offensive behavior when he clamored for American interests. Hawaiian animosity rose to the point that officials refused to recognize him as the American consul.

Upon learning of Ten Eyck's failure to obtain a treaty and of alleged French ambitions in the islands, the new secretary of state, John M. Clayton, determined that the concerns of the monarchy and those of the American commercial interests were similar. In late 1849, Hawaiian and American officials in Washington signed a treaty that Hawaiians found more to their liking. Although it contained a few concessions for American whaling ships, it eliminated most of the offensive economic and criminal justice provisions of the British and French treaties.

After their troublesome encounters with Paulet and Laplace, Hawaiian ministers concluded that they must reorganize their government to fit a western model, or a foreign power would install its own administration. To conform to foreigners' demands for a fee simple system of land ownership, the king, the chiefs, and the government reluctantly agreed to a land division among themselves in 1848, which became known as the Great Mahele. Each group was given fee simple title to roughly a third of the lands. The hopes of missionaries and other foreigners to convert common Hawaiians (*makaainana*) into independent family farmers resulted in *kuleana* grants, authorized by the government in 1849. The kuleanas, typically small plots of fertile, irrigated land, were used by the commoners to grow taro, a staple Hawaiian crop. In 1850, after much debate, the legislature passed a law allowing foreigners to own land. This law, opposed by many Hawaiians, was forced by fears of a French takeover or an overthrow instigated by California "filibusters" and by local planters who were eager to export sugar to rapidly growing markets on the West Coast. Within

two decades, foreigners gained what they sought, the most desirable Hawaiian farm lands, with fee simple titles.

Fears of a French takeover intensified in 1848 following the arrival of French foreign consul, G. P. Dillon, presumably to settle French grievances. His list of demands included the lowering of import duties on alcoholic beverages and the repeal of laws that required customs-house documents to be printed in either English or Hawaiian. Dillon believed the requirement discriminated against the French language. Inadequate response from the Hawaiian government brought two French warships captained by Admiral Legoarant de Tromelin to Honolulu Harbor. After further negotiations proved unsatisfactory, French soldiers marched ashore and occupied the government buildings and the fort. They also confiscated the king's schooner, the *Kamehameha,* to ensure compliance with their demands.

Government ministers and American residents feared the French would seize the islands despite the U.S. treaty in 1849 that supported Hawaiian sovereignty. Anxious officials sent Dr. Judd to Washington, Paris, and London to seek support for the Hawaiian government. In the event of armed invasion by the French, the king resolved to put the islands under American protection. In Paris, Judd sought a political compromise, financial compensation for the ship *Kamehameha,* and damages for government property. French officials would not budge. Later, in Washington, Judd received further assurances of American support. The impasse lasted for nearly two years, during which American influence grew on the islands and on the U.S. West Coast. In 1851, France gave up any designs it may have held for the islands and agreed to a compromise.

Reciprocity with the United States

The efforts of Native Hawaiians and some *haoles* (non-Hawaiians) to preserve Hawaiian sovereignty met further hardship during the 1850s. European diseases continued to shrink the Native Hawaiian population. The major revenue source for the islands, the whaling industry, leveled off and started to decline, seriously threatening the economy. Planters understood the potential for agriculture, particularly sugar, but were discouraged by high foreign tariffs and a labor shortage. In 1855, the recent shift of power in the north Pacific toward Washington led to the refusal of the United States to endorse a joint protectorate with Great Britain and France that guaranteed Hawaii's independence. The United States emerged as a new and more potent threat to Hawaiian sovereignty.

Under these conditions, the business and foreign communities sought annexation with the United States, but their efforts failed to survive the objection of Kamehameha IV. In 1855, the king and business interests sought a reciprocity treaty that would allow Hawaii to export sugar and other agricultural products into the United States duty free. Opponents in Congress, at the behest of sugar planters in the South and wool interests in Vermont, defeated the treaty. Some feared that cheap sugar from the Philippines or China could be smuggled into the United States through Hawaii.

In 1866, the arrival of a pro-reciprocity U.S. minister, coupled with the continued stagnation of Hawaiian agriculture, encouraged high government officials to renew their efforts to attain a reciprocity treaty. U.S. Secretary of State William Seward supported the treaty, but he and other advocates faced a Congress preoccupied with Reconstruction. Opponents of reciprocity saw no need to fatten Hawaiian sugar planters at the expense of the U.S. Treasury. The argument that economic ties were needed to increase American influence in the islands fell upon deaf ears. According to a leading opponent, Senator William Fessenden of Maine, U.S. influence was already "sufficient to assure the concessions of whatever naval and commercial privileges are needed in the islands . . ." (Kuykendall 1953, 220), and American capital was needed at home. Some annexation supporters in the United States also opposed the treaty. They hoped that sugar planters, already in desperate condition, would rally Hawaiian support for annexation should reciprocity fail to pass Congress.

Other annexationists in the United States supported reciprocity, believing that American interests were not yet strong enough to procure the islands without the use of force. They preferred to further strengthen economic ties, believing that an influx of American businessmen and capital would eventually lead to American control of the government. The next economic depression in Hawaii (perhaps caused by nonrenewal of the prospective reciprocity treaty) would lead this enlarged American group to clamor for the security of annexation. A similar scenario would gradually unfold and then climax with the destruction of the monarchy forty years later.

Foreigners and haoles feverishly debated annexation in the latter 1860s. To planters, annexation offered a permanent solution to their export problems instead of the temporary seven years specified by the prospective reciprocity treaty. They also saw the Hawaii Constitution of 1864 as dictatorial and did not like the ministers Hawaiian sovereigns chose to help run the government. Native Hawaiians, still the vast majority on the islands, also suffered a loss of rights under the constitution but remained patriotic to the king and would not support annexation.

In 1870, the decline of whaling and the lack of markets for agricultural products continued to depress the economy and worry Hawaiian officials. Some observers in the United States feared a revolution if a reciprocity treaty could not be obtained or if a peaceful succession for the ailing and childless King Kamehameha V did not occur. The British commissioner wrote, "There is a great feeling of insecurity lest the King himself in a moment of weakness should be persuaded to sell his throne" (Kuykendall 1953, 247).

When Kamehameha V died in late 1872, two American warships remained in Honolulu Harbor to keep peace during the election of King Lunalilo. A year later, Lunalilo's death without a successor opened a struggle between dowager Queen Emma, an opponent of reciprocity and a favorite of traditional Hawaiians, and David Kalakaua, a strong advocate of Hawaiian independence who saw cooperation with foreigners as a way to achieve that end. The presence of three foreign warships in Honolulu Harbor served as a stabilizing influence during the election of Kalakaua but did not prevent rioting by Queen Emma's supporters afterward.

King Kalakaua's well-publicized and successful tour of the United States in 1875 reopened treaty negotiations. His delegation warned the State Department that, if a treaty could not be negotiated, Hawaii would turn to Great Britain, New Zealand, or Australia. Reciprocity with Hawaii continued to face staunch opposition from special interest groups in the United States. Sugar plantations in the South could not produce sugar as cheaply, East Coast sugar refiners did not wish to compete with West Coast refiners fed by cheap Hawaiian sugar, and labor advocates condemned the terrible working conditions of Asian contract labor. Other opponents abhorred the idea of enriching Hawaiian planters and West Coast refiners at the expense of the federal government.

Nor was the treaty universally popular in Hawaii. The British faction correctly feared that the government would raise duties on British imported goods to make up for the loss of tax revenue resulting from American reciprocity. The most important opposition came from Native Hawaiians led by Queen Emma, who feared the loss of sovereignty, as a sugar boom would surely attract more foreigners. Even King Kalakaua feared the growing American influence and sought assurance from the British consul that Britain would support the monarchy in the event of an insurrection led by resident American annexationists.

Treaty proponents in Congress pointed to the location of the islands in the central Pacific as an economic gateway to Asia. Expanded commercial ties would bring Hawaii further within America's sphere of influence. At this time, many of the proponents sought not eventual annexation but rather an extension of the Monroe Doctrine.

The reciprocity initiative proved successful; the treaty was ratified by Congress and went into effect September 9, 1876. The agreement provided for the duty-free exchange of agricultural goods (most notably sugar), basic materials, and manufactured items between the two countries. It also limited Hawaiian sovereignty by restricting the nation from leasing any of its harbors or by agreeing to reciprocity with any other foreign power. Its ultimate impact upon the sugar industry was enormous; acreage planted in sugar increased tenfold between 1874 and 1898.

Conflict between the Hawaiian Government and the Business Community

During the 1880s, Honolulu businessmen and the foreign community increasingly railed against government corruption. Many believed that King Kalakaua's government paid too little attention to the constitution, employed sycophants in the civil service, packed the legislature, and was bankrupting the kingdom. The king also balked at ceding Pearl Harbor to the United States in return for a renewal of the reciprocity treaty. Discontented businessmen, led mostly by descendants of Protestant missionaries, formed the Hawaiian League, which numbered four hundred by 1887. They engaged the services of the Honolulu Rifles, an all-white, volunteer militia, which, according to historian Gavan Daws, was the "only well-organized military company" in Hawaii (Daws 1968, 246). Backed by the U.S. minister and the Honolulu Rifles, the league forced King Kalakaua to consent to a new cabinet, composed of league members, and a new constitution in which his authority was reduced greatly. The Bayonet Constitution, as it was called, removed certain voting

rights of most Native Hawaiians and extended the franchise to most foreigners. The constitution never achieved ratification by popular vote.

In 1891, U.S. President Benjamin Harrison signed into law the McKinley Act, which eliminated tariffs from sugar imported into the United States and subsidized sugar grown domestically. As American purchasers could now buy sugar cheaper in certain other countries than in Hawaii, the act effectively nullified the reciprocity treaty and led to an economic depression in the islands.

The following year, the slowdown began to exact a severe toll upon the government, which faced declining tax revenues and demands that it stimulate the economy. The legislative session in 1892, the longest on record, was marked by quarrels among haoles, Native Hawaiians, several political groups, and Queen Liliuokalani, who still possessed veto power over bills that failed to pass by a two-thirds majority. The queen ultimately won passage of two controversial bills, a lottery act and an opium licensing act, which she hoped would raise government revenues.

The most visible aspect of the conflict between Liliuokalani and the business community was the legislative struggle for control of the queen's cabinet. The Constitution of 1887 left the sovereign monarch the right to choose a cabinet but allowed the legislature, with sufficient votes, to disband it. In 1892, members of the legislature voted on seven no-confidence motions, four of which succeeded. On each occasion, the queen simply appointed a new cabinet.

The Overthrow of the Hawaiian Government

Most foreigners and haoles greatly feared Queen Liliuokalani's support of a new constitution that would restore power to the monarchy and voting rights to Native Hawaiians. In early January 1893, when it appeared that the queen was planning to proclaim such a constitution, a handful of insurrectionists created the Committee of Public Safety, the purpose of which was to eliminate the monarchy and then to create a provisional government that would exist until annexation with the United States could be achieved. They appealed to the U.S. minister to Hawaii, John L. Stevens, for military protection. Stevens, a rabid expansionist, obliged. On January 16, he arranged for approximately 160 well-armed troops to march through the streets of Honolulu to a town hall located across the street from the government building and in sight of the queen's palace. Although the Hawaiian foreign minister protested their presence to Stevens, the public remained unaware of the troops' motives. Under the protection of American guns, members of the Committee for Public Safety read a statement on the steps of the government building. Attracting a small gathering of spectators, the committee declared the overthrow of the monarchy and the establishment of a provisional government. Stevens immediately recognized the new government, even though it was a paper entity having no control over the government bureaucracy, including the treasury, archives, or police. He also ignored the wishes of Native Hawaiians, nearly all of whom staunchly opposed a pro-annexation government.

Queen Liliuokalani yielded power "to the superior force of the United States of America" only after being informed that Stevens supported the provisional government. To prevent loss of life and to avoid diplomatic questions involved in firing on American troops, she surrendered under protest and in the belief that higher American authorities would reinstate her later.

The committee worked quickly. Several members rushed to Washington, compiled an annexation treaty with the help of the outgoing William Henry Harrison administration, and submitted it to the Senate a month later. The treaty emphatically stated that the United States had played no part in the overthrow of the monarchy. Because this and other annexationist claims contradicted the queen's story, incoming president Grover Cleveland withdrew the treaty and sent Congressman James H. Blount of Georgia to investigate the revolt.

Blount's report detailed a deliberate conspiracy between Stevens and annexationist planters and businessmen to overthrow the kingdom. Blount found that the troops were landed not to guard American life and property but to assist in removing the existing government. Cleveland withdrew the treaty. Stevens was replaced by Albert Willis, who, in accordance with instructions from Cleveland, offered to restore the throne on the condition that amnesty be given to the conspirators. At first, the queen refused, believing they should be subject to Hawaiian law and punished, but a month later she relented. By this time, Cleveland had submitted the restoration question to a hostile Congress, a move that undoubtedly strengthened the provisional government. When Willis asked the provisional government to step down, its officers refused, claiming the president lacked the authority to intervene in

Hawaii's internal affairs. Cleveland was not inclined to force the matter, given the strength of the annexationists in Congress. In early 1894, the U.S. Senate Foreign Relations Committee held its own hearings in Washington and afterward issued the Morgan Report, which cleared Stevens and the marines of any moral improprieties.

Annexation

Expecting that Hawaii would not be annexed during Cleveland's term, in mid-1894 leaders of the provisional government declared a constitutional republic with Sanford Dole as its president. A year later, Robert Wilcox, a mixed-blood Hawaiian, led an unsuccessful rebellion in which authorities arrested Queen Liliuokalani for her alleged involvement. The new government forced her to sign a statement abdicating her throne in exchange for reducing the punishment of Wilcox and other conspirators.

With the ascension of pro-annexation William McKinley to the presidency in 1898, expansionists again brought a Hawaii annexation treaty before Congress. The queen issued a formal protest, stating that the treaty ignored (1) the Blount report; (2) the wishes of Native Hawaiians (who at that time numbered about forty thousand, compared to the three thousand foreigners who supported the revolt); (3) compensation for lands ceded to the United States; (4) all previous treaties between the United States and the Kingdom of Hawaii; and (5) the violation of international law. More than thirty thousand Native Hawaiians signed a petition opposing the treaty. Some congressmen were undoubtedly moved by the protest and recent publicity citing the bad treatment of American Indians. The treaty failed to attain the two-thirds majority required to pass the Senate. But annexationists reintroduced the measure as a joint resolution (the Newlands Resolution), which required only a simple majority. The resolution passed and was signed into law. It scrapped all existing treaties of the Hawaiian republic and placed the new territory under the coverage of U.S. treaties. It also transferred to the United States lands belonging to the Hawaiian Crown and government and all rights of sovereignty.

Use of a joint resolution instead of a treaty to annex Hawaii was considered unconstitutional by some congressmen. But annexationists pointed to the Republic of Texas, which had been annexed by joint resolution, as sufficient precedent. However, the residents of Texas had clearly stated their preference for annexation at the polls. The large number of signatures protesting Hawaiian annexation provided strong evidence to the contrary for Hawaii.

Congress established a territorial government by passage of the Hawaiian Organic Act of 1900. The new government preserved most of the laws enacted under the old kingdom, including the recognition of Hawaiian tradition and custom and limited land rights. Except for land used for military purposes, the 1.8 million acres of Crown and government lands obtained by the Newlands Resolution were placed under control of the territorial government.

The end of the kingdom was a direct result of U.S. policy as reflected in its treaties with Hawaii. The last two treaties, the reciprocity of 1875 and the extension of reciprocity in 1884, created a tidal wave of American capital and Asian immigrants. As Native Hawaiian groups had feared, the reciprocity period (1876–1900) saw a drastic decline in the Native Hawaiian population as a percent of the total. In 1876, the population of the islands numbered 55,000, of which 89.2 percent were Hawaiian. By 1900, immigration for plantation labor had swelled the number to 154,000, of which Hawaiians constituted 26 percent. This shrinking percentage, along with the widespread belief that Native Hawaiians would become extinct, inevitably undermined the foreign community's support for what they considered an expensive and inefficient monarchy. After annexation, the major forum for Native Hawaiians to regain their rights, land, and sovereignty would be the U.S. legal system.

The Aftermath of Annexation

In 1910, Queen Liliuokalani sued the United States for the return of the Crown lands. The U.S. Court of Claims ruled that the lands were originally part of the public lands of the kingdom, not the queen's private property. The court relied on a case in 1864, *In re Estate of Kamehameha IV* (2 *Haw.* 1864, 715), which held that the king's land was not his private property but "belonged to the chiefs and people in common."

After annexation, the population and welfare of Native Hawaiians continued to deteriorate. Numbering an estimated 300,000 at the time of Cook's visit in 1778, the population of full-blood Hawaiians had dwindled to 23,723 by 1920. Soon after annexation, advocates for Native Hawaiian rights led by Kuhio Kalaniana'ole, Hawaii Territory's delegate to Congress, started lobbying Congress to restore some of the ceded lands (former Crown and government lands) to Native Hawaiian ownership. They obtained some leverage in 1910, when certain land provisions of the Hawaiian Organic Act were amended to encourage homesteaders at the expense of sugar growers. In 1921, a compromise that granted sugar interests the best agricultural lands allowed the passage of the Hawaiian Homes Commission Act. The act removed from the ceded lands about 200,000 acres, to be held in trust for Native Hawaiians who wished to homestead. Advocates hoped that the relocation of Native Hawaiians to the land as independent family farmers would save them from extinction as a race. This ideology supported the distribution of kuleanas seventy years earlier and, for Native Americans, the General Allotment Act of 1887 and the removal of the Five Civilized Tribes in the 1830s.

The 200,000 acres were poor lands; most of the land lacked water for irrigation, and nearly one-third was either barren lava or steep mountain slope. Native Hawaiians saw little satisfaction in the administration of the land trust, first by the territory and later by the state. Lack of federal and state funding to oversee the program, to settle Hawaiians on the land, and to provide water forced administrators to collect revenue by leasing the lands. Some of the original 200,000 acres were transferred to various government agencies, mostly the military. Native Hawaiians were kept on a long waiting list, which by 1998 totaled 7,503 persons. By this time, about 20 percent of the trust lands had been homesteaded.

In 1959, the State of Hawaii, as a condition of its admission to the Union, agreed to take control of the ceded lands from the federal government and to lease them under a public land trust for five specific uses, including public education, the betterment of the conditions of Native Hawaiians, and the increase of home and farm ownership. From 1959 until 1978, the state allocated most of the money to public education.

In 1978, the state held a constitutional convention in which its trust obligation to Native Hawaiians was further clarified. The convention established the Office of Hawaiian Affairs (OHA), a new state agency to lobby for Native Hawaiians and improve their conditions. The agency would receive funds, land, and resources held in trust for or intended for use by Native Hawaiians. Controlled by a board of trustees consisting of at least nine Native Hawaiians, it would allocate those assets and formulate policy for Native Hawaiians.

Authorizing such an agency was one thing, but funding it was another. Following the initiative of the constitutional convention, two years later the legislature specified a funding source of 20 percent of all funds derived from the ceded lands. This act proved difficult to enforce and thus formed the foundation for uncertainty and litigation that has yet to be resolved. In 1983, the OHA sued the state of Hawaii for its share of revenue from sand mining, the Honolulu International Airport, harbors, and other uses of ceded lands. Four years later, the Hawaii Supreme Court dismissed the case, essentially saying that the 20 percent revenue provision was too vague for court interpretation and that such funding needed further legislative definition.

In 1990, the legislature responded with Act 304, which again stated that "twenty percent of all revenues derived from the public land trust shall be expended by [OHA] for the betterment of the conditions of Native Hawaiians." The act defined "revenues" to include rents, charges, and fees from the use of the ceded lands. As a result, the state and the OHA negotiated a settlement for $130 million for claims dated between 1980 and 1991.

In 1994, OHA sued to settle claims for past revenue from other sources, including the Waikiki duty-free shop, public housing, and the Hilo Hospital. In spite of public outcries that the potential liabilities could bankrupt the state, the state district court ruled in favor of the OHA. The state appealed to the Hawaii Supreme Court.

Shortly afterward, the U.S. Department of Transportation threw opponents of Act 304 what would soon become a legal life raft. Department officials determined that state payments to OHA violated a federal law, the Airport and Airway Improvement Act of 1982. This act required all monies collected by owners from airport sources to be used for airport development, not to fund other projects. One implication of the ruling was that the state would have to find another source of money to pay OHA for airport use. In further negotiations, the state offered $250 million and revenue-producing lands, but OHA trustees rejected the offer.

In September 2001, the Hawaii Supreme Court ruled in favor of the state, reversing the district court. The judges decided that the revenue provision of Act 304 directly conflicted with federal law. As the legislators had written the act as nonseverable, the court ruled the act vacated. The court did acknowledge the state's obligation to Native Hawaiians and exhorted the legislature to see that they benefited from the ceded lands trust.

The Sovereignty Movement

Coinciding with Indian and Alaska Native activism in the 1960s and 1970s, Native Hawaiians formed various nationalistic organizations focusing on numerous issues such as Native land rights threatened by intensive development of the islands, reform of the Hawaiian Homelands program, Native access to beaches and trails, ceded land disputes, desecration of burial grounds, and the desecration of the volcano goddess Pele by drilling geothermal wells in the Kilauea volcano.

In the mid-1980s, Native Hawaiians stepped up their efforts to receive federal recognition as a sovereign nation, similar to the recognition received by more than five hundred Indian and Alaskan Native groups. Hawaiian activists formed numerous sovereignty and self-determination groups; some of the largest include Aboriginal Lands of Hawaiian Ancestry (ALOHA), Hui Ala Loa, and Kingdom of Hawai'i.

Enactment of a congressional joint resolution (107 *Stat.* 1510) in 1993 apologizing for the overthrow of the monarchy marked a major milestone for the sovereignty movement. The apology acknowledged that the Kingdom of Hawaii had been an independent nation, to which the United States had extended "full and complete diplomatic recognition" and with which the United States had entered into several treaties. Congress admitted the illegality of the overthrow and the contribution of the United States to it. The significance of the joint resolution lay in its recognition that Native Hawaiians had never relinquished sovereignty over their lands, a point that could be vital for future litigation. Also important, it urged the president to support reconciliation efforts between the United States and the Native Hawaiian people.

As part of the reconciliation process, the U.S. Departments of Interior and Justice, at the request of Hawaii's Senator Daniel Akaka, held hearings with Native Hawaiians to determine direction and consensus. Their report recommended that Native Hawaiians, through congressional action, should possess limited sovereignty within the framework of federal law, as do Native American tribes. The United States should recognize a Native Hawaiian governing body similar to those of Native American tribes in order to initiate a government-to-government relationship.

The largest and best-funded Hawaiian governing body at that time was the OHA. But the ability of the OHA to act as a legitimate government was crippled in 2000 by the U.S. Supreme Court ruling in *Rice v. Cayetano* (528 U.S. 2000, 495), which held that the state law restricting the election and membership of OHA trustees to Native Hawaiians was unconstitutional. By expanding the electorate and elected trustees to include non-Native Hawaiians, the decision negated the credibility of OHA and its effectiveness as a Native Hawaiian representative body. The decision left open the possibility of a congressional solution, that of bringing OHA and other Hawaiian programs under federal supervision. Such an approach has since been proposed in Congress but has yet to pass.

Linda S. Parker

References and Further Reading

Adams, Jacob. 2002. "Native Lands Key Factor in State's Growth." *Resource Review Newsletter* (August): 6.

Alaska Natives Commission. 1994. *Final Report. Vol 1: Healing Harmony Hope*. 3 vols. Anchorage: Alaska Natives Commission.

Andrade, Ernest. 1996. *Unconquerable Rebel: Robert W. Wilcox and Hawaiian Politics, 1880–1903*. Boulder: University Press of Colorado.

Berger, Thomas R. 1995. *Village Journey: The Report of the Alaska Native Review Commission*. Rev. ed. New York: Hill and Wang.

Case, David. 1984. *Alaska Natives and American Laws*. Fairbanks: University of Alaska Press.

Daws, Gavan. 1968. *Shoal of Time: A History of the Hawaiian Islands*. Honolulu: University of Hawaii Press.

Dudley, Michael, and Kenoni Agard. 1990. *A Call for Hawaiian Sovereignty*. Honolulu: Na Kane O Ka Malo Press.

Kuykendall, Ralph. 1938. *The Hawaiian Kingdom*, vol. 1, *1778–1854, Foundation and Transformation*. Honolulu: University Press of Hawaii.

Kuykendall, Ralph. 1953. *The Hawaiian Kingdom*, vol. 2, *1854–1974, Twenty Critical Years*. Honolulu: University Press of Hawaii.

Kuykendall, Ralph. 1967. *The Hawaiian Kingdom*, vol. 3, *1874–1893, The Kalakaua Dynasty*. Honolulu: University Press of Hawaii.

Liliuokalani. 1898. *Hawaii's Story: By Hawaii's Queen*. Boston: Lothrop, Lee & Shepard.

McClanahan, Alexandra. 2000. *Growing Up Native in Alaska*. Anchorage: AK: The Ciri Foundation.

Merry, Sally. 2000. *Colonizing Hawaii: The Cultural Power of Law.* Princeton, NJ: Princeton University Press.

Mitchell, Donald. 1997. *Sold American: The Story of Alaska Natives and Their Land, 1867–1959.* Hanover, NH: University Press of New England.

Mitchell, Donald. 2001. *Take My Land, Take My Life: The Story of Congress's Historic Settlement of Alaska Native Claims, 1960–1971.* Fairbanks: University of Alaska Press.

Osorio, Jonathan. 2002. *Dismembering Lahui: A History of the Hawaiian Nation to 1887.* Honolulu: University of Hawaii Press.

Parker, Linda. 1989. *Native American Estate: The Struggle over Indian and Hawaiian Lands.* Honolulu: University of Hawaii Press.

Tate, Merze. 1965. *The United States and the Hawaiian Kingdom: A Political History.* New Haven, CT: Yale University Press.

Tate, Merze. 1968. *Hawaii: Reciprocity or Annexation.* East Lansing: Michigan State University Press.

U.S. Department of State. 1895. *Papers Relating to the Foreign Relations of the United States for 1894. Appendix 2.* Washington, DC: Government Printing Office.

Canadian Indian Treaties

Introduction

In what is now called Canada, treaty making has been the primary means of fostering colonization since the 1600s. Although it has been the cornerstone of the largely peaceful Indian-settler relationship for the past four centuries, its enduring benefits have been overwhelmingly one sided. Treaty making was the approach preferred by the First Nations as well as the European parties to sort out the essential terms of how colonists and their governments would relate to the original owners of the land throughout most of North America. The history of negotiating treaties, their political and legal significance up to the present day, and the many disputes that continue to arise regarding their meaning create a situation that is, however, markedly different from that found in the United States. Understanding the place of treaties in modern Canada is possible only through a full appreciation of the different types of treaties signed over the years, the history of treaty formation, and the evolving legal importance that treaties have acquired more recently. One must also recognize that Indian perspectives on the function of treaties and the precise rights they contain have differed dramatically from the views held by Canadian governments over the intervening decades, and that considerable conflict, disappointment, anger, and frustration have been the result.

Recent judicial interpretations, along with the entrenchment of the protection of treaty rights in Canada's constitution in 1982 [Section 35(1) of the Constitution Act, 1982, states, "The existing aboriginal and treaty rights of the aboriginal peoples of Canada are hereby recognized and affirmed."], have resurrected the importance of historic Indian treaties as well as the necessity for new treaties to be negotiated with Indian, Inuit, and Métis peoples. The Inuit (still called Eskimos by many in the United States) did not share the precontact treaty-making tradition, nor was their interaction with newcomers regulated in this fashion. The Métis—reflecting the emergence of a new people springing from the merger, then reformulation, of both European and Indian cultures and origins—were often shunted aside during treaty negotiations. Occasionally, the Métis were included within the scope of Crown-Indian treaties as individual beneficiaries or as communities adhering to its terms rather than through separate agreements. Both Inuit and Métis peoples have adopted the treaty model in recent years to develop major land claim settlements and new governance arrangements within Canada.

France was the first significant colonizing presence from Europe; it also sought peaceful trading relationships with the Indian nations and negotiated some treaties to encourage such opportunities. The displacement of the French regime from the Maritimes in 1713 and from Quebec in 1763 by Great Britain meant that the latter's legal system and emphasis on treaties has dominated the experience throughout North America. As both Canada and the United States were established predominantly as British colonies, with the same common-law legal system and the same initial approach to dealing with the Indian nations encountered by European settlers, it is not surprising that both countries today share many common perceptions of treaty relationships. American case law, with its far greater volume and earlier vintage, has had considerable influence on the development of Canadian thinking in this regard. In fact, some of the earliest treaties relating to Indian nations resident in Canada were actually negotiated in the American colonies, particularly in Boston. The border between the two countries also bisects the traditional territory of various Indian nations from coast to coast to coast.

The content of the common law and official government policy of Great Britain in the 1600s were both shaped largely by the emerging international law doctrines first enunciated by Spanish theologians and legal thinkers, especially Francisco de Vitoria, and within the Roman Catholic Church in the mid-sixteenth century. After extensive debate and a period of controversy, international law came to recognize the indigenous peoples of the so-called New World as human beings with souls who were entitled to respect and to protection from physical violence. The developing theory of international law also recognized them as "peoples," who constituted sovereign nations with ownership rights over their territories.

Even though Europeans did not appreciate it at the time of contact, indigenous states practiced treaty making extensively before they ever encountered people from the other side of the Atlantic Ocean. A wide variety of treaty relationships existed among many of the Indian nations in North America, in some places extending over immense distances. Trading of natural resources and produced goods could occur over thousands of miles. Military alliances also were forged in opposition to common enemies, and military conflict was frequently resolved through the creation of new peace and friendship commitments accompanied by solemn treaty promises.

From the perspective of Indian nations, turning to the institution of treaties as the primary peaceful method for dealing with newcomers was logical—the only alternatives were war or complete avoidance of contact, both of which were also pursued at various locales and times. However, the flood of migrants from overseas, coupled with their attractive trade goods, quickly led the Indian nations along the Atlantic coast to conclude that peaceful relations were the preferred choice. Likewise, from the European perspective, treaties were a logical device to regulate future relationships, as that was how Europeans themselves attempted to organize their own internal relationships among competing states.

Treaty making, therefore, worked well as a common vehicle for both sides to pursue the establishment of new relations based upon clear understandings. Each party was able to pursue its separate interests within a shared construct. The pure act of negotiating out of self-interest brought together leading representatives in a context of equal status with the common objective of reaching agreement. Treaties became the best way to cement a relationship inspired by desires for peace and friendship, to encourage trading patterns that were economically beneficial to both sides, and to create potentially powerful military alliances against common enemies, be they other European colonial powers or Indian nations.

It should be understood that control over treaty making on the European side rested exclusively with the empire. That is, the imperial government possessed the sole prerogative to decide when to negotiate new treaties, with whom to seek such relationships, and on what terms. Only the Crown could appoint representatives with a mandate to bind the government. The people on the ground—the colonists—could enter into private contracts of trade, but they had no authority whatsoever as private individuals or as communities to negotiate formal treaties or to acquire land directly from Indian nations.

The individual Indian nation that occupied particular territory was viewed as the rightful owner of that soil in accordance with the terms of its own rules or laws. According to those laws, land was usually held with collective or communal title and could not be individually conveyed or sold. This meant that the "discovering" European nation could not claim exclusive title to the "new" lands but merely the sole right, vis-à-vis other European countries, to enter into treaty relations regarding trade and military alliances or to acquire land for settlement from a willing Indian nation. International law did, however, recognize a principle of conquest such that a victor in war obtained the legal right to seize territory and substitute its sovereignty for that of the defeated nation. Local law would remain in force, however, until the conqueror chose to impose any changes, including a decision to establish new governments.

The Evolution of Treaty Making in Canada

Canada has experienced four distinct eras in which treaties were negotiated: (1) from the earliest days of contact to the American Revolution, (2) from 1790 to independence in 1867, (3) from 1867 to 1930, and (4) the modern era, from 1975 to the present. Each period is considered in turn.

Peace and Friendship Treaties

The primary focal points of treaty relations in the 1600s and 1700s—and of international or intergovernmental relationships in general among Europeans and Indian nations at this time—were on trade, military alliances, and peaceful interaction so as to permit colonies to flourish and to generate maximum economic wealth for the mother countries. Early agreements often involved some small land conveyances by the Indian partners for trading posts, military forts, and modest colonial settlements while also establishing a pattern of gift giving on the part of the Crown. The offering of presents, which was to become a common element in almost all later treaties, made sense to Europeans as well as to indigenous peoples in the Americas, as each was accustomed to presenting tokens of esteem and recognition on formal occasions. Nevertheless, the clear majority of the gifts presented came from the European emissaries.

The first formal treaty between the British Crown and the Iroquois Confederacy, the Treaty of Albany of September 24, 1664—also known as the Two Row Wampum—typifies a number of these elements. The Iroquois, then consisting of five distinct nations but later increasing to six when the Tuscarora Nation joined the Confederacy early in the eighteenth century, were a major military force and far more numerous than the British in the region. They had previously been allies of the Dutch, who transferred their interest in New Netherlands (renamed New York) to the British in 1664. The Iroquois were also long-standing adversaries of the Huron Nation, who had previously forged an alliance with the French colony of New France in the St. Lawrence River valley that included the provision of rifles. Treaty negotiations between the Iroquois Confederacy and the British representatives extended over several days, resulting in separate agreements on September 24 and 25 that consisted of the following key elements:

1. "[T]hat the Indian Princes above named and their subjects, shall have all such wares and commodities from the English for the future, as heretofore they had from the Dutch."
2. Each party pledged to capture and punish any fugitive committing any injury or violence to a person under the other's protection so that all due satisfaction would be given to the victim.
3. The English were mandated to "make peace for the Indian Princes, with the Nations down the River."
4. The English promised not to assist the three nations of the Abenaki Confederacy and to provide accommodation to the Iroquois if they should be beaten by those nations. (O'Callaghan 1853–61:3, 67–68)

The treaty was recorded in English, and an official version on parchment was given to the Iroquois. The treaty was also recorded on a wampum belt, which was delivered to Colonel George Cartwright (on behalf of the Duke of York). The Iroquois method of recording the significance of important events involved the sewing together of beads made from seashells on animal skins in pictorial patterns unique to that particular event. Thus, each party followed its traditional practice of acknowledging the importance of this historic and solemn occasion in a manner that reflected its culture while making mutual assurances to honor in perpetuity the promises made.

Treaty making was rapidly adopted as the preferred strategy of Great Britain, as it expanded Great Britain's colonial and trading empire either through being welcomed by Indian nations into their territory or through acquiring the European claims of its predecessors. A number of treaties were negotiated with the Wabanaki Confederacy (the Mi'kmaq, Maliseet, Penobscot, and Passamaquoddy Nations), in northern New England and the Maritime colonies from 1678 until 1761. These treaties often followed political withdrawals by the Wabanaki's former ally, France. Their purpose, more generally, was the commitment of both partners to peaceful and friendly relations, to exclusivity in trade, to nonmolestation of each other's citizens, to respect for criminal and civil jurisdiction, to the release of prisoners, and to the refusal to aid deserters.

The early success of the treaty mechanism (and the absence of an economically and politically attractive alternative) caused it to be used over and over again to meet immediate needs as well as for longer-term objectives, including the end of any hostilities that may have arisen, so as to restore peace and foster trade. Treaties were negotiated by Britain all along the Atlantic seaboard, from Georgia to Nova Scotia and as far west as the Appalachian Mountain range, from 1664 to the end of the American Revolution.

The emphasis upon England retaining control and the importance of treaty making overall to imperial strategy was later confirmed by the Royal Proclamation issued by King George III on October 7, 1763, after the Seven Years' War between France and Great Britain ended through the Treaty of Versailles. One major objective was to create new colonial governments for the former French colonies (in what later became the provinces of Quebec and Prince Edward Island) as well as for the former Spanish colony of Florida. The Royal Proclamation also sought to confirm the position of Indian nations by declaring that they were to be left unmolested by colonists in their remaining territories inside of the British colonies unless they were willing to sell their lands to properly appointed Crown representatives, who would negotiate the purchase through public meetings resulting in formal treaty arrangements. Outside the colonial borders, largely to the west of the Appalachian Mountains, was expressly confirmed by the king as preserved as Indian country for their continued exclusive use.

American Independence to Canadian Independence

The American Revolution quickly changed everything both for the United States and for Canada. The land demands of colonists had been one of the driving forces underlying the American Revolution; hence the desires of land speculators—including George Washington, military veterans, and others in search of farmland—were able to flourish without the imperial constraints that previously had required the colonies' adherence to treaty promises and had restricted treaty making to the Crown. Although some Indian nations joined with those rebelling and others remained neutral, many tribes had honored their military alliance with the British and were now on the losing side without the continuing protection of the Crown or the existence of prior treaties.

The birth of the new country meant, of course, that all residents needed to decide for themselves where their future lay. Many colonists who had remained loyal to the Crown, the so-called United Empire Loyalists (or UELs), chose to flee the United States and move to what remained of British North America, namely, Canada. They suddenly needed massive quantities of land on which to resettle, a factor that immediately changed the pattern of the prior Indian-Crown relationship on the Canadian side of the border, where colonial settlement had been limited.

The American victory also encouraged a major relocation of many tribes from the eastern coast of the new United States; these Indians moved westward and, in some cases, fled northward into Canada along with the UELs.

Although victorious, the United States was an extremely vulnerable country, its economy in tatters and the solidity of its success in the Revolution uncertain, with no guarantee against future British invasion. The French Revolution, which occurred only a few years later, provided some political comfort but effectively robbed the United States of its major European ally. Thus, the United States wanted to create peaceful relations with outside powers and to stabilize its domestic situation. To meet these objectives, it wisely sought to inherit the benefits of the treaty relationships possessed by the British within American territory and to form new ones. The United States could not merely succeed to existing British treaties, because they stemmed from the defeated empire; the young country had to form new relationships of its own, which began with the Treaties of Hopewell with the Cherokee, Choctaw, and Chickasaw Nations in 1785 and 1786. Similarly, the United States did not wish publicly to be perceived to be merely following British policies, such that it needed to demonstrate its independence from its former mother country. Therefore, British decrees had to be modified and given new birth as American instruments. The Royal Proclamation of 1763 was transformed by the U.S. Congress into the Non-Intercourse Act, passed on July 22, 1790, although the orientation was largely the same.

A direct effect of the Revolution was an unleashing of pent-up demand for Indian land, thereby weakening the Indian nations that remained within American borders in political terms as well as economic and military ones. A by-product of the necessity for tribes to make peace with their far more populous neighbor was to look to the U.S. judiciary as a potential mechanism for their ongoing protection. Because they could no longer realistically appeal to the British Crown as an ally, and in the face of their declining military and trading importance to the American government, the only available alternative to leaving their traditional territory became the American court system.

This choice also presented serious challenges for Indian nations who saw themselves as fully sovereign. How could they invoke the protection of a foreign court operating in a totally different legal system and in a foreign language? This was not an attractive option by any means, or one that many Indian nations chose, although a few did. What they discovered, not surprisingly, was a judicial system that was itself relatively fragile, a new institution primarily concerned about its own place within the American system of government and the vulnerability of this new country.

Through three key decisions in the 1820s and 1830s, the U.S. Supreme Court, under the leadership of Chief Justice John Marshall, sought to develop a principled legal foundation for what was essentially a political compromise that justified the imposition of U.S. might and law on sovereign, independent countries. The stark options essentially available to the Court were either the continuation of a fully Indian, independent-nation sovereignty theory, or a complete absorption of Indian people into the body politic. The former could threaten American stability, as it would mean that Indian nations would retain the capacity to form treaties with European nations of their choosing—including the British to the north, whom they had defeated on two occasions, the French and Spanish to the south, and potentially others. That possibility, obviously, was not attractive from an American perspective.

On the other hand, to deny all Indian sovereignty would contradict the treaty history that existed in North America, as well as the initial post-Revolution efforts of the U.S. government to form peaceful, treaty-based relationships with Indian nations. Such a legal position would also undermine the federal government's own constitutional authority, as the Constitution's division of powers with state governments had not precisely addressed the question of who possessed jurisdiction to engage in law-making and other aspects of noncommercial Indian affairs. Denying Indian sovereignty also could have the consequence of making the Indian people subjects or, potentially, citizens with a right to vote. Framed in a different fashion, the latter legal analysis would have meant that the federal government did not have the capacity to regulate the important economic domain of Indian trade, to deal with potential military threats, and to control vital revenue matters. It must be noted that one of the most significant methods of raising revenue before the introduction of the income tax system was the sale of government land. If the federal government controlled the acquisition of land from Indian nations through treaties, then it would acquire the revenue from the resale of those lands to settlers and thereby could direct the growth of populations and the creation of new states.

Therefore, the status of Indian nations and their treaty relationships held grave importance for the U.S. Supreme Court, which was intent on flexing its legal muscles as it strove to confirm its identity as the ultimate arbiter of the U.S. Constitution. Chief Justice John Marshall's response to these opportunities was to develop a hybrid approach—neither full acceptance nor full denial of the competing legal streams. He decided, instead, to construct a legal doctrine that transformed formerly independent Indian sovereignty into a continuing but internal variation through the concept of domestic dependent nationhood. Indian nations were defined as "domestic" in the sense that they were declared to have lost international status or the capacity to form relations with foreign countries. Their governments and their traditional territories were simply stated to be internal to the United States. They were further deemed to be "dependent" in that their authority was rendered subject to some initially undefined power on the part of Congress and the executive branch to infringe upon their autonomy. Marshall also drew upon the imagery that Indian nations, by virtue of being dependent, were somehow like wards in relation to the U.S. government as their protector or guardian.

The source of Marshall's thinking was largely his assessment of the tides of history, in which he drew heavily upon his own research conducted for the preparation of a mammoth biography of George Washington. This was coupled with his desire to draft a compromise that advanced federal interests while simultaneously respecting some recognition of the reality of Indian nations as distinct, self-governing peoples who were the rightful original owners of the soil. His theory indicates that Indian sovereignty remains in existence yet is constrained, such that what remains of the formerly complete sovereignty is the residue that is subject to further intrusions by Congress in the future. This residual sovereignty includes the continuing power to negotiate treaties, but only with the United States, and to surrender territory for sale.

The landmark litigation before the Supreme Court in *Cherokee Nation v. Georgia* (1831) and *Worcester v. Georgia* (1832) did not, in fact, protect the Cherokee Nation; on the orders of President Andrew Jackson, they, among others, were forcibly dispossessed of their territory and marched west of the Mississippi—the infamous Trail of Tears.

The Canadian experience during this same time period involved less drama; however, its consequences for many Indian nations were no less dramatic. The pressure for land to accommodate the arriving UELs and allied Indian nations required treaty making to switch emphasis from encouraging trade and peace to obtaining land on a massive scale for settlement and agriculture. Clearing the land in the south for farming meant a drastic reduction in the wildlife population's capacity to support the traditional economy and reduced the importance of the fur trade, causing much of the trapping to relocate north and westward. The new wave of land cession treaties began in the late 1780s in southern Ontario, following the procedures of the Royal Proclamation of 1763 but focusing on acquiring clear legal title to land, in a form of property conveyance in return for a lump-sum payment that consisted of a combination of money and trade goods. Promises were made to reassure the Indian negotiators that they would continue to receive regular presents, would be able to hunt, fish, and trap as before, would be able to harvest wild or grown foods, and would retain some of their traditional lands. Little was said, however, about how the influx of white colonists would drastically reshape the landscape. By 1818, imperial officials were complaining that the cost of treaty payments was becoming too onerous for the local colony to bear; this led to the substitution of a scheme for annual payments (annuities). This effectively meant that an installment payment plan was used, in which Indian nations were compensated for their land out of a small portion of the money that actually came from the resale of Indian land to settlers and speculators, leaving the sizable profits to defray the cost of colonial government.

The next significant development in the nature of treaties in Canada occurred through the negotiation of the Robinson-Huron and Robinson-Superior Treaties, which affected the upper Great Lakes region. Not only did these two treaties operate on a far larger geographic scale (affecting more than twice the territory of all prior land surrender treaties combined), but they also introduced the concept of creating Indian reserves for individual communities out of small portions of the territory surrendered under treaty. These reserves were then set aside, after the extinguishment of aboriginal title, for the exclusive use of individual Indian communities, and the underlying title was claimed by the Crown. The Robinson Treaties effectively set the stage for all of the post-confederation treaties until the modern era.

Treaties from 1867 to 1930

Canada was formally confirmed as a semi-independent country in 1867, with Great Britain retaining ultimate control over all foreign affairs until the Statute of Westminster was passed by the United Kingdom Parliament in 1931; even then, the parliament's approval was required to amend Canada's constitution until 1982. Canada considerably expanded its territorial base in 1870 by acquiring western and northern lands held by the Crown and those lands owned by the private Hudson's Bay Company under a royal charter issued two hundred years earlier. The new national government of Canada immediately launched upon a campaign to negotiate treaties with the Indian nations in the southern portions of these areas to allow agriculture, forestry, and mining on a large scale while setting the stage for an expected massive influx of new settlers from Europe and the building of a national railway system.

The so-called numbered treaties (numbered from 1 to 11 as they were negotiated from 1871 to 1921, with adhesions to Treaty 9 signed as late as 1930) followed the pattern set by the two Robinson Treaties of 1850. The written form of each treaty (in English only) involved the surrender of vast tracts of traditional territory to the federal Crown by Indian leaders on behalf of their populations. In return, the Indians were promised small parcels of land to be set aside as exclusive Indian reserves for particular communities, annual payments to each member, guarantees of continued hunting and fishing rights, and occasional other benefits (such as schools, farming implements, ammunition, and medical supplies).

The indigenous version of the treaty negotiations, the oral promises made during the discussions, and the content of the final agreement are consistently asserted to differ dramatically from the "official" text. Many Indian elders have relayed stories of the negotiations as having focused on sharing the territory with the newcomers rather than surrendering the land absolutely, as Mother Earth could not be "sold." Many others allege that only the surface of the land "to the depth of a plough" was being shared or given but not the subsurface resources, and that the territory was to be left undamaged.

Few of the Indian participants could anticipate the large-scale settlements that were to occur in many of the treaty areas or how the influx of farmers and foresters would fundamentally alter the landscape in a way that would virtually destroy the traditional economy in the southern portion of the Prairies in only a few years. The thrust of the federal vision was that treaties would open up the region for immigrants and Canadians moving westward, whereas Indian people would disappear or be converted over time into farmers with their own plots of land so as to be assimilated into the general agrarian society. This policy was maintained even in northern areas that were completely ill-suited for agriculture with the technology available at the time.

The establishment of the residential school system in the 1880s and its removal of all school-age children, enforced vigorously through pass (permission to leave the reserve) restrictions by police and government officials, coupled with the drastic reduction in wildlife harvesting opportunities and trapping income, left many Indian communities devastated—economically, socially, politically and spiritually. The Métis Nation was left in an even more destitute situation, as no communal land base was provided for their survival under treaty or otherwise. A federal statutory scheme, started in Manitoba in 1871 to offer individual entitlements to blocks of land or cash (called scrip) to Métis families

in lieu of treaty benefits, generated little tangible gain, as most recipients were quickly defrauded by land speculators.

The passage of time led to a significant shift in federal governmental attitudes, as Indian people were thought to face either extinction as a race (in part through the massive death toll from imported diseases) or complete absorption into Canadian society as an underclass of farm workers and domestic laborers. Indian reserves became the means to "smooth the dying pillow" or to serve as a laboratory for social re-engineering and assimilation. This perception was far removed from the former view of sovereign Indian nations as military allies and valuable trading partners. Over time, treaties came to be viewed by nonaboriginal citizens as anachronistic documents that had outlived their purpose and were to be neither renewed nor replicated elsewhere. All of this was to change, however, with the decision in 1973 of the Supreme Court of Canada in *Calder v. Attorney General of British Columbia.*

The Modern Treaty Era

The *Calder* case was launched by the Nisga'a Nation of northwestern British Columbia as the latest salvo in their century-long struggle to have their land rights recognized by the Crown. They went to court to assert their rights over their traditional territory through the common-law doctrine of aboriginal title and drew heavily upon the Marshall decisions of the U.S. Supreme Court to support their argument. They lost at trial, before the provincial court of appeal and again before the Supreme Court of Canada, ultimately on the procedural basis that they did not have the consent (or "fiat") of the provincial government they were suing at a time when Crown immunity was still absolute. Nevertheless, six of the seven judges who addressed the case on its merits concluded that the doctrine of aboriginal title was still good law in Canada. Both leading judgments relied primarily on American jurisprudence to support their positions. Although these six judges were evenly split on whether or not the aboriginal title of the Nisga'a had been effectively extinguished by general public lands legislation during the colonial era, they all were of the view that the Nisga'a had never surrendered their title by treaty or lost it through conquest. The judges declared that aboriginal title could only have been extinguished by unilateral Crown action, and they differed on the level of explicitness required to meet the test for extinguishment. Even the leading opinion of Justice Wilfred Judson, which ruled against the Nisga'a continuing to possess aboriginal title, still stated, "[T]the fact is, that when the settlers came, the Indians were there, organized in societies and occupying the land as their forefathers had done for centuries."

The fallout of this landmark decision for the federal government was immense, for it compelled both a complete reversal of its previous views and acceptance of the fact that aboriginal title likely still existed in large parts of Canada where no historic treaty had previously been negotiated. The government of Canada issued a major policy pronouncement in August 1973, in which it proposed to negotiate "comprehensive land claims agreements" based on unextinguished aboriginal title in the form of modern treaties. Litigation immediately ensued in the Northwest Territories and Quebec to block major proposed petroleum pipelines and hydroelectric projects. An agreement-in-principle was reached on November 15, 1974, among the Grand Council of the Cree, the Northern Quebec Inuit Association (now called the Makivik Corporation), the federal and provincial governments, Hydro-Quebec, and the James Bay Development Corporation, as the first major land claims agreement in the modern era. The parties concluded the final 455-page agreement the following November; over the next two years, legislation was passed by the National Assembly of Quebec and the Parliament of Canada to give the agreement added legal force.

Major modern land-claim settlements have been negotiated between the government of Canada, the relevant provincial or territorial government, and the aboriginal titleholders over the past thirty years, as follows:

- The James Bay and Northern Quebec Agreement (1975)
- The Northeastern Quebec Agreement (1978)
- The Inuvialuit (or Western Arctic) Final Agreement (1984)
- The Gwich'in Final Agreement (1991)
- The Nunavut Land Claims Agreement (1993)
- The Sahtu Dene and Métis Comprehensive Land Claim Agreement (1993)
- The Nisga'a Final Agreement (2000)
- Eleven individual Yukon First Nation Final Agreements based on the Council for Yukon Indians-Canada-Yukon Umbrella Final Agreement (1993), starting in 1995 and ending with the last one ratified in 2005

The Tlicho (Dogrib) Land Claims and Self-Government Agreement (2003)
The Labrador Inuit Land Claims Agreement (2003)

The enabling legislation for the last two agreements on this list was proclaimed law in 2005. These settlements are all modern treaties that confirm exclusive land rights for the Indian, Inuit, and Métis participants of the relevant agreements that exist in Quebec, British Columbia, Yukon, Northwest Territories, Nunavut Territory, and Labrador, totaling more than 600,000 square kilometers (or more than 230,000 square miles). Many of them also include detailed descriptions of self-government jurisdiction. In addition, six large Métis settlements were established by the provincial government of Alberta in the 1930s for the exclusive use of those communities. As a result, almost 7 percent of Canada today is recognized as exclusively in aboriginal hands; however, these territories are not equitably distributed; many aboriginal communities are still without recognized lands.

The ongoing effort to negotiate new treaties in Canada is a long way from a conclusion for many First Nations and Métis peoples, although the process is now completed for the Inuit all across northern Canada. Aboriginal communities in many parts of the country are still struggling for recognition that their traditional territory remains in their exclusive hands. Unresolved aboriginal title claims are in negotiation in southern parts of the Northwest Territories, the Yukon, Labrador, Quebec, the Ottawa valley region of Ontario, and throughout much of British Columbia. Ownership or title and jurisdiction of Canadian portions of the Great Lakes and the offshore waters remain outstanding. One can also anticipate that similar land claims will begin at some stage in the future in other parts of British Columbia and in the rest of Atlantic Canada concerning First Nations as well as the Labrador Métis. Negotiations have finally begun in Nova Scotia concerning the continuing legal and political significance of the treaties of peace and friendship of the early eighteenth century between the Mi'kmaq Nation and the British Crown in the aftermath of the *Marshall* commercial fishing decisions of 1999. Similar discussions may soon commence in New Brunswick and Prince Edward Island involving the Mi'kmaq and Malecite Nations.

The issue of Métis land rights, in regard to instances of extensive fraud under the nineteenth century scrip system in the Prairies and also based on aboriginal title, has yet to find a sympathetic ear among nonaboriginal governments in Canada (other than the negotiations involving the South Slave Métis Tribal Council, Canada, and the government of the Northwest Territories). The 2003 decision of the Supreme Court of Canada in *R v. Powley* may advance the thinking in this regard, although the existence of aboriginal title for the Métis has yet to be brought to court.

Also vigorously pursued by most First Nations is another type of land claim. *Specific claims* relate to unfulfilled treaty promises for the creation of reserves and other breaches of lawful obligations concerning reserve lands and natural resources. Whereas comprehensive land claims are based upon unextinguished aboriginal title, specific claims focus upon the loss of specific reserve lands, federal maladministration of band funds, and failure to fulfill or honor treaty promises in a manner that could be considered to breach Canadian law or equity. More than six hundred specific land claims are currently in negotiation, are under review by the federal Departments of Indian and Northern Affairs and Justice, or have been appealed to the Indian Specific Claims Commission. More than two hundred other claims have been settled over the past thirty years. A further three hundred claims are still in early stages of the assessment process, whereas estimates of one thousand to two thousand more claims not yet filed have been suggested.

A further reality is that federal and provincial governments are slowly recognizing that First Nations and Métis communities are not only entitled to govern themselves but should be allowed to get on with doing so. Thus, First Nations are confirming their jurisdictions in various parts of the country, with the concurrence of federal, provincial, and territorial governments, through negotiating self-government agreements that can take the form of treaties. Perhaps the best-known, most controversial example in this regard has been the Nisga'a treaty in British Columbia, the validity of which has been unsuccessfully challenged in a number of lawsuits. Eleven self-government agreements are in place in the Yukon (with three more under negotiation), one in the Northwest Territories, and one in Labrador. There are also agreements-in-principle or final agreements on self-government with the Meadow Lake Tribal Council in Saskatchewan, the Sioux Valley First Nation in Manitoba, the United Anishnabeg Council in Ontario, and Deline First

Nation in the Northwest Territories as well as a number of sectoral agreements with the Mohawks of Kahnawake.

The Position of Aborginal Peoples

The 2001 census report on the status of aboriginal peoples indicates that slightly more than 1.3 million people have some aboriginal ancestry, with 976,305 individuals defining themselves as being North American Indian (608,850), Métis (292,310) or Inuit (45,070) (Canada 2003a). The latest data demonstrate that the level of self-identification directly as an aboriginal person grew by 22.2 percent from 1996 to 2001. At least half of this growth stems from personal redefinition, that is, individuals choosing to redefine themselves as to their aboriginal identity. This redefinition can be seen, for example, in the Métis population, as it increased by 43 percent during this short period. The official population of Indian people recognized as such by federal statute (the Indian Act) has also grown at an extremely rapid and varied rate, rising from only 323,782 registered Indians in 1981 to 690,101 twenty years later (Canada 2003b). This growth, however, is inconsistent, as the Indian population grew at an overall annual rate of more than 7 percent from 1986 to 1999 but only 1.9 percent per year from 1991 to 1996 (Guimond 1999).

A number of possible explanations exist for this excessive and varied growth. First, it is clear that higher birth rates and longer life spans have naturally increased the aboriginal population. Nevertheless, natural population growth alone is incapable of explaining levels that far exceed the theoretical maximum of 5.5 percent for natural annual population increase (Guimond 1999). A second possible explanation can be attributed to the changing legal status and definition of the designation *Indian*. The 1985 amendments to the federal Indian Act have caused the percent change in the registered Indian population growth rate to fluctuate considerably, nearly quadrupling between 1985 and 1986 before returning to preamendment levels (Canada 2002). As of December 31, 2001, a total of 112,306 Indians were registered based on the legislative amendments of 1985 and made up 16 percent of the Indian Register (Canada 2002). A third possible explanation may also be attributed to ethnic mobility, a phenomenon whereby the ethnic identity chosen and reported by individuals changes over time (Guimond 1999).

This growing aboriginal population is becoming increasingly urbanized, while social problems are still very common, unfortunately, in First Nations communities. The number of status Indian children kept in nonparental care increased by 50 percent during the 1990s. Statistics regarding the state of health among aboriginal peoples are also highly discouraging; however, there are signs of improvement. Since 1975, the life expectancy for an aboriginal male has increased from 59.2 years to 68.9 years in 2000. Similarly, aboriginal women are now expected to live to 76.6 years, whereas in 1975 the life expectancy was only 65.9 years (Canada 2002). Although life expectancy for aboriginal peoples is expected to continue to rise and to draw nearer to that of the general Canadian population, there continues to be a gap between these two groups of approximately 6.3 years (Canada 2002). In comparison to nonaboriginals, the much higher rates of illness, injury, and death among aboriginal peoples serve as a constant reminder of the disparities that exist within Canada. Suicide rates for both male and female registered Indian youth are five and seven times higher, respectively, than the Canadian average; these youth suicide rates represent some of the highest in the world (Guimond 2002). In 1997, the rate of tuberculosis in First Nations was approximately eight times that of the rest of Canada (Canada 2002). Moreover, registered Indians in Canada continue to suffer from far higher rates of diabetes, heart disease, hypertension, arthritis, and violent death.

The rate of incarceration of aboriginal peoples in Canada remains extraordinarily high and disproportionate with respect to the remainder of the nonaboriginal Canadian population. Although Canada already possesses one of the highest incarceration rates among developed countries at 129 per 100,000 Canadians, adult aboriginal people are imprisoned at more than eight times the national rate. High unemployment continues to plague aboriginal communities and ensures that a large segment of the population remains on social assistance. Almost 38 percent of reserve residents (or 148,236 Indian people, on a monthly average) depended upon social assistance payments for survival in 2000–2001 (Canada 2002). Many more relied largely on employment insurance, old age pensions, and payments from the Canada Pension Plan. In this way, the largest source of income for a majority of on-reserve residents came directly from individual federal payments. There were, however, post-secondary education rates of more than 27,000

status Indians per year; 35 percent were over thirty years old, and two-thirds of them were women. It should also be noted that $5 billion from the Department of Indian and Northern Affairs and an additional $2 billion from other federal departments is provided annually; 90 percent of this funding targets only First Nations and Inuit groups. This causes a growing number of complaints and litigation from the Métis and nonstatus Indians, who feel they deserve equivalent attention.

Despite the statistics indicating a growing population, severe societal issues, and highly economically dependent communities, the national land base set aside exclusively as Indian reserves remains at only three million hectares, or approximately 0.3 percent of Canada. This small reserve space provides a thoroughly inadequate natural resource base, creating substantial pressure on most First Nations, who find it increasingly difficult to accommodate their populations and support their economies. Métis peoples face an even more restrictive situation, as fewer than 5 percent have access to the six Métis settlements in Alberta. This dire situation has increased significantly the importance placed, in recent years, on the proper fulfillment of treaty commitments made in historic treaties by the Crown, on settling outstanding land claims, and on negotiating new treaties to reflect current realities and future aspirations. Those aboriginal communities who have successfully concluded modern treaties in recent years face a far brighter future than those without such agreements. It should be appreciated, however, that achieving even a modern treaty is not an end in itself. Ongoing struggles also arise for Inuit, Métis, and First Nations parties in their efforts to seek full implementation of the fundamental commitments made in the new treaties by governments and to ensure that, this time, the relevant government signatories will honor the terms of these solemn promises.

The Modern Legal Status of Treaties

Treaty negotiations have been heavily affected in several critical respects by the jurisprudence that has evolved over the last twenty years. As discussed following, the courts have articulated a clear set of principles that must guide all efforts to interpret the proper meaning to be given to historic as well as modern treaties. The Supreme Court has also definitively established the existence of a fiduciary relationship between the Crown and aboriginal peoples, which has received constitutional elevation through Section 35 of the Constitution Act, 1982. Each of these basic tenets is having a profound impact on the way in which both federal and provincial governments must interrelate with Indian, Inuit, and Métis communities.

Legal Interpretation Principles for Treaties

The current chief justice of Canada, Beverly McLachlin, summarized the jurisprudence developed by Canadian courts over the prior three decades in the leading treaty fishing-rights case of *Regina v. Marshall (No 1)* in 1999. She listed the following as the proper legal guidelines to be used in interpreting treaty provisions (at paragraph 78 with sources deleted):

1. Aboriginal treaties constitute a unique type of agreement and attract special principles of interpretation.
2. Treaties should be liberally construed and ambiguities or doubtful expressions should be resolved in favour of the aboriginal signatories.
3. The goal of treaty interpretation is to choose from among the various possible interpretations of common intention the one which best reconciles the interests of both parties at the time the treaty was signed.
4. In searching for the common intention of the parties, the integrity and honour of the Crown is presumed.
5. In determining the signatories' respective understanding and intentions, the court must be sensitive to the unique cultural and linguistic differences between the parties.
6. The words of the treaty must be given the sense which they would naturally have held for the parties at the time.
7. A technical or contractual interpretation of treaty wording should be avoided.
8. While construing the language generously, courts cannot alter the terms of the treaty by exceeding what "is possible on the language" or realistic.
9. Treaty rights of aboriginal peoples must not be interpreted in a static or rigid way. They are not frozen at the date of signature. The interpreting court must update treaty rights

> to provide for their modern exercise. This involves determining what modern practices are reasonably incidental to the core treaty right in its modern context.

It is important to note, however, that these principles may be subject to modification when interpreting a modern treaty, as the circumstances are drastically different. The aboriginal party has received the full benefit of legal counsel and is negotiating highly detailed documents through a lengthy period of time in a language with which they are comfortable. The federal court of appeal has suggested that modern treaties should be viewed quite differently and more akin to other contractual agreements among relatively equal parties. The Quebec Court of Appeal has adopted a somewhat hybrid approach and has suggested that modern treaties should be interpreted according to the intentions of all the parties, rather than automatically assuming that any ambiguities will be resolved in favor of the indigenous signatory. At the same time, the court also noted the fundamental importance of the subject matter in that case—education—to the Cree. The court concluded that a liberal, generous interpretation was warranted for the provisions concerning the participation of the Cree in discussions establishing the annual budget for the Cree school board.

Jurisprudence thus indicates that the Crown and its representatives, in dealing with all historic treaties, must adhere to the general treaty principles elaborated by the courts over the last forty-two years since the leading decision of the British Columbia Court of Appeal in *Regina v. White and Bob* in 1964. In the intervening years, these principles have become somewhat modified—but only slightly—in the effort to ascertain the true meaning of the language used in modern treaties and other agreements reached between aboriginal peoples and federal or provincial governments.

The primary focal point for conflicts between First Nations and other governments, resulting in frequent litigation, is the assertion of treaty-protected harvesting rights running afoul of general legislation aimed at regulating natural resources on Crown (federal or provincial government-owned) lands. These conflicts became commonplace in the 1950s with the more vigorous enforcement of hunting and fishing laws in rural and northern areas. The amount of litigation escalated considerably in the 1960s with the imposition of more detailed statutory restrictions on impermissible locations for harvesting fish and wildlife, allowed methods and equipment for harvesting, establishment of licensing requirements, identification of precluded and permitted harvesting times, and regulation of the sale of harvested goods. Asserting treaty rights as a ground of defense has been a common strategy in many parts of Canada since the 1970s, and the volume of charges laid for allegedly illegal activity by First Nations members has yet to abate noticeably, even though treaty rights obtained constitutional protection in 1982. It has also become more common of late for Métis and nonrecognized Indian people to be charged with such violations and for them to seek to assert an aboriginal or treaty right to hunt or fish free from such statutory restraints. A major reason for this continuing conflict is that the federal and provincial legislation in this sector has rarely been designed to accommodate the unique legal situation of aboriginal harvesters and treaty rights. As a result, governments have sought to impose a uniform natural resource management regime upon aboriginal peoples, who firmly believe they have an inherent right to maintain their traditional activities free from external regulation. The latter perspective is often further supported, in many parts of the country, by solemn Crown commitments, given in express language in individual treaties, that the Indian parties and their descendants would be free to hunt, fish, and trap forever as they had done for untold number of generations.

In recent years, similar conflicts have extended beyond wildlife to include disputes over aboriginal and treaty rights to log trees on Crown land for personal use, to use in the production of goods, and for sale as raw logs. The Supreme Court of Canada in July 2005 overturned appellate courts in Nova Scotia and New Brunswick that had previously upheld treaty rights to commercial logging (*Regina v. Marshall* and *Regina v. Bernard* respectively). The Supreme Court decided that the specific language in the treaty in question guaranteed only a right to trade goods today that were proven to have been actively traded with the British at the time the treaty was signed in 1760–1761. Because there was some limited trade in wood products at that time but not in raw logs themselves, the defendants did not have the treaty right to harvest trees on Crown land and then sell the logs without provincial government permission in the form of a license. Many other natural resource claims have yet to be pursued on a treaty basis.

Rights have also been asserted through reliance on particular treaty terms for exemption from income tax, for guarantees of financial support for university education, for the provision of free and comprehensive health care, for the availability of adequate housing, and regarding other important governmental initiatives. Efforts have also been made to resist the application of gun control and other laws to First Nations through reliance on treaty commitments. These efforts have met with mixed success.

A further recent development in treaty litigation in Canada has been the complaints of First Nations and Inuit peoples, with either modern or historic treaties, that other governments have not consulted with them effectively prior to making decisions that may have a major impact upon their daily lives and territories. This concern has arisen in relation to federal or provincial proposals to launch new policies or programs—or to change existing ones—in allocating natural-resource harvesting rights to companies; in approving planned mines and petroleum developments; and in considering potential environmental impacts of energy projects, the building of new roads, and the like. Similar protests have been launched by First Nations seeking to negotiate new treaty agreements who believe that their position will inevitably be altered for the worse prior to reaching such arrangements if governments authorize large-scale logging, mining, oil drilling, electricity generating, and other such projects on land that is subject to aboriginal title claims. The same strategy has been used to challenge aquaculture operations (fish farms) and other activities in coastal waters, by insisting upon full First Nations' involvement in decision making so as to protect the environment. The Supreme Court of Canada, in the *Haida Nation* case, has confirmed that the federal and provincial governments have a legally enforceable duty to respect the honor of the Crown by consulting meaningfully with aboriginal communities when their unique aboriginal or treaty rights might be negatively impacted. This duty may also require the government to seek to accommodate legitimate aboriginal concerns by altering its proposals or requiring changes from third parties before authorizing the planned activities to proceed if these constitutionally protected rights might be infringed.

Conclusion

Over the past four centuries, Canada has been reasonably successful in forging peaceful relationships within its external borders between the descendants of European settlers (as well as immigrants from the rest of the world) and the original sovereign owners of this land, as succeeded by the First Nations, Inuit, and Métis peoples of today. In many parts of Canada, these relationships have been built upon the foundation of mutually binding commitments in the form of treaties. Canada has been far less successful, however, in ensuring that a common understanding of the fundamental purpose of these treaty compacts, along with a mutual acceptance of the precise meaning of the treaty terms, remained alive among—and were honored by—subsequent generations. Oral histories of the actual treaty negotiations and the words agreed upon are very much a part of the fabric of regular life for many First Nations communities. Most nonaboriginal Canadians, however, have virtually no knowledge whatsoever of the significance of Crown-Indian treaties in their own lives as a critical source of the rights and benefits that they enjoy as members of Canadian society and as the source of much of the prosperity on which the Canadian economy has been built. The ongoing need to negotiate treaties for the first time in some parts of the country, along with the need to revitalize and renew the historic treaty commitments from generations ago, will continue to be a noteworthy aspect of domestic development for quite some years to come. Through devoting greater attention to the import of treaties, whether they result from hands extended in friendship several centuries ago or through the flourish of pens at signing ceremonies yesterday and tomorrow, hopefully Canadians will develop a greater appreciation of their unique opportunity to create a truly modern nation based on profound respect and partnership.

Bradford W. Morse

References and Further Reading

Court Cases

Calder v. Attorney General of British Columbia, SCR 313 (1973).

Cherokee Nation v. Georgia, 30 U.S. 1 (1831).

Haida Nation v. British Columbia (Minister of Forests), 3 SCR 511 (2004).

Johnson v. M'Intosh, 21 U.S. 543 (1823).

Mikisew Cree First Nation v. Canada (Minister of Canadian Heritage), 1 CNLR 78 (2006).

Regina v. Marshall (No. 1), 3 SCR 456 (1999).

Regina v. Marshall (No. 2), 3 SCR 533 (1999).

Regina v. Marshall; Regina v. Bernard, 3 CNLR 214 (2005).

Regina v. Powley, 4 CNLR 321(SCC) (2003).

Regina v. White and Bob, 50 DLR (2d) 193 (B.C.C.A.) (1964).

Worcester v. Georgia, 31 U.S. 515 (1832).

Books and Articles

Alfred, Taiaiake. 1999. *Peace, Power and Righteousness: An Indigenous Manifesto.* Don Mills, ON: Oxford University Press.

Asch, Michael, ed. 1998. *Aboriginal and Treaty Rights in Canada.* Vancouver: University of British Columbia Press.

Bell, Catherine, and Karin Buss. 2000. "The Promise of Marshall on the Prairies: A Framework for Analyzing Unfulfilled Treaty Promises." *Saskatchewan Law Review* 63(2): 667.

Bird, John, Lorraine Land, and Murray MacAdam, eds. 2002. *Nation to Nation: Aboriginal Sovereignty and the Future of Canada*, 2nd ed. Toronto: Iwin.

Borrows, John. 1992. "Negotiating Treaties and Land Claims: The Impact of Diversity within First Nations Property Interests." *Windsor Yearbook of Access to Justice* 12: 179.

Borrows, John. 2005. "Creating an Indigenous Legal Community." *McGill Law Journal* 50: 153.

Brown, George, and Ron Maguire. 1979. *Indian Treaties in Historical Perspective.* Ottawa: Research Branch, Indian and Northern Affairs Canada.

Canada. 2002, March. Department of Indian Affairs and Northern Development, *Basic Departmental Data 2001.* Ottawa: Public Works and Government Services. Online: <http://www.ainc-inac.gc.ca/pr/sts/bdd01/bdd01_e.pdf>, at 2.

Canada. 2003a, January. *Census: Aboriginal Peoples of Canada: A Semographic Profile* Ottawa: Minister of Industry. Online: Statistics Canada<http://www12statcan.ca/english/census01/Products/Analytic/companion/abor/contents.cfm?>

Canada. 2003b, March. Department of Indian Affairs and Northern Development, *Basic Departmental Data 2002.* Ottawa: Public Works and Government Services. Online: http://www.ainc-inac.go.ca/prsts/bdd02/bidd02_c.pdfat3

Coates, Ken. 2000. *The Marshall Decision and Native Rights.* Montreal: McGill-Queen's University Press.

Guimond, Eric. 1999. "Ethnic Mobility and the Demographic Growth of Canada's Aboriginal Populations from 1986 to 1996." In *Report on the Demographic Situation in Canada, 1998–1999.* Ottawa: Statistics Canada.

Guimond, Eric. 2002. "Aboriginal Profile 2001." Unpublished. Hull, ON: Indian and Northern Affairs Canada.

Groves, Robert K., and Bradford W. Morse. 2004. "Constituting Aboriginal Collectivities: Avoiding New Peoples 'In Between.'" *Saskatchewan Law Review* 67(1): 257.

Henderson, James [Sakej] Youngblood. 1997. "Interpreting Sui Generis Treaties." *Alberta Law Review* 36(1)1: 46.

Henderson, James [Sakej] Youngblood. 2000. "Constitutional Powers and Treaty Rights." *Saskatchewan Law Review* 63(2): 719.

Indian Treaties and Surrenders from 1680–1890. 1905. Ottawa: S. E. Dawson. Reprint, Saskatoon, SK: Fifth House, 1992.

Imai, Shin. 1999. *Aboriginal Law Handbook*, 2nd ed. Scarborough, ON: Carswell.

Isaac, Thomas. 2001. *Aboriginal and Treaty Rights in the Maritimes: The Marshall Decision and Beyond.* Saskatoon, SK: Purich.

Mainville, Robert. 2001. *An Overview of Aboriginal and Treaty Rights and Compensation for Their Breach.* Saskatoon, SK: Purich.

Morse, Bradford. 2004. "Aboriginal and Treaty Rights in Canada." In *Canadian Charter of Rights and Freedoms/Charte canadienne des droits et libertés*, 4th ed., eds. Gérald-A. Beaudoin and Errol Mendes, 1171–1257. Markham, ON: LexisNexis Butterworths.

O'Callaghan, Edmund Bailey, ed. 1853–1861. *Documents Relative to the Colonial History of the State of New York.* Albany, NY: Weed, Parsons.

Price, Richard, ed. 1979. *The Spirit of the Alberta Indian Treaties.* Montreal: Institute for Research on Public Policy.

Purich, Donald. 1988. *The Métis.* Toronto: James Lorimer & Company.

Royal Commission on Aboriginal Peoples. 1995. *Treaty Making in the Spirit of Co-Existence: An Alternative to Extinguishment.* Ottawa: Canada Communication Group.

Royal Commission on Aboriginal Peoples. 1996. *Report of the Royal Commission on Aboriginal Peoples.* Ottawa: Canada Communication Group.

Slattery, Brian. 2000. "Making Sense of Aboriginal and Treaty Rights." *Canadian Bar Review* 79: 196.

Treaty 7 Elders and Tribal Council with Walter Hildebrandt, Sarah Carter, and Dorothy First Rider. 1996. *The True Spirit and Original Intent of Treaty 7.* Montreal: McGill-Queen's University Press.

Upton, Leslie F. S. 1979. *Micmacs and Colonists: Indian-White Relations in the Maritimes, 1713–1867.* Vancouver: University of British Columbia Press.

Wicken, William C. 2002. *Mi'kmaq Treaties on Trial: History, Land and Donald Marshall Junior.* Toronto: University of Toronto Press.

Williams, Robert A., Jr. 1997. *Linking Arms Together: American Indian Treaty Visions of Law and Peace, 1600–1800.* New York: Oxford University Press.

Regional Essays

California, Hawaii, and the Pacific Northwest

Introduction

Native Americans of the far West entered into treaty making with the United States during the 1850s. By this time, the U.S. government had established procedures for acquiring Native land title by treaty. Nevertheless, large portions of the far West remain nontreaty areas. In this essay, the states of Washington, Oregon, Idaho, and California are discussed in relation to the Indian treaties of the Northwest, Plateau, and California culture areas. In addition, treaties made by the Native peoples of the Kingdom of Hawaii prior to annexation by the United States in 1898 are discussed.

The Pacific Northwest

By the Treaty of Oregon, the United States gained control over what are now the states of Washington, Oregon, and Idaho. The Oregon Territory was created two years later, and in 1853 Washington Territory was separated. Most ratified treaties in the Pacific Northwest were negotiated in the mid-1850s, but there were earlier attempts that resulted in a number of nonratified treaties. Prior to the Treaty of Oregon of 1846, which established the boundary between British North America and the United States, the Pacific Northwest was jointly claimed by the two nations. Considerable numbers of Americans immigrated to the Pacific Northwest from 1843 to 1846, primarily settling in the Willamette Valley of Oregon. The federal government established a treaty process in 1850 when Anson Dart was appointed superintendent of Indian affairs for the Oregon Territory. Dart's task was to remove the Native groups in the vicinity of European American settlement, preferably to the eastern portion of the territory. He quickly realized that such a proposition would be unacceptable to the Native peoples and instead sought to create small reservations near their settlements and fishing locations. Native peoples west of the Cascade Range were particularly adamant about not moving to the drier east side of the territory (Coan 1921, 57).

Between June 1850 and March 1853, twenty-three treaties were negotiated with various tribes of western Oregon Territory. None of these treaties were ratified. Different federal representatives negotiated on behalf of the U.S. government. In June 1850, the governor of Oregon Territory, Joseph Lane, negotiated a peace treaty with the Takelma of the Rogue River valley in order to protect settlers in the area. In the spring of 1851, six treaties were signed with the Kalapuya and the Molala of the Willamette Valley by a commission that included Lane and Dart. When it was discovered that it would be impossible to remove the tribes from the Willamette Valley without resorting to force, the commission abandoned its work. Unbeknownst to the commissioners, the Willamette Valley Treaty Commission had been abolished by Congress prior to the time they had begun negotiating treaties. As a result, these six treaties were never ratified. Another peace treaty with the Takelma was negotiated by Governor John Gaines in July 1851. Then, in August, Indian superintendent Anson Dart initiated a treaty program with the groups around the mouth of the Columbia River for the express purpose of "extinguishing Indian land title" and moving them to reservations. Dart became painfully aware that his task was hopeless. He could not persuade the Indians to leave their village sites and burial grounds, nor could he persuade them to agree to annuity payments beyond a ten-year span. Dart came to understand their reasoning, "fully aware of the rapidity with which, as a people, they are wasting away . . . they could not be persuaded to fix a time beyond ten years to receive all of their money in exchange for their lands" (Boxberger and Taylor 1991, 42).

Although signed and forwarded to Washington, D.C., none of the thirteen treaties negotiated by Dart were ever ratified. The settlers were opposed to them because they did not provide for removal. Governor Joseph Lane, subsequently territorial representative to Congress, possibly lobbied against them because they did not provide for removal east of the Cascade Range, a policy he recommended while governor of Oregon Territory. Ultimately, the Senate refuse to ratify the treaties, reasoning that they had been made with "insignificant tribes" (Boxberger and Taylor 1991, 42).

Another peace treaty, with the Rogue River tribes in September 1853, and further negotiations with the Willamette Valley tribes completed the attempts at treaty making that never came to fruition in Oregon Territory.

Joel Palmer replaced Anson Dart as superintendent of Indian affairs in 1853. At the same time, Washington Territory was separated from Oregon Territory, and Isaac I. Stevens was appointed governor and superintendent of Indian affairs for Washington Territory, which included the present-day states of Washington and Idaho and parts of Montana and Wyoming. Both Palmer and Stevens initiated comprehensive treaty negotiations for their respective territories; where tribal lands crossed territorial boundaries, they conducted joint negotiations.

Seven treaties with the coastal and Willamette Valley tribes of western Oregon were negotiated between September 1854 and December 1855 (see Table 2, page 230). The Cow Creek and Rogue River treaties (Treaty with the Umpqua-Cow Creek Band, Treaty with the Kalapuya, Etc.) provided for reservations in southwest Oregon, but hostilities between the settlers and the tribes persuaded Palmer to remove them to the Grande Ronde and Siletz Reservations farther north along the coast.

The Palmer treaties were indicative of U.S. treaty policy in the 1850s. The numerous small tribes and bands were "confederated" for convenience, and "chiefs and headmen" were appointed by the government representatives to facilitate the negotiation process. Numerous tribes were consolidated on the two reservations, often becoming neighbors with groups with whom they had hostilities. Although treaty tribes were placed on the Grande Ronde and the Siletz, these were executive order reservations and thereby subject to reduction. The removal process was traumatic; many groups were forced to the reservations under military escort. The reservations had no provisions for food, housing, or medical assistance. As a result, starvation and disease took their toll.

When Isaac I. Stevens assumed the governorship of Washington Territory in 1853, his responsibilities included entering into treaties with the Native people. Stevens would eventually negotiate ten treaties between December 1854 and January 1856, all of which were ratified. Stevens's contact with Indians prior to his appointment as governor had been limited; as such, his policy was shaped by the prevailing attitude of the commissioner of Indian affairs, George Manypenny. Manypenny believed that Indians should be assimilated into the dominant society, and consequently the policies of his administration reflected this viewpoint. Manypenny especially advocated the allotment of reservation lands to individual tribal members as a means of expediting the "civilizing process." This policy was written into the nine treaties Manypenny was in the midst of personally negotiating with the tribes just west of the Mississippi River between March and June 1854. He strongly urged Stevens to follow this policy when he suggested that Stevens use two of these treaties, the Treaty with the Omaha and the Treaty with the Oto and Missouri, as models for the treaties in Washington Territory.

Stevens began the treaty process in December 1854 by appointing a commission to review the Oto and Missouri and Omaha treaties and adapt them accordingly. It was decided that additional provisions would be necessary, especially provisions reserving the right to access fishing locations and creating numerous small reservations, as opposed to a single large reservation. The first treaty negotiation was held at Medicine Creek with the Nisqually, Puyallup, and others in December 1854. Within twelve months, Stevens had secured a total of ten treaties. The Medicine Creek treaty was ratified just three months later, but the outbreak of hostilities delayed the ratification of the subsequent treaties until 1859. Stevens was gone from Washington Territory shortly after the treaty-making years. Elected territorial representative to Congress in 1857, Stevens was himself responsible for seeing that the treaties were ratified by the Senate.

After the negotiations at Medicine Creek, Stevens set about securing treaties with the rest of the tribes in western Washington. Things went smoothly; there were negotiations at Point Elliott, Point No Point, and Neah Bay, all in January 1855. These four treaties covered most of western Washington, but the final treaty, with the tribes of the southwest portion of the territory, did not go well. At the Chehalis River in February 1855, Stevens sought to negotiate with the Chehalis, Cowlitz, Chinook, Quinalt, and other tribes of southwest Washington, some of whom had earlier negotiated treaties with Anson Dart when the area was still part of Oregon Territory. Knowing that Dart's treaties were turned down because they failed to remove the Indians from the area of densest settler population, Stevens was adamant that all the tribes remove to a single reservation on the central Washington coast. The only tribe willing to sign the treaty was the Quinalt, primarily because the proposed reservation was in their territory. The treaty negotiations broke down because Stevens would not give in to the request to establish separate reservations in the different tribal

territories. The following January, the Quinalt and Quileute signed the Treaty of Olympia, which created reservations on the central Washington coast. Subsequently, executive order reservations were created for the Chehalis and the Chinook, but they remain nontreaty tribes.

In the summer and fall of 1855, treaty councils were held with the Indians of eastern Washington and Oregon Territories. The first was at Walla Walla in May and June. This council was attended by Stevens and Palmer, as some of the tribes in attendance claimed traditional lands in both Oregon and Washington Territories. On June 9, two treaties were signed: the Yakima treaty with fourteen tribes and bands, now known as the Confederated Tribes and Bands of the Yakama Indian Reservation, and the Walla Walla treaty, with the Walla Walla, Cayuse, and Umatilla, which was jointly negotiated by Stevens and Palmer. Two days later, the various bands of the Nez Perce tribe signed a treaty with Stevens and Palmer that created a large reservation in what is now southeast Washington, northeast Oregon, and central Idaho. The Nez Perce Reservation was reduced in size by two subsequent treaties. In June 1863, the Treaty of Lapwai reduced the Nez Perce Reservation from 7.7 million acres to just over 750,000 acres; the Nez Perce refer to this as the "thief treaty." In 1868, the third Nez Perce treaty clarified the harvest of timber on the reservation. This was the last treaty between the U.S. government and an Indian tribe before treaty making was abandoned as Indian policy in 1871.

After the Walla Walla treaty council, Stevens left to negotiate further treaties in eastern Washington Territory, and Palmer left to negotiate with other tribes of eastern Oregon. Palmer met with a number of tribes from north central Oregon near The Dalles in June 1855, concluding with the Treaty of Middle Oregon. Like the previous treaties, this treaty created a reservation for several bands. The Warm Springs Reservation of north central Oregon was to become the home of the western Columbia River Sahaptin and the Upper Chinook bands. Similar to the other Pacific Northwest treaties, this treaty contained a provision establishing the right to fish at usual and accustomed places and to hunt and gather on open and unclaimed lands. The subsequent superintendent of Indian affairs for Oregon, J. W. Perit Huntington, secured a treaty in November 1865 that was designed to limit off-reservation subsistence activities and encourage on-reservation agriculture.

In July 1855, Stevens met with the Flathead, Kutenai, and Pend d'Oreille at Hell Gate in the Bitterroot Valley. The Hell Gate treaty created the Flathead Indian Reservation in what is now Montana (Bigart and Woodcock 1996). From Hell Gate, Stevens traveled to Fort Benton to meet with the Blackfeet. This treaty created a Blackfeet Territory over a huge portion of the northwest plains.

Subsequent attempts at treaty making in eastern Washington Territory were suspended when hostilities broke out among the tribes' signatory to the Yakima and Medicine Creek treaties. The Indian War of 1855–1856, sometimes referred to as the Yakima War, was the direct result of the dissatisfaction with the Stevens treaties. For three years, this war consisted of skirmishes, raids, and indecisive battles. In September 1858, the Native leaders of the war were decisively defeated at the Battle of Four Lakes, which brought hostilities to an end. This war caused the delay of the ratification of the Stevens and Palmer treaties until 1859. Another impact of the war was that Stevens's plans to negotiate with the tribes of the northeast portion of Washington State were interrupted, and thus they have never been party to a treaty. The Colville, Spokane, and Kalispel Reservations were later created by executive order, but these tribes remain nontreaty tribes.

The tribes of south central Oregon met with J. W. Perit Huntington in October 1864 and concluded the Treaty with the Klamath. This treaty included the Klamath, Modoc, and Yahooskin Band of Northern Paiute. The Treaty with the Klamath created the Klamath Indian Reservation. The Modoc and Yahooskin were dissatisfied with the Klamath Reservation and soon left. Efforts to force them to return resulted in military action, culminating in the Modoc War of 1872–1873. After an extended standoff at Captain Jack's Stronghold near Tule Lake in California, the Modoc War was concluded, and the Modoc were exiled to Indian Territory (present-day Oklahoma) until after 1900, when they were permitted to return to Oregon. In 1954, when Congress initiated legislation to terminate tribes deemed capable of managing their own affairs, the Klamath was one of the first reservations to be terminated.

One more treaty deserves mention here, as it included groups whose territory extended into southern Idaho and for whom an executive order reservation was subsequently established. The Fort Bridger treaty of July 1868 with the Shoshone and the Bannock established the Wind River Reservation in Wyoming and provided for a reservation for the

western Shoshone and Bannock "whenever the Bannacks desire" (Kappler 1904, 1020). By executive order, the Fort Hall Reservation in south central Idaho was established in July 1869 as the one contemplated in the Fort Bridger treaty. Previous attempts at treaty making in southern Idaho had failed. The Soda Springs treaty of 1863, the Treaty of Fort Boise in 1864, and the Bruneau River Treaty of 1864 were never ratified.

California

On September 30, 1850, the U.S. Senate authorized the negotiation of treaties with the Native peoples of California. After the completion of eighteen treaties, the Senate chose on July 8, 1852, not to ratify any of them. As a result, the Native peoples of California have remained nontreaty tribes to this day. During the Spanish occupation from 1769 to 1821 and the Mexican rule from 1821 to 1846, treaties were not a matter of policy. Both the Spanish and the Mexicans considered the Native people subjects of the Crown and, through the system of missions, attempted to incorporate them into the dominant society. This approach had been used throughout Mexico but did not meet with much success in the northern outposts of the Spanish empire. At least two treaties of peace were made by Mexican authorities with the Wappo in 1836 and 1837 (Heizer 1978, 701), but these do not appear to have been formal treaty relationships.

During the American period, local government agents signed treaties that were never authorized and never considered for ratification. General Mariano Vallejo secured the agreement of eleven groups of Pomo and Miwok in 1848. In the same year, J. A. Sutter secured an agreement with the Nisenan, who resided in the area where gold was discovered. Both of these documents were dismissed by government officials as unofficial governmental actions.

The movement of large numbers of Americans into California was precipitated by the discovery of gold. By the end of 1849, more than one hundred thousand settlers and gold seekers had streamed into the territory. California became a state in September 1850, and the Senate immediately authorized the negotiation of treaties. From 1850 to 1880, the American citizens of California engaged in a process of genocide against Native peoples. Voluntary militias and groups of vigilantes systematically hunted down and slaughtered thousands of Native people. Although the United States government did not condone this action, it did nothing to stop it. By 1890, only twenty thousand Native people remained in the state of California out of a pre-Columbian population some estimate to have been as high as one million. In the midst of these acts of genocide, a commission of three agents was sent to negotiate treaties. These treaties were to secure title to the land and to remove the California Natives from contact with miners and settlers. In all, eighteen treaties were negotiated and signed by Native representatives and the agents of the U.S. government. Each of the treaties set aside a tract of land for a reservation and other concessions, such as agricultural instruction, food rations, and annuities.

Early in the treaty-making process, the commissioners decided that, if they attempted to work together, they could never meet with the vast number of tribal groups. Splitting up, each of the three took a section of the state and set about securing acceptance of a model treaty they developed. Redick McKee covered the area north of San Francisco, George Barbour the San Joaquin Valley south, and O. M. Wozencraft took the Coast Range from south of San Francisco to the Sacramento River. In all, 139 tribes were listed in the treaties. Later analyses found that many of these tribes were listed erroneously. Heizer and Kroeber determined that, of the 139 tribes, 67 were identifiable as tribelets, 45 were village names, 14 were duplicates with different spellings, and 13 were either personal names or unidentifiable (Heizer 1978, 703).

In July 1852, the Senate rejected the California treaties, and no further treaty negotiations were authorized. Congress established seven reservations in California between 1853 and 1855. Beset by corruption that led to destitution and continued annihilation of Native peoples, these reservations were reduced in size or abandoned altogether. Subsequently, reservations and rancherias were established by executive order, purchase, or other means. Eventually, 117 reservations and rancherias would be established; nearly half of them would be terminated in the 1950s and 1960s.

The Kingdom of Hawaii

At the time Europeans first arrived in the Hawaiian Islands in 1778, there existed a number of chiefdoms under the control of local elite rulers. The hierarchical system included the *ali'i* (nobility), the *Konohiki* (land managers), and the *Maka'ainana* (commoners). Beginning in 1791, the chief of the island of Hawaii,

Kamehameha, began a campaign to unite the islands under a single kingdom, which was nearly complete by 1795. In 1810, with the joining of Kauai, the Kingdom of Hawaii was established.

Kamehameha ruled Hawaii from 1810 to 1819. Over the next eighty years, there would be a total of eight rulers of the kingdom. Kamehameha II ruled from 1819 to 1824. During his reign, the ancient *kapui* system—the set of laws regulating societal behavior—underwent revision, especially the kapui on women and men eating together. Coinciding with the arrival of missionaries in 1820, the breakdown of the kapui paved the way for new religious beliefs to be incorporated into Hawaiian life. Kamehameha III assumed the throne in 1825 and ruled for thirty years. In 1840, Kamehameha III introduced Hawaii's first constitution. The constitution defined the powers of the monarch and distributed the King's absolute powers among the monarchy, the House of Nobles, and the House of Representatives. The constitution also provided for a court system. Kamehameha III sent delegations to the United States and Europe to secure treaties and established Hawaii's sovereignty. In 1842, President John Tyler gave his assurance that Hawaii would be recognized as an independent nation by the United States. Similarly, Queen Victoria issued a decree that the United Kingdom recognized Hawaii as an independent state. As a result of recognition, Hawaii began entering into treaties with a number of nations. Between 1826 and 1887, Hawaii signed thirty treaties and agreements with the United States, the United Kingdom, France, Germany, Spain, Russia, Japan, and a number of other nations. Four treaties were entered into with the United States. In 1898, when the United States annexed

Table 1
Non-Ratified Treaties, Pacific Northwest

Tribe	*U.S. Negotiator*	*Date*
Takelma	Joseph Lane	June 1850
Santiam Kalapuya	Willamette Valley Treaty Commission	April 1851
Tualatim Kalapuya		April 1851
Yamhill Kalapuya		May 1851
Lakmiut Kalapuya		May 1851
Molala		May 1851
Santiam Molala		May 1851
Takelma	John Gaines	July 1851
Lower Band of Chinook	Anson Dart	August 1851
Wheelapa Band of Chinook		August 1851
Quillequeoqua Band of Chinook		August 1851
Waukikum Band of Chinook		August 1851
Konnack Band of Chinook		August 1851
Klatskania Band of Chinook		August 1851
Kathlamet Band of Chinook		August 1851
Wallooska (Personal Name) Band of Chinook		August 1851
Clatsop Band of Chinook		August 1851
Tillamook Band of Chinook		August 1851
Port Orford Treaties (2)		September 1851
Clackamas		September 1851
Rogue River Indians	Joseph Lane	September 1853
Tualatin Kalapuya	Joel Palmer	March 1854
Coastal Tribes		August September 1855

Source: Kappler 1904, Vol. II

Table 2
Ratified Treaties, Pacific Northwest

Tribe	*U.S. Negotiator*	*Date*	*Ratified*
Rogue River Indians	Joel Palmer	September 1854	April 1854
Cow Creek Band of Umpqua		September 1854	April 1854
Takelma		November 1854	March 1855
Chasta, Scoton, Takelma		November 1854	March 1855
Upper Umpqua, Yoncalla Kalapuya		November 1854	March 1855
Confederated Bands of Kalapuya		January 1855	March 1855
Molala		December 1855	March 1859
Medicine Creek	Isaac Stevens	December 1854	March 1855
Point Elliott		January 1855	March 1859
Point No Point		January 1855	March 1859
Makah		January 1855	March 1859
Quinalt, Quileute		January 1856	March 1859
Confederated Tribes of Yakama		June 1855	March 1859
Walla Walla, Umatilla, Cayuse	Isaac Stevens and Joel Palmer	June 1855	March 1859
Nez Perce		June 1855	March 1859
Tribes of Middle Oregon	Joel Palmer	June 1855	March 1859
Hell Gate	Isaac Stevens	July 1855	March 1859
Blackfeet		October 1855	April 1859
Nez Perce (Lapwai)	C. H. Hale, Charles Hutchins, S. D. Howe	June 1863	April 1867
Klamath, Modoc,Paiute	J. W. Perit Huntington, William Logan	October 1864	July 1866
Middle Oregon Tribes, 1865	J. W. Perit Huntington	November 1865	March 1867
Nez Perce	Nathaniel G. Taylor	August 1868	February 1869

Source: Kappler 1904, Vol. II

Hawaii, Congressional Joint Resolution No. 55 stated, "The existing treaties of the Hawaiian Islands with foreign nations shall forthwith cease . . . being replaced by such treaties as may exist, or as may be hereafter concluded, between the United States and such foreign nations."

The Great Mahele of 1848 introduced a new system of land tenure. Previously, the king had owned all the land; now he relinquished control, title passed to the island chiefs, and each commoner received three acres. Land reform had effectively opened Hawaiian land to developers, who quickly stepped in and obtained large portions of land, which were converted to plantations. As the sugar industry boomed and introduced diseases took their toll on the Native Hawaiian population, large numbers of immigrants came to Hawaii to work the plantations. In 1851, the legislature of the Kingdom of Hawaii passed a resolution calling for a revision of the constitution of 1840. This constitution, adopted in 1852, further restricted the role of the monarch and created a constitutional monarchy.

With the death of Kamehameha III in 1854, Kamehameha IV ascended the throne. During his short reign from 1854 to 1863, further legal changes included new naturalization laws, which allowed non-Native Hawaiians to become citizens of the nation. With the death of Kamehameha IV, Kamehameha V assumed the throne. His primary legacy was to call for a constitutional convention to revise the constitution of 1852. The constitution of 1864 returned some of the powers to the monarch and restricted the right to vote. Under the constitution, the monarch was to name his successor during his

Table 3
Non-Ratified Treaties, California

Tribe	*U.S. Negotiator*	*Date*
Treaty with the Si-Yan-Te, etc.	Redick McKee	March 1851
Treaty with the Howechees, etc.	Redick McKee	April 1851
Treaty with the Taches, Cahwai, etc.	George W. Barbour	May 1851
Treaty with the Ko-Yate, Wo-A-Si, etc.	George W. Barbour	May 1851
Treaty with the Iou-Ol-umnes, Wethillas, etc.	O. M. Wozencraft	May 1851
Treaty with the Chu-Nuts, Wo-Woz, etc.	George W. Barbour	June 1851
Treaty with the Castake, Texon, etc.	George W. Barbour	June 1851
Treaty with the Das-Pia, Ya-Ma-Do, etc.	O. M. Wozencraft	July 1851
Treaty with the Mi-Chop-Da, Es-Kun, etc.	O. M. Wozencraft	August 1851
Treaty with the Noe-Ma, etc.	O. M. Wozencraft	August 1851
Treaty with the Ca-La Na-Po, etc.	Redick McKee	August 1851
Treaty with the Sai-Nell, Yu-Ki-As, etc.	Redick McKee	August 1851
Treaty with the Colus, Willays, etc.	O. M. Wozencraft	September 1851
Treaty with the Cu-Zu, Yas-Si, etc.	O. M. Wozencraft	September 1851
Treaty with the Pohlik or Lower Klamath, etc.	Redick McKee	October 1851
Treaty with the Upper Klamath, Shasta, and Scott's River	Redick McKee	November 1851
Treaty with the San Luis Rey, etc.	O. M. Wozencraft	January 1852
Treaty with the Diegunio	O. M. Wozencraft	January 1852

Source: Kappler 1929, Vol. IV: 1081-1128

Table 4
Treaties with the Kingdom of Hawaii and the United States of America

Treaty	*Signators*	*Date*
Articles of Agreement	King Kamehameha III Thomas ap Catesby Jones	December 1826
Treaty with the Hawaiian Islands	King Kamehameha III President Zachary Taylor	December 1849
Treaty of Reciprocity	Elisha P. Allen (Chancellor of Hawaii) President Ulysses S. Grant	January 1875
Convention of 1884	King Kalakaua Ratified by United States Senate	December 1884

Source: Hawaiian Kingdom, "International Treaties"

lifetime. When Kamehameha V died unexpectedly in 1872, he left no successor and had no heirs. Kamehameha was the last monarch directly descended through the Kamehameha line. Under the constitution, when no successor to the throne was named, a general election was to be held to choose the constitutional monarch from among the ali'i. William Lunalilo was elected in 1873 but died just one year later. Although his reign was short, Lunalilo's government was instrumental in establishing important relationships with the United States. In exchange for duty-free sugar exports to the United States, Hawaii agreed to allow duty-free imports of American products.

In 1877, David Kalakaua was elected king. King Kalakaua brought about a revival of Hawaiian customs and tried to strengthen Native Hawaiian self-rule. He traveled to the United States, where he met with President Ulysses S. Grant to negotiate a treaty of reciprocity, which continued the duty-free import of sugar and other Hawaiian products in exchange for the exclusive use of Pearl Harbor by the United States.

In 1887, a group of Hawaiian citizens, mostly Americans, organized a takeover of the Hawaiian government. Under threat of harm, King Kalakaua was forced to accept a new constitution that dramatically decreased the power of the monarchy and limited suffrage to property owners. Known as the Bayonet Constitution, this action initiated a series of events that would eventually result in Hawaii's becoming a territory of the United States. Despite organized resistance by Native Hawaiians, the new constitution remained in effect. When David Kalakaua died in 1891, he was succeeded by his sister, Lydia Kamaka'eha Dominic, who became known as Queen Lili'uokalani.

The reign of Queen Lili'uokalani was constantly under siege. In January 1893, U.S. military personnel conspired with American landowners to overthrow the government of Hawaii and annex Hawaii to the United States. When a treaty of annexation was forwarded to President Grover Cleveland, he was informed that the overthrow was illegal, and he subsequently withdrew the treaty. When William McKinley was elected president in 1896, a new treaty of annexation was forwarded. Protests submitted by Queen Lili'uokalani and Hawaiian Natives delayed ratification. In 1898, due to the need for a Pacific Ocean military base during the Spanish-American War, the United States opted to annex Hawaii by congressional joint resolution.

The treaties between the Kingdom of Hawaii and the United States of America were similar to other international treaties the United States entered into during the 1800s. The Article of Agreement of 1826 established peace and friendship between the two nations and allowed U.S. trade into Hawaii. While apparently never ratified as a formal treaty, the Articles of Agreement did establish government-to-government relations and was respectful of Hawaiian sovereignty.

The Treaty with the Hawaiian Islands of 1849 was ratified by the Senate and the president of the United States. This treaty of "friendship, commerce and navigation" allowed duty-free entry of U.S. ships, among other provisions, for a period of ten years.

The two subsequent treaties were a continuation of the treaties of commerce. The Treaty of Reciprocity of 1875 allowed for the duty-free import of U.S. goods into Hawaii and the duty-free import of Hawaiian goods, most importantly sugar, into the United States for a period of seven years. The treaty of 1875 was extended by the convention in 1884. The treaty of 1884 allowed seven more years to be added to the reciprocal trade between Hawaii and the United States, in addition to granting the United States exclusive use of Pearl Harbor.

When Hawaii was annexed in 1898, no provisions were made for Native Hawaiians separately from non-Native residents of the kingdom. Certain rights for Native Hawaiians are written into the state constitution of Hawaii, but a federal relationship like that of Native Americans on the mainland does not exist. The relationship between the U.S. government and Native Hawaiians has always been different from its relationship with other Native peoples. Ever since annexation, there has been a strong Native political movement to return Native Hawaiian sovereignty. Today, several organizations are working toward that goal. On November 23, 1993, President Clinton signed Public Law 103–150, the Apology Resolution, which states that Congress "apologizes to Native Hawaiians on behalf of the people of the United States for the overthrow of the Kingdom of Hawaii . . . and the deprivation of the rights of Native Hawaiians to self-determination."

Daniel L. Boxberger

References and Further Reading

Bigart, Robert, and Clarence Woodcock. 1996. *In the Name of the Salish and Kootenai Indians: The 1855 Hell Gate Treaty and the Origin of the Flathead Indian Reservation.* Seattle: University of Washington Press.

Boxberger, Daniel L. 1979. *Handbook of Western Washington Indian Treaties.* Lummi Island, WA: Lummi Indian School of Aquaculture and Fisheries.

Boxberger, Daniel L., and Herbert C. Taylor. 1991. "Treaty or Non-Treaty Status." *Columbia,* 5(3): 40–45.

Buck, Elizabeth. 1993. *Paradise Remade: The Politics of Culture and History in Hawai'i.* Philadelphia: Temple University Press.

Coan, C. F. 1921. "The First Stage of the Federal Indian Policy in the Pacific Northwest, 1849–1852." *Oregon Historical Quarterly,* 22 (1): 46–89.

Heizer, Robert F. 1978. "Treaties." In *Handbook of North American Indians*, vol. 8, *California*, ed. Robert F. Heizer, 701–704. Washington, DC: Smithsonian Institution Press.

Kappler, Charles J., ed. 1904. *Indian Affairs: Laws and Treaties*, vol. 2. Washington, DC: U.S. Government Printing Office.

Kappler, Charles J., ed. 1929. *Indian Affairs: Laws and Treaties*, vol. 4. Washington, DC: U.S. Government Printing Office.

Records Relating to Treaties. "Records of the Proceedings of the Commission to Hold Treaties with the Indian Tribes in Washington Territory and the Blackfoot Country." File Microcopies of Record in the National Archives: No. 5, Roll 26. *Records Relating to Treaties.* Washington, DC: National Archives and Records Service.

Kirch, Patrick V., and Marshall D. Sahlins. 1992. *Anahulu: The Anthropology of History in the Kingdom of Hawaii.* Chicago: University of Chicago Press.

Canada

Treaties in Canada can be divided into seven categories according to time, purpose, region, and negotiating parties. These seven categories are French nonaggression pacts, British treaties of peace and friendship, British treaties of neutrality, Hudson's Bay Company land purchases, Upper Canada land surrenders, the numbered treaties, and contemporary comprehensive and specific claims treaties. The large geographic area that eventually became Canada first was under the colonial rule of France, then of Great Britain. Northern and Pacific coastal regions belonged to a royal charter company, the Hudson's Bay Company, from 1670 to the mid-nineteenth century. After the 1867 union of four British North American colonies (known as confederation), six other provinces joined, culminating with the adhesion of Newfoundland in 1949. Historically, however, a much vaster area of North America was ruled from Quebec.

The colony of New France (1524–1763) was made up of several regions that included a wide range of bands and tribes: the Atlantic coastal region known as Acadia, governed from Port Royal and later Louisbourg; the St. Lawrence valley and Great Lakes region known as Canada, with its "upper country," governed from Quebec; the Illinois country, which included the Ohio and Mississippi valleys, attached first to Canada and later to Louisiana; Louisiana, which took in a vast area on both sides of the Mississippi, governed from New Orleans; the Mer de l'Ouest (Western Sea), which encompassed all of the northern Great Plains to the foothills of the Rockies, administered from Fort Kaministiquia (Thunder Bay). Much of this continental empire, although under an umbrella of French sovereignty proclaimed against British and Spanish rivals, was inhabited by independent, self-governing Native bands and tribes, many of them formal allies of the French. Apart from a restricted area of French colonization in the St. Lawrence valley between Montreal and Quebec and along the Bay of Fundy in Acadia, French settlements were widely dispersed, largely near trading posts, military forts, and mission stations located throughout the hinterland with specific permission from Native people on their acknowledged territory.

The French in Acadia and Canada neither displaced Native inhabitants to make way for European settlement nor waged war to conquer Native territory. The only displacement of peoples was voluntary, as Iroquoian and Algonkian people, many of them Catholic converts or Abenaki refugees from Maine, came to live on the *réductions* (later reserves) near Quebec, Trois Rivières, and Montreal. All the bands and tribes were recognized as independent and autonomous, usually allies, and in full possession of their territories. Only the Five Nations Iroquois—under Dutch and, later, English influence—were regarded as enemies until the Great Peace of Montreal in 1701. The few treaties signed with Native peoples were nonaggression pacts. New France passed from French to British rule in 1763. Native possessory rights, as observed under the French regime, were guaranteed by the British Crown by the Royal Proclamation of October 1763. Only the Crown could negotiate the acquisition of land belonging to the Native people, officially designated as their "hunting territories." This prevented settler encroachment on Native land, dispossession, and frontier violence.

The maritime region of French Acadia was claimed and frequently attacked by the English and American colonists. It was therefore not uncommon for them to enter into treaties of peace and friendship, a practice originating with Powhatan in 1608 with the Mi'kmaq, Maliseet, and Abenaki bands. Peninsular Acadia (Nova Scotia) was ceded to Britain in 1713. The last treaty of this type was signed in July 1766 with the Ottawa, Potawatomi, and Ojibwa, the former Three Fires Confederacy of the Great Lakes region, which was allied to the French.

In 1670, a vast northern region inhabited largely by Cree and Ojibwa was granted to the Hudson's Bay Company by royal charter, for the exploitation of the fur trade. When settlement was planned at Red River (Manitoba) in 1812 and later in British Columbia, Vancouver Island, and Oregon Territory, company officials negotiated land purchase treaties.

Following the loss of thirteen of its sixteen North American colonies in 1783, the British were forced to negotiate a series of land surrender treaties in Upper Canada (Ontario) to clear the way for the settlement of refugees from the United States, the United Empire Loyalists, and immigrants from the British Isles. These were remaining lands reserved to the Native population as hunting territories under the terms of the Royal Proclamation of 1763. The Upper Canadian land surrender treaties followed the model developed in Maryland in 1634. This, in fact, relegated Natives to restricted areas known as land *reserves.* The aboriginal inhabitants in Canada were never considered aliens, and therefore their common designation is now First Nations people.

In 1860, Great Britain handed over responsibility for Indian affairs to its several British North American colonies. When Nova Scotia, New Brunswick, and the United Canadas (Quebec and Ontario) joined in a federal union in 1867, "Indians, and Lands reserved for Indians" were assigned to the federal government in Ottawa. Indian treaties, therefore, given this political evolution over several centuries, could be negotiated by the Crown in the right of France, Great Britain, the distinct colonies, or the Dominion of Canada. The federal government used the constitutional authority defined in the British North America Act, 1867, to negotiate eleven "numbered" treaties of land surrender between 1871 and 1921 with Assiniboine Cree, Sioux, Blackfoot (including Blood and Piegan), Sarcee, Chipewyan, and Athapaskan for most of the western and northern regions that eventually entered the federal union.

A final category includes the contemporary comprehensive and specific claims treaties. Treaty making is a continuing process in Canada, especially since the federal government launched a comprehensive and specific claims process in 1973. Comprehensive land claims are negotiated in areas where aboriginal title has not been addressed clearly by treaty or other legal means. Since 1995, an inherent right policy allows simultaneous negotiation for self-government. As most of the lands and resources subject to comprehensive claim negotiations are under provincial jurisdiction, provincial negotiators participate in the negotiation of agreements with aboriginal groups. Specific claims deal with grievances of First Nations about the implementation or interpretation of existing treaties. Treaty rights now belong to inhabitants of *reserves,* or designated territories, but not to at least half the First Nations people who live in urban centers where no bands or community organizations with treaty rights exist.

The French Nonaggression Treaties

The French Crown signed no treaties of land surrender, because limited European settlement required no displacement of original inhabitants. Cooperation persisted between indigenous inhabitants and colonists through the fur trade, fishing, and resistance to Iroquois and American incursions. Royal instructions in 1665 stated explicitly that no colonists were to "take the lands on which they [Natives] are living under pretext that it would be better and more suitable if they were [possessed by] French." Native possessory and territorial rights were acknowledged in the official correspondence by such phrases as "these nations govern themselves" and "they must be deemed free everywhere on their lands." In 1755, a Ministry of War directive reminded serving officers in the colony, "The natives are jealous of their liberty, and one could not without committing an injustice take away from them *the primitive right of property* to the Lands on which Providence has given them birth and located them."

The few treaties the French signed with Native peoples were neither land surrenders nor international treaties between sovereign powers belonging to the "family of nations" as understood in European diplomatic circles. The nonaggression treaties of the seventeenth century were all concluded with the Iroquois, who, following Champlain's participation in an intertribal expedition against the Mohawks in 1609, became hostile toward the colonists. The treaties negotiated were as follows:

1. The Treaty of Trois Rivières, 1645, between Governor Montmagny and Mohawk delegates, ending hostilities and pledging peace
2. The Montreal Conference of 1653, in which the French agreed to remain neutral in the event of an Iroquois attack on the Algonquians and Montagnais
3. The Quebec Agreements of 1665 to 1667 with each of the Five Nations Iroquois, following a French military expedition, restoring peace
4. The Treaty of La Famine, 1684, following a disastrous military expedition led by Governor La Barr against the Seneca, in which the French agreed to remain neutral in the event of war between the Iroquois and the Illinois
5. The Great Peace of Montreal, 1701, a series of agreements between the French, the Five Nations Iroquois, the tribes of the Three Fires Confederacy, the "domiciled" Natives of the Seven Nations of Canada, and the Wabanaki Confederacy, including the Mi'kmaq and Maliseet

The French were mediators in this general peace and resumption of trade relations, which recognized the Five Nations Iroquois as neutral in international conflicts, a status later confirmed in the international Treaty of Utrecht in 1713. This celebration, held with all the pomp of cross-cultural diplomacy, marked the end of Iroquois-French feuding. This was followed by orders in 1716 to restrict settlement above Montreal and to avoid "war against the Natives which can never have any utility." It will be noted that the nonaggression treaties often stipulated French neutrality in an intertribal conflict.

Nevertheless, the French did not forget their Native allies when forced to capitulate to superior British forces at Montreal in September 1760. The property rights and liberty of these allied nations were specifically protected in Article 40 of the Capitulation of Montreal and reiterated in Article 4 of the Treaty of Paris in 1763, by which Canada became a British colony. It was a well-established principle of international law that the civil rights of subjects acquired by conquest or cession continued in force. In other words, the ancestral rights of Canada's Native peoples were protected by international treaty in 1763. Not surprisingly, the First Nations were accorded special mention in the subsequent Treaty of Paris (1783), Jay Treaty (1794), and Treaty of Ghent (1815).

The British Treaties of Peace and Friendship

In Nova Scotia, occupied in 1710, the British negotiated a number of treaties of peace and friendship with the chiefs of various maritime bands to safeguard incoming settlers and commerce. The first treaties, which included some Maliseet and Mi'kmaq bands, were negotiated in Massachusetts in December 1725 with unspecified "Eastern Indians," ending Dummer's War. It provided for "peaceable possession" of their unceded territories and the privilege of "fishing, hunting, and fowling as formerly." This could be interpreted as the rights they enjoyed under French rule prior to the cession of 1713. Native possession excluded lands "conveyed or sold to or possessed by any of the English subjects."

Treaty 239 was signed with representatives of the St. John and Cape Sable bands. It acknowledged British "jurisdiction and dominion over the territories" and made submission to the Crown "in as ample a manner as we have formerly done to the Most Christian King." This raised more questions than it settled. Only a few bands were party to the agreement, and the legitimacy of the Maliseet and Mi'kmaq delegates to make such general agreements remained problematical. Moreover, the provision for continuation of the relationship they had enjoyed under French rule did not ensure much submission. The important understanding was that the Mi'kmaq and Maliseet would not attack Annapolis Royal but would remain neutral in the event of another war with France.

In 1727, several other bands adhered to the treaty negotiated two years earlier at a special ceremony at Casco Bay.

In 1728, it was deemed necessary for the St. John band to adhere to the treaty of 1725 at a convocation at Annapolis Royal, thereby confirming their neutrality in the event of war between Britain and France. But the Maliseet and Mi'kmaq joined the French in four attacks on Annapolis Royal and other settlements during the War of 1744–1748. Governor Edward Cornwallis decided to exterminate the bands, but orders from London advocated a more conciliatory policy.

Peace overtures were made by some Mi'kmaq at Halifax in 1749 and 1752. Jean-Baptiste Cope, self-styled chief of the Shubenaccadie band, asked for a renewal of treaty terms and payment "for the land the English have settled upon in this country." On September 15, 1752, the Nova Scotia Council drew up a formal treaty in English and French for Cope to take back to his band; the treaty made no mention of compensation for land taken for settlement. Cope was presented with a golden belt and two lace hats as his reward. He returned with the agreement of his small band, and peace was confirmed on November 24, 1752. But within a year, some English attacked his band. Cope threw his copy of the treaty into the fire, and his warriors killed the crew of a government supply ship.

In 1754, French missionaries influenced the Mi'kmaq to present their own peace proposal, which caused the creation of an independent and neutral Mi'kmaq enclave that included most of eastern Nova Scotia and would serve as a buffer between the British on the Bay of Fundy and the French on Cape Breton and Prince Edward Island. The next year, war broke out between Britain and France. Nova Scotian authorities proceeded to deport the Acadian French population to the southern American colonies, depriving the Natives of a valued ally. Following the defeat of the French, a Maliseet delegation came to Halifax to sign a treaty acknowledging British rule,

accepting blame for having broken the peace, and welcoming a truckhouse on the St. John River.

Throughout 1760–1761, various bands of Mi'kmaq made their peace with the British. The final treaty was signed in November 1761 at La Have. With the elimination of a French presence, British authorities concentrated on keeping peace by abiding by treaty terms. In 1762, a government order forbade settlement on or trespass of certain lands claimed by the Native population.

In 1778, the Mi'kmaq renounced their alliance with the Americans. At Windsor on September 22, 1779, delegates from the New Brunswick and Gulf of St. Lawrence regions affirmed their loyalty to Britain and promised to win over the Mi'kmaq bands to the British cause. In return, they were promised freedom to hunt and fish without hindrance and the immediate supply of "ammunition, clothing and other necessary stores." Hunting and fishing rights promised in these treaties have continued to be claimed into the twenty-first century.

A Mi'kmaq band in the Miramichi region of the colony of New Brunswick adhered to a treaty of friendship in 1794, in which King George III promised, "[H]enceforth I will provide for you and for the future generation so long as the sun rises and river flows." By these treaties, most of the maritime band chiefs had recognized a British protectorate without at the same time surrendering lands or other rights.

The British Treaties of Neutrality

The Seven Fires or Nations of Canada had been important allies of the French in the late seventeenth and early eighteenth centuries. But, as New France's defenses began to collapse, these allies began to seek amicable agreements with the advancing British forces. Three treaties were negotiated during the closing days of the Seven Years' War (French and Indian War).

On August 30, 1760, a treaty was concluded at Oswegatchie, or Fort La Galette, with General Amherst. In effect, the Indians would not assist the French and would not permit the invaders to advance down the St. Lawrence to Montreal. Also, if Canada remained in British hands, they would enjoy the same privileges as "in the time of the French, but still more and greater," the possession of their lands, their hunting grounds, and the free exercise of the Catholic religion.

On September 5, the Hurons of Lorette signed a separate treaty at Longueuil with Major General James Murray, by which they were granted safe passage back to their village, amnesty, the free exercise of their religion and customs, and freedom of trade.

These treaties were reconfirmed and ratified by William Johnson, superintendent of the Indian Department, at a special congress at the Kahnawake reserve during September 15–16, 1760.

The Hudson's Bay Company Treaties

The Hudson's Bay Company, a London royal charter company founded in 1670, administered all the lands draining into Hudson Bay, as well as the coastal lands of British Columbia and Vancouver Island, known as the Oregon Territory.

In 1812, the company granted the Earl of Selkirk permission to bring settlers to the Red River Valley. To avoid opposition from the Cree and the Saulteaux, Selkirk proposed to purchase a bloc of land in return for "a small annual present, in the nature of a quit rent, or acknowledgment of their right." The Selkirk treaty was signed on July 18, 1817, granting the local bands two hundred pounds of tobacco annually. When the Canadian government acquired Rupert's Land and the Northwest Territories in 1870, the order-in-council stipulated that "any claims of Indians to compensation for lands required for purposes of settlement shall be disposed of by the Canadian government in communication with the Imperial government; and the company (HBCo) shall be relieved of all responsibility in respect of them. . . ."

On Vancouver Island, Governor James Douglas, acting for the Hudson's Bay Company as well as the crown colony, entered into six land surrender treaties with the Songhees in April 1850, two treaties with the Klallam in May 1850, a treaty with the Sooke in May 1850, two treaties with the Saanich in February 1852, and one treaty in 1854 with the Saalequun tribe. Two further purchases were made, at Fort Rupert in 1851 and Nanaimo in 1854. These fourteen Fort Victoria treaties promised reserve lands for "village sites and enclosed fields," hunting rights "over the unoccupied lands," and fishing rights "as formerly." In return, Douglas paid the least acceptable amount "in woollen goods which they prefer to money."

On the mainland of British Columbia, Douglas asked the various communities to "point out" their

habitation and hunting territories, which were defined as reserves, but they were offered no treaty protection. British Columbia entered confederation with mainland reserves without treaties.

The Upper Canada Treaties of Land Surrender

The Royal Proclamation of 1763 reserved the right of acquisition of Native lands in Upper Canada [Ontario] to the Crown. A series of land surrender treaties were negotiated to open large tracts to settlement by refugees and immigrants. To simplify the complex process, six categories can be discerned.

Three treaties were lost or never properly registered: the Collins Purchase along Lake Simcoe, the Oswegatchie lands on the Upper St. Lawrence, and the Crawford Purchase on the north shore of Lake Ontario east of the Trent River.

Two surrenders by Mississauga chiefs for the Etobicoke River tract and the southern Lake Simcoe tract were effected by signing blank deeds that were never properly recorded. This was not regularized until 1923 in the Williams treaty.

Thirty-seven documented treaties were signed between 1781 and 1836, covering much of the southern region north of Lake Ontario and Lake Erie. Twenty-four of these provided a payment of a one-time fixed sum to the Mississauga and the Ojibwa. From the ceded lands, two Indian reserves were created for Iroquois Loyalists—the Six Nations Reserve on the Grand River for Joseph Brant's people and the Bay of Quinte Reserve for John Deserontyon's people. Some of the treaties lacked precision, such as the Gunshot Treaty (1787), which defined the ceded tract as running back from designated points on Lake Ontario "as far as a gunshot can be heard on a clear day."

After the war of 1812–1814, with tribes demoralized by declining numbers and marginalization in military strategy, seven more land cessions were signed before 1830 to make way for immigrants from the British Isles. The Indians were offered small reserves, fixed annuities, and some farm instructors, blacksmiths, and doctors.

The Robinson Superior and the Robinson Huron Treaties in 1850 ceded northern land to gain access to forest reserves, mineral deposits, and transportation corridors along the northern shores of Lake Huron and Lake Superior. The objective was to acquire from the Ojibwa bands twice as much land as had been ceded in the southern region for as little as possible. The appended schedules of reserves stipulated that title remain vested in the Crown. The annuities were much less than those offered in the southern part of the province, because the land was not judged suitable for agriculture.

Two further treaties, involving smaller areas—the Saugeen peninsula and an eastern portion of Manitoulin Island—were signed in 1854 and 1862, respectively, to facilitate exploitation of the Lake Huron fisheries.

The Numbered Treaties

Acquisition of land west of Quebec to British Columbia, including the unceded lands of northwestern Ontario and the Great Plains, proceeded by a series of numbered treaties from 1870 to 1929 negotiated by representatives of the government of Canada.

Treaty 1, the Stone Fort treaty, negotiated at Fort Garry in 1871, set the pattern for cession of all rights and title in return for annuities in perpetuity and reserves for the Indians' own use. It covered the fertile lands of the Red River Valley.

Treaty 2, also made in 1871, completed the cession of southern Manitoba and granted special gifts for the chiefs and the promise of farm animals and implements when farming was taken up on the reserved land.

Treaty 3, the Northwest Angle treaty, negotiated in 1873 with the Ojibwa, covered northwestern Ontario to Lake Superior. It included the Métis in its terms but stipulated that those who received benefits as Indians could not also hold scrip lands under the provisions of the Manitoba Act. The area ceded was crucial to the right-of-way for a transcontinental railway and was of interest to mining and lumbering companies. The chiefs inquired about mineral rights and were told these were held on the reserves by the Crown for their benefit.

Treaty 4, negotiated in 1874, provided for the cession of most of the agricultural land of southern Saskatchewan at a time when the bands were facing starvation and had little choice but to accept the reserves and annuities offered them. Hunting and fishing rights were subject to government regulations.

Treaty 5, negotiated in 1875, covered north central Manitoba; it included less favorable terms but was signed speedily at the urging of the missionaries, who acted as diplomatic agents.

Treaty 6, negotiated in 1876 and covering much of what became central Saskatchewan and Alberta, provided for a "medicine chest," which the Indian agents were to keep available to deal with epidemics or "general famine." The Plains Cree, in this case, faced starvation and were threatened with withdrawal of government food rations if they did not make treaty. The medicine chest provision has been interpreted as full Medicare coverage (1984) both on and off reserves, including optical and dental care, prescription drugs, and transportation to medical care centers.

Treaty 7, negotiated in 1877 in what became southern Alberta, saw the intervention of both missionaries and the Northwest Mounted Police in the negotiation process, inasmuch as they had a direct interest in avoiding discontent and frontier violence. Provision was made for schools, agricultural supplies and implements, and farm instructors, and liquor was prohibited on reserves. The chiefs were now aware that "outside promises," or verbal promises not specifically written into the treaties, had little validity.

Treaty 8, negotiated in 1899 and covering northern Alberta and British Columbia, was the first of the northern resource development treaties to deal with an influx of miners into the Yukon and adjacent areas.

Treaty 9, negotiated in 1905, came as a response to Native demands for protection of some of their lands in view of mining developments and railway construction in northern Ontario. It was negotiated jointly by the federal and Ontario provincial governments with Native bands because the province controlled natural resources.

Treaty 10, completed in 1906 in northern Saskatchewan, was negotiated solely by the federal government because the province did not yet have jurisdiction over its natural resources.

Treaty 11 was made in 1921 following the discovery of oil in the Mackenzie Valley. The Dene obtained a guarantee of complete freedom to hunt, trap, and fish. The building of the Alaska Highway undermined that promise.

Contemporary Agreements

The major recent agreements occurred in the early 1970s and continued to be made until the end of the twentieth century.

The James Bay and Northern Quebec Agreements were negotiated in 1975 and 1978. In 1971, the Quebec government announced a plan for a massive hydroelectric development involving the diversion of four rivers and dammed reservoirs on La Grande Rivière. Through the courts and the media, the Cree and Inuit of the eastern James Bay region forced the federal and Quebec provincial governments to consider their aboriginal rights. The treaty, negotiated in 1975 and implemented in 1990, provided some exclusive hunting, fishing, and trapping territories for each of the Cree and Inuit, $135 million for the Cree, $90 million for the Inuit (both amounts have been paid in full), an income security program for hunters and trappers, self-government under Quebec's Cree-Naskapi Act, and participation in an environmental and social protection regime. In 1978, the Northeastern Quebec Agreement amended the James Bay Agreement to provide the Naskapi with comparable benefits.

The Inuvialuit Agreement of Northwest Territories was completed in 1984. It was the second comprehensive agreement with the 2,500 Inuvialuit of the Mackenzie Delta and Beaufort Sea area, renowned for its oil and gas reserves. The agreement provided for a land base, some of which included mineral rights, wildlife harvesting rights, and participation in environmental management, in addition to substantial allocation of funds to an economic enhancement fund and a social development fund.

The Dene and Métis Agreements were completed in 1992 and 1994. They were separate regional settlements with the Gwich'in and Sahtu Dene and the Métis of the Mackenzie Valley in the Northwest Territories. The agreements provided for land reserves with mineral rights, wildlife harvesting rights, and participation in decision-making bodies dealing with renewable resources, land use, environmental assessment, and regulation of land and water use.

The Nunavut Agreement of 1999 resulted from previous dealings. In 1992, the federal government and territorial government of the Northwest Territories agreed on the eventual creation of the self-governing Nunavut Territory in the eastern Arctic. The new territory, with a population of just under twenty thousand and its capital at Iqaluit, has a highly decentralized government to respond to the specific needs of its twenty-eight Inuit communities.

The Nisga'a Treaty was completed in 2000. In April 1999, the British Columbia legislature ratified terms of a land settlement with the Nisga'a Tribal Council. The federal parliament passed the necessary legislation a year later, providing for ownership and self-government of about two thousand square kilometers of land in the Nass River Valley and a cash payment of $190 million. It is the first modern-day treaty in British Columbia.

Cornelius J. Jaenen

References and Further Reading

Canada. 1971. *Indian Treaties and Surrenders, from 1680 to 1890.* 3 vols. Ottawa: Queen's Printer.

Daugherty, W. E. 1981. *Maritime Indian Treaties in Historical Perspective.* Ottawa: Indian and Northern Affairs Canada.

Duff, Wilson. 1969. "The Fort Victoria Treaties." *BC Studies* 3.

Jaenen, Cornelius J. 2001. "Aboriginal Rights and Treaties in Canada." In *The Native North American Almanac,* ed. Duane Champagne. Los Angeles: University of California Press.

Morris, Alexander. 1880. *The Treaties of Canada with the Indians of Manitoba and the North-West Territories,* Repr., Toronto: Coles, 1971.

Price, Richard. 1979. *The Spirit of the Alberta Indian Treaties.* Edmonton: Institute for Research on Public Policy.

Surtees, Robert J. 1988. "Canadian Indian Treaties." In *History of Indian White Relations,* Wilcomb E. Washburn. Washington, DC: Smithsonian Institution.

Tobias, J. L. 1977. "Indian Reserves in Western Canada." In *Approaches to Indian History in Canada,* ed. D. A. Muise. Ottawa: National Museum of Man.

Northeast and the Great Lakes

Because they resided in regions that from an early period were accessible to Europeans, the tribal people of the Northeast and Great Lakes have a long history of treaty negotiations with the colonial powers and with both state and federal governments. These treaties encompass a broad spectrum of issues, but most focus upon five major themes: they delineate the manner in which formal relations between the governments of European American and Native American communities will be conducted; they establish a formal peace after periods of warfare; they provide for the transfer of land ownership from one community to the other; and they establish procedures through which Native American people were removed from their former homelands to regions farther west. In addition, several of the treaties contain articles that delineate hunting and fishing rights for tribes in the Great Lakes region. Although tribal hunting and fishing rights were not envisioned as a major issue when these treaties were negotiated in the nineteenth century, these rights have emerged as a focal point of controversy for tribal people and non-Indians in the late twentieth century. Many treaties encompass and address more than one of these issues.

Unquestionably, the most important series of treaties that delineated and prescribed the relationship between Native American and non-Indian communities in the Northeast was the Covenant Chain. Originating in the aftermath of Metacom's War (King Philip's War), the Covenant Chain was forged at a treaty signed in April 1677 at Albany, New York, in which delegates from the Mohawks and the Mahicans (both British allies during the late conflict) met with representatives from New York, Massachusetts Bay, and Connecticut. In the treaty, the British colonies in New England agreed that the colony of New York should be the conduit through which all British "Indian affairs" in the region would be conducted, whereas the Mahicans and Mohawks (and, in turn, the Iroquois Confederacy) would be the negotiating agents for the tribes in the Northeast. As the Mohicans continued to decline in numbers and influence, the Iroquois Confederacy (often led by Mohawk spokespeople) emerged as the dominant Native American entity through which British Indian policy was implemented to neighboring tribes.

During the eighteenth century, as French influence increased in Ohio and western Pennsylvania, the Mohawks were hard pressed to keep other members of the Iroquois Confederacy closely tied to British officials at Albany, and in 1726 the Senecas readily negotiated with the French, permitting French engineers to build Fort Niagara at the mouth of the Niagara River. But the Iroquois used the Covenant Chain agreement to dominate the Delawares and Susquehannas living in Pennsylvania, negotiating with British officials in their behalf and readily surrendering lands that ostensibly belonged to these two tribes in the Delaware and Susquehanna River valleys. When the Delawares protested the sale, the Iroquois informed them that they now were "women" and could no longer speak for themselves in negotiations with the British. The Iroquois forced the Delawares to move to northern and western Pennsylvania, regions abutting Iroquois territories, while the British claimed and occupied the former Delaware lands they had purchased through the Iroquois.

By the 1750s, the Covenant Chain lay in disarray as political unity within the Iroquois Confederacy crumbled. Meanwhile, many of the Delawares and associated eastern Algonquian tribes moved to southwestern Pennsylvania and eastern Ohio, at the very edge of Iroquois (particularly Mohawk) hegemony. Although the Mohawks remained tied to New York, many of the other Iroquois league members periodically negotiated with the French, whereas the Senecas exercised an independent influence (apart from the Mohawks) over the tribes near the forks of the Ohio. In 1753, Theyanoguin (Hendrick), a Mohawk chief, admitted to officials in New York that the Covenant Chain had been broken. Five years later, it was partially reforged when delegates from the Delawares and Iroquois met with officials from the British colonies at Easton in Pennsylvania, and the Delawares agreed to support the British against the French, who had occupied Fort Duquesne (at modern Pittsburgh) and seemed to pose a threat to the Delawares in western Pennsylvania. In exchange for Iroquois support, the Delawares reluctantly agreed to allow the Iroquois again to exercise some control over their diplomacy. The French withdrew from Fort Duquesne, but when the British occupied the post, the Delawares charged

that they again had been betrayed, and the renewed Covenant Chain finally ended.

The Covenant Chain, which originally had shaped diplomacy between Native Americans and Europeans in the northeastern United States, emerged from a series of treaties that had ended a period of significant military conflict: Metacom's War. Other treaties during the colonial and Early National Period that also terminated periods of warfare had a significant impact upon both Native American and non-Indian people.

The most important of these colonial peace treaties in the Great Lakes region was the intertribal treaty associated with the Great Peace of 1701. Since the middle of the seventeenth century, the Iroquois Confederacy had warred intermittently with both the French and their Indian allies from the western Great Lakes. Initially, the Iroquois had been successful, driving many tribes, such as the Miamis, Sauks, and Potawatomis, from their homelands in Michigan, Indiana, and Ohio into Wisconsin. Because the warfare disrupted the fur trade, the French had assisted the western tribespeople, providing them with arms, ammunition, and other military assistance. By the 1690s, however, the tide of warfare had turned; the Iroquois had overextended themselves, and the western tribesmen struck back. Joined by French troops, they carried the conflict to the Seneca homeland, and during the 1690s the Iroquois sent envoys to Montreal to ask for a peace. French officials initially refused, but the western tribes also sought peace, so in 1699–1700 Louis-Hector de Callieres met with small delegations from several tribes, inviting them to reassemble in the summer of 1701 to negotiate a "lasting" peace between both sides.

More than 1,300 Indians, both Iroquois and allies of New France, assembled at Montreal in July and August 1701. The treaty proceedings reflected both the French desire for intertribal peace and their knowledge that Native American diplomacy was surrounded by elaborate ceremony. Delegations from both the Iroquois and the western tribes arrived by canoe and were saluted by salvos of cannon fire. They walked up from the river bank on broad red carpets, met under canopies of evergreen boughs, and were wined and dined on brandy and boiled oxen. French officials and tribal spokesmen alike dressed in their finest clothing and delivered formal speeches before throngs of assembled warriors, French citizens, and soldiers. After speeches, negotiations, and ceremonies lasting more than three weeks, both sides agreed to return all their captives and to live in peace. French officials and tribal leaders affixed their names or clan totems on the treaty document on August 5, 1701.

The Great Peace of 1701 marked a turning point in the history of the Great Lakes region. In a tacit acknowledgement that their military and political power was finite, the Iroquois pulled back from their expansion into the western Great Lakes. The Senecas continued to exercise a limited hegemony over western Pennsylvania and eastern Ohio, but the peace also illustrated that western members of the Iroquois Confederacy, particularly the Senecas, had adopted a realpolitik approach to the French and were willing to come to terms with French military power if necessary. In contrast, the Mohawks, still staunchly allied through the Covenant Chain to New York, refused to attend the proceedings. Obviously, the Iroquois Confederacy was split by this treaty, and although the Mohawks grudgingly accepted it, the myth of Iroquois unity and loyalty to the British had been shattered.

The treaty also provided renewed opportunities for the western tribes. Ostensibly at peace with the Iroquois, tribes such as the Miamis, Shawnees, and Miamis who had fled to Illinois or Wisconsin now returned to their old homes in Ohio and Michigan. At first, the French welcomed their reoccupation of these regions, but their rebuilt villages soon became targets for British merchants eager to envelop them in the growing network of a British trade offensive. These tribespeople welcomed cheaper British trade goods, but French officials feared the political ties that such economic dependency might engender among these tribes.

Finally, the festivities surrounding the Great Peace of 1701 were characteristic of major treaty negotiations during the eighteenth and early nineteenth centuries. Tribal people expected treaties to be negotiated amid considerable feasting, ceremony, and presents. Unquestionably, the French were more lavish in their treaty making than the British. Throughout the eighteenth century, in contrast, the British remained relatively parsimonious in their distribution of food and presents at such occasions, a practice that did not bode well for their relationship with the Great Lakes Indians. Ironically, after 1783, the Americans learned from the French example. American leaders were quite willing to disburse food, drink, and presents, particularly if they were trying to purchase land from the Native Americans.

The second major treaty that established peace between tribal people in the Northeast and the Great

Lakes region and Europeans or Americans was the Treaty of Greenville. Signed in 1795, the Treaty of Greenville ended almost half a century of internecine warfare between Indian people, the colonial powers, and, finally, the new United States. Throughout much of the seventeenth and eighteenth centuries, the western Iroquois and Ohio tribes had successfully played off the British and French, periodically shifting their allegiance from one side to the other to prevent either colonial power from achieving sufficient power to dominate the Ohio Valley and Lake Erie region. Although the British had vanquished the French during the Seven Years' War (1756–1763), tribespeople remained a significant military and political power in the region and during the British attempt to enforce new trade regulations in the conflict's aftermath. Native Americans had risen during Pontiac's Revolt (1763) and had forced British officials to reconsider their Indian policies. A decade later, when colonial settlers from Virginia attempted to occupy Kentucky, the Shawnees and Mingoes rebelled against colonial authority, and, although they had been beaten in Lord Dunsmore's War (1774), they remained a significant factor in any attempts to control the upper Ohio Valley. When the Crown and the colonists went to war in the American Revolution, the Ohio tribes sided with the British, renewed their attacks upon Kentucky, and fought the Americans to a standstill. Yet at the Treaty of Paris (1783), which ended the American Revolution (and which was not signed by Native Americans), Britain officially acknowledged American control over the Ohio Valley, and the tribes felt betrayed. When the Americans attempted to occupy the region, Miamis, Shawnees, and other tribes opposed their entrance, attacking settlers and inflicting decisive defeats upon two American armies (Harmar's defeat, 1790; St. Clair's defeat, 1791) before suffering a major setback at the Battle of Fallen Timbers (August 1794). In the aftermath of Fallen Timbers, the tribes were forced to sign the Treaty of Greenville, in which they acknowledged federal control over the region (see next paragraph) and agreed to remain at peace with the Americans.

The Treaty of Greenville was the death knell for Native American political autonomy in the Ohio Valley and the Great Lakes region. Although many midwestern tribespeople would support Tecumseh's and the Shawnee Prophet's effort to defend Indian lands and autonomy in the years preceding the War of 1812, the Shawnee brothers' movement was doomed to failure. By 1812, newly settled Americans in the region so outnumbered the tribespeople and their reluctant British allies that Tecumseh and his followers had little chance of success. Moreover, significant numbers of Indians (including many Shawnees) sided with the federal government against the Shawnee war chief. The treaty and its aftermath marked a significant turning point for Indian people in the Great Lakes region.

In many ways, the Treaty of Greenville also exemplified those treaties that transferred lands from Indian people to Europeans or Americans. Treaties enabling such transactions started early in the colonial period. Often associated with the termination of warfare, they were characterized by Native Americans losing significant areas of lands and agreeing to occupy small, restricted regions within their former homelands. The Treaty of Hartford, which ended the Pequot War in 1638, transferred Pequot lands to the British and assigned those Pequots not sold into slavery to two small village sites; the Treaty of Albany, signed in 1677, not only established the Covenant Chain (discussed previously) but also provided for the formal consignment of former tribal lands to the British.

Other land treaties were conducted during periods of relative peace but also were fraught with coercion. The most famous of these took place in 1734—the notorious Walking Purchase, through which the Delawares surrendered a large tract of land in eastern Pennsylvania. During the early 1700s, officials in Pennsylvania repeatedly had attempted to purchase Delaware lands in the Delaware Valley, but the Delawares steadfastly had refused to sell. Because the Delawares were enmeshed in the Covenant Chain, the Pennsylvanians then went to the Iroquois, who supposedly spoke for the Delawares, and purchased small tracts of Delaware land from the confederacy. But as growing numbers of recently arrived Scotch-Irish settlers moved into Pennsylvania, the colony's demands for Indian lands increased, and in 1734 colonial officials produced a forged document in which they claimed that in 1700 the Delawares had agreed to sell to Pennsylvania all the land west of the Delaware River that a man could walk across in a day and half. Delaware leaders protested that they had never signed such an agreement, but in 1734 Pennsylvania hired two specially trained colonists to walk as far and as fast as possible. The two men walked continually but in relays, and they covered almost sixty-five miles. When the colony's surveyors finished with their measurement, Pennsylvania claimed that the

Delawares had relinquished almost 1,200 square miles. The Delawares protested, but the Iroquois interceded on the colonists' behalf, and the lands passed into the hands of Pennsylvania.

The Walking Purchase provides an interesting case study of another facet of treaties and land purchases in the northeast: the sale of Native American lands by tribes having little claim to the region. Several tribes participated in this dubious practice, but the Iroquois were particularly vulnerable to such charges. Not only were their claims to eastern Pennsylvania certainly questionable, but the confederacy also readily sold land in Ohio and Kentucky. Two treaties signed at Fort Stanwix provide good case studies. In 1768, the Iroquois, claiming to speak for the Shawnees and Cherokees as well as the Delawares, signed a treaty at Fort Stanwix in Pennsylvania in which they ceded to the British these tribes' claims to much of Kentucky. Iroquois claims to the region were spurious, and none of the three tribes whom the Iroquois supposedly represented were notified of the negotiations prior to the treaty signing. Incensed, both the Cherokees and Shawnees denounced the agreement, and when British colonists attempted to occupy the region, the Shawnees struck back, eventually triggering Lord Dunmore's War, a precursor to the American Revolution in the region. At the second Treaty of Fort Stanwix, signed in 1784 at the same location, the Iroquois also gave up all their claims to lands west of Pennsylvania (Ohio), a region over which their claim and control in the post-revolutionary period were tenuous, at best. Ironically, by 1784, Iroquois influence in Ohio had so diminished that the western tribes scoffed at the agreement, and even federal officials who had negotiated the purchase admitted that they knew they would be forced to also purchase Ohio from other tribes.

They soon attempted to do so, but again they negotiated with tribes or tribal leaders who had no authority to cede the region. Intent on clearing Indian title from Ohio, in 1785 (Treaty of Fort McIntosh) and 1786 (Treaty of Fort Finney), federal officials negotiated two treaties with tribes from Detroit or with Shawnee and Wyandot tribesmen who had no authority to make such agreements. The treaties supposedly surrendered tribal control of lands in eastern Ohio, but they were denounced by most Native Americans in Ohio and only increased their determination to form a multitribal confederacy in opposition to further land sales and any American attempt to occupy lands north of the Ohio River. In 1788, federal officials again attempted to lure tribal leaders to renewed negotiations, but the resulting Treaty of Fort Harmar was a farce. John Heckewelder, a Moravian missionary who attended the proceedings, commented that the treaty signatures did not include "the name of even one Great Chief," while George Morgan, an American Indian agent, admitted,

> "Few of the natives attended and none were fully represented; here the treaty was negotiated . . . in the French language through a Canadian interpreter who had to guess at the meaning for he can neither speak or write the language as to make himself understood in any matter of that importance."

Native American rejection of these treaties and their determination to retain Ohio led to the border warfare that raged through the early 1790s. In 1794 at Fallen Timbers, the Americans finally gained the upper hand, and the subsequent Treaty of Greenville (discussed previously) formally marked the cessation of hostilities. The treaty also contained one of the most important Native American land cessions in American history. At Greenville, the twelve tribes in attendance not only relinquished their claims to all lands in southern and eastern Ohio but also agreed to the construction of American forts at strategic locations (Fort Wayne, Chicago, Peoria, etc.) within their remaining homelands.

Anthony Wayne, who led the American negotiators, promised that the government would protect the tribes within their remaining territories, but American settlers violated the new boundary lines before they could even be surveyed, and white hunters repeatedly crossed over onto Indian lands to kill game and run trap lines. As American settlement spread into Illinois, Indiana, and northern Ohio, federal officials admitted that Native Americans were being subjected to "injustices and wrongs of the most provoking character, . . . they are abused, cheated, robbed, plundered, and murdered at pleasure."

Between 1795 and 1809, federal negotiators conducted sixteen additional treaties with tribes in Ohio, Michigan, Indiana, and Illinois. Led by William Henry Harrison, the governor of Indiana Territory, the government obtained the acreages on a piecemeal basis, buying smaller tracts from cooperative leaders among the individual bands or tribes. On some occasions, tribal claims overlapped, and

the government was forced to purchase the same lands from different tribal communities. The loss of lands alienated many more traditional tribespeople, and by 1808 they had rallied to Tecumseh and his brother, the Shawnee Prophet, who opposed the land sales and denounced those chiefs who sold the lands as traitors. In 1809, after Harrison had purchased much of southern Indiana from friendly chiefs at the Treaty of Fort Wayne, he was confronted by Tecumseh, who warned Americans not to occupy the recently ceded territories.

Land cession treaties in this region ceased for almost a decade, as both sides became embroiled in the War of 1812, but following the conflict white settlement poured into the region, and the government renewed its purchases. During the next thirty years, federal officials met repeatedly with tribal leaders and acquired almost all of the remaining agricultural lands in the Old Northwest. Vast tracts of Illinois, Indiana, southern and central Michigan and Wisconsin, and northwestern Ohio passed into government hands. Yet many of the treaties marking the transfer of these lands reflected the growing sophistication of the tribes who negotiated with the United States. Leaders among the Potawatomis and Miamis bargained aggressively with federal agents and secured numerous small plots of land (usually between one and two square miles in area) for individual Indians or for chiefs of tribal villages set aside within the purchased territories. These small reserves often were located at strategic locations (crossroads, fords across streams, mill sites, or fertile bottomlands) which continued to serve as residential regions for tribespeople who remained within their old homelands. For example, in a treaty signed with federal agents on September 27, 1832, Potawatomi leaders ceded a large tract of land in northern Indiana and southern Michigan, but only after federal officials had agreed to establish eighty-eight separate individual or village reservations totaling more than 101,000 acres. Miami land cession treaties signed in 1826 and 1835 contain similar provisions.

Ironically, as the ceded lands filled with American settlers, the real estate value of these small remaining reserves appreciated. American land speculators clamored for the sale of the remaining lands, while federal officials were dismayed that the reserves provided a haven for those tribespeople who resisted the government's efforts to remove the Indians to the West. Yet when federal agents attempted to purchase the remaining reserves, they found that their Indian owners were aware of the lands' new market value and demanded an increased price. Most of these reserves eventually were sold, but their owners received a handsome price. Some of these recipients then left for the West, but others, usually people of mixed Native American-European lineage, remained in the Midwest, where they settled among remaining Indian communities in Wisconsin or Michigan, or joined with other Indian people and "hid in plain sight" amid the general American population in the region.

Not all the land ceded by Native Americans in the Northeast after 1783 was ceded to the federal government; some land initially was ceded or sold to private companies or states. Although the Indian Trade and Intercourse Act of 1790 forbade tribes from selling land to any entity other than the federal government, in 1794 the Commonwealth of Massachusetts purchased about twelve million acres from the Pasamaquoddy and Penoboscot tribes. The lands were contained within the modern boundaries of the state of Maine, which remained part of Massachusetts prior to becoming a separate state. Because the federal government had never consented to the sale of the lands, in the 1970s the two tribes forced the federal government to reluctantly sue the state of Maine for the return of the land, as the U.S. court of appeals ruled that the federal government maintained a trust relationship for the two tribes and was responsible for the tribes' welfare. Litigation of the case, which extended through the late 1970s, threatened to cloud the legal title to real estate holdings in Maine and prevent the state from issuing bonds. The Carter administration intervened, and Congress passed the Maine Indian Claims Settlement Act, which awarded the tribes $27 million and created a $54 million fund to finance additional land purchases by these Indians.

In the mid-1820s, the sale of tribal lands by Seneca leaders to the Ogden Land Company, a private firm in New York, also violated the Indian Trade and Intercourse Act of 1790, but the Senate refused to ratify the agreements, and a later legal challenge similar to the claims case in Maine was averted.

After 1830, almost all the treaties negotiated by the tribes residing in Illinois, Indiana, and southern Michigan and Wisconsin focused on the tribes' removal from these areas and their relocation to new homes, either in northern regions of Wisconsin or Michigan or to new lands in the West. Indeed, provisions for Indian removal, usually absent from or

peripheral to land cession treaties prior to the 1820s, became a focal point for negotiations in the following decade. The treaties providing for the removal of the Great Lakes tribes followed a format similar to other removal treaties of the era. After ceding the final portions of their homeland, the tribes usually agreed to assemble within six to twelve months at an embarkation camp, where they would join federal removal agents and government contractors employed to provide them with food and other provisions for their journey to the West.

Most removals were scheduled to begin in the early fall, when the summer heat had subsided, newly harvested foodstuffs were available, and rivers were sufficiently low to make then readily fordable. Wagons usually were provided for at least a portion of the tribespeople's belongings and to transport the ill, the elderly, or those tribespeople who needed assistance. Sometimes horses were furnished to some of the Indian emigrants, but often they were expected to make the trek westward on foot. The removal party, accompanied by their contractors and agents, camped each night along the route, sometimes near frontier settlements where additional food or supplies were purchased. If things went as planned, the removal party would reach their new homes in the West (usually western Iowa, Kansas, or Indian Territory) late in the fall but before winter arrived.

The treaty signed by the Senecas (and Cayugas) residing near Sandusky, Ohio, in 1831 provides a good case study. At the treaty, the Senecas ceded their remaining lands along the Sandusky River to the United States. In exchange, the government awarded the tribe lands in Indian Territory, promised the tribe that they would "be removed in a convenient and suitable manner," and agreed to support the tribe for one year in the West. Federal officials also promised to help them erect houses and establish farms, furnish them with livestock and farm utensils, and provide them with a blacksmith, a gristmill, and a sawmill. In addition, tribal leaders were furnished with presents, and federal agents assured them that all future annuities would be paid to them at their new home in the West. Obviously, from the government's perspective, the treaty was designed to lure the Sandusky Senecas from Ohio to the West.

As with many other removal treaties, the actual removal that resulted from the 1831 Sandusky Seneca treaty did not go as planned. The removal was scheduled for September 1, 1831, but due to bureaucratic bickering the Indians did not depart until early October. One party traveled to Dayton, then was carried by barges and steamboats to St. Louis, where they disembarked, then marched to the Cuivre River in eastern Missouri, where they spent the winter. The second party traveled overland but proceeded no farther than the Muncie, Indiana, region, where, short of food and blankets, they were abandoned by their removal agent and spent a miserable winter among the Delawares. In May 1832, the Senecas and Cayugas from Indiana joined their kinsmen on the Cuivre River, but as the combined parties of emigrants journeyed toward Indian Territory, they were plagued with measles and were forced to wait for days before ferries could carry them across the flooded Missouri and Grand rivers. Their ranks were decimated by exhaustion and disease, but they finally reached Indian Territory on July 4, 1832, six months after their projected arrival date.

In retrospect, most of the removal treaties combined a curious mixture of well-intentioned altruism with political opportunism. Unquestionably, some American reformers believed that, if tribal people removed west of the Mississippi, they could be isolated from alcohol and corrupting influences in American society, but the removal treaties also were motivated by frontier politicians who simply wanted access to Indian lands. Moreover, regardless of the motivation, most removals were conducted amid so much fraud and corruption that the tribespeople who participated in them suffered considerably. Tribes from the Great Lakes region probably suffered less than the Cherokees or Choctaws, but hundreds died during the removal process. The Potawatomis, in particular, still remember their removal from northern Indiana to eastern Kansas in the fall of 1838 as "the Trail of Death."

Several treaties signed between tribes residing in Michigan and Wisconsin that ceded lands to the government also contained clauses that engendered considerable controversy in the final decades of the twentieth century. For example, in treaties signed with federal officials in 1837, 1842, and 1854, Ojibwe leaders relinquished control of large acreages in these states, but the treaties stated that "the privilege of hunting, fishing, and gathering the wild rice, upon the lands, the rivers, and the lakes included in the territory ceded, is guaranteed to the Indians, during the pleasure of the President of the United States." Initially, this provision engendered little attention, but as tourism and recreational hunting and fishing grew in importance during the late nineteenth and early twentieth centuries, state governments in both Michigan and Wisconsin began to restrict the rights of Native Americans to hunt and fish, both on and off their established reservations. In 1879, the Wisconsin Supreme Court ruled that Native Americans were subject to state laws on their reservations, including laws governing game and fisheries, and in 1899 the state required Indians to purchase hunting licenses. In 1908, the Wisconsin Supreme Court (*State v. Morrin*) ruled that all "off-reservation rights" of Indians in the state had been abrogated in 1848 when Wisconsin became a state.

Ojibwe hunters and fishermen periodically "violated" the state's restrictions, and their activities attracted the attention of state game wardens, but most of their hunting or fishing took place on reservation lands until the late 1960s and generally was ignored by non-Indians. In contrast, during the 1970s many Ojibwes in Michigan and especially Wisconsin began to hunt and fish "out of season" on nonreservation land. They were prosecuted, but in 1983 the U.S. court of appeals ruled in *LCO v. Voigt* that the State of Wisconsin must negotiate with the tribes to clarify the specific hunting and fishing rights of the Ojibwes. The state reluctantly agreed, and the Indians were allowed to spearfish for walleyed pike in off-reservation waters. The resulting reassertion of Native American hunting and (particularly) fishing rights resulted in the Walleye War, a series of confrontations between Indians and non-Indians in Wisconsin and Michigan that has continued into the twenty-first century.

In retrospect, treaties between Native American people and European, colonial, or federal governments have markedly affected the course of history in the Northeast and Great Lakes regions. These treaties have shaped the lives of Native American people, but they also continue to shape the relationship between Native Americans and non-Indians.

R. David Edmunds

References and Further Reading

American State Papers, Indian Affairs. 1832. 2 vols. Washington, DC: Gales and Seaton.

Edmunds, R. David. 1978. *The Potawatomis: Keepers of the Fire*. Norman: University of Oklahoma Press.

Jennings, Francis. 1984. *Ambiguous Empire: The Covenant Chain Confederation of Indian Treaties With the English Colonies; Its Beginnings to the Lancaster Treaty of 1744*. New York: Norton.

Kappler, Charles J., comp. and ed. 1972. *Indian Affairs: Laws and Treaties*. Mattituck, NY: Amereon House. (Orig. pub in 1903).

Nesper, Larry. 2002. *The Walleye War: The Struggle for Ojibwe Spearfishing and Treaty Rights*. Lincoln: University of Nebraska Press.

Prucha, Francis Paul. 1994. *American Indian Treaties: The History of a Political Anomaly*. Berkeley: University of California Press.

Richter, Daniel, and James Merrell, eds. 1987. *Beyond the Covenant Chain: The Iroquois and Their Neighbors in Indian North America, 1600–1800*. Syracuse, NY: Syracuse University Press.

Satz, Ronald. 1975. *American Indian Policy in the Jacksonian Era*. Lincoln: University of Nebraska Press.

White, Richard. 1991. *The Middle Ground: Indians, Empires, and Republics, 1650–1815*. New York: Cambridge University Press.

Northern Plains

Treaty making in the northern Great Plains region of the United States has a long, fascinating, and ultimately disturbing history that begins with the Lewis and Clark expedition of 1804–1806 and ends with the federal government's unethical abrogation, or abandonment, of the Treaty of Fort Laramie of 1868 in 1877. Between 1804 and 1871, when Congress rejected formal treaty making, Indian peoples of the northern plains restructured their political organizations to negotiate with the increasingly powerful U.S. government and fought to retain their national sovereignty—and, ultimately, their future as individual nations of people, as Sioux or Arapaho or Blackfeet, with distinct cultural traditions. In the midst of great demographic, cultural, and economic change, treaties became the principal vehicle for securing and maintaining peace and friendship between American officials and Indian leaders to allow for peaceful trade relations. Although treaties embedded Native Americans' political culture in a framework of European American legal and diplomatic principles, scholar Maureen Konkle notes that they signified "the autonomy of Native political formations and the equality of those political entities to other political entities and of Native peoples to other peoples" (Konkle 2004, 5). The tragic story of violence on the northern plains that unfolded between the 1850s and 1870s is in large measure the story of the breakdown of this spirit of friendship, reciprocity, and equality established in the early 1800s.

Because the treaty-making process is in many ways based on a foundation of cultural interactions, it is helpful to begin the story of the northern plains in the early years of the United States, especially during the presidency of Thomas Jefferson, as his vision and his policies helped to shape the negotiations that led to a series of treaties between Native Americans and white Americans and redefined the geography of the United States in the mid-nineteenth century.

After the American Revolution ended, American politicians came to understand that violence on the western frontier resulted largely from a steadily encroaching stream of American settlers. These federal officials also believed that extinction of Native Americans was possible under such conditions unless the Indians made an effort to adopt elements of white "civilization." *Civilization* was, in fact, the word used, set off against the stages of "savagery" and "barbarism" that were part of the vocabulary of Enlightenment-era conceptions of racial difference. Contained within this idea was the notion that Native Americans had the capacity to rise above their "savage" or "barbarous" condition and achieve the state of civilization.

In an effort to reduce frontier conflict and thus the chance of continual war, the federal government assumed control of negotiating with Indian nations and wrote into its treaties provisions for "civilization" programs. The Treaty of Holston of 1791, signed with the Cherokee of the Southeast, included the following passage: "That the Cherokee nation may be led to a greater degree of civilization, and to become herdsmen and cultivators, instead of remaining in a state of hunters, the United States will furnish the said nation with useful implements of farming" (Perdue and Green 1995, 11). The Trade and Intercourse Act of 1793 extended this program to all Indian nations, setting in motion the civilization program, which eventually grew to include educational and religious instruction; the civilization program would remain at the heart of federal Indian policy into the twentieth century. At the same time, federal officials believed that Native Americans would have to sell much of their territory to meet white settlers' constant demand for land. Helping Native Americans become "civilized" would enable them to remain on their homelands, shrunken but intact, with the eventual goal of shedding their Indian skin for American citizenship.

This set of ideas gave rise to the notion of American expansion with honor. In short, expansion was inevitable, a notion that eventually grew into the idea of Manifest Destiny, which was used to justify the conquest of the American West; it was preordained that white Christians would expand west across the country and "be fruitful, multiply, and replenish the Earth." Whether it would happen honorably, without tainting the new American nation's Christian conscience, would depend on whether or not the Indians embraced "civilization."

As president, Thomas Jefferson expanded the federal civilization program and supported the factory system developed under George Washington, a system of government-managed trading posts in which federal agents regulated prices to minimize antagonism between white traders and Indian trappers. After Jefferson negotiated the purchase of the Louisiana Territory from France, the United States found itself with an enormous territory, roughly one million square miles, which stretched from the Mississippi River to the Rocky Mountains and northward from the Gulf of Mexico to Canada. Jefferson sent his personal secretary, Meriwether Lewis, to explore this new territory, including the northern plains, in order to establish diplomatic relations with Indian groups living within it and to facilitate the spread of the civilization program to them.

On May 14, 1804, the expedition, led by Lewis and his good friend William Clark, left St. Louis. After traveling nearly eight thousand miles over two years, Lewis and Clark returned with extensive knowledge of the geography and the Indian peoples of the American West. Their route followed the Missouri River north from St. Louis into what became the states of South Dakota, North Dakota, Montana, and northern Wyoming, bringing them into contact with most of the major tribal groups of the northern plains, which include the various divisions of the Sioux of South and North Dakota, the Blackfeet, Flathead, and Crow of Montana, the Shoshone (Snake) and Arapaho of Wyoming, the Mandan and Hidatsa of North Dakota, and the Northern Cheyenne of South Dakota and Wyoming.

Lewis and Clark brought dozens of medals to award to Native leaders. Their goal was not only to establish diplomatic relations but to reshape the very political structure of Native American society by creating different ranks of "chiefs," who, by accepting the medals, would accept the supreme authority of the United States as the "Great Father" of the northern plains and of the American West in general. Lewis and Clark also arranged for a delegation of Native leaders to visit the president of the United States, the "Great Father." In 1806, Jefferson addressed a visiting delegation of tribes from the Missouri River region, explaining that, as France, England, and Spain had agreed to "retire from all the country which you & we hold between Canada & Mexico," that the Americans "are now your fathers" (Jefferson's Speech to a Delegation of Indian Chiefs, January 4, 1806). He told them of his plans to expand the factory system to facilitate the expansion of the fur trade into the American West. Trade would benefit all parties, he told them, but only if peaceful relations were maintained:

> You are all my children, and I wish you to live in peace & friendship with one another as brethren of the same family ought to do. If you will cease to make war on one another, if you will live in friendship with all mankind, you can employ all of your time in providing food & clothing for yourselves and you families. . . . Your numbers will be increased, instead of diminishing, and you will live in plenty & in quiet. (ibid.)

But he also warned them of Americans' power, both their strength in numbers and their weapons: "My children, we are strong, we are numerous as the stars in the heavens, & we are all gun-men." Responding to Jefferson's speech, leaders of the Osage, Missouri, Oto, Pani, Cansa, Ayowai, and Sioux Nations accepted U.S. authority, promised peace and friendship, but also asserted their right to defend themselves from violent white settlers if the "Great Father" did not use his power wisely and fairly:

> You say that you are numerous as the stars in the skies, & as strong as numerous. So much the better, fathers, tho', if you are so . . . you may tell to your white Children on our lands, to follow your orders, & do not as they please, for they do not keep your word. . . . Our hearts are good, though we are powerfull & strong, & we know how to fight, we do not wish to fight but shut the mouth of your Children who speak war, stop the arm of those who rise the tomahawk over our heads and Crush those who strike first, then we will Confess that we have good fathers who wish to make their red Children happy and peace maintained among them. For when we are at peace . . . , our wives and Children Do not stand in want.

In Jefferson's speech and in these Native leaders' response, we can find the major themes of U.S.-Native American diplomatic relations in the nineteenth century. And it is within this general framework of diplomatic relations that the history of treaty making with Native Americans of the northern plains evolves. From the perspective of the U.S. government, Indians needed to allow settlement and trade to proceed without Indian resistance. From the Native American perspective, peace was impossible unless the federal government used its power to compel its "white children" to honor the agreements of the "Great Father." It was the "white children" who raised the tomahawk and struck against Native Americans, initiating a cycle of violence in which Native Americans retaliated in defense, which triggered a more violent response from U.S. troops.

When Lewis and Clark entered the northern plains, they encountered a world that was undergoing rapid change. The expansion of trade between Native groups and Europeans in the late eighteenth century had engendered several major changes. Trade spread disease, particularly smallpox, which devastated the Native nations of the northern plains. The smallpox epidemics of 1779–1781 and 1801–1802 led to extraordinary death rates among the Arikara, Mandan, Hidatsa, Shoshone, and other groups of the northern plains, making them vulnerable to incursions from more nomadic groups, such as the Sioux, who quickly became the dominant force on the plains. Competition of Native groups with the Sioux for trade and for survival helped to militarize the plains, leading to the increased use of horses and guns, remaking Native American societies in the process.

American traders in great numbers pushed into the Missouri River basin of the northern plains after the Lewis and Clark expedition. Although the Sioux, in particular, welcomed the trade, other tribes did not and created barriers to the expansion of American fur traders based in St. Louis, which led to clashes between federal troops and nations such as the Arikara. At the behest of Missouri senator Thomas Hart Benson, Congress developed a new initiative to create stability and promote expansion, especially on the northern plains. The Act of May 25, 1824, authorized the president of the United States to make "treaties of trade and friendship with the Indian tribes beyond the Mississippi" (Prucha 2000, 38). The diplomatic effort targeted the upper Missouri River region, where much of the fur trade was concentrated. Federal agents were to make treaties with as many Indian nations as possible and to designate specific sites where federal officials could regulate trade between white traders and Native trappers, in a sense continuing the old factory system while abandoning federal control over prices. As a result, a new pair of Americans, Brigadier General Henry Atkinson and U.S. Indian agent Major Benjamin O'Fallon, ventured forth, as had Lewis and Clark twenty years earlier, to redefine federal-Indian relations through the written instrument of the treaty. On this 1825 expedition, however, Atkinson and Fallon were accompanied by 476 troops, a show of force designed to demonstrate to Native Americans that the United States was the dominant power in the region and that resistance would be met with resolve.

The Atkinson and Fallon mission resulted in the signing of a series of treaties that framed Indian-white diplomatic relations in the northern plains before the advent of the California gold rush triggered a new round of white settlement, Indian-white conflict, and treaty making. In August 1825, Atkinson and O'Fallon negotiated treaties with the Crow, Mandan, Oto and Missouri, Arikara, Chayenne (Cheyenne), Pawnee, and Sioux. Importantly, the American negotiators had written the treaties in advance. Thus, the treaties themselves were not the product of a negotiation between two parties but Native Americans' acceptance of the Americans' explanation of the treaty terms in combination with a gift of trade goods.

As an example of these meetings, the Crow gathered with Atkinson and Fallon in a Hidatsa town on the Missouri River on August 3, 1825, eight days after receiving an invitation to meet with them. A large group of Crow, led by Red Plume, arrived in the town to negotiate with the Americans. However, a separate group of Crow refused to acknowledge American sovereignty or accept American gifts; tribal divisions would become common in the nineteenth century, as some Native American factions grew to distrust the U.S. government's intentions, a distrust aggravated by that government's failures to honor previous treaties. On August 4, Red Plume and other Crow chiefs in attendance signed the treaty and accepted the Americans' gift of trade goods. But trouble developed when the Americans made additional demands on the Crow delegation that were not specified in the treaty, which insulted Red Plume and other Crow, who believed that the negotiations had ended. Violence was narrowly averted. The following day, the American delegation made amends by providing more gifts. The incident demonstrated the ways in which Native groups such as the Crow had to conform to the new political and economic realities of the northern plains. As the Sioux, Cheyenne, and Arapaho had grown stronger and more capable of expansion by forging extensive trading links with Americans, nations such as the Crow had to keep pace by remaining within the orbit of American traders in order to secure guns and other tools with which to resist incursion onto their lands by white settlers as well as other Native groups. Thus, as historian Frederick Hoxie relates, the Red Plume delegation resolved that "their wounds were covered and they would throw all that had passed behind them" (Hoxie 1995, 65). The insult was forgotten in the interest of preventing violence and preserving trade relations integral to the Crow Nation's survival.

The treaties of August 1825 were virtually identical in language and in scope. The treaty that the Crow signed on August 4, for example, contained the following:

> It is admitted by the Crow tribe of Indians, that they reside within the territorial limits of the United States, acknowledge their supremacy, and claim their protection.—The said tribe also admit the right of the United States to regulate all trade and intercourse with them. . . . The United States agrees to receive the Crow tribe of Indians into their friendship, and under their protection, and to extend to them, from time to time, such benefits and acts of kindness as may be convenient, and seem just and proper to the President of the United States.

The Crow, as well as the Sioux and other Native groups that signed similar treaties in August 1825, accepted American supremacy, at least on paper, and granted to the United States the authority to regulate trade. They also agreed to work within a European American framework of justice, which required Native leaders, in the event of a "crime," to "deliver up the [Native] person or persons against whom the complaint is made, to the end that he or they may be punished, agreeably to the laws of the United States" (ibid.). Thus, the treaties not only circumscribed the place where economic relations would be conducted but undermined Native Americans' sovereignty, their ability to define justice within their own territories. For the Crow, especially, but also for other Native groups, 1825 marked an end to their isolation and the beginning of increasingly complex relations with the United States: territorial boundaries were established, social behavior was defined, and economic relations were regulated in accordance with the imperatives of powerful white traders.

It remained to be seen, however, whether or not Native Americans would continue to accept the terms of these new intercultural relations. As the group of chiefs had told Jefferson in 1806, it was incumbent upon the "Great Father" to prevent his many "white children" from raising the tomahawk and instigating violence that prompted Native Americans to exercise sovereignty and defend themselves. After the gold rush of 1848–1849 triggered massive waves of white settlers, this effort to reduce violence and maintain justice became problematic. In 1848, when Mexico finally gave up its claim to U.S. land north of its current border, the United States controlled all land westward from the Rockies to the Pacific Coast, as well as territory that stretched from the Rio Grande River north to the 49th parallel. The gold rush in California accelerated the process of frontier settlement. Between 1850 and 1870, nearly five million Americans, as well as many Europeans, crossed the Mississippi River and headed west. In their search for the mother lode, these white settlers trespassed on Native Americans' Mother Earth, creating a crisis of sovereignty for Native Americans, who had been promised protection from white settlers' depredations. Although Hollywood and accounts common to the time depicted the Indians as perpetrators of "massacres" against innocent women and children, the historical record shows that settlers traveling the Bozeman Trail and the Oregon Trail (the two main trails across the northern plains) trespassed on Native lands without consulting Native leaders, slaughtered buffalo on those lands, and left smallpox, cholera, measles, and scarlet fever in their wake. Between 1840 and 1860, only 362 emigrants crossing the plains died as a result of Native American attacks (Calloway 2004, 267). The cost to Native Americans was much higher.

As a result of this increased emigration and federal officials' need to protect American citizens, the U.S. government initiated another round of treaty making to try to keep the peace. For three weeks in September 1851, federal negotiators, led by the superintendent of Indian affairs (at St. Louis), David D. Mitchell, a former fur trader in the region, and the Indian agent Thomas Fitzpatrick, met with representatives of the Crow and ten bands of the Sioux, Cheyenne, Arapaho, Assiniboine, Hidatsa, Mandan, and Arikara at Fort Laramie in present-day Wyoming. All told, nearly ten thousand Native Americans assembled for the treaty council, the largest such gathering in the history of Indian-white relations. Federal treaty commissioners spent a total of eight days meeting with these tribal representatives, who spent an additional eight days discussing the various treaty provisions among themselves.

Ethnohistorian Raymond DeMallie, who has studied extensively the plains treaty councils, identified three main stages in the negotiations: ritual, delineation of demands, and gift giving. The intercultural relations that led to the signing of the Fort Laramie treaty on September 17 first featured the employment of specific rituals by each side to set the stage for the detailed negotiations. To begin and end the daily discussions, treaty commissioners and Indian leaders performed the ceremony of the smoking of the pipe; to call the meeting to order, U.S. representatives fired one of their cannons and raised the American flag, symbolically asserting their power. The second stage involved presenting the specific provisions of the treaty, most of which had been written before the commissioners arrived in Wyoming. In the third stage, the negotiations were sealed with presents brought by the American commissioners, which were distributed by tribal leaders as a means of solidifying their political authority and their social standing as providers to the community. In return for smoking the pipe, American commissioners required Native American leaders to "touch the pen," or sign the treaty document, despite the fact that Native negotiators found that step unnecessary, given the trust established by the ritual of smoking the pipe. The three stages of ritual, negotiation, and gift giving represented continuity with previous councils stretching back to the Lewis and Clark expedition and would remain the pattern for negotiations beyond 1851.

As was the case during the Lewis and Clark negotiations, U.S. commissioners forced Native Americans to nominate one leader to represent all the constituencies of a tribe, and in the case of the Sioux, to unite all the bands into one nation and have just one Sioux chief, the "head chief," to represent all the diverse bands. For Native Americans used to consensus building, this was a traumatic restructuring of political culture that reflected their declining sovereignty.

The treaty, signed for the purpose of "establishing and confirming peaceful relations" among the assembled Indian nations to protect white settlers, outlined new rules of engagement on the northern plains. Native Americans would permit the construction of forts and roads in their territory; in return, the United States would "bind themselves to protect the aforesaid Indian nations against the commission of all depredations by the people of the said United States." Additionally, the United States promised to provide annual payments worth $50,000 for ten years, in the form of "provisions, merchandize, domestic animals, and agricultural implements." Thus, the United States intended to sustain the civilization program whether Native Americans wanted it or not.

The treaty also stipulated that each Indian nation would subscribe to specific new boundaries determined by the United States; this was the most contentious and controversial part of the treaty. The Sioux, in particular, had no interest in being told where they could live and hunt. Rejecting the notion of a restricted territory, Black Hawk of the Oglala band of Sioux told U.S. commissioners, "These lands once belonged to the Kiowa and the Crow, but we whipped those nations out of them, and in this we did what the white men do when they want the lands of the Indians" (White 1978, 342). As historian Richard White contends, the Sioux had the upper hand in 1851 and had no intention of accepting U.S. domination on the northern plains. The same year as the Fort Laramie treaty of 1851, U.S. officials negotiated with the Dakota (Santee) Sioux of present-day Minnesota, producing the Treaty of Traverse des Sioux (Treaty with the Sioux–Sisseton and Wahpeton Bands–July 23, 1851), in which the Dakota Sioux gave up their claim to much of their territory and accepted a reservation as their new homeland. A second treaty, signed in 1858, shrank that homeland even further. For this land, the U.S. government agreed to provide blacksmith, farming, and education assistance, as well as annual payments. The sale of Sioux land to white settlers, many of whom treated the Sioux poorly and thus upset a delicate system of interethnic relations formed during the colonial era fur trade, helped fuel resentment among Sioux. This resentment became explosive in 1862, when the federal government failed to produce annuities on time, which led to widespread starvation. The result was the Sioux Uprising, which involved brutal violence on both sides and the hanging of thirty-eight Sioux, the largest mass execution in U.S. history. It is critical to understand this violence as a product of the Dakota Sioux's belief that the spirit of the treaties had been violated, which meant that they now viewed the Americans' entire value system as corrupt, as the treaty itself embodied cultural values such as trust and reciprocity. This dynamic of resentment and violence would be repeated after the Lakota Sioux and other Northern Plains tribes signed the second Treaty of Fort Laramie in 1868.

Between 1851 and 1868, the U.S. government negotiated a series of treaties with Native groups of the northern plains and other regions of the American West, including treaties with the Blackfeet and the Flathead, signed in 1855, that circumscribed their territory. After the Civil War ended, the U.S. government concentrated on ending Indian-white violence in the southern and the northern plains regions. The United States Indian Peace Commission, comprising military officers, ministers, and civilian reformers, formed in 1867 to end hostilities and accelerate the "concentration" and "domestication" of Native Americans on reservations through a reborn civilization program. The Peace Commission first negotiated treaties with Native American nations of the southern plains before turning its attention to those of the northern plains, in particular the Sioux, who remained intent on defending their territory against settlers on the Bozeman Trail and against hordes of white hunters who slaughtered buffalo herds from railroad cars. In late April 1868, after agreeing to the demands of the great Sioux leader Red Cloud that the U.S. abandon its forts on the Bozeman Trail, the Peace Commission gathered with Red Cloud and other Sioux chiefs to negotiate a major treaty at Fort Laramie, Wyoming, in an effort to end the so-called Red Cloud War. Similar negotiations with the Crow Nation and the Cheyenne and Arapaho followed in May 1868, which produced treaties similar to the Sioux treaty signed on April 29. In contrast to the negotiations at Fort Laramie in 1851, the United States held the upper hand at Fort Laramie in 1868. At the council with the Brule Sioux on April 28, General John B. Sanborn told the Sioux chiefs, "If you continue to fight the whites you can not expect the President nor your friends among them to protect you in your country from those who are waiting to go there in large numbers. If you continue at war your country will soon be all overrun by white people . . . Your game and yourselves will be destroyed." General William S. Harney added, "We do not want to go to war with you because you are a small nation, a handful compared with us, and we want you to live." Harney and Sanborn tried to persuade the Sioux that one large army after another would engage the Sioux until hostilities ended. This treaty council was, as Sanborn put it, "the last effort of the President to make peace with you and save for you a country and a home" (Calloway 2004, 301–302).

The treaty signed on April 29 had numerous provisions, the most important of which confirmed that the United States would abandon its forts in Sioux territory, granted to the Sioux the "Great Sioux Reservation" in present-day South Dakota, and guaranteed access to and hunting rights in "unceded Indian territory" adjacent to the reservation, which included the Black Hills. In addition, the treaty provided annuities to the Sioux for the purpose of expanding the civilization program and remaking the Sioux in the image of the Christian yeoman farmer. For example, Article 7 read as follows: "In order to insure the civilization of the Indians . . . , the necessity of education is admitted . . . , and [the Sioux] therefore pledge themselves to compel their children, male and female . . . to attend school." Thus, the treaty laid the foundation of a program of coercive assimilation that would cause great social and cultural trauma for the Sioux, even as it sowed the seeds of future military conflict over the status of the Black Hills, considered sacred ground to the Sioux. The treaty, in short, failed to produce peace. And the United States failed to uphold its honor to maintain it.

In 1871, Congress resolved that "hereafter no Indian nation or tribe within the territory of the United States shall be acknowledged or recognized as an independent nation, tribe, or power with whom the United States may contract by treaty" (Prucha 2000, 135). Believing that all barriers to expansion had been removed, American politicians no longer felt an obligation to conduct diplomacy with Native groups as sovereign nations. The spirit of equality was shattered. However, as during the early national period, Congress expressed the intent to expand with honor, noting that, although it would stop making new treaties, it would also continue to honor those treaties already ratified. Such noble sentiments melted away during the spring thaw in South Dakota, as white gold miners by the hundreds descended on Sioux lands near the Black Hills, engendering resistance on the part of Sioux who believed they had the right by treaty to defend themselves. Not only did the federal government fail to honor the Treaty of Fort Laramie of 1868, it sent federal troops led by General George Custer to protect the gold miners. This clear violation of the spirit and the letter of the law led to the militarization of Sioux, Cheyenne, and Arapaho forces, which destroyed Custer's troops in July 1876 at the Battle of Greasy Grass, as the Sioux called the Battle of Little Bighorn.

But it was a short-lived victory for the Sioux. In 1877, they were forced by federal officials' threats of starvation to give up the Black Hills. This immoral action on the part of federal officials was simply one of a series of occasions on which the U.S. government invalidated existing treaties when it became economically useful to do so. But the larger problem, as military historian John Gray has pointed out,

stemmed from the duplicitous ways in which federal treaty commissioners negotiated the treaty documents in the first place, embedding a set of contradictions in the language that Native American negotiators could not foresee would produce future conflict. As Gray writes of the Fort Laramie Treaty of 1868,

> Here is a solemn treaty that cedes territory admittedly unceded; that confines the Indian to a reservation while allowing him to roam elsewhere, and that guarantees against trespass, unless a trespasser appears! . . . It was the Commission that wrote in the contradictions. There can be only one explanation—they designed one set of provisions to beguile and another to enforce.

The treaty itself, Gray concluded, was "so exclusively a white man's device . . . that it served primarily as an instrument of chicanery and a weapon of aggression" (Calloway, 2004, 296–297). In short, the U.S. government engineered a dishonorable expansion in the northern plains and across the continent.

Ever since 1877, the Sioux have fought to reclaim the Black Hills. In 1950, the Sioux filed a claim with the Indian Claims Commission, established in 1946 to facilitate the adjudication of treaty violations, which awarded the Sioux $17.5 million after determining that the taking of the Black Hills in 1877 was unconstitutional. In the 1980 case *United States v. Sioux Nation*, the U.S. Supreme Court upheld the award while granting the Sioux interest on the original judgment of $17.5 million, which raised the total to more than $100 million. In doing so, the Supreme Court noted, "A more ripe and rank case of dishonorable dealings will never, in all probability, be found in our history. . . ." However, the Sioux wanted land, not money, and have yet to claim the Court's monetary compensation. The Sioux continue to fight for the return of the Black Hills. Treaties signed well over one hundred years ago continue to animate, define, and shape Indian-white relations for the Sioux and for many other Native American groups.

Paul C. Rosier

References and Further Reading

Calloway, Colin G. 2004. *First Peoples: A Documentary Survey of American Indian History.* Boston: Bedford/St. Martin's.

Deloria, Vine, Jr. 1985. *Behind the Trail of Broken Treaties: An Indian Declaration of Independence.* Austin: University of Texas Press.

Deloria, Vine, Jr., and Raymond DeMallie, eds. 1975. *Proceedings of the Great Peace Commission of 1867–1868.* Washington, DC: Institute for the Development of Indian Law.

Deloria, Vine, Jr., and David E. Wilkins. 2000. *Tribes, Treaties, and Constitutional Tribulations.* Austin: University of Texas Press.

DeMallie, Raymond J. 1980. "Touching the Pen: Plains Indian Treaty Councils in Ethnohistorical Perspective." In *Ethnicity on the Great Plains,* ed. Fredrick C. Luebke, 38–51. Lincoln: University of Nebraska Press.

Hoxie, Frederick E. 1995. *Parading through History: The Making of the Crow Nation in America, 1805–1935.* New York: Cambridge University Press.

Konkle, Maureen. 2004. *Writing Indian Nations: Native Intellectuals and the Politics of Historiography, 1827–1863.* Chapel Hill: University of North Carolina Press.

Lazarus, Edward. 1991. *Black Hills/White Justice: The Sioux Nation Versus the United States, 1775 to the Present.* New York: HarperCollins.

Perdue, Theda, and Michael Green, eds. 1995. *The Cherokee Removal: A Brief History with Documents.* Boston: Bedford Books.

Prucha, Francis Paul. 1986. *The Great Father: The United States Government and the American Indian.* Lincoln: University of Nebraska Press.

Prucha, Francis Paul. 1997. *American Indian Treaties: The History of a Political Anomaly.* Berkeley: University of California Press.

Prucha, Francis Paul, ed. 2000. *Documents of United States Indian Policy.* Lincoln: University of Nebraska Press.

White, Richard. 1978. "The Winning of the West: The Expansion of the Western Sioux in the Eighteenth and Nineteenth Centuries." *Journal of American History* 65 (September): 319–343.

Wilkinson, Charles. 1987. *American Indians, Time, and the Law.* New Haven, CT: Yale University Press.

Southeast and Florida

Diplomacy in the Native Southeast

The Native American peoples in the southeastern quadrant of North America and Florida participated in diplomatic relations long before the arrival of Europeans. Indian communities held diplomatic councils to create and maintain trade relations, negotiated agreements to acquire materials and products not indigenous to their territory, and made arrangements to ensure safe passage for their trade representatives through the territories of other tribes. Indian peoples also used diplomatic arrangements to construct intertribal confederacies, to set up military alliances, and to establish peace with enemies after periods of war.

Southeastern Indians followed diplomatic protocols familiar to most Eastern Woodlands peoples. From the beginning of an intertribal council, which for some peoples began with an elaborate procession to the council grounds, the host people established a hospitable atmosphere by warmly greeting the visiting representatives, offering them food and drink, and ensuring that they were comfortable. The parties smoked a peace pipe, or calumet, to symbolically open a clear line of communication between the two peoples and exchanged gifts such as furs, feathers, and pipes to prove their sincerity.

The negotiations began with orations from each side. In a peace negotiation, for example, the representatives might express their sadness that relations had been broken by war, announce their desire to restore peace, and describe the vision of the future that would be created if the parties came to agreement. The parties spoke in a common diplomatic language that enabled peoples who spoke distinct languages and dialects to communicate; they couched their discussions in metaphors, stories, and symbols designed to signify their expectations in a clear but polite fashion. Early European records indicate that Indians participating in diplomatic negotiations used language that encouraged their counterparts to "think good thoughts of peace," "bury the hatchet," "link arms together," and "eat out of the same bowl." When Indian communities established diplomatic arrangements, they often created fictive kinship relations with their negotiating partners and described their counterparts in familiar kinship terms. A small, less powerful group, for instance, might refer to a militarily stronger people as their "older brother." This signified that they expected to be protected, just as a young boy is defended by his elder sibling.

Treaties in the Colonial Era

The European imperial and colonial governments established the practice of dealing with the Native American nations by means of the diplomatic treaty. Over time, European negotiators in America adopted many of the same diplomatic procedures and formalities that Indian peoples had used in the past, including the exchanging of gifts, the passing of the peace pipe, and the use of Indian metaphors and allusions. The British and colonial governments used treaties to make peace with, acquire territory from, and establish trade relations with the Southeastern Indian nations. For example, in 1715 the Yamasee, Catawba, and other Indian tribes in the region attacked the town of Charleston after becoming frustrated by unscrupulous traders who captured indebted tribal members and sold them into slavery. After bitter fighting, in 1717 the Yamasee and Catawba made peace with the English; the parties used a diplomatic treaty to bring hostilities to an end.

The British also used treaties to acquire land from the tribes and impose their vision of territorial order. For example, in 1765 the British and the Choctaw signed a treaty at Mobile establishing the Choctaw border at the Alabama and Cahaba rivers. The British also promised to keep English settlers from crossing into Choctaw territory. The European nations also used treaty negotiations to attack the interests of their colonial rivals. In the Treaty of Grandpré (1750), French agents persuaded the Choctaw to wage war against the Chickasaw, who were aligned with Great Britain. In that agreement, the French threatened to execute any Choctaw who killed a French subject or invited an English subject into their village.

Treaty Relations during the American Revolution

During the Revolutionary War, the American colonies unsuccessfully competed with Great Britain to conclude treaties that secured the military assistance or neutrality of the Indian nations in the Southeast. The major tribal nations in the Southeast—the Cherokee, the Choctaw, the Chickasaw, and the Muscogee Creek—feared that an American victory would only encourage the intrusion of settlers into their lands and remained hostile to the colonies. American military efforts were more successful in bringing about Indian neutrality. In 1776, militia forces from Virginia, North Carolina, South Carolina, and Georgia invaded the Cherokee Nation, destroyed Cherokee crops and villages, and cowed the Cherokee and the rest of the southeastern tribes into neutrality for the remainder of the war. After the conclusion of the Cherokee War of 1776, the states involved in the war opened separate negotiations with the Cherokee within their borders. On May 20, 1777, the Lower Cherokee signed a treaty with South Carolina and Georgia at DeWitt's Corner, South Carolina. The Cherokee agreed to return their American prisoners and ceded their territory east of the Unicoi Mountains; Georgia and South Carolina promised to keep their citizens from crossing into Cherokee territory and agreed to provide the Cherokee people with trade goods. In the Treaty of Long Island of Holston, concluded on June 20, 1777, the Overhill Cherokee concluded peace negotiations with similar provisions with North Carolina and Virginia. In August 1783, a dissident faction of the Creek Nation, rejecting the British alliance arranged by Alexander McGillivray, ceded a portion of their territory to Georgia in the Treaty of Augusta. In that same year, the Chickasaw signed a treaty with Virginia that established peace and borders between the two peoples.

The fact that these treaties were concluded with the states rather than the Continental Congress demonstrates the confusion that existed over which government held jurisdiction over Indian relations. The southern states argued that the Articles of Confederation gave the states complete jurisdiction over Indian affairs, and they continued to conclude separate treaties with the Indians within their borders. Those who favored a stronger central government argued that Indian relations were a concern of all of the states and therefore a matter to be handled by the Continental Congress. The Constitutional Convention of 1787 clarified the wording of the national government's authority somewhat by endowing Congress with the power "to regulate commerce with foreign nations, and among the several States, and with the Indian tribes," although many southerners continued to claim the power to treat with Indian nations.

The Hopewell Treaties

In 1783, soon after the signing of the Treaty of Paris, which concluded the American Revolutionary War, the Continental Congress directed treaty commissioners to make peace with the Indian nations and inform them that the United States had acquired sovereignty over them with its victory over Great Britain. The Indian nations in the Southeast refused to accept this argument. The Cherokee, Chickasaw, Choctaw, and Muscogee Creek continued to possess formidable military forces, and the latter three nations preferred to continue playing off the United States against Spain for their own benefit. In 1784 the Creek, Chickasaw, and Choctaw Nations signed treaties with the Spanish government. These treaties raised serious concerns among American policymakers that the southeastern nations might ally with Spain and attack the southern and western flank of the United States.

In 1785, the United States accelerated its efforts to establish peaceful relations with the southeastern tribes. In November of that year, treaty commissioners sent by the Congress met with Cherokee leaders at Hopewell, a plantation on the Keowee River in northwestern South Carolina. After lengthy negotiations, the United States and the Cherokee Nation concluded a treaty that established peace and agreed upon formal boundaries.

Some provisions of the agreement suggested that the Cherokee had surrendered aspects of national sovereignty to the United States. The Cherokee, for instance, acknowledged that they would thereafter live "under the protection of the United States of America, and of no other sovereign, whosoever." Another article stated that "the United States in Congress assembled shall have the sole and exclusive right of regulating the trade with the Indians, and managing all their affairs in such manner as they think proper." The Hopewell agreement also prohibited the Cherokee from engaging in diplomatic or trade relations with other nations. (Despite this provision, the Cherokee signed a treaty with Spain in 1792. The Choctaw, the Chickasaw, and the Muscogee Creek also signed treaties with Spain that year; these agreements seemed to violate the United States' efforts at Hopewell and, later, in the treaty with the Creek in New York, to prohibit the tribes from conducting trade or diplomacy with European nations).

Other provisions of the treaty implied that the United States recognized the Cherokee people as an independent, sovereign nation. Along with establishing borders for the Cherokee, the treaty required American settlers to leave Cherokee territory. Those who did not leave, the treaty stated, would fall subject to Cherokee law. The treaty also provided the Cherokee with the right to send a "deputy of their choice, whenever they think fit, to Congress." Some scholars have argued that this provision was an admission on the part of the United States that the Cherokee constituted an independent sovereign nation; others have argued that the American treaty commissioners intended the Cherokee eventually to assimilate into the United States.

As the U.S. commissioners were preparing to depart, they received word that treaty delegations from the Choctaw and Chickasaw Nations were on their way to Hopewell. On January 3, 1786, the United States and the Choctaw reached treaty terms. The Chickasaw concluded their agreement with the United States on January 10. The Choctaw and Chickasaw treaties were almost identical to the U.S.-Cherokee accord, except that the Choctaw and Chickasaw did not receive permission to send a deputy to the U.S. Congress.

Treaties and the Civilization Program

In 1789, President George Washington appointed Henry Knox, his artillery commander during the Revolutionary War, as his secretary of war. In letters to Washington, Knox argued that the United States should recognize that the Indian tribes were sovereign peoples possessing a legitimate claim to their land. By recognizing the rights of the Indian nations, Knox continued, the United States could establish peace along its western frontier, institute an orderly process for territorial expansion, and demonstrate that it was a just nation that dealt honorably with its indigenous population. Knox persuaded Washington to his view, and together, through executive orders, treaties, and legislation, they implemented the secretary's suggestions. In 1790, Congress enacted the first in a series of statutes called the Trade and Intercourse Acts, which provided, among other things, that land purchases from Indians be acquired in treaties negotiated by tribal leaders and federal commissioners appointed by the president.

Knox did not believe that the tribes would remain forever sovereign, and he argued that the United States had a duty to prepare Native Americans for their eventual assimilation. He proposed a civilization program in which the government would teach Indians to read, write, and till the soil like American yeomen farmers. Knox believed that, once Native Americans abandoned hunting for European American-styled farming, their "hunting grounds," or national territory, could be purchased by the United States and sold to and developed by Americans. Over time, Knox predicted, acculturated Indians would assimilate into the American society that slowly engulfed them. Congress appropriated money to supply Indians with plows, spinning wheels, and other tools and implements, and began posting agents among the tribes to instruct individual Indians in their use.

The Muscogee Creek Nation became the first southeastern tribe to conclude a treaty that included civilization provisions. On August 7, 1790, the Muscogee Creek and the United States signed the Treaty of New York, which contained provisions similar to those set forth in the Hopewell treaties and reaffirmed, to a considerable extent, the Creek borders established in treaties made with Georgia at Augusta (1783), Galphinton (1785), and Shoulderbone (1786). The civilization article of the treaty declared that the United States would assist the Creek on the path toward "a greater degree of civilization," teach them to become "herdsmen and cultivators," and provide them "useful domestic animals and implements of husbandry." The United States also promised to respect the borders of the remaining Creek territory and to provide the Creek with trade goods and an annuity of $1,500. Annuities, an annual cash payment to the tribe, became common in U.S.-Indian treaties. In a set of secret provisions, which also became commonplace in federal-Indian treaties, the United States agreed to pay the Creek Chief Alexander McGillivray $1,200 a year, made him the federal agent for the Creek Nation, and appointed him a brigadier general in the U.S. Army. With this treaty, and with the treaties at Fort Harmar with several tribes from north of the Ohio, George Washington's administration established the precedent of sending concluded treaties to the Senate for ratification. Proponents of the idea that the tribes were sovereign nations subsequently used this

development to bolster their argument, for the Constitution required the Senate to consent to treaties the president negotiated with foreign states.

The United States also persuaded the other major southeastern tribes to sign treaties implementing the civilization program. On July 2, 1791, at the Holston River near what is now Knoxville, the Cherokee reaffirmed the peace and protection clauses of the Hopewell agreement and ceded a tract of territory settled by Americans. This pattern, in which settlers encroached on Indian land, which was then acquired by the United States by treaty, was forced on the Cherokee and the other southeastern tribes over and over again. In return, the United States agreed to provide funds and instruction to lead the Cherokee toward acculturation.

Jefferson and the Southeast Nations

When Thomas Jefferson was elected president of the United States, he quickly set out to acquire Indian land in the Southeast. Although the Cherokee at first tried to resist U.S. demands, they eventually surrendered cessions in treaties at Wafford's Settlement (1804), Tellico (1804–1805), and Washington (1806). The Creek, Choctaw, and Chickasaw Nations also ceded territory to the United States during this era. These nations had incurred enormous debts to the British trading firm of Panton, Leslie, and Company. The three nations offered up land and rights-of-way through their territory to the United States; in exchange, the federal government paid the Indians' debts. Between 1801 and 1805, in three treaties at Fort Adams, Fort Confederation, and Hoe Buckintoopa, the Choctaw ceded to the United States approximately seven million acres and the right to build a federal road through their territory. In 1805, the Chickasaw ceded all their lands north of the Tennessee River to the United States; most of the annuities the Indians received were paid directly to their creditors at Chickasaw Bluffs. That same year, the Creek surrendered territory east of the Ocmulgee River and authorized the United States to build a road through their nation to Mobile.

In 1803, Jefferson's administration completed the Louisiana Purchase. The acquisition of this vast territory gave Jefferson the opportunity to implement an idea he had contemplated for many years: the relocation of the Indian nations in the East beyond the Mississippi River. There, Jefferson suggested, Native Americans could acculturate at their own pace, retain their autonomy, and live free from the trespasses of American settlers. Jefferson attempted to persuade Indian leaders to take their people to the West. Although the southeastern tribes generally rejected the president's overtures, in 1808 the federal government did conclude a removal and exchange treaty with a group of disaffected Cherokee. By 1810, about one thousand members of that dissident group had migrated to the Arkansas River valley.

Treaties after the War of 1812

During the War of 1812, American militia forces under Andrew Jackson destroyed the Nativist Redstick Creek revolt at Horseshoe Bend (1814). In the Treaty of Fort Jackson (1814), Jackson forced the Muscogee Creek Nation to surrender more than twenty million acres, even though many of the Creek had fought with Jackson against the Redsticks. The treaty also required the Muscogee Creek Nation to end its relations with Spain and Great Britain and authorized the United States to build roads, forts, and trading posts in Creek territory.

After the war, Jackson and John C. Calhoun, the secretary of war under President James Monroe, called for the United States to end the use of treaties and what Jackson called the "absurdity" of dealing with the Indian tribes as sovereign nations. In 1817, a congressional committee advised Monroe to embrace Jefferson's removal idea and relocate the southeastern tribes to the West. During Monroe's administration, the Creek, Cherokee, Choctaw, and Chickasaw all ceded land to the United States; treaties with the Cherokee in 1817 and 1819, the Choctaw in 1820, the Chickasaw in 1816 and 1818, and the Creek in 1825 all included articles providing inducements for tribe members to emigrate west of the Mississippi. In the Treaty of Doak's Stand (1820), the Choctaw traded more than five million acres in Alabama and Mississippi for thirteen million acres in what is now western Arkansas and eastern Oklahoma. When surveyors arrived to mark out the new western territory, however, the Choctaw learned that white settlers had already moved into the area. When the Choctaw leadership protested, the United States asked them to send a delegation to Washington to renegotiate the boundaries of their cession. There, the Choctaw chief Moshulatubbee agreed to the Treaty of Washington City, which required the Choctaw to surrender approximately two million acres of the land they

had acquired at Doak's Stand. Although Calhoun and federal officials urged the Choctaw to move en masse to the West, only a few small groups chose to remove.

The Chickasaw also surrendered cessions in 1816 and 1818, although they did not agree to provisions for removal at this time. In the treaties of 1805, 1816, and 1818, the Chickasaw gave up almost twenty million acres of their national territory. The Seminole, a nation comprising remnant indigenous groups and Creek Redsticks who had fled into the region after the Creek Civil War, also ceded territory to the United States. In 1823, at Moultrie Creek, Florida, the Seminole ceded their lands in northern Florida and along the coasts and agreed to remain in the interior of the state. After surrendering thirty million acres, the Seminole retained only five million acres in the central part of the peninsula.

In 1825, federal commissioners and Georgia officials persuaded a small group of Muscogee Creek, led by a chief named William McIntosh, to sign the Treaty of Indian Springs (1825), which required the Creek to abandon their territory in Georgia and a large tract in Alabama. The Creek council had earlier passed a law imposing the death penalty for anyone who sold national lands without the consent of the government; and on April 30, 1825, a number of Creek warriors representing their government killed McIntosh. The Creek government also sent representatives to the United States capital to protest the treaty. In 1827, the Creek Nation and the United States signed the Treaty of Washington, which voided the Treaty of Indian Springs. The new treaty and a subsequently signed revision, however, still resulted in the surrender of all Creek territory in Georgia.

The Removal Treaties

These agreements did not satisfy the southern state governments. In the 1820s, politicians in Georgia called for the expulsion of all Indians from the state. The demands for removal were a product of the profitability of cotton agriculture in the Southeast, the concomitant demand for arable land, and the emerging racial prejudice on the part of many white southerners. Beginning in 1827, Georgia passed a series of laws designed to coerce the Cherokee to leave the state. The Georgia legislature extended the state's jurisdiction over the Cherokee Nation, passed laws purporting to abolish the Cherokee laws and government, and set in motion a process to seize the Cherokee national territory, divide it up into parcels, and offer it in a lottery to white Georgians. Alabama, Mississippi, and Tennessee followed Georgia's lead and passed laws extending state jurisdiction over the Indians in their borders. In 1828, Andrew Jackson was elected president of the United States, and he set out to achieve a general removal of the eastern tribes. In 1830, Congress passed the Indian Removal Act, which authorized the president to negotiate removal and cession treaties with the Indian tribes in the East.

The Cherokee, however, refused to remove. John Ross, the principal chief of the Cherokee, argued to the American public that the Cherokee Nation was a sovereign nation, that Georgia's efforts to exert its jurisdiction over the Cherokee violated both the U.S. Constitution and international law, and that the federal government had a duty under the Treaty of Hopewell and subsequent U.S.-Cherokee treaties to protect his nation from Georgia's attacks. Ross understood that the Cherokees' only hope for survival in the East was to force the United States to abide by its treaty commitments, and he consistently reminded federal leaders of their nation's longstanding recognition of the Cherokees' national sovereignty in those agreements.

With Congress and the president now promoting a removal policy, the Cherokee asked the U.S. Supreme Court to intervene in their behalf and recognize the Cherokee Nation as a separate, sovereign nation. In *Cherokee Nation v. Georgia* (1831), Chief Justice John Marshall wrote that the Cherokee constituted a distinct state and that the United States had historically recognized the sovereignty of their nation in numerous treaties. However, Marshall said, the Cherokee Nation was not a foreign state; it was a "domestic dependent nation" under the protection of the United States. A year later, in *Worcester v. Georgia*, Marshall offered a stronger pronouncement in favor of the sovereignty of the Indian tribes. Though the Cherokee Nation had placed itself under the protection of the United States at Hopewell, Marshall held, it remained a distinct and separate nation. The efforts by Georgia to extend its laws over the Cherokee, Marshall concluded, violated the sovereignty of the Cherokee Nation and unconstitutionally intruded into the special treaty relationship between the Cherokee and the United States. Andrew Jackson was determined not to enforce the decision in *Worcester*, however, and allowed Georgia to continue its efforts to force the Cherokee out of the state. At the same time, Jackson, now empowered by

the Indian Removal Act, moved to relocate all of the Indian nations from the East.

The removal of the southeastern Indian nations was accomplished through the use of the treaty. Ironically, even as the U.S. government worked to coerce the Indian nations to surrender their land in the East, it continued to use the mechanism that suggested that the tribes were sovereign. The removal treaties typically provided for an exchange of remaining national territory in the East for new lands west of the Mississippi, reimbursements for the loss of buildings and fixtures, the costs of emigration, funds to help the removed Indians acclimate to their new environment, and cash or annuities. The United States also promised to honor the title of the Indian nation's new land in the West, to respect its political autonomy once there, and to protect the tribe from future trespasses.

On September 18, 1830, about six thousand Choctaw met with federal treaty officials at Dancing Rabbit Creek in eastern Mississippi and signed a removal treaty with the United States. In an effort to coerce the Choctaw into removing, federal agents plied the Indians with alcohol and warned them they would forfeit their existence as a tribe and fall under the authority of Mississippi if they refused to sign. Many Choctaw refused to be bullied and left the council. On September 27, however, Greenwood LeFlore, Mushulatubbee, and 170 other Choctaw leaders signed a treaty that called for the wholesale removal of the Choctaw Nation. The treaty also provided that LeFlore and other Choctaw families could remain in the East if they accepted individual allotments of land. The treaty effectively divided the Choctaw Nation in two. In 1831, the first group of Choctaw emigrated to their new homes in the West. The majority of Choctaw moved on to the Indian Territory, yet perhaps as many as six thousand remained in Mississippi. Only sixty-nine of those who remained took allotments; most of the Mississippi Choctaw were left landless and destitute.

In 1832, the Creek government agreed to surrender its territory east of the Mississippi. In return, the United States provided the Creek Nation with territory in what is now east central Oklahoma. In addition, Creek individuals received allotments of land; they could either retain the tract and remain where they were or sell their land and emigrate to the West. Most of the individuals who received an allotment lost them through fraudulent schemes to white Americans. The Creek, now overrun by American settlers and speculators, removed to the West.

In 1830, the Chickasaw agreed to a cession and removal treaty at Franklin, Tennessee. When the Chickasaw visited their new territory, they were dissatisfied with the land and nullified the Treaty of Franklin. White settlers, however, continued to flood into the Chickasaw Nation; and local and state authorities began to arrest and imprison individual Chickasaw on false or minor charges. In addition, federal negotiators threatened to withhold annuities from the Chickasaw if they did not agree to remove. In October 1832, the Chickasaw signed another removal treaty at their council house at Pontotoc Creek. The Treaty of Pontotoc provided that the Chickasaw Nation's land would be surveyed, divided up into tracts, and allotted to individual Chickasaw adults. The Chickasaw would remove to their new lands in the West, and the remaining Chickasaw land would be sold by the federal government and placed in a tribal fund. After the signing of the treaty, the Chickasaw immediately began to protest the manner in which it had been pressed upon them, and they began sending delegations to Washington to demand its nullification. In 1834, the federal government agreed to amend the treaty and allow the individual owners of each allotment to receive the proceeds from the sale of their land. In the Treaty of Doaksville (1837), the Chickasaw accepted an invitation from the Choctaw to move onto an area between the Canadian and Red rivers that the latter nation had acquired in their removal treaty. The treaty also provided that Chickasaws could accept citizenship in the Choctaw Nation.

In May 1832, the Seminole agreed to emigrate to the West in the Treaty of Payne's Landing if they had an opportunity to visit and approve of the land the federal government was offering in exchange. In November, seven Seminole leaders visited the proposed territory, where they signed the removal Treaty of Fort Gibson without receiving the authority of the Seminole council. The seven who signed later claimed that they had been tricked and intimidated into agreeing to the treaty. Almost all the Seminole refused to recognize the treaty and resolved to oppose removal by force. When the time set for their removal passed, on January 1, 1836, the U.S. Army moved into Seminole territory. When the Second Seminole War ended in 1842, all but a very small population of the Seminole had been either killed or forcibly removed. The remnant that remained became the core of the vibrant Seminole nations that reemerged in the twentieth century.

The Cherokee were the last nation to remove to the West. After Jackson allowed the *Worcester* decision to go unenforced, the Cherokee Nation became divided between those who refused to remove and those who wanted the Cherokee to get the best deal they could and remove to the West. In 1835, a dissident group of Cherokee led by Major Ridge, John Ridge, and Elias Boudinot signed the removal Treaty of New Echota. The treaty required the Cherokee Nation to surrender its remaining territory in the East for a parcel in the recently established Indian Territory and to remove within two years from the signing of the agreement. Even though it was completed without the sanction of the Cherokee national government, the U.S. Senate ratified the treaty. In 1838, the U.S. Army rounded up as many Cherokee as they could into temporary stockades; and during the winter of 1838–1839, the Cherokee traveled the Trail of Tears to the Indian Territory. Scholars estimate that one-quarter of the Cherokee Nation died on the forced emigration to the West. Once in the Indian Territory, a group of men who had opposed removal attacked and killed the two Ridges and Boudinot for violating a law that prohibited the sale of Cherokee land without their government's consent.

With the departure of most of the remaining Seminole in 1842, the United States had, by treaty, forced all of the major southeastern Indian tribes out of the region. In the West, the Indian nations continued to receive federal funds and instruction toward civilization; and there, for many years, they continued to exist as separate, sovereign nations.

Tim Alan Garrison

References and Further Reading

Carson, James T. 1999. *Searching for the Bright Path: The Mississippi Choctaws from Prehistory to Removal.* Lincoln: University of Nebraska Press.

Champagne, Duane. 1992. *Social Order and Political Change: Constitutional Governments among the Cherokee, the Choctaw, the Chickasaw, and the Creek.* Stanford, CA: Stanford University Press.

Garrison, Tim Alan. 2002. *The Legal Ideology of Removal: The Southern Judiciary and the Sovereignty of Native American Nations.* Athens: University of Georgia Press.

Gibson, Arrell M. 1981. *The Chickasaws.* Norman: University of Oklahoma Press.

Green, Michael D. 1982. *The Politics of Indian Removal: Creek Government and Society in Crisis.* Lincoln: University of Nebraska Press.

Hudson, Charles. 1976. *The Southeastern Indians.* Knoxville: University of Tennessee Press.

McLoughlin, William G. 1992. *Cherokee Renascence in the New Republic.* Princeton, NJ: Princeton University Press.

O'Brien, Greg. 2002. *Choctaws in a Revolutionary Age, 1750–1830.* Lincoln: University of Nebraska Press.

Perdue, Theda. 1979. *Slavery and the Evolution of Cherokee Society, 1540–1866.* Knoxville: University of Tennessee Press.

Prucha, Francis Paul. 1984. *The Great Father: The United States Government and the American Indians.* Lincoln: University of Nebraska Press.

Prucha, Francis Paul. 1994. *American Indian Treaties: The History of a Political Anomaly.* Berkeley: University of California Press.

Reid, John Phillip. 1976. *A Better Kind of Hatchet: Law, Trade, and Diplomacy in the Cherokee Nation during the Early Years of European Contact.* State College: Pennsylvania State University Press.

Satz, Ronald N. 1975. *American Indian Policy in the Jacksonian Era.* Lincoln: University of Nebraska Press.

Swanton, John R. 1946. *The Indians of the Southeastern United States.* Washington, DC: Smithsonian Institution Press.

Wallace, Anthony F. C. 2001. *Jefferson and the Indians: The Tragic Fate of the First Americans.* Cambridge, MA: Harvard University Press.

Williams, Robert A., Jr. 1999. *Linking Arms Together: American Indian Treaty Visions of Law and Peace, 1600–1800.* New York: Routledge.

Wright, J. Leitch. 1990. *Creeks and Seminoles: Destruction and Regeneration of the Muscogulge People.* Lincoln: University of Nebraska Press.

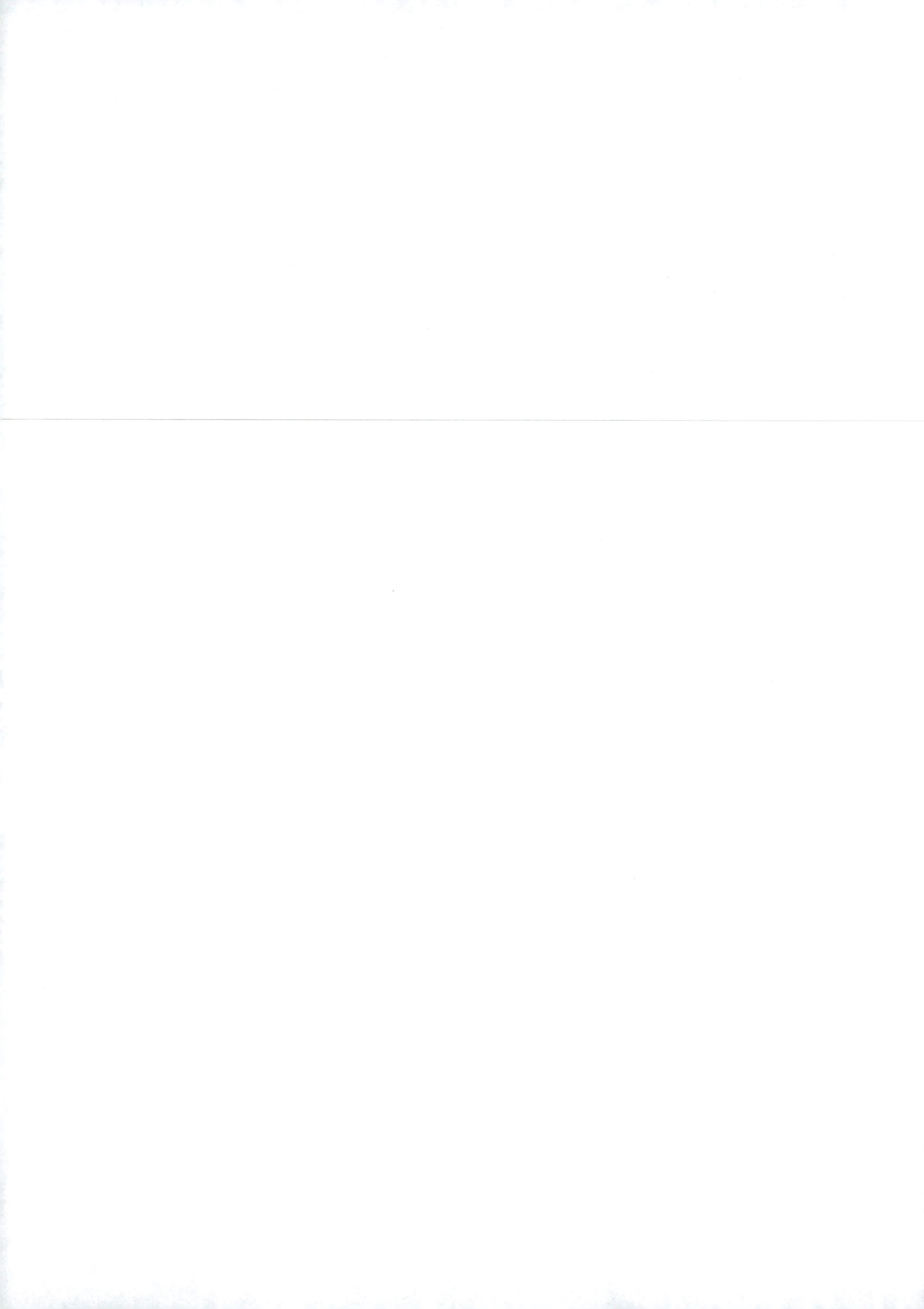

Southern Plains and the Southwest

In the Southwest, Indians first dealt with the Spanish government in Mexico, then with the Republic of Mexico after 1821, and with the United States after 1846. The approaches of all three of these colonial powers were rather consistent, seeking to protect colonists from Indian attacks and to open new lands for trade and settlement, but only the United States was able to provide the consistent military presence that finally put an end to the resistance of the Comanche, Apache, Navajo, and other tribes to this encroachment.

Frequent treaties with the nomadic Comanche, Apache, and Navajo were a sign of recurrent hostilities. Colonial governments usually could not or would not stop the continued encroachment on Indian lands that brought on new conflicts. The lack of treaties, as with the less nomadic groups, especially the Pueblo Indians of New Mexico in the nineteenth and twentieth centuries, indicated that there was less armed conflict with the colonial powers. A continued problem with treaty making was that the "tribes" with which the treaties were made tended to be loosely affiliated kinship groups speaking the same language or dialect and sharing similar customs. Making an agreement with one part of the "tribe" often did not bind other members, leading the colonial governments to accuse the "tribe" of bad faith.

The first treaties in the Southwest were made with the Spanish government. Spanish treaties with the Navajo were made in 1786, 1805, and 1819. At the 1786 conference, two Comanche were used to exhort "the Navajo to be careful to be faithful in their promises," and the Navajos were called on to help in the fight with the Gilas (Deloria and DeMallie 1999, 133). The treaty of 1805 resulted in an exchange of captives and called for peace; the 1819 treaty again called for peace, including peace with the Hopi Pueblos, and for Navajo hostages to ensure that the treaty was honored.

Mexican treaties with Navajo were made in 1822, 1823, 1839, 1841, and 1844. The large number of treaties indicates continued raids. The treaty of 1823 is typical in its call for peace and its provisions for the handing over of captives and stolen property. It also included a vain request that Navajos become Catholic and settle in pueblos.

The United States picked up where the Mexicans left off. An agreement in 1846 with Colonel Alexander W. Doniphan, which was never submitted to Congress and which called for peace, mutual trade, and mutual restoration of prisoners and stolen property, was agreed to by fourteen Navajo chiefs, including Sandoval, Narbona, and Manuelito. A second such agreement was made in 1848 with Colonel E. W. B. Newby, with similar provisions.

Seven treaties were negotiated with the Navajo between 1846 and 1868. However, there was no central Navajo government to enforce treaties signed by particular headmen. Only three were ratified by the U.S. Senate, the first one in 1850, but a treaty with some Navajo leaders could not prevent the raiding of the Navajos and the counterraiding of New Mexicans. Renewed raiding between the New Mexico settlers and the Pueblos and Navajos erupted soon after each treaty was signed. When Kit Carson was assigned to round up the Navajos, he learned from past efforts; taking drastic measures, he used a winter scorched-earth campaign that included burning cornfields and chopping down peach trees.

The trauma of the five years of captivity away from their homeland that resulted from Carson's campaign helped to unite the Navajo and led to the signing of a permanent peace treaty in 1868, negotiated by peace commissioners General William T. Sherman and Colonel Lewis Tappan, which allowed the Navajo to return home. That treaty included articles on mutual friendship, reservation boundaries, agency buildings, starting farming, education, construction of roads and railroads, and the purchase of sheep, goats, cattle, and corn. The U.S. government had wanted to move the Navajos to Indian Territory, but the Navajos' continued objections led to their being allowed to return home. Historian Peter Iverson writes that "the signing of the Navajo treaty of June 1, 1868, defined the heart of a homeland rather than ripping the heart out of a people" (Iverson 2002, 37). Repeated executive orders between 1878 and 1934 greatly expanded the size of the Navajo Reservation, as the Navajo population soared after 1868.

The Apache, whose language is closely related to the Navajo language, were arguably the most troublesome Indians for all three of the colonial

powers in the Southwest; relations with the Apache led to treaty after treaty. The first treaty recorded by Spain with the Apache was concluded in 1790. The Gila Apache pledged not to attack El Paso and to take part in campaigns against other hostile Apaches. Mexico made treaties with various groups of Apaches in 1835, 1836, 1839, 1842, and 1843. In these treaties, the cessation of raiding and the return of captives and stolen property were major issues, as they also were in Comanche and Navajo treaties. The Treaty of Guadalupe Hidalgo of 1848 between the United States and Mexico ceded to the United States much of the land in which Apaches lived.

A treaty made in 1851 in Santa Fe with eastern Apache by Governor James S. Calhoun, which was not presented to Congress, called for unconditional submission to the United States and good behavior. A convention in 1873 with the Jicarilla Apache laid out for them the boundaries of a reservation, pledged them to "induce their children, male and female, between the ages of seven and eighteen, to attend school," and provided 160-acre allotments to any heads of families who desired to commence farming. The U.S. Army was still fighting the Apache in the 1880s, and Geronimo did not surrender until 1886. An agreement with the Apache, Mohave, and Yuma of San Carlos Reservation in 1896 ceded land.

Living east of the Navajo and the Apache on the southern Great Plains, the Comanche, too, fought with the Spanish throughout the eighteenth century and later with Mexico, Texas, and the United States. A treaty of 1785 between eastern (Texas) Comanche and Spaniards called for annual gifts to the Comanche, the cessation of hostilities, the return of captives, exclusive trading rights, and opposition to the common enemy, the Lipan Apache. The following year, a treaty was made that included the Comanche in New Mexico.

The treaty of 1822, formalized in Mexico City with the newly independent Mexican government, called for trade, for putting past conflicts with the Spanish government behind, for the return of prisoners, and for controlled access to each other's territory. It also provided for twelve Comanche youth to go to Mexico City every four years to be educated. Another treaty with the Comanche was signed in 1826. The United States signed a treaty in Indian Territory with the Comanche and Witchetaw Indians and their associated bands in 1835. It gave the tribes hunting rights throughout the western possessions of the United States and declared, "Every injury or act of hostility by one or either of the contracting parties on the other, shall be mutually forgiven and forever forgot."

In 1837, the Kiowa Apache (under the name Kataka) made their first treaty with the U.S. government. Their subsequent history is that of the Kiowa. In 1853, they are mentioned as a warlike band ranging the waters of the Canadian River in the same area of the Great Plains occupied by the Comanche, whom they often joined in raiding expeditions.

Twelve treaties between Indian nations and the Republic of Texas were made between 1836 and 1845. These included a treaty of peace and perpetual friendship made in 1838 between the republic and the Lipan Apache, in which the Apache surrendered their sovereignty, making them subject to the laws of the Republic of Texas. The same year, Texas made a "Treaty of Peace and Amity" with the Comanche, who let the Republic of Texas prosecute whites who infringed on Comanche rights. A second treaty with the Comanche in 1843 called for the exchange of prisoners and "temporary peace" until a council could be held. In 1844, the Treaty of Tehuacana Creek between Texas and the Comanche, Kitsai, Waco, Caddo, Anadarko, Hainai, Delaware, Shawnee, Cherokee, Lipan Apache, and Tawakoni called for peace, for the establishment of trading houses by Texas with exclusive rights, for a prohibition on the sale of alcohol, for the provision of blacksmiths and schoolmasters, and for the mutual surrendering of prisoners.

In 1845, Texas and the Tawakoni, Waco, Wichita, and Kitsai agreed to a treaty of peace, friendship, and commerce. The previous year, the Comanche and other tribes had pledged peace and agreed to trade only with Texas. In addition, no alcohol was to be sold to Indians, and schoolmasters and farmers might be sent to teach them. After Texas became part of the United States, the Butler and Lewis treaty of 1846 put the Comanche under the protection of the United States. A treaty concluded in 1850 with the Comanche, Caddo, Lipan Apache, Quapaw, Tawakoni, and Waco was never presented to Congress. In that agreement, lawbreakers were to be given up to the officer commanding Fort Martin Scott, and captive whites and runaway Negro slaves were to be returned. Additionally, horse stealing was to end, liquor was outlawed, and blacksmiths were to be provided to repair guns and farm utensils. The possibility of sending schoolteachers was also broached.

The treaty of 1853 with the Comanche, Kiowa, and Apache allowed U.S. citizens to travel through their lands and promised indemnification for damages caused by that transit. It also pledged an annuity of $18,000 per year in goods and supplies for at least ten years, and the tribes pledged not to raid Mexico or fight each other. The 1863 treaty of perpetual "peace, friendship, and unity" with the same tribes, signed in Washington, D.C., was rejected by Congress. It was designed to allow unrestricted passage on the Overland Mail Route from Kansas City, Missouri, to Santa Fe, New Mexico, and in return promised $25,000 per year for five years to be given in goods, merchandise, provisions, agricultural implements, and so on, with a possible extension by the president for another five years. A treaty with the Kiowa and Comanche, negotiated in 1865 by John B. Sanborn, William S. Harney, Thomas Murphy, Kit Carson, William W. Bent, Jesse H. Leavenworth, and James Steele, provided annuities and sought to build roads through the tribes' territory that would be safe for passage. During the Civil War, nine treaties also were made between Indian nations and the Confederate States of America, including two with the Comanche.

North of the Comanche, the Southern Cheyenne saw their lives change drastically starting in the 1840s, as pandemics sharply reduced their numbers at the same time that their major food supply, the buffalo, followed a similar path to near extinction. As the Treaty of Fort Laramie in 1851 described:

> The territory of the Cheyennes and Arrapahoes, commencing at the Red Bute, or the place where the road leaves the north fork of the Platte River; thence up the north fork of the Platte River to its source; thence along the main range of the Rocky Mountains to the head-waters of the Arkansas River; thence down the Arkansas River to the crossing of the Santa Fé road; thence in a northwesterly direction to the forks of the Platte River, and thence up the Platte River to the place of beginning.

The U.S. government promised supplies and reserved the right to build roads and military posts.

In the 1861 Treaty of Fort Wise with the Arapaho and the Cheyenne, the Indian signers were not told all the terms written into the treaty. They were no longer to hold land in common and were promised annuities, but spending would be controlled by Indian Office officials, who supplied inferior goods. They were assigned barren lands that the whites did not want at the time, and their hunting rights were restricted to the plains of eastern Colorado. Unique to the 1965 treaty with the Cheyenne and Arapaho negotiated on the banks of the Little Arkansas River was an apology, in Article 6, for "the gross and wanton outrages perpetrated" by Chivington's Colorado Volunteers in their massacre at Sand Creek in 1864. The tribes were again assigned marginal land taken from other tribes in the Oklahoma panhandle. The treaty included hunting rights, defined reservation boundaries, provided annuities of $20 per person before removal to a reservation and $40 thereafter for forty years, and contained no education provisions. The majority of both tribes rejected this treaty. In 1890, an agreement with the Cheyenne and Arapaho paid for ceded land and called for allotment. Similar agreements were made with the Wichita and Kickapoo in 1891 and the Comanche, Kiowa, and Apache in 1892.

Sharing the southern Great Plains with the Cheyenne, Comanche, and Arapaho were the Pawnee and the Kiowa. Treaties with the Pawnee in 1818, negotiated with William Clark and Auguste Choteau, acknowledged that the Pawnee were under the protection of the United States and called for perpetual peace. In 1833, at the Grand Pawnee village on the Platte River, the United States agreed "to allow one thousand dollars a year for ten years, for schools to be established for the benefit of said four bands at the discretion of the President" and agreed "to furnish two blacksmiths and two strikers, with shop, tools and iron, for ten years . . . at an expense not exceeding two thousand dollars in the whole annually." In the treaty of 1857 with the Pawnee, negotiated at Table Creek in Nebraska Territory, a large amount of land was ceded to the United States in return for $40,000 per year for five years and then $30,000 per year "as a perpetual annuity, at least one-half of which annual payments shall be made in goods, and such articles as may be deemed necessary for them." Two manual labor schools were also promised. An agreement with the Pawnee in 1892 also called for a perpetual annuity of $30,000 per year. An agreement was made in 1909 to replace that perpetual annuity with a $600,000 lump sum payment.

Whereas southwestern Indians, especially those located in the present state of New Mexico, have a long history of colonial imposition dating back to the early seventeenth century, the Indians of the southern plains, in contrast, lived relatively unrestricted lives until repeated discoveries of gold in various parts of the West from 1848 on brought a steady flow of immigrants through Indian lands who demanded military protection. Then, in the 1860s, the rapid extension of railroads brought a massive influx of settlers.

Treaties made before the Civil War tended to focus on provisions for trading and safe passage of immigrants; after the Civil War and the passage of the Homestead Act of 1862, they focused on either removing of Indians from arable lands or "civilizing" them and giving them small homesteads (allotments) of their own in order to open up the remaining land for speculators and settlers.

Even before the Indian Civilization Act of 1819, the United States had sought to transform nomadic Indians into Christian, English-speaking farmers who would live in peace alongside colonists. Schooling was an integral part of this plan, first to be undertaken by missionaries but, starting in the late nineteenth century, implemented by teachers who were directly employed by the government. However, establishing schools among the various tribes was futile until the tribes gave up their nomadic existence. For the Plains Indians, this was largely accomplished by the destruction of the buffalo herds on which they relied for their survival.

The movement of the U.S. Indian Office from the War Department to the Department of the Interior in 1849 is symbolic of the increased military strength of the United States after a shaky beginning in which it had lost some major Indian battles. However, during the Civil War, that military dominance on the Great Plains was threatened, as troops were pulled east. Drastic measures were taken to protect settlers and immigration routes, such as Christopher (Kit) Carson's scorched-earth campaign against the Navajo and their imprisonment for five years on the New Mexico-Texas border. Prolonged military campaigns under harsh winter conditions helped break the back of Indian resistance, but the campaigns were costly.

For the more warlike tribes, it was cheaper for the U.S. government to try to buy land cessions with annuities than to fight for them. Critics of the military approach to Indian pacification complained that it cost a million dollars to kill one hostile Indian. The increasing cost of annuities agreed to by the Senate in treaties, but which had to be paid for with appropriation bills initiated in the House of Representatives, led to the ending of treaty making in 1871. Annuities were doubly important to tribes displaced by treaties because the tribes were often assigned barren lands that were the least attractive to white settlement. However, a reluctant Congress and corruption within the Indian Office meant that rations promised in treaties were not always delivered or were inferior to what was promised, which created a situation ripe for the renewal of hostilities.

The goal of treaty after treaty for perpetual peace and friendship was also undermined by the continued encroachment of settlers on Indian lands, and the continued warfare did not end until the Indians were confined to relatively small reservations. The colonial powers were greatly aided in their work of dispossessing Indians of their lands by the catastrophic decreases in the Indian population caused by recurring pandemics of smallpox, measles, and other diseases to which they had little or no immunity.

Some Indian tribes took advantage of the withdrawal of troops from the West to fight in the Civil War (1861–1865), to renew warfare. At the end of the Civil War, some of the eastern reformers who had worked to abolish slavery turned their attention to ending the mistreatment of Indians and stopping the Indian wars. In 1865, the Republican-controlled Congress approved a Joint Special Committee on the Conduct of the Indian Tribes, known as the Doolittle Committee after its chairman. The committee divided into three groups and toured the West. Their report of 1867 noted a precipitous decline in Indian population outside of the Indian territories and found "that in a large majority of cases Indian wars are to be traced to the aggressions of lawless white men" (Prucha 2000, 102). The committee recommended a "civilization policy" that included providing schools and persuading Indians to become farmers.

In 1867, the Arapaho and Southern Cheyenne were living between the Platte and Arkansas Rivers, and the Comanche and Kiowa were living to the south of the Arkansas River. The Plains tribes were being starved into submission, as professional hunters helped wipe out the vast buffalo herds on which the Indians depended for food, and they were beaten into submission by protracted military campaigns that continued through the harsh plains winters. Railroads were rapidly being built through the southern buffalo hunting grounds and, in the north, had already reached Cheyenne, Wyoming. Using the new Homestead Act of 1862, settlers were coming in on the new railroads and increasingly were pushing into Indian hunting grounds, creating continued friction and warfare. Settlers called on the military to protect them.

The need for continued expensive military expeditions against the various Plains tribes, along with the same humanitarian impulses that had led to the freeing of slaves, impelled Congress on July 20, 1867, to authorize President Andrew Johnson to appoint a Peace Commission to treat with Indian tribes. Its congressional mandate was to develop "a system for civilizing the Indians," and it had

> the power and authority to call together the chiefs and headmen of such bands or tribes of Indians as are now waging war against the United States or committing depredations upon the people thereof, to ascertain the alleged reasons for their acts of hostility, and in their discretion, under the direction of the President, to make and conclude with said bands or tribes such treaty stipulations, subject to the action of the Senate, as may remove all just cause of complaint on their part, and at the same time establish security for person and property along the lines of railroad now being construction to the Pacific and other thoroughfares of travel to the western Territories, and such as will most likely insure civilization for the Indians and peace and safety for the whites. (St. Germain 2001, 48)

Major General Winfield Scott Hancock ordered a halt to offensive warfare in 1867 to give the Great Peace Commission a chance to deal with hostile tribes. The commission was made up of Nathaniel G. Taylor, Senator John B. Henderson, Samuel F. Tappan, John Sanborn, and Generals William T. Sherman, William Harney, and Alfred Terry. Appointed by President Johnson as Commissioner of Indian Affairs, Taylor was a former Methodist minister and a military officer who was in favor of a peace policy. He had seen the devastation caused by the military during the Civil War in his home state of Tennessee and had some sympathy for the Indians. Sanborn and Harney had previously negotiated treaties while serving on the Peace Commission of 1865, and Sanborn had also co-chaired the commission that investigated the Fetterman Massacre. Tappan was an ardent abolitionist who had been actively involved in the Underground Railroad, helping escaped slaves before the Civil War. He saw U.S. Indian policy as a "national sin" and chaired a commission that investigated the Sand Creek Massacre.

Three months after the commission's authorization, the commissioners brought presents for an estimated five thousand Indians and negotiated the Treaty of Medicine Lodge Creek. They were accompanied by nine newspaper reporters and guarded by two companies of the Seventh Cavalry, supported by a Gatling gun unit. The Seventh Cavalry was temporarily without its commander, Lieutenant Colonel George Armstrong Custer, who had been arrested for leaving his troops to visit his wife without authorization. The commission met first with the Comanche and the Kiowa, then with the Apache, and finally with the Arapaho and the Cheyenne. The tribes gave up claims to some 90 million acres in return for 2.9 million acres in Indian Territory that had been taken from the Five Civilized Tribes because some had sided with the Confederacy during the Civil War. The treaty also contained provisions for hunting outside the new reservation, schooling of their children, and annuities. It could not be altered except by a vote of three-fourths of the adult male population of the tribes.

This treaty was no more successful than the subsequent Treaty of Fort Laramie negotiated by the Peace Commission, and sporadic fighting continued till 1875. When the Jerome Commission sought to open a portion of the reservation of 1867 to whites, the tribes objected, and the new agreement did not receive the approval of three-fourths of the Kiowa. However, the tribe failed in its effort to enforce compliance with the treaty in the Supreme Court decision *Lone Wolf v. Hitchcock* in 1903.

In the spring following the negotiation of the Treaty of Medicine Lodge Creek, the Peace Commission negotiated an equally ill-fated treaty with the Sioux at Fort Laramie and then in the summer had much better luck with the previously described treaty with the Navajo. In late 1868, the Peace Commission members agreed among themselves that tribes should not be considered independent nations, and this helped to end treaty making in 1871. In its final report of 1868 to President Andrew Johnson, the commission declared, "The history of the Government connections with the Indians is a shameful record of broken treaties and unfulfilled promises" and declared their treatment to be "unjust and iniquitous beyond the power of words to express." The commission's report stated, "The history of the border white man's connection with the Indians is a sickening record of murder, outrage, robbery, and wrongs committed by the former as the rule, and occasional savage outbreaks and unspeakable barbarous deeds of retaliation by the latter as the exception" (*Annual Report* 1869, 7).

When General Ulysses S. Grant, who had served in the army in the West, became president in 1869, he continued a peace policy that reflected the reports of the previous Peace Commissions. In his first inaugural address he declared, "The proper treatment of the original occupants of this land—the Indians—is one deserving of careful study. I will favor any course toward them which tends to their civilization and ultimate citizenship" (Richardson 1910, 3962). He appointed a Seneca Indian as his commissioner of Indian affairs, his Civil War aide Brigadier General Ely S. Parker, who served from 1869 to 1871. As a measure to halt Indian Office corruption and promote peace, Grant also appointed a Board of Indian Commissioners to supervise the appointment of Indian agents, teachers, and farmers as well as the buying of supplies. This board continued to operate until 1933; however, it soon lost most of its power. The board divided up Indian agencies among thirteen different religious groups. However, it was the Civil Service reforms of the 1890s that finally ended the spoils system, which based the appointment of Indian agents and other government positions on political support rather than job qualifications.

While the Navajo, Apache, and Comanche generated the most treaties, other tribes lived in the Southwest as well. The Pueblo Indians of New Mexico and Arizona, who lived in permanent villages, did not fit the stereotype of the nomadic Indian. When the Spanish retook New Mexico after the Pueblo Revolt of 1680, the Pueblos resigned themselves to the presence of colonists; because of this, peace treaties were never signed. Although squatters infringed on their traditional lands, these tribes did not suffer the massive displacement that more nomadic tribes continued to face as settlers. Similarly, the many smaller tribes of Arizona, including the Pima, Maricopa, Hualapai, Mojave, Havasupai, and Hopi, never made treaties with the United States.

A year after the United States invaded New Mexico in 1846, the new territorial legislature recognized each Pueblo village as a separate group and basically confirmed the old Spanish land grants, which were again confirmed in the Treaty of Guadalupe Hidalgo of 1848, which ended the war with Mexico. A Pueblo Indian agency was established in 1849. However, in 1876 the U.S. Supreme Court ruled that Pueblos of New Mexico were not Indians. In *U.S. v. Joseph* (94 U.S. 614), the Court declared that the Pueblo Indians "had nothing in common" with the Navajo, Apache, and Comanche, were not wards of the government subject to control of U.S. Indian agents, and could sell their property as they saw fit. This decision was reversed in 1913 in *U.S. v. Sandoval*, and in 1924 Congress established the Pueblo Lands Board to resolve claims of non-Indians to Pueblo lands.

A treaty in 1848 with the Zuni, which was not submitted to Congress, required the Zuni to obey the laws of the United States and the Territory of New Mexico in return for being "protected in the full enjoyment of all its rights of personal property and religion." Another treaty not submitted to Congress was made in 1850 by Indian agent James S. Calhoun with ten other Pueblos, who agreed to being "governed by their own laws and customs, and such authorities as they may prescribe, subject only to the controlling power of the Government of the United States."

The United States also made treaties with various bands of Ute in 1855, 1865, and 1866, which the Senate failed to ratify. Initially given the whole of eastern Colorado for a reservation, the discovery of gold there in the 1860s brought a quick reduction in territory. The treaty with the Ute in 1865 provided for the cession of land in exchange for the entire valley of the Unitah River in Utah, plus $25,000 per year for ten years, then $20,000 for twenty years, and thereafter $15,000 per year, based on an estimated population of five thousand Ute. The treaty also banned liquor and provided for the establishment and maintenance of a manual labor school for ten years.

In 1878, an agreement with the Capote, Muache, and Weeminuche bands of Ute, consented to by the Yampa, Grand River, Uintah, and Tabequache bands, also ceded lands. An agreement of 1911 with the Wiminuche band of Southern Ute traded land to get them to relinquish claims to land in Mesa Verde National Park in Colorado.

Besides the treaties with Spain, Mexico, Texas, and the United States, there were also treaties made between Indian nations. In 1858, a treaty of permanent peace and friendship was made at the Ute agency in Taos, New Mexico, between the Arapaho, Cheyenne, and Apache, represented by an Arapaho named Guatanamo, and the Muahuache Ute, Jicarilla Apache, and Pueblo of Taos. The treaty was signed in the presence of Christopher (Kit) Carson, the Ute Indian agent. Another treaty, made at Fort

Yuma, California, in 1863 between the Mojave, Pima, Papago, Maricopa, Yuma, Chemehuevi, and Hualapai called for these tribes to be at peace with each other, to join in war against the Apaches, and to protect Americans.

The United States had a consistent policy of opening relatively sparsely populated, fertile Indian lands to white settlement. This policy was tempered by the cost of the Indian wars caused by this continued encroachment of setters, and, especially after the Civil War, by a humanitarian desire to civilize the Indian. Treaty after treaty tried to stop unrestricted encroachment by settlers on Indian lands and to control the sale of liquor to Indians, but the U.S. government had no more success with these efforts to pacify the frontier than it has today in trying to stem the influx of illegal immigrants and drugs.

Jon Reyhner

References and Further Reading

Annual Report of the Commissioner of Indian Affairs. 1869. Washington, DC: U.S. Government Printing Office.

Deloria, Vine, Jr., and Raymond J. DeMallie. 1999. *Documents of American Indian Diplomacy: Treaties, Agreements, and Conventions, 1775–1979.* Norman: University of Oklahoma Press.

Iverson, Peter. 2002. *Diné: A History of the Navajo.* Albuquerque: University of New Mexico Press.

Jones, Douglas C. 1966. *The Treaty of Medicine Lodge: The Story of the Great Treaty Council as Told by Eyewitnesses.* Norman: University of Oklahoma Press.

Kavanagh, Thomas W. 1996. *The Comanches: A History 1706–1875.* Lincoln: University of Nebraska Press.

Prucha, Francis Paul. 1984. *The Great Father: The United States Government and the American Indians.* Lincoln: University of Nebraska Press.

Prucha, Francis Paul. ed. 2000. *Documents of United States Indian Policy,* 3rd ed. Lincoln: University of Nebraska Press.

Richardson, James D., ed. 1910. *A Compilation of the Messages and Papers of the Presidents.* Washington, DC: Bureau of National Literature and Art.

St. Germain, Jill. 2001. *Indian Treaty-Making Policy in the United States and Canada,* 1867–1877. Lincoln: University of Nebraska Press.

Resources

Alternate Tribal Names and Spellings

Tribal Name	Alternate Tribal Name(s)
Abenaki (western)	Alnonba, Abnaki
Absaroke	Crow
Adai	Nateo
Adamstown	Upper Mattaponi
Alabama	Alibamu
Aleut	Alutiiq, Unangan
Anadarko	Nadaco
Anishinabe	Chippewa, Ojibwa
Apache	N de,Tinneh, Dine, Tinde, Unde, Shis Inde, Aravaipa, Bedonkohe, Chihene, Chiricahua, Chokonen, Cibecue, Jicarilla, Kiowa, Lipan, Mescalero, Mimbres, Nednhi, Tonto, Yuma
Apache Mohave	Yavapai
Appomattoc	Apamatuks
Arapahoe	Inunaina, Atsina
Arikara	Northern Pawnee, Ricara, Ree
Assiniboine	Hohe
Athapaskan	Dene
Atsina	Haaninin
Aztec	Nahua, Nahuatl
Bannock	Panaiti
Bear River Indians	Niekeni
Bellabella	Heiltsuqu, Heiltsuk
Bellacoola	Nuxalk
Beothuk	Beathunk, Betoukuag, Macquajeet, Red Indians, Skraelling, Ulno
Blackfeet/Blackfoot	Niitsitapi, Nitsi-tapi, Piegan, Ahpikuni, Pikuni (northern); Siksika, Sisaka (southern), Sihasapa, Ahkainah
Blood	Kainai, Ahkainah
Boothroyd	Chomok
Brule Sioux	Si can gu
Caddo	Adai, Eyeish, Hasinai, Hainai, Kadohodacho, Kadohadacho Confederacy, Natchitoches
Cahuilla	Agua Caliente, Cabazon, Kawasic, Morongo, Los Coyotes, Painakic, Wanikik
Calusa	Caloosa, Calos, Calosa, Carlos, Muspa
Campo	Kumeyaay
Carrier	Dakelh, Wet'suwet'en
Catawba	Esaw, Iswa, Iyeye, Nieye, Ushery
Cayuga	Kweniogwen, Iroquois
Cayuse	Wailetpu, Te-taw-ken
Chakchiuma	Shaktci Homma
Chehalis	Copalis, Humptulips, Qwaya, Satsop, Sts'Ailes, Wynoochee
Chemainus	Tsa-mee-nis

Alternate Tribal Names and Spellings (cont.)

Tribal Name	Alternate Tribal Name(s)
Chemehuevi	Nuwu, Tantawats
Chetco	Tolowa
Cherokee	Tsa-la-gi, Ani-yun-wiya, Anikituhwagi, Keetowah
Cheyenne	Dzi tsi stas, Sowonia (southern), O mi sis (northern), Tse-tsehese-staestse
Chilcotin	Esdilagh, Tl'esqox, Tl'etinqox, Xeni Gwet'in
Chimakum	Aqokdlo
Chippewa	Anishinabe, Ojibwa
Chitimacha	Chawasha, Pantch-pinunkansh, Washa, Yagenechito
Choctaw	Chakchiuma, Chatot, Cha'ta
Chumash	Santa Barbara Indians
Clackamas	Guithlakimas
Clallam	S'klallam, Nusklaim, Tlalem
Cocopah	Xawitt Kunyavaei
Coeur d'Alene	Skitswish, Schee chu'umsch, Schitsu'umsh
Comanche	Detsanayuka, Kotsoteka, Nermernuh, Noconi, Nokoni, Numunuu, Padouca (Sioux word), Penateka, Pennande, Quahadi, Yamparika
Comox	Catloltx
Copane	Kopano, Quevenes
Cora	Nayarit
Coree	Coranine
Coushatta	Koasati, Acoste
Cree	Kenistenoag, Iyiniwok, Nehiawak or Nay-hee-uh-wuk (Plains Cree), Sah-cow-ee-noo-wuk (bush Cree)
Creek	Muscogee, Abihika, Abeika, Hitchiti, Homashko
Crow	Absaroke, Apsaalooke
Cupenos	Kuupangaxwichem
Cuthead	Pabaksa
Dakelh	Carrier
Delaware	Lenni Lenape, Lenape, Abnaki, Alnanbai, Wampanoag, Munsee, Unami, Unalachitgo, Powhatan-Renápe
Dieguenos	Comeya, Tipai, Ipai, Kumeyaay
Ditidaht	Nitinaht
Eskimo	Inuit, Inupiat, Inuvialuit, Yupik, Alutiiq
Equimalt	Is-Whoy-Malth
Fox	Mesquaki, Meskwaki, Mshkwa'kiitha
Gabrieleno	Tongva
Ganawese	Conoys, Piscataways
Gitanyow	Kitwancool
Gitxsan	Tsimshian
Goshute	Kusiutta
Gros Ventre	Atsina (prairie), Hidatsa (Missouri), A'ani', Ah-ah-nee-nin, Minnetaree
Gwich'in	Loucheux
Hainai	Ioni
Havasupai	Suppai
Heiltsuk	Hailhazakv
Hidatsa	Gros Venture
Hohokam	Hoo-hoogam
Hopi	Hopitu, Hopitu Shinumu, Moqui, Hapeka
Hualapai	Hwal'bay, Walapai
Huichol	Wirrarika, Wixalika

Alternate Tribal Names and Spellings (cont.)

Tribal Name	Alternate Tribal Name(s)
Hupa	Natinnohhoi
Huron	Wendat, Wyandot
Ingalik Athapaskans	Deg Het'an
Iowa	Pahodja
Iroquois	Haudenosaunee, Hodenosaunee, Ongwanosionni, Hotinonshonni
Jemez	Tuwa
Jicarilla Apache	Tinde
Kalispel	Pend d'Oreilles
Kamia	Tipai
Kansa	Hutanga, Kansas, Kanza, Kaw,
Kato	Tlokeang
Keres	Pueblo, Acoma, Cochiti, Isleta, Laguna, San Felipe, Santa Ana, Santo Domingo, Zia
Kickapoo	Kiwigapawa
Kiowa	Kwuda, Tepda, Tepkinago, Gaigwu, Kompabianta, Kauigu
Kiowa Apache	Nadiisha Dena
Klamath	Eukshikni Maklaks, Auksni
Klickitat	Qwulhhwaipum
Kootenai	Kuronoqa, Kutenai, Kootenay, Yaqan nukiy, Akun'kunik', Ktunaxa
Koso	Panamint
Karok	Karuk, Arra-arra
Ktunaxa	Kootenay
Kumeyaay	Diegueño, Barona, Sycuan, Viejas, Campo, Cuyapaipe, Ewiiaapaayp
Kutchin	Gwich'in
Kutenai	Asanka
Lancandon	Maya, Hach Winik
Lemhi Shoshone	Agaidika, Salmon Eaters, Tukudika, Sheep Eater
Loucheux	Gwich'in
Lillooet	Lil'wat, St'át'imc, T'it'kit
Lipan	Naizhan
Lower Sioux	Mdewakanton, Wahpekute
Luiseño	Ataxum, La Jolla, Pechanga, Soboba, Quechnajuichom
Lumbee	Cheraw
Maicopa	Xalychidom Piipaash, Pipatsji
Makah	Kwenetchechat, Kwi-dai-da'ch
Mandan	Metutahanke or Mawatani (after 1837), Numakaki (before 1837)
Manhattan	Rechgawawank
Manso	Maise, Mansa, Manse, Manxo, Gorreta, Gorrite, Tanpachoa
Maricopa	Xalychidom Piipaash, Xalchidom Pii-pash, Pipatsje, Pee-posh
Miami	Twightwis, Twa-h-twa-h, Oumameg, Pkiiwileni
Micmac	Mi'kmaq
Miniconjou	Mnikawozu, Mnikowoju, Minnicoujou
Mi'kmaq	Lnu'k, L'nu'k
Missouri	Niutachi
Mixtec	Ñusabi, Nusabi
Moapa	Moapariats
Modoc	Moatokni, Okkowish
Mohave	Mojave, Tzinamaa, Ahamakav, Hamakhava
Mohawk	Kanienkahaka, Kaniengehage, Abenaki, Iroquois, Akwesasne
Mohican	Muh-he-con-neok, Mahikan, Mahican
Molala	Latiwe

Alternate Tribal Names and Spellings (cont.)

Tribal Name	Alternate Tribal Name(s)
Mono	Monache
Moratoc	Nottoway
Mosopelea	Ofom
Munsee	Minasinink, Homenethiki
Muscogee	Creek, Homashko
Nanticoke	Unalachtgo, Onehtikoki
Navajo	Diné, Dineh, Tenuai, Navaho
Nez Perce	Nee-me-poo, Nimipu, Kamuinu, Tsutpeli, Sahaptin, Chopunnish
Nisga'a	Tsimshian
Nootka	Nuu-chah-nulth
Northern Ojibwa	Saulteaux, Sauteux
Nuu-chah-nulth	Nootka
Nuxalk	Kimsquit, Kwalhnmc, South Bentick Sutslmc, Taliyumc
Ogallala	Okandanda
Ojibwa	Chippewa, Anishinabe, Missisauga, Odjbway, Saginaw
Okanagon	Isonkuaili
Omaha	UmonHon
Oneida	Iroquois
Onondaga	Iroquois
Oohenupa	Two Kettle, Oohenonpa
Osage	Wa-Shah-She, Wakon, Wazhazhe
Ottawa	Adawe, Otawaki
Otto	Chewaerae
Oulaouaes	Necariages
Oweekeno	Kwakiutl, Oweehena
Pacheenaht	Nootka
Paiute	Numa, Nuwuvi, Kuyuiticutta
Papagos	Tohono O'odham, Ak-chin, Yohono Au'autam
Parianuc	White River Utes
Passamaquoddy	Peskedemakddi
Patchogue	Unkechaug
Pawnee	Pariki, Panyi, Chahiksichahiks, Ckirihki Kuruuriki
Pechanga	Luiseño
Pecos	Pueblos from Jemez
Pend d'Oreilles	Kalispel
Penobscot	Pannawanbskek, Penaubsket
Petun	Khionontateronon, Tionontati
Piegan	Blood, Kainai, Pikuni, Pigunni, Ahpikuni
Pima	Onk Akimel Au-authm, Akimel O'odham, A-atam, Akimul Au'autam, Tohono O'odham (incorrectly)
Piro	Tortuga
Pit River	Achomawi, Atsugewi
Poosepatuck	Unkechaug
Popolucas	Chochos
Pyramid Lake Paiute	Kuyuidokado
Quapaw	Quapah, Akansea, Ouaguapas, Ugakhpa
Quechan	Yuma
Quileute	Quil-leh-ute
Quinault	Qui-nai-elts
Sac and Fox	Sauk, Asakiwaki, Meshkwakihug, Fox
Sahwnee	Shawadasay

Alternate Tribal Names and Spellings (cont.)

Tribal Name	Alternate Tribal Name(s)
Salish	Okinagan, Slathead
Saanich	Pauquachin, Tsawout, Tsartlip, Tseycum, Malahat
Sans Arc	Itazipco
Santee	Sisseton
Saponi	Monasukapanough
Sauk	Hothaaki, Sac, Sack, Sock, Thakiki
Scioto	(Five Nations of the Scioto Plains) Shawnee, Wyandot, Delaware, Munsee, Seneca
Seminole	Ikaniuksalgi, Alachua, Mikasuki
Seneca	Iroquois
Serrano	Cowangachem, Mohineyam, Qawishwallanavetum, Yuhavitam
Shawnee	Savannah, Chillicothe, Hathawekela, Mequachake, Piqua
Shoshone	Shoshoni, Snake, Nimi, Tukudeka, Agaidika
Sioux	Brule, Dakota, Hunkpapa, Isanyati, Itazipco, Lakota, Mnikawozu, Mnikowoju, Nakota, Ocheti Shakowin, Oglala, Oohenunpa, Sicangu, Sihasapa, Sisseton, Sisitonwan, Teton, Titunwan
Sissipahaw	Haw
Skagit	Humaluh
Skoskomish	Twana
Squinamish	Swinomish
Slotas	Red River Metis
Songish	Lkungen
Southern Paiute	Numa
St. Francis	Abenaki
St. Mary's Indian Band	A'qam, Ktunaxa
St. Regis Mohawk	Akwesasne, Kaniengehage
Stockbridge	Mahican
Snuneymuxw	Nanaimo
Susquehanna	Susquehannock, Conestoga, Minqua, Andaste
Taidnapam	Upper Cowlitz
Tarahumara	Raramuri
Taviwac	Uncompahgre Ute
Tejas	Hasinai, Cenis
Tenino	Melilema
Tequistlatecos	Chontales of Oaxaca
Teton	Brule, Hunkpapa, Itazipco, Mnikowoju, Oglala, Oohenunpa, Sicangu, Sihasapa, Titunwan
Tewa	Pueblo, Nambe, Pojoaque, San Ildefonso, San Juan, Santa Clara, Tesuque
Thompson	Nlaka'pamux
Tigua	Pueblo, Tiwa, Tortuga
Tillamook	Killamuck
Timucua	Utina, Acuera
T'it'kit	Lillooet
Tiwa	Pueblo, Tortuga
Tlaoquiaht	Clayoquot
Tlatlasikwala	Nuwitti
Tobacco	Khionontateronon, Tionontati
Toltec	Chiaimeca Mochanecatoca
Tonkawa	Titskan Watitch, Titskanwatitch, Tonkaweya
Tubatulabal	Bahkanapul, Kern River

Alternate Tribal Names and Spellings (cont.)

Tribal Name	Alternate Tribal Name(s)
Tunica	Yoron
Tuscarora	Skarure, Iroquois, Coree
Tututni	Tolowa
Twana	Tuadhu
Two Kettle	Oohenonpa, Oohenupa
Umpqua	Etnemitane
Uncompahgre Ute	Taviwac
Upper Chehalis	Kwaiailk
Upper Sioux	Sisseton, Wahpeton
Ute	Noochi, Notch, Nuciu, Yamparka, Parianuc, Taviwac, Wiminuc, Kapota, Muwac, Cumumba, Tumpanuwac, Uinta-ats, Pahvant, San Pitch, and Sheberetch
Viejas	Quimi
Wampanoag	Pokanoket
Wappo	Ashochimi
Warm Springs	Tilkuni
Wasco	Galasquo
Watlala	Katlagakya
Wea	Eel River, Gros, Kilataks, Mangakekis, Pepicokia, Peticotias, Piankeshaw, Wawiyatanwa
Whilkut	Redwood Indians
Winnebago	Winipig
Wichita	Kitikiti'sh, Wia Chitch (Choctaw word)
Winik	Maya
Wishram	Ilaxluit, Tlakluit
Wyandot	Huron, Talamatans
Yakama	Waptailmin, Pakiutlema, Yakima
Yaqui	Yoeme, Surem, Hiakim
Yazoo	Chakchiuma
Yoncalla	Tchayankeld
Yuchi	Chisa
Yuma	Quechan, Euqchan
Zapotec	Binigulaza
Zuni	Ashiwi, Taa Ashiwani

Source: Phil Konstantin

Tribal Name Meanings

Tribal Name	Meaning
A'ani'	white clay people
Abnaki	those living at the sunrise (easterners)
Achomawi	river, people that live at the river
Acolapissa	those who listen and see
Agaidika	salmon eaters
Ahousaht	facing opposite from the ocean, people living with their backs to the land and mountains
Ahtena	ice people
Aitchelitz	bottom
Akun'kunik'	people of the place of the flying head
Akwesasne	land where the partridge drums
Alabama	I clear the thicket
Apache	enemy (Zuni word)
Apalachicola	people of the other side
Apalachee	people of the other side
A'qam	people of the dense forest or brush
Arikara	horns or elk people, or corn eaters
Assiniboine	ones who cook using stones (Ojibwa word)
Atakapa	man eater
Atsina	white clay people
Atsugewi	hat creek indians
Avoyel	people of the rocks
Bayogoula	people of the bayou
Bedonkohe (Apache)	in front at the end people
Bidai	brushwood (Caddo word)
Binigulaza	people of the clouds
Brule	burned thighs
Caddo	true chiefs
Cahuilla	leader, master, powerful nation (all questionable)
Calusa	fierce people
Canim	canoe, broken rock
Catawba	river people
Cayuga	place where boats were taken out, place locusts were taken out, people at the mucky land
Cayuse	people of the stones or rocks (French-Canadian word)
Chakchiuma	red crawfish people
Cheam	wild strawberry place, the place to always get strawberries
Chehalis	sand, beating heart
Chemehuevi	those that play with fish (Mojave word)
Cherokee	cave people (Choctaw word), people of different speech (Creek word)
Cheslatta	top of a small mountain, small rock mountain at the east side
Chetco	close to the mouth of the stream
Cheyenne	red talkers (Dakota word), little Cree (Lakota word)
Chickahominy	hominy people
Chihene (Apache)	red paint people
Chilcotin	young man river
Chipewyan	pointed skins (Cree word)
Chitimacha	men altogether red, they have cooking vessels
Chokonen (Apache)	rising sun people
Chontal	stranger (Nahuatl word)
Choula	fox

Tribal Name Meanings (cont.)

Tribal Name	Meaning
Chowanoc	people at the south
Chumash	people who make the shell bead money
Clallam	strong people
Clatsop	dried salmon
Clayoquot	people of other tribes
Cocopah	river people
Coeur d'Alene	those who are found here or heart of an awl (French words)
Comanche	anyone who wants to fight me all the time (Ute word)
Comox	place of abundance
Cowichan	warm country, land warmed by the sun
Crow	crow, sparrowhawk, bird people, people of the large-beaked bird
Dakelh	people who travel by water
Dakota	allie
Ehdiitat Gwich'in	people who live among timber or spruce
Erie	long tail or cat people (Iroquois word)
Eskimo	eaters of raw meat (Algonquin or Cree word)
Esquimalt	the place of gradually shoaling water
Fox	red earth people
Gingolx	the place of the skulls
Gitanmaax	people who fish with burning torches
Gitwangak	place of rabbits
Gwich'in	people who live at a certain place
Gros Ventre	big bellies, one who cooks with a stone, he cooks by roasting (see Atsina)
Hach winik	true people
Hagwilget	gentle or quiet people
Han	those who live along the river
Haudenosaunee	people of the long house, people of the extended lodge
Havasupai	people of the blue green water
Heiltsuk	to speak or act correctly
Hesquiaht	people of the sound made by eating herring eggs off eel grass
Hidatsa	willow (speculation)
Hiute	bowmen
Hohokam	those who have gone
Honniasont	wearing something around the neck
Hopi	peaceful ones, people who live in a peaceful way
Houma	red
Hualapai	people of the tall pines
Huchnom	mountain people
Huichol	healers
Hul'qumi'num	those who speak the same language
Hunkpapa	campers at the opening of the circle
Hupa	trinity river
Huron	ruffian (French word)
Hwal'bay (Hualapai)	people of the tall pines
Ihanktonwan	dwellers at the end
Ihanktonwana	little dwellers at the end
Iowa	sleepy ones (Dakota word)
Iroquois	real adders (Algonquian word) or we of the extended lodge
Jatibonicu	people of the great sacred high waters
Jatibonuco	great people of the sacred high waters

Tribal Name Meanings (cont.)

Tribal Name	Meaning
Jicaque	ancient person (Nahuatl word)
Jicarilla	little basket weaver (Spanish word)
Kainai	many chiefs
Kamloops	the meeting of the waters
Kan-hatki	white earth
Kanienkahaka	people of the place of flint
Kanza	people of the south wind
Karok	upstream
Kaskaskia	he scrapes it off by means of a tool
Kato	lake
Kawchottine	people of the great hares
Ketsei	going in wet sand
Kickapoo	he stands about
Kiowa	principal people, pulling out, coming out, people of the large tent flaps
Kispiox	people of the hiding place
Kitamaat	people of the falling snow
Kitkatla	people of the salt, village by the sea
Kitselas	people of the canyon
Kitsumkalum	people of the plateau
Klallam	strong people
Klamath	people of the lake
Klickitat	beyond (Chinook word)
Kluskus	place of small whitefish
Kotsoteka	buffalo eaters
Kutcha-kutchin	those who live on the flats
Kuupangaxwichem	people who slept here
Kuyuidokado	cui-ui eaters
Kwalhioqua	lonely place in the woods (Chinook word)
Kwayhquitlum	stinking fish slime
Kwuda	people coming out
Lakota	friend or ally (same with Dakota and Nakota)
Latgawa	those living in the uplands
Lenni Lenape	genuine men
Lheidli T'enneh	people of the confluence of the two rivers
Lillooet	wild onion
Loucheux	people with slanted or crossed eyes
Machapunga	bad dust
Mahican	wolf (incorrect translation per the Mohican Nation, Stockbridge-Munsee Band)
Makah	cape people
Malahat	infested with caterpillars, place where one gets bait
Maliseet	broken talkers
Maricopa	people who live toward the water
Massachuset	at the hills
Matsqui	easy portage, easy travelling
Mdewankantonwan	dwellers of the spirit lake
Menominee	wild rice men
Metlakatla	a passage connecting two bodies of salt water
Miami	people on the peninsula, cry of the crane
Michigamea	great water
Mimbres (Apache)	willow (Spanish word)

Tribal Name Meanings (cont.)

Tribal Name	Meaning
Miniconjou	planters by water
Minnetaree	they crossed the water
Minqua	stealthy
Missouri	great muddy, people with wooden canoes
Moapa	mosquito creek people
Moatokni	southerners
Modoc	southerners
Mohave	three mountains, people of the water/river
Mohawk	the possessors of the flint, coward or man eater (Abenaki words)
Mohegan	wolf
Mohican	the people of the waters that are never still
Moneton	big water people
Munsee	at the place where the stones are gathered together
Musqueam	place always to get iris plant root
Nahane	people of the west
Nak'azdli	when arrows were flying
Narragansett	people of the small point
Nanticoke	people of the tidewaters
Nanoose	to push forward
Natsit-kutchin	those who live off the flats
Navajo	cultivated field in an arroyo (Tewa word)
Nehalem	where the people live
Nicomen	level part
Nihtat Gwich'in	people living together as a mixture
Nipmuck	freshwater fishing place
Nokoni	those who turn back
Nooksack	mountain men
Nootka	along the coast
Nusabi	people of the clouds
Oglala	scatters their own
Ojibwa	to roast till puckered up
Okanagan	head, top of head
Okelousa	blackwater
Okmulgee	where water boils up
Omaha	upstream people or people going against the current
Oneida	a boulder standing up, people of the standing stone
Onondaga	people on top of the hills
Opata	hostile people (Pima word)
Ottawa	to trade
Otto	lechers
Oweekeno	those who carry on the back, people talking right
Pahodja	dusty nones
Pakiutlema	people of the gap
Pamunkey	rising upland
Pantch-pinunkansh	men altogether red
Papagos	desert people, bean people
Pascagoula	bread people
Passamaquoddy	plenty of pollock
Paugusset	where the narrows open out
Pawnee	horn people, men of men, look like wolves
Pechanga	place where the water drips

Tribal Name Meanings (cont.)

Tribal Name	Meaning
Penateka	honey eaters
Penelakut	something buried
Pennacook	down hill
Penobscot	it forks on the white rocks or the descending ledge place, at the stone place
Pensacola	hair people
Penticton	permanent place, always place
People of the lakes	tribes near the great lakes
Peoria	carrying a pack on his back
Pequot	fox people or destroyers
Piegan	scabby robes
Piikani	poor robe
Pilthlako	big swamp
Pima	river people
Pojoaque	drinking place
Potawatomi	people of the place of the fire, keepers of the fire (fire nation, fire people)
Powhatan	falls in a current of water
Pshwanwapam	stony ground
Puyallup	shadow
Qawishwallanavetum	people that live among the rocks
Quahadi	antelope
Qualicum	where the dog salmon run
Quapaw	downstream people
Quatsino	downstream people
Qwulhhwaipum	prairie people
Raramuri	foot runner
Sac (Sauk)	people of the yellow earth or people of the outlet
Salish	flatheads
Sans Arc	without bows
Schaghticoke	at the river forks
Schitsu'umsh	the ones that were found here
Sekani	dwellers on the rocks
Semiahmoo	half moon
Seminole	separatist or breakaway, peninsula people
Seneca	place of stone, people of the standing rock, great hill people
Shawnee	south or southerners
Sicangu	burned thighs
Sihasapa Sioux	blackfeet
Siksika	blackfeet
Sioux	snake (French version of other tribe's name)
Sisitonwan	dwellers of the fish ground
Siska	uncle, lots of cracks in the rocks
Skidegate	red paint stone
Skokomish	river people
Skookumchuck	strong water
Snuneymuxw	people of many names
Spallumcheen	flat along edge
Spokane	sun people or children of the sun (generally accepted)
Spuzzum	little flat
Sts'Ailes	the beating heart

Tribal Name Meanings (cont.)

Tribal Name	Meaning
Sumas	big flat opening
Tahltan	something heavy in the water
Taino	we the good people
Takelma	those living along the river
Tamarois	out tail
Tanima	liver eaters
Tangipahoa	corn gatherers
Tantawats	southern men
Tarahumara	foot runner
Tatsanottine	people of the copper water
Tawakoni	river bend among red hills
Teetl'it Gwich'in	people who live at the head of the waters
Tejas	friendly
Tenawa	down stream
Tennuth-ketchin	middle people
Teton	dwellers of the prairie
Tewa	moccasins
Thlingchadinne	dog-flank people
Titonwan	dwellers of the plains
Tl'azt'en	people by the edge of the bay
Toltec	master builders (Nahuatl word)
Tonawanda	confluent stream
Tonkawa	they all stay together or most human of people
Toquaht	people of the narrow place in front, people of the narrow channel
Tsa-mee-nis	bitten breast
Tsattine	lives among the beavers
Tsawout	houses raised up
Tsawwassen	beach at the mouth, facing the sea
Tsay Keh Dene	people of the mountains
Tsetsaut	people of the interior (Niska word)
Tseycum	clay people
Tsleil-Waututh	people of the inlet
Tubatulabal	pinenut eaters (Shoshone word)
Tukudika	sheep eater
Tuscarora	hemp gatherers, the shirt wearing people
Two Kettle	two boilings
Uchuckledaht	there inside the bay
Ulkatcho	good feeding place where animals get fat
Unalachtgo	tidewater people
Viniintaii Gwich'in	people who live on or by the caribou trail
Vuntut Gwitch'in	dwellers among the lakes
Vvunta-ketchin	those who live among the lakes
Wahpekute	shooters amoung the leaves
Wahpetonwan	dwellers amoung the leaves
Wailaki	north language (Wintun word)
Wakokai	blue heron breeding place
Walapai	pine tree people
Wallawalla	little river
Wampanoag	eastern people
Wappo	brave
Waptailmin	people of the narrow river

Tribal Name Meanings (cont.)

Tribal Name	Meaning
Wasco	cup, those who have the cup
Wea	the forest people, light-skinned ones, people who live near the river eddy
Whel mux	people of spirit, people of breath
Wichita	big arbor (Choctaw word)
Winnebago	filthy water people
Wiwohka	roaring water
Wyandot	people of the peninsula, islanders
Yakama	runaway
Yamparika	rooteaters or yapeaters
Yaqan nukiy	the people where the rock is standing
Yavapai	people of the sun, crooked mouth people
Yoncalla	those living at ayankeld
Yuchi	situated yonder
Yuhavitam	people of the pines
Yuki	stranger (Wintun word)
Yurok	downstream (Karok word)

Source: Phil Konstantin

Treaties by Tribe

Tribe	Treaty Name
Aionai	Treaty with the Comanche, Aionai, Anadarko, Caddo, Etc., 1846
Anadarko	Treaty with the Comanche, Aionai, Anadarko, Caddo, Etc., 1846
Apache	Treaty with the Apache, 1852 Treaty with the Apache, Cheyenne, and Arapaho, 1865 Treaty with the Cheyenne and Arapaho, 1865 Treaty with the Comanche, Kiowa, and Apache, 1853 Treaty with the Kiowa, Comanche, and Apache, 1867
Appalachicola	Treaty with the Appalachicola Band, 1832 Treaty with the Appalachicola Band, 1833
Arapaho	Treaty with the Apache, Cheyenne, and Arapaho, 1865 Treaty with the Arapaho and Cheyenne, 1861 Treaty with the Cheyenne and Arapaho, 1865 Treaty with the Cheyenne and Arapaho, 1867 Treaty with the Northern Cheyenne and Northern Arapaho, 1868 Treaty of Fort Laramie with Sioux, Etc., 1851 Treaty with the Sioux—Brulé, Oglala, Miniconjou, Yanktonai, Hunkpapa, Blackfeet, Cuthead, Two Kettle, Sans Arcs, and Santee—and Arapaho
Arikara	Treaty with the Arikara Tribe, 1825 Agreement at Fort Berthold, 1866 Treaty of Fort Laramie with Sioux, Etc., 1851
Assinaboine	Treaty of Fort Laramie with Sioux, Etc., 1851
Bannock	Treaty with the Eastern Band Shoshoni and Bannock, 1868
Belantse-Etoa or Minitaree	Treaty with the Belantse-Etoa or Minitaree Tribe, 1825
Blackfeet	Treaty with the Blackfeet, 1855 Treaty with the Blackfeet Sioux, 1865
Blood	Treaty with the Blackfeet, 1855
Brothertown	Treaty with the New York Indians, 1838
Caddo	Treaty with the Caddo, 1835 Treaty with the Comanche, Aionai, Anadarko, Caddo, Etc., 1846
Cahokia	Treaty with the Peoria, Etc., 1818

Treaties by Tribe (cont.)

Tribe	Treaty Name
Cayuga	Agreement with the Five Nations of Indians, 1792
	Treaty with the Six Nations, 1784
	Treaty with the New York Indians, 1838
	Treaty with the Six Nations, 1789
	Treaty with the Six Nations, 1794
Cayuse	Treaty with the Walla-Walla, Cayuse, Etc., 1855
Chasta	Treaty with the Chasta, Etc., 1854
Cherokee	Treaty with the Cherokee, 1785
	Treaty with the Cherokee, 1791
	Treaty with the Cherokee, 1794
	Treaty with the Cherokee, 1798
	Treaty with the Cherokee, 1804
	Treaty with the Cherokee, 1805
	Treaty with the Cherokee, 1805
	Treaty with the Cherokee, 1806
	Treaty with the Cherokee, 1816
	Treaty with the Cherokee, 1816
	Treaty with the Cherokee, 1816
	Treaty with the Cherokee, 1817
	Treaty with the Cherokee, 1819
	Treaty with the Western Cherokee, 1828
	Treaty with the Western Cherokee, 1833
	Treaty with the Cherokee, 1835
	Treaty with the Cherokee, 1846 [Western Cherokee]
	Treaty with the Cherokee, 1866
	Treaty with the Cherokee, 1868
	Agreement with the Cherokee, 1835 (Unratified)
	Agreement with the Cherokee and Other Tribes in the Indian Territory, 1865
	Treaty with the Comanche, Etc., 1835
Cheyenne	Treaty with the Apache, Cheyenne, and Arapaho, 1865
	Treaty with the Arapaho and Cheyenne, 1861
	Treaty with the Cheyenne Tribe, 1825
	Treaty with the Cheyenne and Arapaho, 1865
	Treaty with the Cheyenne and Arapaho, 1867
	Treaty with the Northern Cheyenne and Northern Arapaho, 1868
	Treaty of Fort Laramie with Sioux, Etc., 1851
Chickasaw	Agreement with the Cherokee and Other Tribes in the Indian Territory, 1865
	Treaty with the Chickasaw, 1786
	Treaty with the Chickasaw, 1801
	Treaty with the Chickasaw, 1805
	Treaty with the Chickasaw, 1816
	Treaty with the Chickasaw, 1818

Treaties by Tribe (cont.)

Tribe	Treaty Name
Chickasaw (cont.)	Treaty with the Chickasaw, 1832
	Treaty with the Chickasaw, 1832
	Treaty with the Chickasaw, 1834
	Treaty with the Chickasaw, 1830
	Treaty with the Choctaw and Chickasaw, 1837
	Treaty with the Chickasaw, 1852
	Treaty with the Choctaw and Chickasaw, 1854
	Treaty with the Choctaw and Chickasaw, 1855
	Treaty with the Choctaw and Chickasaw, 1866
Chippewa	Treaty with the Chippewa, Etc., 1808
	Treaty with the Chippewa, 1819
	Treaty with the Chippewa, 1820
	Treaty with the Ottawa and Chippewa, 1820
	Treaty with the Chippewa, 1826
	Treaty with the Chippewa, Etc., 1827
	Treaty with the Chippewa, Etc., 1829
	Treaty with the Chippewa, Etc., 1833
	Treaty with the Chippewa, 1836
	Treaty with the Chippewa, 1837
	Treaty with the Chippewa, 1837
	Treaty with the Chippewa, 1837
	Treaty with the Chippewa, 1838
	Treaty with the Chippewa, 1839
	Treaty with the Chippewa, 1842
	Treaty with the Chippewa of the Mississippi and Lake Superior, 1847
	Treaty with the Chippewa, 1854
	Treaty with the Chippewa, 1855
	Treaty with the Chippewa of Saginaw, Etc., 1855
	Treaty with the Chippewa, Etc., 1859
	Treaty with the Chippewa of the Mississippi and the Pillager and Lake Winnibigoshish Bands, 1863
	Treaty with the Chippewa—Red Lake and Pembina Bands, 1863
	Treaty with the Chippewa—Red Lake and Pembina Bands, 1864
	Treaty with the Chippewa, Mississippi, and Pillager and Lake Winnibigoshish Bands, 1864
	Treaty with the Chippewa of Saginaw, Swan Creek, and Black River, 1864
	Treaty with the Chippewa—Bois Forte Band, 1866
	Treaty with the Chippewa of the Mississippi, 1867
	Treaty with the Ottawa, Etc., 1807
	Treaty with the Ottawa, Etc., 1816
	Treaty with the Ottawa, Etc., 1821
	Treaty with the Ottawa, Etc., 1836
	Treaty with the Ottawa and Chippewa, 1855
	Treaty with the Pillager Band of Chippewa Indians, 1847
	Treaty with the Potawatomi Nation, 1846
	Treaty with the Chippewa of Sault Ste. Marie, 1855
	Treaty with the Sioux, Etc., 1825
	Treaty with the Winnebago, Etc., 1828

Treaties by Tribe (cont.)

Tribe	Treaty Name
Chippewa (cont.)	Treaty with the Wyandot, Etc., 1785 Treaty with the Wyandot, Etc., 1789 Treaty with the Wyandot, Etc., 1795 Treaty with the Wyandot, Etc., 1805 Treaty with the Wyandot, Etc., 1815 Treaty with the Wyandot, Etc., 1817 Treaty with the Wyandot, Etc., 1818
Choctaw	Agreement with the Cherokee and Other Tribes in the Indian Territory, 1865 Treaty with the Choctaw and Chickasaw, 1837 Treaty with the Choctaw, 1786 Treaty with the Choctaw, 1801 Treaty with the Choctaw, 1802 Treaty with the Choctaw, 1803 Treaty with the Choctaw, 1805 Treaty with the Choctaw, 1816 Treaty with the Choctaw, 1820 Treaty with the Choctaw, 1825 Treaty with the Choctaw, 1830 Treaty with the Choctaw and Chickasaw, 1854 Treaty with the Choctaw and Chickasaw, 1855 Treaty with the Choctaw and Chickasaw, 1866 Treaty with the Comanche, Etc., 1835 Treaty with the Comanche and Kiowa, 1865
Clack-A-Mas	Treaty with the Kalapuya, Etc., 1855
Columbia	Agreement with the Columbia and Colville, 1883
Colville	Agreement with the Columbia and Colville, 1883
Comanche	Treaty with the Comanche, Etc., 1835 Treaty with the Comanche, Aionai, Anadarko, Caddo, Etc., 1846 Treaty with the Comanche, Kiowa, and Apache, 1853 Treaty with the Kiowa and Comanche, 1867 Treaty with the Kiowa, Comanche, and Apache, 1867
Creeks	Agreement with the Cherokee and Other Tribes in the Indian Territory, 1865 Treaty with the Comanche, Etc., 1835 Treaty with the Creeks, 1790 Treaty with the Creeks, 1796 Treaty with the Creeks, 1802 Treaty with the Creeks, 1805 Treaty with the Creeks, 1814 Treaty with the Creeks, 1818 Treaty with the Creeks, 1821 Treaty with the Creeks, 1821 Treaty with the Creeks, 1825 Treaty with the Creeks, 1826

Treaties by Tribe (cont.)

Tribe	Treaty Name
Creeks (cont.)	Treaty with the Creeks, 1827
	Treaty with the Creeks, 1832
	Treaty with the Creeks, 1833
	Treaty with the Creeks, 1838
	Treaty with the Creeks and Seminole, 1845
	Treaty with the Creeks, 1854
	Treaty with the Creeks, Etc., 1856
	Treaty with the Creeks, 1866
	Agreement with the Creeks, 1825 (Unratified)
Crow	Treaty with the Crow Tribe, 1825
	Treaty with the Crows, 1868
	Agreement with the Crows, 1880 (Unratified)
	Treaty of Fort Laramie with Sioux, Etc., 1851
Dakota	Treaty with the Blackfeet Sioux, 1865
	Treaty of Fort Laramie with Sioux, Etc., 1851
De Chutes	Treaty with the Middle Oregon Tribes, 1865
	Treaty with the Tribes of Middle Oregon, 1855
Delaware	Treaty with the Delawares, 1778
	Treaty with the Delawares, Etc., 1803
	Treaty with the Delawares, 1804
	Treaty with the Delawares, Etc., 1805
	Treaty with the Delawares, Etc., 1809
	Treaty with the Delawares, 1818
	Treaty with the Delawares, 1829
	Treaty with the Delawares, 1829
	Treaty with the Delawares, 1854
	Treaty with the Delawares, 1860
	Treaty with the Delawares, 1861
	Treaty with the Delawares, 1866
	Agreement with the Delawares and Wyandot, 1843
	Supplementary Treaty with the Miami, Etc., 1809
	Treaty with the Shawnee, Etc., 1832
	Treaty with the Wyandot, Etc., 1785
	Treaty with the Wyandot, Etc., 1789
	Treaty with the Wyandot, Etc., 1795
	Treaty with the Wyandot, Etc., 1805
	Treaty with the Wyandot, Etc., 1814
	Treaty with the Wyandot, Etc., 1815
	Treaty with the Wyandot, Etc., 1817
	Treaty with the Wyandot, Etc., 1818
Dwamish	Treaty with the Dwamish, Suquamish, Etc., 1855
Eel River	Treaty with the Delawares, Etc., 1803
	Treaty with the Delawares, Etc., 1805
	Treaty with the Delawares, Etc., 1809
	Treaty with the Eel River, Etc., 1803

Treaties by Tribe (cont.)

Tribe	Treaty Name
Eel River (cont.)	Supplementary Treaty with the Miami, Etc., 1809 Treaty with the Miami, 1828 Treaty with the Wyandot, Etc., 1795
Five Nations	Agreement with the Five Nations of Indians, 1792
Flathead	Treaty with the Blackfeet, 1855 Treaty with the Flatheads, Etc., 1855
Fox	Treaty with the Foxes, 1815
Gros Ventres	Treaty with the Blackfeet, 1855 Agreement at Fort Berthold, 1866 Treaty of Fort Laramie with Sioux, Etc., 1851
Illinois	Treaty with the Kaskaskia, Etc., 1832 Treaty with the Peoria, Etc., 1818
Iowa	Treaty with the Iowa, 1815 Treaty with the Iowa, 1824. Treaty with the Iowa, Etc., 1836. Treaty with the Iowa, 1837 Treaty with the Iowa, 1838 Treaty with the Iowa, 1854 Treaty with the Sauk and Fox, Etc., 1830 Treaty with the Sauk and Fox, Etc., 1861 Treaty with the Sioux, Etc., 1825
Kalapuya	Treaty with the Kalapuya, Etc., 1855 Treaty with the Umpqua and Kalapuya, 1854
Kansa	Treaty with the Kansa, 1815 Treaty with the Kansa, 1825 Treaty with the Kansa, 1825 Treaty with Kansa Tribe, 1846 Treaty with the Kansa Tribe, 1859 Treaty with the Kansa Indians, 1862
Kaskaskia	Treaty with the Delawares, Etc., 1803 Treaty with the Eel River, Etc., 1803 Treaty with the Kaskaskia, 1803 Treaty with the Kaskaskia, Etc., 1832 Treaty with the Kaskaskia, Peoria, Etc., 1854 Treaty with the Peoria, Etc., 1818 Treaty with the Seneca, Mixed Seneca and Shawnee, Quapaw, Etc., 1867 Treaty with the Wyandot, Etc., 1795
Ka-Ta-Ka	Treaty with the Kiowa, Etc., 1837
Keechy	Treaty with the Comanche, Aionai, Anadarko, Caddo, Etc., 1846

Treaties by Tribe (cont.)

Tribe	Treaty Name
Kickapoo	Treaty with the Delawares, Etc., 1803
	Treaty with the Eel River, Etc., 1803
	Treaty with the Kickapoo, 1809
	Treaty with the Kickapoo, 1815
	Treaty with the Wea and Kickapoo, 1816
	Treaty with the Kickapoo, 1819
	Treaty with the Kickapoo, 1819
	Treaty with the Kickapoo, 1820
	Treaty with the Kickapoo of the Vermilion 1820
	Treaty with the Kickapoo, 1832
	Treaty with the Kickapoo, 1854
	Treaty with the Kickapoo, 1862
	Treaty with the Wyandot, Etc., 1795
Kik-Ial-Lus	Treaty with the Dwamish, Suquamish, Etc., 1855
Kiowa	Treaty with the Comanche, Kiowa, and Apache, 1853
	Treaty with the Comanche and Kiowa, 1865
	Treaty with the Kiowa, Etc., 1837
	Treaty with the Kiowa and Comanche, 1867
	Treaty with the Kiowa, Comanche, and Apache, 1867
Klamath	Treaty with the Klamath, Etc., 1864
Kootenay	Treaty with the Blackfeet, 1855
	Treaty with the Flatheads, Etc., 1855
Lepan	Treaty with the Comanche, Aionai, Anadarko, Caddo, Etc., 1846
Long-Wha	Treaty with the Comanche, Aionai, Anadarko, Caddo, Etc., 1846
Lummi	Treaty with the Dwamish, Suquamish, Etc., 1855
Makah	Treaty with the Makah, 1815
	Treaty with the Makah Tribe, 1825
	Treaty with the Makah, 1855
Mandan	Agreement at Fort Berthold, 1866
	Treaty with the Mandan Tribe, 1825
	Treaty of Fort Laramie with Sioux, Etc., 1851
Me-Sek-Wi-Guilse	Treaty with the Dwamish, Suquamish, Etc., 1855
Menominee	Treaty with the Chippewa, Etc., 1827
	Treaty with the Menominee, 1817
	Treaty with the Menominee, 1831
	Treaty with the Menominee, 1831
	Treaty with the Menominee, 1832
	Treaty with the Menominee, 1836
	Treaty with the Menominee, 1848
	Treaty with the Menominee, 1854

Treaties by Tribe (cont.)

Tribe	Treaty Name
Menominee (cont.)	Treaty with the Menominee, 1856
	Treaty with the Sioux, Etc., 1825
Miami	Treaty with the Delawares, Etc., 1803
	Treaty with the Delawares, Etc., 1805
	Treaty with the Delawares, Etc., 1809
	Supplementary Treaty with the Miami, Etc., 1809
	Treaty with the Miami, 1818
	Treaty with the Miami, 1826
	Treaty with the Miami, 1828
	Treaty with the Miami, 1834
	Treaty with the Miami, 1838
	Treaty with the Miami, 1840
	Treaty with the Miami, 1854
	Treaty with the Seneca, Mixed Seneca and Shawnee, Quapaw, Etc., 1867
	Treaty with the Wyandot, Etc., 1795
	Treaty with the Wyandot, Etc., 1814
	Treaty with the Wyandot, Etc., 1815
Middle Oregon Tribes	Treaty with the Middle Oregon Tribes, 1865
	Treaty with the Tribes of Middle Oregon, 1855
Minitaree or Belantse-Etoa	Treaty with the Belantse-Etoa or Minitaree Tribe, 1825
Mitchigamia	Treaty with the Peoria, Etc., 1818
Modoc	Treaty with the Klamath, Etc., 1864
Mohawk	Treaty with the Mohawk, 1797
	Treaty with the Six Nations, 1784
	Treaty with the Six Nations, 1789
	Treaty with the Six Nations, 1794
Molala	Treaty with the Kalapuya, Etc., 1855
	Treaty with the Molala, 1855
Muscogee	Treaty with the Comanche, Etc., 1835
Munsee	Treaty with the Chippewa, Etc., 1859
	Treaty with the New York Indians, 1838
	Treaty with the Stockbridge and Munsee, 1839
	Treaty with the Stockbridge and Munsee, 1856
	Treaty with the Wyandot, Etc., 1805
Navajo	Treaty with the Navaho, 1849
	Treaty with the Navaho, 1868
New York Indians	Treaty with the New York Indians, 1838
Nez Percé	Treaty with the Blackfeet, 1855

Treaties by Tribe (cont.)

Tribe	Treaty Name
Nex Percé (cont.)	Treaty with the Nez Percé, 1855 Treaty with the Nez Percé, 1863 Treaty with the Nez Percé, 1868
Nisqually	Treaty with the Nisqualli, Puyallup, Etc., 1854
Noo-Wha-Ha	Treaty with the Dwamish, Suquamish, Etc., 1855
Omaha	Treaty with the Omaha, 1854 Treaty with the Omaha, 1865 Treaty with the Oto, Etc., 1836 Treaty with the Sauk and Fox, Etc., 1830
Oneida	Agreement with the Five Nations of Indians, 1792 Treaty with the Six Nations, 1784 Treaty with the New York Indians, 1838 Treaty with the Oneida, Etc., 1794 Treaty with the Oneida, 1838 Treaty with the Six Nations, 1789 Treaty with the Six Nations, 1794
Onondaga	Agreement with the Five Nations of Indians, 1792 Treaty with the Six Nations, 1784 Treaty with the New York Indians, 1838 Treaty with the Six Nations, 1789 Treaty with the Six Nations, 1794
Osage	Agreement with the Cherokee and Other Tribes in the Indian Territory, 1865 Treaty with the Comanche, Etc., 1835 Treaty with the Osage, 1808 Treaty with the Osage, 1815 Treaty with the Osage, 1818 Treaty with the Osage, 1822 Treaty with the Osage, 1825 Treaty with the Great and Little Osage, 1825 Treaty with the Osage, 1839 Treaty with the Osage, 1865
Oto	Treaty with the Oto, 1817
Oto & Missouri	Treaty with the Confederated Oto and Missouri, 1854 Treaty with the Oto and Missouri Tribe, 1825 Treaty with the Oto and Missouri, 1833 Treaty with the Oto, Etc., 1836 Treaty with the Oto and Missouri, 1854 Treaty with the Sauk and Fox, Etc., 1830
Ottawa	Treaty with the Chippewa, Etc., 1808 Treaty with the Ottawa and Chippewa, 1820 Treaty with the Chippewa, Etc., 1829

Treaties by Tribe (cont.)

Tribe	Treaty Name
Ottawa (cont.)	Treaty with the Chippewa, Etc., 1833
	Treaty with the Ottawa, Etc., 1807
	Treaty with the Ottawa, Etc., 1816
	Treaty with the Ottawa, Etc., 1821
	Treaty with the Ottawa, 1831
	Treaty with the Ottawa, 1833
	Treaty with the Ottawa, Etc., 1836
	Treaty with the Ottawa and Chippewa, 1855
	Treaty with the Ottawa of Blanchard's Fork and Roche De Bœuf, 1862
	Treaty with the Potawatomi Nation, 1846
	Treaty with the Seneca, Mixed Seneca and Shawnee, Quapaw, Etc., 1867
	Treaty with the Sioux, Etc., 1825
	Treaty with the Winnebago, Etc, 1828
	Treaty with the Wyandot, Etc., 1785
	Treaty with the Wyandot, Etc., 1789
	Treaty with the Wyandot, Etc., 1795
	Treaty with the Wyandot, Etc., 1805
	Treaty with the Wyandot, Etc., 1815
	Treaty with the Wyandot, Etc., 1817
	Treaty with the Wyandot, Etc., 1818
Pawnee	Treaty with the Grand Pawnee, 1818
	Treaty with the Noisy Pawnee, 1818
	Treaty with the Pawnee Republic, 1818
	Treaty with the Pawnee Marhar, 1818
	Treaty with the Pawnee Tribe, 1825
	Treaty with the Pawnee, 1833
	Treaty with the Pawnee—Grand, Loups, Republicans, Etc., 1848
	Treaty with the Pawnee, 1857
Peoria	Treaty with the Kaskaskia, Etc., 1832
	Treaty with the Kaskaskia, Peoria, Etc., 1854
	Treaty with the Peoria, Etc., 1818
	Treaty with the Seneca, Mixed Seneca and Shawnee, Quapaw, Etc., 1867
Piankeshaw	Treaty with the Delawares, Etc., 1803
	Treaty with the Eel River, Etc., 1803
	Treaty with the Kaskaskia, Peoria, Etc., 1854
	Treaty with the Piankeshaw, 1804
	Treaty with the Piankashaw, 1805
	Treaty with the Piankashaw, 1815
	Treaty with the Piankashaw and Wea, 1832
	Agreement with the Piankeshaw, 1818 (Unratified)
	Treaty with the Seneca, Mixed Seneca and Shawnee, Quapaw, Etc., 1867
	Treaty with the Wyandot, Etc., 1795
Piegan	Treaty with the Blackfeet, 1855

Treaties by Tribe (cont.)

Tribe	Treaty Name
Ponca	Treaty with the Ponca, 1817
	Treaty with the Ponca, 1825
	Treaty with the Ponca, 1858
	Treaty with the Ponca, 1865
Potawatomi	Treaty with the Chippewa, Etc., 1808
	Treaty with the Chippewa, Etc., 1829
	Treaty with the Chippewa, Etc., 1833
	Treaty with the Delawares, Etc., 1803
	Treaty with the Delawares, Etc., 1805
	Treaty with the Delawares, Etc., 1809
	Supplementary Treaty with the Miami, Etc., 1809
	Treaty with the Ottawa, Etc., 1807
	Treaty with the Ottawa, Etc., 1816
	Treaty with the Ottawa, Etc., 1821
	Treaty with the Potawatomi, 1815
	Treaty with the Potawatomi, 1818
	Treaty with the Potawatomi, 1826
	Treaty with the Potawatomi, 1827
	Treaty with the Potawatomi, 1828
	Treaty with the Potawatomi, 1832
	Treaty with the Potawatomi, 1832
	Treaty with the Potawatomi, 1832
	Treaty with the Potawatomi, 1834
	Treaty with the Potawatomi, 1834
	Treaty with the Potawatomi, 1834
	Treaty with the Potawatomi, 1834
	Treaty with the Potawatomi, 1836
	Treaty with the Potawatomi, 1836
	Treaty with the Potawatomi, 1836
	Treaty with the Potawatomi, 1836
	Treaty with the Potawatomi, 1836
	Treaty with the Potawatomi, 1836
	Treaty with the Potawatomi, 1836
	Treaty with the Potawatomi, 1836
	Treaty with the Potawatomi, 1836
	Treaty with the Potawatomi, 1837
	Treaty with the Potawatomi Nation, 1846
	Treaty with the Potawatomi, 1861
	Treaty with the Potawatomi, 1866
	Treaty with the Potawatomi, 1867
	Treaty with the Sioux, Etc., 1825
	Treaty with the Winnebago, Etc, 1828
	Treaty with the Wyandot, Etc., 1789
	Treaty with the Wyandot, Etc., 1795
	Treaty with the Wyandot, Etc., 1805
	Treaty with the Wyandot, Etc., 1815
	Treaty with the Wyandot, Etc., 1817
	Treaty with the Wyandot, Etc., 1818

Treaties by Tribe (cont.)

Tribe	Treaty Name
Puyallup	Treaty with the Nisqualli, Puyallup, Etc., 1854
Quapaw	Agreement with the Cherokee and Other Tribes in the Indian Territory, 1865
	Treaty with the Comanche, Etc., 1835
	Treaty with the Quapaw,1818
	Treaty with the Quapaw, 1824
	Treaty with the Quapaw, 1833
	Treaty with the Seneca, Mixed Seneca and Shawnee, Quapaw, Etc., 1867
Qui-Nai-Elt	Treaty with the Quinaielt, Etc., 1855
Quil-Leh-Ute	Treaty with the Quinaielt, Etc., 1855
Ricara	Treaty with the Arikara Tribe, 1825
	Agreement at Fort Berthold, 1866
	Treaty of Fort Laramie with Sioux, Etc., 1851
Rogue River	Treaty with the Rogue River, 1853
	Treaty with the Rogue River, 1854
	Agreement with the Rogue River, 1853 (Unratified)
Sac & Fox	Treaty with the Fox, 1815
	Treaty with the Iowa, Etc., 1836.
	Treaty with the Sauk and Fox, 1804
	Treaty with the Sauk, 1815
	Treaty with the Sauk, 1816
	Treaty with the Sauk and Fox, 1822
	Treaty with the Sauk and Fox, 1824
	Treaty with the Sauk and Fox, Etc., 1830
	Treaty with the Sauk and Fox, 1832
	Treaty with the Sauk and Fox Tribe, 1836
	Treaty with the Sauk and Fox, 1836
	Treaty with the Sauk and Fox, 1836
	Treaty with the Sauk and Fox, 1837
	Treaty with the Sauk and Fox, 1837
	Treaty with the Sauk and Fox, 1842
	Treaty with the Sauk and Fox of Missouri, 1854
	Treaty with the Sauk and Fox, 1859
	Treaty with the Sauk and Fox, Etc., 1861
	Treaty with the Sauk and Fox, 1867
	Treaty with the Sioux, Etc., 1825
	Treaty with the Wyandot, Etc., 1789
Sa-Heh-Wamish	Treaty with the Nisqualli, Puyallup, Etc., 1854
Sah-Ku-Meh-Hu	Treaty with the Dwamish, Suquamish, Etc., 1855
Scotons	Treaty with the Chasta, Etc., 1854

Treaties by Tribe (cont.)

Tribe	Treaty Name
Seminole	Agreement with the Cherokee and Other Tribes in the Indian Territory, 1865
	Treaty with the Creeks and Seminole, 1845
	Treaty with the Creeks, Etc., 1856
	Treaty with the Florida Tribes of Indians, 1823
	Treaty with the Seminole, 1832
	Treaty with the Seminole, 1833
	Treaty with the Seminole, 1866
Seneca	Agreement with the Cherokee and Other Tribes in the Indian Territory, 1865
	Treaty with the Comanche, Etc., 1835
	Agreement with the Five Nations of Indians, 1792
	Treaty with the Six Nations, 1784
	Treaty with the New York Indians, 1838
	Treaty with the Seneca, 1802
	Treaty with the Seneca, 1802
	Treaty with the Seneca, 1831
	Treaty with the Seneca, Etc., 1831
	Treaty with the Seneca and Shawnee, 1832
	Treaty with the Seneca, 1842
	Treaty with the Seneca, Tonawanda Band, 1857.
	Treaty with the Seneca, Mixed Seneca and Shawnee, Quapaw, Etc., 1867
	Agreement with the Seneca, 1797
	Agreement with the Seneca, 1823 (Unratified)
	Treaty with the Six Nations, 1789
	Treaty with the Six Nations, 1794
	Treaty with the Wyandot, Etc., 1814
	Treaty with the Wyandot, Etc., 1815
	Treaty with the Wyandot, Etc., 1817
	Treaty with the Wyandot, Etc., 1818
Seven Nations of Canada	Treaty with the Seven Nations of Canada, 1796
Shawnee	Agreement with the Cherokee and Other Tribes in the Indian Territory, 1865
	Treaty with the Chippewa, Etc., 1808
	Treaty with the Delawares, Etc., 1803
	Treaty with the Seneca, Etc., 1831
	Treaty with the Seneca and Shawnee, 1832
	Treaty with the Seneca, Mixed Seneca and Shawnee, Quapaw, Etc., 1867
	Treaty with the Shawnee, 1786
	Treaty with the Shawnee, 1825
	Treaty with the Shawnee, 1831
	Treaty with the Shawnee, Etc., 1832
	Treaty with the Shawnee, 1854
	Treaty with the Wyandot, Etc., 1795
	Treaty with the Wyandot, Etc., 1805
	Treaty with the Wyandot, Etc., 1814

Treaties by Tribe (cont.)

Tribe	Treaty Name
Shawnee (cont.)	Treaty with the Wyandot, Etc., 1815 Treaty with the Wyandot, Etc., 1817 Treaty with the Wyandot, Etc., 1818
S'homamish	Treaty with the Nisqualli, Puyallup, Etc., 1854
Shoshoni	Treaty with the Eastern Shoshoni, 1863 Treaty with the Shoshoni—Northwestern Bands, 1863 Treaty with the Western Shoshoni, 1863 Treaty with the Eastern Band Shoshoni and Bannock, 1868
Shoshoni-Goship	Treaty with the Shoshoni-Goship, 1863
Sioux	Treaty with the Blackfeet Sioux, 1865 Treaty with the Hunkpapa Band of the Sioux Tribe, 1825 Treaty with the Sioune and Oglala Tribes, 1825 (Also Ogallala) Treaty with the Oto, Etc., 1836 — Yankton and Santee Bands Treaty with the Sauk and Fox, Etc., 1830 — Medawah-Kanton, Wahpacoota, Wahpeton, Sissetong [Sisseton], Yanckton [Yancton] and Santie Bands Treaty with the Sioux of the Lakes, 1815 Treaty with the Sioux of St. Peter's River, 1815 Treaty with the Sioux, 1816 Treaty with the Teton, Etc., Sioux, 1825 — Teton, Yancton and Yanctonies Bands Treaty with the Sioux, Etc., 1825 Treaty with the Sioux, 1836 Treaty with the Sioux, 1836 Treaty with the Sioux, 1837 Treaty with the Sioux—Sisseton and Wahpeton Bands, 1851 Treaty with the Sioux—Mdewakanton and Wahpakoota Bands, 1851 (Also Med-ay-wa-kan-toan and Wah-pay-koo-tay) Treaty of Fort Laramie with Sioux, Etc., 1851 Treaty with the Sioux, 1858 — Mendawakanton and Wahpahoota Bands Treaty with the Sioux, 1858 — Sisseeton and Wahpaton Bands Treaty with the Sioux—Miniconjou Band, 1865 (Also Minneconjon) Treaty with the Sioux—Lower Brulé Band, 1865 Treaty with the Sioux—Two-Kettle Band, 1865 Treaty with the Sioux—Sans Arcs Band, 1865 Treaty with the Sioux—Hunkpapa Band, 1865 (Also Onkpahpah) Treaty with the Sioux—Yanktonai Band, 1865 Treaty with the Sioux—Upper Yanktonai Band, 1865 Treaty with the Sioux—Oglala Band, 1865 (Also Ogallala; O'Galla) Treaty with the Sioux—Sisseton and Wahpeton Bands, 1867 (Also Sissiton) Treaty with the Sioux—Brulé, Oglala, Miniconjou, Yanktonai, Hunkpapa, Blackfeet, Cuthead, Two Kettle, Sans Arcs, and Santee—and Arapaho, Treaty with the Sioux, 1805

Treaties by Tribe (cont.)

Tribe	Treaty Name
Sioux (cont.)	Agreement with the Sisseton and Wahpeton Bands of Sioux Indians, 1872 (Unratified) Amended Agreement with Certain Sioux Indians, 1873 — Sisseton and Wahpeton Bands Agreement with the Sioux of Various Tribes, 1882–83 (Unratified) — Pine Ridge, Rosebud, Standing Rock, Cheyenne River, and Lower Brulé Agencies Treaty with the Yankton Sioux, 1815 Treaty with the Yankton Sioux, 1837 Treaty with the Yankton Sioux, 1858
Six Nations	Treaty with the Six Nations, 1784 Treaty with the Six Nations, 1789 Treaty with the Six Nations, 1794
Skai-Wha-Mish	Treaty with the Dwamish, Suquamish, Etc., 1855
Skagit	Treaty with the Dwamish, Suquamish, Etc., 1855
S'klallam	Treaty with the S'Klallam, 1855
Sk-Tah-Le-Jum	Treaty with the Dwamish, Suquamish, Etc., 1855
Snake	Treaty with the Klamath, Etc., 1864 Treaty with the Snake, 1865
Snohomish	Treaty with the Dwamish, Suquamish, Etc., 1855
Snoqualmoo	Treaty with the Dwamish, Suquamish, Etc., 1855
Squawskin	Treaty with the Nisqualli, Puyallup, Etc., 1854
Squi-Aitl	Treaty with the Nisqualli, Puyallup, Etc., 1854
Squin-Ah-Nush	Treaty with the Dwamish, Suquamish, Etc., 1855
St. Regis	Treaty with the New York Indians, 1838 Treaty with the Seven Nations of Canada, 1796
Stehchass	Treaty with the Nisqualli, Puyallup, Etc., 1854
Steilacoom	Treaty with the Nisqualli, Puyallup, Etc., 1854
Stockbridge	Agreement with the Five Nations of Indians, 1792 Treaty with the New York Indians, 1838 Treaty with the Oneida, Etc., 1794 Treaty with the Stockbridge and Munsee, 1839 Treaty with the Stockbridge Tribe, 1848 Treaty with the Stockbridge and Munsee, 1856
Suquamish	Treaty with the Dwamish, Suquamish, Etc., 1855

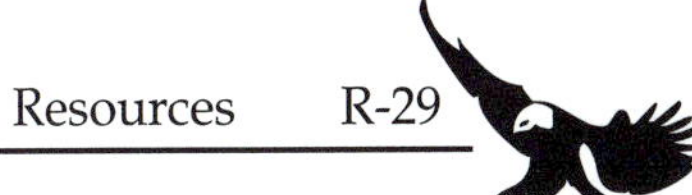

Treaties by Tribe (cont.)

Tribe	Treaty Name
Swinamish	Treaty with the Dwamish, Suquamish, Etc., 1855
Tah-Wa-Carro	Treaty with the Comanche, Aionai, Anadarko, Caddo, Etc., 1846 Treaty with the Kiowa, Etc., 1837
Tamarois	Treaty with the Peoria, Etc., 1818
Tenino	Treaty with the Middle Oregon Tribes, 1865 Treaty with the Tribes of Middle Oregon, 1855
Teton	Treaty with the Teton, 1815
Tonkawa	Treaty with the Comanche, Aionai, Anadarko, Caddo, Etc., 1846
T'peek-Sin	Treaty with the Nisqualli, Puyallup, Etc., 1854
Tum-Waters	Treaty with the Kalapuya, Etc., 1855
Tuscarora	Agreement with the Five Nations of Indians, 1792 Treaty with the Six Nations, 1784 Treaty with the New York Indians, 1838 Treaty with the Oneida, Etc., 1794 Treaty with the Six Nations, 1789 Treaty with the Six Nations, 1794
Umatilla	Treaty with the Walla-Walla, Cayuse, Etc., 1855
Umpqua	Treaty with the Chasta, Etc., 1854 Treaty with the Umpqua—Cow Creek Band, 1853 Treaty with the Umpqua and Kalapuya, 1854
Upper Pend D'oreille	Treaty with the Blackfeet, 1855 Treaty with the Flatheads, Etc., 1855
Utah	Treaty with the Utah, 1849 Treaty with the Utah—Tabeguache Band, 1863
Ute	Treaty with the Ute, 1868
Waco	Treaty with the Comanche, Aionai, Anadarko, Caddo, Etc., 1846
Walla-Walla	Treaty with the Middle Oregon Tribes, 1865 Treaty with the Tribes of Middle Oregon, 1855 Treaty with the Walla-Walla, Cayuse, Etc., 1855
Wasco	Treaty with the Middle Oregon Tribes, 1865 Treaty with the Tribes of Middle Oregon, 1855
Wea	Treaty with the Delawares, Etc., 1803 Treaty with the Delawares, Etc., 1805 Treaty with the Kaskaskia, Peoria, Etc., 1854

Treaties by Tribe (cont.)

Tribe	Treaty Name
Wea (cont.)	Treaty with the Wea and Kickapoo, 1816
	Supplementary Treaty with the Miami, Etc., 1809
	Treaty with the Piankashaw and Wea, 1832
	Treaty with the Seneca, Mixed Seneca and Shawnee, Quapaw, Etc., 1867
	Treaty with the Wea, 1809
	Treaty with the Wea, 1818
	Treaty with the Wea, 1820
	Treaty with the Wyandot, Etc., 1795
Winnebago	Treaty with the Chippewa, Etc., 1827
	Treaty with the Sioux, Etc., 1825
	Treaty with the Winnebago, 1816
	Treaty with the Winnebago, Etc, 1828
	Treaty with the Winnebago, 1829
	Treaty with the Winnebago, 1832
	Treaty with the Winnebago, 1837
	Treaty with the Winnebago, 1846
	Treaty with the Winnebago, 1855
	Treaty with the Winnebago, 1859
	Treaty with the Winnebago, 1865
Witchetaw	Treaty with the Comanche, Etc., 1835
	Treaty with the Comanche, Aionai, Anadarko, Caddo, Etc., 1846
Wyandot	Treaty with the Chippewa, Etc., 1808
	Agreement with the Delawares and Wyandot, 1843
	Treaty with the Eel River, Etc., 1803
	Treaty with the Ottawa, Etc., 1807
	Treaty with the Seneca, Mixed Seneca and Shawnee, Quapaw, Etc., 1867
	Treaty with the Wyandot, Etc., 1785
	Treaty with the Wyandot, Etc., 1789
	Treaty with the Wyandot, Etc., 1795
	Treaty with the Wyandot, Etc., 1805
	Treaty with the Wyandot, Etc., 1814
	Treaty with the Wyandot, Etc., 1815
	Treaty with the Wyandot, Etc., 1817
	Treaty with the Wyandot, Etc., 1818
	Treaty with the Wyandot, 1818
	Treaty with the Wyandot, 1832
	Treaty with the Wyandot, 1836
	Treaty with the Wyandot, 1842
	Treaty with the Wyandot, 1850
	Treaty with the Wyandot, 1855
Yakima	Treaty with the Yakima, 1855

Source: Charles J. Kappler, *Indian Affairs: Laws and Treaties* (Washington DC: Government Printing Office, 1904). Digital copy courtesy of the Oklahoma State University Library Electronic Publishing Center

Common Treaty Names

Common Name	Full Treaty Name
Albany, Treaty of	Treaty of Albany with the Five Nations–July 31, 1684
Canandaigua Treaty	Treaty with the Six Nations–November 11, 1794
Chicago, Treaty of	Treaty with the Chippewa, Etc.–September 26, 1833
Dancing Rabbit Creek, Treaty of	Treaty with the Choctaw–September 27, 1830
Doak's Stand, Treaty of	Treaty with the Choctaw–October 18, 1820
Doaksville, Treaty of	Treaty with the Choctaw and Chickasaw–January 17, 1837
Fort Bridger, Treaty of	Treaty with the Eastern Band Shoshone and Bannock–July 3, 1868
Fort Harmar, Treaty of	Treaty with the Wyandot, Etc.–January 9, 1789 Treaty with the Six Nations–January 9, 1789 (Addendum) Treaty with the Cherokee–June 26, 1794
Fort Laramie, Treaty of	Treaty of Fort Laramie with the Sioux, Etc.–September 17, 1851
Fort McIntosh, Treaty of	Treaty with the Wyandot, Etc.–January 21, 1785
Fort Stanwix, Treaty of	Treaty Conference with the Six Nations at Fort Stanwix–November 5, 1768 Treaty with the Six Nations–October 22, 1784
Greenville, Treaty of	Treaty with the Wyandot, Etc.–August 3, 1795
Holston, Treaty of	Treaty with the Cherokee–July 2, 1791
Hopewell, Treaty of	Treaty with the Cherokee–November 28, 1785
Medicine Creek, Treaty of	Treaty with the Nisqually, Puyallup, Etc.–December 26, 1854
Medicine Lodge Creek, Treaty of	Treaty with the Cheyenne and Arapaho-–October 28, 1867
New Echota, Treaty of	Treaty with the Cherokee–December 29, 1835
Northwest Angle Treaty	Canadian Indian Treaty 3–October 3, 1873
Prairie du Chien, Treaty of	Treaty with the Sioux, Etc.–August 19, 1825
Qu'Appelle Treaty	Canadian Indian Treaty 4–September 15, 1874
St. Louis, Treaty of	Treaty with the Sauk and Fox–November 3, 1804

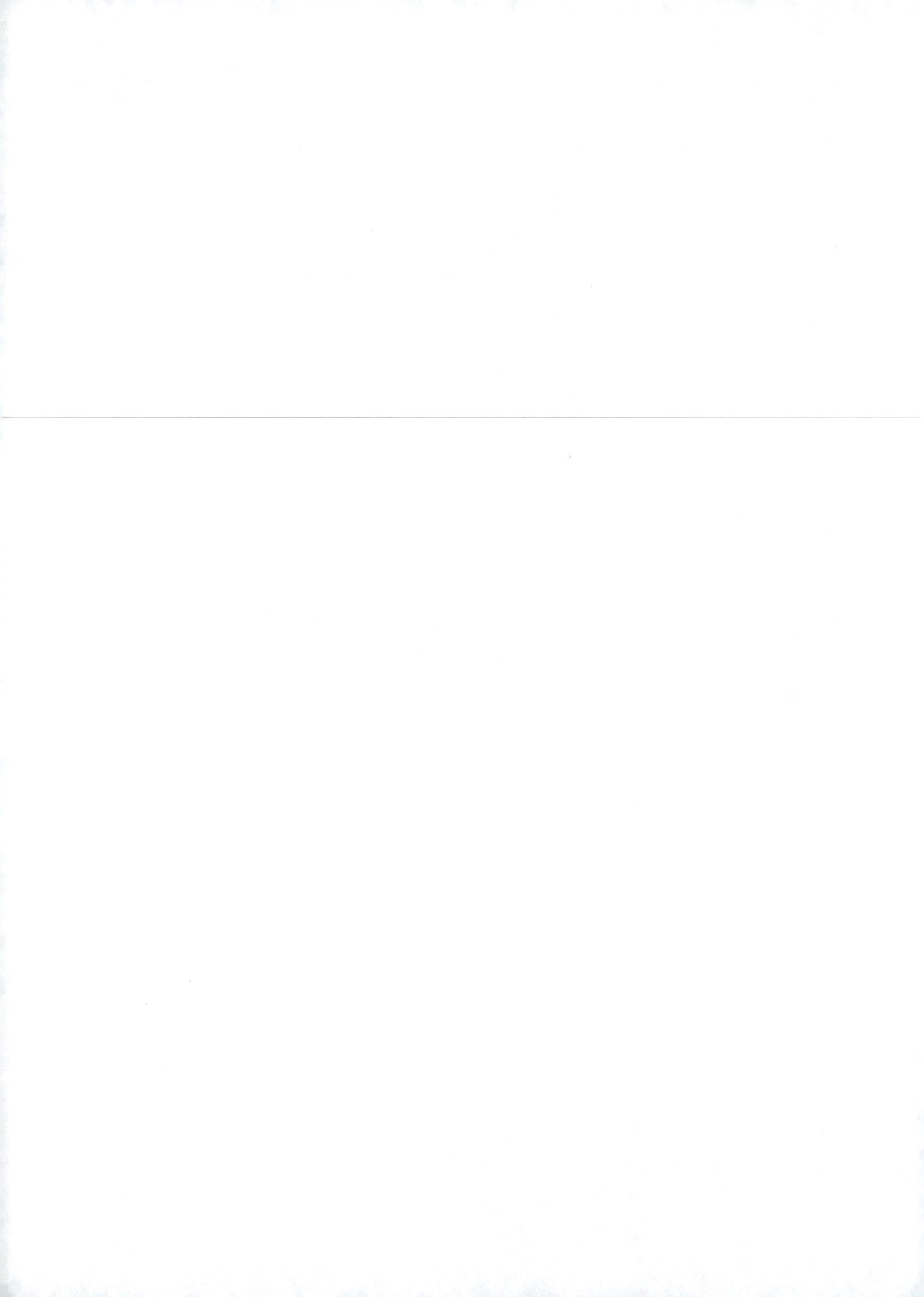

Selected Bibliography

Abele, Charles A. 1969. "The Grand Indian Council and Treaty of Prairie du Chien, 1825," Ph.D. dissertation, Loyola University of Chicago.

Anderson, George E., W. H. Ellison, and Robert F. Heizer. 1978. *Treaty Making and Treaty Rejection by the Federal Government in California, 1850–1852.* Socorro, NM: Ballena Press.

Anderson, George E., and Robert F. Heizer. 1978. "Treaty-making by the Federal Government in California 1851–1852." In *Treaty Making and Treaty Rejection by the Federal Government in California, 1850–1852,* eds. George E. Anderson, W. H. Ellison, and Robert F. Heizer, 1–36. Socorro, NM: Ballena Press.

Anderson, Harry. 1956. "The Controversial Sioux Amendment to the Fort Laramie Treaty of 1851." *Nebraska History* 37 (September): 201–220.

Asch, Michael, ed. 1998. *Aboriginal and Treaty Rights in Canada.* Vancouver: University of British Columbia Press.

Balman, Gail. 1970. "The Creek Treaty of 1866." *Chronicles of Oklahoma* 48 (Summer): 184–196.

Barce, Elmore. 1915. "Governor Harrison and the Treaty of Fort Wayne, 1809." *Indiana Magazine of History* 11 (December): 352–367.

Barnes, Lela. 1936. "Isaac McCoy and the Treaty of 1821." *Kansas Historical Quarterly* 5 (May): 122–142.

Bell, Catherine, and Karin Buss. 2000. "The Promise of Marshall on the Prairies: A Framework for Analyzing Unfulfilled Treaty Promises." *Saskatchewan Law Review* 63(2): 667.

Bigart, Robert, and Clarence Woodcock, eds. 1996. *In the Name of the Salish and Kootenai Nation: The 1885 Hell Gate Treaty and the Origin of the Flathead Indian Reservation.* Pablo, MT: Salish Kootenai College Press/University of Washington Press.

Bird, John, Lorraine Land, and Murray MacAdam, eds. 2002. *Nation to Nation: Aboriginal Sovereignty and the Future of Canada,* 2nd ed. Toronto: Irwin.

Bischoff, William N., and Charles M. Gates, eds. 1943. "The Jesuits and the Coeur D'Alene Treaty of 1858." *Pacific Northwest Quarterly* 34 (April): 169–181.

Borrows, John. 1992. "Negotiating Treaties and Land Claims: The Impact of Diversity within First Nations Property Interests." *Windsor Yearbook of Access to Justice* 12: 179.

Borrows, John. 2005. "Creating an Indigenous Legal Community." *McGill Law Journal* 50: 153.

Boxberger, Daniel L. 1979. *Handbook of Western Washington Indian Treaties.* Lummi Island, WA: Lummi Indian School of Aquaculture and Fisheries.

Boxberger, Daniel L., and Herbert C. Taylor. 1991. "Treaty or Non-Treaty Status." *Columbia,* 5(3): 40–45.

Boyd, Mark F. 1958. "Horatio S. Dexter and Events Leading to the Treaty of Moultrie Creek with the Seminole Indians." *Florida Anthropologist,* 11 (September): 65–95.

Brooks, Drex, and Patricia Nelson Limerick. 1995. *Sweet Medicine: Sites of Indian Massacres, Battlefields, and Treaties.* Albuquerque: University of New Mexico Press.

Brown, George, and Ron Maguire. 1979. *Indian Treaties in Historical Perspective.* Ottawa: Research Branch, Indian and Northern Affairs Canada.

Bugge, David, and J. Lee Corell. 1971. *The Story of the Navajo Treaties.* Window Rock, AZ: Research Section, Navajo Parks and Recreation Department, Navajo Tribe.

Burns, Robert Ignatius, ed. 1952. "A Jesuit at the Hell Gate Treaty of 1855." *Mid-American* 34 (April): 87–114. Report of Adrian Hoechen.

Bushnell, David I., Jr. 1916. "The Virginia Frontier in History–1778." Part 5, "The Treaty of Fort Pitt." *Virginia Magazine of History and Biography* 24 (April): 168–179.

Campisi, Jack. 1988. "From Stanwix to Canandaigua: National Policy, States' Rights, and Indian Land." In *Iroquois Land Claims,* eds. Christopher Vecsey and William A. Starna, 49–65. Syracuse, NY: Syracuse University Press.

Campisi, Jack. 1988. "The Oneida Treaty Period, 1783–1838." In *The Oneida Indian Experience: Two Perspectives,* eds. Jack Campisi and Laurence M. Hauptman, 48–64. Syracuse, NY: Syracuse University Press.

Canada. 1905. *Indian Treaties and Surrenders from 1680–1890.* Ottawa: S. E. Dawson. Repr., Saskatoon: Fifth House, 1992.

Canada. 1971. *Indian Treaties and Surrenders from 1680 to 1890.* 3 vols. Ottawa: Queen's Printer.

Clark, Blue. 1994. *Lone Wolf v. Hitchcock: Treaty Rights and Indian Law at the End of the Nineteenth Century.* Lincoln: University of Nebraska Press.

Clifton, James A. 1980. "Chicago, September 14, 1833: The Last Great Indian Treaty in the Old Northwest." *Chicago History* 9 (Summer): 86–97.

Cohen, Fay G. 1986. *Treaties on Trial: The Continuing Controversy over Northwest Indian Fishing Rights.* With contributions by Joan La France and Vivian L. Bowden. Seattle: University of Washington Press.

Cohen, Felix S. 1942. "Indian Treaties." In Cohen, *Handbook of Federal-Indian Law,* ed. Felix Cohen. Washington, DC: U.S. Government Printing Office.

Cohen, Felix S. 2005. *Handbook of Federal Indian Law.* Newark, NJ: LexisNexis.

Colby, Bonnie G., John E. Thorson, and Sarah Britton. 2005. *Negotiating Tribal Water Rights: Fulfilling Promises in the Arid West.* Tucson: University of Arizona Press.

Commissioner of Indian Affairs. 1975. *Article Six, Treaties between the United States and the Several Indian Tribes from 1778 to 1837.* Millwood, NY: Kraus Reprint.

Costo, Rupert, and Jeannette Henry. 1977. *Indian Treaties: Two Centuries of Dishonor.* San Francisco: Indian Historian Press.

Danziger, Edmund J., Jr. 1973. "They Would Not Be Moved: The Chippewa Treaty of 1854." *Minnesota History* 43 (Spring): 174–185.

Daugherty, W. E. 1981. *Maritime Indian Treaties in Historical Perspective.* Ottawa: Indian and Northern Affairs Canada.

Decker, Craig A. 1977. "The Construction of Indian Treaties, Agreements, and Statutes." *American Indian Law Review* 5(2): 299–311.

Deloria, Vine, Jr. 1974. *Behind the Trail of Broken Treaties: An Indian Declaration of Independence.* New York: Delacorte Press.

Deloria, Vine, Jr. 1996. "Reserving to Themselves: Treaties and the Powers of Indian Tribes." *Arizona Law Review* 38(3): 963–980.

Deloria, Vine, Jr., and David E. Wilkins. 1999. *Tribes, Treaties, and Constitutional Tribulations.* Austin: University of Texas Press.

DeMallie, Raymond J. 1977. "American Indian Treaty Making: Motives and Meanings." *American Indian Journal* 3 (January): 2–10.

DeMallie, Raymond J. 1980. "Touching the Pen: Plains Indian Treaty Councils in Ethnohistorical Perspective." In *Ethnicity in the Great Plains,* ed. Frederick C. Luebke, 38–51. Lincoln: University of Nebraska Press.

DePuy, H. 1917. *A Bibliography of the English Colonial Treaties with the American Indians: Including a Synopsis of Each Treaty.* New York: Lennox Club.

Downes, Randolph C. 1977. *Council Fires on the Upper Ohio: A Narrative of Indian Affairs in the Upper Ohio Valley until 1795.* Pittsburgh, PA: University of Pittsburgh Press.

Duff, Wilson. 1969. "The Fort Victoria Treaties." *BC Studies* 3 (Fall), 3–57.

Dustin, Fred. 1920. "The Treaty of Saginaw, 1819." *Michigan History Magazine* 4 (January): 243–278.

Edmunds, R. David. 1978. "'Nothing Has Been Effected': The Vincennes Treaty of 1792." *Indiana Magazine of History* 74 (March): 23–35.

Ellison, William H. 1978. "Rejection of California Indian Treaties: A Study in Local Influence on National Policy." In *Treaty Making and Treaty Rejection by the Federal Government in California, 1850–1852,* eds. George E. Anderson, W. H. Ellison, and Robert F. Heizer, 50–70. Socorro, NM: Ballena Press.

Fay, George Emory. 1971. *Treaties Between the Potawatomi Tribe of Indians and the United States of America, 1789–1867.* Greeley, CO: Museum of Anthropology: University of Northern Colorado.

Fay, George Emory. 1972. *Treaties and Land Cessions Between the Bands of the Sioux and the United States of America, 1805–1906.* Greeley, CO: Museum of Anthropology: University of Northern Colorado.

Fay, George Emory. 1977. *Treaties Between the Tribes of the Great Plains and the United States of America: Cheyenne and Arapaho, 1825–1900 Etc.* Greeley, CO: Museum of Anthropology: University of Northern Colorado.

Fay, George Emory. 1982. *Treaties Between the Tribes of the Great Plains and the United States of America: Comanche and Kiowa, Arikara, Gros Ventre, and Mandan, 1835–1891*. Greeley, CO: Museum of Anthropology, University of Northern Colorado.

Ferguson, Clyde R. 1979. "Confrontation at Coleraine: Creeks, Georgians and Federalist Indian Policy." *South Atlantic Quarterly* 78 (Spring): 224–243.

Ferguson, Robert B. 1985. "Treaties between the United States and the Choctaw Nation." In *The Choctaw before Removal*, ed. Carolyn Keller Reeves, 214–230. Jackson: University Press of Mississippi.

Fielder, Betty. 1955. "The Black Hawk Treaty." *Annals of Iowa* 32 (January): 535–540.

Fisher, Andrew H. 1999. "This I Know from the Old People: Yakama Indian Treaty Rights as Oral Tradition." *Montana, The Magazine of Western History* 49 (Spring): 2–17.

Fisher, Andrew H. 2004. "Tangled Nets: Treaty Rights and Tribal Identities at Celilo Falls." *Oregon Historical Quarterly* 105 (Summer): 178–211.

Fisher, Robert L. 1933. "The Treaties of Portage des Sioux." *Mississippi Valley Historical Review* 19 (March): 495–508.

Fixico, Donald L. 1984. "As Long as the Grass Grows . . . The Cultural Conflicts and Political Strategies of United States-Indian Treaties." In *Ethnicity and War*, ed. Winston A. Van Horne, 128–149. Milwaukee: University of Wisconsin System, American Ethnic Studies Committee/Urban Corridor Consortium.

Foreman, Carolyn Thomas. 1955. "The Lost Cherokee Treaty." *Chronicles of Oklahoma* 33 (Summer): 238–245.

Foreman, Grant, ed. 1936. "The Journal of the Proceedings of Our First Treaty with the Wild Indians, 1835." *Chronicles of Oklahoma* 14 (December): 394–418.

Foreman, Grant. 1948. "The Texas Comanche Treaty of 1846." *Southwestern Historical Quarterly* 51 (April): 313–332.

Franks, Kenny A. 1972–1973. "An Analysis of the Confederate Treaties with the Five Civilized Tribes." *Chronicles of Oklahoma* 50 (Winter): 458–473.

Franks, Kenny A. 1973. "The Impeachment of the Confederate Treaties with the Five Civilized Tribes." *Chronicles of Oklahoma* 51 (Spring): 21–33.

Gates, Charles M., ed. 1955. "The Indian Treaty of Point No Point." *Pacific Northwest Quarterly* 46 (April): 52–58.

Gerwing, Anselm J. 1964. "The Chicago Indian Treaty of 1838." *Journal of the Illinois State Historical Society* 57 (Summer): 117–142.

Getches, David H., and Charles F. Wilkinson. 1998. *Federal Indian Law: Cases and Materials*, 4th ed. St. Paul: West.

Gibson, Ronald V. 1977. *Jefferson Davis and the Confederacy and Treaties Concluded by the Confederate States with Indian Tribes*. Dobbs Ferry, NY: Oceana Publications.

Gold, Susan Dudley. 1997. *Indian Treaties*. New York: Twenty-First Century Books.

Goodman, Edmund Clay. 2002. "Indian Reserved Rights." In *Nontimber Forest Products in the United States*, eds. Eric T. Jones, Rebecca J. McLain, and James Weigand, 273–281. Lawrence: University Press of Kansas.

Hagan, William T. 1956. "The Sauk and Fox Treaty of 1804." *Missouri Historical Review* 51 (October): 1–7.

Haines, Francis. 1964. "The Nez Perce Tribe versus the United States." *Idaho Yesterdays* 8 (Spring): 18–25.

Halbert, Henry S. 1902. "The Story of the Treaty of Dancing Rabbit Creek." *Publications of the Mississippi Historical Society* 6: 373–402.

Harmon, George D. 1929. "The North Carolina Cherokees and the New Echota Treaty of 1835." *North Carolina Historical Review* 6 (July): 237–253.

Harring, Sidney L. 1994. *Crow Dog's Case: American Indian Sovereignty, Tribal Law, and United States Law in the Nineteenth Century*. New York: Cambridge University Press.

Hawkinson, Ella. 1934. "The Old Crossing Chippewa Treaty and Its Sequel." *Minnesota History* 15 (September): 282–300.

Hawley, Donna Lea. 1990. *The Annotated 1990 Indian Act: Including Related Treaties, Statutes, and Regulations*. Toronto: Carswell.

Hayden, Ralston. 1920. *The Senate and Treaties, 1789–1817: The Development of the Treaty-Making Functions of the United States Senate during Their Formative Period*. New York: Macmillan.

Heilbron, Bertha L. 1941. "Frank B. Mayer and the Treaties of 1851." *Minnesota History* 22 (June): 133–156.

Heizer, Robert F. 1978. "Treaties." In *Handbook of North American Indians*, vol. 8, *California*, ed. Robert F. Heizer, 701–704. Washington, DC: Smithsonian Institution.

Henderson, Archibald. 1931. "The Treaty of Long Island of Holston, July, 1777." *North Carolina Historical Review* 8 (January): 55–116.

Henderson, James [Sakej] Youngblood. 1997. "Interpreting Sui Generis Treaties." *Alberta Law Review* 36(1): 46.

Henderson, James [Sakej] Youngblood. 2000. "Constitutional Powers and Treaty Rights." *Saskatchewan Law Review* 63(2): 719.

Henslick, Harry. 1970. "The Seminole Treaty of 1866." *Chronicles of Oklahoma* 48 (Autumn): 280–294.

Hill, Burton S. 1966. "The Great Indian Treaty Council of 1851." *Nebraska History* 47 (March): 85–110.

Holmes, Jack. 1969. "Spanish Treaties with West Florida Indians, 1784–1802." *Florida Historical Society*, 48 (140–154).

Hoover, Herbert T. 1989. "The Sioux Agreement of 1889 and Its Aftermath." *South Dakota History* 19 (Spring): 56–94.

Horsman, Reginald. 1961. "The British Indian Department and the Abortive Treaty of Lower Sandusky, 1793." *Ohio Historical Quarterly* 70 (July): 189–213.

Hosen, Fredrick E. 1985. *Rifle, Blanket, and Kettle: Selected Indian Treaties and Laws*. Jefferson, NC: McFarland.

Hough, Franklin B., ed. 1861. *Proceedings of the Commissioners of Indian Affairs, Appointed by Law for the Extinguishment of Indian Titles in the State of New York*. 2 vols. Albany, NY: Joel Munsell.

Hryniewicki, Richard J. 1964. "The Creek Treaty of Washington, 1826." *Georgia Historical Quarterly* 48 (December): 425–441.

Hryniewicki, Richard J. 1968. "The Creek Treaty of November 15, 1827." *Georgia Historical Quarterly* 52 (March): 1–15.

Humphreys, A. Glen. 1971. "The Crow Indian Treaties of 1868: An Example of Power Struggle and Confusion in United States Indian Policy." *Annals of Wyoming* 43 (Spring): 73–90.

Ibbotson, Joseph D. 1938. "Samuel Kirkland, the Treaty of 1792, and the Indian Barrier State." *New York History* 19 (October): 374–391.

Imai, Shin. 1999. *Aboriginal Law Handbook*. 2nd ed. Scarborough, ON: Carswell.

Isaac, Thomas. 2001. *Aboriginal and Treaty Rights in the Maritimes: The Marshall Decision and Beyond*. Saskatoon: Purich.

Jaenen, Cornelius J. 2001. "Aboriginal Rights and Treaties in Canada." In *The Native North American Almanac*, ed. Duane Champagne, 1–6. Los Angeles: University of California Press.

Jennings, Francis, ed. 1985. *The History and Culture of Iroquois Diplomacy: An Interdisciplinary Guide to the Treaties of the Six Nations and Their League*. Syracuse, NY: Syracuse University Press.

Jones, Dorothy V. 1982. *License for Empire: By Treaty in Early America*. Chicago: University of Chicago Press.

Jones, Douglas C. 1966. *The Treaty of Medicine Lodge: The Story of the Great Treaty Council as Told by Eyewitnesses*. Norman: University of Oklahoma Press.

Jones, Douglas C. 1969. "Medicine Lodge Revisited." *Kansas Historical Quarterly* 35 (Summer): 130–142.

Josephy, Alvin M., Jr. 1965. "A Most Satisfactory Council." *American Heritage* 16 (October): 26–31, 70–76.

Kane, Lucile M. 1951. "The Sioux Treaties and the Traders." *Minnesota History* 32 (June): 65–80.

Keller, Robert H. 1971. "On Teaching Indian History: Legal Jurisdiction in Chippewa Treaties." *Ethnohistory* 19 (Summer): 209–218.

Keller, Robert H. 1978. "An Economic History of Indian Treaties in the Great Lakes Region." *American Indian Journal* 4 (February): 2–20.

Keller, Robert H. 1989. "America's Native Sweet: Chippewa Treaties and the Right to Harvest Maple Sugar." *American Indian Quarterly* 13 (Spring): 117–135.

Kellogg, Louise Phelps. 1931. "The Menominee Treaty at the Cedars, 1836." *Transactions of the Wisconsin Academy of Sciences, Arts and Letters* 26: 127–135.

Kelsey, Harry. 1973. "The California Indian Treaty Myth." *Southern California Quarterly* 55 (Fall): 225–238.

Kessell, John L. 1981. "General Sherman and the Navajo Treaty of 1868: A Basic and Expedient Misunderstanding." *Western Historical Quarterly* 12 (July): 251–272.

Kickingbird, Kirke, Lynn Kickingbird, Alexander Tallchief Skibine, and Charles Chibitty. 1980. *Indian Treaties.* Washington, DC: Institute for the Development of Indian Law.

Kickingbird, Lynn, and Curtis Berkey. 1975. "American Indian Treaties—Their Importance Today." *American Indian Journal* 1 (October): 3–7.

Kinnaird, Lucia Burk. 1932. "The Rock Landing Conference of 1789." *North Carolina Historical Review* 9 (October): 349–365.

Kvasnicka, Robert M. 1988. "United States Indian Treaties and Agreements." In *Handbook of North American Indians,* vol. 4, *History of Indian–White Relations,* ed. Wilcomb E. Washburn, 195–201. Washington, DC: Smithsonian Institution.

Lambert, Paul F. 1973. "The Cherokee Reconstruction Treaty of 1866." *Journal of the West* 12 (July): 471–489.

Lanchart, David. 1985. "Regaining Dinetah: The Navajo and the Indian Peace Commission at Fort Sumner." In *Working in the Range: Essays on the History of Western Land Management and the Environment,* ed. John R. Wunder, 25–38. Westport, CT: Greenwood Press.

Landau, Jack L. 1980. "Empty Victories: Indian Treaty Fishing Rights in the Pacific Northwest." *Environmental Law* 10: 413–456.

Lane, Barbara. 1977. "Background of Treaty Making in Western Washington." *American Indian Journal* 3 (April): 2–11.

Larson, Gustive O. 1974. "Uintah Dream: The Ute Treaty—Spanish Fork, 1865." *Brigham Young University Studies* 14 (Spring): 361–381.

Laurence, Robert. 1991. "The Abrogation of Indian Treaties by Federal Statutes Protective of the Environment." *Natural Resources Journal,* 31 (Fall): 859–886.

Lehman, J. David. 1990. "The End of the Iroquois Mystique: The Oneida Land Cession Treaties of the 1790s." *William and Mary Quarterly,* 47(4): 523–547.

Leonard, Stephen J. 1990. "John Nicolay in Colorado: A Summer Sojourn and the 1863 Ute Treaty." *Essays and Monographs in Colorado History* 11, 25–54.

Lindquist, G. E. E. 1948–1949. "Indian Treaty Making." *Chronicles of Oklahoma* 26 (Winter): 416–448.

Litton, Gaston L., ed. 1939. "The Negotiations Leading to the Chickasaw-Choctaw Agreement, January 17, 1837." *Chronicles of Oklahoma* 17 (December): 417–427.

Madill, Dennis. 1981. *British Columbia Indian Treaties in Historical Perspective.* Ottawa: Indian and Northern Affairs Canada.

Mahan, Bruce E. 1925. "The Great Council of 1825." *Palimpsest* 6 (September): 305–318.

Mahan, Bruce E. 1929. "Making the Treaty of 1842." *Palimpsest* 10 (May): 174–180.

Mahon, John K. 1962. "The Treaty of Moultrie Creek, 1823." *Florida Historical Quarterly* 40 (April): 350–372.

Mahon, John K. 1962. "Two Seminole Treaties: Payne's Landing, 1882, and Ft. Gibson, 1833." *Florida Historical Quarterly* 41 (July): 1–21.

Mainville, Robert. 2001. *An Overview of Aboriginal and Treaty Rights and Compensation for Their Breach.* Saskatoon: Purich.

Manley, Henry S. 1838. "Buying Buffalo from the Indians." *New York History* 28 (July 1947): 313–329, Buffalo Creek Treaty.

Manley, Henry S. 1932. *The Treaty of Fort Stanwix, 1784.* Rome, NY: Rome Sentinel.

Martin, John Henry. 1975. *List of Documents Concerning the Negotiation of Ratified Indian Treaties, 1801–1869.* Millwood, NY: Kraus Reprint.

McCool, Daniel. 2002. *Native Waters: Contemporary Indian Water Settlements and the Second Treaty Era.* Tucson: University of Arizona Press.

McCullar, Marion Ray. 1973. "The Choctaw-Chickasaw Reconstruction Treaty of 1866." *Journal of the West* 12 (July): 462–470.

McKenney, Thomas L. 1827. *Sketches of a Tour to the Lakes, of the Character and Customs of the Chippeway Indians, and of Incidents Connected with the Treaty of Fond du Lac.* Baltimore: Fielding Lucas, Jr.

McNeil, Kinneth. 1964–65. "Confederate Treaties with the Tribes of Indian Territory." *Chronicles of Oklahoma* 42 (Winter): 408–420.

Morris, Alexander. 1880. *The Treaties of Canada with the Indians of Manitoba and the North-West Territories.* Repr., Toronto: Coles, 1971.

Morse, Bradford. 2004. "Aboriginal and Treaty Rights in Canada." In *Canadian Charter of Rights and Freedoms/Charte Canadienne des droits et Libertés,* 4th ed., eds. Gérald-A. Beaudoin and Errol Mendes, 1171–1257. Markham, ON: LexisNexis Butterworths.

Nesper, Larry. 2002. *The Walleye War: The Struggle for Ojibwe Treaty and Spearfishing Rights.* Lincoln: University of Nebraska Press.

Parker, Arthur C. 1924. "The Pickering Treaty." *Rochester Historical Society Publication Fund Series* 3: 79–91.

Partoll, Albert J., ed. 1937. "The Blackfoot Indian Peace Council." *Frontier and Midland: A Magazine of the West* 17 (Spring): 199–207.

Partoll, Albert J. 1938. "The Flathead Indian Treaty Council of 1855." *Pacific Northwest Quarterly* 29 (July): 283–314.

Perdue, Theda, and Michael D. Green, eds. 1995. *The Cherokee Removal: A Brief History with Documents.* Boston: Bedford Books of St. Martin's Press.

Phillips, Charles, and Alan Axelrod. 2000. *Encyclopedia of Historical Treaties and Alliances.* New York: Facts on File.

Phillips, Edward Hake. 1966. "Timothy Pickering at His Best: Indian Commissioner, 1790–1794." *Essex Institute Historical Collections* 102 (July): 185–192.

Pittman, Philip M., and George M. Covington. 1992. *Don't Blame the Treaties: Native American Rights and the Michigan Indian Treaties.* West Bloomfield, MI: Altwerger and Mandel.

Powless, Irving, and G. Peter Jemison. 2000. *Treaty of Canandaigua 1794: 200 Years of Treaty Relations Between the Iroquois Confederacy and the United States.* Santa Fe, NM: Clear Light.

Price, Monroe E., and Robert N. Clinton. 1983. *Law and the American Indian: Readings, Notes and Cases.* Charlottesville, VA: Michie.

Price, Richard, ed. 1979. *The Spirit of the Alberta Indian Treaties.* Montreal: Institute for Research on Public Policy. Repr., Edmonton: University of Alberta Press, 1999.

Prucha, Francis Paul, ed. 1975. *Documents of United States Indian Policy.* Lincoln and London: University of Nebraska Press.

Prucha, Francis Paul. 1994. *American Indian Treaties: The History of a Political Anomaly.* Berkeley, Los Angeles, and London: University of California Press.

Quaife, Milo M., ed. 1918. "The Chicago Treaty of 1833." *Wisconsin Magazine of History* 1 (March): 287–303.

Quinn, William W., Jr. 1990. "Federal Acknowledgment of American Indian Tribes: The Historical Development of a Legal Concept," *American Journal of Legal History* 34 (October): 331–364.

Rakove, Jack N. 1984. "Solving a Constitutional Puzzle: The Treatymaking Clause as a Case Study." *Perspectives in American History,* s.n., 1: 233–281.

Roberts, Gary L. 1975. "The Chief of State and the Chief." *American Heritage* 26 (October): 28–33, 86–89. Creek Treaty of New York, 1790.

Royal Commission on Aboriginal Peoples. 1995. *Treaty Making in the Spirit of Co-Existence: An Alternative to Extinguishment.* Ottawa: Canada Communication Group.

Royal Commission on Aboriginal Peoples. 1996. *Report of the Royal Commission on Aboriginal Peoples.* Ottawa: Canada Communication Group.

Royce, Charles C. 1899. *Indian Land Cessions in the United States.* Washington, DC: U.S. Government Printing Office.

Rutland, Robert A. 1949–1950. "Political Background of the Cherokee Treaty of New Echota." *Chronicles of Oklahoma* 27 (Winter): 389–406.

Satz, Ronald N. 1991. "Chippewa Treaty Rights: The Reserve Rights of Wisconsin's Chippewa Indians in Historical Perspective." *Transactions of the Wisconsin Academy of Sciences, Arts and Letters,* 79(1). Madison: Wisconsin Academy of Sciences, Arts and Letters.

Schwartzman, Grace M., and Susan K. Barnard. 1991. "A Trail of Broken Promises: Georgians and the Muscogee/Creek Treaties, 1796–1826." *Georgia Historical Quarterly* 75 (Winter): 697–718.

Silliman, Sue I. 1922. "The Chicago Indian Treaty of 1821." *Michigan History Magazine* 6(1): 194–197.

Slattery, Brian. 2000. "Making Sense of Aboriginal and Treaty Rights." *Canadian Bar Review* 79: 196.

Smith, Dwight L. 1954. "Wayne and the Treaty of Greene Ville." *Ohio State Archaeological and Historical Quarterly* 63 (January): 1–7.

Smith, Dwight L. 1978. "The Land Cession Theory: A Valid Instrument of Transfer of Indian Title." In *This Land Is Ours: The Acquisition of the Public Domain,* 87–102. Indianapolis: Indiana Historical Society.

St. Germain, Jill. 2001. *Indian Treaty-Making Policy in the United States and Canada, 1867–1877.* Lincoln and London: University of Nebraska Press.

Stanley, Henry M. 1967. "A British Journalist Reports the Medicine Lodge Peace Council of 1867." *Kansas Historical Quarterly* 33 (Autumn): 249–320.

Stern, Theodore. 1956. "The Klamath Indians and the Treaty of 1864." *Oregon Historical Quarterly* 57 (September): 229–273.

Sullivan, Julie E. 2004. "Legal Analysis of the Treaty Violations That Resulted in the Nez Perce War of 1877," 40 *Idaho Law Review* 657.

Surtees, Robert J. 1988. "Canadian Indian Treaties." In *History of Indian White Relations,* ed. Wilcomb E. Washburn, 202–210. Washington, DC: Smithsonian Institution.

Taylor, Alfred A. 1924. "Medicine Lodge Peace Council." *Chronicles of Oklahoma* 2 (June): 98–117.

Townsend, Michael. 1989. "Congressional Abrogation of Indian Treaties: Reevaluation and Reform." *Yale Law Journal,* 98 (February): 793–812.

Trafzer, Clifford E., ed. 1986. *Indians, Superintendents, and Councils: Northwestern Indian Policy, 1850–1855.* Lanham, MD: University Press of America.

Treaty 7 Elders and Tribal Council with Walter Hildebrandt, Sarah Carter, and Dorothy First Rider. 1996. *The True Spirit and Original Intent of Treaty 7.* Montreal: McGill-Queen's University Press.

Van Doren, Carl, and Julian P. Boyd. 1938. *Indian Treaties Printed by Benjamin Franklin, 1736–1762.* Philadelphia: Historical Society of Pennsylvania.

Vaugeois, Denis. 2002. *The Last French and Indian War: An Inquiry into a Safe-Conduct Issued in 1760 That Acquired the Value of a Treaty in 1990.* Montreal: McGill-Queens University Press/Septentrion.

Vaughan, Alden T. 1979. *Early American Indian Documents: Treaties and Laws, 1607– 1789.* Washington, DC: University Publications of America.

Vipperman, Carl J. 1989. "The Bungled Treaty of New Echota: The Failure of Cherokee Removal, 1836–38." *Georgia Historical Quarterly* 73 (Fall): 540–558.

Watts, Charles W. 1959. "Colbert's Reserve and the Chickasaw Treaty of 1818." *Alabama Review* 12 (October): 272–280.

Watts, Tim J. 1991. *American Indian Treaty Rights: A Bibliography.* Monticello, IL: Vance Bibliographies.

Wells, Samuel J. 1983–1984. "Rum, Skins, and Powder: A Choctaw Interpreter and the Treaty of Mount Dexter." *Chronicles of Oklahoma* 61 (Winter): 422–428.

Wells, Samuel J. 1986. "International Causes of the Treaty of Mount Dexter, 1805." *Journal of Mississippi History* 48 (August): 177–185.

Wicken, William C. 2002. *Mi'kmaq Treaties on Trial: History, Land and Donald Marshall Junior.* Toronto: University of Toronto Press.

Wilkins, David E. 1996. "Indian Treaty Rights: Sacred Entitlements or 'Temporary Privileges?'" *American Indian Culture and Research Journal* 20(1): 87–129.

Wilkins, David E., and K. Tsianina Lomawaima. 2001. *Indian Sovereignty and Federal Law.* Norman: University of Oklahoma Press.

Wilkinson, Charles F. 1991. "To Feel the Summer in the Spring: The Treaty Fishing Rights of the Wisconsin Chippewa." *Wisconsin Law Review* (May–June): 375– 414.

Wilkinson, Charles F. 2000. *Messages from Frank's Landing: A Story of Salmon, Treaties, and the Indian Way.* Seattle: University of Washington Press.

Wilkinson, Charles F., and John M. Volkman. 1975. "Judicial Review of Indian Treaty Abrogation: 'As Long as Water Flows, or Grass Grows upon the Earth'—How Long a Time Is That?" *California Law Review* 63 (May): 601–661.

Williams, C. Herb, and Walt Neubrech. 1976. *Indian Treaties: American Nightmare.* Seattle: Outdoor Empire.

Wright, J. Leitch, Jr. 1967. "Creek-American Treaty of 1790: Alexander McGillivray and the Diplomacy of the Old Southwest." *Georgia Historical Quarterly* 51 (December): 379–400.

Wrone, David R. 1986–1987. "Indian Treaties and the Democratic Idea." *Wisconsin Magazine of History* 70 (Winter): 83–106.

Wunder, John R. 1985. "No More Treaties: The Resolution of 1871 and the Alteration of Indian Rights to Their Homelands." In *Working the Range: Essays on the History of Western Land Management and the Environment,* ed. John R. Wunder, 39–56. Westport, CT: Greenwood Press.

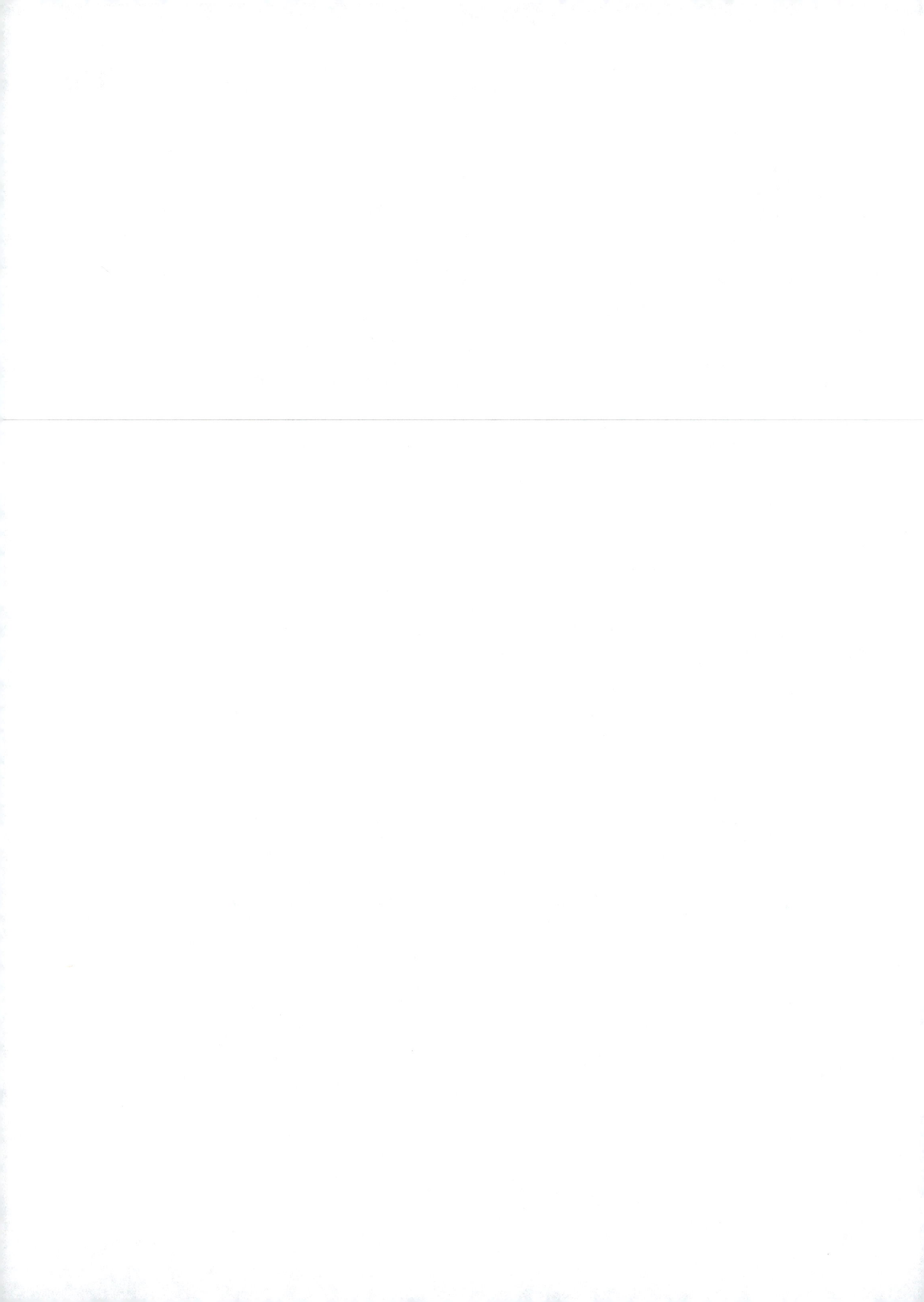

Index

Note: Page locators in **boldface** type indicate the location of a main encyclopedia entry.